Management

Course:
22INTB380
International Business

Instructor:
Ratee Apana

University of Cincinnati

McGraw-Hill/Irwin

A Division of The McGraw-Hill Companies

McGraw–Hill Primis

ISBN–10: 0–39–095948–0
ISBN–13: 978–0–39–095948–5

Text:

Global Business Today, Sixth Edition
Hill

This book was printed on recycled paper.

Management

http://www.primisonline.com

111   MANGGEN   ISBN–10: 0–39–095948–0   ISBN–13: 978-0-39-095948-5

Management

Contents

Hill • *Global Business Today, Sixth Edition*

preface

Global Business Today is intended for the first international business course at either the undergraduate or MBA level. My goal in writing this book has been to set a new standard for international business textbooks. I have attempted to write a book that

1. Is comprehensive and up-to-date.
2. Goes beyond an uncritical presentation and shallow explanation of the body of knowledge.
3. Maintains a tight, integrated flow between chapters.
4. Focuses on managerial implications.
5. Makes important theories accessible and interesting to students.
6. Incorporates ancillary resources that enliven the text and make it easier to teach.

Over the years, and through now six editions, I have worked hard to adhere to these goals. It has not always been easy. An enormous amount has happened over the last decade, both in the real world of economics, politics, and business, and in the academic world of theory and empirical research. Often I have had to significantly rewrite chapters, scrap old examples, bring in new ones, incorporate new theory and evidence into the book, and phase out older theories that are increasingly less relevant to the modern and dynamic world of international business. That process continues in the current edition. As noted later, there have been significant changes in this edition, and that will no doubt continue to be the case in the future. In deciding what changes to make, I have been guided not only by my own reading, teaching, and research, but also by the invaluable feedback I receive from professors and students around the world who use the book, from reviewers, and from the editorial staff at McGraw-Hill/Irwin. My thanks go out to all of them.

Comprehensive and Up-to-Date

To be comprehensive, an international business textbook must

- Explain how and why the world's countries differ.
- Present a thorough review of the economics and politics of international trade and investment.
- Explain the functions and form of the global monetary system.
- Examine the strategies and structures of international businesses.
- Assess the special roles of an international business's various functions.

I have always endeavored to do all of these things. Too many other texts have paid insufficient attention to the strategies and structures of international businesses and to the implications of international business for firms' various functions. This omission has been a serious deficiency. Many of the students in these international business courses will soon be working in international businesses, and they will be expected to understand the implications of international business for their organization's strategy, structure, and functions. This book pays close attention to these issues.

Comprehensiveness and relevance also require coverage of the major theories. It has always been my goal to incorporate the insights gleaned from recent academic work into the text. Consistent with this goal, over the last six editions I have added insights from the following research:

- The new trade theory and strategic trade policy.
- The work of Nobel Prize–winning economist Amartya Sen on economic development.
- The work of Hernando de Soto on the link between property rights and economic development.
- Samuel Huntington's influential thesis on the "clash of civilizations."
- The new growth theory of economic development championed by Paul Romer and Gene Grossman.
- Empirical work by Jeffrey Sachs and others on the relationship between international trade and economic growth.
- Michael Porter's theory of the competitive advantage of nations.
- Robert Reich's work on national competitive advantage.
- The work of Nobel Prize–winner Douglas North and others on national institutional structures and the protection of property rights.
- The market imperfections approach to foreign direct investment that has grown out of Ronald Coase and Oliver Williamson's work on transaction cost economics.
- Bartlett and Ghoshal's research on the transnational corporation.
- The writings of C. K. Prahalad and Gary Hamel on core competencies, global competition, and global strategic alliances.
- Insights for international business strategy that can be derived from the resource-based view of the firm.
- Paul Samuelson's critique of free trade theory.

In addition to including leading-edge theory, in light of the fast-changing nature of the international business environment, I have made every effort to ensure that the book was as up-to-date as possible when it went to press. A significant amount has happened in the world since I first began work on this book. The Uruguay Round of GATT negotiations was successfully concluded and the World Trade Organization was established. In 2001, the WTO embarked upon another major round of talks aimed to reduce barriers to trade, the Doha Round. The European Union moved forward with its post-1992 agenda to achieve a closer economic and monetary union, including the establishment of a common currency in January 1999. The North American Free Trade Agreement passed into law, and Chile indicated its desire to become the next member of the free trade area. The Asia-Pacific Economic Cooperation forum emerged as the kernel of a possible future Asia Pacific free trade area. The former Communist states of Eastern Europe and Asia continued on the road to economic and political reform. As they did, the euphoric mood that followed the collapse of communism in 1989 was slowly replaced with a growing sense of realism about the hard path ahead for many of these countries. The global money market continued its meteoric growth. By 2007, more than $3 trillion per day was flowing across national borders. The size of such flows fueled concern about the ability of short-term speculative shifts in global capital markets to destabilize the world economy. The World Wide Web emerged from nowhere to become the backbone of an emerging global network for electronic commerce. The world continued to become more global. Several Asian Pacific economies, most notably China, continued to grow their economies at a rapid rate. Outsourcing of service functions to places like China and India emerged as a major issue in developed Western nations. New multinationals continued to emerge from developing nations in addition to the world's established industrial powers. Increasingly, the globalization of the world economy affected a wide range of firms of all sizes, from the very large to the very small. And unfortunately, in the wake of the terrorist attacks on the United States that took place on September 11, 2001, global terrorism and the attendant geopolitical risks emerged as a threat to global economic integration and activity.

What's New in the Sixth Edition

The success of the first five editions of *Global Business Today* was based in part upon the incorporation of leading-edge research into the text, the use of the up-to-date examples and statistics to illustrate global trends and enterprise strategy, and the discussion of current events within the context of the appropriate theory. Building on these strengths, my goals for this revision have been threefold:

1. Incorporate new insights from recent scholarly research wherever appropriate.
2. Make sure the content of the text covers all appropriate issues.
3. Make sure the text is as up-to-date as possible with regard to current events, statistics, and examples.

As part of the overall revision process, *changes have been made to every chapter in the book*. All material and statistics are as up-to-date as possible as of 2008. I have added discussion of current events wherever appropriate. For example, the dramatic fall in the value of the dollar that we witnessed in 2006–2008 is discussed in Chapter 10; the trade tensions caused by China's export-led growth are discussed in Chapter 6, as is the current state of play with regard to the Doha Round of trade negotiations undertaken by the World Trade Organization; while in Chapter 8 I discuss the continuing evolution and enlargement of the European Union. The opening and closing cases to each chapter are also new, and many new boxed examples have been added within chapters. I have also changed the positioning of discussion on the balance-of-payments accounts. Previously this was not introduced until Chapter 7 on foreign direct investment, which was probably not the best location. In this edition I have added an Appendix on International Trade and the Balance of Payments to Chapter 5. This includes a discussion of the significance of a deficit on the current account of the balance of payments, which has become something of a political issue in the United States, which has been running record deficits.

Beyond Uncritical Presentation and Shallow Explanation

Many issues in international business are complex and thus necessitate considerations of pros and cons. To demonstrate this to students, I have adopted a critical approach that presents the arguments for and against economic theories, government policies, business strategies, organizational structures, and so on.

Related to this, I have attempted to explain the complexities of the many theories and phenomena unique to international business so the student might fully comprehend the statements of a theory or the reasons a phenomenon is the way it is. I believe that these theories and phenomena are explained in more depth in this book than they are in competing textbooks, which seem to use the rationale that a shallow explanation is little better than no explanation. In international business, a little knowledge is indeed a dangerous thing.

To help students go a step farther in expanding their understanding of international business, each chapter incorporates two globalEDGE research tasks designed and written by Tunga Kiyak and the team at Michigan State University's globalEDGE. msu.edu site to dovetail with the content just covered.

globalEDGE

The globalEDGE task for Chapter 3 asks students to research and list cultural differences they may encounter during a business partnership with a Mexican distributor.

Research Task ⚪ globalEDGE   http://globalEDGE.msu.edu

Use the globalEDGE Resource Desk (http://globalEDGE.msu.edu/ResourceDesk) to complete the following exercises:

1. You have been assigned to negotiate a business deal with the representatives of a potential distributor in Mexico. Since having *intercultural skills* is critical for a successful international experience, you consider collecting information regarding the local culture before your departure. Prepare a short description of the

most striking cultural characteristics involved in communicating with the local people that may affect business interactions in this country.

2. Asian cultures exhibit significant differences in *business etiquette* when compared to Western cultures. For example, in China, large hand movements are usually distracting and in fact it is considered offensive to point while speaking. Find five similar tips regarding the business etiquette of India.

iGLOBE

iGLOBE is McGraw-Hill/Irwin's revolutionary new Web-based video archive, incorporating international business news clips from PBS's *The News Hour*. New clips are added every month, and teaching notes are available for you to use in integrating the segments with your classroom. Students can also subscribe for individual access. (www.mhhe.com/iglobe preview)

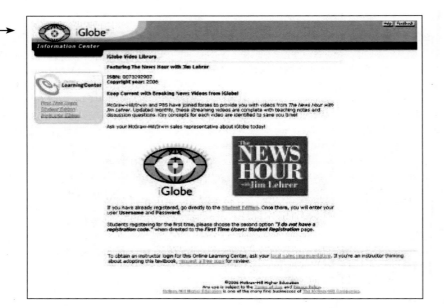

Integrated Progression of Topics

A weakness of many texts is that they lack a tight, integrated flow of topics from chapter to chapter. In Chapter 1 of this book, students will learn how the book's topics are related to each other. I've achieved integration by organizing the material so that each chapter builds on the material of the previous ones in a logical fashion.

PART ONE   Chapter 1 provides an overview of the key issues to be addressed and explains the plan of the book.

PART TWO   Chapters 2 and 3 focus on national differences in political economy and culture, and Chapter 4 examines ethical issues in international business. Most international business textbooks place this material at a later point, but I believe it is vital to discuss national differences first. After all, many of the central issues in international trade and investment, the global monetary system, international business strategy and structure, and international business operations arise out of national differences in political economy and culture. To fully understand these issues, students must first appreciate the differences in countries and cultures. Ethical issues are dealt with at this juncture primarily because many ethical dilemmas flow out of national differences in political systems, economic systems, and culture.

PART THREE   Chapters 5 through 8 investigate the political economy of international trade and investment. The purpose of this part is to describe and explain the trade and investment environment in which international business occurs.

PART FOUR   Chapters 9 and 10 describe and explain the global monetary system, laying out in detail the monetary framework in which international business transactions are conducted.

PART FIVE   In Chapters 11 through 16, attention shifts from the environment to the firm. Here the book examines the strategies that firms adopt to compete effectively in the international business environment and explains how firms can perform key functions—production, marketing, R&D, human resource management, accounting, and finance—to compete and succeed in the international business environment.

Throughout the book, the relationship of new material to topics discussed in earlier chapters is pointed out to the students to reinforce their understanding of how the material comprises an integrated whole.

Focus on Managerial Implications

I have always believed that it is important to show students how the material covered in the text is relevant to the actual practice of international business. This is explicit in the later chapters of the book, which focus on the practice of international business, but it is not always obvious in the first half of the book, which considered many macroeconomic and political issues, from international trade theory and foreign direct investment flows to the IMF and the influence of inflation rates on foreign exchange quotations. Accordingly, at the end of each chapter in Parts Two, Three, and Four—where the focus is on the environment of international business, as opposed to particular firms—there is a section titled "Focus on Managerial Implications." In this section, the managerial implications of the material discussed in the chapter are clearly explained.

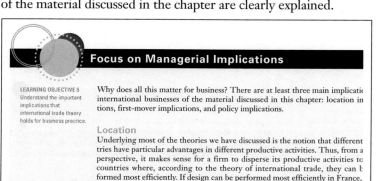

Focus of Managerial Implications

For example, Chapter 5, "International Trade Theory," ends with a detailed discussion of the various trade theories' implications for international business management. See page 188 for the rest of this feature.

In addition, each chapter begins with an **opening case** that sets the stage for the chapter content and familiarizes students with how real international companies conduct business.

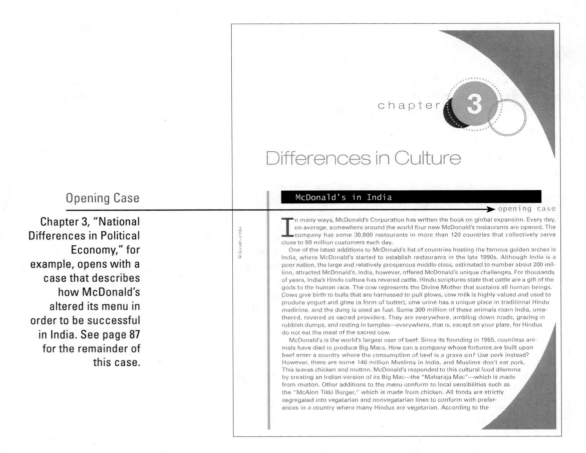

Opening Case

Chapter 3, "National Differences in Political Economy," for example, opens with a case that describes how McDonald's altered its menu in order to be successful in India. See page 87 for the remainder of this case.

I have also added a **closing case** to each chapter. These cases are also designed to illustrate the relevance of chapter material for the practice of international business as well as to provide continued insight into how real companies handle those issues.

Closing Case

The closing case to Chapter 2, for example, explains how the political economy of Venezuela is changing under the leadership of Hugo Chavez and what this might mean for foreign investors. To see the rest of this case, turn to page 84.

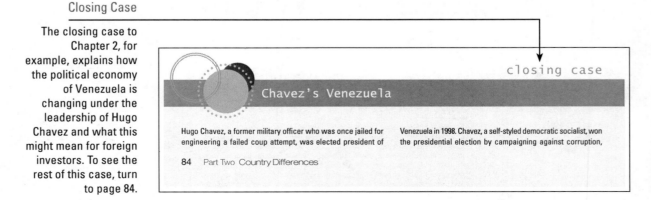

Another tool that I have used to focus on managerial implications are **Management Focus** boxes. There is at least one Management Focus in most chapters. Like the opening cases, the purpose of these boxes is to illustrate the relevance of chapter material for the practice of international business.

Management FOCUS

DMG-Shanghai

In 1993, New Yorker Dan Mintz moved to China as a freelance film director with no contacts, no advertising experience, and no Mandarin. By 2006, the company he subsequently founded in China, DMG, had emerged as one of China's fastest growing advertising agencies with a client list that includes Budweiser, Unilever, Sony, Nabisco, Audi, Volkswagen, China Mobile, and dozens of other Chinese brands. Mintz attributes his success in part to what the Chinese call guanxi.

Guanxi literally means relationships, although in business settings it can be better understood as connections. *Guanxi* has its roots in the Confucian philosophy of valuing social hierarchy and reciprocal obligations. Confucian ideology has a 2,000-year-old history in China. Confucianism stresses the importance of relationships, both within the family and between master and servant. Confucian ideology teaches that people are not created equal. In Confucian thought, loyalty and obligations to one's superiors (or to family) are regarded as a sacred duty, but at the same time, this loyalty has its price. Social superiors are obligated to reward the loyalty of their social inferiors by bestowing "blessings" upon them; thus, the obligations are reciprocal.

Today, Chinese will often cultivate a *guanxiwang*, or "relationship network," for help. Reciprocal obligations are the glue that holds such networks together. If those obligations are not met—if favors done are not paid back or reciprocated—the reputation of the transgressor is tarnished, and he or she will be less able to draw on his or her *guanxiwang* for help in the future. Thus, the implicit threat

acknowledgment that if you have the right *guanxi*, legal rules can be broken, or at least bent.

Mintz, who is now fluent in Mandarin, cultivated his *guanxiwang* by going into business with two young Chinese who had connections, Bing Wu and Peter Xiao. Bing Wu, who works on the production side of the business, was a former national gymnastics champion, which translates into prestige and access to business and government officials. Peter Xiao comes from a military family with major political connections. Together, these three have been able to open doors that long-established Western advertising agencies have not. They have done it in large part by leveraging the contacts of Wu and Xiao, and by backing up their connections with what the Chinese call *Shi li*, the ability to do good work.

A case in point was DMG's campaign for Volkswagen, which helped the German company to become ubiquitous in China. The ads used traditional Chinese characters, which had been banned by Chairman Mao during the Cultural Revolution in favor of simplified versions. To get permission to use the characters in film and print ads—a first in modern China—the trio had to draw on high-level government contacts in Beijing. They won over officials by arguing that the old characters should be thought of as art. Later, they shot TV spots for the ad on Shanghai's famous Bund, a congested boulevard that runs along the waterfront of the old city. Drawing again on government contacts, they were able to shut down the Bund to make the shoot. Steven Spielberg had been able to close down only a portion of the street when he filmed *Empire of the Sun* there in 1986. DMG has also filmed inside Beijing's Forbidden City, even though

Management Focus

The Management Focus in Chapter 2, for example, looks at how Dan Mintz, founder of DMG in China used *guanxi* to create a successful business. See page 108 for the rest of this focus.

Accessible and Interesting

The international business arena is fascinating and exciting, and I have tried to communicate my enthusiasm for it to the student. Learning is easier and better if the subject matter is communicated in an interesting, informative, and accessible manner. One technique I have used to achieve this is weaving interesting anecdotes into the narrative of the text, that is, stories that illustrate theory. The use of **Another Perspective** boxes also serves to provide additional context for the chapter topics.

Another Perspective

More on Aristotle

In addition to believing that the means of production should be privately owned, Aristotle thought that if we were to abolish private property, we would do moral harm to ourselves. Without private property, there would be no need to exercise generosity. "Without private property, no man will be seen to be liberal and no man will ever do any act of liberality; for only in the use of money is liberality made effective." (*The Politics*, Book 2, Ch. 5, trans. T.A. Sinclair)

The Peruvian economist Hernando De Soto develops Aristotle's point in the argument that the underlying, basic source of poverty and underdevelopment is the lack of a legal system that allows for transferable, titled, private property. (*The Mystery of Capital: Why Capitalism Triumphs in the West and Fails Everywhere Else*, Basic Books, 2000)

Another Perspective

For example, this Another Perspective box in Chapter 2 gives a good sense of the scale of economic and demographic measures that this chapter describes. See page 45 for the rest of the picture.

In addition to the Management Focus feature, most chapters also have a **Country Focus** box that provides background on the political, economic, social, or cultural aspects of countries grappling with an international business issue.

Country Focus

In Chapter 2, for example, discusses emerging property rights in China. See page 67 for more details.

Country FOCUS

Emerging Property Right in China

On October 1, 2007, a new property law took effect in China. The law, the culmination of 14 years of effort, granted rural and urban landholders far more secure property rights. The law was a much-needed response to changes in China's economy over the past 30 years as it transitions from a centrally planned system to a dynamic market-based economy where two thirds of economic activity is in the hands of private enterprises.

Although all land in China still technically belongs to the state—an ideological necessity in a country where the government still claims to be guided by Marxism—urban landholders previously had been granted 40- to 70-year leases to use the land, while rural farmers had 30-year leases. However, the lack of legal title to their land meant that landholders were at the whim of the state. Over the last few years, large-scale appropriation of rural land for housing and factory construction has rendered millions of farmers landless. Many have been given little or no compensation, and they have drifted to the cities where they are adding to a growing underclass. In both urban and rural areas, property and land disputes had become a leading cause of social unrest. According to government sources, in 2006 there were about 23,000 "mass incidents" of social unrest in China, many related to disputes over property rights.

The new law, which was fought by left-wing Communist Party activists who objected to it on ideological grounds, gives urban and rural land users the right to automatic renewal of their leases after the expiration of the 30- to 70-year terms. In addition, the law requires that land users be fairly compensated if the land is required for other purposes, and it gives individuals the same legal protection for their property as the state. Taken together with a 2004 change in China's constitution, which stated that private property "was not to be encroached upon," the new law significantly strengthens property rights in China.

Nevertheless, the law has its limitations. Most notably, it still falls short of giving peasants marketable ownership rights to the land they farm. If they could sell their land, tens of millions of underemployed farmers might find more productive work elsewhere. Those that stayed could acquire bigger land holdings that could be used more efficiently. Also, farmers might be able to use their land holdings as security against which they could borrow funds for investments to boost productivity.

Sources: "China's Next Revolution—Property Rights in China," *The Economist*, March 10, 2007, p. 11; "Caught Between the Right and Left," *The Economist*, March 10, 2007, pp. 25–27; and Z. Keliang and L. Ping, "Rural Land Rights under the PRC Property Law," *China Law and Practice*, November 2007, pp. 10–15.

Ancillary Resources That Enliven the Text and Make It Easier to Teach

For instructors, this text offers a number of materials to help them keep their students active and engaged in the learning process. In addition to the course cartridge, International Business DVD, and iGLOBE resources, the **Instructor's Resource CD-ROM** is a one-stop place for several key instructor aids, including the following:

- **Instructor's Manual.** The Instructor's Manual, prepared by Veronica Horton, contains course outlines; chapter teaching resources, including chapter overviews and outlines, teaching suggestions, chapter objectives, teaching suggestions for opening cases, lecture outlines, answers to critical discussion questions, teaching suggestions for the closing case, and two student activities (some with Internet components); and expanded Video Notes with discussion questions for each video. The answers to globalEDGE research tasks will also be included here.
- **Test Bank.** The test bank contains approximately 100 true-false, multiple-choice, and essay questions per chapter. The test bank questions are also categorized by Bloom's taxonomy levels of learning and how they meet various AACSB objectives.

- **EZ Test.** A computerized version of the test bank is available, allowing the instructor to generate random tests and to add his or her own questions.
- **PowerPoint®.** Re-created for this edition by Veronica Horton, the PowerPoint program consists of approximately 500 slides featuring original materials not found in the text in addition to reproductions and illuminations of key text figures, tables, and maps. Quiz questions to keep students on their toes during classroom presentations are also included, along with instructor notes.
- **Online Learning Center (www.mhhe.com/hill/gbt6e).** A password-protected portion of the book's Web site will be available to adopters of *Global Business Today*, featuring online access to the Instructor's Manual, PowerPoints, Video Cases, and globalEDGE answers. Instructors can also view student resources to make more effective supplementary assignments.

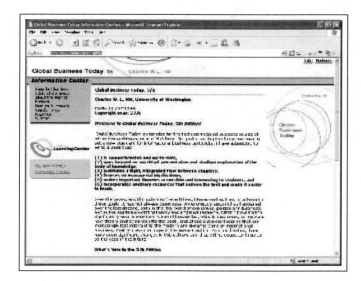

For students, this book also provides rich interactive resources to help them learn how to practice international business.

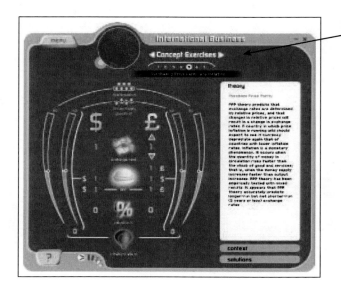

Concept Exercises

Concept Exercises help students learn how to solve realistic problems by exploring Flash modules, linked to the appropriate chapter, of the Hofstede study, absolute and comparative advantage, foreign direct investment, balance of payments, purchasing power parity and inflation, historical exchange rates, and export and import financing.

The Online Learning Center (www.mhhe.com/hillgbt6e) for students includes chapter quizzes, student PowerPoints, and chapter overviews. Students can also access the text glossary as well as all *Global Business Today* interactive modules, including the following.

Concept Videos

The eight Concept Videos, complemented by cases and discussion questions written by Charles Hill, are also exclusive to these online activities. Students can watch and learn more when they access this activity for the appropriate chapter.

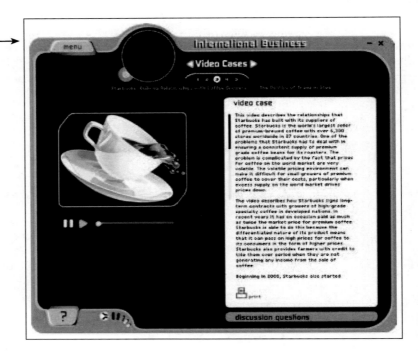

Global Business Plan

The Global Business Plan helps students take it one step further into applications, allowing them to build their own business plan one section at a time to prepare for entering a foreign market.

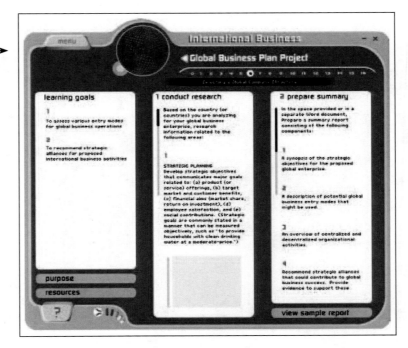

Acknowledgments

Numerous people deserve to be thanked for their assistance in preparing this book. First, I want to thank all the people at McGraw-Hill/Irwin who have worked with me on this project:

Paul Ducham, Publisher

John Weimeister, Sponsoring Editor

Megan Richter, Developmental Editor

Natalie Zook, Marketing Manager

Michael Gedatus, Marketing Coordinator

Lynn Bluhm, Media Project Manager

Bruce Gin, Project Manager

Matt Baldwin, Designer

Michael McCormick, Production Supervisor

Jeremy Cheshareck, Photo Researcher

Second, my thanks go to the reviewers, who provided good feedback that helped shape this edition of the book:

Dr. R. Apanna, *University of Cincinnati*

Claudia E. Browning, *Mesa Community College*

Gretchen Carroll, *Owens Community College*

Macgorine Cassell, *Fairmont State University*

Ken Chinen, *California State University, Sacramento*

Susan Hansen, *University of Wisconsin-Platteville*

DeAnn Hurtado, *Sinclair Community College*

J. Leslie Jankovich, *San Jose State University*

Tomasz Lenartowicz, *Florida Atlantic University*

Daniel Rajaratnam, *Baylor University*

Diane Scott, *Wichita State University*

Christina Scott-Young, *Penn State University, Erie*

Part 1   Introduction and Overview

LEARNING OBJECTIVES

After you have read this chapter you should:

1   Understand what is meant by the term *globalization.*

2   Be familiar with the main drivers of globalization.

3   Appreciate the changing nature of the global economy.

4   Understand the main arguments in the debate over the impact of globalization.

5   Appreciate how the process of globalization is creating opportunities and challenges for business managers.

c h a p t e r 1

Globalization

Globalization at General Electric

opening case

General Electric, the company that Thomas Edison founded and now the largest industrial conglomerate in America, produces a wide array of goods and services, from medical equipment, power generators, jet engines, and home appliances, to financial services and even television broadcasting (GE owns NBC, one of the big three U.S. network broadcasters). This giant company with annual revenues of close to $180 billion is no stranger to international business. GE has been operating and selling overseas for decades. During the tenure of legendary Chief Executive Officer Jack Welch, GE's main goal was to be number one or two globally in every business in which it participated. To further this goal, Welch sanctioned an aggressive and often opportunistic foreign direct investment strategy. GE took advantage of economic weakness in Europe in 1989–1995 to invest $17.5 billion in the region, half of which was used to acquire some 50 companies. When the Mexican peso collapsed in value in 1995, GE took advantage of the economic uncertainty to purchase companies throughout Latin America. And when Asia slipped into a major economic crisis in 1997–1998, due to turmoil in the Asian currency markets, GE's Welch urged his managers to view it as a buying opportunity. In Japan alone, the company spent $15 billion on acquisitions in just six months. As a result, by the end of Welch's tenure in 2001, GE was producing more than 40 percent of its revenues from international sales, up from 20 percent in 1985.

Welch's GE, however, was still very much an American company doing business abroad. Under the leadership of his successor, Jeffery Immelt, GE seems to be intent on becoming a true global company. International revenues continue to grow faster than domestic revenues, passing 50 percent of the total in 2007. This expansion increasingly is being powered by the dynamic economies of Asia, particularly India and China. GE now sells more engines for wide-body jets to India than in the United States, and GE is a major beneficiary of the huge infrastructure investments now occurring in China as that country invests rapidly in airports, railways, and power stations. By 2012, analysts estimate that GE will be generating 55 to 60 percent of its business internationally.

To reflect the shifting center of gravity, Immelt has changed the way GE is organized and operates. Until 2004, all of GE's major businesses had head offices in the United States and were tightly controlled from the center. Then, GE moved the head office of its health care business from the United States to London, the home of Amersham, a company GE had just bought. Next, the headquarters for the unit that sales equipment to oil and gas companies was relocated to Florence, Italy. And in 2008, the headquarters for GE Money was moved to London. In addition, country managers have been given more power. Why is GE doing this? Because the company believes that to succeed internationally, it must be close to its customers. The move of GE Money to London, for example, was prompted by a desire to be closer to customers in Europe and Asia. Executives at GE Health Care like London because it allows for easier flights to anywhere in the world.

GE has also shifted research overseas. Since 2004 it has opened research and development centers in Munich, Germany; Shanghai, China; and Bangalore, India. The belief is that by locating in those economies where it is growing rapidly, GE can better design equipment that is best-suited to local needs. For example, GE Health Care makes MRI scanners that cost $1.5 million each, but its Chinese research center is designing MRI scanners that can be priced for $500,000 and are more likely to gain sales in the developing world.

GE is also rapidly internationalizing its senior management. Once viewed as a company that preferred to hire managers from the Midwest because of their strong work ethic, foreign accents are now frequently heard among the higher ranks. Country managers, who in the past were often American expatriates, increasingly come from the regions where they work. GE has found that local nationals are invaluable when trying to sell to local companies and governments, where a deep understanding of local language and culture is often critical. In China, for example, the government is a large customer, and working closely with government bureaucrats requires a cultural sensitivity that is difficult for outsiders to gain. In addition to the internationalization of the management ranks, GE's American managers are increasingly traveling overseas for management training and company events. In 2008, in a highly symbolic gesture, GE Transportation, which is based in Erie, Pennsylvania, moved its annual sales meeting to Sorrento, Italy, from Florida. "It was time that the Americans learnt to deal with jet lag," according to the head of the unit. ●

Sources: C.H. Deutsch, "At Home in the World," *The New York Times,* February 14, 2008, pp. C1, C4; V.J. Racanelli, "GE's Moment," *Barron's,* June 4, 2007, pp. 25–29; "General Electric: The Immelt Way," *BusinessWeek,* September 11, 2006, p. 30; and F. Guerrera, "GE Money Moves Its HQ to London," *Financial Times,* February 8, 2008, p. 18.

Introduction

A fundamental shift is occurring in the world economy. We are moving away from a world in which national economies were relatively self-contained entities, isolated from each other by barriers to cross-border trade and investment; by distance, time zones, and language; and by national differences in government regulation, culture, and business systems. And we are moving toward a world in which barriers to cross-border trade and investment are declining; perceived distance is shrinking due to advances in transportation and telecommunications technology; material culture is starting to look similar the world over; and national economies are merging into an interdependent, integrated global economic system. The process by which this is occurring is commonly referred to as globalization.

In today's interdependent global economy, an American might drive to work in a car designed in Germany that was assembled in Mexico by Ford from components made in the United States and Japan that were fabricated from Korean steel and Malaysian rubber. She may have filled the car with gasoline at a BP service station owned by a British multinational company. The gasoline could have been made from oil pumped out of a well off the coast of Africa by a French oil company that transported it to the United States in a ship owned by a Greek shipping line. While driving to work, the American might talk to her stockbroker on a Nokia cell phone that was designed in Finland and assembled in Texas using chip sets produced in Taiwan that were designed by Indian engineers working for Texas Instruments. She could tell the stockbroker to purchase shares in Deutsche Telekom, a German telecommunications firm that was transformed from a former state-owned monopoly into a global company by an energetic Israeli CEO. She may turn on the car radio, which was made in Malaysia by a Japanese firm, to hear a popular hip-hop song composed by a Swede and sung by a group of Danes in English who signed a record contract with a French music company to promote their record in America. The driver might pull into a drive-through coffee shop run by a Korean immigrant and order a "single, tall, nonfat latte" and chocolate-covered biscotti. The coffee beans came from Brazil and the chocolate from Peru, while the biscotti was made locally using an old Italian recipe. After the song ends, a news announcer might inform the American listener that antiglobalization protests at a meeting of the World Economic Forum in Davos, Switzerland, have turned violent. One protester has been killed. The announcer then turns to the next item, a story about how fear of interest rate hikes in the United States has sent Japan's Nikkei stock market index down sharply.

This is the world in which we live. It is a world where the volume of goods, services, and investment crossing national borders has expanded faster than world output consistently for more than half a century. It is a world where some $3 trillion in foreign exchange transactions are made every day, where more than $12 trillion of goods and almost $3 trillion of services are sold across national borders.[1] It is a world in which international institutions such as the World Trade Organization and gatherings of leaders from the world's most powerful economies have called for even lower barriers to cross-border trade and investment. It is a world where the symbols of material and popular culture are increasingly global: from Coca-Cola and Starbucks to Sony PlayStations, Nokia cell phones, MTV shows, Disney films, IKEA stores, and Apple iPods and iPhones. It is a world in which products are made from inputs that come from all over the world. It is a world in which an economic crisis in Asia can cause a recession in the United States, and the threat of higher interest rates in the United States really did help drive Japan's Nikkei index down in the spring of 2006. It is also a world in which vigorous and vocal groups protest against globalization, which they blame for a list of ills, from unemployment in developed nations to environmental

 Another Perspective

The United States in Perspective
The United States has the highest level of output in the world, with the GDP valued at more than $12.5 trillion in 2005. The U.S. GDP per capita is $42,129. With around 4.6 percent of the world's population, the United States produces about 20.4 percent of the global GDP. (*The Economist,* May 1, 2006; Factsheet, CIA Factbook)

degradation and the Americanization of popular culture. And yes, these protests have on occasion turned violent.

For businesses, this process has produced many opportunities. Firms can expand their revenues by selling around the world and/or reduce their costs by producing in nations where key inputs, including labor, are cheap. The global expansion of enterprises has been facilitated by favorable political and economic trends. Since the collapse of communism at the end of the 1980s, the pendulum of public policy in nation after nation has swung toward the free market end of the economic spectrum. Regulatory and administrative barriers to doing business in foreign nations have come down, while those nations have often transformed their economies, privatizing state-owned enterprises, deregulating markets, increasing competition, and welcoming investment by foreign businesses. This has allowed businesses both large and small, from both advanced nations and developing nations, to expand internationally.

General Electric, which was profiled in the opening case, exemplifies this trend. Although long an international businesses, GE's international revenues have grown from 20 percent of the total in 1985 to over 50 percent today, and may hit 60 percent by the early years of the next decade. Today GE sees its main growth drivers not in the United States, but in the developing nations of the world, particularly India and China. In response to this, it is traveling down a road that many other companies, large and small, are also following. It is become more of a global business, with significant operations all over the world (including research centers in the United States, Europe, India, and China), an international workforce, and managers who are global in outlook, sophisticated in their understanding of national cultures, and recruited and promoted based on their ability, irrespective of their national origin.

At the same time, globalization has created new threats for businesses accustomed to dominating their domestic markets. Foreign companies have entered many formerly protected industries in developing nations, increasing competition and driving down prices. For three decades, U.S. automobile companies have been battling foreign enterprises, as Japanese, European, and now Korean companies have taken business from them. General Motors has seen its U.S. market share decline from more than 50 percent to about 25 percent, while Japan's Toyota has surpassed first Ford, and now GM, to become the largest automobile company in the world and the second largest producer in the United States behind GM.

As globalization unfolds, it is transforming industries and creating anxiety among those who believed their jobs were protected from foreign competition. Historically, while many workers in manufacturing industries worried about the impact foreign competition might have on their jobs, workers in service industries felt more secure. Now this too is changing. Advances in technology, lower transportation costs, and the rise of skilled workers in developing countries imply that many services no longer need to be performed where they are delivered. For example, accounting work is being outsourced from America to India. In 2005, some 400,000 individual tax returns were compiled in India. Indian accountants, trained in U.S. tax rules, perform work for U.S. accounting firms.[2] They access individual tax returns stored on computers in the United States, perform routine calculations, and save their work so that it can be inspected by a U.S. accountant, who then bills clients. As the best-selling author Thomas Friedman has argued, the world is becoming flat.[3] People living in developed nations no longer have the playing field tilted in their favor. Increasingly, enterprising individuals based in India, China, or Brazil have the same opportunities to better themselves as those living in Western Europe, the United States, or Canada—which is why GE has moved significant operations overseas to tap into that talent (see the opening case).

In this book we will take a close look at the issues introduced here, and at many more besides. We will explore how changes in regulations governing international trade and investment, when coupled with changes in political systems and technology, have dramatically altered the competitive playing field confronting many businesses. We will discuss the resulting opportunities and threats and review the different strategies that managers can pursue to exploit the opportunities and counter the threats. We will consider whether globalization benefits or harms national economies. We will look at what economic theory has to say about the outsourcing of manufacturing and service jobs to places such as India and China, and at the benefits and costs of outsourcing, not just to business firms and their employees, but also to entire economies. First, though, we need to an overview of the nature and process of globalization, and that is the function of Chapter 1.

What Is Globalization?

As used in this book, **globalization** refers to the shift toward a more integrated and interdependent world economy. Globalization has several facets, including the globalization of markets and the globalization of production.

LEARNING OBJECTIVE 1
Understand what is meant by the term *globalization*.

Globalization
The shift toward a more integrated and interdependent world economy.

THE GLOBALIZATION OF MARKETS The **globalization of markets** refers to the merging of historically distinct and separate national markets into one huge global marketplace. Falling barriers to cross-border trade have made it easier to sell internationally. It has been argued for some time that the tastes and preferences of consumers in different nations are beginning to converge on some global norm, thereby helping to create a global market.[4] Consumer products such as Citigroup credit cards, Coca-Cola soft drinks, Sony PlayStation video games, McDonald's hamburgers, Starbucks coffee, and IKEA furniture are frequently held up as prototypical examples of this trend. Firms such as those just cited are more than just benefactors of this trend; they are also facilitators of it. By offering the same basic product worldwide, they help to create a global market.

A company does not have to be the size of these multinational giants to facilitate, and benefit from, the globalization of markets. In the United States, for example, nearly 90 percent of firms that export are small businesses employing less than 100 people, and their share of total U.S. exports has grown steadily over the last decade to now exceed 20 percent.[5] Firms with less than 500 employees accounted for 97 percent of all U.S. exporters and almost 30 percent of all exports by value.[6] Typical of these is Hytech, a New York-based manufacturer of solar panels that generates 40 percent of its $3 million in annual sales from exports to five countries, or B&S Aircraft Alloys, another New York company whose exports account for 40 percent of its $8 million annual revenues.[7] The situation is similar in several other nations. In Germany, for example, which is one of the world's largest exporter, a staggering 98 percent of small and midsize companies have exposure to international markets, either via exports or international production.[8]

Despite the global prevalence of Citigroup credit cards, McDonald's hamburgers, Starbucks coffee, and IKEA stores, it is important not to push too far the view that national markets are giving way to the global market. As we shall see in later chapters, significant differences still exist among national markets along many relevant dimensions, including consumer tastes and preferences, distribution channels, culturally embedded

Globalization of Markets
The merging of historically distinct and separate national markets into one huge global marketplace.

value systems, business systems, and legal regulations. These differences frequently require companies to customize marketing strategies, product features, and operating practices to best match conditions in a particular country.

The most global markets currently are not markets for consumer products—where national differences in tastes and preferences are still often important enough to act as a brake on globalization—but markets for industrial goods and materials that serve a universal need the world over. These include the markets for commodities such as aluminum, oil, and wheat; for industrial products such as microprocessors, DRAMs (computer memory chips), and commercial jet aircraft; for computer software; and for financial assets from U.S. Treasury bills to eurobonds and futures on the Nikkei index or the Mexican peso.

In many global markets, the same firms frequently confront each other as competitors in nation after nation. Coca-Cola's rivalry with PepsiCo is a global one, as are the rivalries between General Motors and Toyota, Boeing and Airbus, Caterpillar and Komatsu in earthmoving equipment, General Electric and Rolls-Royce in aero engines, and Sony, Nintendo, and Microsoft in video games. If a firm moves into a nation not currently served by its rivals, many of them are sure to follow to prevent their competitor from gaining an advantage.[9] As firms follow each other around the world, they bring with them many of the assets that served them well in other national markets—including their products, operating strategies, marketing strategies, and brand names—creating some homogeneity across markets. Thus, greater uniformity replaces diversity. In an increasing number of industries, it is no longer meaningful to talk about "the German market," "the American market," "the Brazilian market," or "the Japanese market"; for many firms there is only the global market.

Globalization of Production
Sourcing goods and services from locations around the globe to take advantage of national differences in the cost and quality of various factors of production.

Factors of Production
Components of production such as labor, energy, land, and capital.

THE GLOBALIZATION OF PRODUCTION
The **globalization of production** refers to the sourcing of goods and services from locations around the globe to take advantage of national differences in the cost and quality of **factors of production** (such as labor, energy, land, and capital). By doing this, companies hope to lower their overall cost structure or improve the quality or functionality of their product offering, thereby allowing them to compete more effectively. Consider Boeing's 777, a commercial jet airliner. Eight Japanese suppliers make parts for the fuselage, doors, and wings; a supplier in Singapore makes the doors for the nose landing gear; three suppliers in Italy manufacture wing flaps; and so on.[10] In total, some 30 percent of the 777, by value, is built by foreign companies. For its most recent jet airliner, the 787, Boeing has pushed this trend even further, with some 65 percent of the total value of the aircraft scheduled to be outsourced to foreign companies, 35 percent of which will go to three major Japanese companies.[11]

Part of Boeing's rationale for outsourcing so much production to foreign suppliers is that these suppliers are the best in the world at their particular activity. A global web of suppliers yields a better final product, which enhances the chances of Boeing winning a greater share of total orders for aircraft than its global rival Airbus Industrie. Boeing also outsources some production to foreign countries to increase the chance that it will win significant orders from airlines based in that country.

For another example of a global web of activities, consider the example of Vizio. Vizio, an American company with just 75 employees, became one of the largest marketers of flat panel TVs in the United States in just four years by coordinating a global web of activities, and bringing together components manufactured in South Korea, China, and the United States; arranging for their assembly in Mexico; and then selling them in the United States.[12]

Early outsourcing efforts were primarily confined to manufacturing activities, such as those undertaken by Boeing and Vizio; increasingly, however, companies are taking

Country FOCUS

Outsourcing American Health Care

Conventional wisdom holds that health care is one of the industries least vulnerable to dislocation from globalization. After all, like many service businesses, health care is delivered where it is purchased, right? If an American goes to a hospital for an MRI scan, won't that scan be read by a local radiologist? And if the MRI scan shows that surgery is required, surely the surgery will be done at a local hospital in the United States. Until recently, this was true, but we are now witnessing the beginnings of globalization in this traditionally most local of industries.

Consider the MRI scan: The United States has a shortage of radiologists, the doctors who specialize in reading and interpreting diagnostic medical images, including X-rays, CT scans, MRI scans, and ultrasounds. Demand for radiologists is reportedly growing twice as fast as the rate at which medical schools are graduating radiologists with the skills and qualifications required to read medical images. This imbalance between supply and demand means that radiologists are expensive; an American radiologist can earn as much as $350,000 a year. In the early 2000s, an Indian radiologist working at the prestigious Massachusetts General Hospital, Dr. Sanjay Saini, thought he had found a clever way to deal with the shortage and expense—beam images over the Internet to India where they could be interpreted by radiologists. This would reduce the workload on America's radiologists and also cut costs. A radiologist in India might earn one-tenth of his or her U.S. counterpart. Plus, because India is on the opposite side of the globe, the images could be interpreted while it was nighttime in the United States and be ready for the attending physician when he or she arrived for work the following morning.

As for the surgery, here too we are witnessing the beginnings of an outsourcing trend. For example, recently Howard Staab, a 53-year-old uninsured self-employed carpenter from North Carolina had surgery to repair a leaking heart valve—in India! Mr. Staab flew to New Delhi, had the operation, and afterward toured the Taj Mahal, the price of which was bundled with that of the surgery. The cost, including airfare, totaled $10,000. If Mr. Staab's surgery had been performed in the United States, the cost would have been $60,000 and there would have been no visit to the Taj Mahal. Howard Staab is not alone. According to one estimate, some 150,000 Americans elected to have surgery outside of the United States in 2006, and predictions call for the numbers to grow rapidly. The management consultancy McKinsey & Co. predicts that medical tourism (overseas trips to have medical procedures performed) could be a $2.3 billion industry in India by 2012.

So will demand for American health services soon collapse as work moves offshore to places like India? That seems unlikely. Regulations, personal preferences, and practical considerations mean that the majority of health services will always be performed in the country where the patient resides. Consider the MRI scan: To safeguard patient care, U.S. regulations require that a radiologist be licensed in the state where the image was made and that he or she be certified by the hospital where care is being given. Given that not many radiologists in India have these qualifications, no more than a small fraction of images can be interpreted overseas. Another complication is that the U.S. government-sponsored medical insurance program, Medicare, will not pay for services done outside of the country. Nor will many private insurance plans, or not yet anyway. Moreover, most people would prefer to have care delivered close to home, and only in exceptional cases, such as when the procedure is not covered by their medical plan, are they likely to consider the foreign option. Still, most experts believe that the trends now in place will continue. Given that health care costs in America are the highest in the world, it seems likely that increasingly, a small but significant percentage of medical service will be performed in a country that is different from the one where the patient resides. The trend will certainly get a big boost if insurance companies start to offer enrollees the option of getting treatment abroad for expensive surgeries, as some are rumored to be considering.

Sources: G. Colvin, "Think Your Job Can't Be Sent to India?" *Fortune,* December 13, 2004, p. 80; A. Pollack, "Who's Reading Your X-Ray," *The New York Times,* November 16, 2003, pp. 1, 9; S. Rai, "Low Costs Lure Foreigners to India for Medical Care," *The New York Times,* April 7, 2005, p. C6; J. Solomon, "Traveling Cure: India's New Coup in Outsourcing," *The Wall Street Journal,* April 26, 2004, p. A1; J. Slater, "Increasing Doses in India," *Far Eastern Economic Review,* February 19, 2004, pp. 32–35; U. Kher, "Outsourcing Your Heart," *Time,* May 29, 2006, pp. 44–47; and "Sun, Sand and Scalpels," *The Economist,* March 10, 2007, p. 62.

advantage of modern communications technology, particularly the Internet, to outsource service activities to low-cost producers in other nations. The Internet has allowed hospitals to outsource some radiology work to India, where images from MRI scans and the like are read at night while U.S. physicians sleep and the results are ready for them in the morning (see the accompanying Country Focus for details). Many software companies, including IBM, now use Indian engineers to perform maintenance functions on software designed in the United States. The time difference allows Indian engineers to run debugging tests on software written in the United States when U.S. engineers sleep, transmitting the corrected code back to the United States over secure Internet connections so it is ready for U.S. engineers to work on the following day. Dispersing value-creation activities in this way can compress the time and lower the costs required to develop new software programs. Other companies, from computer makers to banks, are outsourcing customer service functions, such as customer call centers, to developing nations where labor is cheaper.

Robert Reich, who served as secretary of labor in the Bill Clinton administration, has argued that as a consequence of the trend exemplified by companies such as Boeing, IBM, and Vizio, in many cases it is becoming irrelevant to talk about American products, Japanese products, German products, or Korean products. Increasingly, according to Reich, the outsourcing of productive activities to different suppliers results in the creation of products that are global in nature, that is, "global products."[13] But as with the globalization of markets, companies must be careful not to push the globalization of production too far. As we will see in later chapters, substantial impediments still make it difficult for firms to achieve the optimal dispersion of their productive activities to locations around the globe. These impediments include formal and informal barriers to trade between countries, barriers to foreign direct investment, transportation costs, and issues associated with economic and political risk. For example, government regulations ultimately limit the ability of hospitals to outsource the process of interpreting MRI scans to developing nations where radiologists are cheaper.

Nevertheless, the globalization of markets and production will continue. Modern firms are important actors in this trend, their very actions fostering increased globalization. These firms, however, are merely responding in an efficient manner to changing conditions in their operating environment—as well they should.

The Emergence of Global Institutions

As markets globalize and an increasing proportion of business activity transcends national borders, institutions are needed to help manage, regulate, and police the global marketplace, and to promote the establishment of multinational treaties to govern the global business system. Over the past 60-plus years, a number of important global institutions have been created to help perform these functions, including the **General Agreement on Tariffs and Trade (GATT)** and its successor, the World Trade Organization (WTO); the International Monetary Fund (IMF) and its sister institution, the World Bank; and the United Nations (UN). All these institutions were created by voluntary agreement between individual nation-states, and their functions are enshrined in international treaties.

The **World Trade Organization** (like the GATT before it) is primarily responsible for policing the world trading system and making sure nation-states adhere to the rules laid down in trade treaties signed by WTO member states. As of 2008, 151 nations that collectively accounted for 97 percent of world trade were WTO members, thereby giving the organization enormous scope and influence. The WTO is also responsible for facilitating the establishment of additional multinational agreements between WTO member states. Over its entire history, and that of the GATT before it, the WTO has promoted the lowering of barriers to cross-border trade and investment. In doing so, the WTO has been the instrument of its member states, which have sought to create a more open global business system unencumbered by barriers to trade and investment between countries. Without an institution such as the WTO, the globalization of markets and production is unlikely to have proceeded as far as it has. However, as we shall see in this chapter and in Chapter 6 when we look closely at

General Agreement on Tariffs and Trade (GATT)
International treaty that committed signatories to lowering barriers to the free flow of goods across national borders; led to the WTO.

World Trade Organization
The organization that succeeded the General Agreement on Tariffs and Trade and now acts to police the world trading system.

the WTO, critics charge that the organization is usurping the national sovereignty of individual nation-states.

The **International Monetary Fund** and the **World Bank** were both created in 1944 by 44 nations that met at Bretton Woods, New Hampshire. The IMF was established to maintain order in the international monetary system; the World Bank was set up to promote economic development. In the 65 years since their creation, both institutions have emerged as significant players in the global economy. The World Bank is the less controversial of the two sister institutions. It has focused on making low-interest loans to cash-strapped governments in poor nations that wish to undertake significant infrastructure investments (such as building dams or roads).

The United Nations has the important goal of improving the well-being of people around the world.

The IMF is often seen as the lender of last resort to nation-states whose economies are in turmoil and currencies are losing value against those of other nations. Repeatedly during the past decade, for example, the IMF has lent money to the governments of troubled states, including Argentina, Indonesia, Mexico, Russia, South Korea, Thailand, and Turkey. IMF loans come with strings attached, however; in return for loans, the IMF requires nation-states to adopt specific economic policies aimed at returning their troubled economies to stability and growth. These requirements have sparked controversy. Some critics charge that the IMF's policy recommendations are often inappropriate; others maintain that by telling national governments what economic policies they must adopt, the IMF, like the WTO, is usurping the sovereignty of nation-states. We shall look at the debate over the role of the IMF in Chapter 10.

The **United Nations** was established October 24, 1945, by 51 countries committed to preserving peace through international cooperation and collective security. Today nearly every nation in the world belongs to the United Nations; membership now totals 191 countries. When states become members of the United Nations, they agree to accept the obligations of the UN Charter, an international treaty that establishes basic principles of international relations. According to the charter, the UN has four purposes: to maintain international peace and security, to develop friendly relations among nations, to cooperate in solving international problems and in promoting respect for human rights, and to be a center for harmonizing the actions of nations. Although the UN is perhaps best known for its peacekeeping role, one of the organization's central mandates is the promotion of higher standards of living, full employment, and conditions of economic and social progress and development—all issues that are central to the creation of a vibrant global economy. As much as 70 percent of the work of the UN system is devoted to accomplishing this mandate. To do so, the UN works closely with other international institutions such as the World Bank. Guiding the work is the belief that eradicating poverty and improving the well-being of people everywhere are necessary steps in creating conditions for lasting world peace.[14]

International Monetary Fund
International institution set up to maintain order in the international monetary system.

World Bank
International organization set up to promote economic development, primarily by offering low-interest loans to cash-strapped governments of poorer nations.

United Nations
An international organization made up of 191 countries charged with keeping international peace, developing cooperation between nations, and promoting human rights.

Drivers of Globalization

Two macro factors underlie the trend toward greater globalization.[15] The first is the decline in barriers to the free flow of goods, services, and capital that has occurred since the end of World War II. The second factor is technological change, particularly the dramatic developments in recent years in communication, information processing, and transportation technologies.

LEARNING OBJECTIVE 2
Be familiar with the main drivers of globalization.

DECLINING TRADE AND INVESTMENT BARRIERS   During the 1920s and 30s many of the world's nation-states erected formidable barriers to international trade and foreign direct investment. **International trade** occurs when a firm exports goods or services to consumers in another country. **Foreign direct investment (FDI)** occurs when a firm invests resources in business activities outside its home country. Many of the barriers to international trade took the form of high tariffs on imports of manufactured goods. The typical aim of such tariffs was to protect domestic industries from foreign competition. One consequence, however, was "beggar thy neighbor" retaliatory trade policies, with countries progressively raising trade barriers against each other. Ultimately, this depressed world demand and contributed to the Great Depression of the 1930s.

Having learned from this experience, the advanced industrial nations of the West committed themselves after World War II to removing barriers to the free flow of goods, services, and capital between nations.[16] This goal was enshrined in the General Agreement on Tariffs and Trade. Under the umbrella of GATT, eight rounds of negotiations among member states (now numbering 151) have worked to lower barriers to the free flow of goods and services. The most recent negotiations to be completed, known as the Uruguay Round, were finalized in December 1993. The Uruguay Round further reduced trade barriers; extended GATT to cover services as well as manufactured goods; provided enhanced protection for patents, trademarks, and copyrights; and established the World Trade Organization to police the international trading system.[17] Table 1.1 summarizes the impact of GATT agreements on average tariff rates for manufactured goods. As can be seen, average tariff rates have fallen significantly since 1950 and now stand at about 4 percent.

In late 2001, the WTO launched a new round of talks aimed at further liberalizing the global trade and investment framework. For this meeting, it picked the remote location of Doha in the Persian Gulf state of Qatar. At Doha, the member states of the WTO staked out an agenda. The talks were scheduled to last three years, although it now looks as if they may go on significantly longer. The agenda includes cutting tariffs on industrial goods, services, and agricultural products; phasing out subsidies to agricultural producers; reducing barriers to cross-border investment; and limiting the use of antidumping laws. The biggest gain may come from discussion on agricultural products; average agricultural tariff rates are still about 40 percent, and rich nations spend some $300 billion a year in subsidies to support their farm sectors. The world's poorer nations have the most to gain from any reduction in agricultural tariffs and subsidies; such reforms would give them access to the markets of the developed world.[18]

In addition to reducing trade barriers, many countries have also been progressively removing restrictions to foreign direct investment. According to the United Nations,

International Trade
Occurs when a firm exports goods or services to consumers in another country.

Foreign Direct Investment (FDI)
Occurs when a firm invests resources in business activities outside its home country.

table 1.1

Average Tariff Rates on Manufactured Products as Percent of Value

Source: 1913–90 data are from "Who Wants to Be a Giant?" *The Economist: A Survey of the Multinationals,* June 24, 1995, pp. 3–4. Copyright © The Economist Books, Ltd. The 2006 data are from World Trade Organization, *2007 World Trade Report* (Geneva: WTO, 2007).

	1913	1950	1990	2006
France	21%	18%	5.9%	3.9%
Germany	20	26	5.9	3.9
Italy	18	25	5.9	3.9
Japan	30	—	5.3	2.3
Holland	5	11	5.9	3.9
Sweden	20	9	4.4	3.9
Great Britain	—	23	5.9	3.9
United States	44	14	4.8	3.2

some 90 percent of the 2,444 changes made worldwide between 1992 and 2006 in the laws governing foreign direct investment created a more favorable environment for FDI.[19] The desire of governments to facilitate FDI also has been reflected in a dramatic increase in the number of bilateral investment treaties designed to protect and promote investment between two countries. As of 2006, 2,573 such treaties involved more than 160 countries, a 12-fold increase from the 181 treaties that existed in 1980.[20]

Such trends have been driving both the globalization of markets and the globalization of production. The lowering of barriers to international trade enables firms to view the world, rather than a single country, as their market. The lowering of trade and investment barriers also allows firms to base production at the optimal location for that activity. Thus, a firm might design a product in one country, produce component parts in two other countries, assemble the product in yet another country, and then export the finished product around the world.

According to WTO data, the volume of world merchandise trade has grown faster than the world economy since 1950 (see Figure 1.1).[21] From 1970 to 2005, the volume of world merchandise trade expanded 28-fold, outstripping the expansion of world production, which grew close to eight times in real terms. (World merchandise trade includes trade in manufactured goods, agricultural goods, and mining products, but not services.) What Figure 1.1 does not show is that since the mid-1980s the value of international trade in services has also grown robustly. Trade in services now accounts for about 20 percent of the value of all international trade. Increasingly, international trade in services has been driven by advances in communications, which allow corporations to outsource service activities to different locations around the globe (see the opening case). Thus, as noted earlier, many corporations in the developed world outsource customer service functions, from software maintenance activities to customer call centers, to developing nations where labor costs are lower.

The data summarized in Figure 1.1 imply several things. First, more firms are doing what Boeing does with the 777 and 787 and Vizio with flat-panel TVs: dispersing parts of their production process to different locations around the globe to drive down production costs and increase product quality. Second, the economies of the world's nation-states are becoming more intertwined. As trade expands, nations are becoming increasingly dependent on each other for important goods and services. Third, the world has become significantly wealthier since 1950, and the implication is that rising trade is the engine that has helped to pull the global economy along.

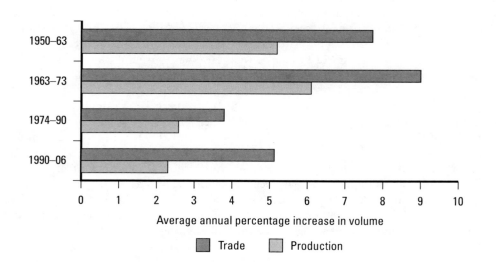

1.1 figure

Growth in World Merchandise Trade and Production, 1950–2006 (Average annual % increase in volume)

Source: Constructed by the author from World Trade Organization, *World Trade Statistics 2007* (Geneva: WTO, 2007).

The evidence also suggests that foreign direct investment is playing an increasing role in the global economy as firms increase their cross-border investments. The average yearly outflow of FDI increased from $25 billion in 1975 to a record $1.2 trillion in 2000. It fell back in the early 2000s, but by 2007 FDI flows hit $1.5 trillion.[22] Over this period, the flow of FDI accelerated faster than the growth in world trade and world output. For example, between 1992 and 2007, the total flow of FDI from all countries increased more than eightfold while world trade by value grew by some 150 percent and world output by around 45 percent.[23] As a result of the strong FDI flow, by 2006 the global stock of FDI exceeded $12 trillion. At least 78,000 parent companies had 780,000 affiliates in foreign markets that collectively employed more than 70 million people abroad and generated value accounting for about one-tenth of global GDP. The foreign affiliates of multinationals had an estimated $25 trillion in global sales, much higher than the value of global exports, which stood at close to $14.1 trillion.[24]

The globalization of markets and production and the resulting growth of world trade, foreign direct investment, and imports all imply that firms are finding their home markets under attack from foreign competitors. This is true in Japan, where U.S. companies such as Kodak, Procter & Gamble, and Merrill Lynch are expanding their presence. It is true in the United States, where Japanese automobile firms have taken market share away from General Motors and Ford. And it is true in Europe, where the once-dominant Dutch company Philips has seen its market share in the consumer electronics industry taken by Japan's JVC, Matsushita, and Sony and Korea's Samsung and LG. The growing integration of the world economy into a single, huge marketplace is increasing the intensity of competition in a range of manufacturing and service industries.

However, declining barriers to cross-border trade and investment cannot be taken for granted. As we shall see in subsequent chapters, demands for "protection" from foreign competitors are still often heard in countries around the world, including the United States. Although a return to the restrictive trade policies of the 1920s and 30s is unlikely, it is not clear whether the political majority in the industrialized world favors further reductions in trade barriers. If trade barriers decline no further, at least for the time being, this will put a brake upon the globalization of both markets and production.

THE ROLE OF TECHNOLOGICAL CHANGE
The lowering of trade barriers made globalization of markets and production a theoretical possibility. Technological change has made it a tangible reality. Since the end of World War II, the world has seen major advances in communication, information processing, and transportation technology, including the explosive emergence of the Internet and World Wide Web. Telecommunications is creating a global audience. Transportation is creating a global village. From Buenos Aires to Boston, and from Birmingham to Beijing, ordinary people are watching MTV, they're wearing blue jeans, and they're listening to iPods as they commute to work.

Microprocessors and Telecommunications
Perhaps the single most important innovation has been development of the microprocessor, which enabled the explosive growth of high-power, low-cost computing, vastly increasing the amount of information that can be processed by individuals and firms. The microprocessor also underlies many recent advances in telecommunications technology. Over the past 30 years, global communications have been revolutionized by developments in satellite, optical fiber, and wireless technologies, and now the Internet and the World Wide Web (WWW). These technologies rely on the microprocessor to encode, transmit, and decode the vast amount of information that flows along these electronic highways. The cost of microprocessors continues to fall, while their power increases (a phenomenon known as **Moore's law,** which predicts that the power of microprocessor technology

Moore's Law
The premise that the power of microprocessor technology doubles and its cost of production drops in half every 18 months.

doubles and its cost of production falls in half every 18 months).[25] As this happens, the cost of global communications plummets, which lowers the costs of coordinating and controlling a global organization. Thus, between 1930 and 1990, the cost of a three-minute phone call between New York and London fell from $244.65 to $3.32.[26] By 1998, it had plunged to just 36 cents for consumers, and much lower rates were available for businesses.[27] Indeed, by using the Internet, the cost of an international phone call is rapidly plummeting toward just a few cents per minute.

The Internet and World Wide Web   The rapid growth of the World Wide Web is the latest expression of this development. In 1990, fewer than 1 million users were connected to the Internet. By 1995, the figure had risen to 50 million. By December 2007, the Internet had 1.3 billion users.[28] The WWW has developed into the information backbone of the global economy. In the United States alone, some $250 billion of goods and services were expected to be sold online to retail customers in 2007, up from almost nothing in 1997.[29] Viewed globally, the Web is emerging as an equalizer. It rolls back some of the constraints of location, scale, and time zones.[30] The Web makes it much easier for buyers and sellers to find each other, wherever they may be located and whatever their size. It allows businesses, both small and large, to expand their global presence at a lower cost than ever before.

Transportation Technology   In addition to developments in communication technology, several major innovations in transportation technology have occurred since World War II. In economic terms, the most important are probably the development of commercial jet aircraft and super-freighters and the introduction of containerization, which simplifies transshipment from one mode of transport to another. The advent of commercial jet travel, by reducing the time needed to get from one location to another, has effectively shrunk the globe. In terms of travel time, New York is now "closer" to Tokyo than it was to Philadelphia in the Colonial days.

Before the advent of containerization, it could take several days and several hundred longshoremen to unload a ship and reload goods onto trucks and trains.

Containerization has revolutionized the transportation business, significantly lowering the costs of shipping goods over long distances. Before the advent of containerization, moving goods from one mode of transport to another was very labor-intensive, lengthy, and costly. It could take days and several hundred longshoremen to unload a ship and reload goods onto trucks and trains. With the advent of widespread containerization in the 1970s and 1980s, the whole process can now be executed by a handful of longshore-men in a couple of days. Since 1980, the world's containership fleet has more than qua-drupled, reflecting in part the growing volume of international trade and in part the switch to this mode of transportation. As a result of the efficiency gains associated with containerization, transportation costs have plummeted, making it much more economical to ship goods around the globe, thereby helping to drive the globalization of markets and production. Between 1920 and 1990, the average ocean freight and port charges per ton of U.S. export and import cargo fell from $95 to $29 (in 1990 dollars).[31] The cost of ship-ping freight per ton-mile on railroads in the United States fell from 3.04 cents in 1985 to 2.3 cents in 2000, largely as a result of efficiency gains from the widespread use of con-tainers.[32] An increased share of cargo now goes by air. Between 1955 and 1999, average air transportation revenue per ton-kilometer fell by more than 80 percent.[33] Reflecting the falling cost of airfreight, by the early 2000s air shipments accounted for 28 percent of the value of U.S. trade, up from 7 percent in 1965.[34]

Implications for the Globalization of Production   As transportation costs associated with the globalization of production declined, dispersal of production to geo-graphically separate locations became more economical. As a result of the technological innovations discussed earlier, the real costs of information processing and communication have fallen dramatically in the past two decades. These developments make it possible for a firm to create and then manage a globally dispersed production system, further facilitat-ing the globalization of production. A worldwide communications network has become essential for many international businesses. For example, Dell uses the Internet to coor-dinate and control a globally dispersed production system to such an extent that it holds only three days' worth of inventory at its assembly locations. Dell's Internet-based system records orders for computer equipment as they are submitted by customers via the com-pany's Web site, then immediately transmits the resulting orders for components to vari-ous suppliers around the world, which have a real-time look at Dell's order flow and can adjust their production schedules accordingly. Given the low cost of airfreight, Dell can use air transportation to speed up the delivery of critical components to meet unantici-pated demand shifts without delaying the shipment of final product to consumers. Dell also has used modern communications technology to outsource its customer service op-erations to India. When U.S. customers call Dell with a service inquiry, they are routed to Bangalore in India, where English-speaking service personnel handle the call.

The Internet has been a major force facilitating international trade in services. It is the Web that allows hospitals in Chicago to send MRI scans to India for analysis, accounting offices in San Francisco to outsource routine tax preparation work to accountants living in the Philippines, and software testers in India to debug code writ-ten by developers in Redmond, Washington, the headquarters of Microsoft. We are probably still in the early stages of this development. As Moore's law continues to advance and telecommunications bandwidth continues to increase, almost any work processes that can be digitalized will be, and this will allow that work to be performed wherever in the world it is most efficient and effective to do so.

The development of commercial jet aircraft has also helped knit together the world-wide operations of many international businesses. Using jet travel, an American man-ager need spend a day at most traveling to his or her firm's European or Asian operations. This enables the manager to oversee a globally dispersed production system.

Implications for the Globalization of Markets In addition to the globalization of production, technological innovations have also facilitated the globalization of markets. Low-cost global communications networks such as the World Wide Web are helping to create electronic global marketplaces. As noted above, low-cost transportation has made it more economical to ship products around the world, thereby helping to create global markets. For example, due to the tumbling costs of shipping goods by air, roses grown in Ecuador can be cut and sold in New York two days later while they are still fresh. This has given rise to an industry in Ecuador that did not exist 20 years ago and now supplies a global market for roses. In addition, low-cost jet travel has resulted in the mass movement of people between countries. This has reduced the cultural distance between countries and is bringing about some convergence of consumer tastes and preferences. At the same time, global communication networks and global media are creating a worldwide culture. U.S. television networks such as CNN, MTV, and HBO are now received in many countries, and Hollywood films are shown the world over. In any society, the media are primary conveyors of culture; as global media develop, we must expect the evolution of something akin to a global culture. A logical result of this evolution is the emergence of global markets for consumer products. The first signs of this are already apparent. It is now as easy to find a McDonald's restaurant in Tokyo as it is in New York, to buy an iPod in Rio as it is in Berlin, and to buy Gap jeans in Paris as it is in San Francisco.

Despite these trends, we must be careful not to overemphasize their importance. While modern communication and transportation technologies are ushering in the "global village," significant national differences remain in culture, consumer preferences, and business practices. A firm that ignores differences between countries does so at its peril. We shall stress this point repeatedly throughout this book and elaborate on it in later chapters.

The Changing Demographics of the Global Economy

Hand in hand with the trend toward globalization has been a fairly dramatic change in the demographics of the global economy over the past 40 years. As late as the 1960s, four stylized facts described the demographics of the global economy. The first was U.S. dominance in the world economy and world trade picture. The second was U.S. dominance in world foreign direct investment. Related to this, the third fact was the dominance of large, multinational U.S. firms on the international business scene. The fourth was that roughly half the globe—the centrally planned economies of the Communist world—were off-limits to Western international businesses. As will be explained below, all four of these qualities either have changed or are now changing rapidly.

LEARNING OBJECTIVE 3 Appreciate the changing nature of the global economy.

THE CHANGING WORLD OUTPUT AND WORLD TRADE PICTURE In the early 1960s, the United States was still by far the world's dominant industrial power. In 1963 the United States accounted for 40.3 percent of world economic activity, measured by gross domestic product (GDP). By 2007, the United States accounted for 20.7 percent of world GDP, still the world's largest industrial power but down significantly in relative size since the 1960s (see Table 1.2). Nor was the United States the only developed nation to see its relative standing slip. The same occurred to Germany, France, and the United Kingdom, all nations that were among the first to industrialize. This change in the U.S. position was not an absolute decline, since the U.S. economy grew at a robust average annual rate of more than 3 percent from 1963 to 2007 (the economies of Germany, France, and the United Kingdom also grew during this time). Rather, it was a relative decline, reflecting the faster economic growth of several other economies, particularly in

table 1.2

The Changing Demographics of World GDP and Trade

Sources: IMF, *World Economic Outlook*, April 2008. Data for 1963 are from N. Hood and J. Young, *The Economics of the Multinational Enterprise* (New York: Longman, 1973). The GDP data are based on purchasing power parity figures, which adjust the value of GDP to reflect the cost of living in various economies.

Country	Share of World Output, 1963	Share of World GDP, 2007	Share of World Exports, 2006
United States	40.3%	20.7	9.8%
Germany	9.7	4.2	8.9
France	6.3	3.1	4.3
Italy	3.4	2.7	3.5
United Kingdom	6.5	3.2	4.6
Canada	3.0	1.9	3.1
Japan	5.5	6.5	5.0
China	NA	11.5	7.2

Asia. For example, as can be seen from Table 1.2, from 1963 to 2007, China's share of world GDP increased from a trivial amount to 11.5 percent. Other countries that markedly increased their share of world output included Japan, Thailand, Malaysia, Taiwan, and South Korea (note that GDP data in Table 1.2 are based on purchasing power parity figures, which adjust the value of GDP to reflect the cost of living in various economies).

By the end of the 1980s, the U.S. position as the world's leading exporter was threatened. Over the past 40 years, U.S. dominance in export markets has waned as Japan, Germany, and a number of newly industrialized countries such as South Korea and China have taken a larger share of world exports. During the 1960s, the United States routinely accounted for 20 percent of world exports of manufactured goods. But as Table 1.2 shows, the U.S. share of world exports of goods and services had slipped to 9.8 percent by 2006. Despite the fall, the United States still remained the world's largest exporter, ahead of Germany, Japan, France, and the fast-rising economic power, China. If China's rapid rise continues, however, it could soon overtake the United States as the world's largest economy and largest exporter.

As emerging economies such as China, India, and Brazil continue to grow, a further relative decline in the share of world output and world exports accounted for by the United States and other long-established developed nations seems likely. By itself, this is not bad. The relative decline of the United States reflects the growing economic development and industrialization of the world economy, as opposed to any absolute decline in the health of the U.S. economy, which by many measures is stronger than ever.

Most forecasts now predict a rapid rise in the share of world output accounted for by developing nations such as China, India, Indonesia, Thailand, South Korea, Mexico, and Brazil, and a commensurate decline in the share enjoyed by rich industrialized countries such as Great Britain, Germany, Japan, and the United States. If current trends continue, the Chinese economy could ultimately be

Another Perspective

India's Tech Export Business Surges and EMC Gains

India's computer-software and services industry, which started out about 20 years ago, undertaking routine outsourced office functions for companies based in the United States and United Kingdom, has extended its scope of operations and grown into a $23.6 billion export business. The industry employed 1.3 million people in 2006, according to the National Association of Software and Service Companies (Nasscom), India's lobbying group. They estimate 382,000 students will graduate with engineering qualifications in 2006–2007.

EMC Corp, the world's biggest maker of storage computers and software, plans to more than double its investment in India to $500 million by 2010 to expand sales, research, and the local market. Research will account for most of EMC's spending because India's primary draw is the quality of the country's technology professionals. Wages are about one-sixth of those in the united States. However, EMC says there are countries lower in cost than India and that the company is going for quality investment. What do you think? (Ashok Bhattacharjee, *Bloomberg News*, June 21, 2006)

Country FOCUS

India's Software Sector

Some 25 years ago a number of small software enterprises were established in Bangalore, India. Typical of these enterprises was Infosys Technologies, which was started by seven Indian entrepreneurs with about $1,000 between them. Infosys now has annual revenues of $22 billion and some 60,000 employees, but it is just one of over a hundred software companies clustered around Bangalore, which has become the epicenter of India's fast-growing information technology sector. From a standing start in the mid-1980s, by 2006 this sector was generating revenues of almost $40 billion, and combined software services, hardware sales, and business process outsourcing exports totaled $31.3 billion. India had also emerged as home to some of the fastest growing software service companies on the planet, including Infosys, Wipro, Tata Consultancy Services, and HCL Technologies.

The growth of the Indian software sector is based on four factors. First, the country has an abundant supply of engineering talent. Every year Indian universities graduate some 400,000 engineers. Second, labor costs in India are low. The cost to hire an Indian graduate is roughly 12 percent of the cost of hiring an American graduate. Third, many Indians are fluent in English, which makes coordination between Western firms and India easier. Fourth, due to time differences, Indians can work while Americans sleep. This means, for example, that software code written in America during the day can be tested in India and shipped back via the Internet to America in time for the start of work the following day. In other words, by utilizing Indian labor and the Internet, software enterprises can create global software development factories that are working 24 hours a day.

Initially Indian software enterprises focused on the low end of the software industry, supplying basic software development and testing services to Western firms. But as the industry has grown in size and sophistication, Indian firms have moved upmarket. Today the leading Indian companies compete directly with the likes of IBM and EDS for large software development projects, business process outsourcing contracts, and information technology consulting services. These markets are booming. Estimates suggested that global spending on information technology outsourcing would rise from $193 billion in 2004 to $260 billion in 2009, with Indian enterprises capturing a larger slice of the pie. One response of Western firms to this emerging competitive threat has been to invest in India to garner the same kind of economic advantages that Indian firms enjoy. IBM, for example, has invested $2 billion in its Indian operations and now has 53,000 employees located there, more than in any other country except America. In early 2007 it announced plans to invest another $6 billion over the next few years in India. Microsoft too has made major investments in India, including an R&D center in Hyderabad that employs 900 people, and was located there specifically to tap into talented Indian engineers who did not want to move to the United States.

Sources: "America's Pain, Indian's Gain: Outsourcing," *The Economist,* January 11, 2003, p. 59; "The World Is Our Oyster," *The Economist,* October 7, 2006, pp. 9–10; and "IBM and Globalization: Hungry Tiger, Dancing Elephant," *The Economist,* April 7, 2007, pp. 67–69.

larger than that of the United States on a purchasing power parity basis, while the economy of India will approach that of Germany. The World Bank has estimated that today's developing nations may account for more than 60 percent of world economic activity by 2020, while today's rich nations, which currently account for more than 55 percent of world economic activity, may account for only about 38 percent. Forecasts are not always correct, but these suggest that a shift in the economic geography of the world is now under way, although the magnitude of that shift is not totally evident. For international businesses, the implications of this changing economic geography are clear: Many of tomorrow's economic opportunities may be found in the developing nations of the world, and many of tomorrow's most capable competitors will probably also emerge from these regions. An example is the dramatic expansion of India's software sector, which is profiled in the accompanying Country Focus.

The Changing Foreign Direct Investment Picture Reflecting the dominance of the United States in the global economy, U.S. firms accounted for 66.3 percent of worldwide foreign direct investment flows in the 1960s. British firms were second, accounting for 10.5 percent, while Japanese firms were a distant eighth, with only 2 percent. The dominance of U.S. firms was so great that books were written about the economic threat posed to Europe by U.S. corporations.[35] Several European governments, most notably France, talked of limiting inward investment by U.S. firms.

However, as the barriers to the free flow of goods, services, and capital fell, and as other countries increased their shares of world output, non-U.S. firms increasingly began to invest across national borders. The motivation for much of this foreign direct investment by non-U.S. firms was the desire to disperse production activities to optimal locations and to build a direct presence in major foreign markets. Thus, beginning in the 1970s, European and Japanese firms began to shift labor-intensive manufacturing operations from their home markets to developing nations where labor costs were lower. In addition, many Japanese firms invested in North America and Europe—often as a hedge against unfavorable currency movements and the possible imposition of trade barriers. For example, Toyota, the Japanese automobile company, rapidly increased its investment in automobile production facilities in the United States and Europe during the late 1980s and early 1990s. Toyota executives believed that an increasingly strong Japanese yen would price Japanese automobile exports out of foreign markets; therefore, production in the most important foreign markets, as opposed to exports from Japan, made sense. Toyota also undertook these investments to head off growing political pressures in the United States and Europe to restrict Japanese automobile exports into those markets.

One consequence of these developments is illustrated in Figure 1.2, which shows how the stock of foreign direct investment by the world's six most important national sources—the United States, the United Kingdom, Germany, the Netherlands, France, and Japan—changed between 1980 and 2006. (The **stock of foreign direct investment** refers to the total cumulative value of foreign investments.) Figure 1.2 also shows the stock accounted for by firms from developing economies. The share of the total stock accounted for by U.S. firms declined from about 38 percent in 1980 to 19.1 percent in 2006. Meanwhile, the shares accounted for by France and the world's developing nations increased markedly. The rise in the share of FDI stock accounted for by developing nations reflects a growing trend for firms from these countries to invest outside their borders. In 2006, firms based in developing nations accounted for

Stock of Foreign Direct Investment
The total accumulated value of foreign-owned assets at a given time.

figure **1.2**

Percentage Share of Total FDI Stock, 1980–2006

Source: UNCTAD, *World Investment Report, 2007* (Geneva: United Nations, 2007).

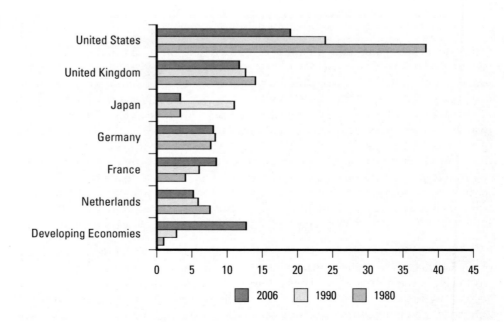

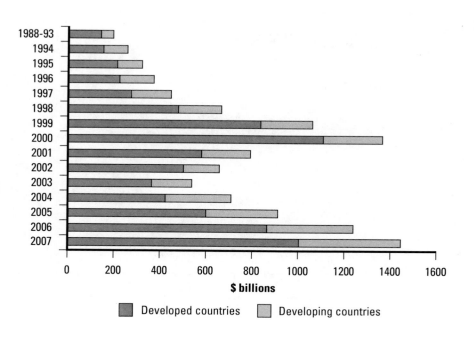

1.3 figure

FDI Inflows, 1988–2007

Source: UNCTAD, *World Investment Report, 2007* (Geneva. United Nations, 2007), and UNCTAD Press release, "FDI Flows Reach New Record in 2007," January 8, 2008.

$ billions

■ Developed countries   ■ Developing countries

12.8 percent of the stock of foreign direct investment, up from only 1.1 percent in 1980. Firms based in Hong Kong, South Korea, Singapore, Taiwan, India, and mainland China accounted for much of this investment.

Figure 1.3 illustrates two other important trends—the sustained growth in cross-border flows of foreign direct investment that occurred during the 1990s and the importance of developing nations as the destination of foreign direct investment. Throughout the 1990s, the amount of investment directed at both developed and developing nations increased dramatically, a trend that reflects the increasing internationalization of business corporations. A surge in foreign direct investment from 1998 to 2000 was followed by a slump from 2001 to 2003 associated with a slowdown in global economic activity after the collapse of the financial bubble of the late 1990s and 2000. However, the growth of foreign direct investment resumed in 2004 and continued through 2007, when it hit record levels. Among developing nations, the largest recipient of foreign direct investment has been China, which in 2004–2007 received $60 billion to $70 billion a year in inflows. As we shall see later in this book, the sustained flow of foreign investment into developing nations is an important stimulus for economic growth in those countries, which bodes well for the future of countries such as China, Mexico, and Brazil, all leading beneficiaries of this trend.

THE CHANGING NATURE OF THE MULTINATIONAL ENTERPRISE

A **multinational enterprise (MNE)** is any business that has productive activities in two or more countries. Since the 1960s, two notable trends in the demographics of the multinational enterprise have been (1) the rise of non-U.S. multinationals and (2) the growth of mini-multinationals.

Multinational Enterprise (MNE)
Any business that has productive activities in two or more countries.

Non-U.S. Multinationals   In the 1960s, global business activity was dominated by large U.S. multinational corporations. With U.S. firms accounting for about two-thirds of foreign direct investment during the 1960s, one would expect most multinationals to be U.S. enterprises. According to the data summarized in Figure 1.4, in 1973, 48.5 percent of the world's 260 largest multinationals were U.S. firms. The second-largest source

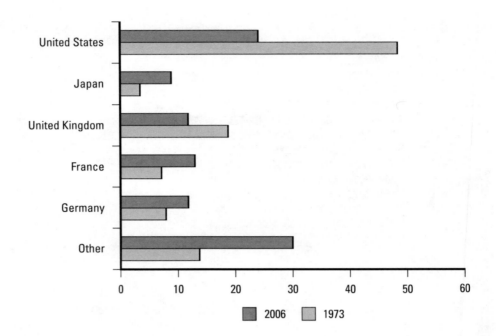

figure 1.4

National Origin of Largest Multinational Enterprises, 1973 and 2006

country was the United Kingdom, with 18.8 percent of the largest multinationals. Japan accounted for 3.5 percent of the world's largest multinationals at the time. The large number of U.S. multinationals reflected U.S. economic dominance in the three decades after World War II, while the large number of British multinationals reflected that country's industrial dominance in the early decades of the 20th century.

By 2006 things had shifted significantly. Some 24 of the world's 100 largest non-financial multinationals were now U.S. enterprises; 13 were French; 12, German; 12, British; and 9, Japanese.[36] Although the 1973 data are not strictly comparable with the later data, they illustrate the trend (the 1973 figures are based on the largest 260 firms, whereas the later figures are based on the largest 100 multinationals). The globalization of the world economy has resulted in a relative decline in the dominance of U.S. firms in the global marketplace.

According to UN data, the ranks of the world's largest 100 multinationals are still dominated by firms from developed economies.[37] However, seven firms from developing economies had entered the UN's list of the 100 largest multinationals by 2006. The largest was Hutchison Whampoa of Hong Kong, China, which ranked 20.[38] The growth in the number of multinationals from developing economies is evident when we look at smaller firms. By 2005, the largest 50 multinationals from developing economies had foreign sales of $323 billion out of total sales of $738 billion and employed 1.1 million people outside of their home countries. Some 64 percent of the largest 100 multinationals from developing nations came from Hong King, Taiwan, Singapore, and mainland China. Other nations with multiple entries on the list included South Korea, Brazil, Mexico, and Malaysia. We can reasonably expect more growth of new multinational enterprises from the world's developing nations. Firms from developing nations can be expected to emerge as important competitors in global markets, further shifting the axis of the world economy away from North America and Western Europe and threatening the long dominance of Western companies. One such rising competitor, Hisense, one of China's premier manufacturers of consumer appliances and telecommunications equipment, is profiled in the accompanying Management Focus.

Management FOCUS

China's Hisense—An Emerging Multinational

Hisense is rapidly emerging as one of China's leading multinationals. Like many other Chinese corporations, Hisense traces its origins back to a state-owned manufacturer, Qingdao No. 2 Radio Factory, which was established in 1969 with just 10 employees. In the 1970s the state-owned factory diversified into the manufacture of TV sets, and by the 1980s it was one of China's leading manufacturers of color TVs, making sets designed by Matsushita under license. In 1992 a 35-year-old engineer named Zhou Houjian was appointed head of the enterprise. In 1994 the shackles of state ownership were relaxed when the Hisense Co. Ltd. was established, with Zhou as CEO (he is now chairman of the board).

Under Zhou's leadership, Hisense entered a period of rapid growth, product diversification, and global expansion. By 2006 the company had sales of $3.3 billion and had emerged as one of China's premier makers of TV sets (with an 11 percent share of the domestic market), air conditioners, refrigerators, personal computers, and telecommunications equipment. In 2006, Hisense sold about 10 million TV sets, 3 million air conditioners, 4 million CDMA wireless phones, 6 million refrigerators, and 1 million personal computers. International sales accounted for $490 million, or more than 15 percent of total revenue. The company had established overseas manufacturing subsidiaries in Algeria, Hungary, Iran, Pakistan, and South Africa and was growing rapidly in developing markets where it was taking share away from long-established consumer electronics and appliance makers.

Hisense seeks to become a global enterprise with a world-class consumer brand. It aims to increase revenue to over $12 billion in 2010, a goal that may be attainable following the 2006 acquisition of its troubled Chinese rival, Kelon. Although Hisense is without question a low-cost manufacturer, it believes its core strength is not in low-cost manufacturing but in rapid product innovation. The company believes that the only way to gain leadership in the highly competitive markets in which it competes is to continuously launch advanced, high-quality, and competitively priced products.

To this end, Hisense established its first R&D center in China in the mid-1990s. This was followed by a South African R&D center in 1997 and a European R&D center in 2007. The company also has plans for an R&D center in the United States. In 2006 these R&D centers filed for some 534 patents.

Hisense's technological prowess is evident in its digital TV business. It introduced set-top boxes in 1999, making it possible to browse the Internet from a TV. In 2002, Hisense introduced its first interactive digital TV set, and in 2005 it developed China's first core digital processing chip for digital TVs, breaking the country's reliance on foreign chip makers for this core technology. In 2006, Hisense launched an innovative line of multimedia TV sets that integrated digital high-definition technology, network technology, and flat-panel displays.

Sources: Harold L. Sirkin, "Someone May Be Gaining on Us," *Barron's*, February 5, 2007, p. 53; "Hisense Plans to Grab More International Sales," *Sino Cast China IT Watch*, November 30, 2006; "Hisense's Wonder Chip", Financial Times Information Limited–Asian Intelligence Wire, October 30, 2006; and Hisense's Web site, www.hisense.com/en/index.jsp, accessed June 14, 2007.

The Rise of Mini-Multinationals

Another trend in international business has been the growth of medium-size and small multinationals (mini-multinationals).[39] When people think of international businesses, they tend to think of firms such as Exxon, General Motors, Ford, Fuji, Kodak, Matsushita, Procter & Gamble, Sony, and Unilever—large, complex multinational corporations with operations that span the globe. Although most international trade and investment is still conducted by large firms, many medium-size and small businesses are becoming increasingly involved in international trade and investment.

Consider Lubricating Systems, Inc., of Kent, Washington. Lubricating Systems, which manufactures lubricating fluids for machine tools, employs 25 people and generates sales of $6.5 million. It's hardly a large, complex multinational, yet more than $2 million of the company's sales are generated by exports to a score of countries, including Japan, Israel, and the United Arab Emirates. Lubricating Systems also has set up a joint venture with a German company to serve the European market.[40] Consider also Lixi, Inc., a small U.S. manufacturer of industrial X-ray equipment; 70 percent of Lixi's $4.5 million in revenues comes from exports to Japan.[41] Or take G. W. Barth, a manufacturer of cocoa-bean roasting machinery based in Ludwigsburg, Germany. Employing just 65 people, this small company has captured 70 percent of the global market for cocoa-bean roasting machines.[42] International business is conducted not just by large firms but also by medium-size and small enterprises.

THE CHANGING WORLD ORDER

Between 1989 and 1991 a series of remarkable democratic revolutions swept the Communist world. For reasons that are explored in more detail in Chapter 2, in country after country throughout Eastern Europe and eventually in the Soviet Union itself, Communist Party governments collapsed like the shells of rotten eggs. The Soviet Union is now receding into history, having been replaced by 15 independent republics. Czechoslovakia has divided itself into two states, while Yugoslavia dissolved into a bloody civil war, now thankfully over, among its five successor states.

Many of the former Communist nations of Europe and Asia seem to share a commitment to democratic politics and free market economics. If this continues, the opportunities for international businesses may be enormous. For half a century, these countries were essentially closed to Western international businesses. Now they present a host of export and investment opportunities. Just how this will play out over the next 10 to 20 years is difficult to say. The economies of many of the former Communist states are still relatively undeveloped, and their continued commitment to democracy and free market economics cannot be taken for granted. Disturbing signs of growing unrest and totalitarian tendencies continue to be seen in several Eastern European and Central Asian states, including Russia, which under the government of Vladimir Putin showed signs of shifting back toward greater state involvement in economic activity.[43] Thus, the risks involved in doing business in such countries are high, but so may be the returns.

In addition to these changes, more quiet revolutions have been occurring in China, other states in Southeast Asia, and Latin America. Their implications for international businesses may be just as profound as the collapse of communism in Eastern Europe. China suppressed its own pro-democracy movement in the bloody Tiananmen Square massacre of 1989. Despite this, China continues to move progressively toward greater free market reforms. If what is occurring in China continues for two more decades, China may move from Third World to industrial superpower status even more rapidly than Japan did. If China's gross domestic product (GDP) per capita grows by an average of 6 to 7 percent, which is slower than the 8 percent growth rate achieved during the last decade, then by 2020 this nation of 1.273 billion people could boast an average income per capita of about $13,000, roughly equivalent to that of Spain's today.

The potential consequences for international business are enormous. On the one hand, with more than 1 billion people, China represents a huge and largely untapped market. Reflecting this, between 1983 and 2007, annual foreign direct investment in China increased from less than $2 billion to $60 billion to $70 billion. On the other hand, China's new firms are proving to be very capable competitors, and they could take global market share away from Western and Japanese enterprises (for example, see the Management Focus about Hisense). Thus, the changes in China are creating both opportunities and threats for established international businesses.

As for Latin America, both democracy and free market reforms also seem to have taken hold. For decades, most Latin American countries were ruled by dictators, many of whom seemed to view

Another Perspective

Economic Freedom and Globalization: A Different Picture

The Frasier Institute's *Economic Freedom of the World Report*, which measures economic freedom using 38 variables, indicates a strong correlation between economic freedom, per capita growth, and life expectancy. In the 2005 report, Hong Kong has the highest rating for economic freedom (8.7 of 10) closely followed by Singapore (8.5). New Zealand, Switzerland, and the United States tied for third with ratings of 8.2. Botswana's ranking of 30 is the highest-ranking African economy and ranks higher than France (38) and Italy (54). See the 2005 report results and data at www.freetheworld.com.

Western international businesses as instruments of imperialist domination. Accordingly, they restricted direct investment by foreign firms. In addition, the poorly managed economies of Latin America were characterized by low growth, high debt, and hyperinflation—all of which discouraged investment by international businesses. In the past two decades much of this had changed. Throughout most of Latin America, debt and inflation are down, governments have sold state-owned enterprises to private investors, foreign investment is welcomed, and the region's economies have expanded. Brazil, Mexico, and Chile have led the way here. These changes have increased the attractiveness of Latin America, both as a market for exports and as a site for foreign direct investment. At the same time, given the long history of economic mismanagement in Latin America, there is no guarantee that these favorable trends will continue. Under left-wing governments, Bolivia and Venezuela have shifted back toward greater state involvement in industry in the last few years, and foreign investment is now less welcome than it was during the 1990s. In both nations, the government has seized control of oil and gas fields from foreign investors and has limited the rights of foreign energy companies to extract oil and gas from their nations. Thus, as in the case of Eastern Europe, substantial opportunities are accompanied by substantial risks.

THE GLOBAL ECONOMY OF THE 21ST CENTURY As discussed, the past quarter century has seen rapid changes in the global economy. Barriers to the free flow of goods, services, and capital have been coming down. The volume of cross-border trade and investment has been growing more rapidly than global output, indicating that national economies are becoming more closely integrated into a single, interdependent, global economic system. As their economies advance, more nations are joining the ranks of the developed world. A generation ago, South Korea and Taiwan were viewed as second-tier developing nations. Now they boast large economies, and their firms are major players in many global industries, from shipbuilding and steel to electronics and chemicals. The move toward a global economy has been further strengthened by the widespread adoption of liberal economic policies by countries that had firmly opposed them for two generations or more. Thus, in keeping with the normative prescriptions of liberal economic ideology, in country after country we have seen state-owned businesses privatized, widespread deregulation adopted, markets opened to more competition, and commitment increased to removing barriers to cross-border trade and investment. This suggests that over the next few decades, countries such as the Czech Republic, Mexico, Poland, Brazil, China, India, and South Africa may build powerful market-oriented economies. In short, current trends indicate that the world is moving rapidly toward an economic system that is more favorable for international business.

But it is always hazardous to use established trends to predict the future. The world may be moving toward a more global economic system, but globalization is not inevitable. Countries may pull back from the recent commitment to liberal economic ideology if their experiences do not match their expectations. Periodic signs, for example, indicate a retreat from liberal economic ideology in Russia. Russia has experienced considerable economic pain as it tries to shift from a centrally planned economy to a market economy. If Russia's hesitation were to become more permanent and widespread, the liberal vision of a more prosperous global economy based on free market principles might not occur as quickly as many hope. Clearly, this would be a tougher world for international businesses.

Another Perspective

Globalization and Complexity

Another way to understand globalization is to think of it as the result of our increasing ability to deal with complexity. Some cultures such as the Chinese, Japanese, and Middle Eastern (see Chapter 3 for high context and high power distance) are inclined to work well with complexity. Will these cultural traits serve as a comparative advantage as globalization proceeds?

Also, greater globalization brings with it risks of its own. This was starkly demonstrated in 1997 and 1998 when a financial crisis in Thailand spread first to other East Asian nations and then in 1998 to Russia and Brazil. Ultimately, the crisis threatened to plunge the economies of the developed world, including the United States, into a recession. We explore the causes and consequences of this and other similar global financial crises in Chapter 10. Even from a purely economic perspective, globalization is not all good. The opportunities for doing business in a global economy may be significantly enhanced, but as we saw in 1997–98, the risks associated with global financial contagion are also greater. Still, as explained later in this book, firms can exploit the opportunities associated with globalization, while at the same time reducing the risks through appropriate hedging strategies.

The Globalization Debate

LEARNING OBJECTIVE 4
Understand the main arguments in the debate over the impact of globalization

Is the shift toward a more integrated and interdependent global economy a good thing? Many influential economists, politicians, and business leaders seem to think so.[44] They argue that falling barriers to international trade and investment are the twin engines driving the global economy toward greater prosperity. They say increased international trade and cross-border investment will result in lower prices for goods and services. They believe that globalization stimulates economic growth, raises the incomes of consumers, and helps to create jobs in all countries that participate in the global trading system. The arguments of those who support globalization are covered in detail in Chapters 5, 6, and 7. As we shall see, there are good theoretical reasons for believing that declining barriers to international trade and investment do stimulate economic growth, create jobs, and raise income levels. As described in Chapters 6 and 7, empirical evidence lends support to the predictions of this theory. However, despite the existence of a compelling body of theory and evidence, globalization has its critics.[45] Some of these critics have become increasingly vocal and active, taking to the streets to demonstrate their opposition to globalization. Here we look at the nature of protests against globalization and briefly review the main themes of the debate concerning the merits of globalization. In later chapters we elaborate on many of the points mentioned herein.

ANTIGLOBALIZATION PROTESTS

Street demonstrations against globalization date to December 1999, when more than 40,000 protesters blocked the streets of Seattle in an attempt to shut down a World Trade Organization meeting being held in the city. The demonstrators were protesting against a wide range of issues, including job losses in industries under attack from foreign competitors, downward pressure on the wage rates of unskilled workers, environmental degradation, and the cultural imperialism of global media and multinational enterprises, which was seen as being dominated by what some protesters called the "culturally impoverished" interests and values of the United States. All of these ills, the demonstrators claimed, could be laid at the feet of globalization. The World Trade Organization was meeting to try to launch a new round of talks to cut barriers to cross-border trade and investment. As such, it was seen as a promoter of globalization and a target for the antiglobalization protesters. The protests turned violent, transforming the normally placid streets of Seattle into a running battle between "anarchists" and Seattle's bemused and poorly prepared police department. Pictures of brick-throwing protesters and armored police wielding their batons were duly recorded by the global media, which then circulated the images around the world. Meanwhile, the World Trade Organization meeting failed to reach agreement, and although the protests outside the meeting halls had little to do with that failure, the impression took hold that the demonstrators had succeeded in derailing the meetings.

Demonstrators at the WTO meeting in Seattle in December 1999 began looting and rioting in the city's downtown area. Why do you think they felt that behavior was necessary?

Emboldened by the experience in Seattle, antiglobalization protesters now turn up at almost every major meeting of a global institution. Smaller scale protests have occurred in several countries, such as France, where antiglobalization activists destroyed a McDonald's restaurant in August 1999 to protest the impoverishment of French culture by American imperialism (see the Country Focus, "Protesting Globalization in France," for details). While violent protests may give the antiglobalization effort a bad name, it is clear from the scale of the demonstrations that support for the cause goes beyond a core of anarchists. Large segments of the population in many countries believe that globalization has detrimental effects on living standards and the environment, and the media have often fed on this fear. For example, CNN news anchor Lou Dobbs has been running TV shows that are highly critical of the trend by American companies to take advantage of globalization and "export jobs" overseas. Both theory and evidence suggest that many of these fears are exaggerated, but this may not have been communicated clearly, and both politicians and businesspeople need to do more to counter these fears. Many protests against globalization are tapping into a general sense of loss at the passing of a world in which barriers of time and distance, and vast differences in economic institutions, political institutions, and the level of development of different nations, produced a world rich in the diversity of human cultures. This world is now passing into history. However, while the rich citizens of the developed world may have the luxury of mourning the fact that they can now see McDonald's restaurants and Starbucks coffeehouses on their vacations to exotic locations such as Thailand, fewer complaints are heard from the citizens of those countries, who welcome the higher living standards that progress brings.

GLOBALIZATION, JOBS, AND INCOME One concern frequently voiced by globalization opponents is that falling barriers to international trade destroy manufacturing jobs in wealthy advanced economies such as the United States and Western Europe. The critics argue that falling trade barriers allow firms to move manufacturing activities to countries where wage rates are much lower.[46] Indeed, due to the entry of China, India, and states from Eastern Europe into the global trading system, along with global population growth, estimates suggest that the pool of global labor may have quadrupled between 1985 and 2005, with most of the increase taking place after 1990.[47] Other things being equal, one might conclude that this enormous expansion in

Country FOCUS

Protesting Globalization in France

One night in August 1999, 10 men under the leadership of local sheep farmer and rural activist Jose Bove crept into the town of Millau in central France and vandalized a McDonald's restaurant under construction, causing an estimated $150,000 damage. These were no ordinary vandals, however, at least according to their supporters, for the "symbolic dismantling" of the McDonald's outlet had noble aims, or so it was claimed. The attack was initially presented as a protest against unfair American trade policies. The European Union had banned imports of hormone-treated beef from the United States, primarily because of fears that it might lead to health problems (although EU scientists had concluded there was no evidence of this). After a careful review, the World Trade Organization stated the EU ban was not allowed under trading rules that the EU and United States were party to, and that the EU would have to lift it or face retaliation. The EU refused to comply, so the U.S. government imposed a 100 percent tariff on imports of certain EU products, including French staples such as foie gras, mustard, and Roquefort cheese. On farms near Millau, Bove and others raised sheep whose milk was used to make Roquefort. They felt incensed by the American tariff and decided to vent their frustrations on McDonald's.

Bove and his compatriots were arrested and charged. They quickly became a focus of the antiglobalization movement in France that was protesting everything from a loss of national sovereignty and "unfair" trade policies that were trying to force hormone-treated beef on French consumers, to the invasion of French culture by alien American values, so aptly symbolized by McDonald's. Lionel Jospin, France's prime minister, called the cause of Jose Bove "just." Allowed to remain free pending his trial, Bove traveled to Seattle in December to protest against the World Trade Organization, where he was feted as a hero of the antiglobalization movement. In France, Bove's July 2000 trial drew some 40,000 supporters to the small town of Millau, where they camped outside the courthouse and waited for the verdict. Bove was found guilty and sentenced to three months in jail, far less than the maximum possible sentence of five years. His supporters wore T-shirts claiming, "The world is not merchandise, and neither am I."

About the same time in the Languedoc region of France, California winemaker Robert Mondavi had reached agreement with the mayor and council of the village of Aniane and regional authorities to turn 125 acres of wooded hillside belonging to the village into a vineyard. Mondavi planned to invest $7 million in the project and hoped to produce top-quality wine that would sell in Europe and the United States for $60 a bottle. However, local environmentalists objected to the plan, which they claimed would destroy the area's unique ecological heritage. Jose Bove, basking in sudden fame, offered his support to the opponents, and the protests started. In May 2001, the Socialist mayor who had approved the project was defeated in local elections in which the Mondavi project had become the major issue. He was replaced by a Communist, Manuel Diaz, who denounced the project as a capitalist plot designed to enrich wealthy U.S. shareholders at the cost of his villagers and the environment. Following Diaz's victory, Mondavi announced he would pull out of the project. A spokesman noted, "It's a huge waste, but there are clearly personal and political interests at play here that go way beyond us."

So are the French opposed to foreign investment? The experience of McDonald's and Mondavi seems to suggest so, as does the associated news coverage, but look closer and a different reality seems to emerge. McDonald's has more than 800 restaurants in France and continues to do very well there. In fact, France is one of the most profitable markets for McDonald's. France has long been one of the most favored locations for inward foreign direct investment, receiving over $180 billion of foreign investment between 2004 and 2006, more than any other European nation with the exception of Britain. American companies have always accounted for a significant percentage of this investment. Moreover, French enterprises have also been significant foreign investors; some 1,100 French multinationals account for around 8 percent of the global stock of foreign direct investment.

Sources: "Behind the Bluster," *The Economist,* May 26, 2001; "The French Farmers' Anti-global Hero," *The Economist,* July 8, 2000; C. Trueheart, "France's Golden Arch Enemy?" *Toronto Star,* July 1, 2000; J. Henley, "Grapes of Wrath Scare Off U.S. Firm," *The Economist,* May 18, 2001, p. 11; and United Nations, *World Investment Report, 2006* (New York and Geneva: United Nations, 2006).

the global labor force, when coupled with expanding international trade, would have depressed wages in developed nations.

This fear is supported by anecdotes. For example, D. L. Bartlett and J. B. Steele, two journalists for the *Philadelphia Inquirer* who gained notoriety for their attacks on free trade, cite the case of Harwood Industries, a U.S. clothing manufacturer that closed its U.S. operations, where it paid workers $9 per hour, and shifted manufacturing to Honduras, where textile workers receive 48 cents per hour.[48] Because of moves

Hill: Global Business
Today, Sixth Edition

1. Globalization

Text

© The McGraw–Hill
Companies, 2009

39

such as this, argue Bartlett and Steele, the wage rates of poorer Americans have fallen significantly over the past quarter of a century.

In the last few years, the same fears have been applied to services, which have increasingly been outsourced to nations with lower labor costs. The popular feeling is that when corporations such as Dell, IBM, or Citigroup outsource service activities to lower-cost foreign suppliers—as all three have done—they are "exporting jobs" to low-wage nations and contributing to higher unemployment and lower living standards in their home nations (in this case, the United States). Some lawmakers in the United States have responded by calling for legal barriers to job outsourcing.

By outsourcing its customer service call centers to India, Dell can reduce its cost structure and pass on the savings to their customers.

Supporters of globalization reply that critics of these trends miss the essential point about free trade—the benefits outweigh the costs.[49] They argue that free trade will result in countries specializing in the production of those goods and services that they can produce most efficiently, while importing goods and services that they cannot produce as efficiently. When a country embraces free trade, there is always some dislocation—lost textile jobs at Harwood Industries, or lost call center jobs at Dell—but the whole economy is better off as a result. According to this view, it makes little sense for the United States to produce textiles at home when they can be produced at a lower cost in Honduras or China (which, unlike Honduras, is a major source of U.S. textile imports). Importing textiles from China leads to lower prices for clothes in the United States, which enables consumers to spend more of their money on other items. At the same time, the increased income generated in China from textile exports increases income levels in that country, which helps the Chinese to purchase more products produced in the United States, such as pharmaceuticals from Amgen, Boeing jets, Intel-based computers, Microsoft software, and Cisco routers.

The same argument can be made to support the outsourcing of services to low-wage countries. By outsourcing its customer service call centers to India, Dell can reduce its cost structure, and thereby its prices for PCs. U.S. consumers benefit from this development. As prices for PCs fall, Americans can spend more of their money on other goods and services. Moreover, the increase in income levels in India allows Indians to purchase more U.S. goods and services, which helps to create jobs in the United States. In this manner, supporters of globalization argue that free trade benefits all countries that adhere to a free trade regime.

If the critics of globalization are correct, the share of national income received by labor, as opposed to the share received by the owners of capital (e.g., stockholders and bondholders), should have declined in advanced nations as a result of downward pressure on wage rates. And this decline in labor's share of national income must be due to moving production to low-wage countries, as opposed to improvement in production technology and productivity. Supporters of globalization argue that, even though labor's share of the economic pie may have declined, this does not mean lower living standards if the size of the total pie has increased sufficiently to offset any decline in labor's share—in other words, economic growth and rising living standards in advanced economies have offset declines in labor's share.

So what does the data say? Several recent studies shed light on these questions.[50] First, the data suggest that over the past two decades the share of labor in national income has declined. The decline in share is much more pronounced in Europe and

Japan (about 10 percentage points) than in the United States and the United Kingdom (where it is 3 to 4 percentage points). However, detailed analysis suggests that the share of national income enjoyed by skilled labor has actually increased, suggesting that the fall in labor's share has been due to a fall in the share taken by unskilled labor. A study of long-term trends in income distribution in the United States concluded:

> Nationwide, from the late 1970s to the late 1990s, the average income of the lowest-income families fell by over 6 percent after adjustment for inflation, and the average real income of the middle fifth of families grew by about 5 percent. By contrast, the average real income of the highest-income fifth of families increased by over 30 percent.[51]

Another study suggested that the earnings gap between workers in skilled and unskilled sectors has widened by 25 percent over the last two decades.[52] In sum, unskilled labor in developed nations has seen its share of national income decline.

However, this does not mean the living standards of unskilled workers in developed nations have declined. Economic growth in developed nations may have offset the fall in the share of national income enjoyed by unskilled workers, raising their living standards. Evidence suggests that real labor compensation has expanded robustly in most developed nations since the 1980s, including the United States. A study by the Organization for Economic Cooperation and Development, whose members include the 20 richest economies in the world, noted that while the gap between the poorest and richest segments of society in some OECD countries had widened, this trend was by no means universal.[53] The OECD study found that while income inequality increased in the United States from the mid-1970s to the mid-1980s, it did not widen further in the next decade. The report also notes that in almost all countries, real income levels rose over the 20-year period looked at in the study, including the incomes of the poorest segment of most OECD societies. To add to the mixed research results, a 2002 U.S. study that included data from 1990 to 2000 concluded that during those years, falling unemployment rates brought gains to low-wage workers and fairly broad-based wage growth, especially in the latter half of the 1990s. The income of the worst-paid 10 percent of the population actually rose twice as fast as that of the average worker during 1998–2000.[54] If such trends continued into the 2000s—and they may not have—the argument that globalization leads to growing income inequality may lose some of its punch.

As noted earlier, globalization critics argue that the decline in unskilled wage rates is due to the migration of low-wage manufacturing jobs offshore and a corresponding reduction in demand for unskilled workers. However, supporters of globalization see a more complex picture. They maintain that the apparent decline in real wage rates of unskilled workers owes far more to a technology-induced shift within advanced economies away from jobs where the only qualification was a willingness to turn up for work every day and toward jobs that require significant education and skills. They point out that many advanced economies report a shortage of highly skilled workers and an excess supply of unskilled workers. Thus, growing income inequality is a result of the wages for skilled workers being bid up by the labor market and the wages for unskilled workers being discounted. In fact, recent evidence suggests that technological change has had a bigger impact than globalization on the declining share of national income enjoyed by labor.[55] This indicates that the solution to the problem of stagnant incomes among the unskilled is to be found not in limiting free trade and globalization, but in increasing society's investment in education to reduce the supply of unskilled workers.[56]

Finally, it is worth noting that the wage gap between developing and developed nations is closing as developing nations experience rapid economic growth. For example, one estimate suggests that wages in China will approach Western levels in about 30 years.[57] To the extent that this is the case, any migration of unskilled jobs to low-wage countries is a temporary phenomenon representing a structural adjustment on the way to a more tightly integrated global economy.

GLOBALIZATION, LABOR POLICIES, AND THE ENVIRONMENT   A second source of concern is that free trade encourages firms from advanced nations to move manufacturing facilities to less developed countries that lack adequate regulations to protect labor and the environment from abuse by the unscrupulous.[58] Globalization critics often argue that adhering to labor and environmental regulations significantly increases the costs of manufacturing enterprises and puts them at a competitive disadvantage in the global marketplace vis-à-vis firms based in developing nations that do not have to comply with such regulations. Firms deal with this cost disadvantage, the theory goes, by moving their production facilities to nations that do not have such burdensome regulations or that fail to enforce the regulations they have.

If this were the case, one might expect free trade to lead to an increase in pollution and result in firms from advanced nations exploiting the labor of less developed nations.[59] This argument was used repeatedly by those who opposed the 1994 formation of the North American Free Trade Agreement (NAFTA) between Canada, Mexico, and the United States. They painted a picture of U.S. manufacturing firms moving to Mexico in droves so that they would be free to pollute the environment, employ child labor, and ignore workplace safety and health issues, all in the name of higher profits.[60]

Supporters of free trade and greater globalization express doubts about this scenario. They argue that tougher environmental regulations and stricter labor standards go hand in hand with economic progress.[61] In general, as countries get richer, they enact tougher environmental and labor regulations.[62] Because free trade enables developing countries to increase their economic growth rates and become richer, this should lead to tougher environmental and labor laws. In this view, the critics of free trade have got it backward—free trade does not lead to more pollution and labor exploitation, it leads to less. By creating wealth and incentives for enterprises to produce technological innovations, the free market system and free trade could make it easier for the world to cope with pollution and population growth. Indeed, while pollution levels are rising in the world's poorer countries, they have been falling in developed nations. In the United States, for example, the concentration of carbon monoxide and sulphur dioxide pollutants in the atmosphere decreased by 60 percent between 1978 and 1997, while lead concentrations decreased by 98 percent—and these reductions have occurred against a background of sustained economic expansion.[63]

A number of econometric studies have found consistent evidence of a hump-shaped relationship between income levels and pollution levels (see Figure 1.5).[64] As an economy grows and income levels rise, initially pollution levels also rise. However, past some point, rising income levels lead to demands for greater environmental protection, and pollution levels then fall. A seminal study by Grossman and Krueger found that the turning point generally occurred before per capita income levels reached $8,000.[65]

While the hump-shaped relationship depicted in Figure 1.5 seems to hold across a wide range of pollutants—from sulphur dioxide to lead concentrations and water quality—carbon dioxide emissions are an important exception, rising steadily with income levels. Given that increased atmospheric carbon dioxide concentrations are a cause of global warming, this should be of serious concern. The solution to the problem, however, is probably not to roll back the trade liberalization efforts that have fostered economic growth and globalization, but to get the nations of the world to agree to tougher standards on limiting carbon emissions. Although UN-sponsored talks have had this as a central aim since the 1992 Earth Summit in Rio de Janeiro, there has been little success in moving toward the ambitious goals for reducing carbon emissions laid down in the Earth Summit and subsequent talks in Kyoto, Japan, in part

figure **1.5**

Income Levels and Environmental Pollution

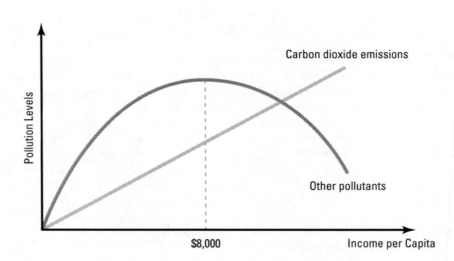

because the largest emitter of carbon dioxide, the United States, has refused to sign global agreements that it claims would unreasonably retard economic growth. In addition China, a country whose carbon emissions are increasing at an alarming rate, has so far shown little appetite to adopt tighter pollution controls.

Notwithstanding this, supporters of free trade point out that it is possible to tie free trade agreements to the implementation of tougher environmental and labor laws in less developed countries. NAFTA, for example, was passed only after side agreements had been negotiated that committed Mexico to tougher enforcement of environmental protection regulations. Thus, supporters of free trade argue that factories based in Mexico are now cleaner than they would have been without the passage of NAFTA.[66]

They also argue that business firms are not the amoral organizations that critics suggest. While there may be some rotten apples, most business enterprises are staffed by managers who are committed to behave in an ethical manner and would be unlikely to move production offshore just so they could pump more pollution into the atmosphere or exploit labor. Furthermore, the relationship between pollution, labor exploitation, and production costs may not be that suggested by critics. In general, a well-treated labor force is productive, and it is productivity rather than base wage rates that often has the greatest influence on costs. The vision of greedy managers who shift production to low-wage countries to exploit their labor force may be misplaced.

GLOBALIZATION AND NATIONAL SOVEREIGNTY   Another concern voiced by critics of globalization is that today's increasingly interdependent global economy shifts economic power away from national governments and toward supranational organizations such as the World Trade Organization, the European Union, and the United Nations. As perceived by critics, unelected bureaucrats now impose policies on the democratically elected governments of nation-states, thereby undermining the sovereignty of those states and limiting the nation's ability to control its own destiny.[67]

The World Trade Organization is a favorite target of those who attack the headlong rush toward a global economy. As noted earlier, the WTO was founded in 1994 to police the world trading system established by the General Agreement on Tariffs and Trade. The WTO arbitrates trade disputes between the 150 states that are signatories to the GATT. The arbitration panel can issue a ruling instructing a member state to change trade policies that violate GATT regulations. If the violator refuses to comply with the ruling, the WTO allows other states to impose appropriate trade sanctions on the transgressor. As a result, according to one prominent critic, U.S. environmentalist, consumer rights advocate, and presidential candidate Ralph Nader:

> Under the new system, many decisions that affect billions of people are no longer made by local or national governments but instead, if challenged by any WTO member nation, would be deferred to a group of unelected bureaucrats sitting behind closed doors in Geneva (which is where the headquarters of the WTO are located). The bureaucrats can decide whether or not people in California can prevent the destruction of the last virgin forests or determine if carcinogenic pesticides can be banned from their foods; or whether European countries have the right to ban dangerous biotech hormones in meat. . . . At risk is the very basis of democracy and accountable decision making.[68]

In contrast to Nader's rhetoric, many economists and politicians maintain that the power of supranational organizations such as the WTO is limited to what nation-states collectively agree to grant. They argue that bodies such as the United Nations and the WTO exist to serve the collective interests of member states, not to subvert those interests. Supporters of supranational organizations point out that the power of these bodies rests largely on their ability to persuade member states to follow a certain action. If these bodies fail to serve the collective interests of member states, those states will withdraw their support and the supranational organization will quickly collapse. In this view, real power still resides with individual nation-states, not supranational organizations.

GLOBALIZATION AND THE WORLD'S POOR   Critics of globalization argue that despite the supposed benefits associated with free trade and investment, over the past hundred years or so the gap between the rich and poor nations of the world has gotten wider. In 1870, the average income per capita in the world's 17 richest nations was 2.4 times that of all other countries. In 1990, the same group was 4.5 times as rich as the rest.[69] While recent history has shown that some of the world's poorer nations are capable of rapid periods of economic growth—witness the transformation that has occurred in some Southeast Asian nations such as South Korea, Thailand, and Malaysia—there appear to be strong forces for stagnation among the world's poorest nations. A quarter of the countries with a GDP per capita of less than $1,000 in 1960 had growth rates of less than zero from 1960 to 1995, and a third had growth rates of less than 0.05 percent.[70] Critics argue that if globalization is such a positive development, this divergence between the rich and poor should not have occurred.

Although the reasons for economic stagnation vary, several factors stand out, none of which have anything to do with free trade or globalization.[71] Many of the world's poorest countries have suffered from totalitarian governments, economic policies that destroyed wealth rather than facilitated its creation, endemic corruption, scant protection for property rights, and war. Such factors help explain why countries such as Afghanistan, Cambodia, Cuba, Haiti, Iraq, Libya, Nigeria, Sudan, Vietnam, and Zaire have failed to improve the economic lot of their citizens during recent decades. A complicating factor is the rapidly expanding populations in many of these countries. Without a major change in government, population growth may exacerbate their problems. Promoters of free trade argue that the best way for these countries to improve their lot is to lower their barriers to free trade and investment and to implement economic policies based on free market economics.[72]

Many of the world's poorer nations are being held back by large debt burdens. Of particular concern are the 40 or so "highly indebted poorer countries" (HIPCs), which are home to some 700 million people. Among these countries, the average government debt burden has been has high as 85 percent of the value of the economy, as measured by gross domestic product, and the annual costs of serving government debt consumed

Even as India makes strides toward economic development, it continues to carry a high budget deficit that cannot meet the needs of its soaring population.

15 percent of the country's export earnings.[73] Servicing such a heavy debt load leaves the governments of these countries with little left to invest in important public infrastructure projects, such as education, health care, roads, and power. The result is the HIPCs are trapped in a cycle of poverty and debt that inhibits economic development. Free trade alone, some argue, is a necessary but not sufficient prerequisite to help these countries bootstrap themselves out of poverty. Instead, large-scale debt relief is needed for the world's poorest nations to give them the opportunity to restructure their economies and start the long climb toward prosperity. Supporters of debt relief also argue that new democratic governments in poor nations should not be forced to honor debts that were incurred and mismanaged long ago by their corrupt and dictatorial predecessors.

In the late 1990s, a debt relief movement began to gain ground among the political establishment in the world's richer nations.[74] Fueled by high-profile endorsements from Irish rock star Bono (who has been a tireless and increasingly effective advocate for debt relief), Pope John Paul II, the Dalai Lama, and influential Harvard economist Jeffrey Sachs, the debt relief movement was instrumental in persuading the United States to enact legislation in 2000 that provided $435 million in debt relief for HIPCs. More important perhaps, the United States also backed an IMF plan to sell some of its gold reserves and use the proceeds to help with debt relief. The IMF and World Bank have now picked up the banner and have embarked on a systematic debt relief program.

For such a program to have a lasting effect, however, debt relief must be matched by wise investment in public projects that boost economic growth (such as education) and by the adoption of economic

Another Perspective

A Question of Debt in Emerging, Poor Economies

The Group of Eight Nations (G-8)—United States, Russia, France, Japan, Germany, Italy, Canada, and the United Kingdom—canceled about $60 billion of debt owed them in 2005 by the world's poorest countries, known as the highly indebted poor countries, or HIPCs. However, in 2006, emerging lenders such as China, India, Brazil, and South Korea are offering preferential loans and export credits to these same poor nations. The emerging lenders want to sell infrastructure-related exports into the HIPCs. China has announced $10 billion in these loans and credits.

These loans and credits don't sit too well with the G-8 finance ministers who have just issued debt relief to these same poor countries. They take the position that it is imperative to prevent the buildup of unsustainable debt in HIPCs. A World Bank study found that eight former HIPCs—including Uganda, Bolivia, Nicaragua. and Ethiopia—are again facing debt problems. The challenge continues: Will this continued debt activity help or hinder HIPC economies? (Michael. Phillips, "G8 Warns China about Loans to Poorest Nations," *The Wall Street Journal,* June 12, 2006, http://online.wsj.com/article/SB115005845957077212.html)

policies that facilitate investment and trade. The rich nations of the world also can help by reducing barriers to the importation of products from the world's poorer nations, particularly tariffs on imports of agricultural products and textiles. High tariff barriers and other impediments to trade make it difficult for poor countries to export more of their agricultural production. The World Trade Organization has estimated that if the developed nations of the world eradicated subsidies to their agricultural producers and removed tariff barriers to trade in agriculture this would raise global economic welfare by $128 billion, with $30 billion of that going to developing nations, many of which are highly indebted. The faster growth associated with expanded trade in agriculture could reduce the number of people living in poverty by as much as 13 percent by 2015, according to the WTO.[75]

Managing in the Global Marketplace

Much of this book is concerned with the challenges of managing in an international business. An **international business** is any firm that engages in international trade or investment. A firm does not have to become a multinational enterprise, investing directly in operations in other countries, to engage in international business, although multinational enterprises are international businesses. All a firm has to do is export or import products from other countries. As the world shifts toward a truly integrated global economy, more firms, both large and small, are becoming international businesses. What does this shift toward a global economy mean for managers within an international business?

As their organizations increasingly engage in cross-border trade and investment, managers need to recognize that the task of managing an international business differs from that of managing a purely domestic business in many ways. At the most fundamental level, the differences arise from the simple fact that countries are different. Countries differ in their cultures, political systems, economic systems, legal systems, and levels of economic development. Despite all the talk about the emerging global village, and despite the trend toward globalization of markets and production, as we shall see in this book, many of these differences are very profound and enduring.

Differences between countries require that an international business vary its practices country by country. Marketing a product in Brazil may require a different approach from marketing the product in Germany; managing U.S. workers might require different skills than managing Japanese workers; maintaining close relations with a particular level of government may be very important in Mexico and irrelevant in Great Britain; the business strategy pursued in Canada might not work in South Korea; and so on. Managers in an international business must not only be sensitive to these differences, but they must also adopt the appropriate policies and strategies for coping with them. Much of this book is devoted to explaining the sources of these differences and the methods for successfully coping with them.

A further way in which international business differs from domestic business is the greater complexity of managing an international business. In addition to the problems that arise from the differences between countries, a manager in an international business is confronted with a range of other issues that the manager in a domestic business never confronts. The managers of an international business must decide where in the world to site production activities to minimize costs and to maximize value added. They must decide whether it is ethical to adhere to the lower labor and environmental standards found in many less developed nations. Then they must decide how best to coordinate and control globally dispersed production activities (which, as we shall see later in the book, is not a trivial problem). The managers in an international business also must decide which foreign markets to enter and which to avoid. They must choose the appropriate mode for entering a particular foreign country. Is it best to export its product to the foreign country? Should the firm allow a local company to produce its product under license in that

LEARNING OBJECTIVE 5
Appreciate how the process of globalization is creating opportunities and challenges for business managers.

International Business
Any firm that engages in international trade or investment.

Hill: Global Business
Today, Sixth Edition

1. Globalization

Text

© The McGraw-Hill
Companies, 2009

country? Should the firm enter into a joint venture with a local firm to produce its product in that country? Or should the firm set up a wholly owned subsidiary to serve the market in that country? As we shall see, the choice of entry mode is critical because it has major implications for the long-term health of the firm.

Conducting business transactions across national borders requires understanding the rules governing the international trading and investment system. Managers in an international business must also deal with government restrictions on international trade and investment. They must find ways to work within the limits imposed by specific governmental interventions. As this book explains, even though many governments are nominally committed to free trade, they often intervene to regulate cross-border trade and investment. Managers within international businesses must develop strategies and policies for dealing with such interventions.

Cross-border transactions also require that money be converted from the firm's home currency into a foreign currency and vice versa. Because currency exchange rates vary in response to changing economic conditions, managers in an international business must develop policies for dealing with exchange rate movements. A firm that adopts a wrong policy can lose large amounts of money, whereas one that adopts the right policy can increase the profitability of its international transactions.

In sum, managing an international business is different from managing a purely domestic business for at least four reasons: (1) countries are different, (2) the range of problems confronted by a manager in an international business is wider and the problems themselves more complex than those confronted by a manager in a domestic business, (3) an international business must find ways to work within the limits imposed by government intervention in the international trade and investment system, and (4) international transactions involve converting money into different currencies.

In this book we examine all these issues in depth, paying close attention to the different strategies and policies that managers pursue to deal with the various challenges created when a firm becomes an international business. Chapters 2 and 3 explore how countries differ from each other with regard to their political, economic, legal, and cultural institutions. Chapter 4 takes a detailed look at the ethical issues that arise in international business. Chapters 5 to 8 look at the international trade and investment environment within which international businesses must operate. Chapters 9 to 10 review the international monetary system. These chapters focus on the nature of the foreign exchange market and the emerging global monetary system. Chapters 11 to 12 explore the strategy of international businesses. Chapters 13 to 16 look at the management of various functional operations within an international business, including production, marketing, and human relations. By the time you complete this book, you should have a good grasp of the issues that managers working within international business have to grapple with on a daily basis, and you should be familiar with the range of strategies and operating policies available to compete more effectively in today's rapidly emerging global economy.

Key Terms

globalization, p. 7

globalization of markets, p. 7

globalization of production, p. 8

factors of production, p. 8

General Agreement on Tariffs and Trade (GATT), p. 10

World Trade Organization, p. 10

International Monetary Fund, p. 11

World Bank, p. 11

United Nations, p. 11

international trade, p. 12

foreign direct investment (FDI), p. 12

Moore's law, p. 14

stock of foreign direct investment, p. 20

multinational enterprise (MNE), p. 21

international business, p. 35

This chapter sets the scene for the rest of the book. It shows how the world economy is becoming more global and reviews the main drivers of globalization, arguing that they seem to be thrusting nation-states toward a more tightly integrated global economy. We looked at how the nature of international business is changing in response to the changing global economy; we discussed some concerns raised by rapid globalization; and we reviewed implications of rapid globalization for individual managers. The chapter made the following points:

1. Over the past two decades, we have witnessed the globalization of markets and production.

2. The globalization of markets implies that national markets are merging into one huge marketplace. However, it is important not to push this view too far.

3. The globalization of production implies that firms are basing individual productive activities at the optimal world locations for the particular activities. As a consequence, it is increasingly irrelevant to talk about American products, Japanese products, or German products, since these are being replaced by "global" products.

4. Two factors seem to underlie the trend toward globalization: declining trade barriers and changes in communication, information, and transportation technologies.

5. Since the end of World War II, barriers to the free flow of goods, services, and capital have been lowered significantly. More than anything else, this has facilitated the trend toward the globalization of production and has enabled firms to view the world as a single market.

6. As a consequence of the globalization of production and markets, in the last decade world trade has grown faster than world output, foreign direct investment has surged, imports have penetrated more deeply into the world's industrial nations, and competitive pressures have increased in industry after industry.

7. The development of the microprocessor and related developments in communication and information processing technology have helped firms link their worldwide operations into sophisticated information networks. Jet air travel, by shrinking travel time, has also helped to link the worldwide operations of international

businesses. These changes have enabled firms to achieve tight coordination of their worldwide operations and to view the world as a single market.

8. In the 1960s, the U.S. economy was dominant in the world, U.S. firms accounted for most of the foreign direct investment in the world economy, U.S. firms dominated the list of large multinationals, and roughly half the world—the centrally planned economies of the Communist world—was closed to Western businesses.

9. By the mid-1990s, the U.S. share of world output had been cut in half, with major shares now being accounted for by Western European and Southeast Asian economies. The U.S. share of worldwide foreign direct investment had also fallen, by about two-thirds. U.S. multinationals were now facing competition from a large number of Japanese and European multinationals. In addition, the emergence of mini-multinationals was noted.

10. One of the most dramatic developments of the past 20 years has been the collapse of communism in Eastern Europe, which has created enormous long-run opportunities for international businesses. In addition, the move toward free market economies in China and Latin America is creating opportunities (and threats) for Western international businesses.

11. The benefits and costs of the emerging global economy are being hotly debated among businesspeople, economists, and politicians. The debate focuses on the impact of globalization on jobs, wages, the environment, working conditions, and national sovereignty.

12. Managing an international business is different from managing a domestic business for at least four reasons: (i) countries are different, (ii) the range of problems confronted by a manager in an international business is wider and the problems themselves more complex than those confronted by a manager in a domestic business, (iii) managers in an international business must find ways to work within the limits imposed by governments' intervention in the international trade and investment system, and (iv) international transactions involve converting money into different currencies.

Critical Thinking and Discussion Questions

1. Describe the shifts in the world economy over the past 30 years. What are the implications of these shifts for international businesses based in Great Britain? North America? Hong Kong?

2. "The study of international business is fine if you are going to work in a large multinational enterprise, but it has no relevance for individuals who are going to work in small firms." Evaluate this statement.

3. How have changes in technology contributed to the globalization of markets and production? Would the globalization of production and markets have been possible without these technological changes?

4. "Ultimately, the study of international business is no different from the study of domestic business. Thus, there is no point in having a separate course on international business." Evaluate this statement.

5. How might the Internet and the associated World Wide Web affect international business activity and the globalization of the world economy?

6. If current trends continue, China may be the world's largest economy by 2020. Discuss the possible implications of such a development for (*a*) the world trading system, (*b*) the world monetary system, (*c*) the business strategy of today's European and U.S.-based global corporations, and (*d*) global commodity prices.

7. Reread the Country Focus "Outsourcing American Healthcare" then answer the following questions:
   a. A decade ago the idea that medical procedures might move offshore was unthinkable. Today it is a reality. What trends have facilitated this process?
   b. Is the globalization of health care good or bad for patients?
   c. Is the globalization of health care good or bad for the American economy?
   d. Who might benefit from the globalization of health care? Who might lose?
   e. Do you think that the U.S. government should restrict the outsourcing of medical procedures to developing nations? What if physicians in those countries are certified by U.S. medical institutions?

Research Task http://globalEDGE.msu.edu

Use the globalEDGE Resource Desk (http://globalEDGE.msu.edu/ResourceDesk/) to complete the following exercises:

1. Your company has developed a new product that is expected to achieve high penetration rates in all the countries in which it is introduced, regardless of the average income status of the local population. Considering the costs of the product launch, the management team has decided to initially introduce the product only in countries that have a sizeable population base. Using the *Population Reference Bureau* as a resource, you are required to prepare a preliminary report with the top 10 countries of the world in terms of population size. Since growth opportunities are another major concern, the average population growth rates should be listed for management's consideration.

2. The United Nations Conference on Trade and Development (UNCTAD) provides ranking of the largest *transnational corporations* (TNCs) in the world, including a ranking of the 100 largest non-financial TNCs from developing countries. Identify the largest 25 TNCs listed in the most recent ranking. What countries are these TNCs from? In what industries are they classified? Do you notice any trends in terms of the countries and industries that are represented in the ranking?

Flat-Panel Televisions and the Global Economy

They begin as glass panels that are manufactured in high technology fabrication centers in South Korean, Taiwan, and Japan. Operating sophisticated tooling in environments that must be kept absolutely clean, these factories produce to exacting specifications sheets of glass twice as large as king-size beds. From there, the glass panels travel to Mexican plants located alongside the U.S. border. There they are cut to size, combined with electronic components shipped in from Asia and the United States, assembled into finished TVs, and loaded onto trucks bound for retail stores in the United States.

It's a huge business. In 2006, U.S. consumers spent some $26.4 billion on flat-panel TVs, a 63 percent increase over the amount spent in 2005. Projections called for U.S. sales to hit $37 billion by 2008; this growth would occur despite continuing decline in prices for flat-panel displays because of intense competition. During 2006, prices for 40-inch flat-panel TVs fell from $3,000 to $1,600, bringing them within the reach of many more consumers. In 2007, half of all TVs sold in the United States were flat-panel TVs.

The underlying technology for flat-panel displays was invented in the United States in the late 1960s by RCA. But after RCA and rivals Westinghouse and Xerox opted not to pursue the technology, the Japanese company Sharp made aggressive investments in flat-panel displays. By the early 1990s Sharp was selling the first flat-panel screens, but as the Japanese economy plunged into a decadelong recession, investment leadership shifted to South Korean companies such as Samsung. Then the 1997 Asian crisis hit Korea hard, and Taiwanese companies seized leadership. Today, Chinese companies are starting to elbow their way into the flat-panel display manufacturing business.

As production for flat-panel displays migrates its way around the globe to low-cost locations, there are clear winners and losers. U.S. consumers have benefited from the falling prices of flat-panel TVs and are snapping them up. Efficient manufacturers have taken advantage of globally dispersed supply chains to make and sell low-cost, high-quality flat-panel TVs. Foremost among these has been the California-based company, Vizio, founded by a Taiwanese immigrant. In just four years, sales of Vizio flat-panel TVs ballooned from nothing to $700 million in 2006. The company was forecasting sales as high as $2 billion for 2007. Vizio, however, has only 75 employees. These workers focus on final product design, sales, and customer service. Vizio outsources most of its engineering work, all of its manufacturing, and much of its logistics. For each of its models, Vizio assembles a team of supplier partners strung across the globe. Its 42-inch flat-panel TV, for example, contains a panel from South Korea, electronic components from China, and processors from the United States, and it is assembled in Mexico. Vizio's managers scour the globe for the cheapest manufacturers of flat-panel displays and electronic components. They sell most of their TVs to large discount retailers such as Costco and Sam's Club. Good order visibility from retailers, coupled with tight management of global logistics, allows Vizio to turn over its inventory every three weeks, twice as fast as many of its competitors, which is a major source of cost saving in a business where prices are falling continually.

On the other hand, the shift to flat-panel TVs has caused pain in certain sectors of the economy, such as those firms that make traditional cathode-ray TVs in high-cost locations. In 2006, for example, Japanese electronics manufacturer Sanyo laid off 300 employees at its U.S. factory and Hitachi closed its TV manufacturing plant in South Carolina, laying off 200 employees. Both Sony and Hitachi still make TVs, but they are flat-panel TVs assembled in Mexico from components manufactured in Asia.

Sources: D.J. Lynch, "Flat Panel TVs Display Effects of Globalization," *USA Today,* May 8, 2007, pp. 1B, 2B; P. Engardio and E. Woyke, "Flat Panels, Thin Margins," *BusinessWeek,* February 26, 2007, p. 50; and B. Womack, "Flat TV Seller Vizio Hits $600 million in Sales, Growing," *Orange County Business Journal,* September 4, 2007, pp. 1, 64.

Case Discussion Questions

1. Why is the manufacturing of flat-panel TVs migrating to different locations around the world?

2. Who benefits from the globalization of the flat-panel display industry? Who are the losers?

3. What would happen if the U.S. government required that flat-panel displays sold in the United States had to also be made in the United States? On balance, would this be a good or a bad thing?

4. What does the example of Vizio tell you about the future of production in an increasingly integrated global economy? What does it tell you about the strategies that enterprises must adopt to thrive in highly competitive global markets?

Part 2 Country Differences

LEARNING OBJECTIVES

After you have read this chapter you should:

1 Understand how the political systems of countries differ.

2 Understand how the economic systems of countries differ.

3 Understand how the legal systems of countries differ.

4 Be able to explain what determines the level of economic development of a nation.

5 Discuss the macro-political and economic changes taking place worldwide.

6 Describe how transition economies are moving toward market-based systems.

7 Articulate the implications for management practice of national difference in political economy.

chapter

2

National Differences in Political Economy

India's Transformation

After gaining independence from Britain in 1947, India adopted a democratic system of government. The economic system that developed in India after 1947 was a mixed economy characterized by a large number of state-owned enterprises, centralized planning, and subsidies. This system constrained the growth of the private sector. Private companies could expand only with government permission. It could take years to get permission to diversify into a new product. Much of heavy industry, such as auto, chemical, and steel production, was reserved for state-owned enterprises. Production quotas and high tariffs on imports also stunted the development of a healthy private sector, as did labor laws that made it difficult to fire employees.

By the early 1990s, it was clear that this system was incapable of delivering the kind of economic progress that many Southeastern Asian nations had started to enjoy. In 1994, India's economy was still smaller than Belgium's, despite having a population of 950 million. Its gross domestic product (GDP) per capita was a paltry $310; less than half the population could read; only 6 million had access to telephones; only 14 percent had access to clean sanitation; the World Bank estimated that some 40 percent of the world's desperately poor lived in India; and only 2.3 percent of the population had a household income in excess of $2,484.

The lack of progress led the government to embark on an ambitious economic reform program. Starting in 1991, much of the industrial licensing system was dismantled, and several areas once closed to the private sector were opened, including electricity generation, parts of the oil industry, steelmaking, air transport, and some areas of the telecommunications industry. Investment by foreign enterprises, formerly allowed only grudgingly and subject to arbitrary ceilings, was suddenly welcomed. Approval was made automatic for foreign equity stakes of up to 51 percent in an Indian enterprise, and 100 percent foreign ownership was allowed under certain circumstances. Raw materials and many industrial goods could be freely imported, and the maximum tariff that could be levied on imports was reduced from 400 percent to 65 percent. The top income tax rate was also reduced, and corporate tax fell from 57.5 percent to 46 percent in 1994, and then to 35 percent in 1997. The government also announced plans to start privatizing India's state-owned businesses, some 40 percent of which were losing money in the early 1990s.

Judged by some measures, the response to these economic reforms has been impressive. The economy expanded at an annual rate of about 6.3 percent from 1994 to 2004, and then accelerated to 9 percent per annum during 2005 to 2007. Foreign investment, a key indicator of how attractive foreign companies thought the Indian economy was, jumped from $150 million in 1991 to $15.3 billion in 2007. Some economic sectors have done particularly well, such as the information technology sector where India has emerged as a vibrant global center for software development with sales of $50 billion in 2007 (about 5.4 percent of GDP) up from just $150 million in 1990. In pharmaceuticals, too, Indian companies are emerging as credible players on the global marketplace, primarily by selling low-cost, generic versions of drugs that have come off patent in the developed world.

However, the country still has a long way to go. Attempts to further reduce import tariffs have been stalled by political opposition from employers, employees, and politicians, who fear that if barriers come down, a flood of inexpensive Chinese products will enter India. The privatization program continues to hit speed bumps—the latest in September 2003 when the Indian Supreme Court ruled that the government could not privatize two state-owned oil companies without explicit approval from the parliament. State-owned firms still account for 38 percent of national output in the non-farm sector, yet India's private firms are 30 to 40 percent more productive than their state-owned enterprises. There has also been strong resistance to reforming many of India's laws that make it difficult for private business to operate efficiently. For example, labor laws make it almost impossible for firms with more than 100 employees to fire workers, creating a disincentive for entrepreneurs to grow their enterprises beyond 100 employees. Other laws mandate that certain products can be manufactured only by small companies, effectively making it impossible for companies in these industries to attain the scale required to compete internationally. ●

Sources: "India's Breakthrough Budget?" *The Economist*, March 3, 2001; Shankar Aiyar, "Reforms: Time to Just Do It," *India Today*, January 24, 2000, p. 47; "America's Pain, India's Gain," *The Economist*, January 11, 2003, p. 57; Joanna Slater, "In Once Socialist India, Privatizations Are Becoming More Like Routine Matters," *The Wall Street Journal*, July 5, 2002, p. A8; "India's Economy: Ready to Roll Again?" *The Economist*, September 20, 2003, pp. 39–40; Joanna Slater, "Indian Pirates Turned Partners," *The Wall Street Journal*, November 13, 2003, p. A14; "The Next Wave: India," *The Economist*, December 17, 2005, p. 67; M. Dell, "The Digital Sector Can Make Poor Nations Prosper," *Financial Times*, May 4, 2006, p. 17; "What's Holding India Back," *The Economist*, March 8th, 2008, p. 11; and "Battling the Babu Raj," *The Economist*, March 8th, 2008, pp. 29–31.

Introduction

International business is much more complicated than domestic business because countries differ in many ways. Countries have different political, economic, and legal systems. Cultural practices can vary dramatically, as can the education and skill level of the population, and countries are at different stages of economic development. All these differences can and do have major implications for the practice of international business. They have a profound impact on the benefits, costs, and risks associated with doing business in different countries; the way in which operations in different countries should be managed; and the strategy international firms should pursue in different countries. A main function of this chapter and the next is to develop an awareness of and appreciation for the significance of country differences in political systems, economic systems, legal systems, and national culture. Another function of the two chapters is to describe how the political, economic, legal, and cultural systems of many of the world's nation-states are evolving and to draw out the implications of these changes for the practice of international business.

The opening case illustrates some of the issues covered in this chapter. Despite having a democratic system of government, for more than four decades after gaining independence in 1947, India's economic development was held back by policies that limited the growth of free enterprise and restricted inward investment by foreigners. This began to change in the early 1990s when the government started to deregulate the economy, removing burdensome regulations that stymied companies and privatizing state-owned enterprises. The consequences have included accelerated economic growth and the emergence of powerful sectors, such as India's booming information technology industry. However, as the opening case makes clear, much remains to be done. Compared to many developed nations, India's economy is still heavily regulated, and a significant proportion of economic activity remains in the hands of inefficient state-owned enterprises. Many would argue that this has to change if India is to stay on its growth path. This analysis has implications for international businesses considering whether to invest in India or another nation where economic policies might be viewed as more favorable.

This chapter focuses on how the political, economic, and legal systems of countries differ. Collectively we refer to these systems as constituting the political economy of a country. We use the term **political economy** to stress that the political, economic, and legal systems of a country are interdependent; they interact and influence each other, and in doing so they affect the level of economic well-being. In addition to reviewing these systems, we also explore how differences in political economy influence the benefits, costs, and risks associated with doing business in different countries, and how they affect management practice and strategy. In the next chapter, we will look at how differences in culture influence the practice of international business. As noted, the political economy and culture of a nation are not independent of each other. As will become apparent in Chapter 3, culture can exert an impact on political economy—on political, economic, and legal systems in a nation—and the converse can also hold true.

Political Economy
The interdependent combination of a country's political, economic, and legal systems.

Political Systems

The political system of a country shapes its economic and legal systems.[1] As such, we need to understand the nature of different political systems before discussing economic and legal systems. By **political system** we mean the system of government in a nation. Political systems can be assessed according to two dimensions. The first is the degree to which they emphasize collectivism as opposed to individualism. The second is the degree to which they are democratic or totalitarian. These dimensions are interrelated;

LEARNING OBJECTIVE 1
Understand how the political systems of countries differ.

Political System
The system of government in any nation.

systems that emphasize collectivism tend toward totalitarian, whereas those that place a high value on individualism tend to be democratic. However, a large gray area exists in the middle. It is possible to have democratic societies that emphasize a mix of collectivism and individualism. Similarly, it is possible to have totalitarian societies that are not collectivist.

COLLECTIVISM AND INDIVIDUALISM

Collectivism

A political system that stresses the primacy of collective goals over individual goals.

Collectivism refers to a political system that stresses the primacy of collective goals over individual goals.[2] When collectivism is emphasized, the needs of society as a whole are generally viewed as being more important than individual freedoms. In such circumstances, an individual's right to do something may be restricted on the grounds that it runs counter to "the good of society" or to "the common good." Advocacy of collectivism can be traced to the ancient Greek philosopher Plato (427–347 BC), who in *The Republic* argued that individual rights should be sacrificed for the good of the majority and that property should be owned in common. Plato did not equate collectivism with equality; he believed that society should be stratified into classes, with those best suited to rule (which for Plato, naturally, were philosophers and soldiers) administering society for the benefit of all. In modern times, the collectivist mantle has been picked up by socialists.

Socialism

Socialism

The political system that believes in state ownership of a country's means of production, distribution, and exchange so that all can benefit.

Modern **socialists** trace their intellectual roots to Karl Marx (1818–83), although socialist thought clearly predates Marx (elements of it can be traced to Plato). Marx argued that the few benefit at the expense of the many in a capitalist society where individual freedoms are not restricted. While successful capitalists accumulate considerable wealth, Marx postulated that the wages earned by the majority of workers in a capitalist society would be forced down to subsistence levels. He argued that capitalists expropriate for their own use the value created by workers, while paying workers only subsistence wages in return. According to Marx, the pay of workers does not reflect the full value of their labor. To correct this perceived wrong, Marx advocated state ownership of the basic means of production, distribution, and exchange (i.e., businesses). His logic was that if the state owned the means of production, the state could ensure that workers were fully compensated for their labor. Thus, the idea is to manage state-owned enterprise to benefit society as a whole, rather than individual capitalists.[3]

Communists

Those who believe that socialism can only be realized through violent revolution and totalitarian dictatorship.

In the early 20th century, the socialist ideology split into two broad camps. The **communists** believed that socialism could be achieved only through violent revolution and totalitarian dictatorship, whereas the **social democrats** committed themselves to achieving socialism by democratic means, turning their backs on violent revolution and dictatorship. Both versions of socialism waxed and waned during the 20th century. The communist version of socialism reached its high point in the late 1970s, when the majority of the world's population lived in communist states. The countries under Communist Party rule at that time included the former Soviet Union; its Eastern European client nations (e.g., Poland, Czechoslovakia, Hungary); China; the Southeast Asian nations of Cambodia, Laos, and Vietnam; various African nations (e.g., Angola and Mozambique); and the Latin American nations of Cuba and Nicaragua. By the mid-1990s, however, communism was in retreat worldwide. The Soviet Union had collapsed and had been replaced by a collection of 15 republics, many of which were at least nominally structured as democracies. Communism was swept out of Eastern Europe by the largely bloodless revolutions of 1989. Although China is still nominally a communist state with substantial limits to individual political freedom, in the economic sphere the country has moved sharply away from strict adherence to communist ideology. Other than China, communism hangs on only in some small fringe states, such as North Korea and Cuba.

Social Democrats

Those who believed in achieving socialism through democratic means.

Social democracy also seems to have passed a high-water mark, although the ideology may prove to be more enduring than communism. Social democracy has had perhaps its greatest influence in a number of democratic Western nations, including Australia, France, Germany, Great Britain, Norway, Spain, and Sweden, where Social Democratic parties have often held political power. Other countries where social democracy has had an important influence include India and Brazil. Consistent with their Marxists roots, many social democratic governments after World War II nationalized private companies in certain industries, transforming them into state-owned enterprises to be run for the "public good rather than private profit." In Great Britain by the end of the 1970s, for example, state-owned companies had a monopoly in the telecommunications, electricity, gas, coal, railway, and shipbuilding industries, as well as substantial interests in the oil, airline, auto, and steel industries.

Another Perspective

More on Aristotle

In addition to believing that the means of production should be privately owned, Aristotle thought that if we were to abolish private property, we would do moral harm to ourselves. Without private property, there would be no need to exercise generosity. "Without private property, no man will be seen to be liberal and no man will ever do any act of liberality; for only in the use of money is liberality made effective." (*The Politics*, Book 2, Ch. 5, trans. T.A. Sinclair)

The Peruvian economist Hernando De Soto develops Aristotle's point in the argument that the underlying, basic source of poverty and underdevelopment is the lack of a legal system that allows for transferable, titled, private property. (*The Mystery of Capital: Why Capitalism Triumphs in the West and Fails Everywhere Else*, Basic Books, 2000)

However, experience demonstrated that state ownership of the means of production ran counter to the public interest. In many countries, state-owned companies performed poorly. Protected from competition by their monopoly position and guaranteed government financial support, many became increasingly inefficient. Individuals paid for the luxury of state ownership through higher prices and higher taxes. As a consequence, a number of Western democracies voted many Social Democratic parties out of office in the late 1970s and early 1980s. They were succeeded by political parties, such as Britain's Conservative Party and Germany's Christian Democratic Party, that were more committed to free market economics. These parties sold state-owned enterprises to private investors (a process referred to as **privatization**). Even where Social Democratic parties have regained the levers of power, as in Great Britain in 1997 when the left-leaning Labor Party won control of the government, they too now seem committed to continued private ownership.

Privatization
The sale of state-owned enterprises to private investors.

Individualism   The opposite of collectivism, **individualism** refers to a philosophy that an individual should have freedom in his or her economic and political pursuits. In contrast to collectivism, individualism stresses that the interests of the individual should take precedence over the interests of the state. Like collectivism, individualism can be traced to an ancient Greek philosopher, in this case Plato's disciple Aristotle (384–322 BC). In contrast to Plato, Aristotle argued that individual diversity and private ownership are desirable. In a passage that might have been taken from a speech by contemporary politicians who adhere to a free market ideology, he argued that private property is more highly productive than communal property and will thus stimulate progress. According to Aristotle, communal property receives little care, whereas property that is owned by an individual will receive the greatest care and therefore be most productive.

Individualism
The philosophy that an individual should have freedom in his or her economic and political pursuits.

Individualism was reborn as an influential political philosophy in the Protestant trading nations of England and the Netherlands during the 16th century. The philosophy was refined in the work of a number of British philosophers, including David Hume (1711–76), Adam Smith (1723–90), and John Stuart Mill (1806–73). Individualism exercised a profound influence on those in the American colonies who sought independence from Great Britain. Indeed, the concept underlies the ideas expressed in the Declaration of Independence. In the 20th century, several Nobel Prize–winning economists, including Milton Friedman, Friedrich von Hayek, and James Buchanan, have championed the philosophy.

Individualism is built on two central tenets. The first is an emphasis on the importance of guaranteeing individual freedom and self-expression. As John Stuart Mill put it,

> The sole end for which mankind are warranted, individually or collectively, in interfering with the liberty of action of any of their number is self-protection. . . . The only purpose for which power can be rightfully exercised over any member of a civilized community, against his will, is to prevent harm to others. His own good, either physical or moral, is not a sufficient warrant. . . . The only part of the conduct of any one, for which he is amenable to society, is that which concerns others. In the part which merely concerns himself, his independence is, of right, absolute. Over himself, over his own body and mind, the individual is sovereign.[4]

The second tenet of individualism is that the welfare of society is best served by letting people pursue their own economic self-interest, as opposed to some collective body (such as government) dictating what is in society's best interest. Or as Adam Smith put it in a famous passage from *The Wealth of Nations*, an individual who intends his own gain is

> led by an invisible hand to promote an end which was no part of his intention. Nor is it always worse for the society that it was no part of it. By pursuing his own interest he frequently promotes that of the society more effectually than when he really intends to promote it. I have never known much good done by those who effect to trade for the public good.[5]

The central message of individualism, therefore, is that individual economic and political freedoms are the ground rules on which a society should be based. This puts individualism in conflict with collectivism. Collectivism asserts the primacy of the collective over the individual; individualism asserts the opposite. This underlying ideological conflict shaped much of the recent history of the world. The Cold War, for example, was in many respects a war between collectivism, championed by the former Soviet Union, and individualism, championed by the United States.

In practical terms, individualism translates into an advocacy for democratic political systems and free market economics. Since the late 1980s, the waning of collectivism has been matched by the ascendancy of individualism. Democratic ideals and free market economics have swept away socialism and communism in many states. The changes of the past 20 years go beyond the revolutions in Eastern Europe and the former Soviet Union to include a move toward greater individualism in Latin America and many of the social democratic states of the West (e.g., Great Britain and Sweden). This is not to claim that individualism has finally won a long battle with collectivism. It has clearly not (indeed, during 2005 and into 2006 there were signs of a swing back toward left-leaning socialist ideas in several countries, most notably in Venezuela and Bolivia). But as a guiding political philosophy, individualism has been on the ascendancy. This is good news for international business because the pro-business and pro-free trade values of individualism create a favorable environment within which international business can thrive.

Democracy
A political system in which government is by the people, exercised either directly or through elected representatives.

Totalitarianism
A political system in which one person or political party exercises absolute control over all spheres of human life and prohibits opposing political parties.

DEMOCRACY AND TOTALITARIANISM

Democracy and totalitarianism are at different ends of a political dimension. **Democracy** refers to a political system in which government is by the people, exercised either directly or through elected representatives. **Totalitarianism** is a form of government in which one person or political party exercises absolute control over all spheres of human life and prohibits opposing political parties. The democratic–totalitarian dimension is not independent of the collectivism–individualism dimension. Democracy and individualism go hand in hand, as do the communist version of collectivism and totalitarianism. However, gray areas exist; it is possible to have a democratic state in which collective values predominate, and it is possible to have a totalitarian state that is hostile to collectivism and in which some degree of individualism—particularly in the economic sphere—is encouraged. For example, China has seen a move toward greater individual freedom in the economic sphere, but the country is still ruled by a totalitarian dictatorship that constrains political freedom.

Democracy

The pure form of democracy, as originally practiced by several city-states in ancient Greece, is based on a belief that citizens should be directly involved in decision making. In complex, advanced societies with populations in the tens or hundreds of millions this is impractical. Most modern democratic states practice **representative democracy.** In a representative democracy, citizens periodically elect individuals to represent them. These elected representatives then form a government, whose function is to make decisions on behalf of the electorate. In a representative democracy, elected representatives who fail to perform this job adequately will be voted out of office at the next election.

To guarantee that elected representatives can be held accountable for their actions by the electorate, an ideal representative democracy has a number of safeguards that are typically enshrined in constitutional law. These include (1) an individual's right to freedom of expression, opinion, and organization; (2) a free media; (3) regular elections in which all eligible citizens are allowed to vote; (4) universal adult suffrage; (5) limited terms for elected representatives; (6) a fair court system that is independent from the political system; (7) a nonpolitical state bureaucracy; (8) a nonpolitical police force and armed service; and (9) relatively free access to state information.[6]

Representative Democracy
A democracy in which citizens periodically elect individuals to represent them in government functions.

Totalitarianism

In a totalitarian country, all the constitutional guarantees on which representative democracies are built—an individual's right to freedom of expression and organization, a free media, and regular elections—are denied to the citizens. In most totalitarian states, political repression is widespread, free and fair elections are lacking, media are heavily censored, basic civil liberties are denied, and those who question the right of the rulers to rule find themselves imprisoned, or worse.

Four major forms of totalitarianism exist in the world today. Until recently, the most widespread was **communist totalitarianism.** Communism, however, is in decline worldwide, and most of the Communist Party dictatorships have collapsed since 1989. Exceptions to this trend (so far) are China, Vietnam, Laos, North Korea, and Cuba, although all these states exhibit clear signs that the Communist Party's monopoly on political power is retreating. In many respects, the governments of China, Vietnam, and Laos are communist in name only since those nations now adhere to market-based economic reforms. They remain, however, totalitarian states that deny many basic civil liberties to their populations. On the other hand, there are signs of a swing back toward communist totalitarian ideas in some states, such as Venezuela where the government of Hugo Chavez is displaying some totalitarian tendencies.

A second form of totalitarianism might be labeled **theocratic totalitarianism.** Theocratic totalitarianism is found in states where political power is monopolized by a party, group, or individual that governs according to religious principles. The most common form of theocratic totalitarianism is based on Islam and is exemplified by states such as Iran and Saudi Arabia. These states limit freedom of political and religious expression with laws based on Islamic principles.

Communist Totalitarianism
A version of collectivism advocating that socialism can only be achieved through a totalitarian dictatorship.

Theocratic Totalitarianism
A political system in which political power is monopolized by a party, group, or individual that governs according to religious principles.

Communist totalitarianism is still the political system in Vietnam, where red banners in the Hanoi marketplace remind citizens and visitors of the government's control.

Tribal Totalitarianism
A political system in which a party, group, or individual that represents the interests of a particular tribe monopolizes political power.

A third form of totalitarianism might be referred to as **tribal totalitarianism.** Tribal totalitarianism has arisen from time to time in African countries such as Zimbabwe, Tanzania, Uganda, and Kenya. The borders of most African states reflect the administrative boundaries drawn by the old European colonial powers rather than tribal realities. Consequently, the typical African country contains a number of tribes. Tribal totalitarianism occurs when a political party that represents the interests of a particular tribe (and not always the majority tribe) monopolizes power. Such one-party states still exist in Africa.

Right-Wing Totalitarianism
A political system in which political power is monopolized by a party, group, or individual that generally permits individual economic freedom but restricts individual political freedom, including free speech, often on the grounds that it would lead to the rise of communism.

A fourth major form of totalitarianism might be described as **right-wing totalitarianism.** Right-wing totalitarianism generally permits some individual economic freedom but restricts individual political freedom, frequently on the grounds that it would lead to the rise of communism. A common feature of many right-wing dictatorships is an overt hostility to socialist or communist ideas. Many right-wing totalitarian governments are backed by the military, and in some cases the government may be made up of military officers. The fascist regimes that ruled Germany and Italy in the 1930s and 1940s were right-wing totalitarian states. Until the early 1980s, right-wing dictatorships, many of which were military dictatorships, were common throughout Latin America. They were also found in several Asian countries, particularly South Korea, Taiwan, Singapore, Indonesia, and the Philippines. Since the early 1980s, however, this form of government has been in retreat. Most Latin American countries are now genuine multiparty democracies. Similarly, South Korea, Taiwan, and the Philippines have all become functioning democracies, as has Indonesia.

Economic Systems

LEARNING OBJECTIVE 2
Understand how the economic systems of countries differ.

It should be clear from the previous section that political ideology and economic systems are connected. In countries where individual goals are given primacy over collective goals, we are more likely to find free market economic systems. In contrast, in countries where collective goals are given preeminence, the state may have taken control over many enterprises; markets in such countries are likely to be restricted rather than free. We can identify three broad types of economic systems—a market economy, a command economy, and a mixed economy.

MARKET ECONOMY

In a pure **market economy,** all productive activities are privately owned, as opposed to being owned by the state. The goods and services that a country produces are not planned by anyone. Production is determined by the interaction of supply and demand and signaled to producers through the price system. If demand for a product exceeds supply, prices will rise, signaling producers to produce more. If supply exceeds demand, prices will fall, signaling producers to produce less. In this system consumers are sovereign. The purchasing patterns of consumers, as signaled to producers through the mechanism of the price system, determine what is produced and in what quantity.

For a market to work in this manner, supply must not be restricted. A supply restriction occurs when a single firm monopolizes a market. In such circumstances, rather than increase output in response to increased demand, a monopolist might restrict output and let prices rise. This allows the monopolist to take a greater profit margin on each unit it sells. Although this is good for the monopolist, it is bad for the consumer, who has to pay higher prices. It also is probably bad for the welfare of society. Since a monopolist has no competitors, it has no incentive to search for ways to lower production costs. Rather, it can simply pass on cost increases to consumers in the form of higher prices. The net result is that the monopolist is likely to become increasingly inefficient, producing high-priced, low-quality goods, and society suffers as a consequence.

Given the dangers inherent in monopoly, the role of government in a market economy is to encourage vigorous free and fair competition between private producers. Governments do this by outlawing monopolies and restrictive business practices designed to monopolize a market (antitrust laws serve this function in the United States). Private ownership also encourages vigorous competition and economic efficiency. Private ownership ensures that entrepreneurs have a right to the profits generated by their own efforts. This gives entrepreneurs an incentive to search for better ways of serving consumer needs. That may be through introducing new products, by developing more efficient production processes, by pursuing better marketing and after-sale service, or simply through managing their businesses more efficiently than their competitors. In turn, the constant improvement in product and process that results from such an incentive has been argued to have a major positive impact on economic growth and development.[7]

Market Economy
An economic system in which the interaction of supply and demand determines the quantity in which goods and services are produced.

COMMAND ECONOMY

In a pure **command economy,** the government plans the goods and services that a country produces, the quantity in which they are produced, and the prices at which they are sold. Consistent with the collectivist ideology, the objective of a command economy is for government to allocate resources for "the good of society." In addition, in a pure command economy, all businesses are state owned, the rationale being that the government can then direct them to make investments that are in the best interests of the nation as a whole rather than in the interests of private individuals. Historically, command economies were found in communist countries where collectivist goals were given priority over individual goals. Since the demise of communism in the late 1980s, the number of command economies has fallen dramatically. Some elements of a command economy were also evident in a number of democratic nations led by socialist-inclined governments. France and India both experimented with extensive government planning and state ownership, although government planning has fallen into disfavor in both countries (see the opening case on India).

While the objective of a command economy is to mobilize economic resources for the public good, the opposite seems to have occurred. In a command economy, state-owned enterprises have little incentive to control costs and be efficient because they

Command Economy
An economic system in which the government plans the allocation of resources, including determination of what goods and services should be produced and in what quantity.

cannot go out of business. Also, the abolition of private ownership means there is no incentive for individuals to look for better ways to serve consumer needs; hence, dynamism and innovation are absent from command economies. Instead of growing and becoming more prosperous, such economies tend to stagnate.

MIXED ECONOMY   Between market economies and command economies can be found mixed economies. In a mixed economy, certain sectors of the economy are left to private ownership and free market mechanisms while other sectors have significant state ownership and government planning. Mixed economies were once common throughout much of the world, although they are becoming much less so. Not long ago, Great Britain, France, and Sweden were mixed economies, but extensive privatization has reduced state ownership of businesses in all three nations. A similar trend can be observed in many other countries where there was once a large state sector, such as Brazil, Italy, and India (in India, the state sector still accounts for 38 percent of non-farm output; see the opening case).

In mixed economies, governments also tend to take into state ownership troubled firms whose continued operation is thought to be vital to national interests. Consider, for example, the French automobile company Renault. The government took over the company when it ran into serious financial problems. The French government reasoned that the social costs of the unemployment that might result if Renault collapsed were unacceptable, so it nationalized the company to save it from bankruptcy. Renault's competitors weren't thrilled by this move because they had to compete with a company whose costs were subsidized by the state.

Legal Systems

LEARNING OBJECTIVE 3
Understand how the legal systems of countries differ.

The **legal system** of a country refers to the rules, or laws, that regulate behavior along with the processes by which the laws are enforced and through which redress for grievances is obtained. The legal system of a country is of immense importance to international business. A country's laws regulate business practice, define the manner in which business transactions are to be executed, and set down the rights and obligations of those involved in business transactions. The legal environments of countries differ in significant ways. As we shall see, differences in legal systems can affect the attractiveness of a country as an investment site or market.

Legal System
Rules that regulate behavior and the processes by which the laws of a country are enforced and through which redress of grievance is obtained.

Like the economic system of a country, the legal system is influenced by the prevailing political system (although it is also strongly influenced by historical tradition). The government of a country defines the legal framework within which firms do business—and often the laws that regulate business reflect the rulers' dominant political ideology. For example, collectivist-inclined totalitarian states tend to enact laws that severely restrict private enterprise, whereas the laws enacted by governments in democratic states where individualism is the dominant political philosophy tend to be pro-private enterprise and pro-consumer.

Here we focus on several issues that illustrate how legal systems can vary—and how such variations can affect international business. First, we look at some basic differences in legal systems. Next we look at contract law. Third, we look at the laws governing property rights with particular reference to patents, copyrights, and trademarks. Then we discuss protection of intellectual property. Finally, we look at laws covering product safety and product liability.

DIFFERENT LEGAL SYSTEMS   There are three main types of legal systems—or legal tradition—in use around the world: common law, civil law, and theocratic law.

Common Law   The common law system evolved in England over hundreds of years. It is now found in most of Great Britain's former colonies, including the United States. **Common law** is based on tradition, precedent, and custom. *Tradition* refers to a country's legal history, *precedent* to cases that have come before the courts in the past, and *custom* to the ways in which laws are applied in specific situations. When law courts interpret common law, they do so with regard to these characteristics. This gives a common law system a degree of flexibility that other systems lack. Judges in a common law system have the power to interpret the law so that it applies to the unique circumstances of an individual case. In turn, each new interpretation sets a precedent that may be followed in future cases. As new precedents arise, laws may be altered, clarified, or amended to deal with new situations.

Common Law
A system of law based on tradition, precedent, and custom, which is flexibly interpreted by judges as it applies to the unique circumstances of each case.

Civil Law   A **civil law system** is based on a detailed set of laws organized into codes. When law courts interpret civil law, they do so with regard to these codes. More than 80 countries, including Germany, France, Japan, and Russia, operate with a civil law system. A civil law system tends to be less adversarial than a common law system, since the judges rely upon detailed legal codes rather than interpreting tradition, precedent, and custom. Judges under a civil law system have less flexibility than those under a common law system. Judges in a common law system have the power to interpret the law, whereas judges in a civil law system have the power only to apply the law.

Civil Law System
A system of law based on a detailed set of written laws and codes.

Theocratic Law   A **theocratic law system** is one in which the law is based on religious teachings. Islamic law is the most widely practiced theocratic legal system in the modern world, although usage of both Hindu and Jewish law persisted into the 20th century. Islamic law is primarily a moral rather than a commercial law and is intended to govern all aspects of life.[8] The foundation for Islamic law is the holy book of Islam, the Koran, along with the Sunnah, or decisions and sayings of the Prophet Muhammad, and the writings of Islamic scholars who have derived rules by analogy from the principles established in the Koran and the Sunnah. Because the Koran and Sunnah are holy documents, the basic foundations of Islamic law cannot be changed. However, in practice Islamic jurists and scholars are constantly debating the application of Islamic law to the modern world. In reality, many Muslim countries have legal systems that are a blend of Islamic law and a common or civil law system.

Theocratic Law System
A system of law based on religious teachings.

Although Islamic law is primarily concerned with moral behavior, it has been extended to cover certain commercial activities. An example is the payment or receipt of interest, which is considered usury and outlawed by the Koran. To the devout Muslim, acceptance of interest payments is seen as a grave sin; the giver and the taker are equally damned. This is not just a matter of theology; in several Islamic states it has also become a matter of law. In the 1990s, for example, Pakistan's Federal Shariat Court, the highest Islamic lawmaking body in the country, pronounced interest to be un-Islamic and therefore illegal and demanded that the government amend all financial laws accordingly. In 1999, Pakistan's Supreme Court ruled that Islamic banking methods should be used in the country after July 1, 2001.[9] By 2007,

Another Perspective

No Interest in Islamic Banking? Why?
How can a banking system operate without interest (*riba* in Arabic)? The basic economic idea is that commercial risk should be shared. In the Western approach, interest guarantees the banker a return, so on a collateralized loan, the banker avoids much of the commercial risk that's inherent in business. No matter what happens to the business, the banker gets a return. In contrast, Islam requires that the banker share this commercial risk. If the business venture is successful, the banker shares the profit. If the venture doesn't do well, neither does the banker. The value of community in Islam is stronger than the value of individual profit. See Chapter 3 for more on this point.

some 500 Islamic financial institutions in the world collectively managed more than $500 billion in assets. In addition to Pakistan, Islamic financial institutions are found in many of the Gulf states, Egypt, and Malaysia.[10]

DIFFERENCES IN CONTRACT LAW   The difference between common law and civil law systems can be illustrated by the approach of each to contract law (remember, most theocratic legal systems also have elements of common or civil law). A **contract** is a document that specifies the conditions under which an exchange is to occur and details the rights and obligations of the parties involved. Some form of contract regulates many business transactions. **Contract law** is the body of law that governs contract enforcement. The parties to an agreement normally resort to contract law when one party feels the other has violated either the letter or the spirit of an agreement.

Because common law tends to be relatively ill specified, contracts drafted under a common law framework tend to be very detailed with all contingencies spelled out. In civil law systems, however, contracts tend to be much shorter and less specific because many of the issues are already covered in a civil code. Thus, it is more expensive to draw up contracts in a common law jurisdiction, and resolving contract disputes can be very adversarial in common law systems. But common law systems have the advantage of greater flexibility and allow for judges to interpret a contract dispute in light of the prevailing situation. International businesses need to be sensitive to these differences; approaching a contract dispute in a state with a civil law system as if it had a common law system may backfire, and vice versa.

When contract disputes arise in international trade, there is always the question of which country's laws to apply. To resolve this issue, a number of countries, including the United States, have ratified the **United Nations Convention on Contracts for the International Sale of Goods (CIGS).** The CIGS establishes a uniform set of rules governing certain aspects of the making and performance of everyday commercial contracts between sellers and buyers who have their places of business in different nations. By adopting the CIGS, a nation signals to other adopters that it will treat the convention's rules as part of its law. The CIGS applies automatically to all contracts for the sale of goods between different firms based in countries that have ratified the convention, unless the parties to the contract explicitly opt out. One problem with the CIGS, however, is that fewer than 70 nations have ratified the convention (the CIGS went into effect in 1988).[11] Many of the world's larger trading nations, including Japan and the United Kingdom, have not ratified the CIGS.

When firms do not wish to accept the CIGS, they often opt for arbitration by a recognized arbitration court to settle contract disputes. The most well known of these courts is the International Court of Arbitration of the International Chamber of Commerce in Paris, which handles more than 500 requests per year for arbitration typically involving over 100 countries.[12]

PROPERTY RIGHTS AND CORRUPTION   In a legal sense, the term *property* refers to a resource over which an individual or business holds a legal title; that is, a resource that it owns. Resources include land, buildings, equipment, capital, mineral rights, businesses, and intellectual property (ideas, which are protected by patents, copyrights, and trademarks). **Property rights** refer to the legal rights over the use to which a resource is put and over the use made of any income that may be derived from that resource.[13] Countries differ in the extent to which their legal systems define and protect property rights. Almost all countries now have laws on their books that protect property rights. Even China, still nominally a Communist state despite its booming market economy, finally enacted a law to protect the rights of private property holders in 2007 (the law gives individuals the same legal protection for their property as the

Contract
A document that specifies the conditions under which an exchange is to occur and details the rights and obligations of the parties involved.

Contract Law
The body of law that governs contract enforcement.

United Nations Convention on Contracts for the International Sale of Goods (CIGS)
A set of rules governing certain aspects of the making and performance of commercial contracts between sellers and buyers who have their places of businesses in different nations.

Property Rights
The bundle of legal rights over the use to which a resource is put and over the use made of any income that may be derived from that resource.

state).[14] However, in many countries these laws are not enforced by the authorities and property rights are violated. Property rights can be violated in two ways—through private action and through public action.

Private Action   In this context, **private action** refers to theft, piracy, blackmail, and the like by private individuals or groups. Although theft occurs in all countries, a weak legal system allows for a much higher level of criminal action in some than in others. For example, in Russia in the chaotic period following the collapse of communism, an outdated legal system, coupled with a weak police force and judicial system, offered both domestic and foreign businesses scant protection from blackmail by the "Russian Mafia." Successful business owners in Russia often had to pay "protection money" to the Mafia or face violent retribution, including bombings and assassinations (about 500 contract killings of businessmen occurred in 1995 and again in 1996).[15]

Private Action
Theft, piracy, blackmail, and the like by private individuals or groups.

Russia is not alone in having Mafia problems (and the situation in Russia has improved significantly since the mid-1990s). The Mafia has a long history in the United States (Chicago in the 1930s was similar to Moscow in the 1990s). In Japan, the local version of the Mafia, known as the *yakuza*, runs protection rackets, particularly in the food and entertainment industries.[16] However, there was a big difference between the magnitude of such activity in Russia in the 1990s and its limited impact in Japan and the United States. This difference arose because the legal enforcement apparatus, such as the police and court system, was so weak in Russia following the collapse of communism. Many other countries from time to time have had problems similar to or even greater than those experienced by Russia.

Public Action and Corruption   **Public action** to violate property rights occurs when public officials, such as politicians and government bureaucrats, extort income, resources, or the property itself from property holders. This can be done through legal mechanisms such as levying excessive taxation, requiring expensive licenses or permits from property holders, taking assets into state ownership without compensating the owners, or redistributing assets without compensating the prior owners. It can also be done through illegal means, or corruption, by demanding bribes from businesses in return for the rights to operate in a country, industry, or location.[17]

Public Action
The extortion of income or resources from property holders by public officials, such as politicians and government bureaucrats.

Corruption has been well documented in every society, from the banks of the Congo River to the palace of the Dutch royal family, from Japanese politicians to Brazilian bankers, and from Indonesian government officials to the New York City Police Department. The government of the late Ferdinand Marcos in the Philippines was famous for demanding bribes from foreign businesses wishing to set up operations in that country.[18] The same was true of government officials in Indonesia under the rule of former president Suharto. No society is immune to corruption. However, there are systematic differences in the extent of corruption. In some countries, the rule of law minimizes corruption. Corruption is seen and treated as illegal, and when discovered, violators are punished by the full force of the law. In other countries, the rule of law is weak and corruption by bureaucrats and politicians is rife. Corruption is so endemic in some countries that politicians and bureaucrats regard it as a perk of office and openly flout laws against corruption.

According to Transparency International, an independent nonprofit organization dedicated to exposing and fighting corruption, businesses and individuals spend some $400 billion a year worldwide on bribes related to government procurement contracts alone.[19] Transparency International has also measured the level of corruption among public officials in different countries.[20] As can be seen in Figure 2.1, the organization rated countries such as Finland and New Zealand as clean; it rated others, such as Russia, India, Indonesia, and Zimbabwe, as corrupt. Somalia ranked last out of all 179 countries in the survey, and Finland and New Zealand ranked first.

figure **2.1**

Rankings of Corruption by Country, 2007

Source: Transparency International, "Global Corruption Report, 2007," www.transparency.org.

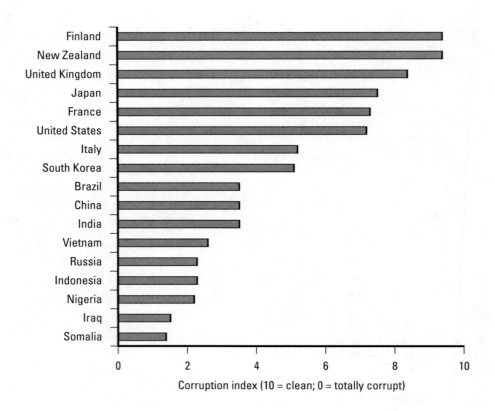

Corruption index (10 = clean; 0 = totally corrupt)

Economic evidence suggests that high levels of corruption significantly reduce the foreign direct investment, level of international trade, and economic growth rate in a country.[21] By siphoning off profits, corrupt politicians and bureaucrats reduce the returns to business investment and, hence, reduce the incentive of both domestic and foreign businesses to invest in that country. The lower level of investment that results hurts economic growth. Thus, we would expect countries such as Indonesia, Nigeria, and Russia to have a much lower rate of economic growth than might otherwise have been the case. A detailed example of the negative effect that corruption can have on economic progress is given in the accompanying Country Focus, which looks at the impact of corruption on economic growth in Nigeria.

Foreign Corrupt Practices Act
U.S. law regulating behavior regarding the conduct of international business in the taking of bribes and other unethical actions.

Foreign Corrupt Practices Act   In the 1970s, the United States passed the **Foreign Corrupt Practices Act** following revelations that U.S. companies had bribed government officials in foreign countries in an attempt to win lucrative contracts. This law makes it illegal to bribe a foreign government official to obtain or maintain business over which that foreign official has authority, and it requires all publicly traded companies (whether or not they are involved in international trade) to keep detailed records that would reveal whether a violation of the act has occurred. Along the same lines, in 1997 trade and finance ministers from the member states of the Organization for Economic Cooperation and Development (OECD), an association of the world's 30 most powerful economies, adopted the Convention on Combating Bribery of Foreign Public Officials in International Business Transactions.[22] The convention obliges member states to make the bribery of foreign public officials a criminal offense.

However, both the U.S. law and OECD convention include language that allows for exceptions known as facilitating or expediting payments (also called *grease payments*

Country FOCUS

Corruption in Nigeria

When Nigeria gained independence from Great Britain in 1960, there were hopes that the country might emerge as an economic heavyweight in Africa. Not only was Nigeria Africa's most populous country, but it also was blessed with abundant natural resources, particularly oil, from which the country earned over $500 billion between 1970 and 2007. Despite this, Nigeria remains one of the poorest countries in the world. According to the Human Development Index compiled by the United Nations, Nigeria ranked 159 out of 177 countries covered. Gross domestic product per capita was just $560, 51 percent of the adult population was illiterate, and life expectancy at birth was only 43 years.

What went wrong? Although there is no simple answer, a number of factors seem to have conspired to damage economic activity in Nigeria. The country is composed of several competing ethnic, tribal, and religious groups, and the conflict among them has limited political stability and led to political strife, including a brutal civil war in the 1970s. With the legitimacy of the government always in question, political leaders often purchased support by legitimizing bribes and by raiding the national treasury to reward allies. Civilian rule after independence was followed by a series of military dictatorships, each of which seemed more corrupt and inept than the last (the country returned to civilian rule in 1999).

During the 1990s, the military dictator, Sani Abacha, openly and systematically plundered the state treasury for his own personal gain. His most blatant scam was the Petroleum Trust Fund, which he set up in the mid-1990s ostensibly to channel extra revenue from an increase in fuel prices into much-needed infrastructure projects and other investments. The fund was not independently audited, and almost none of the money that passed through it was properly accounted for. It was, in fact, a vehicle for Abacha and his supporters to spend at will a sum that in 1996 was equivalent to some 25 percent of the total federal budget. Abacha, aware of his position as an unpopular and unelected leader, lavished money on personal security and handed out bribes to those whose support he coveted. With examples like this at the very top of the government, it is not surprising that corruption could be found throughout the political and bureaucratic apparatus.

Some of the excesses were simply astounding. In the 1980s an aluminum smelter was built on the orders of the government, which wanted to industrialize Nigeria. The cost of the smelter was $2.4 billion, some 60 to 100 percent higher than the cost of comparable plants elsewhere in the developed world. This high cost was widely interpreted to reflect the bribes that had to be paid to local politicians by the international contractors that built the plant. The smelter has never operated at more than a fraction of its intended capacity.

Has the situation in Nigeria improved since the country returned to civilian rule in 1999? In 2003, Olusegun Obasanjo was elected president on a platform that included a promise to fight corruption. By some accounts, progress has been seen. His anticorruption chief, Nuhu Ribadu, claimed that whereas 70 percent of the country's oil revenues were being stolen or wasted in 2002, by 2004 the figure was "only" 40 percent. But in its most recent survey, Transparency International still ranked Nigeria among the most corrupt countries in the world in 2007 (see Figure 2.1), suggesting that the country still has long way to go. In an effort to move things along, in 2007 the country's top anticorruption body, the Economic and Financial Crimes Commission, sent letters to political parties listing 130 candidates for upcoming elections who it stated would soon be charged with corruption. Several parties responded by removing candidates identified as corrupt from their lists. Others argued that the list was itself influenced by political motives and in particular a desire to strengthen the position of President Obasanjo and his handpicked successor, President Umaru Yar'Adua, by blacklisting opponents.

Sources: "A Tale of Two Giants," *The Economist*, January 15, 2000, p. 5; J. Coolidge and S. Rose Ackerman, "High Level Rent Seeking and Corruption in African Regimes," World Bank policy research working paper no. 1780, June 1997; D.L. Bevan, P. Collier, and J.W. Gunning, *Nigeria and Indonesia: The Political Economy of Poverty, Equity and Growth* (Oxford: Oxford University Press, 1999); "Democracy and Its Discontents," *The Economist*, January 29, 2005, p. 55; A. Field, "Can Reform Save Nigeria?" *Journal of Commerce*, November 21, 2005, p. 1; "A Blacklist to Bolster Democracy," *The Economist*, February 17, 2007, p. 59; and J.P. Luna, "Back on Track: Nigeria's Hard Path towards Reform," *Harvard International Review* 29, no. 3 (2007), p. 7.

or *speed money*), the purpose of which is to expedite or to secure the performance of a routine governmental action.[23] For example, they allow for small payments made to speed up the issuance of permits or licenses, process paperwork, or just get vegetables off the dock and on their way to market. The explanation for this exception to general antibribery provisions is that while grease payments are, technically, bribes, they are distinguishable from (and, apparently, less offensive than) bribes used to obtain or maintain business, because they merely facilitate performance of duties that the recipients are already obligated to perform.

THE PROTECTION OF INTELLECTUAL PROPERTY

Intellectual Property
Property that is the product of intellectual activity.

Patent
A legal device that grants the inventor of a new product or process exclusive rights for a defined period to the manufacture, use, or sale of that invention.

Copyrights
Exclusive legal rights of authors, composers, playwrights, artists, and publishers to publish and dispose of their work as they see fit.

Trademarks
Designs and names, often officially registered, by which merchants or manufacturers designate and differentiate their products.

World Intellectual Property Organization
An international organization whose members sign treaties to agree to protect intellectual property.

Paris Convention for the Protection of Industrial Property
The oldest international treaty concerning protection of intellectual property, which has been signed by 170 nations.

Intellectual property refers to property that is the product of intellectual activity, such as computer software, a screenplay, a music score, or the chemical formula for a new drug. Patents, copyrights, and trademarks establish ownership rights over intellectual property. A **patent** grants the inventor of a new product or process exclusive rights for a defined period to the manufacture, use, or sale of that invention. **Copyrights** are the exclusive legal rights of authors, composers, playwrights, artists, and publishers to publish and disperse their work as they see fit. **Trademarks** are designs and names, often officially registered, by which merchants or manufacturers designate and differentiate their products (e.g., Christian Dior clothes). In the high-technology "knowledge" economy of the 21st century, intellectual property has become an increasingly important source of economic value for businesses. Protecting intellectual property has also become increasingly problematic, particularly if it can be rendered in a digital form and then copied and distributed at very low cost via pirated CDs or over the Internet (e.g., computer software, music and video recordings).[24]

The philosophy behind intellectual property laws is to reward the originator of a new invention, book, musical record, clothes design, restaurant chain, and the like, for his or her idea and effort. Such laws stimulate innovation and creative work. They provide an incentive for people to search for novel ways of doing things, and they reward creativity. For example, consider innovation in the pharmaceutical industry. A patent will grant the inventor of a new drug a 20-year monopoly in production of that drug. This gives pharmaceutical firms an incentive to undertake the expensive, difficult, and time-consuming basic research required to generate new drugs (it can cost $800 million in R&D and take 12 years to get a new drug on the market). Without the guarantees provided by patents, companies would be unlikely to commit themselves to extensive basic research.[25]

The protection of intellectual property rights differs greatly from country to country. Although many countries have stringent intellectual property regulations on their books, the enforcement of these regulations has often been lax. This has been the case even among many of the 183 countries that are now members of the **World Intellectual Property Organization,** all of which have signed international treaties designed to protect intellectual property, including the oldest such treaty, the **Paris Convention for the Protection of Industrial Property,** which dates to 1883 and has been signed by some 170 nations as of 2007. Weak enforcement encourages the piracy (theft) of intellectual property. China and Thailand have recently been among the worst offenders in Asia. Pirated computer software is widely available in China. Similarly, the streets of Bangkok, Thailand's capital, are lined with stands selling pirated copies of Rolex watches, Levi Strauss jeans, videotapes, and computer software.

Piracy in music recordings is rampant. The International Federation of the Phonographic Industry claims that about one-third of all recorded music products sold worldwide are pirated (illegal) copies, suggesting that piracy costs the industry more than $4.5 billion annually.[26] The computer software industry also suffers from lax enforcement of intellectual property rights. Estimates suggest that violations of intellectual property rights cost personal computer software firms revenues equal to $40 billion in 2006.[27] According to the Business Software Alliance, a software industry association, in 2006 some 35 percent of all software applications used in the world were pirated. The worst region was Central and Eastern Europe where the piracy rate was 68 percent (see Figure 2.2). One of the worst countries was China, where the piracy rate in 2006 ran at 82 percent and cost the industry more than $5.42 billion in lost sales, up from $444 million in 1995. The piracy rate in the United States was much lower at 21 percent; however, the value of sales lost was more significant because of the size of the U.S. market, reaching an estimated $7.3 billion in 2006.[28]

International businesses have a number of possible responses to violations of their intellectual property. They can lobby their respective governments to push for international agreements to ensure that intellectual property rights are protected and that the law is enforced. Partly as a result of such actions, international laws are being strengthened. As we shall see in Chapter 6, the most recent world trade agreement, signed in 1994, for the first time extends the scope of the General Agreement on Tariffs and Trade to cover intellectual property. Under the new agreement, known as the Trade Related Aspects of Intellectual Property Rights (or TRIPS), as of 1995 a council of the World Trade Organization is overseeing enforcement of much stricter intellectual property regulations. These regulations oblige WTO members to grant and enforce patents lasting at least 20 years and copyrights lasting 50 years. Rich countries had to comply with the rules within a year. Poor countries, in which such protection generally was much weaker, had five years of grace, and the very poorest had 10 years.[29] (For further details of the TRIPS agreement, see Chapter 6.)

A security guard stands near a pile of pirated CDs and DVDs before they were destroyed at a ceremony in Beijing on Saturday, February 26, 2005. Thousands of pirated items were destroyed in the event.

In addition to lobbying governments, firms can file lawsuits on their own behalf. For example, Starbucks recently won a landmark trademark copyright case in China against a copycat (see the Management Focus for details). Firms may also choose to stay out of countries where intellectual property laws are lax, rather than risk having their ideas stolen by local entrepreneurs. Firms also need to be on the alert to ensure that pirated copies of their products produced in countries with weak intellectual property laws don't turn up in their home market or in third countries. U.S. computer software giant Microsoft, for example, discovered that pirated Microsoft software, produced illegally in Thailand, was being sold worldwide as the real thing.

PRODUCT SAFETY AND PRODUCT LIABILITY   **Product safety laws** set certain safety standards to which a product must adhere. **Product liability** involves holding a firm and its officers responsible when a product causes injury, death, or damage. Product liability can be much greater if a product does not conform to required safety standards. Both civil and criminal product liability laws exist. Civil laws call for payment and monetary damages. Criminal liability laws result in fines or imprisonment. Both civil and criminal liability laws are probably more extensive in the United States than in any other country, although many other Western nations also have comprehensive liability

Product Safety Laws
Laws that set certain safety standards to which a product must adhere.

Product Liability
Involves holding a firm and its officers responsible when a product causes injury, death, or damage to its users.

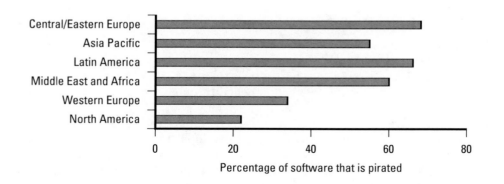

2.2 figure

Regional Piracy Rates for Software, 2006

Source: Business Software Alliance, "Fourth Annual BSA and IDC Global Software Piracy Study," May 2007, www.bsa.org.

Percentage of software that is pirated

Management FOCUS

Starbucks Wins Key Trademark Case in China

Starbucks has big plans for China. It believes the fast-growing nation will become the company's second largest market after the United States. Starbucks entered the country in 1999, and by the end of 2007 it had more than 300 storefronts. Copycats of well-established Western brands are common in China, and Starbucks was no exception. Shanghai Xing Ba Ke Coffee Shop closely matched the Starbucks format, right down to a green-and-white Xing Ba Ke circular logo that mimics Starbucks' ubiquitous logo. Also, the name mimics the standard Chinese translation for Starbucks. *Xing* means "star" and *Ba Ke* sounds like "bucks."

In 2003, Starbucks sued Xing Ba Ke in Chinese court for trademark violations. Xing Ba Ke's general manager responded by claiming it was just an accident that the logo and name were so similar to that of Starbucks. He claimed the right to use the logo and name because Xing Ba Ke had registered as a company in Shanghai in 1999, before Starbucks entered the city. "I hadn't heard of Starbucks at the time," the manager said, "so how could I imitate its brand and logo?"

However, in January 2006 a Shanghai court ruled that Starbucks had precedence, in part because it had registered its Chinese name in 1998. The court stated that Xing Ba Ke's use of the name and similar logo was "clearly malicious" and constituted improper competition. The court ordered Xing Ba Ke to stop using the name and to pay Starbucks $62,000 in compensation. While the money involved here may be small, the precedent is not. In a country where violation of trademarks is common, the courts seem to be signaling a shift toward greater protection of intellectual property rights. This is perhaps not surprising because foreign governments and the World Trade Organization have been pushing China hard recently to start respecting intellectual property rights.

Sources: M. Dickie, "Starbucks Wins Case against Chinese Copycat," *Financial Times,* January 3, 2006, p. 1; "Starbucks: Chinese Court Backs Company over Trademark Infringement," *The Wall Street Journal,* January 2, 2006, p. A11; and "Starbucks Calls China Its Top Growth Focus," *The Wall Street Journal,* February 14, 2006, p. 1.

laws. Liability laws are typically least extensive in less developed nations. A boom in product liability suits and awards in the United States resulted in a dramatic increase in the cost of liability insurance. Many business executives argue that the high costs of liability insurance make American businesses less competitive in the global marketplace.

In addition to the competitiveness issue, country differences in product safety and liability laws raise an important ethical issue for firms doing business abroad. When product safety laws are tougher in a firm's home country than in a foreign country or when liability laws are more lax, should a firm doing business in that foreign country follow the more relaxed local standards or should it adhere to the standards of its home country? While the ethical thing to do is undoubtedly to adhere to home-country standards, firms have been known to take advantage of lax safety and liability laws to do business in a manner that would not be allowed at home.

The Determinants of Economic Development

LEARNING OBJECTIVE 4
Explain what determines the level of economic development of a nation.

The political, economic, and legal systems of a country can have a profound impact on the level of economic development and hence on the attractiveness of a country as a possible market or production location for a firm. Here we look first at how countries differ in their level of development. Then we look at how political economy affects economic progress.

Gross National Income (GNI)
The yardstick for measuring economic activity of a country, this measures the total annual income of a nation's residents.

DIFFERENCES IN ECONOMIC DEVELOPMENT   Different countries have dramatically different levels of economic development. One common measure of economic development is a country's **gross national income (GNI)** per head of population. GNI is regarded as a yardstick for the economic activity of a country; it measures the total annual income received by residents of a nation. Map 2.1 summarizes

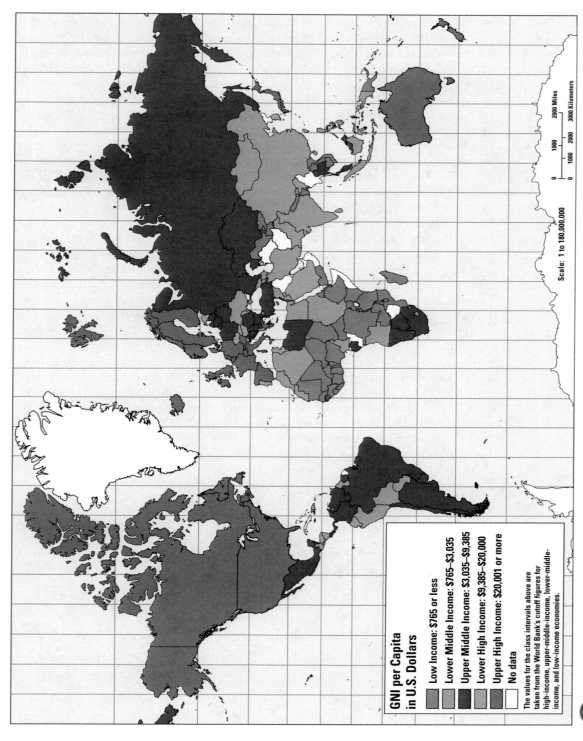

GNI per Capita in U.S. Dollars

Low Income: $765 or less
Lower Middle Income: $765–$3,035
Upper Middle Income: $3,035–$9,385
Lower High Income: $9,385–$20,000
Upper High Income: $20,001 or more
No data

The values for the class intervals above are taken from the World Bank's cutoff figures for high-income, upper-middle-income, lower-middle-income, and low-income economies.

Scale: 1 to 180,000,000

map GNI per Capita, 2006

Source: Data from World Bank. *World Development Indicators Online*, 2003. Reprinted by permission from the International Bank for Reconstruction and Development. © 2003 by the World Bank.

the GNI per capita of the world's nations in 2006. As can be seen, countries such as Japan, Sweden, Switzerland, and the United States are among the richest on this measure, whereas the large countries of China and India are among the poorest. Japan, for example, had a 2006 GNI per capita of $38,410, but China achieved only $2,010 and India just $820.[30]

GNI per person figures can be misleading because they don't consider differences in the cost of living. For example, although the 2006 GNI per capita of Switzerland at $57,230 exceeded that of the United States, which was $44,970, the higher cost of living in Switzerland meant that U.S. citizens could actually afford more goods and services than Swiss citizens. To account for differences in the cost of living, one can adjust GNI per capita by purchasing power. Referred to as a **purchasing power parity (PPP)** adjustment, it allows for a more direct comparison of living standards in different countries. The base for the adjustment is the cost of living in the United States. The PPP for different countries is then adjusted (up or down) depending upon whether the cost of living is lower or higher than in the United States. For example, in 2006 the GNI per capita for China was $2,010, but the PPP per capita was $7,740 suggesting that the cost of living was lower in China and that $2,010 in China would buy as much as $7,740 in the United States. Table 2.1 gives the GNI per capita measured at PPP in 2006 for a selection of countries, along with their GNI per capita and their growth rate in gross domestic product (GDP) from 1997 to 2006. Map 2.2 summarizes the GNI PPP per capita in 2006 for the nations of the world.

As can be seen, there are striking differences in the standards of living between countries. Table 2.1 suggests that the average Indian citizen can afford to consume only 8.6 percent of the goods and services consumed by the average U.S. citizen on a PPP basis. Given this, one might conclude that, despite having a population of 1.1 billion, India is unlikely to be a very lucrative market for the consumer products produced by many Western international businesses. However, this would be incorrect because India has a fairly wealthy middle class of close to 200 million people, despite its large number of very poor. Moreover, in absolute terms the Indian economy is now larger than that of Brazil, Poland, and Russia (see Table 2.1).

Purchasing Power Parity (PPP)
An adjustment in gross domestic product per capita to reflect differences in the cost of living.

table **2.1**

Economic Data for Select Countries

Source: World Development Indicators Online, 2008.

Country	GNI per Capita, 2006 ($)	GNI PPP per Capita, 2006 ($)	GDP Growth Rate, 1997–2006 (%)	Size of Economy GDP, 2006 ($ billions)
Brazil	$ 4,730	$ 8,800	2.54	$ 1,067
China	2,010	7,740	9.15	2,669
Germany	36,620	31,830	1.56	2,907
India	820	3,800	6.57	906
Japan	38,410	33,150	1.17	4,340
Nigeria	640	1,050	4.45	114
Poland	8,190	14,830	4.18	339
Russia	5,780	11,630	4.99	987
Switzerland	57,230	40,930	1.74	380
United Kingdom	40,180	35,580	2.80	2,345
United States	44,970	44,260	3.28	13,202

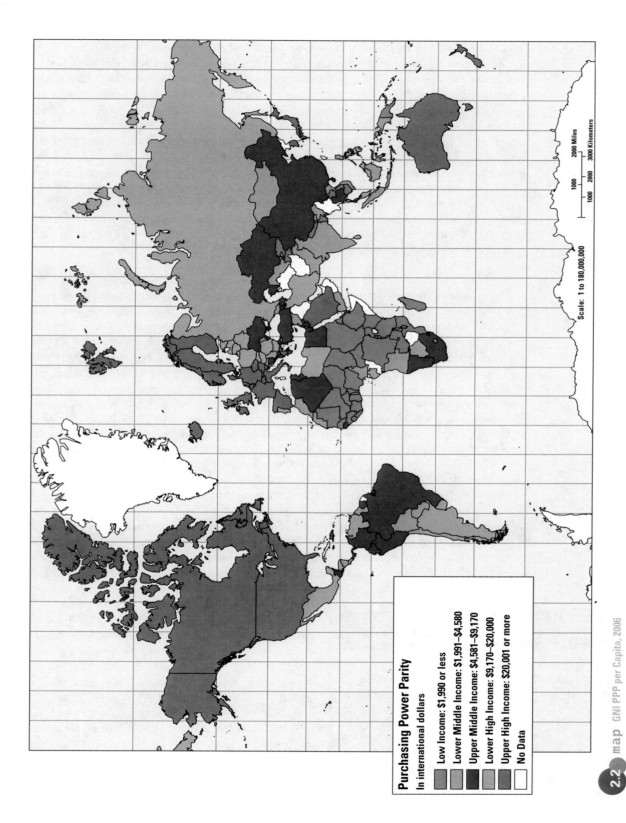

Purchasing Power Parity
In international dollars

Low Income: $1,990 or less
Lower Middle Income: $1,991–$4,580
Upper Middle Income: $4,581–$9,170
Lower High Income: $9,170–$20,000
Upper High Income: $20,001 or more
No Data

Scale: 1 to 180,000,000

1000   2000   3000 Kilometers
1000   2000 Miles

2.2 map GNI PPP per Capita, 2006

Source: Data from World Bank, *World Development Indicators Online.* 2003. Reprinted by permission from the International Bank for Reconstruction and Development. © 2003 by the World Bank.

The GNI and PPP data give a static picture of development. They tell us, for example, that China is much poorer than the United States, but they do not tell us if China is closing the gap. To assess this, we have to look at the economic growth rates achieved by countries. Table 2.1 gives the rate of growth in gross domestic product (GDP) achieved by a number of countries between 1997 and 2006. Map 2.3 summarizes the growth rate in GDP from 1997 to 2006. Although countries such as China and India are currently poor, their economies are already large in absolute terms and growing more rapidly than those of many advanced nations. They are already huge markets for the products of international businesses. If it maintains its growth rates, China in particular will be larger than all but that of the United States within a decade, and India too will be among the largest economies in the world. Given that potential, many international businesses are trying to gain a foothold in these markets now. Even though their current contributions to an international firm's revenues might be relatively small, these nation's future contributions could be much larger.

BROADER CONCEPTIONS OF DEVELOPMENT: AMARTYA SEN The Nobel Prize–winning economist Amartya Sen has argued that development should be assessed less by material output measures such as GNI per capita and more by the capabilities and opportunities that people enjoy.[31] According to Sen, development should be seen as a process of expanding the real freedoms that people experience. Hence, development requires the removal of major impediments to freedom: poverty as well as tyranny, poor economic opportunities as well as systematic social deprivation, neglect of public facilities as well as the intolerance of repressive states. In Sen's view, development is not just an economic process, but it is a political one too, and to succeed requires the "democratization" of political communities to give citizens a voice in the important decisions made for the community. This perspective leads Sen to emphasize basic health care, especially for children, and basic education, especially for women. Not only are these factors desirable for their instrumental value in helping to achieve higher income levels, but they are also beneficial in their own right. People cannot develop their capabilities if they are chronically ill or woefully ignorant.

Human Development Index (HDI)
An attempt by the UN to assess the impact of a number of factors on the quality of human life in a country.

Sen's influential thesis has been picked up by the United Nations, which has developed the **Human Development Index (HDI)** to measure the quality of human life in different nations. The HDI is based on three measures: life expectancy at birth (a function of health care), educational attainment (measured by a combination of the adult literacy rate and enrollment in primary, secondary, and tertiary education), and whether average incomes, based on PPP estimates, are sufficient to meet the basic needs of life in a country (adequate food, shelter, and health care). As such, the HDI comes much closer to Sen's conception of how development should be measured than narrow economic measures such as GNI per capita—although Sen's thesis suggests that political freedoms should also be included in the index, and they are not. The HDI is scaled from 0 to 1. Countries scoring less than 0.5 are classified as having low human development (the quality of life is poor); those scoring from 0.5 to 0.8 are classified as having medium human development; and those that score above 0.8 are classified as having high human development. Map 2.4 summarizes the HDI scores for 2005, the most recent year for which data are available.

Another Perspective

If We Were a Community of 100 People
To get a good sense of the scale of economic and demographic measures that this chapter describes, consider this: If we were a community of 100, 61 of us would be Asian, 12 European, 13 North and South American, 13 African, and 1 Australian. Six of us would own 59 percent of the community's wealth. Thirteen would be hungry or malnourished, 14 could not read, and 7 would be educated (to the secondary level). Thirty would have bank accounts and 53 would live on $2 a day or less. To learn more and to see the video that offers these meaningful metrics, visit www.miniature-earth.com.

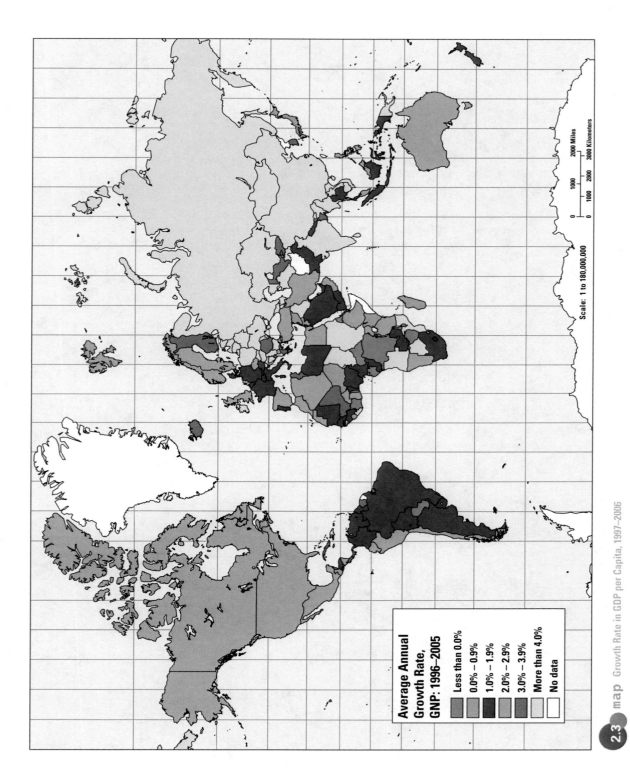

2.3 map Growth Rate in GDP per Capita, 1997–2006

Average Annual Growth Rate, GNP: 1996–2005

- Less than 0.0%
- 0.0% – 0.9%
- 1.0% – 1.9%
- 2.0% – 2.9%
- 3.0% – 3.9%
- More than 4.0%
- No data

Scale: 1 to 180,000,000

Source: Data from World Bank, *World Development Indicators Online*, 2005. Reprinted by permission from the International Bank for Reconstruction and Development. © 2003 by the World Bank.

Levels of Human Development

High Human Development 0.800–1.00

Medium Human Development 0.799–0.500

Low Human Development Less than 0.499

No Data

Scale: 1 to 180,000,000

2000 Miles

3000 Kilometers

2.4 map Human Development Indicators, 2005

Source: Data from United Nations, *Human Development Report, 2004, Human Development Index, 2003.*

POLITICAL ECONOMY AND ECONOMIC PROGRESS

It is often argued that a country's economic development is a function of its economic and political systems. What then is the nature of the relationship between political economy and economic progress? This question has been the subject of vigorous debate among academics and policymakers for some time. Despite the long debate, this remains a question for which an unambiguous answer is impossible. However, it is possible to untangle the main threads of the arguments and make a few generalizations as to the nature of the relationship between political economy and economic progress.

Innovation and Entrepreneurship Are the Engines of Growth

There is wide agreement that innovation and entrepreneurial activity are the engines of long-run economic growth.[32] Those who make this argument define **innovation** broadly to include not just new products but also new processes, new organizations, new management practices, and new strategies. Thus, the Toys "R" Us strategy of establishing large warehouse-style toy stores and then engaging in heavy advertising and price discounting to sell the merchandise can be classified as an innovation because it was the first company to pursue this strategy. Innovation and entrepreneurial activity help to increase economic activity by creating new products and markets that did not previously exist. Also, innovations in production and business processes lead to an increase in the productivity of labor and capital, which further boosts economic growth rates.[33]

> **Innovation**
> Development of new products, processes, organizations, management practices, and strategies.

Innovation is also seen as the product of entrepreneurial activity. Often, **entrepreneurs** first commercialize innovative new products and processes, and entrepreneurial activity provides much of the dynamism in an economy. For example, the U.S. economy has benefited greatly from a high level of entrepreneurial activity, which has resulted in rapid innovation in products and process. Firms such as Cisco Systems, Dell, Microsoft, and Oracle were all founded by entrepreneurial individuals to exploit new technology, and all these firms created significant economic value and boosted productivity by helping to commercialize innovations in products and processes. Thus, one can conclude that if a country's economy is to sustain long-run economic growth, the business environment must be conducive to the consistent production of product and process innovations and to entrepreneurial activity.

> **Entrepreneurs**
> Those who first commercialize innovations.

Innovation and Entrepreneurship Require a Market Economy

This leads logically to a further question: What is required for the business environment of a country to be conducive to innovation and entrepreneurial activity? Those who have considered this issue highlight the advantages of a market economy.[34] It has been argued that the economic freedom associated with a market economy creates greater incentives for innovation and entrepreneurship than either a planned or a mixed economy. In a market economy, any individual who has an innovative idea is free to try to make money out of that idea by starting a business (by engaging in entrepreneurial activity). Similarly, existing businesses are free to improve their operations through innovation. To the extent that they are successful, both individual entrepreneurs and established businesses can reap rewards in the form of high profits. Thus, market economies contain enormous incentives to develop innovations.

Another Perspective

A World without Poverty: Grameen Bank

Imagine a bank that grants loans without requiring collateral. That's Grameen Bank, founded in Bangladesh by Muhammad Yunus in 1983. Yunus turned conventional banking policy on its ear by creating an innovative lending system based on the principle of *microcredit*. The bank's small loans fight poverty and give "the poorest of the poor" the means to become self-sustaining.

In 2008 the bank had more than 2,500 branches and served nearly 82,000 villages. Of its over 7 million borrowers, 97 percent are women.

Grameen Bank has won accolades from numerous agencies, including the World Bank and the International Food Research Policy Institute, and in 2006 Yunus won the Nobel Peace Prize.

For more information, visit www.grameen-info.com.

In a planned economy, the state owns all means of production. Consequently, entrepreneurial individuals have few economic incentives to develop valuable new innovations because it is the state, rather than the individual, that captures most of the gains. The lack of economic freedom and incentives for innovation was probably a main factor in the economic stagnation of many former communist states and led ultimately to their collapse at the end of the 1980s. Similar stagnation occurred in many mixed economies in those sectors where the state had a monopoly (such as health care and telecommunications in Great Britain). This stagnation provided the impetus for the widespread privatization of state-owned enterprises that we witnessed in many mixed economies during the mid-1980s and is still going on today (*privatization* refers to the process of selling state-owned enterprises to private investors).

A study of 102 countries over a 20-year period provided evidence of a strong relationship between economic freedom (as provided by a market economy) and economic growth.[35] The study found that the more economic freedom a country had between 1975 and 1995, the more economic growth it achieved and the richer its citizens became. The six countries that had persistently high ratings of economic freedom from 1975 to 1995 (Hong Kong, Switzerland, Singapore, the United States, Canada, and Germany) were also all in the top 10 in terms of economic growth rates. In contrast, no country with persistently low economic freedom achieved a respectable growth rate. In the 16 countries for which the index of economic freedom declined the most during 1975 to 1995, gross domestic product fell at an annual rate of 0.6 percent.

Innovation and Entrepreneurship Require Strong Property Rights   Strong legal protection of property rights is another requirement for a business environment to be conducive to innovation, entrepreneurial activity, and hence economic growth.[36] Both individuals and businesses must be given the opportunity to profit from innovative ideas. Without strong property rights protection, businesses and individuals run the risk that the profits from their innovative efforts will be expropriated, either by criminal elements or by the state. The state can expropriate the profits from innovation through legal means, such as excessive taxation, or through illegal means, such as demands from state bureaucrats for kickbacks in return for granting an individual or firm a license to do business in a certain area (i.e., corruption). According to the Nobel Prize–winning economist Douglass North, throughout history many governments have displayed a tendency to engage in such behavior. Inadequately enforced property rights reduce the incentives for innovation and entrepreneurial activity—because the profits from such activity are "stolen"—and hence reduce the rate of economic growth.

The influential Peruvian development economist Hernando de Soto has argued that much of the developing world will fail to reap the benefits of capitalism until property rights are better defined and protected.[37] De Soto's arguments are interesting because he claims that the key problem is not the risk of expropriation but the chronic inability of property owners to establish legal title to the property they own. As an example of the scale of the problem, he cites the situation in Haiti where individuals must take 176 steps over 19 years to own land legally. Because most property in poor countries is informally "owned," the absence of legal proof of ownership means that property holders cannot convert their assets into capital, which could then be used to finance business ventures. Banks will not lend money to the poor to start businesses because the poor possess no proof that they own property, such as farmland, that can be used as collateral for a loan. By de Soto's calculations, the total value of real estate held by the poor in Third World and former communist states amounted to more than $9.3 trillion in 2000. If those assets could be converted into capital, the result could be an economic revolution that would allow the poor to bootstrap their way out

Country FOCUS

Emerging Property Right in China

On October 1, 2007, a new property law took effect in China. The law, the culmination of 14 years of effort, granted rural and urban landholders far more secure property rights. The law was a much-needed response to changes in China's economy over the past 30 years as it transitions from a centrally planned system to a dynamic market-based economy where two thirds of economic activity is in the hands of private enterprises.

Although all land in China still technically belongs to the state—an ideological necessity in a country where the government still claims to be guided by Marxism—urban landholders previously had been granted 40- to 70-year leases to use the land, while rural farmers had 30-year leases. However, the lack of legal title to their land meant that landholders were at the whim of the state. Over the last few years, large-scale appropriation of rural land for housing and factory construction has rendered millions of farmers landless. Many have been given little or no compensation, and they have drifted to the cities where they are adding to a growing underclass. In both urban and rural areas, property and land disputes had become a leading cause of social unrest. According to government sources, in 2006 there were about 23,000 "mass incidents" of social unrest in China, many related to disputes over property rights.

The new law, which was fought by left-wing Communist Party activists who objected to it on ideological grounds, gives urban and rural land users the right to automatic renewal of their leases after the expiration of the 30- to 70-year terms. In addition, the law requires that land users be fairly compensated if the land is required for other purposes, and it gives individuals the same legal protection for their property as the state. Taken together with a 2004 change in China's constitution, which stated that private property "was not to be encroached upon," the new law significantly strengthens property rights in China.

Nevertheless, the law has its limitations. Most notably, it still falls short of giving peasants marketable ownership rights to the land they farm. If they could sell their land, tens of millions of underemployed farmers might find more productive work elsewhere. Those that stayed could acquire bigger land holdings that could be used more efficiently. Also, farmers might be able to use their land holdings as security against which they could borrow funds for investments to boost productivity.

Sources: "China's Next Revolution—Property Rights in China," *The Economist*, March 10, 2007, p. 11; "Caught Between the Right and Left," *The Economist*, March 10, 2007, pp. 25–27; and Z. Keliang and L. Ping, "Rural Land Rights under the PRC Property Law," *China Law and Practice*, November 2007, pp. 10–15.

of poverty. Interestingly, the Chinese seem to have taken de Soto's arguments to heart. Despite still being nominally a communist country, in October 2007 the government passed a law that gave private property owners the same rights as the state, and significant improved the rights of urban and rural landowners to the land that they use (see the accompanying Country Focus for details).

The Required Political System   Much debate surrounds which kind of political system best achieves a functioning market economy with strong protection for property rights.[38] People in the West tend to associate a representative democracy with a market economic system, strong property rights protection, and economic progress. Building on this, we tend to argue that democracy is good for growth. However, some totalitarian regimes have fostered a market economy and strong property rights protection and have experienced rapid economic growth. Five of the fastest growing economies of the past 30 years—China, South Korea, Taiwan, Singapore, and Hong Kong—had one thing in common at the start of their economic growth: undemocratic governments. At the same time, countries with stable democratic governments, such as India, experienced sluggish economic growth for long periods. In 1992, Lee Kuan Yew, Singapore's leader for many years, told an audience, "I do not believe that democracy necessarily leads to development. I believe that a country needs to develop discipline more than democracy. The exuberance of democracy leads to undisciplined and disorderly conduct which is inimical to development."[39]

However, those who argue for the value of a totalitarian regime miss an important point: If dictators made countries rich, then much of Africa, Asia, and Latin America should have been growing rapidly during 1960 to 1990, and this was not the case. Only a totalitarian regime that is committed to a free market system and strong protection of property rights is capable of promoting economic growth. Also, there is no guarantee that a dictatorship will continue to pursue such progressive policies. Dictators are rarely so benevolent. Many are tempted to use the apparatus of the state to further their own private ends, violating property rights and stalling economic growth. Given this, it seems likely that democratic regimes are far more conducive to long-term economic growth than are dictatorships, even benevolent ones. Only in a well-functioning, mature democracy are property rights truly secure.[40] Nor should we forget Amartya Sen's arguments that we reviewed earlier. Totalitarian states, by limiting human freedom, also suppress human development and therefore are detrimental to progress.

Economic Progress Begets Democracy   While it is possible to argue that democracy is not a necessary precondition for a free market economy in which property rights are protected, subsequent economic growth often leads to establishment of a democratic regime. Several of the fastest growing Asian economies adopted more democratic governments during the past two decades, including South Korea and Taiwan. Thus, although democracy may not always be the cause of initial economic progress, it seems to be one consequence of that progress.

A strong belief that economic progress leads to adoption of a democratic regime underlies the fairly permissive attitude that many Western governments have adopted toward human rights violations in China. Although China has a totalitarian government in which human rights are violated, many Western countries have been hesitant to criticize the country too much for fear that this might hamper the country's march toward a free market system. The belief is that once China has a free market system, greater individual freedoms and democracy will follow. Whether this optimistic vision comes to pass remains to be seen.

GEOGRAPHY, EDUCATION, AND ECONOMIC DEVELOPMENT   While a country's political and economic systems are probably the big engine driving its rate of economic development, other factors are also important. One that has received attention recently is geography.[41] But the belief that geography can influence economic policy, and hence economic growth rates, goes back to Adam Smith. The influential Harvard University economist Jeffrey Sachs argues

> that throughout history, coastal states, with their long engagements in international trade, have been more supportive of market institutions than landlocked states, which have tended to organize themselves as hierarchical (and often military) societies. Mountainous states, as a result of physical isolation, have often neglected market-based trade. Temperate climes have generally supported higher densities of population and thus a more extensive division of labor than tropical regions.[42]

Sachs's point is that by virtue of favorable geography, certain societies were more likely to engage in trade than others and were thus more likely to be open to and develop market-based economic systems, which in turn would promote faster economic growth. He also argues that, irrespective of the economic and political institutions a country adopts, adverse geographical conditions, such as the high rate of disease, poor soils, and hostile climate that afflict many tropical countries, can have a negative impact on development. Together with colleagues at Harvard's Institute for International Development, Sachs tested for the impact of geography on a country's economic growth rate between 1965 and 1990. He found that landlocked countries grew more slowly than coastal economies and that being entirely landlocked reduced a country's growth rate by roughly 0.7 percent per year. He also found that tropical countries grew 1.3 percent more slowly each year than countries in the temperate zone.

Education emerges as another important determinant of economic development (a point that Amartya Sen emphasizes). The general assertion is that nations that invest more in education will have higher growth rates because an educated population is a more productive population. Anecdotal comparisons suggest this is true. In 1960, Pakistanis and South Koreans were on equal footing economically. However, just 30 percent of Pakistani children were enrolled in primary schools, while 94 percent of South Koreans were. By the mid-1980s, South Korea's GNP per person was three times that of Pakistan's.[43] A survey of 14 statistical studies that looked at the relationship between a country's investment in education and its subsequent growth rates concluded investment in education did have a positive and statistically significant impact on a country's rate of economic growth.[44] Similarly, the work by Sachs discussed above suggests that investments in education help explain why some countries in Southeast Asia, such as Indonesia, Malaysia, and Singapore, have been able to overcome the disadvantages associated with their tropical geography and grow far more rapidly than tropical nations in Africa and Latin America.

States in Transition

The political economy of many of the world's nation-states has changed radically since the late 1980s. Two trends have been evident. First, during the late 1980s and early 1990s, a wave of democratic revolutions swept the world. Totalitarian governments collapsed and were replaced by democratically elected governments that were typically more committed to free market capitalism than their predecessors had been. Second, there has been a strong move away from centrally planned and mixed economies and toward a more free market economic model. We shall look first at the spread of democracy and then turn our attention to the spread of free market economics.

LEARNING OBJECTIVE 5
Discuss the macro-political and economic changes taking place worldwide.

THE SPREAD OF DEMOCRACY   One notable development of the past 15 years has been the spread of democracy (and, by extension, the decline of totalitarianism). Map 2.5 reports on the extent of totalitarianism in the world as determined by Freedom House.[45] This map charts political freedom in 2007, grouping countries into three broad groupings, free, partly free, and not free. In "free" countries, citizens enjoy a high degree of political and civil freedoms. "Partly free" countries are characterized by some restrictions on political rights and civil liberties, often in the context of corruption, weak rule of law, ethnic strife, or civil war. In "not free" countries, the political process is tightly controlled and basic freedoms are denied.

Freedom House classified some 90 countries as free in 2007, accounting for some 47 percent of the world's nations. These countries respect a broad range of political rights. Another 60 countries accounting for 31 percent of the world's nations were classified as partly free, while 43 countries representing some 22 percent of the world's nations were classified as not free. The number of democracies in the world has increased from 69 nations in 1987 to 121 in 2007, slightly below the 2006 total of 123. But not all democracies are free, according to Freedom House, because some democracies still restrict certain political and civil liberties. For example, Russia was rated "not free." According to Freedom House,

> Russia's step backwards into the Not Free category is the culmination of a growing trend under President Vladimir Putin to concentrate political authority, harass and intimidate the media, and politicize the country's law-enforcement system.[46]

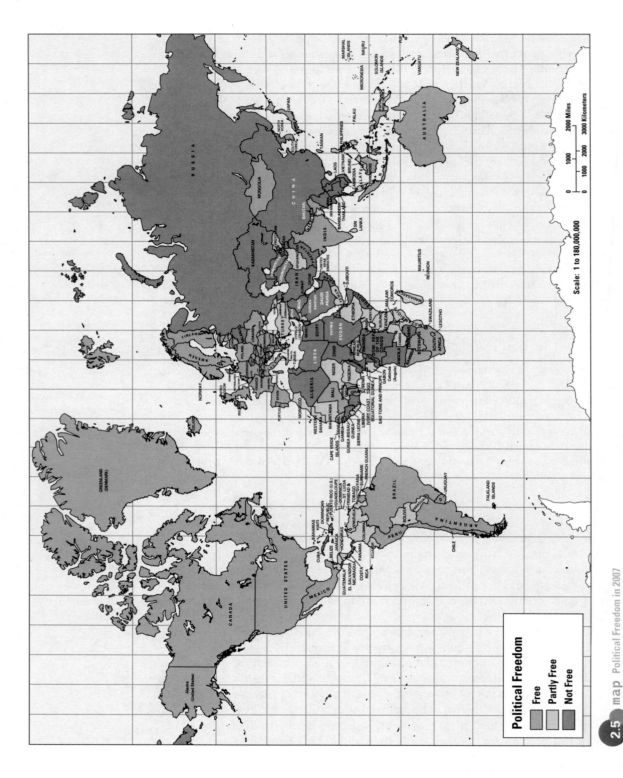

2.5 map **Political Freedom in 2007**

Political Freedom

- Free
- Partly Free
- Not Free

Scale: 1 to 180,000,000

Source: Map data from Freedom House, *Freedom in the World 2005: The Annual Survey of Political Rights and Civil Liberties*, www.freedomhouse.org. Reprinted with permission.

Similarly, Freedom House argues that democracy is being restricted in Venezuela under the leadership of Hugo Chavez.

Many of the newer democracies are to be found in Eastern Europe and Latin America, although there also have been notable gains in Africa during this time, such as in South Africa. Entrants into the ranks of the world's democracies include Mexico, which held its first fully free and fair presidential election in 2000 after free and fair parliamentary and state elections in 1997 and 1998; Senegal, where free and fair presidential elections led to a peaceful transfer of power; Yugoslavia, where a democratic election took place despite attempted fraud by the incumbent; and Ukraine, where popular unrest following widespread ballot fraud in the 2004 presidential election resulted in a second election, the victory of a reform candidate, and a marked improvement in civil liberties.

Three main reasons account for the spread of democracy.[47] First, many totalitarian regimes failed to deliver economic progress to the vast bulk of their populations. The collapse of communism in Eastern Europe, for example, was precipitated by the growing gulf between the vibrant and wealthy economies of the West and the stagnant economies of the Communist East. In looking for alternatives to the socialist model, the populations of these countries could not have failed to notice that most of the world's strongest economies were governed by representative democracies. Today, the economic success of many of the newer democracies, such as Poland and the Czech Republic in the former Communist bloc, the Philippines and Taiwan in Asia, and Chile in Latin America, has strengthened the case for democracy as a key component of successful economic advancement.

Second, new information and communication technologies, including shortwave radio, satellite television, fax machines, desktop publishing, and, most important, the Internet, have reduced the state's ability to control access to uncensored information. These technologies have created new conduits for the spread of democratic ideals and information from free societies. Today, the Internet is allowing democratic ideals to penetrate closed societies as never before.[48]

Third, in many countries the economic advances of the past quarter century have led to the emergence of increasingly prosperous middle and working classes who have pushed for democratic reforms. This was certainly a factor in the democratic transformation of South Korea. Entrepreneurs and other business leaders, eager to protect their property rights and ensure the dispassionate enforcement of contracts, are another force pressing for more accountable and open government.

Despite this, it would be naive to conclude that the global spread of democracy will continue unchallenged. Democracy is still rare in large parts of the world. In sub-Saharan Africa in 2007, only 11 countries were considered free, 23 were partly free, and 14 were not free. Among the 27 post-Communist countries in Eastern and Central Europe, 7 are still not electoral democracies and Freedom House classifies only 13 of these states as free (primarily in Eastern Europe). And there are no free states among the 16 Arab nations of the Middle East and North Africa.

THE NEW WORLD ORDER AND GLOBAL TERRORISM   The end of the Cold War and the "new world order" that followed the collapse of communism in Eastern Europe and the former Soviet Union, taken together with the demise of many authoritarian regimes in Latin America, have given rise to intense speculation about the future shape of global geopolitics. Author Francis Fukuyama has argued, "We may be witnessing . . . the end of history as such: that is, the end point of mankind's ideological evolution and the universalization of Western liberal democracy as the final form of human government."[49] Fukuyama goes on to say that the war of ideas may be at an end and that liberal democracy has triumphed.

Others question Fukuyama's vision of a more harmonious world dominated by a universal civilization characterized by democratic regimes and free market capitalism. In a controversial book, the influential political scientist Samuel Huntington argues that there is no "universal" civilization based on widespread acceptance of Western liberal democratic ideals.[50] Huntington maintains that while many societies may be modernizing—they are adopting the material paraphernalia of the modern world, from automobiles to Coca-Cola and MTV—they are not becoming more Western. On the contrary, Huntington theorizes that modernization in non-Western societies can result in a retreat toward the traditional, such as the resurgence of Islam in many traditionally Muslim societies. He writes,

> The Islamic resurgence is both a product of and an effort to come to grips with modernization. Its underlying causes are those generally responsible for indigenization trends in non-Western societies: urbanization, social mobilization, higher levels of literacy and education, intensified communication and media consumption, and expanded interaction with Western and other cultures. These developments undermine traditional village and clan ties and create alienation and an identity crisis. Islamist symbols, commitments, and beliefs meet these psychological needs, and Islamist welfare organizations, the social, cultural, and economic needs of Muslims caught in the process of modernization. Muslims feel a need to return to Islamic ideas, practices, and institutions to provide the compass and the motor of modernization.[51]

Thus, the rise of Islamic fundamentalism is portrayed as a response to the alienation produced by modernization.

In contrast to Fukuyama, Huntington sees a world that is split into different civilizations, each of which has its own value systems and ideology. In addition to Western civilization, Huntington predicts the emergence of strong Islamic and Sinic (Chinese) civilizations, as well as civilizations based on Japan, Africa, Latin America, Eastern Orthodox Christianity (Russian), and Hinduism (Indian). Huntington also sees the civilizations as headed for conflict, particularly along the "fault lines" that separate them, such as Bosnia (where Muslims and Orthodox Christians have clashed), Kashmir (where Muslims and Hindus clash), and the Sudan (where a bloody war between Christians and Muslims has persisted for decades). Huntington predicts conflict between the West and Islam and between the West and China. He bases his predictions on an analysis of the different value systems and ideology of these civilizations, which in his view tend to bring them into conflict with each other. While some commentators originally dismissed Huntington's thesis, in the aftermath of the terrorist attacks on the United States on September 11, 2001, Huntington's views received new attention.

If Huntington's views are even partly correct—and there is little doubt that the events surrounding September 11 added more weight to his thesis—they have important implications for international business. They suggest many countries may be increasingly difficult places in which to do business, either because they are shot through with violent conflicts or because they are part of a civilization that is in conflict with an enterprise's home country. Huntington's views are speculative and controversial. It is not clear that his predictions will come to pass. More likely is the evolution of a global political system that is positioned somewhere between Fukuyama's universal global civilization based on liberal democratic ideals and Huntington's vision of a fractured world. That would still be a world, however, in which geopolitical forces periodically limit the ability of business enterprises to operate in certain foreign countries.

In Huntington's thesis, global terrorism is a product of the tension between civilizations and the clash of value systems and ideology. Others point to terrorism's roots in long-standing conflicts that seem to defy political resolution, the Palestinian, Kashmir, and Northern Ireland conflicts being obvious examples. It should also be noted that a substantial amount of terrorist activity in some parts of the world, such as Colombia, has been interwoven with the illegal drug trade. The attacks of September 11, 2001, created the impression that global terror is on the rise, although accurate statistics on this are hard to come by. What we do know is that according to data from the U.S. Department of State, in 2006 there were some 14,388 terrorist attacks worldwide, a 25 percent increase over 2005. These attacks resulted in 20,498 deaths in 2006, a 40 percent increase over 2005. Iraq alone, however, accounted for 45 percent of the attacks and 65 percent of the fatalities.[52] Other global hot spots for terrorist incidents in 2006 included the Sudan, Nigeria, and Afghanistan. As former U.S. Secretary of State Colin Powell has maintained, terrorism represents one of the major threats to world peace and economic progress in the 21st century.[53]

THE SPREAD OF MARKET-BASED SYSTEMS

Paralleling the spread of democracy since the 1980s has been the transformation from centrally planned command economies to market-based economies. More than 30 countries that were in the former Soviet Union or the Eastern European Communist bloc have changed their economic systems. A complete list of countries where change is now occurring also would include Asian states such as China and Vietnam, as well as African countries such as Angola, Ethiopia, and Mozambique.[54] There has been a similar shift away from a mixed economy. Many states in Asia, Latin America, and Western Europe have sold state-owned businesses to private investors (privatization) and deregulated their economies to promote greater competition.

The rationale for economic transformation has been the same the world over. In general, command and mixed economies failed to deliver the kind of sustained economic performance that was achieved by countries adopting market-based systems, such as the United States, Switzerland, Hong Kong, and Taiwan. As a consequence, even more states have gravitated toward the market-based model. Map 2.6, based on data from the Heritage Foundation, a politically conservative U.S. research foundation, gives some idea of the degree to which the world has shifted toward market-based economic systems. The Heritage Foundation's index of economic freedom is based on 10 indicators, such as the extent to which the government intervenes in the economy, trade policy, the degree to which property rights are protected, foreign investment regulations, and taxation rules. A country can score between 1 (most free) and 5 (least free) on each of these indicators. The lower a country's average score across all 10 indicators, the more closely its economy represents the pure market model. According to the 2008 index, which is summarized in Map 2.6, the world's freest economies are (in rank order) Hong Kong, Singapore, Ireland, Australia, United States, New Zealand, Canada, Chile, Switzerland, and the United Kingdom in the top 10. Japan came in at 17, Mexico at 44, France at 48, Brazil, 101; India, 115; China, 126;

Another Perspective

Business Students Visualize World Peace Through Commerce

Interested in world peace? Business students worldwide can participate in Peace Through Commerce, an integrated program that shows how business schools can promote peace. The program is sponsored by the Association to Advance Collegiate Schools of Business (AACSB), the global accrediting organization of business schools. Peace Through Commerce is built on the premise that commerce represents the most overlooked—yet most effective—means of facilitating widespread peace.

The idea of encouraging peace through commerce isn't new; it was espoused by philosophers as early as the 1700s. Again after World War II, the concept of world peace through commerce gained momentum when the United Nations was formed. It's also a basic tenet of the European Union: Countries that trade together don't go to war.

As the AACSB puts it: "If we educate students that it's their responsibility to advance society, over a generation we may be able to have more impact than governments have had." For more information, visit www.peacethroughcommerce.com.

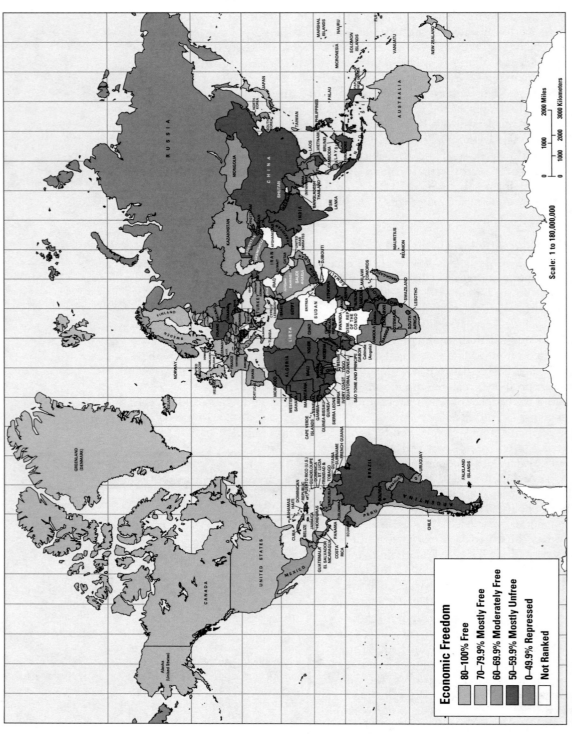

Economic Freedom

- 80–100% Free
- 70–79.9% Mostly Free
- 60–69.9% Moderately Free
- 50–59.9% Mostly Unfree
- 0–49.9% Repressed
- Not Ranked

Scale: 1 to 180,000,000

 map Distribution of Economic Freedom in 2008

Source: Heritage Foundation, www.heritage.org/index/.

and Russia, 134. The economies of Cuba, Laos, Iran, Venezuela, and North Korea are to be found near the bottom of the rankings.[55]

Economic freedom does not necessarily equate with political freedom, as detailed in Map 2.6. For example, the two top states in the Heritage Foundation index, Hong Kong and Singapore, cannot be classified as politically free. Hong Kong was reabsorbed into Communist China in 1997, and the first thing Beijing did was shut down Hong Kong's freely elected legislature. Singapore is ranked as only partly free on Freedom House's index of political freedom due to practices such as widespread press censorship.

The Nature of Economic Transformation

The shift toward a market-based economic system often entails a number of steps: deregulation, privatization, and creation of a legal system to safeguard property rights.[56]

LEARNING OBJECTIVE 6
Describe how transition economies are moving towards market based systems

DEREGULATION
Deregulation involves removing legal restrictions to the free play of markets, the establishment of private enterprises, and the manner in which private enterprises operate. Before the collapse of communism, the governments in most command economies exercised tight control over prices and output, setting both through detailed state planning. They also prohibited private enterprises from operating in most sectors of the economy, severely restricted direct investment by foreign enterprises, and limited international trade. Deregulation in these cases involved removing price controls, thereby allowing prices to be set by the interplay between demand and supply; abolishing laws regulating the establishment and operation of private enterprises; and relaxing or removing restrictions on direct investment by foreign enterprises and international trade.

Deregulation
The process of removing legal restrictions to the free play of markets, the establishment of private enterprises, and the manner in which private enterprises operate.

In mixed economies, the role of the state was more limited; but here too, in certain sectors the state set prices, owned businesses, limited private enterprise, restricted investment by foreigners, and restricted international trade (for example, see the opening case on India). For these countries, deregulation has involved the same kind of initiatives that we have seen in former command economies, although the transformation has been easier because these countries often had a vibrant private sector.

PRIVATIZATION
Hand in hand with deregulation has come a sharp increase in privatization. Privatization, as we discussed earlier in this chapter, transfers the ownership of state property into the hands of private individuals, frequently by the sale of state assets through an auction.[57] Privatization is seen as a way to stimulate gains in economic efficiency by giving new private owners a powerful incentive—the reward of greater profits—to search for increases in productivity, to enter new markets, and to exit losing ones.[58]

The privatization movement started in Great Britain in the early 1980s when then Prime Minister Margaret Thatcher started to sell state-owned assets such as the British telephone company, British Telecom (BT). In a pattern that has been repeated around the world, this sale was linked with the deregulation of the British telecommunications industry. By allowing other firms to compete head-to-head with BT, deregulation ensured that privatization did not simply replace a state-owned monopoly with a private monopoly. Since the 1980s, privatization has become a worldwide phenomenon. More than 8,000 acts of privatization were completed around the world between 1995 and 1999.[59] Some of the most dramatic privatization programs occurred in the economies of the former Soviet Union and its Eastern European satellite states. In the Czech Republic, for example, three-quarters of all state-owned enterprises were privatized between 1989 and 1996, helping to push the share of gross domestic product accounted for by the private sector up from 11 percent in 1989 to 60 percent in 1995.[60]

As privatization has proceeded around the world, it has become clear that simply selling state-owned assets to private investors is not enough to guarantee economic growth. Studies of privatization in central Europe have shown that the process often fails to deliver predicted benefits if the newly privatized firms continue to receive subsidies from the state and if they are protected from foreign competition by barriers to international trade and foreign direct investment.[61] In such cases, the newly privatized firms are sheltered from competition and continue acting like state monopolies. When these circumstances prevail, the newly privatized entities often have little incentive to restructure their operations to become more efficient. For privatization to work, it must also be accompanied by a more general deregulation and opening of the economy. Thus, when Brazil decided to privatize the state-owned telephone monopoly, Telebras Brazil, the government also split the company into four independent units that were to compete with each other and removed barriers to foreign direct investment in telecommunications services. This action ensured that the newly privatized entities would face significant competition and thus would have to improve their operating efficiency to survive.

The ownership structure of newly privatized firms also is important.[62] Many former command economies, for example, lack the legal regulations regarding corporate governance that are found in advanced Western economies. In advanced market economies, boards of directors are appointed by shareholders to make sure managers consider the interests of shareholders when making decisions and try to manage the firm in a manner that is consistent with maximizing the wealth of shareholders. However, some former communist states still lack laws requiring corporations to establish effective boards. In such cases, managers with a small ownership stake can often gain control over the newly privatized entity and run it for their own benefit, while ignoring the interests of other shareholders. Sometimes these managers are the same Communist Party bureaucrats who ran the enterprise before privatization. Because they have been schooled in the old ways of doing things, they often hesitate to take drastic action to increase the efficiency of the enterprise. Instead, they continue to run the firm as a private fiefdom, seeking to extract whatever economic value they can for their own betterment (in the form of perks that are not reported) while doing little to increase the economic efficiency of the enterprise so that shareholders benefit. Such developments seem less likely to occur, however, if a foreign investor takes a stake in the newly privatized entity. The foreign investor, who usually is a major provider of capital, is often able to use control over a critical resource (money) to push through needed change.

LEGAL SYSTEMS   As noted earlier in this chapter, a well-functioning market economy requires laws protecting private property rights and providing mechanisms for contract enforcement. Without a legal system that protects property rights, and without the machinery to enforce that system, the incentive to engage in economic activity can be reduced substantially by private and public entities, including organized crime, that expropriate the profits generated by the efforts of private-sector entrepreneurs. When communism collapsed, many of these countries lacked the legal structure required to protect property rights, all property having been held by the state. Although many nations have made big strides toward instituting the required system, it will be many more years before the legal system is functioning as smoothly as it does in the West. For example, in most Eastern European nations, the title to urban and agricultural property is often uncertain because of incomplete and inaccurate records, multiple pledges on the same property, and unsettled claims resulting from demands for restitution from owners in the pre-Communist era. Also, although most countries have improved their commercial codes, institutional weaknesses still undermine contract enforcement. Court capacity is often inadequate, and procedures for resolving contract disputes out of court are often lacking or poorly developed.[63] Nevertheless, progress is being made. In 2004, for example, China amended its constitution to state that "private property was not to be encroached upon," and in 2007 it enacted a new law on property rights that gave private property holders many of the same protections as those enjoyed by the state (see the accompanying Country Focus).[64]

Implications of Changing Political Economy

The global changes in political and economic systems discussed above have several implications for international business. The long-standing ideological conflict between collectivism and individualism that defined the 20th century is less in evidence today. The West won the Cold War, and Western ideology has never been more widespread than it is now. Although command economies remain and totalitarian dictatorships can still be found around the world, the tide has been running in favor of free markets and democracy.

LEARNING OBJECTIVE 7
Articulate the implications for management practice of national difference in political economy.

The implications for business are enormous. For nearly 50 years, half of the world was off-limits to Western businesses. Now all that is changing. Many of the national markets of Eastern Europe, Latin America, Africa, and Asia may still be undeveloped and impoverished, but they are potentially enormous. With a population of more than 1.2 billion, the Chinese market alone is potentially bigger than that of the United States, the European Union, and Japan combined. Similarly India, with its nearly 1.1 billion people, is a potentially huge market. Latin America has another 400 million potential consumers. It is unlikely that China, Russia, Vietnam, or any of the other states now moving toward a free market system will attain the living standards of the West soon. Nevertheless, the upside potential is so large that companies need to consider making inroads now. For example, if China and Japan continue to grow at the rates they did during 1996–2007, China will surpass Japan and become the world's second largest national economy behind the United States in 2015. Figure 2.3 estimates the future size of five major national economies, based on projecting growth rates attained during the last 10 years forward for another 10. The United States, Japan, and Germany are currently the three largest national economies in the world. As can be seen in the figure, China surges, surpassing Germany in 2008 and Japan in 2015, while by 2025 India will be closing in on Germany.[65]

However, just as the potential gains are large, so are the risks. There is no guarantee that democracy will thrive in many of the world's newer democratic states, particularly if these states have to grapple with severe economic setbacks. Totalitarian dictatorships could return, although they are unlikely to be communist. Although the bipolar world of the Cold War era has vanished, it may be replaced by a multipolar world dominated by a number of civilizations. In such a world, much of the economic promise inherent in the global shift toward market-based economic systems may stall in the face of conflicts between civilizations. While the long-term potential for economic gain from investment in the world's new market economies is large, the risks associated with any such investment are also substantial. It would be foolish to ignore these. The financial system in China, for example, is not transparent, and many suspect that Chinese banks hold a high proportion of nonperforming loans on their books. If true, these bad debts could trigger a significant financial crisis during the next decade in China, which would dramatically lower growth rates and render invalid the projections given in Figure 2.3.

figure **2.3**

The World's Largest National Economies, 2005–2025 (GDP $ billions)

Note: Projections are based on nominal GDP and extrapolate past growth rates into the future.

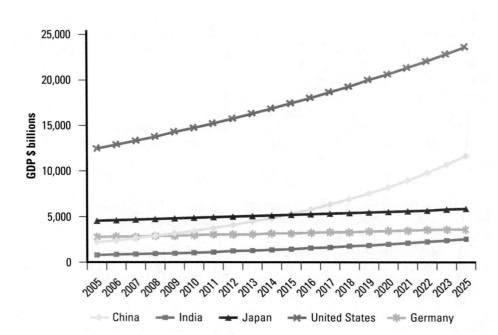

Focus on Managerial Implications

The material discussed in this chapter has two broad implications for international business. First, the political, economic, and legal systems of a country raise important ethical issues that have implications for the practice of international business. For example, what ethical implications are associated with doing business in totalitarian countries where citizens are denied basic human rights, corruption is rampant, and bribes are necessary to gain permission to do business? Is it right to operate in such a setting? A full discussion of the ethical implications of country differences in political economy is reserved for Chapter 4, where we explore ethics in international business in much greater depth.

Second, the political, economic, and legal environments of a country clearly influence the attractiveness of that country as a market or investment site. The benefits, costs, and risks associated with doing business in a country are a function of that country's political, economic, and legal systems. The overall attractiveness of a country as a market or investment site depends on balancing the likely long-term benefits of doing business in that country against the likely costs and risks. Below we consider the determinants of benefits, costs, and risks.

Benefits

In the most general sense, the long-run monetary benefits of doing business in a country are a function of the size of the market, the present wealth (purchasing power) of consumers in that market, and the likely future wealth of consumers. While some markets are very large when measured by number of consumers (e.g., China and India), low living standards may imply limited purchasing power and therefore a relatively small market when measured in economic terms. International businesses need to be aware of this distinction, but they also need to keep in mind the likely future prospects of a country. In 1960, South Korea was viewed as just another impoverished Third World nation. By 2006 it was the world's 11th-largest economy, measured in terms of GDP. International firms that recognized South Korea's potential in 1960 and began to do business in that country may have reaped greater benefits than those that wrote off South Korea.

By identifying and investing early in a potential future economic star, international firms may build brand loyalty and gain experience in that country's business practices. These will pay back substantial dividends if that country achieves sustained high economic growth rates. In contrast, late entrants may find that they lack the brand loyalty and experience necessary to achieve a significant presence in the market. In the language of business strategy, early entrants into potential future economic stars may be able to reap substantial first-mover advantages, while late entrants may fall victim to late-mover disadvantages.[66] (**First-mover advantages** are the advantages that accrue to early entrants into a market. **Late-mover disadvantages** are the handicaps that late entrants might suffer.) This kind of reasoning has been driving significant inward investment into China, which may become the world's second largest economy by 2015 if it continues growing at current rates (China is already the world's sixth-largest economy). For more than a decade, China has been the largest recipient of foreign direct investment in the developing world as international businesses ranging from General Motors and Volkswagen to Coca-Cola and Unilever try to establish a sustainable advantage in this nation.

A country's economic system and property rights regime are reasonably good predictors of economic prospects. Countries with free market economies in which property rights are protected tend to achieve greater economic growth rates than command economies or economies where property rights are poorly protected. It follows that a country's economic system, property rights regime, and market size (in terms of population) probably constitute reasonably good indicators of the potential long-run benefits of doing business in a country. In contrast, countries where property rights are not well respected and where corruption is rampant tend to have lower levels of economic growth. One must be careful about generalizing too much from this, however, since both China and India have achieved high growth rates despite relatively weak property rights regimes and high levels of corruption. In both countries, the shift toward a market-based economic system has produced large gains despite weak property rights and endemic corruption.

First-Mover Advantages Advantages accruing to the first to enter a market.

Late-Mover Disadvantages Handicaps experienced by being a late entrant to a market.

Costs

A number of political, economic, and legal factors determine the costs of doing business in a country. With regard to political factors, a company may have to pay off politically powerful entities in a country before the government allows it to do business there. The need to pay what are essentially bribes is greater in closed totalitarian states than in open democratic societies where politicians are held accountable by the electorate (although this is not a hard-and-fast distinction). Whether a company should actually pay bribes in return for market access should be determined on the basis of the legal and ethical implications of such action. We discuss this consideration in Chapter 4, when we look closely at the issue of business ethics.

With regard to economic factors, one of the most important variables is the sophistication of a country's economy. It may be more costly to do business in relatively primitive or undeveloped economies because of the lack of infrastructure and supporting businesses. At the extreme, an international firm may have to provide its own infrastructure and supporting business, which obviously raises costs. When McDonald's decided to open its first restaurant in Moscow, it found that to serve food and drink indistinguishable from that served in McDonald's restaurants elsewhere, it had to vertically integrate backward to supply its own needs. The quality of Russian-grown potatoes and meat was too poor. Thus, to protect the quality of its product, McDonald's set up its own dairy farms, cattle ranches, vegetable plots, and food processing plants within Russia. This raised the cost of doing business in Russia, relative to the cost in more sophisticated economies where high-quality inputs could be purchased on the open market.

As for legal factors, it can be more costly to do business in a country where local laws and regulations set strict standards with regard to product safety, safety in the workplace, environmental pollution, and the like (since adhering to such regulations is costly). It can also be more costly to do business in a country like the United States, where the absence of a cap on damage awards has meant spiraling liability insurance rates. It can be more costly to do business in a country that lacks well-established laws for regulating business practice (as is the case in many of the former communist nations). In the absence of a well-developed body of business contract law, international firms may find no satisfactory way to resolve contract disputes and, consequently, routinely face large losses from contract violations. Similarly, local laws that fail to adequately protect intellectual property can lead to the theft of an international business's intellectual property and lost income.

Risks

Political Risk
The likelihood that political forces will cause drastic changes in a country's business environment that will adversely affect the profit and other goals of a particular business enterprise.

As with costs, the risks of doing business in a country are determined by a number of political, economic, and legal factors. **Political risk** has been defined as the likelihood that political forces will cause drastic changes in a country's business environment that adversely affect the profit and other goals of a business enterprise.[67] So defined, political risk tends to be greater in countries experiencing social unrest and disorder or in countries where the underlying nature of a society increases the likelihood of social unrest. Social unrest typically finds expression in strikes, demonstrations, terrorism, and violent conflict. Such unrest is more likely to be found in countries that contain more than one ethnic nationality, in countries where competing ideologies are battling for political control, in countries where economic mismanagement has created high inflation and falling living standards, or in countries that straddle the "fault lines" between civilizations.

Social unrest can result in abrupt changes in government and government policy or, in some cases, in protracted civil strife. Such strife tends to have negative economic implications for the profit goals of business enterprises. For example, in the aftermath of the 1979 Islamic revolution in Iran, the Iranian assets of numerous U.S. companies were seized by the new Iranian government without compensation. Similarly, the violent disintegration of the Yugoslavian federation into warring states, including Bosnia, Croatia, and Serbia, precipitated a collapse in the local economies and in the profitability of investments in those countries.

More generally, a change in political regime can result in the enactment of laws that are less favorable to international business. In Venezuela, for example, the populist socialist politician Hugo Chavez won power in 1998, was reelected as president in 2000, and was reelected in 2006. Chavez has declared himself to be a "Fidelista," a follower of Cuba's Fidel Castro. He has pledged to improve the lot of the poor in Venezuela through government intervention in private business and has frequently railed against U.S. imperialism, all of which is of concern to Western enterprises doing business in the country. Among other actions, he increased the royalties foreign oil companies operating in Venezuela have to pay the government from 1 to 30 percent of sales.

Economic Risk
The likelihood that events, including economic mismanagement, will cause drastic changes in a country's business environment that adversely affect the profit and other goals of a particular business enterprise.

Other risks may arise from a country's mismanagement of its economy. An **economic risk** can be defined as the likelihood that economic mismanagement will cause drastic changes in a country's business environment that hurt the profit and other goals of a particular business enterprise. Economic risks are not independent of political risk. Economic mismanagement may give rise to significant social unrest and hence political risk. Nevertheless, economic risks are worth emphasizing as a separate category because there is not always a one-to-one relationship between economic mismanagement and social unrest. One visible indicator of economic mismanagement tends to be a country's inflation rate. Another is the level of business and government debt in the country.

In Asian states such as Indonesia, Thailand, and South Korea, businesses increased their debt rapidly during the 1990s, often at the bequest of the government, which was encouraging them to invest in industries deemed to be of "strategic importance" to the country. The result was overinvestment, with more industrial (factories) and commercial capacity (office space) being built than could be justified by demand conditions. Many of these investments turned out to be uneconomic. The borrowers failed to generate the profits necessary to service their debt payment obligations. In turn, the banks that had lent money to these businesses suddenly found that they had rapid increases in nonperforming loans on their books. Foreign investors, believing that many local companies and banks might go bankrupt, pulled their money out of these countries, selling local stock, bonds, and currency. This action precipitated the 1997–98 financial crises in Southeast Asia. The crisis included a precipitous decline in the value of Asian stock markets, which in some cases exceeded 70 percent; a similar collapse in the value of many Asian currencies against the U.S. dollar; an implosion of local demand; and a severe economic recession that will affect many Asian countries for years to come. In short, economic risks were rising throughout Southeast Asia during the 1990s. Astute foreign businesses and investors limited their exposure in this part of the world. More naive businesses and investors lost their shirts.

On the legal front, risks arise when a country's legal system fails to provide adequate safeguards in the case of contract violations or to protect property rights. When legal safeguards are weak, firms are more likely to break contracts or steal intellectual property if they perceive it as being in their interests to do so. Thus, a **legal risk** can be defined as the likelihood that a trading partner will opportunistically break a contract or expropriate property rights. When legal risks in a country are high, an international business might hesitate entering into a long-term contract or joint-venture agreement with a firm in that country. For example, in the 1970s when the Indian government passed a law requiring all foreign investors to enter into joint ventures with Indian companies, U.S. companies such as IBM and Coca-Cola closed their investments in India. They believed that the Indian legal system did not provide for adequate protection of intellectual property rights, creating the very real danger that their Indian partners might expropriate the intellectual property of the American companies— which for IBM and Coca-Cola amounted to the core of their competitive advantage.

Legal Risk
The likelihood that a trading partner will opportunistically break a contract or expropriate intellectual property rights.

Overall Attractiveness

The overall attractiveness of a country as a potential market or investment site for an international business depends on balancing the benefits, costs, and risks associated with doing business in that country (see Figure 2.4). Generally, the costs and risks associated with doing business in a foreign country are typically lower in economically advanced and politically stable democratic nations and greater in less developed and politically unstable nations. The calculus is complicated, however, because the potential long-run benefits are dependent not only upon a nation's current stage of economic development or political stability but also on likely future economic growth rates. Economic growth appears to be a function of a free market system and a country's capacity for growth (which may be greater in less developed nations). This leads one to conclude that, other things being equal, the benefit–cost–risk trade-off is likely to be most favorable in politically stable developed and developing nations that have free market systems and no dramatic upsurge in either inflation rates or private-sector debt. It is likely to be least favorable in politically unstable developing nations that operate with a mixed or command economy or in developing nations where speculative financial bubbles have led to excess borrowing.

figure 2.4

Country Attractiveness

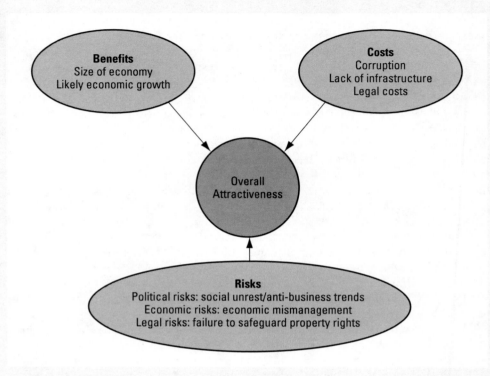

Benefits
Size of economy
Likely economic growth

Costs
Corruption
Lack of infrastructure
Legal costs

Overall
Attractiveness

Risks
Political risks: social unrest/anti-business trends
Economic risks: economic mismanagement
Legal risks: failure to safeguard property rights

Key Terms

political economy, p. 43

political system, p. 43

collectivism, p. 44

socialists, p. 44

communists, p. 44

social democrats, p. 44

privatization, p. 45

individualism, p. 45

democracy, p. 46

totalitarianism, p. 46

representative democracy, p. 47

communist totalitarianism, p. 47

theocratic totalitarianism, p. 47

tribal totalitarianism, p. 48

right-wing totalitarianism, p. 48

market economy, p. 49

command economy, p. 49

legal system, p. 50

common law, p. 51

civil law system, p. 51

theocratic law system, p. 51

contract, p. 52

contract law, p. 52

United Nations Convention on Contracts for the International Sale of Goods (CIGS), p. 52

property rights, p. 52

private action, p. 53

public action, p. 53

Foreign Corrupt Practices Act, p. 54

intellectual property, p. 56

patent, p. 56

copyrights, p. 56

trademarks, p. 56

World Intellectual Property Organization, p. 56

Paris Convention for the Protection of Industrial Property, p. 56

product safety laws, p. 57

product liability, p. 57

gross national income (GNI), p. 58

purchasing power parity (PPP), p. 60

Human Development Index (HDI), p. 62

innovation, p. 65

entrepreneurs, p. 65

deregulation, p. 75

first-mover advantages, p. 79

late-mover disadvantages, p. 79

political risk, p. 80

economic risk, p. 80

legal risk, p. 81

Summary

This chapter has reviewed how the political, economic, and legal systems of countries vary. The potential benefits, costs, and risks of doing business in a country are a function of its political, economic, and legal systems. The chapter made the following points:

1. Political systems can be assessed according to two dimensions: the degree to which they emphasize collectivism as opposed to individualism, and the degree to which they are democratic or totalitarian.

2. Collectivism is an ideology that views the needs of society as being more important than the needs of the individual. Collectivism translates into an advocacy for state intervention in economic activity and, in the case of communism, a totalitarian dictatorship.

3. Individualism is an ideology that is built on an emphasis of the primacy of individual's freedoms in the political, economic, and cultural realms. Individualism translates into an advocacy for democratic ideals and free market economics.

4. Democracy and totalitarianism are at different ends of the political spectrum. In a representative democracy, citizens periodically elect individuals to represent them and political freedoms are guaranteed by a constitution. In a totalitarian state, political power is monopolized by a party, group, or individual, and basic political freedoms are denied to citizens of the state.

5. There are three broad types of economic systems: a market economy, a command economy, and a mixed economy. In a market economy, prices are free of controls and private ownership is predominant. In a command economy, prices are set by central planners, productive assets are owned by the state, and private ownership is forbidden. A mixed economy has elements of both a market economy and a command economy.

6. Differences in the structure of law between countries can have important implications for the practice of international business. The degree to which property rights are protected can vary dramatically from country to country, as can product safety and product liability legislation and the nature of contract law.

7. The rate of economic progress in a country seems to depend on the extent to which that country has a well-functioning market economy in which property rights are protected.

8. Many countries are now in a state of transition. There is a marked shift away from totalitarian governments and command or mixed economic systems and toward democratic political institutions and free market economic systems.

9. The attractiveness of a country as a market and/or investment site depends on balancing the likely long-run benefits of doing business in that country against the likely costs and risks.

10. The benefits of doing business in a country are a function of the size of the market (population), its present wealth (purchasing power), and its future growth prospects. By investing early in countries that are currently poor but are nevertheless growing rapidly, firms can gain first-mover advantages that will pay back substantial dividends in the future.

11. The costs of doing business in a country tend to be greater where political payoffs are required to gain market access, where supporting infrastructure is lacking or underdeveloped, and where adhering to local laws and regulations is costly.

12. The risks of doing business in a country tend to be greater in countries that are politically unstable, subject to economic mismanagement, and lacking a legal system to provide adequate safeguards in the case of contract or property rights violations.

Critical Thinking and Discussion Questions

1. Free market economies stimulate greater economic growth, whereas state-directed economies stifle growth. Discuss.

2. A democratic political system is an essential condition for sustained economic progress. Discuss.

3. What is the relationship between corruption in a country (i.e., bribe taking by government officials) and economic growth? Is corruption always bad?

4. The Nobel Prize–winning economist Amartya Sen argues that the concept of development should be broadened to include more than just economic development. What other factors does Sen think should be included in an assessment of development? How might adoption of Sen's views influence government policy? Do you think Sen is correct that development is about more than just economic development? Explain.

5. You are the CEO of a company that has to choose between making a $100 million investment in Russia or the Czech Republic. Both investments promise the same long-run return, so your choice is driven by risk considerations. Assess the various risks of doing business in each of these nations. Which investment would you favor and why?

6. Read the opening case on India and answer the following questions:

   a. What kind of economic system did India operate under during 1947 to 1990? What kind of system is it moving toward today? What are the impediments to completing this transformation?

   b. How might widespread public ownership of businesses and extensive government regulations have impacted (*i*) the efficiency of state and private businesses, and (*ii*) the rate of new business formation in India during 1947–90? How do you think these factors affected the rate of economic growth in India during this time?

   c. How would privatization, deregulation, and the removal of barriers to foreign direct investment affect the efficiency of business, new business formation, and the rate of economic growth in India during the post-1990 time period?

   d. India now has pockets of strengths in key high-technology industries such as software and pharmaceuticals. Why do you think India is developing strength in these areas? How might success in these industries help to generate growth in other sectors of the Indian economy?

   e. Given what is now occurring in the Indian economy, do you think the country represents an attractive target for inward investment by foreign multinationals selling consumer products? Why?

Research Task globalEDGE   http://globalEDGE.msu.edu

Use the globalEDGE Resource Desk (http://globalEDGE.msu.edu/ResourceDesk/) to complete the following exercises:

1. You work for a manufacturing company that has operations in the U.S. and Western Europe. However, increasing competition has prompted the firm to examine the option of shifting production to a lower-cost location. You have narrowed the list of potential countries down to Taiwan, South Africa, and Argentina. Based on the political and economic *risk ratings*, how would you rate the attractiveness of these three countries for your company? Prepare a brief report summarizing your assessment, including a detailed rundown of risks for your top country choice.

2. The *Market Potential Index* (MPI) is an indexing study conducted by the Michigan State University Center for International Business Education and Research (MSU-CIBER) to compare emerging markets on a variety of dimensions. Provide a description of the indicators used in the indexing procedure. Which of the indicators should have greater importance for a company that markets laptop computers? Considering the MPI rankings, which developing countries would you advise a company selling laptops to enter first?

closing case

Chavez's Venezuela

Hugo Chavez, a former military officer who was once jailed for engineering a failed coup attempt, was elected president of Venezuela in 1998. Chavez, a self-styled democratic socialist, won the presidential election by campaigning against corruption, economic mismanagement, and the "harsh realities" of global capitalism. When he took office in February 1999, Chavez claimed that he had inherited the worst economic situation in the country's recent history. He wasn't far off the mark. A collapse in the price of oil, which accounted for 70 percent of the country's exports, left Venezuela with a large budget deficit and forced the economy into a deep recession.

Soon after taking office, Chavez consolidated his hold over the apparatus of government. A constituent assembly, dominated by Chavez followers, drafted a new constitution that strengthened the powers of the presidency and allowed Chavez (if reelected) to stay in office until 2012. Subsequently, the national congress, which was controlled by Chavez supporters, approved a measure allowing the government to remove and appoint Supreme Court justices, effectively increasing Chavez's power over the judiciary. Chavez also extended government control over the media. By 2007, Freedom House, which annually assesses political and civil liberties worldwide, concluded Venezuela was only "partly free" and that freedoms were being progressively curtailed.

On the economic front, things remained rough. The economy shrank by 9 percent in 2002 and another 8 percent in 2003. Unemployment remained persistently high at 15 to 17 percent and the poverty rate rose to more than 50 percent of the population. A 2003 study by the World Bank concluded that Venezuela was one of the most regulated economies in the world and that state controls over business activities gave public officials ample opportunities to enrich themselves by demanding bribes in return for permission to expand operations or enter new lines of business. Despite Chavez's anticorruption rhetoric, Transparency International, which ranks the world's nations according to the extent of public corruption, reported that corruption has increased under Chavez. In 2007, Transparency International ranked Venezuela 162 out of 179 nations, down from 114 in 2004. Consistent with his socialist rhetoric, Chavez has taken various enterprises into state ownership and has required that other enterprises be restructured as "workers' cooperatives" in return for government loans. In addition, the government has begun to seize large rural farms and ranches that Chavez claims are not sufficiently productive, turning them into state-owned cooperatives.

In 2004, the world oil market bailed Chavez out of mounting economic difficulties. Oil prices started to surge, and Venezuela, the world's fifth largest producer, started to reap a bonanza. On the back of surging oil exports, the economy grew by 18 percent in 2004, 9 percent in 2005, 10.5 percent in 2006, and 8.5 percent in 2007. Chavez's reaction to the oil price increase was to use oil revenues to boost government spending on social programs, many of them modeled after programs

in Cuba. As a result, the government's share of GDP increased from 20 percent at the end of the 1990s to 38 percent in 2007. Chavez also extended government control over foreign oil producers doing business in Venezuela, which he accused of making outsized profits at the expense of a poor nation. In 2005, he increased the government's royalties on oil sales to 30 percent, from 1 percent, and he raised the sales tax rate to 50 percent, from 34 percent. In 2006, he announced plans to reduce the stakes held by foreign companies in oil projects in the Orinoco region and to give the state-run oil company, Petroleos de Venezuela SA, a majority position. However, despite strong global demand, oil production in Venezuela appears to be slipping, having fallen for six successive quarters between mid-2006 and late 2007.

Riding a wave of popularity at home, in December 2006 Chavez won reelection as president. He celebrated his victory by stepping on the revolutionary accelerator. Parliament gave him the power to legislate by decree for 18 months, and a committee of his supporters started to draft a constitutional reform to turn Venezuela into an avowedly socialist country and to allow the president to stand for reelection indefinitely. However, in a sign that Chavez's popularity may have crested, in a December 2, 2007, nationwide referendum, Venezuelan voters narrowly rejected a revised constitution that would have placed more power in Chavez's hands.

Sources: D. Luhnow and P. Millard, "Chavez Plans to Take More Control of Oil away from Foreign Firms," *The Wall Street Journal*, April 24, 2006, p. A1; R. Gallego, "Chavez's Agenda Takes Shape," *The Wall Street Journal*, December 27, 2005, p. A12; "The Sickly Stench of Corruption: Venezuela," *The Economist*, April 1, 2006, p. 50; "Chavez Squeezes the Oil Firms," *The Economist*, November 12, 2005, p. 61; "Glimpsing the Bottom of the Barrel: Venezuela," *The Economist*, February 3, 2007, p. 51; and "The Wind Goes out of the Revolution—Defeat for Hugo Chavez," *The Economist*, December 8, 2007, pp. 30–32.

Case Discussion Questions

1. Under Hugo Chavez's leadership, what kind of economic system is being put in place in Venezuela? How would you characterize the political system?

2. How will Chavez's unilateral changes to contracts with foreign oil companies impact future investment by foreigners in Venezuela?

3. How will the high level of public corruption in Venezuela impact future growth rates?

4. Currently Venezuela is benefiting from a boom in oil prices. What do you think might happen if oil prices retreat from their current high level?

5. What is the long-run prognosis for the Venezuelan economy? Is this a country that is attractive to international businesses?

Part 2 Country Differences

LEARNING OBJECTIVES

After you have read this chapter you should:

1 Know what is meant by the culture of a society.

2 Identify the forces that lead to differences in social culture.

3 Identify the business and economic implications of differences in culture.

4 Understand how differences in social culture influence values in the workplace.

5 Develop an appreciation for the economic and business implications of cultural change.

chapter **3**

Differences in Culture

McDonald's in India

opening case

In many ways, McDonald's Corporation has written the book on global expansion. Every day, on average, somewhere around the world four new McDonald's restaurants are opened. The company has some 30,000 restaurants in more than 120 countries that collectively serve close to 50 million customers each day.

One of the latest additions to McDonald's list of countries hosting the famous golden arches is India, where McDonald's started to establish restaurants in the late 1990s. Although India is a poor nation, the large and relatively prosperous middle class, estimated to number about 200 million, attracted McDonald's. India, however, offered McDonald's unique challenges. For thousands of years, India's Hindu culture has revered cattle. Hindu scriptures state that cattle are a gift of the gods to the human race. The cow represents the Divine Mother that sustains all human beings. Cows give birth to bulls that are harnessed to pull plows, cow milk is highly valued and used to produce yogurt and ghee (a form of butter), cow urine has a unique place in traditional Hindu medicine, and the dung is used as fuel. Some 300 million of these animals roam India, untethered, revered as sacred providers. They are everywhere, ambling down roads, grazing in rubbish dumps, and resting in temples—everywhere, that is, except on your plate, for Hindus do not eat the meat of the sacred cow.

McDonald's is the world's largest user of beef. Since its founding in 1955, countless animals have died to produce Big Macs. How can a company whose fortunes are built upon beef enter a country where the consumption of beef is a grave sin? Use pork instead? However, there are some 140 million Muslims in India, and Muslims don't eat pork. This leaves chicken and mutton. McDonald's responded to this cultural food dilemma by creating an Indian version of its Big Mac—the "Maharaja Mac"—which is made from mutton. Other additions to the menu conform to local sensibilities such as the "McAloo Tikki Burger," which is made from chicken. All foods are strictly segregated into vegetarian and nonvegetarian lines to conform with preferences in a country where many Hindus are vegetarian. According to the head of McDonald's Indian operations, "We had to reinvent ourselves for the Indian palate." Indeed, 75 percent of the menu is Indianized.

For a while, this seemed to work. Then in 2001 McDonald's was blindsided by a class-action lawsuit brought against it in the United States by three Indian businessmen living in Seattle. The businessmen, all vegetarians and two of whom were Hindus, sued McDonald's for "fraudulently concealing" the existence of beef in McDonald's French fries! McDonald's had said it used only 100 percent vegetable oil to make French fries, but the company soon admitted that it used a "minuscule" amount of beef extract in the oil. McDonald's settled the suit for $10 million and issued an apology, which read, "McDonald's sincerely apologizes to Hindus, vegetarians, and others for failing to provide the kind of information they needed to make informed dietary decisions at our U.S. restaurants." Going forward, the company pledged to do a better job of labeling the ingredients of its food and to find a substitute for the beef extract used in its oil.

However, news travels fast in the global society of the 21st century, and the revelation that McDonald's used beef extract in its oil was enough to bring Hindu nationalists onto the streets in Delhi, where they vandalized one McDonald's restaurant, causing $45,000 in damage; shouted slogans outside of another; picketed the company's headquarters; and called on India's prime minister to close McDonald's stores in the country. McDonald's Indian franchise holders quickly issued denials that they used oil that contained beef extract, and Hindu extremists responded by stating they would submit McDonald's oil to laboratory tests to see if they could detect beef extract.

The negative publicity seemed to have little impact on McDonald's long-term plans in India, however. The company continued to open restaurants, and by late 2007 had more than 130 restaurants in the country with plans to triple the number by 2011. When asked why they frequented McDonald's restaurants, Indian customers noted that their children enjoyed the "American" experience, the food was of a consistent quality, and the toilets were always clean! ●

Sources: Luke Harding, "Give Me a Big Mac—But Hold the Beef," *The Guardian,* December 28, 2000, p. 24; Luke Harding, "Indian McAnger," *The Guardian,* May 7, 2001, p. 1; A. Dhillon, "India Has No Beef with Fast Food Chains," *Financial Times,* March 23, 2002, p. 3; "McDonald's Plans More Outlets in India," *Associated Press Worldstream,* December 24, 2004; D. Dutta, "The Perishable Food Chain in India," *Just Food,* September 2005, pp. 22–29; and R. Verma, "Branded Foods in India," *Just Food,* November 2007, pp. 14–17.

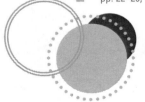

Introduction

As McDonald's has long known, international business is different from domestic business because countries are different. As detailed in the opening case, to succeed in India, McDonald's has had to customize its offerings to the tastes and preferences of a Hindu culture that venerates the cow, will not eat beef, and has a large vegetarian population. In Chapter 2, we saw how national differences in political, economic, and legal systems influence the benefits, costs, and risks associated with doing business in different countries. In this chapter, we will explore how differences in culture across and within countries can affect international business.

Several themes run through this chapter. The first theme is that business success in a variety of countries requires cross-cultural literacy. By **cross-cultural literacy**, we mean an understanding of how cultural differences across and within nations can affect the way business is practiced. In these days of global communications, rapid transportation, and worldwide markets, when the era of the global village seems just around the corner, it is easy to forget just how different various cultures really are. Underneath the veneer of modernism, deep cultural differences often remain. Westerners in general, and Americans in particular, are quick to conclude that because people from other parts of the world also wear blue jeans, listen to Western popular music, eat at McDonald's, and drink Coca-Cola, they also accept the basic tenets of Western (or American) culture. However, this is not true. For example, take the Chinese. Increasingly, they are embracing the material products of modern society. Anyone who has visited Shanghai cannot fail to be struck by how modern the city seems, with its skyscrapers, department stores, and freeways. Yet beneath the veneer of Western modernism, long-standing cultural traditions rooted in a 2,000-year-old ideology continue to have an important influence on the way business is transacted in China. For example, in China, *guanxi*, or a network of social relationships with others backed by reciprocal obligations, are central to getting business done. Firms that lack sufficient *guanxi* may find themselves at a disadvantage when doing business in China. The lesson: To succeed in China you have to play by Chinese rules, just as McDonald's found that to succeed in India you have to play by Indian rules. More generally, in this chapter, we shall argue that it is important for foreign businesses to gain an understanding of the culture that prevails in those countries where they do business, and that success requires a foreign enterprise to adapt to the culture of its host country.[1]

Another theme developed in this chapter is that a relationship may exist between culture and the cost of doing business in a country or region. Different cultures are more or less supportive of the capitalist mode of production and may increase or lower the costs of doing business. For example, some observers have argued that cultural factors lowered the costs of doing business in Japan and helped to explain Japan's rapid economic ascent during the 1960s, '70s, and '80s.[2] Similarly, cultural factors can sometimes raise the costs of doing business. Historically, class divisions were an important aspect of British culture, and for a long time, firms operating in Great Britain found it difficult to achieve cooperation between management and labor. Class divisions led to a high level of industrial disputes in that country during the 1960s and 1970s and raised the costs of doing business relative to the costs in countries such as Switzerland, Norway, Germany, or Japan, where class conflict was historically less prevalent.

The British example, however, brings us to another theme we will explore in this chapter. Culture is not static. It can and does evolve, although the rate at which culture can change is the subject of some dispute. Important aspects of British culture have changed significantly over the past 20 years, and this is reflected in weaker class distinctions and a lower level of industrial disputes. Between 1995 and 2005, the number of days lost per 1,000 workers due to strikes in the United Kingdom was on average 28 each year, significantly less than in the United States (33 each year), Ireland (81), and Canada (168).[3] Finally, it is important to note that multinational enterprises can themselves be engines of cultural change. In India, for example, McDonald's and other Western fast-food companies may help to change the dinning culture of that nation, drawing them away from traditional restaurants and toward fast-food outlets.

Cross-Cultural Literacy
An understanding of how cultural differences across and within nations can affect the way business is practiced.

What Is Culture?

LEARNING OBJECTIVE 1
Know what is meant by the culture of a society.

Culture
A system of values and norms that are shared among a group of people and that when taken together constitute a design for living.

Values
Abstract ideas about what a group believes to be good, right, and desirable.

Norms
The social rules and guidelines that prescribe appropriate behavior in particular situations.

Society
A group of people who share a common set of values and norms.

Scholars have never been able to agree on a simple definition of *culture*. In the 1870s, the anthropologist Edward Tylor defined culture as "that complex whole which includes knowledge, belief, art, morals, law, custom, and other capabilities acquired by man as a member of society."[4] Since then hundreds of other definitions have been offered. Geert Hofstede, an expert on cross-cultural differences and management, defined culture as "the collective programming of the mind which distinguishes the members of one human group from another. . . . Culture, in this sense, includes systems of values; and values are among the building blocks of culture."[5] Another definition of culture comes from sociologists Zvi Namenwirth and Robert Weber, who see culture as a system of ideas and argue that these ideas constitute a design for living.[6]

Here we follow both Hofstede and Namenwirth and Weber by viewing **culture** as a system of values and norms that are shared among a group of people and that when taken together constitute a design for living. By **values** we mean abstract ideas about what a group believes to be good, right, and desirable. Put differently, values are shared assumptions about how things ought to be.[7] By **norms** we mean the social rules and guidelines that prescribe appropriate behavior in particular situations. We shall use the term **society** to refer to a group of people who share a common set of values and norms. While a society may be equivalent to a country, some countries harbor several societies (i.e., they support multiple cultures), and some societies embrace more than one country.

VALUES AND NORMS Values form the bedrock of a culture. They provide the context within which a society's norms are established and justified. They may include a society's attitudes toward such concepts as individual freedom, democracy, truth, justice, honesty, loyalty, social obligations, collective responsibility, the role of women, love, sex, marriage, and so on. Values are not just abstract concepts; they are invested with considerable emotional significance. People argue, fight, and even die over values such as freedom. Values also often are reflected in the political and economic systems of a society. As we saw in Chapter 2, democratic free market capitalism is a reflection of a philosophical value system that emphasizes individual freedom.

Norms are the social rules that govern people's actions toward one another. Norms can be subdivided further into two major categories: folkways and mores. **Folkways** are the routine conventions of everyday life. Generally, folkways are actions of little moral significance. Rather, they are social conventions concerning things such as the appropriate dress code in a particular situation, good social manners, eating with the correct utensils, neighborly behavior, and the like. Although folkways define the way people are expected to behave, violation of them is not normally a serious matter. People who violate folkways may be thought of as eccentric or ill-mannered, but they are not usually considered

Another Perspective

Knowing the Culture: "When in Rome . . ."
It's important to know the cultural norms of other countries. For example, unlike English, many languages have informal and formal forms of address. Speakers use the informal form with peers but the formal form with their elders or to signify respect. This is true of the native languages of India. As a result, English-speaking Indians often use "sir" or "ma'am" or include titles such as "Mr.," "Ms.," or "Professor" when they talk to convey respect.

Americans, on the other hand, tend to be informal and use first names. But beware! In many countries, using a first name without being invited to do so may be perceived as impolite—especially if you're younger than your host. ("Doing Business in India: 20 Cultural Norms You Need to Know," *Business Intelligence Lowdown,* March 6, 2007, www.businessintelligencelowdown.com)

to be evil or bad. In many countries, foreigners may initially be excused for violating folkways.

> **Folkways**
> The routine conventions of everyday life.

A good example of folkways concerns attitudes toward time in different countries. People are keenly aware of the passage of time in the United States and Northern European cultures such as Germany and Britain. Businesspeople are very conscious about scheduling their time and are quickly irritated when their time is wasted because a business associate is late for a meeting or if they are kept waiting. They talk about time as though it were money, as something that can be spent, saved, wasted, and lost.[8] Alternatively, in Arab, Latin, and Mediterranean cultures, time has a more elastic character. Keeping to a schedule is viewed as less important than finishing an interaction with people. For example, an American businesswoman might feel slighted if she is kept waiting for 30 minutes outside the office of a Latin American executive before a meeting, but the Latin American may simply be completing an interaction with an associate and view the information gathered from this as more important than sticking to a rigid schedule. The Latin American executive intends no disrespect, but due to a mutual misunderstanding about the importance of time, the American may see things differently. Similarly, Saudi attitudes to time have been shaped by their nomadic Bedouin heritage, in which precise time played no real role and arriving somewhere tomorrow might mean next week. Like Latin Americans, many Saudis are unlikely to understand the American obsession with precise time and schedules, and Americans need to adjust their expectations accordingly.

Folkways include rituals and symbolic behavior. Rituals and symbols are the most visible manifestations of a culture and constitute the outward expression of deeper values. For example, upon meeting a foreign business executive, a Japanese executive will hold his business card in both hands and bow while presenting the card to the foreigner.[9] This ritual behavior is loaded with deep cultural symbolism. The card specifies the rank of the Japanese executive, which is a very important piece of information in a hierarchical society such as Japan (Japanese often have business cards with Japanese printed on one side, and English printed on the other). The bow is a sign of respect, and the deeper the angle of the bow, the greater the reverence one person shows for the other. The person receiving the card is expected to examine it carefully, which is a way of returning respect and acknowledging the card giver's position in the hierarchy. The foreigner is also expected to bow when taking the card, and to return the greeting by presenting the Japanese executive with his own card, similarly bowing in the process. To not do so, and to fail to read the card that he has been given, instead casually placing it in his jacket, violates this important folkway and is considered rude.

> **Mores**
> Norms that are seen as central to the functioning of a society and to its social life.

Mores are norms that are seen as central to the functioning of a society and to its social life. They have much greater significance than folkways. Accordingly, violating mores can bring serious retribution. Mores include such factors as indictments against theft, adultery, incest, and cannibalism. In many societies, certain mores have been enacted into law. Thus, all advanced societies have laws against theft, incest, and cannibalism. However, there are also many differences between cultures. In America, for example, drinking alcohol is widely accepted, whereas in Saudi Arabia the consumption of alcohol is viewed as violating important social mores and is punishable by imprisonment (as some Western citizens working in Saudi Arabia have discovered).

CULTURE, SOCIETY, AND THE NATION-STATE

We have defined a society as a group of people that share a common set of values and norms; that is,

Another Perspective

Online View of Other Cultures

Visit the online versions of some English-language foreign newspapers in major international cities to get a sense of their cultural values, social structure, and markets. Look at the ads and business names. Check out the classifieds. A good list link is at www.newhopepa.com/News/Intl_News/default.htm.

people who are bound together by a common culture. There is not a strict one-to-one correspondence between a society and a nation-state. Nation-states are political creations. They may contain a single culture or several cultures. While the French nation can be thought of as the political embodiment of French culture, the nation of Canada has at least three cultures—an Anglo culture, a French-speaking "Quebecois" culture, and a Native American culture. Similarly, many African nations have important cultural differences between tribal groups, as exhibited in the early 1990s when Rwanda dissolved into a bloody civil war between two tribes, the Tutsis and Hutus. Africa is not alone in this regard. India is composed of many distinct cultural groups. During the first Gulf War, the prevailing view presented to Western audiences was that Iraq was a homogenous Arab nation. However, since then we have learned that several different societies exist within Iraq, each with its own culture. The Kurds in the north do not view themselves as Arabs and have their own distinct history and traditions. There are two Arab societies: the Shiites in the South and the Sunnis who populate the middle of the country and who ruled Iraq under the regime of Saddam Hussein (the terms *Shiites* and *Sunnis* refer to different sects within the religion of Islam). Among the southern Sunnis is another distinct society of 500,000 Marsh Arabs who live at the confluence of the Tigris and Euphrates rivers, pursuing a way of life that dates back 5,000 years.[10]

At the other end of the scale are cultures that embrace several nations. Several scholars argue that we can speak of an Islamic society or culture that is shared by the citizens of many different nations in the Middle East, Asia, and Africa. As you will recall from the last chapter, this view of expansive cultures that embrace several nations underpins Samuel Huntington's view of a world that is fragmented into different civilizations, including Western, Islamic, and Sinic (Chinese).[11]

To complicate things further, it is also possible to talk about culture at different levels. It is reasonable to talk about "American society" and "American culture," but there are several societies within America, each with its own culture. One can talk about African-American culture, Cajun culture, Chinese-American culture, Hispanic culture, Indian culture, Irish-American culture, and Southern culture. The relationship between culture and country is often ambiguous. Even if a country can be characterized as having a single homogenous culture, often that national culture is a mosaic of subcultures.

LEARNING OBJECTIVE 2
Identify the forces that lead to differences in social culture.

THE DETERMINANTS OF CULTURE The values and norms of a culture do not emerge fully formed. They are the evolutionary product of a number of factors, including the prevailing political and economic philosophies, the social structure of a society, and the dominant religion, language, and education (see Figure 3.1). We discussed political and economic philosophies at length in Chapter 2. Such philosophies clearly influence the value systems of a society. For example, the values found in Communist North Korea toward freedom, justice, and individual achievement are clearly different from the values found in the United States, precisely because each society operates according to different political and economic philosophies. Below we will discuss the influence of social structure, religion, language, and education. The chain of causation runs both ways. While factors such as social structure and religion clearly influence the values and norms of a society, the values and norms of a society can influence social structure and religion.

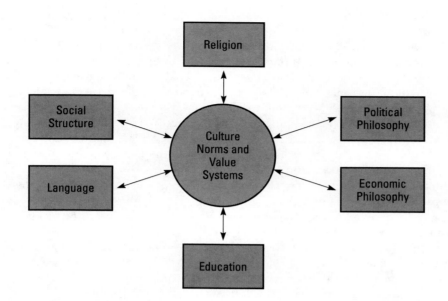

3.1 figure

The Determination of Culture

Social Structure

A society's **social structure** refers to its basic social organization. Although social structure consists of many different aspects, two dimensions are particularly important when explaining differences between cultures. The first is the degree to which the basic unit of social organization is the individual, as opposed to the group. In general, Western societies tend to emphasize the primacy of the individual, whereas groups tend to figure much larger in many other societies. The second dimension is the degree to which a society is stratified into classes or castes. Some societies are characterized by a relatively high degree of social stratification and relatively low mobility between strata (e.g., Indian); other societies are characterized by a low degree of social stratification and high mobility between strata (e.g., American).

INDIVIDUALS AND GROUPS   A **group** is an association of two or more individuals who have a shared sense of identity and who interact with each other in structured ways on the basis of a common set of expectations about each other's behavior.[12] Human social life is group life. Individuals are involved in families, work groups, social groups, recreational groups, and so on. However, while groups are found in all societies, societies differ according to the degree to which the group is viewed as the primary means of social organization.[13] In some societies, individual attributes and achievements are viewed as being more important than group membership; in others the reverse is true.

The Individual   In Chapter 2, we discussed individualism as a political philosophy. However, individualism is more than just an abstract political philosophy. In many Western societies, the individual is the basic building block of social organization. This is reflected not just in the political and economic organization of society but also in the way people perceive themselves and relate to each other in social and business settings. The value systems of many Western societies, for example, emphasize individual achievement. The social standing of individuals is not so much a function

Social Structure
The basic social organization of a society.

Group
An association of two or more individuals who have a shared sense of identity and who interact with each other in structured ways on the basis of a common set of expectations about each other's behavior.

of whom they work for as of their individual performance in whatever work setting they choose.

LEARNING OBJECTIVE 3
Identify the business and economic implications of differences in culture.

The emphasis on individual performance in many Western societies has both beneficial and harmful aspects. In the United States, the emphasis on individual performance finds expression in an admiration of rugged individualism and entrepreneurship. One benefit of this is the high level of entrepreneurial activity in the United States and other Western societies. New products and new ways of doing business (e.g., personal computers, photocopiers, computer software, biotechnology, supermarkets, and discount retail stores) have repeatedly been created in the United States by entrepreneurial individuals. One can argue that the dynamism of the U.S. economy owes much to the philosophy of individualism.

Individualism also finds expression in a high degree of managerial mobility between companies, and this is not always a good thing. Although moving from company to company may be good for individual managers who are trying to build impressive résumés, it is not necessarily a good thing for American companies. The lack of loyalty and commitment to an individual company, and the tendency to move on for a better offer, can result in managers who have good general skills but lack the knowledge, experience, and network of interpersonal contacts that come from years of working within the same company. An effective manager draws on company-specific experience, knowledge, and a network of contacts to find solutions to current problems, and American companies may suffer if their managers lack these attributes. One positive aspect of high managerial mobility is that executives are exposed to different ways of doing business. The ability to compare business practices helps U.S. executives identify how good practices and techniques developed in one firm might be profitably applied to other firms.

The emphasis on individualism may also make it difficult to build teams within an organization to perform collective tasks. If individuals are always competing with each other on the basis of individual performance, it may be difficult for them to cooperate. A study of U.S. competitiveness by the Massachusetts Institute of Technology suggested that U.S. firms are being hurt in the global economy by a failure to achieve cooperation both within a company (e.g., between functions; between management and labor) and between companies (e.g., between a firm and its suppliers). Given the emphasis on individualism in the American value system, this failure is not surprising.[14] The emphasis on individualism in the United States, while helping to create a dynamic entrepreneurial economy, may raise the costs of doing business due to its adverse impact on managerial stability and cooperation.

The Group   In contrast to the Western emphasis on the individual, the group is the primary unit of social organization in many other societies. For example, in Japan, the social status of an individual is determined as much by the standing of the group to which he or she belongs as by his or her individual performance.[15] In traditional Japanese society, the group was the family or village to which an individual belonged. Today, the group has frequently come to be associated with the work team or business organization to which an individual belongs. In a now-classic study of Japanese society, Nakane noted how this expresses itself in everyday life:

> When a Japanese faces the outside (confronts another person) and affixes some position to himself socially he is inclined to give precedence to institution over kind of occupation. Rather than saying, "I am a typesetter" or "I am a filing clerk," he is likely to say, "I am from B Publishing Group" or "I belong to S company."[16]

LEARNING OBJECTIVE 3
Identify the business and economic implications of differences in culture.

Nakane goes on to observe that the primacy of the group to which an individual belongs often evolves into a deeply emotional attachment in which identification with the group becomes all-important in one's life. One central value of Japanese culture is

Hill: Global Business
Today, Sixth Edition

3. Differences in Culture

Text

© The McGraw–Hill
Companies, 2009

105

the importance attached to group membership. This may have beneficial implications for business firms. Strong identification with the group is argued to create pressures for mutual self-help and collective action. If the worth of an individual is closely linked to the achievements of the group (e.g., firm), as Nakane maintains is the case in Japan, this creates a strong incentive for individual members of the group to work together for the common good. Some argue that the success of Japanese enterprises in the global economy has been based partly on their ability to achieve close cooperation between individuals within a company and between companies. This has found expression in the widespread diffusion of self-managing work teams within Japanese organizations, the close cooperation among different functions within Japanese companies (e.g., among manufacturing, marketing, and R&D), and the cooperation between a company and its suppliers on issues such as design, quality control, and inventory reduction.[17] In all of these cases, cooperation is driven by the need to improve the performance of the group (i.e., the business firm).

The primacy of the value of group identification also discourages managers and workers from moving from company to company. Lifetime employment in a particular company was long the norm in certain sectors of the Japanese economy (estimates suggest that between 20 and 40 percent of all Japanese employees have formal or informal lifetime employment guarantees). Over the years, managers and workers build up knowledge, experience, and a network of interpersonal business contacts. All these things can help managers perform their jobs more effectively and achieve cooperation with others.

However, the primacy of the group is not always beneficial. Just as U.S. society is characterized by a great deal of dynamism and entrepreneurship, reflecting the primacy of values associated with individualism, some argue that Japanese society is characterized by a corresponding lack of dynamism and entrepreneurship. Although the long-run consequences are unclear, the United States could continue to create more new industries than Japan and continue to be more successful at pioneering radically new products and new ways of doing business.

SOCIAL STRATIFICATION

All societies are stratified on a hierarchical basis into social categories—that is, into **social strata.** These strata are typically defined on the basis of characteristics such as family background, occupation, and income. Individuals are born into a particular stratum. They become a member of the social category to which their parents belong. Individuals born into a stratum toward the top of the social hierarchy tend to have better life chances than those born into a stratum toward the bottom of the hierarchy. They are likely to have better education, health, standard of living, and work opportunities. Although all societies are stratified to some degree, they differ in two related ways. First, they differ from each other with regard to the degree of mobility between social strata; second, they differ with regard to the significance attached to social strata in business contexts.

Social Mobility

The term **social mobility** refers to the extent to which individuals can move out of the strata into which they are born. Social mobility varies significantly from society to society. The most rigid system of stratification is a caste system. A **caste system** is a closed system of stratification in which social position is determined by the family into which a person is born, and change in that position is usually not possible during an individual's lifetime. Often a caste position carries with it a specific occupation. Members of one caste might be shoemakers, members of another might be butchers, and so on. These occupations are embedded in the caste and passed down through the family to succeeding generations. Although the number of societies with caste systems diminished rapidly during the 20th century, one partial example

Social Strata
The hierarchical categories within a society, defined on the basis of such elements as family background, income, and occupation.

Social Mobility
The extent to which individuals can move out of the strata into which they are born.

Caste System
A closed system of stratification in which social position is determined by the family into which a person is born, and change out of that strata is usually not possible during a person's lifetime.

Country FOCUS

Breaking India's Caste System

Modern-day India is a country of dramatic contrasts. Its information technology sector is among the most vibrant in the world, with companies such as Infosys and Wipro emerging as powerful global players. India's caste system, long an impediment to social mobility, is a fading memory among the educated urban middle-class Indians who make up the majority of employees in the high-tech economy. However, the same is not true in rural India where 70 percent of the population still resides. There caste remains a pervasive influence. In 1950, the national constitution reserved 22.5 percent of jobs for people from the lower castes, or *dalits* (also known as "untouchables") and for tribal people. In 1990, an additional 27 percent of jobs were set aside for what were called "other backward castes." Some Indian states set higher quotas, including Tamil Nadu, which reserves 69 percent of government jobs for lower castes and other needy groups. Despite these long-standing policies, anecdotal and hard evidence suggests castes still plays an important role in daily life.

For example, a young female engineer at Infosys who grew up in a small rural village and is a *dalits* recounts how she never entered the house of a *Brahmin*, India's elite priestly cast, even though half of her village was *Brahmin*. When a *dalit* was hired to cook at the school in her native village, *Brahmins* withdrew their children from the school. The engineer herself is the beneficiary of a charitable training scheme for *dalit* that Infosys launched in 2006. Her caste is among the poorest in India, with some 91 percent making less than $100 a month, compared to 65 percent of Brahmins.

To try to correct this historic inequality, politicians have talked for years about extending the employment quota system to private enterprises. The government has told private companies to hire more *dalits* and members of tribal communities, and warned that "strong measures" will be taken if companies do not comply. Private employers are resisting attempts to impose quotas, arguing with some justification that people who are guaranteed a job by a quota system are unlikely to work very hard. At the same time, progressive employers realize that they need to do something to correct the inequalities, and that, unless India taps into the lower castes, it may not be able to find the employees required to staff rapidly growing high-technology enterprises. Thus, the Confederation of Indian Industry recently introduced a package of *dalit*-friendly measures, including scholarships. Building on this, Infosys is leading the way among high-tech enterprises. The company provides special training to low-caste engineering graduates who have failed to get a job after graduation. While the training does not promise employment, so far almost all graduates who completed the seven-month training program have been hired by Infosys and other enterprises.

Sources: "With Reservations: Business and Caste in India," *The Economist*, October 6, 2007, pp. 81–83; and Eric Bellman, "Reversal of Fortune Isolates India's Brahmins," *The Wall Street Journal*, December 24, 2007, p. 4.

---

still remains. India has four main castes and several thousand subcastes. Even though the caste system was officially abolished in 1949, two years after India became independent, it is still a force in rural Indian society where occupation and marital opportunities are still partly related to caste (for more details, see the accompanying Country Focus on the caste system in India today).[18]

Class System
A less rigid social stratification system, in which mobility is possible depending on a person's achievements or even just luck.

A **class system** is a less rigid form of social stratification in which social mobility is possible. It is a form of open stratification in which the position a person has by birth can be changed through his or her own achievements or luck. Individuals born into a class at the bottom of the hierarchy can work their way up; conversely, individuals born into a class at the top of the hierarchy can slip down.

While many societies have class systems, social mobility within a class system varies from society to society. For example, some sociologists have argued that Britain has a more rigid class structure than certain other Western societies, such as the United States.[19] Historically, British society was divided into three main classes: the upper class, which was made up of individuals whose families for generations had wealth, prestige, and occasionally power; the middle class, whose members were involved in professional, managerial, and clerical occupations; and the working class, whose members earned their living from manual occupations. The middle class was further subdivided into the upper-middle class, whose members were involved in important managerial occupations and the prestigious professions (e.g., lawyers, accountants, doctors), and the lower-middle class, whose members were involved in clerical work (e.g., bank tellers) and the less prestigious professions (e.g., schoolteachers).

Historically, the British class system exhibited significant divergence between the life chances of members of different classes. The upper and upper-middle classes typically sent their children to a select group of private schools, where they wouldn't mix with lower-class children and where they picked up many of the speech accents and social norms that marked them as being from the higher strata of society. These same private schools also had close ties with the most prestigious universities, such as Oxford and Cambridge. Until fairly recently, Oxford and Cambridge guaranteed a certain number of places for the graduates of these private schools. Having been to a prestigious university, the offspring of the upper and upper-middle classes then had an excellent chance of being offered a prestigious job in companies, banks, brokerage firms, and law firms run by members of the upper and upper-middle classes.

In contrast, the members of the British working and lower-middle classes typically went to state schools. The majority left at 16, and those who went on to higher education found it more difficult to get accepted at the best universities. When they did, they found that their lower-class accent and lack of social skills marked them as being from a lower social stratum, which made it more difficult for them to get access to the most prestigious jobs.

Because of this, the class system in Britain perpetuated itself from generation to generation, and mobility was limited. Although upward mobility was possible, it could not normally be achieved in one generation. While an individual from a working-class background may have established an income level that was consistent with membership in the upper-middle class, he or she may not have been accepted as such by others of that class due to accent and background. However, by sending his or her offspring to the "right kind of school," the individual could ensure that his or her children were accepted.

According to many commentators, modern British society is now rapidly leaving this class structure behind and moving toward a classless society. However, sociologists continue to dispute this finding and present evidence that this is not the case. For example, a study reported that in the mid-1990s, state schools in the London suburb of Islington, which has a population of 175,000, had only 79 candidates for university, while one prestigious private school alone, Eton, sent more than that number to Oxford and Cambridge.[20] This, according to the study's authors, implies that "money still begets money." They argue that a good school means a good university, a good university means a good job, and merit has only a limited chance of elbowing its way into this tight little circle.

The class system in the United States is less extreme than in Britain and mobility is greater. Like Britain, the United States has its own upper, middle, and working classes. However, class membership is determined to a much greater degree by individual economic achievements, as opposed to background and schooling. Thus, an individual can, by his or her own economic achievement, move smoothly from the working class to the upper class in a lifetime. Successful individuals from humble origins are highly respected in American society.

Another society where class divisions have historically been of some importance has been China, where there has been a long-standing difference between the life chances of the rural peasantry and urban dwellers. Ironically, this historic division was strengthened during the high point of Communist rule because of a rigid system of household registration that restricted most Chinese to the place of their birth for their lifetime. Bound to collective farming, peasants were cut off from many urban privileges—compulsory education, quality schools, health care, public housing, varieties of foodstuffs, to name

Until the late 1970s, social mobility in China was very limited, but now sociologists believe a new class system is emerging in China based less on the rural-urban divide and more on urban occupation.

only a few—and they largely lived in poverty. Social mobility was thus very limited. This system crumbled following reforms of the late 1970s and early 1980s, and as a consequence, migrant peasant laborers have flooded into China's cities looking for work. Sociologists now hypothesize that a new class system is emerging in China based less on the rural-urban divide and more on urban occupation.[21]

LEARNING OBJECTIVE 3
Identify the business and economic implications of differences in culture.

Class Consciousness
A condition where people tend to perceive themselves in terms of their class background, shaping how they relate with members of other classes.

Significance   From a business perspective, the stratification of a society is significant if it affects the operation of business organizations. In American society, the high degree of social mobility and the extreme emphasis on individualism limit the impact of class background on business operations. The same is true in Japan, where most of the population perceives itself to be middle class. In a country such as Great Britain, however, the relative lack of class mobility and the differences between classes have resulted in the emergence of class consciousness. **Class consciousness** refers to a condition where people tend to perceive themselves in terms of their class background, and this shapes their relationships with members of other classes.

This has been played out in British society in the traditional hostility between upper-middle-class managers and their working-class employees. Mutual antagonism and lack of respect historically made it difficult to achieve cooperation between management and labor in many British companies and resulted in a relatively high level of industrial disputes. However, as noted earlier, the last two decades have seen a dramatic reduction in industrial disputes, which bolsters the arguments of those who claim the country is moving toward a classless society (the level of industrial disputes in the United Kingdom is now lower than in the United States). Alternatively, as noted earlier, class consciousness may be reemerging in urban China, and it may ultimately prove to be significant there.

An antagonistic relationship between management and labor classes, and the resulting lack of cooperation and high level of industrial disruption, tends to raise the costs of production in countries characterized by significant class divisions. In turn, this can make it more difficult for companies based in such countries to establish a competitive advantage in the global economy.

Religious and Ethical Systems

Religion may be defined as a system of shared beliefs and rituals that are concerned with the realm of the sacred.[22] **Ethical systems** refer to a set of moral principles, or values, that are used to guide and shape behavior. Most of the world's ethical systems are the product of religions. Thus, we can talk about Christian ethics and Islamic ethics. However, there is a major exception to the principle that ethical systems are grounded in religion. Confucianism and Confucian ethics influence behavior and shape culture in parts of Asia, yet it is incorrect to characterize Confucianism as a religion.

The relationship among religion, ethics, and society is subtle and complex. Among the thousands of religions in the world today, four dominate in terms of numbers of adherents: Christianity with 1.7 billion adherents, Islam with around 1 billion adherents, Hinduism with 750 million adherents (primarily in India), and Buddhism with 350 million adherents (see Map 3.1). Although many other religions have an important influence in certain parts of the modern world (for example, Judaism, which has 18 million adherents), their numbers pale in comparison with these dominant religions (however, as the precursor of both Christianity and Islam, Judaism has an indirect influence that goes beyond its numbers). We will review these four religions, along with Confucianism, focusing on their business implications. Some scholars have argued that the most important business implications of religion center on the extent to which different religions shape attitudes toward work and entrepreneurship and the degree to which the religious ethics affect the costs of doing business in a country.

It is hazardous to make sweeping generalizations about the nature of the relationship between religion and ethical systems and business practice. While some scholars argue that there is a relationship between religious and ethical systems and business practice in a society, in a world where nations with Catholic, Protestant, Muslim, Hindu, and Buddhist majorities all show evidence of entrepreneurial activity and sustainable economic growth, it is important to view such proposed relationships with a degree of skepticism. The proposed relationships may exist, but their impact is probably small compared to the impact of economic policy. Alternatively, recent research by economists Robert Barro and Rachel McCleary does suggest that strong religious beliefs, and particularly beliefs in heaven, hell, and an afterlife, have a positive impact on economic growth rates, irrespective of the particular religion in question.[23] Barro and McCleary looked at religious beliefs and economic growth rates in 59 countries during the 1980s and 1990s. Their conjecture was that higher religious beliefs stimulate economic growth because they help to sustain aspects of individual behavior that lead to higher productivity.

CHRISTIANITY Christianity is the most widely practiced religion in the world. Approximately 20 percent of the world's people identify themselves as Christians. The vast majority of Christians live in Europe and the Americas, although their numbers are growing rapidly in Africa. Christianity grew out of Judaism. Like Judaism, it is a monotheistic religion (monotheism is the belief in one god). A religious division in the 11th century led to the establishment of two major Christian organizations—the Roman Catholic Church and the Orthodox Church. Today, the Roman Catholic Church accounts for more than half of all Christians, most of whom are found in southern Europe and Latin America. The Orthodox Church, while less influential, is still of

Religion
A system of shared beliefs and rituals that are concerned with the realm of the sacred.

Ethical System
A set of moral principles, or values, that are used to guide and shape behavior.

LEARNING OBJECTIVE 3
Identify the business and economic implications of differences in culture.

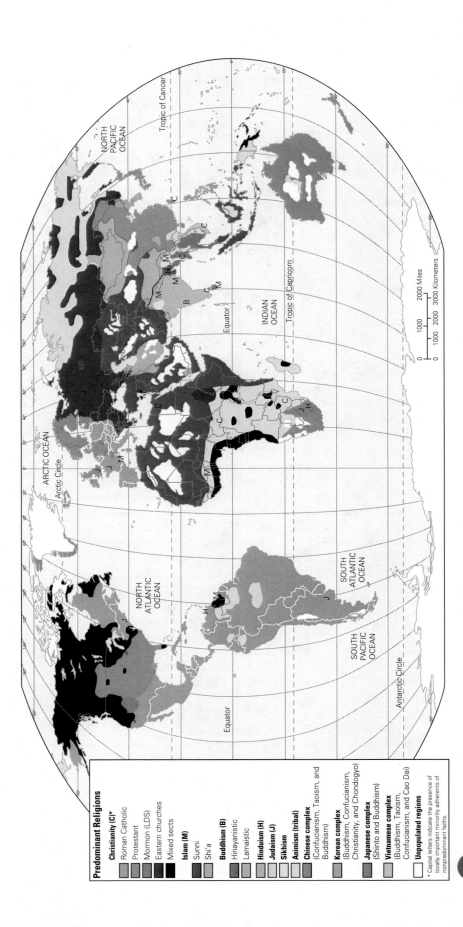

Predominant Religions

Christianity (C)*
Roman Catholic
Protestant
Mormon (LDS)
Eastern churches
Mixed sects

Islam (M)
Sunni
Shi'a

Buddhism (B)
Hinayanistic
Lamaistic

Hinduism (H)
Judaism (J)
Sikhism
Animism (tribal)
Chinese complex
(Confucianism, Taoism, and Buddhism)
Korean complex
(Buddhism, Confucianism, Christianity, and Chondogyo)
Japanese complex
(Shinto and Buddhism)
Vietnamese complex
(Buddhism, Taoism, Confucianism, and Cao Dai)
Unpopulated regions

* Capital letters indicate the presence of locally important minority adherents of nonpredominant faiths.

3.1 map World Religions

Source: John L. Allen, *Student Atlas of World Politics*, 7e, map 8. © 2006 by the McGraw-Hill Companies, Inc. All rights reserved. Reprinted by permission of McGraw-Hill Contemporary Learning Series.

major importance in several countries (e.g., Greece and Russia). In the 16th century, the Reformation led to a further split with Rome; the result was Protestantism. The nonconformist nature of Protestantism has facilitated the emergence of numerous denominations under the Protestant umbrella (e.g., Baptist, Methodist, Calvinist).

Economic Implications of Christianity: The Protestant Work Ethic   Several sociologists have argued that of the main branches of Christianity—Catholic, Orthodox, and Protestant—the latter has the most important economic implications. In 1904, a German sociologist, Max Weber, made a connection between Protestant ethics and "the spirit of capitalism" that has since become famous.[24] Weber noted that capitalism emerged in Western Europe, where

> business leaders and owners of capital, as well as the higher grades of skilled labor, and even more the higher technically and commercially trained personnel of modern enterprises, are overwhelmingly Protestant.[25]

Weber theorized that there was a relationship between Protestantism and the emergence of modern capitalism. He argued that Protestant ethics emphasize the importance of hard work and wealth creation (for the glory of God) and frugality (abstinence from worldly pleasures). According to Weber, this kind of value system was needed to facilitate the development of capitalism. Protestants worked hard and systematically to accumulate wealth. However, their ascetic beliefs suggested that rather than consuming this wealth by indulging in worldly pleasures, they should invest it in the expansion of capitalist enterprises. Thus, the combination of hard work and the accumulation of capital, which could be used to finance investment and expansion, paved the way for the development of capitalism in Western Europe and subsequently in the United States. In contrast, Weber argued that the Catholic promise of salvation in the next world, rather than this world, did not foster the same kind of work ethic.

Protestantism also may have encouraged capitalism's development in another way. By breaking away from the hierarchical domination of religious and social life that characterized the Catholic Church for much of its history, Protestantism gave individuals significantly more freedom to develop their own relationship with God. The right to freedom of form of worship was central to the nonconformist nature of early Protestantism. This emphasis on individual religious freedom may have paved the way for the subsequent emphasis on individual economic and political freedoms and the development of individualism as an economic and political philosophy. As we saw in Chapter 2, such a philosophy forms the bedrock on which entrepreneurial free market capitalism is based. Building on this, some scholars claim there is a connection between individualism, as inspired by Protestantism, and the extent of entrepreneurial activity in a nation.[26] Again, one must be careful not to generalize too much from this historical sociological view. While nations with a strong Protestant tradition such as Britain, Germany, and the United States were early leaders in the industrial revolution, nations with Catholic or Orthodox majorities show significant and sustained entrepreneurial activity and economic growth in the modern world.

ISLAM   With around 1 billion adherents, Islam is the second largest of the world's major religions. Islam dates back to AD 610 when the prophet Muhammad began spreading the word, although the Muslim calendar begins in AD 622 when, to escape growing opposition, Muhammad left Mecca for the oasis settlement of Yathrib, later known as Madina. Adherents of Islam are referred to as Muslims. Muslims constitute a majority in more than 35 countries and inhabit a nearly contiguous stretch of land from the northwest coast of Africa, through the Middle East, to China and Malaysia in the Far East.

Islam has roots in both Judaism and Christianity (Islam views Jesus Christ as one of God's prophets). Like Christianity and Judaism, Islam is a monotheistic religion. The central principle of Islam is that there is but the one true omnipotent God. Islam requires unconditional acceptance of the uniqueness, power, and authority of God and the understanding that the objective of life is to fulfill the dictates of his will in the hope of admission to paradise. According to Islam, worldly gain and temporal power are an illusion. Those who pursue riches on earth may gain them, but those who forgo worldly ambitions to seek the favor of Allah may gain the greater treasure—entry into paradise. Other major principles of Islam include (1) honoring and respecting parents, (2) respecting the rights of others, (3) being generous but not a squanderer, (4) avoiding killing except for justifiable causes, (5) not committing adultery, (6) dealing justly and equitably with others, (7) being of pure heart and mind, (8) safeguarding the possessions of orphans, and (9) being humble and unpretentious.[27] Obvious parallels exist with many of the central principles of both Judaism and Christianity.

Islam is an all-embracing way of life governing the totality of a Muslim's being.[28] As God's surrogate in this world, a Muslim is not a totally free agent but is circumscribed by religious principles—by a code of conduct for interpersonal relations—in social and economic activities. Religion is paramount in all areas of life. The Muslim lives in a social structure that is shaped by Islamic values and norms of moral conduct. The ritual nature of everyday life in a Muslim country is striking to a Western visitor. Among other things, orthodox Muslim ritual requires prayer five times a day (business meetings may be put on hold while the Muslim participants engage in their daily prayer ritual), requires that women should be dressed in a certain manner, and forbids the consumption of pork and alcohol.

Islamic Fundamentalism   The past three decades have witnessed the growth of a social movement often referred to as Islamic fundamentalism.[29] In the West, Islamic fundamentalism is associated in the media with militants, terrorists, and violent upheavals, such as the bloody conflict occurring in Algeria, the killing of foreign tourists in Egypt, and the September 11, 2001, attacks on the World Trade Center and Pentagon in the United States. This characterization is misleading. Just as Christian fundamentalists are motivated by sincere and deeply held religious values firmly rooted in their faith, so are Islamic fundamentalists. The violence that the Western media associates with Islamic fundamentalism is perpetrated by a small minority of radical "fundamentalists" who have hijacked the religion to further their own political and violent ends. (Some Christian "fundamentalists" have done exactly the same, including Jim Jones and David Koresh.) The vast majority of Muslims point out that Islam teaches peace, justice, and tolerance, not violence and intolerance, and that Islam explicitly repudiates the violence that a radical minority practices.

The rise of fundamentalism has no one cause. In part, it is a response to the social pressures created in traditional Islamic societies by the move toward modernization and by the influence of Western ideas, such as liberal democracy, materialism, equal rights for women, and attitudes toward sex, marriage, and alcohol. In many Muslim countries, modernization has been accompanied by a growing gap between a rich urban minority and an impoverished urban and rural majority. For the impoverished majority, modernization has offered little in the way of tangible economic progress, while threatening the traditional value system. Thus, for a Muslim who cherishes his or her traditions and feels that his or her identity is jeopardized by the encroachment of alien Western values, Islamic fundamentalism has become a cultural anchor.

Fundamentalists demand a rigid commitment to traditional religious beliefs and rituals. The result has been a marked increase in the use of symbolic gestures that confirm Islamic values. In areas where fundamentalism is strong, women have resumed

The rise of Islamic fundamentalism as a reaction against globalization and the prevalence of Western cultural ideas has sent many scrambling to try to understand Muslim culture and promote greater dialogue.

wearing floor-length, long-sleeved dresses and covering their hair; religious studies have increased in universities; the publication of religious tracts has increased; and public religious orations have risen.[30] Also, the sentiments of some fundamentalist groups are often anti-Western. Rightly or wrongly, Western influence is blamed for a range of social ills, and many fundamentalists' actions are directed against Western governments, cultural symbols, businesses, and even individuals.

In several Muslim countries, fundamentalists have gained political power and have used this to try to make Islamic law (as set down in the Koran, the bible of Islam) the law of the land. There are good grounds for this in Islam. Islam makes no distinction between church and state. It is not just a religion; Islam is also the source of law, a guide to statecraft, and an arbiter of social behavior. Muslims believe that every human endeavor is within the purview of the faith—and this includes political activity—because the only purpose of any activity is to do God's will.[31] (Some Christian fundamentalists also share this view.) Muslim fundamentalists have been most successful in Iran, where a fundamentalist party has held power since 1979, but they also have had an influence in many other countries, such as Algeria, Afghanistan (where the Taliban established an extreme fundamentalist state until removed by the U.S.-led coalition in 2002), Egypt, Pakistan, the Sudan, and Saudi Arabia.

Economic Implications of Islam   The Koran establishes some explicit economic principles, many of which are pro-free enterprise.[32] The Koran speaks approvingly of free enterprise and of earning legitimate profit through trade and commerce (the prophet Mohammed was once a trader). The protection of the right to private property is also embedded within Islam, although Islam asserts that all property is a favor from Allah (God), who created and so owns everything. Those who hold property are regarded as trustees rather than owners in the Western sense of the word. As trustees they are entitled to receive profits from the property but are admonished to use it in a

LEARNING OBJECTIVE 3
Identify the business and economic implications of differences in culture.

Country FOCUS

Islamic Capitalism in Turkey

For years now, Turkey has been lobbying the European Union to allow it to join. If the EU says yes, Turkey will be the first Muslim state in the free trade bloc. Many critics in the EU worry that Islam and Western-style capitalism do not mix well and that, as a consequence, allowing Turkey into the EU would be a mistake. However, a close look at what is going on in Turkey suggests this view may be misplaced. Consider the area around the city of Kayseri in central Turkey. Many dismiss this poor, largely agricultural region of Turkey as a non-European backwater, far removed from the secular bustle of Istanbul. It is a region where traditional Islamic values hold sway. And yet, it is also a region that has produced so many thriving Muslim enterprises that it is sometimes called the "Anatolian Tiger." Businesses based here include large food manufacturers, textile companies, furniture manufacturers, and engineering enterprises, many of which export a substantial percentage of their production.

Local business leaders attribute the success of companies in the region to an entrepreneurial spirit that they say is part of Islam. They point out that the prophet Muhammad, who was himself a trader, preached merchant honor and commanded that 90 percent of a Muslim's life be devoted to work in order to put food on the table. Outsider observers have gone further, arguing that Kayseri is an example of Islamic Calvinism, a fusion of traditional Islamic values and the work ethic often associated with Protestantism in general and Calvinism in particular.

Within Kayseri, the influence of Islam is plain to see. Many companies set aside rooms and time for 15-minute prayer breaks. Most of the older businessmen have been to Mecca on the Hajj, the pilgrimage that all Muslims are meant to make at least once in a lifetime. Few of the cafés and restaurants in Kayseri serve alcohol, and most women wear a head scarf.

At the Kayseri sugar factory, one of the most profitable in the region, a senior manager says Islam has played a large part in improving the profitability of the enterprise. For a long time the factory bought most of its sugar beet from a single monopoly supplier, who charged a high price. But because Islam preaches equal opportunity in business, managers at the sugar factory decided the Islamic thing to do was diversify the supply base and encourage small producers to sell beets to them. Today the factory buys sugar beets from 20,000 small growers. Competition between them has lowered prices and boosted the factory's profitability. The same manager also noted, "If you are not a good Muslim, don't pray five times a day and don't have a wife who wears a head scarf, it can be difficult to do business here."

However, not everyone agrees that Islam is the driving force behind the region's success. Saffet Arslan, the managing director of Ipek, the largest furniture producer in the region (which exports to more than 30 countries), says another force is at work—globalization! According to Arslan, over the last three decades local Muslims who once eschewed making money in favor of focusing on religion are now making business a priority. They see the Western world, and Western capitalism, as a model, not Islam, and because of globalization and the opportunities associated with it, they want to become successful. Arslan is a practicing Muslim who has built a mosque in the basement of Ipec's headquarters building so that people can pray while at work.

If there is a weakness in the Islamic model of business that is emerging in places like Kayseri, some say it can be found in traditional attitudes toward the role of women in the workplace and the low level of female employment in the region. According to a report by the European Stability Initiative, the same group that holds up the Kayseri region as an example of Islamic Calvinism, the low participation of women in the local workforce is the Achilles' heel of the economy and may stymie the attempts of the region to catch up with the countries of the European Union.

Sources: D. Bilefsky, "Turks Knock on Europe's Door with Evidence that Islam and Capitalism Can Coexist," *The New York Times*, August 27, 2006, p. 4; and European Stability Initiative, *Islamic Calvinists*, September 19, 2005; www.esiweb.org.

righteous, socially beneficial, and prudent manner. This reflects Islam's concern with social justice. Islam is critical of those who earn profit through the exploitation of others. In the Islamic view of the world, humans are part of a collective in which the wealthy and successful have obligations to help the disadvantaged. Put simply, in Muslim countries, it is fine to earn a profit, so long as that profit is justly earned and not based on the exploitation of others for one's own advantage. It also helps if those making profits undertake charitable acts to help the poor. Furthermore, Islam stresses the importance of living up to contractual obligations, of keeping one's word, and of abstaining from deception. For a closer look at how Islam, capitalism and globalization can coexist, see the accompanying Country Focus on the region around Kayseri in central Turkey.

Given the Islamic proclivity to favor market-based systems, Muslim countries are likely to be receptive to international businesses as long as those businesses behave in a manner that is consistent with Islamic ethics. Businesses that are perceived as making an unjust profit through the exploitation of others, by deception, or by breaking contractual obligations are unlikely to be welcomed in an Islamic country. In addition, in Islamic countries where fundamentalism is on the rise, hostility toward Western-owned businesses is likely to increase.

In the previous chapter, we noted that one economic principle of Islam prohibits the payment or receipt of interest, which is considered usury. This is not just a matter of theology; in several Islamic states, it is also becoming a matter of law. The Koran clearly condemns interest, which is called *riba* in Arabic, as exploitative and unjust. For many years, banks operating in Islamic countries conveniently ignored this condemnation, but starting about 30 years ago with the establishment of an Islamic bank in Egypt, Islamic banks started to open in predominantly Muslim countries. By 2006, some 200 Islamic financial institutions worldwide managed more than $400 billion in assets, making an average return on capital of more than 16 percent.[33] Even conventional banks are entering the market—both Citigroup and HSBC, two of the world's largest financial institutions, now offer Islamic financial services. While only Iran and the Sudan enforce Islamic banking conventions, in an increasing number of countries customers can choose between conventional banks and Islamic banks.

Conventional banks make a profit on the spread between the interest rate they have to pay to depositors and the higher interest rate they charge borrowers. Because Islamic banks cannot pay or charge interest, they must find a different way of making money. Islamic banks have experimented with two different banking methods—the *mudarabah* and the *murabaha*.[34]

A *mudarabah* contract is similar to a profit-sharing scheme. Under *mudarabah*, when an Islamic bank lends money to a business, rather than charging that business interest on the loan, it takes a share in the profits that are derived from the investment. Similarly, when a business (or individual) deposits money at an Islamic bank in a savings account, the deposit is treated as an equity investment in whatever activity the bank uses the capital for. Thus, the depositor receives a share in the profit from the bank's investment (as opposed to interest payments) according to an agreed-on ratio. Some Muslims claim this is a more efficient system than the Western banking system, since it encourages both long-term savings and long-term investment. However, there is no hard evidence of this, and many believe that a *mudarabah* system is less efficient than a conventional Western banking system.

The second Islamic banking method, the *murabaha* contract, is the most widely used among the world's Islamic banks, primarily because it is the easiest to implement. In a *murabaha* contract, when a firm wishes to purchase something using a loan—let's say a piece of equipment that costs $1,000—the firm tells the bank after having negotiated the price with the equipment manufacturer. The bank then buys the equipment for $1,000, and the borrower buys it back from the bank at some later date for, say, $1,100, a price that includes a $100 markup for the bank. A cynic might point out that such a markup is functionally equivalent to an interest payment, and it is the similarity between this method and conventional banking that makes it so much easier to adopt.

HINDUISM   Hinduism has approximately 750 million adherents, most of them on the Indian subcontinent. Hinduism began in the Indus Valley in India more than 4,000 years ago, making it the world's oldest major religion. Unlike Christianity and Islam, its founding is not linked to a particular person. Nor does it have an officially sanctioned sacred book such as the Bible or the Koran. Hindus believe that a moral force in society requires the acceptance of certain responsibilities, called *dharma*. Hindus believe in reincarnation, or rebirth into a different body, after death. Hindus also believe in *karma*, the spiritual progression of each person's soul. A person's karma is affected by the way he or she lives. The moral state of an individual's karma determines the challenges he or she will face in the next life. By perfecting the soul in each new life, Hindus believe that an individual can eventually achieve *nirvana*, a state of complete spiritual perfection that renders reincarnation no longer necessary. Many Hindus believe that the way to achieve nirvana is to lead a severe ascetic lifestyle of material and physical self-denial, devoting life to a spiritual rather than material quest.

One of the interesting aspects of Hindu culture is the reverence for the cow, which Hindus see as a gift of the gods to the human race. The sacred status of the cow created some unique problems for McDonald's when it entered India in the 1990s, since devout Hindus do not eat beef (and many are also vegetarians). The opening case looked at how McDonald's dealt with that challenge.

LEARNING OBJECTIVE 3
Identify the business and economic implications of differences in culture.

Economic Implications of Hinduism   Max Weber, famous for expounding on the Protestant work ethic, also argued that the ascetic principles embedded in Hinduism do not encourage the kind of entrepreneurial activity in pursuit of wealth creation that we find in Protestantism.[35] According to Weber, traditional Hindu values emphasize that individuals should be judged not by their material achievements but by their spiritual achievements. Hindus perceive the pursuit of material well-being as making the attainment of nirvana more difficult. Given the emphasis on an ascetic lifestyle, Weber thought that devout Hindus would be less likely to engage in entrepreneurial activity than devout Protestants.

Mahatma Gandhi, the famous Indian nationalist and spiritual leader, was certainly the embodiment of Hindu asceticism. It has been argued that the values of Hindu asceticism and self-reliance that Gandhi advocated had a negative impact on the economic development of postindependence India.[36] But one must be careful not to read too much into Weber's arguments. Modern India is a very dynamic entrepreneurial society, and millions of hardworking entrepreneurs form the economic backbone of the country's rapidly growing economy.

Historically, Hinduism also supported India's caste system. The concept of mobility between castes within an individual's lifetime makes no sense to traditional Hindus. Hindus see mobility between castes as something that is achieved through spiritual progression and reincarnation. An individual can be reborn into a higher caste in his or her next life if he or she achieves spiritual development in this life. Although the caste system has been abolished in India, it still casts a long shadow over Indian life, according to many observers. In so far as the caste system limits individuals' opportunities to adopt positions of responsibility and influence in society, the economic consequences of this religious belief are negative. For example, within a business organization, the most able individuals may find their route to the higher levels of the organization blocked simply because they come from a lower caste. By the same token, individuals may get promoted to higher positions within a firm as much because of their caste background as because of their ability.

BUDDHISM   Buddhism was founded in India in the sixth century BC by Siddhartha Gautama, an Indian prince who renounced his wealth to pursue an ascetic lifestyle and spiritual perfection. Siddhartha achieved nirvana but decided to remain on earth to teach his followers how they too could achieve this state of spiritual enlightenment. Siddhartha became known as the Buddha (which means "the awakened one"). Today,

Buddhism has 350 million followers, most of whom are found in Central and Southeast Asia, China, Korea, and Japan. According to Buddhism, suffering originates in people's desires for pleasure. Cessation of suffering can be achieved by following a path for transformation. Siddhartha offered the Noble Eightfold Path as a route for transformation. This emphasizes right seeing, thinking, speech, action, living, effort, mindfulness, and meditation. Unlike Hinduism, Buddhism does not support the caste system. Nor does Buddhism advocate the kind of extreme ascetic behavior that is encouraged by Hinduism. Nevertheless, like Hindus, Buddhists stress the afterlife and spiritual achievement rather than involvement in this world.

Economic Implications of Buddhism   The emphasis on wealth creation that is embedded in Protestantism is not found in Buddhism. Thus, in Buddhist societies, we do not see the same kind of historical cultural stress on entrepreneurial behavior that Weber claimed could be found in the Protestant West. But unlike Hinduism, the lack of support for the caste system and extreme ascetic behavior suggests that a Buddhist society may represent a more fertile ground for entrepreneurial activity than a Hindu culture.

LEARNING OBJECTIVE 3
Identify the business and economic implications of differences in culture.

CONFUCIANISM   Confucianism was founded in the fifth century BC by K'ung-Fu-tzu, more generally known as Confucius. For more than 2,000 years until the 1949 Communist revolution, Confucianism was the official ethical system of China. While observance of Confucian ethics has been weakened in China since 1949, more than 200 million people still follow the teachings of Confucius, principally in China, Korea, and Japan. Confucianism teaches the importance of attaining personal salvation through right action. Although not a religion, Confucian ideology has become deeply embedded in the culture of these countries over the centuries and, through that, has an impact on the lives of many millions more. Confucianism is built around a comprehensive ethical code that sets down guidelines for relationships with others. High moral and ethical conduct and loyalty to others are central to Confucianism. Unlike religions, Confucianism is not concerned with the supernatural and has little to say about the concept of a supreme being or an afterlife.

Economic Implications of Confucianism   Some scholars maintain that Confucianism may have economic implications as profound as those Weber argued were to be found in Protestantism, although they are of a different nature.[37] Their basic thesis is that the influence of Confucian ethics on the culture of China, Japan, South Korea, and Taiwan, by lowering the costs of doing business in those countries, may help explain their economic success. In this regard, three values central to the Confucian system of ethics are of particular interest: loyalty, reciprocal obligations, and honesty in dealings with others.

LEARNING OBJECTIVE 3
Identify the business and economic implications of differences in culture.

In Confucian thought, loyalty to one's superiors is regarded as a sacred duty—an absolute obligation. In modern organizations based in Confucian cultures, the loyalty that binds employees to the heads of their organization can reduce the conflict between management and labor that we find in more class-conscious societies. Cooperation between management and labor can be achieved at a lower cost in a culture where the virtue of loyalty is emphasized in the value systems.

However, in a Confucian culture, loyalty to one's superiors, such as a worker's loyalty to management, is not blind loyalty. The concept of reciprocal obligations is important. Confucian ethics stress that superiors are obliged to reward the loyalty of their subordinates by bestowing blessings on them. If these "blessings" are not forthcoming, then neither will be the loyalty. This Confucian ethic is central to the Chinese concept of *guanxi*, which refers to relationship networks supported by reciprocal

Management FOCUS

DMG-Shanghai

In 1993, New Yorker Dan Mintz moved to China as a freelance film director with no contacts, no advertising experience, and no Mandarin. By 2006, the company he subsequently founded in China, DMG, had emerged as one of China's fastest growing advertising agencies with a client list that includes Budweiser, Unilever, Sony, Nabisco, Audi, Volkswagen, China Mobile, and dozens of other Chinese brands. Mintz attributes his success in part to what the Chinese call guanxi.

Guanxi literally means relationships, although in business settings it can be better understood as connections. *Guanxi* has its roots in the Confucian philosophy of valuing social hierarchy and reciprocal obligations. Confucian ideology has a 2,000-year-old history in China. Confucianism stresses the importance of relationships, both within the family and between master and servant. Confucian ideology teaches that people are not created equal. In Confucian thought, loyalty and obligations to one's superiors (or to family) are regarded as a sacred duty, but at the same time, this loyalty has its price. Social superiors are obligated to reward the loyalty of their social inferiors by bestowing "blessings" upon them; thus, the obligations are reciprocal.

Today, Chinese will often cultivate a *guanxiwang,* or "relationship network," for help. Reciprocal obligations are the glue that holds such networks together. If those obligations are not met—if favors done are not paid back or reciprocated—the reputation of the transgressor is tarnished, and he or she will be less able to draw on his or her *guanxiwang* for help in the future. Thus, the implicit threat of social sanctions is often sufficient to ensure that favors are repaid, obligations are met, and relationships are honored. In a society that lacks a strong rule-based legal tradition, and thus legal ways of redressing wrongs such as violations of business agreements, *guanxi* is an important mechanism for building long-term business relationships and getting business done in China. There is a tacit acknowledgment that if you have the right *guanxi,* legal rules can be broken, or at least bent.

Mintz, who is now fluent in Mandarin, cultivated his *guanxiwang* by going into business with two young Chinese who had connections, Bing Wu and Peter Xiao. Bing Wu, who works on the production side of the business, was a former national gymnastics champion, which translates into prestige and access to business and government officials. Peter Xiao comes from a military family with major political connections. Together, these three have been able to open doors that long-established Western advertising agencies have not. They have done it in large part by leveraging the contacts of Wu and Xiao, and by backing up their connections with what the Chinese call *Shi li,* the ability to do good work.

A case in point was DMG's campaign for Volkswagen, which helped the German company to become ubiquitous in China. The ads used traditional Chinese characters, which had been banned by Chairman Mao during the Cultural Revolution in favor of simplified versions. To get permission to use the characters in film and print ads—a first in modern China—the trio had to draw on high-level government contacts in Beijing. They won over officials by arguing that the old characters should be thought of as art. Later, they shot TV spots for the ad on Shanghai's famous Bund, a congested boulevard that runs along the waterfront of the old city. Drawing again on government contacts, they were able to shut down the Bund to make the shoot. Steven Spielberg had been able to close down only a portion of the street when he filmed *Empire of the Sun* there in 1986. DMG has also filmed inside Beijing's Forbidden City, even though it is against the law to do so. Using his contacts, Mintz persuaded the government to lift the law for 24 hours. As Mintz noted, "We don't stop when we come across regulations. There are restrictions everywhere you go. You have to know how get around them and get things done."

Sources: J. Bryan, "The Mintz Dynasty," *Fast Company,* April 2006, pp. 56–62; and M. Graser, "Featured Player," *Variety,* October 18, 2004, p. 6.

obligations.[38] *Guanxi* means relationships, although in business settings it can be better understood as connections. Today, Chinese will often cultivate a *guanxiwang*, or "relationship network," for help. Reciprocal obligations are the glue that holds such networks together. If those obligations are not met—if favors done are not paid back or reciprocated—the reputation of the transgressor is tarnished and the person will be less able to draw on his or her *guanxiwang* for help in the future. Thus, the implicit threat of social sanctions is often sufficient to ensure that favors are repaid, obligations are met, and relationships are honored. In a society that lacks a rule-based legal tradition, and thus legal ways of redressing wrongs such as violations of business agreements, *guanxi* is an important mechanism for building long-term business relationships and getting business done in China. For an example of the importance of *guanxi*, read the accompanying Management Focus on DMG-Shanghai.

A third concept found in Confucian ethics is the importance attached to honesty. Confucian thinkers emphasize that, although dishonest behavior may yield short-term benefits for the transgressor, dishonesty does not pay in the long run. The importance attached to honesty has major economic implications. When companies can trust each other not to break contractual obligations, the costs of doing business are lowered. Expensive lawyers are not needed to resolve contract disputes. In a Confucian society, people may be less hesitant to commit substantial resources to cooperative ventures than in a society where honesty is less pervasive. When companies adhere to Confucian ethics, they can trust each other not to violate the terms of cooperative agreements. Thus, the costs of achieving cooperation between companies may be lower in societies such as Japan relative to societies where trust is less pervasive.

For example, it has been argued that the close ties between the automobile companies and their component parts suppliers in Japan are facilitated by a combination of trust and reciprocal obligations. These close ties allow the auto companies and their suppliers to work together on a range of issues, including inventory reduction, quality control, and design. The competitive advantage of Japanese auto companies such as Toyota may in part be explained by such factors.[39] Similarly, the combination of trust and reciprocal obligations is central to the workings and persistence of *guanxi* networks in China. Someone seeking and receiving help through a *guanxi* network is then obligated to return the favor and faces social sanctions if that obligation is not reciprocated when it is called upon. If the person does not return the favor, his or her reputation will be tarnished and he or she will be unable to draw on the resources of the network in the future. It is claimed that these relationship-based networks can be more important in helping to enforce agreements between businesses than the Chinese legal system. Some claim that *guanxi* networks are a substitute for the legal system.[40]

Language

One obvious way in which countries differ is language. By language, we mean both the spoken and the unspoken means of communication. Language is one of the defining characteristics of a culture.

SPOKEN LANGUAGE   Language does far more than just enable people to communicate with each other. The nature of a language also structures the way we perceive the world. The language of a society can direct the attention of its members to certain features of the world rather than others. The classic illustration of this phenomenon is that whereas the English language has but one word for snow, the language of the Inuit (Eskimos) lacks a general term for it. Instead, because distinguishing different forms of snow is so important in the lives of the Inuit, they have 24 words that describe different types of snow (e.g., powder snow, falling snow, wet snow, drifting snow).[41]

Because language shapes the way people perceive the world, it also helps define culture. Countries with more than one language often have more than one culture. Canada has an English-speaking culture and a French-speaking culture. Tensions between the two can run quite high, with a substantial proportion of the French-speaking minority demanding independence from a Canada "dominated by English speakers." The same phenomenon can be observed in many other countries. Belgium is divided into Flemish and French speakers, and tensions between the two groups exist; in Spain, a Basque-speaking minority with its own distinctive culture has been agitating for independence from the Spanish-speaking majority for decades; on the Mediterranean island of Cyprus, the culturally diverse Greek- and Turkish-speaking populations of the island engaged in open conflict in the 1970s, and the island is now partitioned into two parts. While it does not necessarily follow that language differences create differences in culture and, therefore, separatist pressures (e.g., witness the harmony in Switzerland, where four languages are spoken), there certainly seems to be a tendency in this direction.[42]

LEARNING OBJECTIVE 3
Identify the business and economic implications of differences in culture.

Chinese is the mother tongue of the largest number of people, followed by English and Hindi, which is spoken in India. However, the most widely spoken language in the world is English, followed by French, Spanish, and Chinese (i.e., many people speak English as a second language). English is increasingly becoming the language of international business. When a Japanese and a German businessperson get together to do business, it is almost certain that they will communicate in English. However, although English is widely used, learning the local language yields considerable advantages. Most people prefer to converse in their own language, and being able to speak the local language can build rapport, which may be very important for a business deal. International businesses that do not understand the local language can make major blunders through improper translation. For example, the Sunbeam Corporation used the English words for its "Mist-Stick" mist-producing hair curling iron when it entered the German market, only to discover after an expensive advertising campaign that *mist* means excrement in German. General Motors was troubled by the lack of enthusiasm among Puerto Rican dealers for its new Chevrolet Nova. When literally translated into Spanish, *nova* means star. However, when spoken it sounds like "no va," which in Spanish means "it doesn't go." General Motors changed the name of the car to Caribe.[43]

UNSPOKEN LANGUAGE Unspoken language refers to nonverbal communication. We all communicate with each other by a host of nonverbal cues. The raising of eyebrows, for example, is a sign of recognition in most cultures, while a smile is a sign of joy. Many nonverbal cues, however, are culturally bound. A failure to understand the nonverbal cues of another culture can lead to a communication failure. For example, making a circle with the thumb and the forefinger is a friendly gesture in the United States, but it is a vulgar sexual invitation in Greece and Turkey. Similarly, while most Americans and Europeans use the thumbs-up gesture to indicate that "it's all right," in Greece the gesture is obscene.

Another aspect of nonverbal communication is personal space, which is the comfortable amount of distance between you and someone you are talking with. In the United States, the customary distance apart adopted by parties in a business discussion is five to eight feet. In Latin America, it is three to five feet. Consequently, many North Americans unconsciously feel that Latin Americans are invading their personal space and can be seen backing away from them during a conversation. Indeed, the American may feel that the Latin is being aggressive and pushy. In turn, the Latin American may

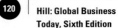

Another Perspective

Making Small Talk
Knowing when—and when not—to make small talk is an important skill for businesspeople traveling outside their country. In the United States, the art of making small talk is considered almost essential to business success. These days, only a few topics—like politics, religion, and sex—are generally considered off-limits among Americans. But in other countries, the rules are different.

In a business setting in Scotland, for example, casually inquiring about another person's family would be considered rude. In Argentina, don't ask what a person does for a living; wait for that information to be volunteered. And, when in Thailand, it's important to begin meetings with small talk before tackling the business agenda. (Gary Stoller, "Doing Business Abroad? Simple Faux Pas Can Sink You," *USA Today*, August 24, 2007, www.usatoday.com; and Sue Fox, *Business Etiquette for Dummies* [New York: Wiley & Sons, Inc., 2000]) interpret such backing away as aloofness. The result can be a regrettable lack of rapport between two businesspeople from different cultures.

Education

Formal education plays a key role in a society. Formal education is the medium through which individuals learn many of the language, conceptual, and mathematical skills that are indispensable in a modern society. Formal education also supplements the family's role in socializing the young into the values and norms of a society. Values and norms are taught both directly and indirectly. Schools generally teach basic facts about the social and political nature of a society. They also focus on the fundamental obligations of citizenship. Cultural norms are also taught indirectly at school. Respect for others, obedience to authority, honesty, neatness, being on time, and so on, are all part of the "hidden curriculum" of schools. The use of a grading system also teaches children the value of personal achievement and competition.[44]

From an international business perspective, one important aspect of education is its role as a determinant of national competitive advantage.[45] The availability of a pool of skilled and educated workers seems to be a major determinant of the likely economic success of a country. In analyzing the competitive success of Japan since 1945, for example, Michael Porter notes that after the war, Japan had almost nothing except for a pool of skilled and educated human resources.

> With a long tradition of respect for education that borders on reverence, Japan possessed a large pool of literate, educated, and increasingly skilled human resources. . . . Japan has benefited from a large pool of trained engineers. Japanese universities graduate many more engineers per capita than in the United States. . . . A first-rate primary and secondary education system in Japan operates based on high standards and emphasizes math and science. Primary and secondary education is highly competitive. . . . Japanese education provides most students all over Japan with a sound education for later education and training. A Japanese high school graduate knows as much about math as most American college graduates.[46]

Porter's point is that Japan's excellent education system is an important factor explaining the country's postwar economic success. Not only is a good education system a determinant of national competitive advantage, but it is also an important factor guiding the location choices of international businesses. The recent trend to outsource information technology jobs to India, for example, is partly due to the presence of significant numbers of trained engineers in India, which in turn is a result of the Indian education system. By the same token, it would make little sense to base production facilities that require highly skilled labor in a country where the education system was so poor that a skilled labor pool wasn't available, no matter how attractive the country might seem on other dimensions. It might make sense to base production operations that require only unskilled labor in such a country.

The general education level of a country is also a good index of the kind of products that might sell in a country and of the type of promotional material that should be used. For example, a country where more than 70 percent of the population is illiterate is unlikely to be a good market for popular books. Promotional material containing written descriptions of mass-marketed products is unlikely to have an effect in a country where almost three-quarters of the population cannot read. It is far better to use pictorial promotions in such circumstances.

LEARNING OBJECTIVE 3
Identify the business and economic implications of differences in culture.

Culture and the Workplace

LEARNING OBJECTIVE 4
Understand how differences in social culture influence values in the workplace.

Of considerable importance for an international business with operations in different countries is how a society's culture affects the values found in the workplace. Management process and practices may need to vary according to culturally determined work-related values. For example, if the cultures of the United States and France result in different work-related values, an international business with operations in both countries should vary its management process and practices to account for these differences.

Probably the most famous study of how culture relates to values in the workplace was undertaken by Geert Hofstede.[47] As part of his job as a psychologist working for IBM, Hofstede collected data on employee attitudes and values for more than 100,000 individuals from 1967 to 1973. These data enabled him to compare dimensions of culture across 40 countries. Hofstede isolated four dimensions that he claimed summarized different cultures—power distance, individualism versus collectivism, uncertainty avoidance, and masculinity versus femininity.

Power Distance
Extent to which a society allows inequalities of physical and intellectual capabilities between people to grow into inequalities of power and wealth.

Hofstede's **power distance** dimension focused on how a society deals with the fact that people are unequal in physical and intellectual capabilities. According to Hofstede, high power distance cultures were found in countries that let inequalities grow over time into inequalities of power and wealth. Low power distance cultures were found in societies that tried to play down such inequalities as much as possible.

Individualism versus Collectivism
Extent to which a society teaches individuals either to prize personal achievement or to conversely look after the interests of their collective first and foremost.

The **individualism versus collectivism** dimension focused on the relationship between the individual and his or her fellows. In individualistic societies, the ties between individuals were loose and individual achievement and freedom were highly valued. In societies where collectivism was emphasized, the ties between individuals were tight. In such societies, people were born into collectives, such as extended families, and everyone was supposed to look after the interest of his or her collective.

Uncertainty Avoidance
Extent to which cultures socialize members to accept ambiguous situations and to tolerate uncertainty.

Hofstede's **uncertainty avoidance** dimension measured the extent to which different cultures socialized their members into accepting ambiguous situations and tolerating uncertainty. Members of high uncertainty avoidance cultures placed a premium on job security, career patterns, retirement benefits, and so on. They also had a strong need for rules and regulations; the manager was expected to issue clear instructions, and subordinates' initiatives were tightly controlled. Lower uncertainty avoidance cultures were characterized by a greater readiness to take risks and less emotional resistance to change.

Masculinity versus Femininity
Extent to which a society differentiates and emphasizes traditional gender and work roles; a masculine characterization means there is more differentiation, whereas a feminine level means there is less.

Hofstede's **masculinity versus femininity** dimension looked at the relationship between gender and work roles. In masculine cultures, sex roles were sharply differentiated and traditional "masculine values," such as achievement and the effective exercise of power, determined cultural ideals. In feminine cultures, sex roles were less sharply distinguished, and little differentiation was made between men and women in the same job.

Hofstede created an index score for each of these four dimensions that ranged from 0 to 100 and scored high for high individualism, high power distance, high uncertainty avoidance, and high masculinity. He averaged the score for all employees from a given country. Table 3.1 summarizes these data for 20 selected countries. Western nations such as the United States, Canada, and Britain score high on the individualism scale and low on the power distance scale. At the other extreme are a group of Latin American and Asian countries that emphasize collectivism over individualism and score high on the power distance scale. Table 3.1 also reveals that Japan's culture

	Power Distance	Uncertainty Avoidance	Individualism	Masculinity
Argentina	49	86	46	56
Australia	36	51	90	61
Brazil	69	76	38	49
Canada	39	48	80	52
Denmark	18	23	74	16
France	68	86	71	43
Germany (F.R.)	35	65	67	66
Great Britain	35	35	89	66
Indonesia	78	48	14	46
India	77	40	48	56
Israel	13	81	54	47
Japan	54	92	46	95
Mexico	81	82	30	69
Netherlands	38	53	80	14
Panama	95	86	11	44
Spain	57	86	51	42
Sweden	31	29	71	5
Thailand	64	64	20	34
Turkey	66	85	37	45
United Sates	40	46	91	62

3.1 table

Work-Related Values for 20 Selected Countries

Source: G. Hofstede, *Culture's Consequences.* © 1980, Sage Publications. Cited in G. Hofstede, "The Cultural Relativity of Organizational Practices and Theories," *Journal of International Business Studies* 14 (Fall 1983), pp. 75–89. Reprinted by permission of Geert Hofstede.

has strong uncertainty avoidance and high masculinity. This characterization fits the standard stereotype of Japan as a country that is male dominant and where uncertainty avoidance exhibits itself in the institution of lifetime employment. Sweden and Denmark stand out as countries that have both low uncertainty avoidance and low masculinity (high emphasis on "feminine" values).

Hofstede's results are interesting for what they tell us in a very general way about differences between cultures. Many of Hofstede's findings are consistent with standard Western stereotypes about cultural differences. For example, many people believe Americans are more individualistic and egalitarian than the Japanese (they have a lower power distance), who in turn are more individualistic and egalitarian than Mexicans. Similarly, many might agree that Latin countries such as Mexico place a higher emphasis on masculine value—they are machismo cultures—than the Nordic countries of Denmark and Sweden.

However, one should be careful about reading too much into Hofstede's research. It has been criticized on a number of points.[48] First, Hofstede assumes there is a one-to-one correspondence between culture and the nation-state, but as we saw earlier, many countries have more than one culture. Hofstede's results do not capture this distinction. Second, the research may have been culturally bound. The research team was composed of Europeans and Americans. The questions they asked of IBM employees and their analysis of the answers may have been shaped by their own cultural biases and concerns. So it is not surprising that Hofstede's results confirm Western stereotypes, because it was Westerners who undertook the research.

Third, Hofstede's informants worked not only within a single industry, the computer industry, but also within one company, IBM. At the time, IBM was renowned for its own strong corporate culture and employee selection procedures, making it possible that the employees' values were different in important respects from the values of the cultures from which those employees came. Also, certain social classes (such as unskilled manual workers) were excluded from Hofstede's sample. A final caution is that Hofstede's work is now beginning to look dated. Cultures do not stand still; they evolve, albeit slowly. What was a reasonable characterization in the 1960s and 1970s may not be so today.

Still, just as it should not be accepted without question, Hofstede's work should not be dismissed either. It represents a starting point for managers trying to figure out how cultures differ and what that might mean for management practices. Also, several other scholars have found strong evidence that differences in culture affect values and practices in the workplace, and Hofstede's basic results have been replicated using more diverse samples of individuals in different settings.[49] Still, managers should use the results with caution, for they are not necessarily accurate.

Hofstede subsequently expanded his original research to include a fifth dimension that he argued captured additional cultural differences not brought out in his earlier work.[50] He referred to this dimension as "Confucian dynamism" (sometimes called *long-term orientation*). According to Hofstede, **Confucian dynamism** captures attitudes toward time, persistence, ordering by status, protection of face, respect for tradition, and reciprocation of gifts and favors. The label refers to these "values" being derived from Confucian teachings. As might be expected, East Asian countries such as Japan, Hong Kong, and Thailand scored high on Confucian dynamism, while nations such as the United States and Canada scored low. Hofstede and his associates went on to argue that their evidence suggested that nations with higher economic growth rates scored high on Confucian dynamism and low on individualism—the implication being Confucianism is good for growth. However, subsequent studies have shown that this finding does not hold up under more sophisticated statistical analysis.[51] During the past decade, countries with high individualism and low Confucian dynamics such as the United States have attained high growth rates, while some Confucian cultures such as Japan have had stagnant economic growth. In reality, while culture might influence the economic success of a nation, it is just one of many factors, and while its importance should not be ignored, it should not be overstated either. The factors discussed in Chapter 2—economic, political, and legal systems— are probably more important than culture in explaining differential economic growth rates over time.

Confucian Dynamism
Extent to which a society adheres to Confucian values about time, persistence, ordering by status, protection of face, respect for tradition, and reciprocation of gifts.

Cultural Change

LEARNING OBJECTIVE 5
Develop an appreciation for the economic and business implications of cultural change.

Culture is not a constant; it evolves over time.[52] Changes in value systems can be slow and painful for a society. In the 1960s, for example, American values toward the role of women, love, sex, and marriage underwent significant changes. Much of the social turmoil of that time reflected these changes. Change, however, does occur and can often be quite profound. For example, at the beginning of the 1960s, the idea that women might hold senior management positions in major corporations was not widely accepted. Many scoffed at the idea. Today, it is a reality, and few in the mainstream of

American society question the development or the capability of women in the business world. American culture has changed (although it is still more difficult for women to gain senior management positions than men). Similarly, the value systems of many ex-communist states, such as Russia, are undergoing significant changes as those countries move away from values that emphasize collectivism and toward those that emphasize individualism. While social turmoil is an inevitable outcome of such a shift, the shift will still probably occur.

Similarly, some claim that a major cultural shift is occurring in Japan, with a move toward greater individualism.[53] The model Japanese office worker, or "salaryman," is characterized as being loyal to his boss and the organization to the point of giving up evenings, weekends, and vacations to serve the organization, which is the collective of which the employee is a member. However, a new generation of office workers does not seem to fit this model. An individual from the new generation is likely to be more direct than the traditional Japanese. He acts more like a Westerner, a *gaijian*. He does not live for the company and will move on if he gets the offer of a better job. He is not keen on overtime, especially if he has a date. He has his own plans for his free time, and they may not include drinking or playing golf with the boss.[54]

Several studies have suggested that economic advancement and globalization may be important factors in societal change.[55] For example, there is evidence that economic progress is accompanied by a shift in values away from collectivism and toward individualism.[56] Thus, as Japan has become richer, the cultural emphasis on collectivism has declined and greater individualism is being witnessed. One reason for this shift may be that richer societies exhibit less need for social and material support

Another Perspective

The Chinese as Conspicuous Consumers?
By all accounts, the growth of consumerism in China would appear to be a gold mine for marketers in the West looking to promote "the next new thing." In her book *Brand New China*, Massachusetts Institute of Technology Professor Jing Wang characterizes this cultural change as "a mockery of the Communist revolution." And although she agrees that Chinese culture is changing, Wang says it's not happening as fast as Western marketers might believe. Traditional Chinese values, she says, have not disappeared altogether, and Wang advises marketers to keep those values in mind when targeting the Chinese market. ("Party Times: Marketing through Events," *BusinessWeek*, June 19, 2007, www.businessweek.com)

The 2006 MTV awards show in India demonstrates the globalization of what was originally American pop culture. Do you think traditional Indian values are at risk from the importation of MTV?

structures built on collectives, whether the collective is the extended family or the paternalistic company. People are better able to take care of their own needs. As a result, the importance attached to collectivism declines, while greater economic freedoms lead to an increase in opportunities for expressing individualism.

The culture of societies may also change as they become richer because economic progress affects a number of other factors, which in turn influence culture. For example, increased urbanization and improvements in the quality and availability of education are both a function of economic progress, and both can lead to declining emphasis on the traditional values associated with poor rural societies. A 25-year study of values in 78 countries, known as the World Values Survey, coordinated by the University of Michigan's Institute for Social Research, has documented how values change. The study linked these changes in values to changes in a country's level of economic development.[57] According to this research, as countries get richer, a shift occurs away from "traditional values" linked to religion, family, and country, and toward "secular rational" values. Traditionalists say religion is important in their lives. They have a strong sense of national pride; they also think that children should be taught to obey and that the first duty of a child is to make his or her parents proud. They say abortion, euthanasia, divorce, and suicide are never justified. At the other end of this spectrum are secular rational values.

Another category in the World Values Survey is quality of life attributes. At one end of this spectrum are "survival values," the values people hold when the struggle for survival is of paramount importance. These values tend to stress that economic and physical security are more important than self-expression. People who cannot take food or safety for granted tend to be xenophobic, are wary of political activity, have authoritarian tendencies, and believe that men make better political leaders than women. "Self-expression" or "well-being" values stress the importance of diversity, belonging, and participation in political processes.

As countries get richer, there seems to be a shift from "traditional" to "secular rational" values, and from "survival values" to "well-being" values. The shift, however, takes time, primarily because individuals are socialized into a set of values when they are young and find it difficult to change as they grow older. Substantial changes in values are linked to generations, with younger people typically being in the vanguard of a significant change in values.

With regard to globalization, some have argued that advances in transportation and communication technologies, the dramatic increase in trade that we have witnessed since World War II, and the rise of global corporations such as Hitachi, Disney, Microsoft, and Levi Strauss, whose products and operations can be found around the globe, are creating conditions for the merging of cultures.[58] With McDonald's hamburgers in China, The Gap in India, iPods in South Africa, and MTV everywhere helping to foster a ubiquitous youth culture, some argue that the conditions for less cultural variation have been created. At the same time, one must not ignore important countertrends, such as the shift toward Islamic fundamentalism in several countries; the separatist movement in Quebec, Canada; or the continuing ethnic strains and separatist movements in Russia. Such countertrends in many ways are a reaction to the pressures for cultural convergence. In an increasingly modern and materialistic world, some societies are trying to reemphasize their cultural roots and uniqueness. Cultural change is not unidirectional, with national cultures converging toward some homogenous global entity. Also, while some elements of culture change quite rapidly—particularly the use of material symbols—other elements change slowly if at all. Thus, just because people the world over wear blue jeans and eat at McDonald's, one should not assume that they have also adopted American values—for more often than not, they have not.

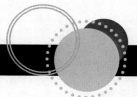

Focus on Managerial Implications

International business is different from national business because countries and societies are different. In this chapter, we have seen just how different societies can be. Societies differ because their cultures vary. Their cultures vary because of profound differences in social structure, religion, language, education, economic philosophy, and political philosophy. Three important implications for international business flow from these differences. The first is the need to develop cross-cultural literacy. There is a need not only to appreciate that cultural differences exist but also to appreciate what such differences mean for international business. A second implication centers on the connection between culture and national competitive advantage. A third implication looks at the connection between culture and ethics in decision making. In this section, we will explore the first two of these issues in depth. The connection between culture and ethics is explored in the next chapter.

LEARNING OBJECTIVE 3
Identify the business and economic implications of differences in culture.

Cross-Cultural Literacy

One of the biggest dangers confronting a company that goes abroad for the first time is the danger of being ill-informed. International businesses that are ill-informed about the practices of another culture are likely to fail. Doing business in different cultures requires adaptation to conform with the value systems and norms of that culture. Adaptation can embrace all aspects of an international firm's operations in a foreign country. The way in which deals are negotiated, the appropriate incentive pay systems for salespeople, the structure of the organization, the name of a product, the tenor of relations between management and labor, the manner in which the product is promoted, and so on, are all sensitive to cultural differences. What works in one culture might not work in another.

To combat the danger of being ill-informed, international businesses should consider employing local citizens to help them do business in a particular culture. They must also ensure that home-country executives are cosmopolitan enough to understand how differences in culture affect the practice of international business. Transferring executives overseas at regular intervals to expose them to different cultures will help build a cadre of cosmopolitan executives. An international business must also be constantly on guard against the dangers of *ethnocentric behavior*. **Ethnocentrism** is a belief in the superiority of one's own ethnic group or culture. Hand in hand with ethnocentrism goes a disregard or contempt for the culture of other countries. Unfortunately, ethnocentrism is all too prevalent; many Americans are guilty of it, as are many French people, Japanese people, British people, and so on. Ugly as it is, ethnocentrism is a fact of life, one that international businesses must be on guard against.

Ethnocentrism
A belief in the superiority of one's own ethnic group or culture.

Simple examples illustrate how important cross-cultural literacy can be. Anthropologist Edward T. Hall has described how Americans, who tend to be informal in nature, react strongly to being corrected or reprimanded in public.[59] This can cause problems in Germany, where a cultural tendency toward correcting strangers can shock and offend most Americans. For their part, Germans can be a bit taken aback by the tendency of Americans to call everyone by their first name. This is uncomfortable enough among executives of the same rank, but it can be seen as insulting when a young and junior American executive addresses an older and more senior German manager by his first name without having been invited to do so. Hall

Social networking and the importance of communal eating are some of the collectivist values Arabs bring to business.

concludes it can take a long time to get on a first-name basis with a German; if you rush the process you will be perceived as overfriendly and rude, and that may not be good for business.

Hall also notes that cultural differences in attitude to time can cause a myriad of problems. He notes that in the United States, giving a person a deadline is a way of increasing the urgency or relative importance of a task. However, in the Middle East, giving a deadline can have exactly the opposite effect. The American who insists an Arab business associate make his mind up in a hurry is likely to be perceived as overly demanding and exerting undue pressure. The result may be exactly the opposite of what the American intended, with the Arab going slow as a reaction to the American's arrogance and rudeness. For his part, the American may believe that an Arab associate is being rude if he shows up late to a meeting because he met a friend in the street and stopped to talk. The American, of course, is very concerned about time and scheduling. But for the Arab, who lives in a society where social networks are a major source of information, and maintaining relationships is important, finishing the discussion with a friend is more important than adhering to a strict schedule. Indeed, the Arab may be puzzled as to why the American attaches so much importance to time and schedule.

Culture and Competitive Advantage

One theme that continually surfaces in this chapter is the relationship between culture and national competitive advantage. Put simply, the value systems and norms of a country influence the costs of doing business in that country. The costs of doing business in a country influence the ability of firms to establish a competitive advantage in the global marketplace. We have seen how attitudes toward cooperation between management and labor, toward work, and toward the payment of interest are influenced by social structure and religion. It can be argued that the class-based conflict between workers and management in class-conscious societies, when it leads to industrial disruption, raises the costs of doing business in that society. Similarly, we have seen how some sociologists have argued that the ascetic "other-worldly" ethics of Hinduism may not be as supportive of capitalism as the ethics embedded in Protestantism and Confucianism. Also, Islamic laws banning interest payments may raise the costs of doing business by constraining a country's banking system.

Japan presents an interesting case study of how culture can influence competitive advantage. Some scholars have argued that the culture of modern Japan lowers the costs of doing business relative to the costs in most Western nations. Japan's emphasis on group affiliation, loyalty, reciprocal obligations, honesty, and education all boost the competitiveness of Japanese companies. The emphasis on group affiliation and loyalty encourages individuals to identify strongly with the companies in which they work. This tends to foster an ethic of hard work and cooperation between management and labor "for the good of the company." Similarly, reciprocal obligations and honesty help foster an atmosphere of trust between companies and their suppliers. This encourages them to enter into long-term relationships with each other to work on inventory reduction, quality control, and design—all of which have been shown to improve an organization's competitiveness. This level of cooperation has often been lacking in the West, where the relationship between a company and its suppliers tends to be a short-term one structured around competitive bidding rather than one based on long-term mutual commitments. In addition, the availability of a pool of highly skilled labor, particularly engineers, has helped Japanese enterprises develop cost-reducing process innovations that have boosted their productivity.[60] Thus, cultural factors may help explain the competitive advantage enjoyed by many Japanese businesses in the global marketplace. The rise of Japan as an economic power during the second half of the twentieth century may be in part attributed to the economic consequences of its culture.

It also has been argued that the Japanese culture is less supportive of entrepreneurial activity than, say, American society. In many ways, entrepreneurial activity is a product of an individualistic mind-set, not a classic characteristic of the Japanese. This may explain why American enterprises, rather than Japanese corporations, dominate industries where entrepreneurship and innovation are highly valued, such as computer software and biotechnology. Of course, obvious and significant exceptions to this generalization exist. Masayoshi Son recognized the potential of software far faster than any of Japan's corporate giants; set up his company, Softbank, in 1981; and has since built it into Japan's top software distributor. Similarly, dynamic entrepreneurial individuals established major Japanese companies such as Sony and Matsushita. But these examples may be the exceptions that prove the rule, for as yet there has been no surge in entrepreneurial high-technology enterprises in Japan equivalent to what has occurred in the United States.

For the international business, the connection between culture and competitive advantage is important for two reasons. First, the connection suggests which countries are likely to produce the most viable competitors. For example, one might argue that U.S. enterprises are likely to see continued growth in aggressive, cost-efficient competitors from those Pacific Rim nations where a combination of free market economics, Confucian ideology, group-oriented social structures, and advanced education systems can all be found (e.g., South Korea, Taiwan, Japan, and, increasingly, China).

Second, the connection between culture and competitive advantage has important implications for the choice of countries in which to locate production facilities and do business. Consider a hypothetical case when a company has to choose between two countries, A and B, for locating a production facility. Both countries are characterized by low labor costs and good access to world markets. Both countries are of roughly the same size (in terms of population) and both are at a similar stage of economic development. In country A, the education system is undeveloped, the society is characterized by a marked stratification between the upper and lower classes, and there are six major linguistic groups. In country B, the education system is well developed, social stratification is lacking, group identification is valued by the culture, and there is only one linguistic group. Which country makes the best investment site?

Country B probably does. In country A, conflict between management and labor, and between different language groups, can be expected to lead to social and industrial disruption, thereby raising the costs of doing business.[61] The lack of a good education system also can be expected to work against the attainment of business goals.

The same kind of comparison could be made for an international business trying to decide where to push its products, country A or B. Again, country B would be the logical choice because cultural factors suggest that in the long run, country B is the nation most likely to achieve the greatest level of economic growth.

But as important as culture is, it is probably less important than economic, political, and legal systems in explaining differential economic growth between nations. Cultural differences are significant, but we should not overemphasize their importance in the economic sphere. For example, earlier we noted that Max Weber argued that the ascetic principles embedded in Hinduism do not encourage entrepreneurial activity. While this is an interesting academic thesis, recent years have seen an increase in entrepreneurial activity in India, particularly in the information technology sector where India is rapidly becoming an important global player. The ascetic principles of Hinduism and caste-based social stratification have apparently not held back entrepreneurial activity in this sector.

Key Terms

cross-cultural literacy, p. 89

culture, p. 90

values, p. 90

norms, p. 90

society, p. 90

folkways, p. 90

mores, p. 91

social structure, p. 93

group, p. 93

social strata, p. 95

social mobility, p. 95

caste system, p. 95

class system, p. 96

class consciousness, p. 98

religion, p. 99

ethical systems, p. 99

power distance, p. 112

individualism versus collectivism, p. 112

uncertainty avoidance, p. 112

masculinity versus femininity, p. 112

Confucian dynamism, p. 114

ethnocentrism, p. 117

Summary

We have looked at the nature of social culture and studied some implications for business practice. The chapter made the following points:

1. Culture is a complex whole that includes knowledge, beliefs, art, morals, law, customs, and other capabilities acquired by people as members of society.

2. Values and norms are the central components of a culture. Values are abstract ideals about what a society believes to be good, right, and desirable. Norms are social rules and guidelines that prescribe appropriate behavior in particular situations.

3. Values and norms are influenced by political and economic philosophy, social structure, religion, language, and education.

4. The social structure of a society refers to its basic social organization. Two main dimensions along which social structures differ are the individual–group dimension and the stratification dimension.

5. In some societies, the individual is the basic building block of social organization. These societies emphasize individual achievements above all else. In other societies, the group is the basic building block of social organization. These societies emphasize group membership and group achievements above all else.

6. All societies are stratified into different classes. Class-conscious societies are characterized by low social mobility and a high degree of stratification. Less class-conscious societies

are characterized by high social mobility and a low degree of stratification.

7. Religion may be defined as a system of shared beliefs and rituals that is concerned with the realm of the sacred. Ethical systems refer to a set of moral principles, or values, that are used to guide and shape behavior. The world's major religions are Christianity, Islam, Hinduism, and Buddhism. Although not a religion, Confucianism has an impact on behavior that is as profound as that of many religions. The value systems of different religious and ethical systems have different implications for business practice.

8. Language is one defining characteristic of a culture. It has both spoken and unspoken dimensions. In countries with more than one spoken language, we tend to find more than one culture.

9. Formal education is the medium through which individuals learn skills and are socialized into the values and norms of a society.

Education plays an important role in the determination of national competitive advantage.

10. Geert Hofstede studied how culture relates to values in the workplace. He isolated four dimensions that he claimed summarized different cultures: power distance, individualism versus collectivism, uncertainty avoidance, and masculinity versus femininity.

11. Culture is not a constant; it evolves. Economic progress and globalization seem to be two important engines of cultural change.

12. One danger confronting a company that goes abroad for the first time is being ill-informed. To develop cross-cultural literacy, international businesses need to employ host-country nationals, build a cadre of cosmopolitan executives, and guard against the dangers of ethnocentric behavior.

13. The value systems and norms of a country can affect the costs of doing business in that country.

Critical Thinking and Discussion Questions

1. Outline why the culture of a country might influence the costs of doing business in that country. Illustrate your answer with examples.

2. Do you think that business practices in an Islamic country are likely to differ from business practices in the United States? If so, how?

3. What are the implications for international business of differences in the dominant religion or ethical system of a country?

4. Choose two countries that appear to be culturally diverse. Compare the cultures of those countries and then indicate how cultural differences influence (*a*) the costs of doing business in each country, (*b*) the likely future economic development of that country, and (*c*) business practices.

5. Reread the Country Focus "Islamic Capitalism in Turkey." Then answer the following questions:
   a. Can you see anything in the value of Islam that is hostile to business?

   b. What does the experience of the region around Kayseri teach us about the relationship between Islam and business?

   c. What are the implications of Islamic values toward business for the participation of a country like Turkey in the global economy?

6. Reread the Management Focus on DMG-Shanghai and answer the follow questions:
   a. Why do you think that it is so important to cultivate guanxi and guanxiwang in China?

   b. What does the experience of DMG tells us about the way things work in China? What would like happen to a business that obeyed all of the rules and regulations, rather than trying to find a way around them as Dan Mintz apparently does?

   c. What are the ethical issues that might arise when drawing upon *guanxiwang* to get things done in China? What does this suggest about the limits of using *guanxiwang* for a Western business committed to high ethical standards?

Research Task  globalEDGE   http://globalEDGE.msu.edu

Use the globalEDGE Resource Desk (http://globalEDGE.msu.edu/ResourceDesk) to complete the following exercises:

1. You have been assigned to negotiate a business deal with the representatives of a potential distributor in Mexico. Since having *intercultural skills* is critical for a successful international experience, you consider collecting information regarding the local culture before your departure. Prepare a short description of the most striking cultural characteristics involved in communicating with the local people that may affect business interactions in this country.

2. Asian cultures exhibit significant differences in *business etiquette* when compared to Western cultures. For example, in China, large hand movements are usually distracting and in fact it is considered offensive to point while speaking. Find five similar tips regarding the business etiquette of India.

closing case

Wal-Mart's Foreign Expansion

Wal-Mart, the world's largest retailer, has built its success on a strategy of every day low prices and highly efficient operations, logistics, and information systems that keep inventory to a minimum and ensure against both overstocking and under-stocking. The company employs some 1.8 million people, operates 3,900 stores in the United States and 2,700 in the rest of the world, and generated sales of $345 billion in fiscal 2007. Of these sales, some $77 billion was generated in 15 nations outside of the United States. Facing a slowdown in growth in the United States, Wal-Mart began its international expansion in the early 1990s when it entered Mexico, teaming up in a joint venture with Cifra, Mexico's largest retailer, to open a series of supercenters that sell both groceries and general merchandise.

Initially the retailer hit headwind in Mexico. It quickly discovered that shopping habits were different. Most people preferred to buy fresh products at local stores, particularly items such as meat, tortillas, and *pan dulce,* which doesn't keep well overnight (many Mexicans lack large refrigerators). Many consumers also lack cars and do not buy in large volumes as in the United States. Wal-Mart adjusted its strategy to meet the local conditions, hiring local managers who understood Mexican culture, letting those managers control merchandising strategy, building smaller stores that people could walk to, and offering more fresh produce. At the same time, the company believed that it could gradually change the shopping culture in Mexico, educating consumers by showing them the benefits of its U.S. merchandising culture. After all, Wal-Mart's managers reasoned, people once shopped at small stores in the United States, but starting in the 1950s they increasingly gravitated toward large stores like Wal-Mart. As it built up its distribution systems in Mexico, Wal-Mart could lower its own costs, and it passed these savings on to Mexican consumers in the form of lower prices. The customization, persistence, and low prices paid off. Mexicans started to change their shopping habits. Today Wal-Mart is Mexico's largest retailer and the country is widely considered to be the company's most successful foreign venture.

Next Wal-Mart expanded into a number of developed nations, including Great Britain, Germany, and South Korea. There its experiences have been less successful. In all three countries it found itself going head-to-head against well-established local rivals who had nicely matched their offerings to local shopping habits and consumer preferences. Also, consumers in all three countries seemed to have a preference for higher quality merchandise and were not as attracted to Wal-Mart's discount strategy as consumers in the United States and Mexico. After years of losses, Wal-Mart pulled out of Germany and South Korea in 2006. At the same time, it continued to look for retailing opportunities elsewhere, particularly in developed nations where it lacked strong local competitors, where it could gradually alter the shopping culture to its advantage, and where its low-price strategy was appealing.

Recently, the centerpiece of its international expansion efforts has been China. Wal-Mart opened its first store in China in 1996, but initially expanded very slowly, and by 2006 had only 66 stores. Wal-Mart discovered that the Chinese are bargain hunters and open to the low-price strategy and wide selection offered at Wal-Mart stores. In terms of their shopping habits, the emerging Chinese middle class seemed more like

Americans than Europeans. But to succeed in China, Wal-Mart also found it had to adapt its merchandising and operations strategy so that it meshes with Chinese culture. For example, Wal-Mart has learned that Chinese consumers insist that food must be freshly harvested or even killed in front of them. Wal-Mart initially offended Chinese consumers by trying to sell them dead fish, as well as meat packed in Styrofoam and cellophane. Shoppers turned their noses up at what they saw as old merchandise. So Wal-Mart began to display the meat uncovered, installed fish tanks into which shoppers could plunge fishing nets to pull out their evening meal, and began selling live turtles for turtle soup. Sales soared.

Wal-Mart has also learned that to succeed in China, the company must embrace unions. While Wal-Mart has vigorously resisted unionization in the United States, Chinese unions don't bargain for labor contracts. Instead, they are an arm of the state, providing funding for the Communist Party and (in the government's view) securing social order. In mid-2006, Wal-Mart broke with its long-standing antagonism to unions and agreed to allow unions for its Chinese employees. Many believe this set the stage for Wal-Mart's purchase in December 2006 of a 35 percent stake in the Trust-Mart chain, which has 101 hypermarkets in 34 cities across China. Now Wal-Mart has proclaimed that China lies at the center of its growth strategy.

Sources: J. Lyons, "In Mexico Wal-Mart Is Defying Its Critics," *The Wall Street Journal,* March 5, 2007, pp. A1, A9; K. Norton, "The Great Wal Mart of China," *Newsweek,* October 30, 2006, pp. 50–51; and E. Rigby, "Smooth Supply in High Demand," *Financial Times,* February 14, 2007, p. 10.

Case Discussion Questions

1. Do you think Wal-Mart could translate its merchandising strategy wholesale to another country and succeed? If not, why not?

2. Why do you think Wal-Mart was successful in Mexico?

3. Why do you think Wal-Mart failed in South Korea and Germany? What are the differences between these countries and Mexico?

4. What must Wal-Mart do to succeed in China? Is it on track?

5. To what extent can a company such as Wal-Mart change the culture of the nation where it is doing business?

Part 2 Country Differences

LEARNING OBJECTIVES

After you have read this chapter you should:

1 Be familiar with the ethical issues faced by international businesses.

2 Recognize an ethical dilemma.

3 Discuss the causes of unethical behavior by managers.

4 Be familiar with the different philosophical approaches to ethics.

5 Know what managers can do to incorporate ethical considerations into their decision making.

chapter 4

Ethics in International Business

Wal-Mart's Chinese Suppliers

opening case

Wal-Mart, the world's largest retailer, built its rise to dominance on the mantra of "every-day low prices." Getting those low prices has required Wal-Mart to source many of the goods it sells from low-cost factories around the world. Increasingly, those factories are in less developed nations, opening Wal-Mart to the charge that it uses sweatshop labor to make the goods it sells to American consumers at low prices. Long cognizant of the fact that working conditions in many parts of the world fall short of Western norms, like many other corporations, Wal-Mart has an ethical supplier code of conduct in place. This mandates, among other things, that suppliers do not employ under-age labor, pay at least the legal minimum wage for that nation, do not make employees work excessive overtime, and adhere to basic safety standards. To put teeth in this code, Wal-Mart regularly audits the factories of its suppliers. In 2006, for example, 16,700 audits were conducted in 8,873 factories around the world. The audits were undertaken by Wal-Mart's own ethical standards auditors and selected third-party firms. Some 26 percent of those audits were unannounced surprise audits. The audits found that 40.3 percent of factories had "high-risk" violations. These factories were re-audited after 120 days to determine if they had corrected any violations. If a factory incurs four "high-risk" violations in a two-year period, it is banned from producing goods for Wal-Mart for one year. In 2006, 2.1 percent of all factories audited fell into this category. Another 0.2 percent of factories were permanently barred from producing goods for Wal-Mart, presumably because they had failed to correct past violations that led them to being banned for a year.

Wal-Mart's auditing scheme seems comprehensive, but critics charge that the audits are not always as successful detecting workplace violations as the company would like to believe. Consider the case of Tang Yinghong, the manager of a Chinese factory that supplies pens, mechanical pencils, and highlight-ers to Wal-Mart. In 2005, Tang learned that Wal-Mart was about to inspect his factory. The factory had already had three "high-risk" violations.

Auditors had found that the factory paid its 3,000 employees less than the legal minimum wage in the province and violated overtime rules. A fourth violation would mean that the relationship with Wal-Mart would end. So Tang hired a Shanghai consulting company, which for $5,000 promised that the factory would get past the audit. The company provided Tang with advice on how to create fake but authentic-looking records and suggested that Tang hustle any workers with grievances out of the factory on the day of the audit. The consulting company also coached Tang on what questions to expect from the auditors and how to answer. Tang followed this advice, and the factory passed the audit, even though it changed none of its practices.

How widespread is this kind of behavior? A compliance manager for a major multinational company who overseas many factory audits stated in an interview with *BusinessWeek* that the percentage of Chinese suppliers caught submitting false payroll records rose from 46 percent to 75 percent between 2002 and 2006. The same manager, who requested anonymity, estimated that only 20 percent of Chinese suppliers complied with wage rules, while just 5 percent obeyed overtime limitations.

A typical example of falsification occurred at Zhongshan Tat Shing Toys Factory, which employs 650 people in southern China and supplies Wal-Mart. When an audit team turned up, factory managers produced time sheets showing each worker put in an eight-hour day and was paid double the local minimum wage of $0.43 cents per hour. However, when auditors interviewed workers some said they were paid less than the minimum wage and that most of them were obliged to work an extra three to five hours a day without overtime pay. Employees told auditors that the factory had a different set of records showing actual overtime hours, and that many employees worked an entire month without a day off. When pressed, factory officials said that many of their records had been destroyed in a fire.

Wal-Mart says its auditing process is state of the art and that the company is getting much more aggressive in its auditing. Factory managers, however, report that Wal-Mart puts constant pressure on them to reduce prices but meeting Wal-Mart's demands regarding working conditions inevitably raises their costs, so falsifying records may be their only option. Recognizing the problem, Wal-Mart is working with some of its suppliers to help them improve productivity through better utilization of technology and better management practices, rather than by keeping pay low and forcing workers to put in extra overtime. ●

Sources: D. Roberts and P. Engardio, "Secrets, Lies and Sweatshops, *BusinessWeek*, November 27, 2006, pp. 50–54; A. Harney, "Falsified Records Show the Flaw in the Social Audit Culture," *Financial Times*, January 11, 2007, p. 1; Wal-Mart, "Sourcing Ethically Through a Socially Responsible Program: 2006 Report on Ethical Sourcing," http://walmartstores.com/GlobalWMStoresWeb/navigate.do?catg=720, accessed January 16, 2008.

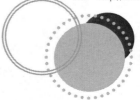

Introduction

As Wal-Mart has discovered, ethical issues can arise when companies do business in different nations. These issues are often a function of differences in economic development, politics, legal systems, and culture. In China, for example, falsification of documents pertaining to employment practices among companies supplying Wal-Mart and other Western corporations is apparently widespread. By falsifying documents, the suppliers hope to pass an audit, while continuing to require excessive overtime from employees and paying wages that are below the legal minimum. For Wal-Mart, the challenge is how to identify falsification of documents and what to do about it. Is it ethical for Wal-Mart to continue to source goods from developed nations where pay is low, working conditions are poor, and falsification of documentation is common? Wal-Mart would argue that it is, and that the company is striving to ensure that suppliers meet Wal-Mart's ethical code of conduct.

As we shall see repeatedly in this chapter, many managers have made poor ethical decisions while engaged in international business. The term *ethics* refers to accepted principles of right or wrong that govern the conduct of a person, the members of a profession, or the actions of an organization. **Business ethics** are the accepted principles of right or wrong governing the conduct of businesspeople, and an **ethical strategy** is a strategy, or course of action, that does not violate these accepted principles. This chapter looks at how ethical issues should be incorporated into decision making in an international business. We start by looking at the source and nature of ethical issues in an international business. Next, we review the reasons for poor ethical decision making. Then we discuss different philosophical approaches to business ethics. We close the chapter by reviewing the processes that managers can adopt to make sure that ethical considerations are incorporated into decision making in an international business firm.

Business Ethics
The accepted principles of right or wrong governing the conduct of businesspeople.

Ethical Strategy
A course of action, that does not violate ethical principles.

Ethical Issues in International Business

Many of the ethical issues in international business are rooted in the variations among nations in their political systems, law, economic development, and culture. What is considered normal practice in one nation may be considered unethical in another. Because they work for an institution that transcends national borders and cultures, managers in a multinational firm need to be particularly sensitive to these differences. In the international business setting, the most common ethical issues involve employment practices, human rights, environmental regulations, corruption, and the moral obligation of multinational corporations.

LEARNING OBJECTIVE 1
Be familiar with the ethical issues faced by international businesses.

EMPLOYMENT PRACTICES When work conditions in a host nation are clearly inferior to those in a multinational's home nation, what standards should be applied? Those of the home nation, those of the host nation, or something in between? While few would suggest that pay and work conditions should be the same across nations, how much divergence is acceptable? For example, while 12-hour workdays, extremely low pay, and a failure to protect workers against toxic chemicals may be common in some developing nations, does this mean it is OK for a multinational to tolerate such working conditions in its subsidiaries there, or to condone it by using local subcontractors.

For example, in the 1990s Nike found itself the center of a storm of protests when news reports revealed that working conditions at many of its subcontractors were very poor. Typical of the allegations were those detailed in a *48 Hours* television program that aired in 1996. The report painted a picture of young women at a Vietnamese

It may have been legal for a Vietnamese contractor to allow employees to work with toxic materials six days a week in poor conditions for 20 cents an hour at a Nike factory. But was it ethical for Nike to use subcontractors who by Western standards clearly exploited their workers?

subcontractor who worked with toxic materials six days a week in poor conditions for only 20 cents an hour. The report also stated that a living wage in Vietnam was at least $3 a day, an income that could not be achieved at the subcontractor without working substantial overtime. Nike and its subcontractors were not breaking any laws, but this report, and others like it, raised questions about the ethics of using sweatshop labor to make what were essentially fashion accessories. It may have been legal, but was it ethical to use subcontractors who by Western standards clearly exploited their workforce? Nike's critics thought not, and the company found itself the focus of a wave of demonstrations and consumer boycotts. The exposé surrounding Nike's use of subcontractors forced the company to reexamine its policies. Realizing that, even though it was breaking no law, its subcontracting policies were perceived as unethical, Nike's management established a code of conduct for Nike subcontractors and instituted annual monitoring by independent auditors of all subcontractors.[1]

As the Nike and Wal-Mart cases demonstrate, a strong argument can be made that it is not OK for a multinational firm to tolerate poor working conditions in its foreign operations or those of subcontractors. However, this still leaves unanswered the question of what standards should be applied. We shall return to and consider this issue in more detail later in the chapter. For now, note that establishing minimal acceptable standards that safeguard the basic rights and dignity of employees, auditing foreign subsidiaries and subcontractors on a regular basis to make sure those standards are met, and taking corrective action if they are not, is a good way to guard against ethical abuses. This is exactly what Wal-Mart is doing. Another Western company, Levi Strauss, has long taken such an approach. The company terminated a long-term contract with one of its large suppliers, the Tan family, after it discovered that the Tans were allegedly forcing 1,200 Chinese and Filipino women to work 74 hours per week in guarded compounds on the Mariana Islands.[2] For another example of problems with working practices among suppliers, see the read the accompany Management Focus that looks at working conditions in a factory that supplied Apple with iPods.

HUMAN RIGHTS   Questions of human rights can arise in international business. Basic human rights still are not respected in many nations. Rights that we take for granted in developed nations, such as freedom of association, freedom of speech, freedom of assembly, freedom of movement, freedom from political repression, and so on, are by no means universally accepted (see Chapter 2 for details). One of the most obvious historic examples was South Africa during the days of white rule and apartheid, which did not end until 1994. The apartheid system denied basic political rights to the majority nonwhite population of South Africa, mandated segregation between whites and nonwhites, reserved certain occupations exclusively for whites, and prohibited blacks from being placed in positions where they would manage whites. Despite the odious nature of this system, Western businesses operated in South Africa. By the 1980s, however, many questioned the ethics of doing so. They argued that inward investment by foreign multinationals, by boosting the South African economy, supported the repressive apartheid regime.

Several Western businesses started to change their policies in the late 1970s and early 1980s.[3] General Motors, which had significant activities in South Africa, was at

Management FOCUS

Making Apple's iPod

In mid-2006, news reports surfaced suggesting systematic labor abuses at the factory in China that made the iconic iPod for Apple Computer. According to the reports, workers at Hongfujin Precision Industries were paid as little as $50 a month to work 15-hour shifts making the iPod. There were also reports of forced overtime and poor living conditions for the workers, many of whom were young women who had migrated in from the countryside to work at the plant and lived in company-owned dormitories. The articles were the work of two Chinese journalists, Wang You and Weng Bao, employed by *China Business News,* a state-run newspaper. The target of the reports, Hongfujin Precision Industries, was reportedly China's largest export manufacturer in 2005 with overseas sales totaling $14.5 billion. Hongfujin is owned by Foxconn, a large Taiwanese conglomerate, whose customers in addition to Apple include Intel, Dell Computer, and Sony Corporation. The Hongfujin factory is a small city in its own right, with clinics, recreational facilities, buses, and 13 restaurants that serve the 200,000 employees.

Upon hearing the news, management at Apple responded quickly, pledging to audit the operations to make sure that Hongfujin was complying with Apple's code on labor standards for subcontractors. Managers at Hongfujin took a somewhat different tack: They filed a defamation suit against the two journalists, suing them for $3.8 million in a local court, which promptly froze the journalists' personal assets pending a trial. Clearly, the management of Hongfujin was trying to send a message to the journalistic community—criticism would be costly. The suit sent a chill through the Chinese news media since Chinese courts have shown a tendency to favor powerful, locally based companies in legal proceedings.

Within six weeks, Apple had completed its audit. The company's report suggested that although workers had not been forced to work overtime and were earning at least the local minimum wage, many had worked more than the 60 hours a week allowed by Apple, and their housing was substandard. Under pressure from Apple, management at Hongfujin agreed to bring practices in line with Apple's code, committing themselves to building new housing for employees and limiting work to 60 hours a week.

However, Hongfujin did not immediately withdraw the defamation suit. In an unusually bold move in a country where censorship is still common, *Chinese Business News* gave its unconditional backing to Wang and Weng. The Shanghai-based news organization issued a statement arguing that what the two journalists did "was not a violation of any rules, laws, or journalistic ethics." The Paris-based group Reporters Without Borders also took up the case of Wang and Weng, writing a letter to Apple's CEO Steve Jobs stating, "We believe that all Wang and Weng did was to report the facts and we condemn Foxconn's reaction. We therefore ask you to intercede on behalf of these two journalists so that their assets are unfrozen and the lawsuit is dropped."

Once again, Apple moved quickly, pressuring Foxconn behind the scenes to drop the suit. Foxconn agreed to do so and issued a statement saying the two sides had agreed to end the dispute after apologizing to each other "for the disturbances brought to both of them by the lawsuit." The experience shed a harsh light on labor conditions in China. At the same time, the response of the Chinese media, and *Chinese Business News* in particular, points toward the emergence of some journalist freedoms in a nation that has historically seen news organizations as a mouthpiece for the state.

Sources: E. Kurtenbach, "The Foreign Factory Factor," *Seattle Times,* August 31, 2006, pp. C1, C3; Elaine Kurtenbach, "Apple Says It's Trying to Resolve Dispute over Labor Conditions at Chinese iPod Factory," *Associated Press Financial Wire,* August 30, 2006; and "Chinese iPod Supplier Pulls Suit," *Associated Press Financial Wire,* September 3, 2006.

the forefront of this trend. GM adopted what came to be called the *Sullivan principles,* named after Leon Sullivan, a black Baptist minister and a member of GM's board of directors. Sullivan argued that it was ethically justified for GM to operate in South Africa so long as two conditions were fulfilled. First, the company should not obey the apartheid laws in its own South African operations (a form of passive resistance). Second, the company should do everything within its power to promote the abolition of apartheid laws. Sullivan's principles were widely adopted by U.S. firms operating in South Africa. Their violation of the apartheid laws was ignored by the South Africa government, which clearly did not want to antagonize important foreign investors.

However, after 10 years, Sullivan concluded that simply following the principles was not sufficient to break down the apartheid regime and that any American company, even those adhering to his principles, could not ethically justify a continued

Another Perspective

Modern-Day Slave Labor

Throughout history, impoverished people have migrated—legally or otherwise—to find work. Today, Uzbekistan's dismal economy and rampant unemployment prompt a daily exodus of Uzbek *gastarbeiters,* or "guest workers," into neighboring Russia and Kazakhstan. An estimated 1.5 million illegal Uzbeks reside in Russia alone, and for many of them, the consequences are dire.

Unskilled workers seeking jobs in agriculture, construction, and other industries, Uzbek illegals are often enslaved by Russians or Kazakhs and sold for as little as 72 euros. Accounts of daily insults, beatings, rapes—even murder—are common. Some escape their captors or are deported. Although human rights agencies work for reform, bureaucracy and corruption hamper progress. (Marina Kozlova, "Slave Laborers in Central Asia," *BusinessWeek,* October 15, 2007, www.businessweek.com)

presence in South Africa. Over the next few years, numerous companies divested their South African operations, including Exxon, General Motors, Kodak, IBM, and Xerox. At the same time, many state pension funds signaled they would no longer hold stock in companies that did business in South Africa, which helped to persuade several companies to divest their South African operations. These divestments, coupled with the imposition of economic sanctions from the U.S. and other governments, contributed to the abandonment of white minority rule and apartheid in South Africa and the introduction of democratic elections in 1994. Thus, adopting an ethical stance was argued to have helped improve human rights in South Africa.[4]

Although change has come in South Africa, many repressive regimes still exist in the world. Is it ethical for multinationals to do business in them? It is often argued that inward investment by a multinational can be a force for economic, political, and social progress that ultimately improves the rights of people in repressive regimes. This position was discussed in Chapter 2, when we noted that economic progress in a nation could create pressure for democratization. In general, this belief suggests it is ethical for a multinational to do business in nations that lack the democratic structures and human rights records of developed nations. Investment in China, for example, is frequently justified on the grounds that although China's human rights record is often questioned by human rights groups, and although the country is not a democracy, continuing inward investment will help boost economic growth and raise living standards. These developments will ultimately create pressures from the Chinese people for more participative government, political pluralism, and freedom of expression and speech.

However, there is a limit to this argument. As in the case of South Africa, some regimes are so repressive that investment cannot be justified on ethical grounds. A current example would be Myanmar (formally known as Burma). Ruled by a military dictatorship for more than 45 years, Myanmar has one of the worst human rights records in the world. Beginning in the mid-1990s, many Western companies exited Myanmar, judging the human rights violations to be so extreme that doing business there cannot be justified on ethical grounds. (In contrast, the accompanying Management Focus looks at the controversy surrounding one company, Unocal, which chose to stay in Myanmar.) A cynic might note that Myanmar has a small economy and that divestment carries no great economic penalty for Western firms, unlike, for example, divestment from China.

Nigeria is another country where serious questions have arisen over the extent to which foreign multinationals doing business in the country have contributed to human rights violations. Most notably, the largest foreign oil producer in the country, Royal Dutch Shell, has been repeatedly criticized.[5] In the early 1990s, several ethnic groups in Nigeria, which was ruled by a military dictatorship, protested against foreign oil companies for causing widespread pollution and failing to invest in the communities from which they extracted oil. Shell reportedly requested the assistance of Nigeria's Mobile Police Force (MPF) to quell the demonstrations. According to the human rights group Amnesty International, the results were bloody. In 1990, the MPF put down protests against Shell in the village of Umuechem, killing 80 people and destroying 495 homes. In 1993, following protests in the Ogoni region of Nigeria that were designed to stop contractors from laying a new pipeline for Shell, the MPF raided the area to quell the unrest. In the chaos that followed, it has been alleged that 27 villages were razed, 80,000 Ogoni people displaced, and 2,000 people killed.

Critics argued that Shell was partly to blame for the massacres. Shell never acknowledged this, and the MPF probably used the demonstrations as a pretext for punishing an ethnic group that had been agitating against the central government for some time. Nevertheless, these events did prompt Shell to look at its own ethics and to set up internal mechanisms to ensure that its subsidiaries acted in a manner that was consistent with basic human rights.[6] More generally, the question remains, what is the responsibility of a foreign multinational when operating in a country where basic human rights are trampled? Should the company be there at all, and if it is there, what actions should it take to avoid the situation Shell found itself in?

ENVIRONMENTAL POLLUTION   Ethical issues arise when environmental regulations in host nations are inferior to those in the home nation. Many developed nations have substantial regulations governing the emission of pollutants, the dumping of toxic chemicals, the use of toxic materials in the workplace, and so on. Those regulations are often lacking in developing nations, and, according to critics, the result can be higher levels of pollution from the operations of multinationals than would be allowed at home. For example, consider again the case of foreign oil companies in Nigeria. According to a 1992 report prepared by environmental activists in Nigeria, in the Niger Delta region:

> Apart from air pollution from the oil industry's emissions and flares day and night, producing poisonous gases that are silently and systematically wiping out vulnerable airborne biota and endangering the life of plants, game, and man himself, we have widespread water pollution and soil/land pollution that results in the death of most aquatic eggs and juvenile stages of the life of fin fish and shell fish on the one hand, whilst, on the other hand, agricultural land contaminated with oil spills becomes dangerous for farming, even where they continue to produce significant yields.[7]

The implication inherent in this description is that pollution controls applied by foreign companies in Nigeria were much laxer than those in developed nations.

Should a multinational feel free to pollute in a developing nation? (To do so hardly seems ethical.) Is there a danger that amoral management might move production to a developing nation precisely because costly pollution controls are not required, and the company is therefore free to despoil the environment and perhaps endanger local people in its quest to lower production costs and gain a competitive advantage? What is the right and moral thing to do in such circumstances—pollute to gain an economic advantage, or make sure that foreign subsidiaries adhere to common standards regarding pollution controls?

These questions take on added importance because some parts of the environment are a public good that no one owns, but anyone can despoil. No one owns the atmosphere or the oceans, but polluting both, no matter where the pollution originates, harms all.[8] The atmosphere and oceans can be viewed as a global commons from which everyone benefits but for which no one is specifically responsible. In such cases, a phenomenon known as the *tragedy of the commons* becomes applicable. The tragedy of the commons occurs when a resource held in common by all, but owned by no one, is overused by individuals, resulting in its degradation. The phenomenon was first named by Garrett Hardin when describing a particular problem in 16th-century England. Large open areas, called commons, were free for all to use as

Management FOCUS

Unocal in Myanmar

In 1995, Unocal, an oil and gas enterprise based in California, took a 29 percent stake in a partnership with the French oil company Total and state-owned companies from both Myanmar and Thailand to build a gas pipeline from Myanmar to Thailand. At the time, the $1 billion project was expected to bring Myanmar about $200 million in annual export earnings, a quarter of the country's total. The gas used domestically would increase Myanmar's generating capacity by 30 percent. This investment was made when a number of other American companies were exiting Myanmar. Myanmar's government, a military dictatorship, had a reputation for brutally suppressing internal dissent. Citing the political climate, the apparel companies Levi Strauss and Eddie Bauer had both withdrawn from the country. However, as far as Unocal's management was concerned, the giant infrastructure project would generate healthy returns for the company and, by boosting economic growth, a better life for Myanmar's 43 million people. Moreover, while Levi Strauss and Eddie Bauer could easily shift production of clothes to another low-cost location, Unocal argued it had to go where the oil and gas were located.

However, Unocal's investment quickly became highly controversial. Under the terms of the contract, the government of Myanmar was contractually obligated to clear a corridor for the pipeline through Myanmar's tropical forests and to protect the pipeline from attacks by the government's enemies. According to human rights groups, the Myanmar army forcibly moved villages and ordered hundreds of local peasants to work on the pipeline in conditions that were no better than slave labor. Those who refused suffered retaliation. News reports cite the case of one woman who was thrown into a fire, along with her baby, after her husband tried to escape from troops forcing him to work on the project. The baby died and she suffered burns. Other villagers report being beaten, tortured, raped, and otherwise mistreated when the alleged slave labor conditions were occurring.

In 1996, human rights activists brought a lawsuit against Unocal in the United States on behalf of 15 Myanmar villagers who had fled to refugee camps in Thailand. The suit claimed that Unocal was aware of what was going on, even if it did not participate or condone it, and that awareness was enough to make Unocal in part responsible for the alleged crimes. The presiding judge dismissed the case, arguing that Unocal could not be held liable for the actions of a foreign government against its own people—although the judge did note that Unocal was indeed aware of what was going on in Myanmar. The plaintiffs appealed, and in late 2003 the case wound up in a superior court. In 2005 the case was settled out of court for an undisclosed amount. Unocal itself was acquired by Chevron in 2005.

Sources: Jim Carlton, "Unocal Trial for Slave Labor Claims Is Set to Start Today," *The Wall Street Journal,* December 9, 2003, p. A19; Seth Stern, "Big Business Targeted for Rights Abuse," *Christian Science Monitor,* September 4, 2003, p. 2; "Trouble in the Pipeline," *The Economist,* January 18, 1997, p. 39; Irtani Evelyn, "Feeling the Heat: Unocal Defends Myanmar Gas Pipeline Deal," *Los Angeles Times,* February 20, 1995, p. D1; and "Unocal Settles Myanmar Human Rights Cases," *Business and Environment,* February 16, 2005, pp. 14–16.

pasture. The poor put out livestock on these commons and supplemented their meager incomes. It was advantageous for each to put out more and more livestock, but the social consequence was far more livestock than the commons could handle. The result was overgrazing, degradation of the commons, and the loss of this much-needed supplement.[9]

In the modern world, corporations can contribute to the global tragedy of the commons by moving production to locations where they are free to pump pollutants into the atmosphere or dump them in oceans or rivers, thereby harming these valuable global commons. While such action may be legal, is it ethical? Again, such actions seem to violate basic societal notions of ethics and social responsibility.

CORRUPTION   As noted in Chapter 2, corruption has been a problem in almost every society in history, and it continues to be one today.[10] There always have been and always will be corrupt government officials. International businesses can and have gained economic advantages by making payments to those officials. A classic example concerns a well-publicized incident in the 1970s. Carl Kotchian, the president of Lockheed, made a $12.5 million payment to Japanese agents and government officials to secure a large order from Nippon Air for Lockheed's TriStar jet. When the payments were discovered, U.S. officials charged Lockheed with falsification of its records and tax violations. Although such payments were supposed to be an accepted business practice in Japan (they might be viewed as an exceptionally lavish form of gift giving), the revelations created a scandal there too. The government ministers in question were criminally charged, one committed suicide, the government fell in disgrace, and the Japanese people were outraged. Apparently, such a payment was not an accepted way of doing business in Japan! The payment was nothing more than a bribe, paid to corrupt officials, to secure a large order that might otherwise have gone to another manufacturer, such as Boeing. Kotchian clearly engaged in unethical behavior, and to argue that the payment was an "acceptable form of doing business in Japan" was self-serving and incorrect.

The Lockheed case was the impetus for the 1977 passage of the **Foreign Corrupt Practices Act** in the United States, which we also discussed in Chapter 2. The act outlawed the paying of bribes to foreign government officials to gain business. Some

A Burmese woman at market. Many activists question Unocal's continued involvement in Myanmar/Burma because the state's dictatorship harshly punishes proponents of democracy.

U.S. businesses immediately objected that the act would put U.S. firms at a competitive disadvantage (there is no evidence that subsequently occurred).[11] The act was subsequently amended to allow for "facilitating payments." Sometimes known as speed money or grease payments, facilitating payments are *not* payments to secure contracts that would not otherwise be secured and nor are they payments to obtain exclusive preferential treatment. Rather they are payments to ensure receiving the standard treatment that a business ought to receive from a foreign government, but might not due to the obstruction of a foreign official.

In 1997, the trade and finance ministers from the member states of the Organization for Economic Cooperation and Development (OECD) followed the U.S. lead and adopted the **Convention on Combating Bribery of Foreign Public Officials in International Business Transactions**.[12] The convention, which took effect in 1999, obliges member states and other signatories to make the bribery of foreign public officials a criminal offense. The convention excludes facilitating payments made to expedite routine government action from the convention. To date, some 36 countries have signed the convention, six of whom are not OECD members.

While facilitating payments, or speed money, are excluded from both the Foreign Corrupt Practices Act and the OECD convention on bribery, the ethical implications of making such payments are unclear. In many countries, payoffs to government officials in the form of speed money are a part of life. One can argue that not investing because government officials demand speed money ignores the fact that such investment can bring substantial benefits to the local populace in terms of income and jobs. From a pragmatic standpoint, giving bribes, although a little evil, might be the price that must be paid to do a greater good (assuming the investment creates jobs where

Foreign Corrupt Practices Act A U.S. act outlawing the payment of bribes to foreign government officials in order to gain business.

Convention on Combating Bribery of Foreign Public Officials in International Business Transactions A convention obliging member states to make the bribery of foreign public officials a criminal offense.

none existed and assuming the practice is not illegal). Several economists advocate this reasoning, suggesting that in the context of pervasive and cumbersome regulations in developing countries, corruption may improve efficiency and help growth! These economists theorize that in a country where preexisting political structures distort or limit the workings of the market mechanism, corruption in the form of black-marketeering, smuggling, and side payments to government bureaucrats to "speed up" approval for business investments may enhance welfare.[13] Arguments such as this persuaded the U.S. Congress to exempt facilitating payments from the Foreign Corrupt Practices Act.

In contrast, other economists have argued that corruption reduces the returns on business investment and leads to low economic growth.[14] In a country where corruption is common, unproductive bureaucrats who demand side payments for granting the enterprise permission to operate may siphon off the profits from a business activity. This reduces businesses' incentive to invest and may retard a country's economic growth rate. One study of the connection between corruption and economic growth in 70 countries found that corruption had a significant negative impact on a country's growth rate.[15]

Given the debate and the complexity of this issue, one again might conclude that generalization is difficult and the demand for speed money creates a genuine ethical dilemma. Yes, corruption is bad, and yes, it may harm a country's economic development, but yes, there are also cases where side payments to government officials can remove the bureaucratic barriers to investments that create jobs. However, this pragmatic stance ignores the fact that corruption tends to corrupt both the bribe giver and the bribe taker. Corruption feeds on itself, and once an individual starts down the road of corruption, pulling back may be difficult if not impossible. This argument strengthens the ethical case for never engaging in corruption, no matter how compelling the benefits might seem.

Many multinationals have accepted this argument. The large oil multinational, BP, for example, has a zero-tolerance approach toward facilitating payments. Other corporations have a more nuanced approach. For example, consider the following from the code of ethics at Dow Corning:

> Dow Corning employees will not authorize or give payments or gifts to government employees or their beneficiaries or anyone else in order to obtain or retain business. Facilitating payments to expedite the performance of routine services are strongly discouraged. In countries where local business practice dictates such payments and there is no alternative, facilitating payments are to be for the minimum amount necessary and must be accurately documented and recorded.[16]

This statement allows for facilitating payments when "there is no alternative," although they are strongly discouraged.

Social Responsibility The idea that businesspeople should consider the social consequences of economic actions and give preference to outcomes with positive social and economic consequences when making business decisions.

MORAL OBLIGATIONS

Multinational corporations have power that comes from their control over resources and their ability to move production from country to country. Although that power is constrained not only by laws and regulations, but also by the discipline of the market and the competitive process, it is nevertheless substantial. Some moral philosophers argue that with power comes the social responsibility for multinationals to give something back to the societies that enable them to prosper and grow. The concept of **social responsibility** refers to the idea that businesspeople should consider the social consequences of economic actions when making business decisions, and that there should be a presumption in favor of decisions that have both good economic and social consequences.[17] In its purest form, social responsibility can be supported for its own sake simply because it is the right way for a business to behave. Advocates of this approach argue that businesses, particularly large successful businesses, need to recognize their *noblesse oblige* and give something back to the societies that have made their success possible. *Noblesse oblige* is a French term that refers to honorable and benevolent behavior considered the responsibility of people of high (noble) birth. In a business setting, it is taken to mean benevolent behavior that is the responsibility of *successful* enterprises. This has long been recognized by many businesspeople, resulting in a substantial and venerable history of corporate giving to society and in businesses making social investments designed to enhance the welfare of the communities in which they operate.

In addition to a commitment to introduce cleaner fuels and renewable energy, BP also supports urban renewal programs, art sponsorships, literacy drives, and conservation programs.

However, there are examples of multinationals that have abused their power for private gain. The most famous historic example relates to one of the earliest multinationals, the British East India Company. Established in 1600, the East India Company grew to dominate the entire Indian subcontinent in the 19th century. At the height of its power, the company deployed over 40 warships, possessed the largest standing army in the world, was the de facto ruler of India's 240 million people, and even hired its own church bishops, extending its dominance into the spiritual realm.[18]

Power itself is morally neutral; how power is used is what matters. It can be used in a positive way to increase social welfare, which is ethical, or it can be used in a manner that is ethically and morally suspect. Consider the case of News Corporation, one of the largest media conglomerates in the world, which is profiled in the accompanying Management Focus. The power of media companies derives from their ability to shape public perceptions by the material they choose to publish. News Corporation founder and CEO Rupert Murdoch has long considered China to be one of the most promising media markets in the world and has sought permission to expand News Corporation's operations in China, particularly the satellite broadcasting operations of Star TV. Some critics believe that Murdoch used the power of News Corporation in an unethical way to attain this objective.

Some multinationals have acknowledged a moral obligation to use their power to enhance social welfare in the communities where they do business. BP, one of the world's largest oil companies, has made it part of the company policy to undertake "social investments" in the countries where it does business.[19] In Algeria, BP has been investing in a major project to develop gas fields near the desert town of Salah. When the company noticed the lack of clean water in Salah, it built two desalination plants to provide drinking water for the local community and distributed containers to residents so they could take water from the plants to their homes. There was no economic reason for BP to make this social investment, but the company believes it is morally obligated to use its power in constructive ways. The action, while a small thing for BP, is a very important thing for the local community.

Management FOCUS

News Corporation in China

Rupert Murdoch built News Corporation into one of the largest media conglomerates in the world with interests that include newspapers, publishing, and television broadcasting. According to critics, however, Murdoch abused his power to gain preferential access to the Chinese media market by systematically suppressing media content that was critical of China and publishing material designed to ingratiate the company with the Chinese leadership.

In 1994, News Corporation excluded BBC news broadcasts from Star TV coverage in the region after it had become clear that Chinese politicians were unhappy with the BBC's continual reference to repression in China, and most notably, the 1989 massacre of student protesters for democracy in Beijing's Tiananmen Square. In 1995, News Corporation's book publishing subsidiary, HarperCollins, published a flattering biography of Deng Xiaoping, the former leader of China, written by his daughter. Then in 1998, HarperCollins dropped plans to publish the memoirs of Chris Patten, the last governor of Hong Kong before its transfer to the Chinese. Patten, a critic of Chinese leaders, had aroused their wrath by attempting to introduce a degree of democracy into the administration of the old British territory before its transfer back to China in 1997.

In a 1998 interview in *Vanity Fair*, Murdoch took another opportunity to ingratiate himself with the Chinese leadership when he described the Dalai Lama, the exiled leader of Chinese-occupied Tibet, as "a very political old monk shuffling around in Gucci shoes." On the heels of this, in 2001 Murdoch's son James, who was in charge of running Star TV, made disparaging remarks about Falun Gong, a spiritual movement involving breathing exercises and meditation that had become so popular in China that the Communist regime regarded it as a political threat, and

suppressed its activities. According to James Murdoch, Falun Gong was a "dangerous," "apocalyptic cult" that "clearly does not have the success of China at heart."

Critics argued that these events were all part of a deliberate effort on the part of News Corporation to curry favor with the Chinese. The company received its reward in 2001 when Star TV struck an agreement with the Chinese government to launch a Mandarin-language entertainment channel for the affluent southern coastal province of Guangdong. Earlier that year, China's leader, Jiang Zemin, had publicly praised Murdoch and Star TV for their efforts to "to present China objectively and to cooperate with the Chinese press."

Once in China, News Corporation was soon tugging at the constraints imposed on it by the Chinese government. Starting in 2002, News Corporation set up shell companies, owned by News Corporation employees, which then resold News Corporation programming to local cable TV networks throughout China, in direct violation of Chinese regulations. Payments, sometimes in the form of briefcases stuffed with cash, were channeled to News Corporation through the shell companies. One such deal involved selling programming through a shell company, known as Runde Investment Corp., to a nationwide satellite TV channel, Qinghai Satellite, based in the remote Qinghai province of China. Runde was partly owned by the son of the former hard-line Communist Party propaganda minister, Ding Guangen. If News Corporation was hoping that its political connections would help it to get away with these actions, it was badly disappointed. In 2005, Chinese authorities raided News Corporation's headquarters and seized documents and equipment. They also quickly terminated the deal with Qinghai Satellite.

Sources: Daniel Litvin, *Empires of Profit* (New York: Texere, 2003); and M. Forney, "Testing Beijing's Limits," *Time*, September 5, 2005, p. 50.

Ethical Dilemmas

LEARNING OBJECTIVE 2
Recognize an ethical dilemma.

The ethical obligations of a multinational corporation toward employment conditions, human rights, corruption, environmental pollution, and the use of power are not always clear-cut. There may be no agreement about accepted ethical principles. From an international business perspective, some argue that what is ethical depends upon one's cultural perspective.[20] In the United States, it is considered acceptable to execute murderers, but in many cultures this is not acceptable—execution is viewed as an affront to human dignity and the death penalty is outlawed. Many Americans find this attitude very strange, but many Europeans find the American approach barbaric. For a more business-oriented example, consider the practice of "gift giving" between the parties to a business negotiation. While this is considered right and proper behavior in many

Asian cultures, some Westerners view the practice as a form of bribery and unethical, particularly if the gifts are substantial.

Managers often confront very real ethical dilemmas where the appropriate course of action is not clear. For example, imagine that a visiting American executive finds that a foreign subsidiary in a poor nation has hired a 12-year-old girl to work on a factory floor. Appalled to find that the subsidiary is using child labor in direct violation of the company's own ethical code, the American instructs the local manager to replace the child with an adult. The local manager dutifully complies. The girl, an orphan, who is the only breadwinner for herself and her 6-year-old brother, is unable to find another job, so in desperation she turns to prostitution. Two years later she dies of AIDS. Meanwhile, her brother takes up begging. He encounters the American while begging outside the local McDonald's. Oblivious that this was the man responsible for his fate, the boy begs him for money. The American quickens his pace and walks rapidly past the outstretched hand into the McDonald's, where he orders a quarter-pound cheeseburger with fries and a cold milk shake. A year later, the boy contracts tuberculosis and dies.

Had the visiting American understood the gravity of the girl's situation, would he still have requested her replacement? Perhaps not! Would it have been better, therefore, to stick with the status quo and allow the girl to continue working? Probably not, because that would have violated the reasonable prohibition against child labor found in the company's own ethical code. What then would have been the right thing to do? What was the obligation of the executive given this ethical dilemma?

There is no easy answer to these questions. That is the nature of **ethical dilemmas**—they are situations in which none of the available alternatives seems ethically acceptable.[21] In this case, employing child labor was not acceptable, but given that she was employed, neither was denying the child her only source of income. What the American executive needed, what all managers need, was a moral compass, or perhaps an ethical algorithm, that would guide him through such an ethical dilemma to find an acceptable solution. Later we will outline what such a moral compass, or ethical algorithm, might look like. For now, it is enough to note that ethical dilemmas exist because many real-world decisions are complex, difficult to frame, and involve first-, second-, and third-order consequences that are hard to quantify. Doing the right thing, or even knowing what the right thing might be, is often far from easy.[22]

Ethical Dilemma
A situation in which none of the available alternatives seems ethically acceptable.

The Roots of Unethical Behavior

As we have seen, examples abound of managers behaving in a manner that might be judged unethical in an international business setting. Why do managers behave in an unethical manner? There is no simple answer to this question, for the causes are complex, but some generalizations can be made (see Figure 4.1).[23]

LEARNING OBJECTIVE 3
Discuss the causes of unethical behavior by managers.

PERSONAL ETHICS   Business ethics are not divorced from *personal ethics*, which are the generally accepted principles of right and wrong governing the conduct of individuals. As individuals, we are typically taught that it is wrong to lie and cheat—it is unethical—and that it is right to behave with integrity and honor, and to stand up for what we believe to be right and true. This is generally true across societies. The personal ethical code that guides our behavior comes from a number of sources, including our parents, our schools, our religion, and the media. Our personal ethical code exerts a profound influence on the way we behave as businesspeople. An individual with a strong sense of personal ethics is less likely to behave in an unethical manner in a business setting. It follows that the first step to

figure 4.1

Determinants of
Ethical Behavior

establishing a strong sense of business ethics is for a society to emphasize strong personal ethics.

Home-country managers working abroad in multinational firms (expatriate managers) may experience more than the usual degree of pressure to violate their personal ethics. They are away from their ordinary social context and supporting culture, and they are psychologically and geographically distant from the parent company. They may be based in a culture that does not place the same value on ethical norms important in the manager's home country, and they may be surrounded by local employees who have less rigorous ethical standards. The parent company may pressure expatriate managers to meet unrealistic goals that can only be fulfilled by cutting corners or acting unethically. For example, to meet centrally mandated performance goals, expatriate managers might give bribes to win contracts or might implement working conditions and environmental controls that are below minimal acceptable standards. Local managers might encourage the expatriate to adopt such behavior. Due to its geographical distance, the parent company may be unable to see how expatriate managers are meeting goals or may choose not to see how they are doing so, allowing such behavior to flourish and persist.

DECISION-MAKING PROCESSES Several studies of unethical behavior in a business setting have concluded that businesspeople sometimes do not realize they are behaving unethically, primarily because they simply fail to ask, "Is this decision or action ethical"?[24] Instead, they apply a straightforward business calculus to what they perceive to be a business decision, forgetting that the decision may also have an important ethical dimension. The fault lies in processes that do not incorporate ethical considerations into business decision making. This may have been the case at Nike when managers originally made subcontracting decisions (see the earlier discussion). Those decisions were probably made based on good economic logic. Subcontractors were probably chosen based on business variables such as cost, delivery, and product quality and the key managers simply failed to ask, "How does this subcontractor treat its workforce?" If they thought about the question at all, they probably reasoned that it was the subcontractor's concern, not theirs. (For another example of a business decision that may have been unethical, see the Management

Focus describing Pfizer's decision to test an experimental drug on children suffering from meningitis in Nigeria.)

ORGANIZATION CULTURE   The climate in some businesses does not encourage people to think through the ethical consequences of business decisions. This brings us to the third cause of unethical behavior in businesses—an organizational culture that deemphasizes business ethics, reducing all decisions to the purely economic. The term **organization culture** refers to the values and norms that are shared among employees of an organization. You will recall from Chapter 3 that *values* are abstract ideas about what a group believes to be good, right, and desirable, while *norms* are the social rules and guidelines that prescribe appropriate behavior in particular situations. Just as societies have cultures, so do business organizations. Together, values and norms shape the culture of a business organization, and that culture has an important influence on the ethics of business decision making.

> **Organization Culture**
> The values and norms that are shared among employees of an organization.

Author Robert Bryce has explained how the organization culture at now-bankrupt multinational energy company Enron was built on values that emphasized greed and deception.[25] According to Bryce, the tone was set by top managers who engaged in self-dealing to enrich themselves and their own families. Bryce tells how former Enron CEO Kenneth Lay made sure his own family benefited handsomely from Enron. Much of Enron's corporate travel business was handled by a travel agency partly owned by Lay's sister. When an internal auditor recommended that the company could do better by using another travel agency, the auditor soon found himself out of a job. In 1997, Enron acquired a company owned by Kenneth Lay's son, Mark Lay, which was trying to establish a business trading paper and pulp products. At the time, Mark Lay and another company he controlled were targets of a federal criminal investigation of bankruptcy fraud and embezzlement. As part of the deal, Enron hired Mark Lay as an executive with a three-year contract that guaranteed him at least $1 million in pay over that period, plus options to purchase about 20,000 shares of Enron. Bryce also details how Lay's grown daughter used an Enron jet to transport her king-sized bed to France. With Kenneth Lay as an example, it is perhaps not surprising that self-dealing soon became endemic at Enron. The most notable example was Chief Financial Officer Andrew Fastow, who set up "off balance sheet" partnerships that not only hid Enron's true financial condition from investors, but also paid tens of millions of dollars directly to Fastow. (Fastow was subsequently indicted by the government for criminal fraud and went to jail.)

UNREALISTIC PERFORMANCE EXPECTATIONS   A fourth cause of unethical behavior has already been hinted at—it is pressure from the parent company to meet unrealistic performance goals that can be attained only by cutting corners or acting in an unethical manner. Again, Bryce discusses how this may have occurred at Enron. Lay's successor as CEO, Jeff Skilling, put a performance evaluation system in place that weeded out 15 percent of underperformers every six months. This created a pressure-cooker culture with a myopic focus on short-run performance, and some executives and energy traders responded to that pressure by falsifying their performance—inflating the value of trades, for example—to make it look as if they were performing better than was actually the case.

The lesson from the Enron debacle is that an organizational culture can legitimize behavior that society would judge as unethical, particularly when this is mixed with a focus on unrealistic performance goals, such as maximizing short-term economic performance, no matter what the costs. In such circumstances, there is a greater than average probability that managers will violate their own personal ethics and engage

Management FOCUS

Pfizer's Drug-Testing Strategy in Nigeria

The drug development process is long, risky, and expensive. It can take 10 years and cost in excess of $500 million to develop a new drug. Also, between 80 and 90 percent of drug candidates fail in clinical trials. Pharmaceutical companies rely upon a handful of successes to pay for their failures. Among the most successful of the world's pharmaceutical companies is New York-based Pfizer. Given the risks and costs of developing a new drug, pharmaceutical companies will jump at opportunities to reduce them, and in 1996 Pfizer thought it saw one.

Pfizer had been developing a novel antibiotic, Trovan, that was proving to be useful in treating a wide range of bacterial infections. Wall Street analysts were predicting that Trovan could be a blockbuster, one of a handful of drugs capable of generating sales of more than $1 billion a year. In 1996, Pfizer was pushing to submit data on Trovan's efficacy to the Food and Drug Administration (FDA) for review. A favorable review would allow Pfizer to sell the drug in the United States, the world's largest market. Pfizer wanted the drug to be approved for both adults and children, but it was having trouble finding sufficient numbers of sick children in the United States to test the drug on. Then in early 1996, a researcher at Pfizer read about an emerging epidemic of bacterial meningitis in Kano, Nigeria. This seemed like a quick way to test the drug on a large number of sick children.

Within weeks a team of six doctors had flown to Kano and were administering the drug, in oral form, to children with meningitis. Desperate for help, Nigerian authorities gave the go-ahead for Pfizer to give the drug to children (the epidemic would ultimately kill nearly 16,000 people). Over the next few weeks, Pfizer treated 198 children. The protocol called for half the patients to get Trovan and half to get a comparison antibiotic already approved for the treatment of children. After a few weeks, the Pfizer team left, the experiment complete. Trovan seemed to be about as effective and safe as the already approved

antibiotic. The data from the trial were put into a package with data from other trials of Trovan and delivered to the FDA.

Questions were soon raised about the nature of Pfizer's experiment. Allegations charged that the Pfizer team kept children on Trovan, even after they failed to show a response to the drug, instead of switching them quickly to another drug. The result, according to critics, was that some children died who might have been saved had they been taken off Trovan sooner. Questions were also raised about the safety of the oral formulation of Trovan, which some doctors feared might lead to arthritis in children. Fifteen children who took Trovan showed signs of joint pain during the experiment, three times the rate of children taking the other antibiotic. Then there were questions about consent. The FDA requires that patient (or parental) consent be given before patients are enrolled in clinical trials, no matter where in the world the trials are conducted. Critics argue that in the rush to get the trial established in Nigeria, Pfizer did not follow proper procedures and that many parents of the infected children did not know their children were participating in a trial for an experimental drug. Many of the parents were illiterate, could not read the consent forms, and had to rely upon the questionable translation of the Nigerian nursing staff. Pfizer rejected these charges and contends that it did nothing wrong.

Trovan was approved by the FDA for use in adults in 1997, but it was never approved for use in children. Launched in 1998, by 1999 there were reports that up to 140 patients in Europe had suffered liver damage after taking Trovan. The FDA subsequently restricted the use of Trovan to those cases where the benefits of treatment outweighed the risk of liver damage. European regulators banned sales of the drug.

Sources: Joe Stephens, "Where Profits and Lives Hang in the Balance," *Washington Post*, December 17, 2000, p. A1; Andra Brichacek, "What Price Corruption?" *Pharmaceutical Executive* 21, no. 11 (November 2001), p. 94; and Scott Hensley, "Court Revives Suit against Pfizer on Nigeria Study," *The Wall Street Journal*, October 13, 2004, p. B4.

---

in unethical behavior. Conversely, an organization culture can do just the opposite and reinforce the need for ethical behavior. At Hewlett-Packard, for example, Bill Hewlett and David Packard, the company's founders, propagated a set of values known as The HP Way. These values, which shape the way business is conducted both within and by the corporation, have an important ethical component. Among other things, they stress the need for confidence in and respect for people, open communication, and concern for the individual employee.

LEADERSHIP   The Enron and Hewlett-Packard examples suggest a fifth root cause of unethical behavior—leadership. Leaders help to establish the culture of an organization, and they set the example that others follow. Other employees in a business often take their cue from business leaders, and if those leaders do not behave in an ethical manner, the employees might not either. It is not what leaders say that matters, but what they do. Enron, for example, had a code of ethics that Kenneth Lay himself often referred to, but Lay's own actions to enrich family members spoke louder than any words.

Enron executive Jeff Skilling has become a well-known example of corporate greed and deception.

Philosophical Approaches to Ethics

We shall look at several approaches to business ethics here, beginning with some that can best be described as straw men, which either deny the value of business ethics or apply the concept in a very unsatisfactory way. Having discussed, and dismissed, the straw men, we then move on to consider approaches that are favored by most moral philosophers and form the basis for current models of ethical behavior in international businesses.

LEARNING OBJECTIVE 4
Be familiar with the different philosophical approaches to ethics.

STRAW MEN   Straw men approaches to business ethics are raised by business ethics scholars primarily to demonstrate that they offer inappropriate guidelines for ethical decision making in a multinational enterprise. Four such approaches to business ethics are commonly discussed in the literature. These approaches can be characterized as the Friedman doctrine, cultural relativism, the righteous moralist, and the naive immoralist. All of these approaches have some inherent value, but all are unsatisfactory in important ways. Nevertheless, sometimes companies adopt these approaches.

The Friedman Doctrine   The Nobel Prize-winning economist Milton Friedman wrote an article in 1970 that has since become a classic straw man that business ethics scholars outline only to then tear down.[26] Friedman's basic position is that the only social responsibility of business is to increase profits, so long as the company stays within the rules of law. He explicitly rejects the idea that businesses should undertake social expenditures beyond those mandated by the law and required for the efficient running of a business. For example, his arguments suggest that improving working conditions beyond the level required by the law *and* necessary to maximize employee productivity will reduce profits and are therefore not appropriate. His belief is that a firm should maximize its profits because that is the way to maximize the returns that accrue to the owners of the firm, its stockholders. If stockholders then wish to use the proceeds to make social investments, that is their right, according to Friedman, but managers of the firm should not make that decision for them.

Although Friedman is talking about social responsibility, rather than business ethics per se, many business ethics scholars equate social responsibility with ethical behavior and thus believe Friedman is also arguing against business ethics. However, the assumption that Friedman is arguing against ethics is not quite true, for Friedman does state,

> There is one and only one social responsibility of business—to use its resources and engage in activities designed to increase its profits so long as it stays within the rules of the game, which is to say that it engages in open and free competition without deception or fraud.[27]

In other words, Friedman states that businesses should behave in an ethical manner and not engage in deception and fraud.

Nevertheless, Friedman's arguments do break down under examination. This is particularly true in international business where the rules of the game are not well-established and differ from country to county. Consider again the case of sweatshop labor. Child labor may not be against the law in a developing nation, and maximizing productivity may not require that a multinational firm stop using child labor in that country, but it is still immoral to use child labor because the practice conflicts with widely held views about what is the right and proper thing to do. Similarly, there may be no rules against pollution in a developed nation and spending money on pollution control may reduce the profit rate of the firm, but generalized notions of morality would hold that it is still unethical to dump toxic pollutants into rivers or foul the air with gas releases. In addition to the local consequences of such pollution, which may have serious health effects for the surrounding population, there is also a global consequence as pollutants degrade those two global commons so important to us all—the atmosphere and the oceans.

Cultural Relativism
The belief that ethics are nothing more than a reflection of a culture and that firms should simply adopt the ethics of the cultures in which they operate.

Cultural Relativism Another straw man often raised by business ethics scholars is **cultural relativism,** which is the belief that ethics are nothing more than the reflection of a culture—all ethics are culturally determined—and that accordingly, a firm should adopt the ethics of the culture in which it is operating.[28] This approach is often summarized by the maxim *when in Rome do as the Romans.* As with Friedman's approach, cultural relativism does not stand up to a closer look. At its extreme, cultural relativism suggests that if a culture supports slavery, it is OK to use slave labor in a country. Clearly, it is not! Cultural relativism implicitly rejects the idea that universal notions of morality transcend different cultures, but, as we shall argue later in the chapter, some universal notions of morality are found across cultures.

While dismissing cultural relativism in its most sweeping form, some ethicists argue there is residual value in this approach.[29] As we noted in Chapter 3, societal values and norms do vary from culture to culture, customs do differ, so it might follow that certain business practices are ethical in one country, but not another. Indeed, the facilitating payments allowed in the Foreign Corrupt Practices Act can be seen as an acknowledgment that in some countries, the payment of speed money to government officials is necessary to get business done, and if not ethically desirable, it is at least ethically acceptable.

Another Perspective

Child Labor: India's Ethical Dilemma

As India strives to become an industrialized nation, it faces an ethical dilemma: tens of millions of its workers are children. While most countries regard child labor as unacceptable, the practice is legal in India, and families depend on their child's earnings for survival.

After the government banned children under 14 from holding certain hazardous jobs, the changes in the law forced many children "underground"—into jobs where monitoring is more difficult and where they may suffer abuse and neglect. The prospect of children on the production floor represents a huge concern for U.S. manufacturers with plants in India.

Believing it will take time to eliminate child labor, advocacy groups in India argue that the government should instead support and protect child workers. (Laurie Goering, "Ending Child Labor Tricky Job for India," *Chicago Tribune,* April 17, 2008, www.chicagotribune.com)

However, not all ethicists or companies agree with this pragmatic view. As noted earlier, oil company BP explicitly states it will not make facilitating payments, no matter what the prevailing cultural norms are. In 2002, BP enacted a zero-tolerance policy for facilitation payments, primarily on the basis that such payments are a low-level form of corruption, and thus cannot be justified because corruption corrupts both the bribe giver and the bribe taker, and perpetuates the corrupt system. As BP notes on its Web site, because of its zero-tolerance policy:

> Some oil product sales in Vietnam involved inappropriate commission payments to the managers of customers in return for placing orders with BP. These were stopped during 2002 with the result that BP failed to win certain tenders with potential profit totalling $300k. In addition, two sales managers resigned over the issue. The business, however, has recovered using more traditional sales methods and has exceeded its targets at year-end.[30]

BP's experience suggests that companies should not use cultural relativism as an argument for justifying behavior that is clearly based upon suspect ethical grounds, even if that behavior is both legal and routinely accepted in the country where the company is doing business.

The Righteous Moralist

A **righteous moralist** claims that a multinational's home-country standards of ethics are the appropriate ones for companies to follow in foreign countries. This approach is typically associated with managers from developed nations. While this seems reasonable at first blush, the approach can create problems. Consider the following example: An American bank manager was sent to Italy and was appalled to learn that the local branch's accounting department recommended grossly underreporting the bank's profits for income tax purposes.[31] The manager insisted that the bank report its earnings accurately, American style. When he was called by the Italian tax department to the firm's tax hearing, he was told the firm owed three times as much tax as it had paid, reflecting the department's standard assumption that each firm underreports its earnings by two-thirds. Despite his protests, the new assessment stood. In this case, the righteous moralist has run into a problem caused by the prevailing cultural norms in the country where he is doing business. How should he respond? The righteous moralist would argue for maintaining the position, while a more pragmatic view might be that in this case, the right thing to do is to follow the prevailing cultural norms, since there is a big penalty for not doing so.

The main criticism of the righteous moralist approach is that its proponents go too far. While there are some universal moral principles that should not be violated, it does not always follow that the appropriate thing to do is adopt home-country standards. For example, U.S. laws set down strict guidelines with regard to minimum wage and working conditions. Does this mean it is ethical to apply the same guidelines in a foreign country, paying people the same as they are paid in the United States, providing the same benefits and working conditions? Probably not, because doing so might nullify the reason for investing in that country and therefore deny locals the benefits of inward investment by the multinational. Clearly, a more nuanced approach is needed.

The Naive Immoralist

A **naive immoralist** asserts that if a manager of a multinational sees that firms from other nations are not following ethical norms in a host nation, that manager should not either. The classic example to illustrate the approach is known as the drug lord problem. In one variant of this problem, an American manager

Righteous Moralist
The belief that a multinational's home-country standards of ethics are the appropriate ones for companies to follow in foreign countries.

Naive Immoralist
The belief that if a manager of a multinational sees that firms from other nations are not following ethical norms in a host nation, that manager should not either.

in Colombia routinely pays off the local drug lord to guarantee that his plant will not be bombed and that none of his employees will be kidnapped. The manager argues that such payments are ethically defensible because everyone is doing it.

The objection is twofold. First, to say that an action is ethically justified if everyone is doing it is not sufficient. If firms in a country routinely employ 12-year-olds and makes them work 10-hour days, is it therefore ethically defensible to do the same? Obviously not, and the company does have a clear choice. It does not have to abide by local practices, and it can decide not to invest in a country where the practices are particularly odious. Second, the multinational must recognize that it does have the ability to change the prevailing practice in a country. It can use its power for a positive moral purpose. This is what BP is doing by adopting a zero-tolerance policy with regard to facilitating payments. BP is stating that the prevailing practice of making facilitating payments is ethically wrong, and it is incumbent upon the company to use its power to try to change the standard. While some might argue that such an approach smells of moral imperialism and a lack of cultural sensitivity, if it is consistent with widely accepted moral standards in the global community, it may be ethically justified.

To return to the drug lord problem, an argument can be made that it is ethically defensible to make such payments, not because everyone else is doing so but because not doing so would cause greater harm (i.e., the drug lord might seek retribution and engage in killings and kidnappings). Another solution to the problem is to refuse to invest in a country where the rule of law is so weak that drug lords can demand protection money. This solution, however, is also imperfect, for it might mean denying the law-abiding citizens of that country the benefits associated with inward investment by the multinational (i.e., jobs, income, greater economic growth and welfare). Clearly, the drug lord problem constitutes one of those intractable ethical dilemmas where there is no obvious right solution, and managers need a moral compass to help them find an acceptable solution to the dilemma.

UTILITARIAN AND KANTIAN ETHICS

In contrast to the straw men just discussed, most moral philosophers see value in utilitarian and Kantian approaches to business ethics. These approaches were developed in the 18th and 19th centuries and although they have been largely superseded by more modern approaches, they form part of the tradition upon which newer approaches have been constructed.

The utilitarian approach to business ethics dates to philosophers such as David Hume (1771–1776), Jeremy Bentham (1784–1832), and John Stuart Mill (1806–1873). **Utilitarian approaches to ethics** hold that the moral worth of actions or practices is determined by their consequences.[32] An action is judged desirable if it leads to the best possible balance of good consequences over bad consequences. Utilitarianism is committed to the maximization of good and the minimization of harm. Utilitarianism recognizes that actions have multiple consequences, some of which are good in a social sense and some of which are harmful. As a philosophy for business ethics, it focuses attention on the need to weigh carefully all of the social benefits and costs of a business action and to pursue only those actions where the benefits outweigh the costs. The best decisions, from a utilitarian perspective, are those that produce the greatest good for the greatest number of people.

Many businesses have adopted specific tools such as cost-benefit analysis and risk assessment that are firmly rooted in a utilitarian philosophy. Managers often weigh the benefits and costs of an action before deciding whether to pursue it. An oil company considering drilling in the Alaskan wildlife preserve must weigh the economic benefits of increased oil production and the creation of jobs against the costs of environmental

Utilitarian Approaches to Ethics
These hold that the moral worth of actions or practices is determined by their consequences.

degradation in a fragile ecosystem. An agricultural biotechnology company such as Monsanto must decide whether the benefits of genetically modified crops that produce natural pesticides outweigh the risks. The benefits include increased crop yields and reduced need for chemical fertilizers. The risks include the possibility that Monsanto's insect-resistant crops might make matters worse over time if insects evolve a resistance to the natural pesticides engineered into Monsanto's plants, rendering the plants vulnerable to a new generation of super bugs.

For all of its appeal, utilitarian philosophy does have some serious drawbacks as an approach to business ethics. One problem is measuring the benefits, costs, and risks of a course of action. In the case of an oil company considering drilling in Alaska, how does one measure the potential harm done to the region's ecosystem? In the Monsanto example, how can one quantify the risk that genetically engineered crops might ultimately result in the evolution of super bugs that are resistant to the natural pesticide engineered into the crops? In general, utilitarian philosophers recognize that the measurement of benefits, costs, and risks is often not possible due to limited knowledge.

The second problem with utilitarianism is that the philosophy omits the consideration of justice. The action that produces the greatest good for the greatest number of people may result in the unjustified treatment of a minority. Such action cannot be ethical, precisely because it is unjust. For example, suppose that in the interests of keeping down health insurance costs, the government decides to screen people for the HIV virus and deny insurance coverage to those who are HIV positive. By reducing health costs, such action might produce significant benefits for a large number of people, but the action is unjust because it discriminates unfairly against a minority.

Kantian ethics are based on the philosophy of Immanuel Kant (1724–1804). **Kantian ethics** hold that people should be treated as ends and never purely as *means* to the ends of others. People are not instruments, like a machine. People have dignity and need to be respected as such. Employing people in sweatshops, making them work long hours for low pay in poor work conditions, is a violation of ethics, according to Kantian philosophy, because it treats people as mere cogs in a machine and not as conscious moral beings that have dignity. Although contemporary moral philosophers tend to view Kant's ethical philosophy as incomplete—for example, his system has no place for moral emotions or sentiments such as sympathy or caring—the notion that people should be respected and treated with dignity still resonates in the modern world.

RIGHTS THEORIES

Developed in the 20th century, **rights theories** recognize that human beings have fundamental rights and privileges that transcend national boundaries and cultures. Rights establish a minimum level of morally acceptable behavior. One well-known definition of a fundamental right construes it as something that takes precedence over or "trumps" a collective good. Thus, we might say that the right to free speech is a fundamental right that takes precedence over all but the most compelling collective goals and overrides, for example, the interest of the state in civil harmony or moral consensus.[33] Moral theorists argue that fundamental human rights form the basis for the *moral compass* that managers should navigate by when making decisions that have an ethical component. More precisely, they should not pursue actions that violate these rights.

The notion that there are fundamental rights that transcend national borders and cultures was the underlying motivation for the United Nations **Universal Declaration of Human Rights,** which has been ratified by almost every country on the planet

Kantian Ethics
The belief that people should be treated as ends and never as means to the ends of others.

Rights Theories
A 20th-century ethical approach based on the belief that human beings have fundamental rights and privileges that transcend national boundaries and cultures.

Universal Declaration of Human Rights
A UN document inspired by Kantian and rights theories and ratified by almost every country on the planet; it lays down basic principles that should always be adhered to, irrespective of the culture in which one is doing business.

and lays down basic principles that should always be adhered to irrespective of the culture in which one is doing business.[34] Echoing Kantian ethics, Article 1 of this declaration states:

> Article 1: All human beings are born free and equal in dignity and rights. They are endowed with reason and conscience and should act towards one another in a spirit of brotherhood.

Article 23 of this declaration, which relates directly to employment, states:

> Everyone has the right to work, to free choice of employment, to just and favorable conditions of work, and to protection against unemployment. Everyone, without any discrimination, has the right to equal pay for equal work.
>
> Everyone who works has the right to just and favorable remuneration ensuring for himself and his family an existence worthy of human dignity, and supplemented, if necessary, by other means of social protection.
>
> Everyone has the right to form and to join trade unions for the protection of his interests.

Clearly, the rights to "just and favorable work conditions," "equal pay for equal work," and remuneration that ensures an "existence worthy of human dignity" embodied in Article 23 imply that it is unethical to employ child labor in sweatshop settings and pay less than subsistence wages, even if that happens to be common practice in some countries. These are fundamental human rights that transcend national borders.

It is important to note that along with *rights* come *obligations*. Because we have the right to free speech, we are also obligated to make sure that we respect the free speech of others. The notion that people have obligations is stated in Article 29 of the Universal Declaration of Human Rights:

> Article 29: Everyone has duties to the community in which alone the free and full development of his personality is possible.

Within the framework of a theory of rights, certain people or institutions are obligated to provide benefits or services that secure the rights of others. Such obligations also fall upon more than one class of moral agent (a moral agent is any person or institution that is capable of moral action such as a government or corporation).

For example, to escape the high costs of toxic waste disposal in the West, in the late 1980s several firms shipped their waste in bulk to African nations, where it was disposed of at a much lower cost. In 1987, five European ships unloaded toxic waste containing dangerous poisons in Nigeria. Workers wearing sandals and shorts unloaded the barrels for $2.50 a day and placed them in a dirt lot in a residential area. They were not told about the contents of the barrels.[35] Who bears the obligation for protecting the rights of workers and residents to safety in a case like this? According to rights theorists, the obligation rests not on the shoulders of one moral agent, but on the shoulders of all moral agents whose actions might harm or contribute to the harm of the workers and residents. Thus, it was the obligation not just of the Nigerian government but also of the multinational firms that shipped the toxic waste to make sure it did no harm to residents and workers. In this case, both the government and the multinationals apparently failed to recognize their basic obligation to protect the fundamental human rights of others.

Just Distribution
A distribution that is considered fair and equitable.

JUSTICE THEORIES Justice theories focus on the attainment of a just distribution of economic goods and services. A **just distribution** is one that is considered fair and equitable. There is no one theory of justice, and several theories of justice conflict with each other in important ways.[36] Here we shall focus on one particular theory of justice that is both very influential and has important ethical implications. The theory is attributed to philosopher John Rawls.[37] Rawls argues that all economic goods and services should be distributed equally except when an unequal distribution would work to everyone's advantage.

According to Rawls, valid principles of justice are those with which all persons would agree if they could freely and impartially consider the situation. Impartiality is guaranteed by a conceptual device that Rawls calls the *veil of ignorance*. Under the veil of ignorance, everyone is imagined to be ignorant of all of his or her particular characteristics, for example, race, sex, intelligence, nationality, family background, and special talents. Rawls then asks what system people would design under a veil of ignorance. Under these conditions, people would unanimously agree on two fundamental principles of justice.

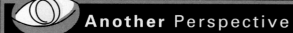

Another Perspective

Ethical Analysis: *In a Different Voice*
In addition to utilitarian, Kantian, rights, and justice approaches to business ethics, Carol Gilligan offers another way to think about our moral actions: as a series of caring relationships that evolve over time, focused first on the self, then on dependent others, and finally, on establishing equality of needs between self and others so that dynamic relationships can replace dependent ones. Such an approach (self, dependent other, dynamic equality) may be a helpful way of thinking about a multinational's evolving corporate involvement in a developing country. (Carol Gilligan, *In a Different Voice*, 1982)

The first principle is that each person be permitted the maximum amount of basic liberty compatible with a similar liberty for others. Rawls takes these to be political liberty (e.g., the right to vote), freedom of speech and assembly, liberty of conscience and freedom of thought, the freedom and right to hold personal property, and freedom from arbitrary arrest and seizure.

The second principle is that once equal basic liberty is assured, inequality in basic social goods—such as income and wealth distribution, and opportunities—is to be allowed *only* if such inequalities benefit everyone. Rawls accepts that inequalities can be just if the system that produces inequalities is to the advantage of everyone. More precisely, he formulates what he calls the *difference principle*, which is that inequalities are justified if they benefit the position of the least-advantaged person. So, for example, wide variations in income and wealth can be considered just if the market-based system that produces this unequal distribution also benefits the least-advantaged members of society. One can argue that a well-regulated, market-based economy and free trade, by promoting economic growth, benefit the least-advantaged members of society. In principle at least, the inequalities inherent in such systems are therefore just (in other words, the rising tide of wealth created by a market-based economy and free trade lifts all boats, even those of the most disadvantaged).

In the context of international business ethics, Rawls's theory creates an interesting perspective. Managers could ask themselves whether the policies they adopt in foreign operations would be considered just under Rawls's veil of ignorance. Is it just, for example, to pay foreign workers less than workers in the firm's home country? Rawls's theory would suggest it is, so long as the inequality benefits the least-advantaged members of the global society (which is what economic theory suggests). Alternatively, it is difficult to imagine that managers operating under a veil of ignorance would design a system where foreign employees were paid subsistence wages to work long hours in sweatshop conditions and where they were exposed to toxic materials. Such working conditions are clearly unjust in Rawls's framework, and therefore, it is unethical to adopt them. Similarly, operating under a veil of ignorance, most people would probably design a system that imparts some protection from environmental degradation to important global commons, such as the oceans, atmosphere, and tropical

LEARNING OBJECTIVE 5
Know what managers can do to incorporate ethical considerations into their decision making.

rain forests. To the extent that this is the case, it follows that it is unjust, and by extension unethical, for companies to pursue actions that contribute toward extensive degradation of these commons. Thus, Rawls's veil of ignorance is a conceptual tool that contributes to the moral compass that managers can use to help them navigate through difficult ethical dilemmas.

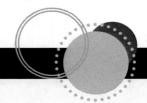

Focus on Managerial Implications

What then is the best way for managers in a multinational firm to make sure that ethical considerations figure into international business decisions? How do managers decide upon an ethical course of action when confronted with decisions pertaining to working conditions, human rights, corruption, and environmental pollution? From an ethical perspective, how do managers determine the moral obligations that flow from the power of a multinational? In many cases, there are no easy answers to these questions, for many of the most vexing ethical problems arise because there are very real dilemmas inherent in them and no obvious correct action. Nevertheless, managers can and should do many things to make sure that basic ethical principles are adhered to and that ethical issues are routinely inserted into international business decisions.

Here we focus on five things that an international business and its managers can do to make sure ethical issues are considered in business decisions. These are (1) favor hiring and promoting people with a well-grounded sense of personal ethics; (2) build an organizational culture that places a high value on ethical behavior; (3) make sure that leaders within the business not only articulate the rhetoric of ethical behavior, but also act in a manner that is consistent with that rhetoric; (4) put decision-making processes in place that require people to consider the ethical dimension of business decisions; and (5) develop moral courage.

Hiring and Promotion

It seems obvious that businesses should strive to hire people who have a strong sense of personal ethics and would not engage in unethical or illegal behavior. Similarly, you would not expect a business to promote people, and perhaps to fire people, whose behavior does not match generally accepted ethical standards. However, actually doing so is very difficult. How do you know that someone has a poor sense of personal ethics? In our society, we have an incentive to hide a lack of personal ethics from public view. Once people realize that you are unethical, they will no longer trust you.

Is there anything that businesses can do to make sure they do not hire people who subsequently turn out to have poor personal ethics, particularly given that people have an incentive to hide this from public view (indeed, the unethical person may lie about his or her nature)? Businesses can give potential employees psychological tests to try to discern their ethical predisposition, and they can check with prior employees regarding someone's reputation (e.g., by asking for letters of reference and talking to people who have worked with the prospective employee). The latter is common and does influence the hiring process. Promoting people who have displayed poor ethics should not occur in a company where the organization culture values the need for ethical behavior and where leaders act accordingly.

Some probing questions to ask about a prospective employer:

1. Is there a formal code of ethics? How widely is it distributed? Is it reinforced in other formal ways such as through decision-making systems?
2. Are workers at all levels trained in ethical decision making? Are they also encouraged to take responsibility for their behavior or to question authority when asked to do something they consider wrong?
3. Do employees have formal channels available to make their concerns known confidentially? Is there a formal committee high in the organization that considers ethical issues?
4. Is misconduct disciplined swiftly and justly within the organization?
5. Is integrity emphasized to new employees?
6. How are senior managers perceived by subordinates in terms of their integrity? How do such leaders model ethical behavior?

4.1 table

A Job Seeker's Ethics Audit

Source: Linda K. Trevino, chair of the Department of Management and Organization, Smeal College of Business, Pennsylvania State University. Reported in K. Maher, "Career Journal. Wanted: Ethical Employer," *The Wall Street Journal*, July 9, 2002, p. B1.

Not only should businesses strive to identify and hire people with a strong sense of personal ethics, but it also is in the interests of prospective employees to find out as much as they can about the ethical climate in an organization. Who wants to work at a multinational such as Enron, which ultimately entered bankruptcy because unethical executives had established risky partnerships that were hidden from public view and that existed in part to enrich those same executives? Table 4.1 lists some questions job seekers might want to ask a prospective employer.

Organization Culture and Leadership

To foster ethical behavior, businesses need to build an organization culture that values ethical behavior. Three things are particularly important in building an organization culture that emphasizes ethical behavior. First, the businesses must explicitly articulate values that emphasize ethical behavior. Many companies now do this by drafting a **code of ethics,** which is a formal statement of the ethical priorities a business adheres to. Often, the code of ethics draws heavily upon documents such as the UN Universal Declaration of Human Rights, which itself is grounded in Kantian and rights-based theories of moral philosophy. Others have incorporated ethical statements into documents that articulate the values or mission of the business. For example, the food and consumer products multinational Unilever has a code of ethics that includes the following points:[38]

Code of Ethics
A formal statement of the ethical priorities to which a business adheres.

> **Employees:** Unilever is committed to diversity in a working environment where there is mutual trust and respect and where everyone feels responsible for the performance and reputation of our company. We will recruit, employ, and promote employees on the sole basis of the qualifications and abilities needed for the work to be performed. We are committed to safe and healthy working conditions for all employees. We will not use any form of forced, compulsory, or child labor. We are committed to working with employees to develop and enhance each individual's skills and capabilities. We respect the dignity of the individual and the right of employees to freedom of association. We will maintain good communications with employees through company-based information and consultation procedures.
>
> **Business Integrity:** Unilever does not give or receive, whether directly or indirectly, bribes or other improper advantages for business or financial gain. No employee may offer, give, or receive any gift or payment which is, or may be construed as being, a bribe. Any demand for, or offer of, a bribe must be rejected

Another Perspective

Putting the "Fair" into "Fair Trade"

Where does your cup of coffee come from? In many cases, from farmers earning subsistence-level wages on sun-drenched land—where lush rain forests used to grow—to ripen beans in a hurry. But some coffee sellers, like Chicago-based Intelligentsia, promote ethical practices through *fair trade* coffee. "Fair trade" guarantees farmers a minimum price over their production costs: at least $1.26 a pound. Intelligentsia pays even more—25 percent or more *above* the fair-trade price—to help farmers invest in their business.

As Intelligentsia's Geoff Watts says, "If you want to begin talking about sustainability, you really have to look at economic stability. Is the farmer getting paid enough to invest in his business? And then you have to look at environmental issues. It goes far beyond whether or not there's shade." (Janet Rausa Fuller, "'Fair Trade' Gives Growers a Fighting Chance," *Chicago Sun-Times*, April 19, 2007, www.suntimes.com)

immediately and reported to management. Unilever accounting records and supporting documents must accurately describe and reflect the nature of the underlying transactions. No undisclosed or unrecorded account, fund, or asset will be established or maintained.

It is clear from these principles, that among other things, Unilever will not tolerate substandard working conditions, use child labor, or give bribes under any circumstances. Note also the reference to respecting the dignity of employees, a statement that is grounded in Kantian ethics. Unilever's principles send a very clear message about appropriate ethics to managers and employees.

Having articulated values in a code of ethics or some other document, leaders in the business must give life and meaning to those words by repeatedly emphasizing their importance *and then acting on them*. This means using every relevant opportunity to stress the importance of business ethics and making sure that key business decisions not only make good economic sense but also are ethical. Many companies have gone a step further, hiring independent auditors to make sure they are behaving in a manner consistent with their ethical codes. Nike, for example, has hired independent auditors to make sure that subcontractors used by the company are living up to Nike's code of conduct.

Finally, building an organization culture that places a high value on ethical behavior requires incentive and reward systems, including promotions that reward people who engage in ethical behavior and sanction those who do not. At General Electric, for example, the former CEO Jack Welch has described how he reviewed the performance of managers, dividing them into several different groups. These included overperformers who displayed the right values and were singled out for advancement and bonuses and overperformers who displayed the wrong values and were let go. Welch was not willing to tolerate leaders within the company who did not act in accordance with the central values of the company, even if they were in all other respects skilled managers.[39]

Decision-Making Processes

In addition to establishing the right kind of ethical culture in an organization, businesspeople must be able to think through the ethical implications of decisions in a systematic way. To do this, they need a moral compass, and both rights theories and Rawls's theory of justice help to provide such a compass. Beyond these theories, some experts on ethics have proposed a straightforward practical guide—or ethical algorithm—to determine whether a decision is ethical.[40] According to these experts, a decision is acceptable on ethical grounds if a businessperson can answer yes to each of these questions:

- Does my decision fall within the accepted values or standards that typically apply in the organizational environment (as articulated in a code of ethics or some other corporate statement)?

- Am I willing to see the decision communicated to all stakeholders affected by it—for example, by having it reported in newspapers or on television?
- Would the people with whom I have a significant personal relationship, such as family members, friends, or even managers in other businesses, approve of the decision?

Others have recommended a five-step process to think through ethical problems (this is another example of an ethical algorithm).[41] In step 1, businesspeople should identify which stakeholders a decision would affect and in what ways. A firm's **stakeholders** are individuals or groups that have an interest, claim, or stake in the company, in what it does, and in how well it performs.[42] They can be divided into internal stakeholders and external stakeholders. **Internal stakeholders** are individuals or groups who work for or own the business. They include all employees, the board of directors, and stockholders. **External stakeholders** are all other individuals and groups that have some claim on the firm. Typically, this group comprises customers, suppliers, lenders, governments, unions, local communities, and the general public.

All stakeholders are in an exchange relationship with the company. Each stakeholder group supplies the organization with important resources (or contributions), and in exchange each expects its interests to be satisfied (by inducements).[43] For example, employees provide labor, skills, knowledge, and time and in exchange expect commensurate income, job satisfaction, job security, and good working conditions. Customers provide a company with its revenues and in exchange they want quality products that represent value for money. Communities provide businesses with local infrastructure and in exchange they want businesses that are responsible citizens and seek some assurance that the quality of life will be improved as a result of the business firm's existence.

Stakeholder analysis involves a certain amount of what has been called *moral imagination*.[44] This means standing in the shoes of a stakeholder and asking how a proposed decision might impact that stakeholder. For example, when considering outsourcing to subcontractors, managers might need to ask themselves how it might feel to be working under substandard health conditions for long hours.

Step 2 involves judging the ethics of the proposed strategic decision, given the information gained in step 1. Managers need to determine whether a proposed decision would violate the *fundamental rights* of any stakeholders. For example, we might argue that the right to information about health risks in the workplace is a fundamental entitlement of employees. Similarly, the right to know about potentially dangerous features of a product is a fundamental entitlement of customers (something tobacco companies violated when they did not reveal to their customers what they knew about the health risks of smoking). Managers might also want to ask themselves whether they would allow the proposed strategic decision if they were designing a system under Rawls's veil of ignorance. For example, if the issue under consideration was whether to outsource work to a subcontractor with low pay and poor working conditions, managers might want to ask themselves whether they would allow for such action if they were considering it under a veil of ignorance, where they themselves might ultimately be the ones to work for the subcontractor.

The judgment at this stage should be guided by various moral principles that should not be violated. The principles might be those articulated in a corporate code of ethics or other company documents. In addition, certain moral principles that we have adopted as members of society—for instance, the prohibition on stealing—should not be violated. The judgment at this stage will also be guided by the decision rule that is chosen to assess the proposed strategic decision. Although maximizing long-run profitability is the decision rule that most businesses stress, it should be applied subject to the

Stakeholders Individuals or groups that have an interest, claim, or stake in a company, what it does, and how well it performs.

Internal Stakeholders Individuals or groups that work for or own the business.

External Stakeholders All other individuals and groups that have some claim on a firm, such as the government, suppliers, and the general public.

Another Perspective

How Do You Know What Is Really Happening? Giving Meaning across Cultures

One of the difficulties in making ethical decisions across cultural borders is that expatriate managers may tend to interpret a local cultural practice in the ways such behavior would be understood in their home culture. If the manager's process of meaning-giving stops there, rather than continue in an attempt to understand the practice's meaning *in the local culture*, the manager may miss a huge step in ethical analysis. For example, if women's covering their heads and faces in conservative Muslim cultures is given meaning in a Western context, it would lead to different conclusions than were it given meaning with knowledge of the specific, local, Muslim context. Remember to consider context when conducting an ethical analysis. In such a process, a local informant can be helpful. At the same time, be aware of the ethical trap of cultural relativism. (Example from H. Lane, M. Maznevski, M. Mendenhall, and J. McNett, *The Blackwell Handbook of Global Management: A Guide to Managing Complexity,* 2004)

constraint that no moral principles are violated—that the business behaves in an ethical manner.

Step 3 requires managers to establish moral intent. This means the business must resolve to place moral concerns ahead of other concerns in cases where either the fundamental rights of stakeholders or key moral principles have been violated. At this stage, input from top management might be particularly valuable. Without the proactive encouragement of top managers, middle-level managers might tend to place the narrow economic interests of the company before the interests of stakeholders. They might do so in the (usually erroneous) belief that top managers favor such an approach.

Step 4 requires the company to engage in ethical behavior. Step 5 requires the business to audit its decisions, reviewing them to make sure they were consistent with ethical principles, such as those stated in the company's code of ethics. This final step is critical and often overlooked. Without auditing past decisions, businesspeople may not know if their decision process is working and if changes should be made to ensure greater compliance with a code of ethics.

Ethics Officers

To make sure that a business behaves in an ethical manner, a number of firms now have ethics officers. These individuals are responsible for making sure that all employees are trained to be ethically aware, that ethical considerations enter the business decision-making process, and that the company's code of ethics is followed. Ethics officers may also be responsible for auditing decisions to make sure they are consistent with this code. In many businesses, ethics officers act as an internal ombudsperson with responsibility for handling confidential inquiries from employees, investigating complaints from employees or others, reporting findings, and making recommendations for change.

United Technologies the maker of Sikorsky helicopters such as the one pictured here, demonstrates its commitment to ethical behavior by employing over 160 business practices officers.

For example, United Technologies, a multinational aerospace company with worldwide revenues of more than $30 billion, has had a formal code of ethics since 1990.[45] There are some 160 business practice officers within United Technologies (this is the company's name for ethics officers). They are responsible for making sure the code is followed. United Technologies also established an ombudsperson program in 1986 that lets employees inquire anonymously about ethics issues. The program has received some 60,000 inquiries since 1986, and over 10,000 cases have been handled by an ombudsperson.

Moral Courage

Finally, it is important to recognize that employees in an international business may need significant *moral courage*. Moral courage enables managers to walk away from a decision that is profitable, but unethical. Moral courage gives an employee the strength to say no to a superior who instructs her to pursue actions that are unethical. Moral courage gives employees the integrity to go public to the media and blow the whistle on persistent unethical behavior in a company. Moral courage does not come easily; there are well-known cases where individuals have lost their jobs because they blew the whistle on corporate behaviors they thought unethical, telling the media about what was occurring.[46]

However, companies can strengthen the moral courage of employees by committing themselves to not retaliate against employees who exercise moral courage, say no to superiors, or otherwise complain about unethical actions. For example, consider the following extract from Unilever's code of ethics:

> Any breaches of the Code must be reported in accordance with the procedures specified by the Joint Secretaries. The Board of Unilever will not criticize management for any loss of business resulting from adherence to these principles and other mandatory policies and instructions. The Board of Unilever expects employees to bring to their attention, or to that of senior management, any breach or suspected breach of these principles. Provision has been made for employees to be able to report in confidence and no employee will suffer as a consequence of doing so.[47]

This statement gives permission to employees to exercise moral courage. Companies can also set up ethics hotlines, which allow employees to anonymously register a complaint with a corporate ethics officer.

Summary of Decision-Making Steps

All of the steps discussed here—hiring and promoting people based upon ethical considerations as well as more traditional metrics of performance, establishing an ethical culture in the organization, instituting ethical decision-making processes, appointing ethics officers, and creating an environment that facilitates moral courage—can help to make sure that when making business decisions, managers are cognizant of the ethical implications and do not violate basic ethical prescripts. At the same time, it must be recognized that not all ethical dilemmas have a clean and obvious solution— that is why they are dilemmas. There are clearly things that international businesses should not do and there are things that they should do, but there are also actions that present managers with true dilemmas. In these cases, a premium is placed on managers' ability to make sense out of complex situations and make balanced decisions that are as just as possible.

Key Terms

cultural relativism, p. 142

righteous moralist, p. 143

naive immoralist, p. 143

utilitarian approaches to ethics, p. 144

Kantian ethics, p. 145

rights theories, p. 145

Universal Declaration of Human Rights, p. 145

just distribution, p. 146

code of ethics, p. 149

stakeholders, p. 151

internal stakeholders, p. 151

external stakeholders, p. 151

Summary

This chapter has discussed the source and nature of ethical issues in international businesses, the different philosophical approaches to business ethics, and the steps managers can take to ensure that ethical issues are respected in international business decisions. The chapter made these points:

1. The term *ethics* refers to accepted principles of right or wrong that govern the conduct of a person, the members of a profession, or the actions of an organization. Business ethics are the accepted principles of right or wrong governing the conduct of businesspeople, and an ethical strategy is one that does not violate these accepted principles.

2. Ethical issues and dilemmas in international business are rooted in the variations among political systems, law, economic development, and culture from nation to nation.

3. The most common ethical issues in international business involve employment practices, human rights, environmental regulations, corruption, and the moral obligation of multinational corporations.

4. Ethical dilemmas are situations in which none of the available alternatives seems ethically acceptable.

5. Unethical behavior is rooted in poor personal ethics, the psychological and geographical distances of a foreign subsidiary from the home office, a failure to incorporate ethical issues into strategic and operational decision making, a dysfunctional culture, and failure of leaders to act in an ethical manner.

6. Moral philosophers contend that approaches to business ethics such as the Friedman doctrine, cultural relativism, the righteous moralist, and the naive immoralist are unsatisfactory in important ways.

7. The Friedman doctrine states that the only social responsibility of business is to increase profits, as long as the company stays within the rules of law. Cultural relativism contends that one should adopt the ethics of the culture in which one is doing business. The righteous moralist monolithically applies home-country ethics to a foreign situation, while the naive immoralist believes that if a manager of a multinational sees that firms from other nations are not following ethical norms in a host nation, that manager should not either.

8. Utilitarian approaches to ethics hold that the moral worth of actions or practices is determined by their consequences, and the best decisions are those that produce the greatest good for the greatest number of people.

9. Kantian ethics state that people should be treated as ends and never purely as *means* to the ends of others. People are not instruments, like a machine. People have dignity and need to be respected as such.

10. Rights theories recognize that human beings have fundamental rights and privileges that transcend national boundaries and cultures. These rights establish a minimum level of morally acceptable behavior.

11. The concept of justice developed by John Rawls suggests that a decision is just and ethical if people would allow for it when designing a social system under a veil of ignorance.

12. To make sure that ethical issues are considered in international business decisions, managers should (*a*) favor hiring and promoting people with a well-grounded sense of personal ethics;

(*b*) build an organization culture that places a high value on ethical behavior; (*c*) make sure that leaders within the business not only articulate the rhetoric of ethical behavior, but also act in a manner that is consistent with that rhetoric; (*d*) put decision-making processes in place that require people to consider the ethical dimension of business decisions; and (*e*) be morally courageous and encourage others to do the same.

Critical Thinking and Discussion Questions

1. A visiting American executive finds that a foreign subsidiary in a poor nation has hired a 12-year-old girl to work on a factory floor, in violation of the company's prohibition on child labor. He tells the local manager to replace the child and tell her to go back to school. The local manager tells the American executive that the child is an orphan with no other means of support, and she will probably become a street child if she is denied work. What should the American executive do?

2. Drawing upon John Rawls's concept of the veil of ignorance, develop an ethical code that will (*a*) guide the decisions of a large oil multinational toward environmental protection, and (*b*) influence the policies of a clothing company to outsourcing of the manufacturing process.

3. Under what conditions is it ethically defensible to outsource production to the developing world where labor costs are lower when such actions also involve laying off long-term employees in the firm's home country?

4. Are facilitating payments ethical?

5. A manager from a developing country is overseeing a multinational's operations in a country where drug trafficking and lawlessness are rife. One day, a representative of a local "big man" approaches the manager and asks for a "donation" to help the "big man" provide housing for the poor. The representative tells the manager that in return for the donation, the "big man" will make sure that the manager has a productive stay in his country. No threats are made, but the manager is well aware that the "big man" heads a criminal organization that is engaged in drug trafficking. He also knows that the big man does indeed help the poor in the run-down neighborhood of the city where he was born. What should the manager do?

6. Reread the Management Focus feature on Unocal and answer the following questions:
   a. Was it ethical for Unocal to enter into a partnership with a brutal military dictatorship for financial gain?
   b. What actions could Unocal have taken, short of not investing at all, to safeguard the human rights of people affected by the gas pipeline project?

Research Task

http://globalEDGE.msu.edu   globalEDGE

Use the globalEDGE Resource Desk (http://globalEDGE.msu.edu/ResourceDesk/) to complete the following exercises:

1. The Organization for Economic Cooperation and Development (OECD) *Guidelines for Multinational Enterprises* are a set of voluntary principles and standards for responsible business conduct addressed by governments to multinational enterprises. They provide recommendations in a number of areas including labor relations, the environment, bribery, competition, and taxation. Find the text of the Guidelines and prepare an outline of the guidelines in the area of employment and industrial relations.

2. The *Corruption Perceptions Index (CPI)* is a comparative assessment of integrity performance in a variety of countries. Provide a description of this index and its ranking. Identify the five countries with the lowest and the highest CPI scores. Do you notice any trends or similarities among the countries listed?

Google in China

Google, the fast-growing Internet search engine company, was established with a clear mission in mind: to organize the world's information and make it universally acceptable and useful. Google has built a highly profitable advertising business on the back of its search engine, which is by far the most widely used in the world. Under the pay-per-click business model, advertisers pay Google every time a user of its search engine clicks on one of the paid links typically listed on the right-hand side of Google's results page.

Google has long operated with the mantra "don't be evil"! When this phrase was originally formulated, the central message was that Google should never compromise the integrity of its search results. For example, Google decided not to let commercial considerations bias its ranking. This is why paid links are not included in its main search results, but listed on the right-hand side of the results page. The mantra "don't be evil," however, has become more than that at Google; it has become a central organizing principle of the company and an ethical touchstone by which managers judge all strategic decisions.

Google's mission and mantra raised hopes among human rights activists that the search engine would be an unstoppable tool for circumventing government censorship, democratizing information, and allowing people in heavily censored societies, such as China, to gain access to information that their governments were trying to suppress.

Google began a Chinese-language service in 2000, although the service was operated from the United States. In 2002, the site was blocked by the Chinese authorities. Would-be users of Google's search engine were directed to a Chinese rival. The blocking took Google's managers by surprise. Reportedly, co-founder Sergey Brin immediately ordered half a dozen books on China and quickly read them in an effort to understand this vast country. Two weeks later, for reasons that have never been made clear, Google's service was restored. Google said it did not change anything about its service, but Chinese users soon found that they could not access politically sensitive sites that appeared in Google's search results, suggesting that the government was censoring more aggressively. (The Chinese government has essentially erected a giant firewall between the Internet in China and the rest of the world, allowing its censors to block sites outside of China that are deemed subversive.)

By late 2004, it was clear to Google that China was a strategically important market. To exploit the opportunities that China offered, however, the company realized that it would have to establish operations in China, including its own computer servers and a Chinese home page. Serving Chinese users from the United States was too slow, and the service was badly degraded by the censorship imposed. This created a dilemma for the company, given the "don't be evil" mantra. Once it established Chinese operations, it would be subject to Chinese regulations, including those censoring information. For perhaps 18 months, senior managers inside the company debated the pros and cons of entering China directly, as opposed to serving the market from its U.S. site. Ultimately, they decided the opportunity was too large to ignore. With over 100 million users, and that number growing quickly, China promised to become the largest Internet market in the world and a major source of advertising revenue for Google. Moreover, Google was at a competitive disadvantage relative to its U.S. rivals, Yahoo! and Microsoft's MSN, which had already established operations in China, and relative to China's homegrown company, Baidu, which leads the market for Internet search in China (in 2006 Baidu had about 40 percent of the search engine market in China, compared to Google's 30 percent share).

In mid-2005, Google established a direct sales presence in China. In January 2006, Google rolled out its Chinese home page, which is hosted on servers based in China and maintained by Chinese employees in Beijing and Shanghai. Upon launch, Google stated that its objective was to give Chinese users "the greatest amount of information possible." It was immediately apparent that this was not the same as "access to all information." In accordance with Chinese regulations, Google engaged in self-censorship, excluding results on such politically sensitive topics as democratic reform, Taiwanese independence, the banned Falun Gong movement, and references to the notorious Tiananmen Square massacre of democratic protesters that occurred in 1989. Human rights activists quickly protested, arguing that Google had abandoned its principles in order to make greater profits. For its part, Google's managers claimed it was better to give Chinese users access to a limited amount of information than to none at all, or to serve the market from the United States and allow the government to continue proactively censoring its search results, which would result in a badly degraded service. Brin justified the Chinese decision by saying, "It will be better for Chinese Web users, because ultimately they will get more information, though not quite all of it." Google also argued that it was the only search engine in

China that let users know if search results had been censored (which is done by the inclusion of a bullet at the bottom of the page indicating censorship).

Sources: Andy Kessler, "Sellout.com," *The Wall Street Journal,* January 31, 2006, p. A14; D. Henninger, "Wonderland: Google in China," *The Wall Street Journal,* March 10, 2006, p. A18; J. Dean, "Limited Search: As Google Pushes into China It Faces Clashes with Censors," *The Wall Street Journal,* December 16, 2005, p. A1; and "The Party, the People, and the Power of Cyber Talk: China and the Internet," *The Economist,* April 29, 2006, pp. 28–30.

Case Discussion Questions

1. What philosophical principle did Google's managers adopt when deciding that the benefits of operating in China outweighed the costs?

2. Do you think Google should have entered China and engaged in self-censorship, given the company's long-standing mantra "Don't be evil"? Is it better to engage in self-censorship than have the government censor for you?

3. If all foreign search engine companies declined to invest directly in China due to concerns over censorship, what do you think the results would be? Who would benefit most from this action? Who would lose the most?

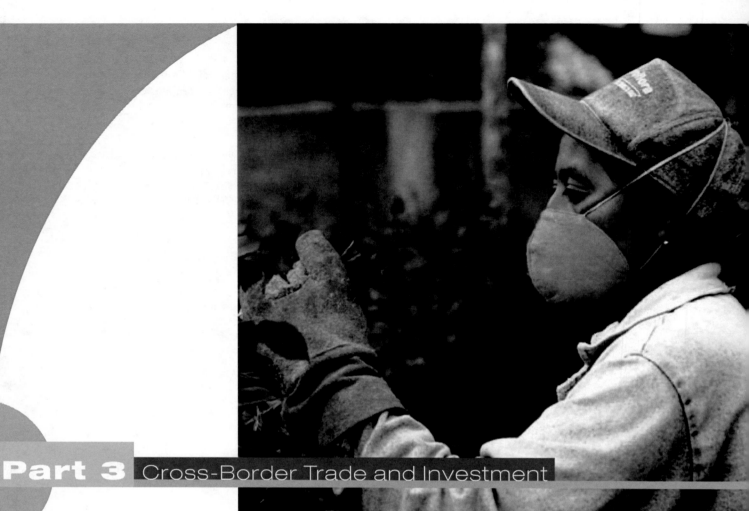

Part 3   Cross-Border Trade and Investment

LEARNING OBJECTIVES

After you have read this chapter you should:

1   Understand why nations trade with each other.

2   Be familiar with the different theories explaining trade flows between nations.

3   Understand why many economists believe that unrestricted free trade between nations will raise the economic welfare of countries that participate in a free trade system.

4   Be familiar with the arguments of those who maintain that government can play a proactive role in promoting national competitive advantage in certain industries.

5   Understand the important implications that international trade theory holds for business practice.

chapter 5

International Trade Theory

The Ecuadorean Rose Industry

opening case

It is 6:20 a.m. February 7 in the Ecuadorean town of Cayambe, and Maria Pacheco has just been dropped off for work by the company bus. She pulls on thick rubber gloves, wraps an apron over her white, traditional embroidered dress, and grabs her clippers, ready for another long day. Any other time of year, Maria would work until 2 p.m., but it's a week before Valentine's Day, and Maria along with her 84 co-workers at the farm are likely to be busy until 5 p.m. By then, Maria will have cut more than 1,000 rose stems.

A few days later, after they have been refrigerated and shipped via aircraft, the roses Maria cut will be selling for premium prices in stores from New York to London. Ecuadorean roses are quickly becoming the Rolls-Royce of roses. They have huge heads and unusually vibrant colors, including 10 different reds, from bleeding heart crimson to a rosy lover's blush.

Most of Ecuador's 460 or so rose farms are located in the Cayambe and Cotopaxi regions, 10,000 feet up in the Andes about an hour's drive from the capital, Quito. The rose bushes are planted in huge flat fields at the foot of snowcapped volcanoes that rise to more than 20,000 feet. The bushes are protected by 20-foot-high canopies of plastic sheeting. The combination of intense sunlight, fertile volcanic soil, an equatorial location, and high altitude makes for ideal growing conditions, allowing roses to flower almost year-round. Ecuador apparently has a comparative advantage in the production of roses.

Ecuador's rose industry started some 20 years ago and has been expanding rapidly since. Ecuador is now the world's fourth largest producer of roses. Roses are the nation's fifth largest export, with customers all over the world. Rose farms generate $240 million in sales and support tens of thousands of jobs. In Cayambe, the population has increased in 10 years from 10,000 to 70,000, primarily as a result of the rose industry. The revenues and taxes from rose growers have helped to pave roads, build schools, and construct sophisticated irrigation systems.

Maria works Monday to Saturday, and earns $210 a month, which she says is an average wage in Ecuador and substantially above the country's $120 a month minimum wage. The farm also provides her with health care and a pension. By employing women such as Maria, the industry has fostered a social revolution in which mothers and wives have more control over their family's spending, especially on schooling for their children.

For all of the benefits that roses have bought to Ecuador, where the gross national income per capita is only $1,080 a year, the industry has come under fire from environmentalists. Large growers have been accused of misusing a toxic mixture of pesticides, fungicides, and fumigants to grow and export unblemished pest-free flowers. Reports claim that workers often fumigate roses in street clothes without protective equipment. Some doctors and scientists say that many of the industry's 50,000 employees have serious health problems as a result of exposure to toxic chemicals. A study by the International Labor Organization reported that women in the industry had more miscarriages than average and that some 60 percent of all workers suffered from headaches, nausea, blurred vision, and fatigue. Still, the critics acknowledge that their studies have been hindered by a lack of access to the farms, and they do not know what the true situation is. The International Labor Organization has also said that some rose growers in Ecuador use child labor, a claim that has been strenuously rejected by both the growers and Ecuadorean government agencies.

In Europe, consumer groups have urged the European Union to press for improved environmental safeguards. In response, some Ecuadorean growers have joined a voluntary program aimed at helping customers identify responsible growers. The certification signifies that the grower has distributed protective gear, trained workers in using chemicals, and hired doctors to visit workers at least weekly. Other environmental groups have pushed for stronger sanctions, including trade sanctions, against Ecuadorean rose growers that are not environmentally certified by a reputable agency. On February 14, however, most consumers are oblivious to these issues; they simply want to show their appreciation to their wives and girlfriends with a perfect bunch of roses. ●

Sources: G. Thompson, "Behind Roses' Beauty, Poor and Ill Workers," *The New York Times,* February 13, 2003, pp. A1, A27; J. Stuart, "You've Come a Long Way Baby," *The Independent,* February 14, 2003, p. 1; V. Marino, "By Any Other Name, It's Usually a Rosa," *The New York Times,* May 11, 2003, p. A9; A. DePalma, "In Trade Issue, the Pressure Is on Flowers," *The New York Times,* January 24, 2002, p. 1; and "The Search for Roses Without Thorns," *The Economist,* February 18, 2006, p. 38.

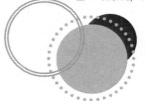

Introduction

The Ecuadorean rose industry is a striking example of the benefits of free trade and globalization. Lower barriers to trade have allowed Ecuador to exploit its comparative advantage in the growing of roses and enabled the country to emerge as one of the world's largest exporters of roses. This benefits Ecuador, where economic growth and personal incomes have been bolstered by the emergence of the rose growing industry. It also benefits consumers in developed nations, who now have access to affordable high-quality roses from Ecuador. February is not exactly the best time for growing roses in New York State, but thanks to free trade, a New Yorker can now buy a bunch of fresh roses for his beloved on February 14 that were picked in Ecuador only 24 hours earlier. It also benefits foreigners who export goods and services to Ecuador, for a stronger Ecuadorean economy can purchase more of those goods and services. If there are losers in this process, they are high-cost rose producers in places like Florida, who have lost business to the Ecuadoreans. In the world of international trade, there are always winners and losers, but as economists have long argued, the benefits to the winners outweigh the costs born by the losers, resulting in a net gain to society. Also, economists argue that in the long run, free trade stimulates economic growth and raises living standards across the board.

The economic arguments surrounding the benefits and costs of free trade in goods and services are not abstract academic ones. International trade theory has shaped the economic policy of many nations for the past 50 years. It was the driver behind the formation of the World Trade Organization and regional trade blocs such as the European Union and the North American Free Trade Agreement (NAFTA). The 1990s, in particular, saw a global move toward greater free trade. It is crucially important to understand, therefore, what these theories are and why they have been so successful in shaping the economic policy of so many nations and the competitive environment in which international businesses compete.

This chapter has two goals that go to the heart of the debate over the benefits and costs of free trade. The first is to review a number of theories that explain why it is beneficial for a country to engage in international trade. The second goal is to explain the pattern of international trade that we observe in the world economy. With regard to the pattern of trade, we will be primarily concerned with explaining the pattern of exports and imports of goods and services between countries. We will not be concerned with the pattern of foreign direct investment between countries; that is discussed in Chapter 7.

An Overview of Trade Theory

We open this chapter with a discussion of mercantilism. Propagated in the 16th and 17th centuries, mercantilism advocated that countries should simultaneously encourage exports and discourage imports. Although mercantilism is an old and largely discredited doctrine, its echoes remain in modern political debate and in the trade policies of many countries. Next, we will look at Adam Smith's theory of absolute advantage. Proposed in 1776, Smith's theory was the first to explain why unrestricted free trade is beneficial to a country. **Free trade** refers to a situation where a government does not attempt to influence through quotas or duties what its citizens can buy from another country, or what they can produce and sell to another country. Smith argued that the invisible hand of the market mechanism, rather than government policy, should determine what a country imports and what it exports. His arguments imply that such a laissez-faire stance toward trade was in the best interests of a country. Building on Smith's work are two additional theories that we shall review. One is the theory of comparative advantage, advanced by the 19th century English economist David Ricardo. This theory is the intellectual basis of the modern argument for unrestricted free trade. In the 20th century, Ricardo's work was refined by two Swedish economists, Eli Heckscher and Bertil Ohlin, whose theory is known as the Heckscher-Ohlin theory.

Free Trade
The absence of government-imposed barriers, such as quotas or duties, that impede the free flow of goods and services between countries.

LEARNING OBJECTIVE 1
Understand why nations trade with each other.

THE BENEFITS OF TRADE   The great strength of the theories of Smith, Ricardo, and Heckscher-Ohlin is that they identify with precision the specific benefits of international trade. Common sense suggests that some international trade is beneficial. For example, nobody would suggest that Iceland should grow its own oranges. Iceland can benefit from trade by exchanging some of the products that it can produce at a low cost (fish) for some products that it cannot produce at all (oranges). Thus, by engaging in international trade, Icelanders are able to add oranges to their diet of fish.

The theories of Smith, Ricardo, and Heckscher-Ohlin go beyond this common-sense notion, however, to show why it is beneficial for a country to engage in international trade *even for products it is able to produce for itself.* This is a difficult concept for people to grasp. For example, many people in the United States believe that American consumers should buy products made in the United States by American companies whenever possible to help save American jobs from foreign competition. The same kind of nationalistic sentiments can be observed in many other countries.

However, the theories of Smith, Ricardo, and Heckscher-Ohlin tell us that a country's economy may gain if its citizens buy certain products from other nations that could be produced at home. The gains arise because international trade allows a country to specialize in the manufacture and export of products that can be produced most efficiently in that country, while importing products that can be produced more efficiently in other countries. Thus it may make sense for the United States to specialize in the production and export of commercial jet aircraft, since the efficient production of commercial jet aircraft requires resources that are abundant in the United States, such as a highly skilled labor force and cutting-edge technological know-how. On the other hand, it may make sense for the United States to import textiles from China since the efficient production of textiles requires a relatively cheap labor force—and cheap labor is not abundant in the United States.

Of course, this economic argument is often difficult for segments of a country's population to accept. With their future threatened by imports, U.S. textile companies and their employees have tried hard to persuade the government to limit the importation of textiles by demanding quotas and tariffs. Although such import controls may benefit particular groups, such as textile businesses and their employees, the theories of Smith, Ricardo, and Heckscher-Ohlin suggest that the economy as a whole is hurt by such action. Limits on imports are often in the interests of domestic producers, but not domestic consumers.

Another Perspective

Outsourcing: Putting Jobs into Growing Markets
Another way of looking at the hollowing out of the American knowledge-based economy through outsourcing is to see the process from the perspective of developing nations. To them, outsourcing brings with it the benefits of trade. It is one of the positive outcomes of globalization. Multinational corporations doing some business in their markets can locate their production in the very markets into which they are selling. As India, the Philippines, and China develop a knowledge-based labor supply, companies like Intel and EMC that are selling into these markets may want to locate some of their research and development and other knowledge-based activities in these markets as a commitment to a local presence, as a way to learn more about the customer, and as a way to establish sustained and sustaining relationships. Yes, there are cost savings, especially on labor, but long term, such cost savings may be secondary.

THE PATTERN OF INTERNATIONAL TRADE   The theories of Smith, Ricardo, and Heckscher-Ohlin help to explain the pattern of international trade that we observe in the world economy. Some aspects of the pattern are easy to understand. Climate and natural resource endowments explain why Ghana exports cocoa, Brazil exports coffee, Saudi Arabia exports oil, and China exports crawfish. However, much of the observed pattern of international trade is more difficult to explain. For example, why does Japan export automobiles, consumer electronics, and machine tools? Why does Switzerland export chemicals, pharmaceuticals, watches, and jewelry? David Ricardo's theory of comparative advantage offers an explanation in terms of international differences in labor productivity. The more sophisticated Heckscher-Ohlin theory emphasizes the interplay between the proportions in which the factors of production (such as land, labor, and capital) are available in different countries and the proportions in which they are needed for producing particular goods. This explanation rests on the assumption that countries have varying endowments of the various factors of production. Tests of this theory, however, suggest that it is a less powerful explanation of real-world trade patterns than once thought.

One early response to the failure of the Heckscher-Ohlin theory to explain the observed pattern of international trade was the product life-cycle theory. Proposed by Raymond Vernon, this theory suggests that early in their life cycle, most new products are produced in and exported from the country in which they were developed. As a new product becomes widely accepted internationally, however, production starts in other countries. As a result, the theory suggests, the product may ultimately be exported back to the country of its original innovation.

In a similar vein, during the 1980s economists such as Paul Krugman developed what has come to be known as the new trade theory. **New trade theory** stresses that in some cases, countries specialize in the production and export of particular products not because of underlying differences in factor endowments, but because in certain industries the world market can support only a limited number of firms. (This is argued to be the case for the commercial aircraft industry.) In such industries, firms that enter the market first are able to build a competitive advantage that is subsequently difficult to challenge. Thus, the observed pattern of trade between nations may be due in part to the ability of firms within a given nation to capture first-mover advantages. The United States is a major exporter of commercial jet aircraft because American firms such as Boeing were first movers in the world market. Boeing built a competitive advantage that has subsequently been difficult for firms from countries with equally favorable factor endowments to challenge (although Europe's Airbus Industries has succeeded in doing that). In a work related to the new trade theory, Michael Porter developed a theory, referred to as the theory of national competitive advantage. This attempts to explain why particular nations achieve international success in particular industries. In addition to factor endowments, Porter points out the importance of country factors such as domestic demand and domestic rivalry in explaining a nation's dominance in the production and export of particular products.

> **New trade theory**
> Theory predicts that nations that are home to firms that gained a first mover advantage in certain products may have an advantage in the trade of those products.

TRADE THEORY AND GOVERNMENT POLICY

Although all these theories agree that international trade is beneficial to a country, they lack agreement in their recommendations for government policy. Mercantilism makes a crude case for government involvement in promoting exports and limiting imports. The theories of Smith, Ricardo, and Heckscher-Ohlin form part of the case for unrestricted free trade. The argument for unrestricted free trade is that both import controls and export incentives (such as subsidies) are self-defeating and result in wasted resources. Both the new trade theory and Porter's theory of national competitive advantage can be interpreted as justifying some limited government intervention to support the development of certain export-oriented industries. We will discuss the pros and cons of this argument, known as strategic trade policy, as well as the pros and cons of the argument for unrestricted free trade, in Chapter 6.

Mercantilism

The first theory of international trade, mercantilism, emerged in England in the mid-16th century. The principle assertion of mercantilism was that gold and silver were the mainstays of national wealth and essential to vigorous commerce. At that time, gold and silver were the currency of trade between countries; a country could earn gold and silver by exporting goods. Conversely, importing goods from other countries would result in an outflow of gold and silver to those countries. The main tenet of **mercantilism** was that it was in a country's best interests to maintain a trade surplus, to export more than it imported. By doing so, a country would accumulate gold and silver and, consequently, increase its national wealth, prestige, and power. As the English mercantilist writer Thomas Mun put it in 1630:

> The ordinary means therefore to increase our wealth and treasure is by foreign trade, wherein we must ever observe this rule: to sell more to strangers yearly than we consume of theirs in value.[1]

Consistent with this belief, the mercantilist doctrine advocated government intervention to achieve a surplus in the balance of trade. The mercantilists saw no virtue in a large volume of trade. Rather, they recommended policies to maximize exports and minimize imports. To achieve this, imports were limited by tariffs and quotas, while exports were subsidized.

Country FOCUS

Is China a Neo-Mercantilist Nation?

China's rapid rise in economic power has been built on export-led growth. The country has taken raw material imports from other countries, and using its cheap labor, converted them into products that it sells to developed nations like the United States. For years, the country's exports have been growing faster than its imports, leading some critics to claim that China is pursuing a neo-mercantilist policy, trying to amass record trade surpluses and foreign currency that will give it economic power over developed nations. This rhetoric reached new heights in 2007 when China's trade surplus hit a record $262 billion and its foreign exchange reserves exceeded $1.5 trillion, some 70 percent of which are held in U.S. dollars. Observers worry that if China ever decides to sell its holdings of U.S. currency, this could depress the value of the dollar against other currencies and increase the price of imports into America.

Throughout 2005, 2006, and most of 2007, China's exports grew much faster than its imports, leading some to argue that China was limiting imports by pursuing an import substitution policy, encouraging domestic investment in the production of products such as steel, aluminum, and paper, which it had historically imported from other nations. The trade deficit with the United States has been a particular cause for concern. In 2007, this reached $240 billion, the largest deficit ever recorded with a single country. At the same time, China has long resisted attempts to let its currency float freely against the U.S. dollar. Many claim that China's currency is too cheap, and that this keeps the prices of China's goods artificially low, which fuels the country's exports.

So is China a neo-mercantilist nation that is deliberately discouraging imports and encouraging exports in order to grow its trade surplus and accumulate foreign exchange reserves, which might give it economic power? The jury is out on this issue. Skeptics suggest that the slowdown in imports to China is temporary and that the country will have no choice but to increase its imports of commodities that it lacks, such as oil. They also note that China did start allowing the value of the *renminbi* (China's currency) to appreciate against the dollar in July 2005, and between then and January 2008 it appreciated 12 percent in value. Also, although China's overall trade surplus was up sharply in 2007, import growth exceeded export growth for the last three months of 2007, suggesting that China's trade surplus may have peaked.

Sources: A. Browne, "China's Wild Swings Can Roil the Global Economy, *The Wall Street Journal,* October 24, 2005, p. A2; S.H. Hanke, "Stop the Mercantilists," *Forbes,* June 20, 2005, p. 164; G. Dyer and A. Balls, "Dollar Threat as China Signals Shift," *Financial Times,* January 6, 2006, p. 1; Tim Annett, "Righting the Balance," *The Wall Street Journal,* January 10, 2007, p. 15; and "China's Trade Surplus Peaks," *Financial Times,* January 12, 2008, p. 1.

Hill: Global Business
Today, Sixth Edition

5. International Trade
Theory

Text

© The McGraw–Hill
Companies, 2009

175

The classical economist David Hume pointed out an inherent inconsistency in the mercantilist doctrine in 1752. According to Hume, if England had a balance-of-trade surplus with France (it exported more than it imported), the resulting inflow of gold and silver would swell the domestic money supply and generate inflation in England. In France, however, the outflow of gold and silver would have the opposite effect. France's money supply would contract, and its prices would fall. This change in relative prices between France and England would encourage the French to buy fewer English goods (because they were becoming more expensive) and the English to buy more French goods (because they were becoming cheaper). The result would be a deterioration in the English balance of trade and an improvement in France's trade balance, until the English surplus was eliminated. Hence, according to Hume, in the long run no country could sustain a surplus on the balance of trade and so accumulate gold and silver as the mercantilists had envisaged.

The flaw with mercantilism was that it viewed trade as a zero-sum game. (A **zero-sum game** is one in which a gain by one country results in a loss by another.) It was left to Adam Smith and David Ricardo to show the shortsightedness of this approach and to demonstrate that trade is a positive-sum game, or a situation in which all countries can benefit. Unfortunately, the mercantilist doctrine is by no means dead. Neo-mercantilists equate political power with economic power and economic power with a balance-of-trade surplus. Critics argue that many nations have adopted a neo-mercantilist strategy that is designed to simultaneously boost exports and limit imports.[2] For example, critics charge that China is pursuing a neo-mercantilist policy, deliberately keeping its currency value low against the U.S. dollar in order to sell more goods to the United States, and thus amass a trade surplus and foreign exchange reserves (see the accompanying Country Focus).

Zero-Sum Game
A situation in which a gain by one country results in a loss by another.

Absolute Advantage

In his 1776 landmark book *The Wealth of Nations*, Adam Smith attacked the mercantilist assumption that trade is a zero-sum game. Smith argued that countries differ in their ability to produce goods efficiently. In his time, the English, by virtue of their superior manufacturing processes, were the world's most efficient textile manufacturers. Due to the combination of favorable climate, good soils, and accumulated expertise, the French had the world's most efficient wine industry. The English had an *absolute advantage* in the production of textiles, while the French had an *absolute advantage* in the production of wine. Thus, a country has an **absolute advantage** in the production of a product when it is more efficient than any other country in producing it.

According to Smith, countries should specialize in the production of goods for which they have an absolute advantage and then trade these for goods produced by other countries. In Smith's time, this suggested that the English should specialize in the production of textiles while the French should specialize in the production of wine. England could get all the wine it needed by selling its textiles to France and buying wine in exchange. Similarly, France could get all the textiles it needed by selling wine to England and buying textiles in exchange. Smith's basic argument, therefore, is that a country should never produce goods at home that it can buy at a lower cost from other countries. Smith demonstrates that, by specializing in the production of goods in which each has an absolute advantage, both countries benefit by engaging in trade.

Consider the effects of trade between two countries, Ghana and South Korea. The production of any good (output) requires resources (inputs) such as land, labor, and capital. Assume that Ghana and South Korea both have the same amount of resources and that these resources can be used to produce either rice or cocoa. Assume further that 200 units of resources are available in each country. Imagine that in Ghana it

LEARNING OBJECTIVE 2
Be familiar with the different theories explaining trade flows between nations.

Absolute Advantage
When one country is more efficient than any other country in producing a particular product.

figure 5.1

The Theory of
Absolute Advantage

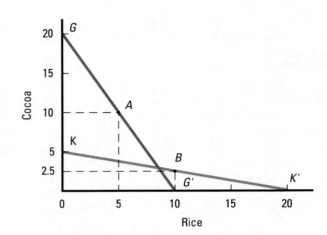

takes 10 resources to produce one ton of cocoa and 20 resources to produce one ton of rice. Thus, Ghana could produce 20 tons of cocoa and no rice, 10 tons of rice and no cocoa, or some combination of rice and cocoa between these two extremes. The different combinations that Ghana could produce are represented by the line GG' in Figure 5.1. This is referred to as Ghana's *production possibility frontier* (PPF). Similarly, imagine that in South Korea it takes 40 resources to produce 1 ton of cocoa and 10 resources to produce 1 ton of rice. Thus, South Korea could produce 5 tons of cocoa and no rice, 20 tons of rice and no cocoa, or some combination between these two extremes. The different combinations available to South Korea are represented by the line KK' in Figure 5.1, which is South Korea's PPF. Clearly, Ghana has an absolute advantage in the production of cocoa. (More resources are needed to produce a ton of cocoa in South Korea than in Ghana.) By the same token, South Korea has an absolute advantage in the production of rice.

Now consider a situation in which neither country trades with any other. Each country devotes half of its resources to the production of rice and half to the production of cocoa. Each country must also consume what it produces. Ghana would be able to produce 10 tons of cocoa and 5 tons of rice (point A in Figure 5.1), while South Korea would be able to produce 10 tons of rice and 2.5 tons of cocoa. Without trade, the combined production of both countries would be 12.5 tons of cocoa (10 tons in Ghana plus 2.5 tons in South Korea) and 15 tons of rice (5 tons in Ghana and 10 tons in South Korea). If each country were to specialize in producing the good for which it had an absolute advantage and then trade with the other for the good it lacks, Ghana could produce 20 tons of cocoa, and South Korea could produce 20 tons of rice. Thus, by specializing, the production of both goods could be increased. Production of cocoa would increase from 12.5 tons to 20 tons, while production of rice would increase from 15 tons to 20 tons. The increase in production that would result from specialization is therefore 7.5 tons of cocoa and 5 tons of rice. Table 5.1 summarizes these figures.

By engaging in trade and swapping 1 ton of cocoa for 1 ton of rice, producers in both countries could consume more of both cocoa and rice. Imagine that Ghana and South Korea swap cocoa and rice on a one-to-one basis; that is, the price of one ton of cocoa is equal to the price of one ton of rice. If Ghana decided to export 6 tons of cocoa to South Korea and import 6 tons of rice in return, its final consumption after trade would be 14 tons of cocoa and 6 tons of rice. This is 4 tons more cocoa than it could have consumed before specialization and trade and 1 ton more rice. Similarly, South Korea's final consumption after trade would be 6 tons of cocoa and 14 tons of

Resources Required to Produce 1 Ton of Cocoa and Rice		
	Cocoa	**Rice**
Ghana	10	20
South Korea	40	10
Production and Consumption without Trade		
	Cocoa	**Rice**
Ghana	10.0	5.0
South Korea	2.5	10.0
Total production	12.5	15.0
Production with Specialization		
	Cocoa	**Rice**
Ghana	20.0	0.0
South Korea	0.0	20.0
Total production	20.0	20.0
Consumption after Ghana Trades 6 Tons of Cocoa for 6 Tons of South Korean Rice		
	Cocoa	**Rice**
Ghana	14.0	6.0
South Korea	6.0	14.0
Increase in Consumption as a Result of Specialization and Trade		
	Cocoa	**Rice**
Ghana	4.0	1.0
South Korea	3.5	4.0

5.1 table

Absolute Advantage and the Gains from Trade

rice. This is 3.5 tons more cocoa than it could have consumed before specialization and trade and 4 tons more rice. Thus, as a result of specialization and trade, output of both cocoa and rice would be increased, and consumers in both nations would be able to consume more. Thus, we can see that trade is a positive-sum game; it produces net gains for all involved.

Comparative Advantage

David Ricardo took Adam Smith's theory one step further by exploring what might happen when one country has an absolute advantage in the production of all goods.[3] Smith's theory of absolute advantage suggests that such a country might derive no benefits from international trade. In his 1817 book *The Principles of Political Economy and Taxation*, Ricardo showed that this was not the case. According to Ricardo's theory of comparative advantage, it makes sense for a country to specialize in the production

LEARNING OBJECTIVE 2
Be familiar with the different theories explaining trade flows between nations.

of those goods that it produces most efficiently and to buy the goods that it produces less efficiently from other countries, even if this means buying goods from other countries that it could produce more efficiently itself.[4] While this may seem counterintuitive, the logic can be explained with a simple example.

Assume that Ghana is more efficient in the production of both cocoa and rice; that is, Ghana has an absolute advantage in the production of both products. In Ghana it takes 10 resources to produce 1 ton of cocoa and $13\frac{1}{3}$ resources to produce 1 ton of rice. Thus, given its 200 units of resources, Ghana can produce 20 tons of cocoa and no rice, 15 tons of rice and no cocoa, or any combination in between on its PPF (the line GG' in Figure 5.2). In South Korea it takes 40 resources to produce 1 ton of cocoa and 20 resources to produce 1 ton of rice. Thus, South Korea can produce 5 tons of cocoa and no rice, 10 tons of rice and no cocoa, or any combination on its PPF (the line KK' in Figure 5.2). Again assume that without trade, each country uses half of its resources to produce rice and half to produce cocoa. Thus, without trade, Ghana will produce 10 tons of cocoa and 7.5 tons of rice (point A in Figure 5.2), while South Korea will produce 2.5 tons of cocoa and 5 tons of rice (point B in Figure 5.2).

In light of Ghana's absolute advantage in the production of both goods, why should it trade with South Korea? Although Ghana has an absolute advantage in the production of both cocoa and rice, it has a comparative advantage only in the production of cocoa: Ghana can produce 4 times as much cocoa as South Korea, but only 1.5 times as much rice. Ghana is *comparatively* more efficient at producing cocoa than it is at producing rice.

Without trade the combined production of cocoa will be 12.5 tons (10 tons in Ghana and 2.5 in South Korea), and the combined production of rice will also be 12.5 tons (7.5 tons in Ghana and 5 tons in South Korea). Without trade each country must consume what it produces. By engaging in trade, the two countries can increase their combined production of rice and cocoa, and consumers in both nations can consume more of both goods.

THE GAINS FROM TRADE   Imagine that Ghana exploits its comparative advantage in the production of cocoa to increase its output from 10 tons to 15 tons. This uses up 150 units of resources, leaving the remaining 50 units of resources to use in producing 3.75 tons of rice (point C in Figure 5.2). Meanwhile, South Korea specializes in the production of rice, producing 10 tons. The combined output of both cocoa and rice has now increased. Before specialization, the combined output was 12.5 tons

figure 5.2

The Theory of Comparative Advantage

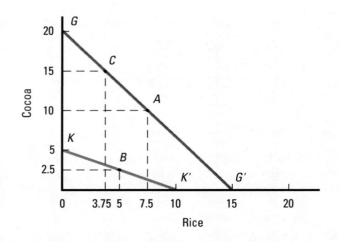

of cocoa and 12.5 tons of rice. Now it is 15 tons of cocoa and 13.75 tons of rice (3.75 tons in Ghana and 10 tons in South Korea). The source of the increase in production is summarized in Table 5.2.

Not only is output higher, but both countries also can now benefit from trade. If Ghana and South Korea swap cocoa and rice on a one-to-one basis, with both countries choosing to exchange 4 tons of their export for 4 tons of the import, both countries are able to consume more cocoa and rice than they could before specialization and trade (see Table 5.2). Thus, if Ghana exchanges 4 tons of cocoa with South Korea for 4 tons of rice, it is still left with 11 tons of cocoa, which is 1 ton more than it had before trade. The 4 tons of rice it gets from South Korea in exchange for its 4 tons of cocoa, when added to the 3.75 tons it now produces domestically, leaves it with a total of 7.75 tons of rice, which is 0.25 of a ton more than it had before specialization. Similarly, after swapping 4 tons of rice with Ghana, South Korea still ends up with 6 tons of rice,

Resources Required to Produce 1 Ton of Cocoa and Rice		
	Cocoa	Rice
Ghana	10	13.33
South Korea	40	20
Production and Consumption without Trade		
	Cocoa	Rice
Ghana	10.0	7.5
South Korea	2.5	5.0
Total production	12.5	12.5
Production with Specialization		
	Cocoa	Rice
Ghana	15.0	3.75
South Korea	0.0	10.0
Total production	15.0	13.75
Consumption after Ghana Trades 4 Tons of Cocoa for 4 Tons of South Korean Rice		
	Cocoa	Rice
Ghana	11.0	7.75
South Korea	4.0	6.0
Increase in Consumption as a Result of Specialization and Trade		
	Cocoa	Rice
Ghana	1.0	0.25
South Korea	1.5	1.0

5.2 table

Comparative Advantage and the Gains from Trade

which is more than it had before specialization. In addition, the 4 tons of cocoa it receives in exchange is 1.5 tons more than it produced before trade. Thus, consumption of cocoa and rice can increase in both countries as a result of specialization and trade.

The basic message of the theory of comparative advantage is that *potential world production is greater with unrestricted free trade than it is with restricted trade*. Ricardo's theory suggests that consumers in all nations can consume more if there are no restrictions on trade. This occurs even in countries that lack an absolute advantage in the production of any good. In other words, to an even greater degree than the theory of absolute advantage, *the theory of comparative advantage suggests that trade is a positive-sum game in which all countries that participate realize economic gains*. As such, this theory provides a strong rationale for encouraging free trade. So powerful is Ricardo's theory that it remains a major intellectual weapon for those who argue for free trade.

LEARNING OBJECTIVE 3
Understand why many economists believe that unrestricted free trade between nations will raise the economic welfare of countries that participate in a free trade system.

QUALIFICATIONS AND ASSUMPTIONS   The conclusion that free trade is universally beneficial is a rather bold one to draw from such a simple model. Our simple model includes many unrealistic assumptions:

1. We have assumed a simple world in which there are only two countries and two goods. In the real world, there are many countries and many goods.
2. We have assumed away transportation costs between countries.
3. We have assumed away differences in the prices of resources in different countries. We have said nothing about exchange rates, simply assuming that cocoa and rice could be swapped on a one-to-one basis.
4. We have assumed that resources can move freely from the production of one good to another within a country. In reality, this is not always the case.
5. We have assumed constant returns to scale; that is, that specialization by Ghana or South Korea has no effect on the amount of resources required to produce one ton of cocoa or rice. In reality, both diminishing and increasing returns to specialization exist. The amount of resources required to produce a good might decrease or increase as a nation specializes in production of that good.
6. We have assumed that each country has a fixed stock of resources and that free trade does not change the efficiency with which a country uses its resources. This static assumption makes no allowances for the dynamic changes in a country's stock of resources and in the efficiency with which the country uses its resources that might result from free trade.
7. We have assumed away the effects of trade on income distribution within a country.

Given these assumptions, can the conclusion that free trade is mutually beneficial be extended to the real world of many countries, many goods, positive transportation costs, volatile exchange rates, immobile domestic resources, nonconstant returns to specialization, and dynamic changes? Although a detailed extension of the theory of comparative advantage is beyond the scope of this book, economists have shown that the basic result derived from our simple model can be generalized to a world composed of many countries producing many different goods.[5] Despite the shortcomings of the Ricardian model, research suggests that the basic proposition that countries will export the goods that they are most efficient at producing is borne out by the data.[6]

However, once all the assumptions are dropped, the case for unrestricted free trade, while still positive, has been argued by some economists associated with the "new trade theory" to lose some of its strength.[7] We return to this issue later in this chapter and in the next when we discuss the new trade theory. In a recent and widely discussed analysis, the Nobel Prize-winning economist Paul Samuelson argued that contrary to the standard interpretation, in certain circumstances the theory of comparative advantage predicts that a rich country might actually be *worse* off by switching to a free trade regime with a poor nation.[8] We will consider Samuelson's critique in the next section.

EXTENSIONS OF THE RICARDIAN MODEL

Let us explore the effect of relaxing three of the assumptions identified earlier in the simple comparative advantage model. Next we relax the assumptions that resources move freely from the production of one good to another within a country, that there are constant returns to scale, and that trade does not change a country's stock of resources or the efficiency with which those resources are utilized.

Immobile Resources

In our simple comparative model of Ghana and South Korea, we assumed that producers (farmers) could easily convert land from the production of cocoa to rice, and vice versa. While this assumption may hold for some agricultural products, resources do not always shift quite so easily from producing one good to another. A certain amount of friction is involved. For example, embracing a free trade regime for an advanced economy such as the United States often implies that the country will produce less of some labor-intensive goods, such as textiles, and more of some knowledge-intensive goods, such as computer software or biotechnology products. Although the country as a whole will gain from such a shift, textile producers will lose. A textile worker in South Carolina is probably not qualified to write software for Microsoft. Thus, the shift to free trade may mean that she becomes unemployed or has to accept another less attractive job, such as working at a fast-food restaurant.

Resources do not always move easily from one economic activity to another. The process creates friction and human suffering too. While the theory predicts that the benefits of free trade outweigh the costs by a significant margin, this is of cold comfort to those who bear the costs. Accordingly, political opposition to the adoption of a free trade regime typically comes from those whose jobs are most at risk. In the United States, for example, textile workers and their unions have long opposed the move toward free trade precisely because this group has much to lose from free trade. Governments often ease the transition toward free trade by helping to retrain those who lose their jobs as a result. The pain caused by the movement toward a free trade regime is a short-term phenomenon, while the gains from trade once the transition has been made are both significant and enduring.

Diminishing Returns

The simple comparative advantage model developed earlier assumes constant returns to specialization. By **constant returns to specialization** we mean the units of resources required to produce a good (cocoa or rice) are assumed to remain constant no matter where one is on a country's production possibility frontier (PPF). Thus, we assumed that it always took Ghana 10 units of resources to produce 1 ton of cocoa. However, it is more realistic to assume diminishing returns to specialization. Diminishing returns to specialization occurs when more units of resources are required to produce each additional unit. While 10 units of resources may be sufficient to increase Ghana's output of cocoa from 12 tons to 13 tons, 11 units of resources may be needed to increase output from 13 to 14 tons, 12 units of resources to increase output from 14 tons to 15 tons, and so on. Diminishing returns implies a convex PPF for Ghana (see Figure 5.3), rather than the straight line depicted in Figure 5.2.

It is more realistic to assume diminishing returns for two reasons. First, not all resources are of the same quality. As a country tries to increase its output of a certain good, it is increasingly likely to draw on more marginal resources whose productivity is not as great as those initially employed. The result is that it requires ever more resources to produce an equal increase in output. For example, some land is more

Constant Returns to Specialization
Costs stay the same as specialization increases.

figure 5.3

Ghana's PPF under Diminishing Returns

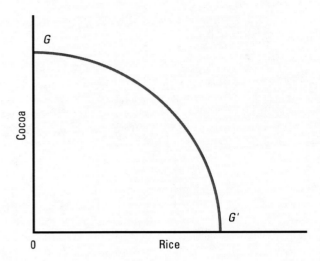

productive than other land. As Ghana tries to expand its output of cocoa, it might have to utilize increasingly marginal land that is less fertile than the land it originally used. As yields per acre decline, Ghana must use more land to produce one ton of cocoa.

A second reason for diminishing returns is that different goods use resources in different proportions. For example, imagine that growing cocoa uses more land and less labor than growing rice, and that Ghana tries to transfer resources from rice production to cocoa production. The rice industry will release proportionately too much labor and too little land for efficient cocoa production. To absorb the additional resources of labor and land, the cocoa industry will have to shift toward more labor-intensive methods of production. The effect is that the efficiency with which the cocoa industry uses labor will decline, and returns will diminish.

Diminishing returns show that it is not feasible for a country to specialize to the degree suggested by the simple Ricardian model outlined earlier. Diminishing returns to specialization suggest that the gains from specialization are likely to be exhausted before specialization is complete. In reality, most countries do not specialize, but instead, produce a range of goods. However, the theory predicts that it is worthwhile to specialize until that point where the resulting gains from trade are outweighed by diminishing returns. Thus, the basic conclusion that unrestricted free trade is beneficial still holds, although because of diminishing returns, the gains may not be as great as suggested in the constant returns case.

LEARNING OBJECTIVE 3
Understand why many economists believe that unrestricted free trade between nations will raise the economic welfare of countries that participate in a free trade system.

Dynamic Effects and Economic Growth   The simple comparative advantage model assumed that trade does not change a country's stock of resources or the efficiency with which it utilizes those resources. This static assumption makes no allowances for the dynamic changes that might result from trade. If we relax this assumption, it becomes apparent that opening an economy to trade is likely to generate dynamic gains of two sorts.[9] First, free trade might increase a country's stock of resources as increased supplies of labor and capital from abroad become available for use within the country. For example, this has been occurring in Eastern Europe since the early 1990s, with many Western businesses have been investing significant capital in the former Communist countries.

Second, free trade might also increase the efficiency with which a country uses its resources. Gains in the efficiency of resource utilization could arise from a number of factors. For example, economies of large-scale production might become available as trade expands the size of the total market available to domestic firms. Trade might make better technology from abroad available to domestic firms; better technology can increase labor productivity or the productivity of land. (The so-called green revolution had this effect on agricultural outputs in developing countries.) Also, opening an economy to foreign competition might stimulate domestic producers to look for ways to increase their efficiency. Again, this phenomenon has arguably been occurring in the once-protected markets of Eastern Europe, where many former state monopolies have had to increase the efficiency of their operations to survive in the competitive world market.

Dynamic gains in both the stock of a country's resources and the efficiency with which resources are utilized will cause a country's PPF to shift outward. This is illustrated in Figure 5.4, where the shift from PPF1 to PPF2 results from the dynamic gains that arise from free trade. As a consequence of this outward shift, the country in Figure 5.4 can produce more of both goods than it did before introduction of free trade. The theory suggests that opening an economy to free trade not only results in static gains of the type discussed earlier, but also results in dynamic gains that stimulate economic growth. If this is so, then one might think that the case for free trade becomes stronger still, and in general it does. However, as noted earlier, in a recent article one of the leading economic theorists of the 20th century, Paul Samuelson, argued that in some circumstances, dynamic gains can lead to an outcome that is not so beneficial.

The Samuelson Critique Paul Samuelson's critique looks at what happens when a rich country—the United States—enters into a free trade agreement with a poor country—China—that rapidly improves its productivity after the introduction of a free trade regime (i.e., there is a dynamic gain in the efficiency with which resources are used in the poor country). Samuelson's model suggests that in such cases, the lower prices that U.S. consumers pay for goods imported from China following the introduction of a free trade regime *may* not be enough to produce a net gain for the U.S. economy if the dynamic effect of free trade is to lower real wage rates in the United States. As he stated in a *New York Times* interview, "Being able to purchase groceries 20 percent cheaper at Wal-Mart (due to international trade) does not necessarily make up for the wage losses (in America)."[10]

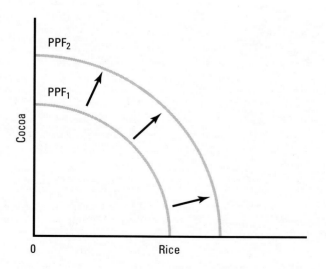

5.4 figure

The Influence of Free Trade on the PPF

Samuelson goes on to note that he is particularly concerned about the ability to off-shore service jobs that traditionally were not internationally mobile, such as software debugging, call center jobs, accounting jobs, and even medical diagnosis of MRI scans (see the accompanying Country Focus for details). Recent advances in communications technology have made this possible, effectively expanding the labor market for these jobs to include educated people in places such as India, the Philippines, and China. When coupled with rapid advances in the productivity of foreign labor due to better education, the effect on middle-class wages in the United States, according to Samuelson, may be similar to mass inward migration into the United States—it will lower the market clearing wage rate, *perhaps* by enough to outweigh the positive benefits of international trade.

However, Samuelson concedes that free trade has historically benefited rich counties (as data discussed later seem to confirm). Also, he notes that introducing protectionist measures (e.g., trade barriers) to guard against the theoretical possibility that free trade may harm the United States in the future may produce a situation that is worse than the disease they are trying to prevent. To quote Samuelson: "Free trade may turn out pragmatically to be still best for each region in comparison to lobbyist-induced tariffs and quotas which involve both a perversion of democracy and nonsubtle deadweight distortion losses."[11]

Some economists have been quick to dismiss Samuelson's fears.[12] While not questioning his analysis, they note that as a practical matter developing nations are unlikely to be able to upgrade the skill level of their workforce rapidly enough to give rise to the situation in Samuelson's model. In other words, they will quickly run into diminishing returns. To quote one such rebuttal: "The notion that India and China will quickly educate 300 million of their citizens to acquire sophisticated and complex skills at stake borders on the ludicrous. The educational sectors in these countries face enormous difficulties."[13] Notwithstanding such rebuttals, however, Samuelson's stature is such that his work will undoubtedly be debated for some time to come.

Evidence for the Link Between Trade and Growth

Many economic studies have looked at the relationship between trade and economic growth.[14] In general, these studies suggest that, as predicted by the standard theory of comparative advantage, countries that adopt a more open stance toward international trade enjoy higher growth rates than those that close their economies to trade (the opening case provides evidence of the link between trade and growth). Jeffrey Sachs and Andrew Warner created a measure of how "open" to international trade an economy was and then looked at the relationship between "openness" and economic growth for a sample of more than 100 countries from 1970 to 1990.[15] Among other findings, they reported:

> We find a strong association between openness and growth, both within the group of developing and the group of developed countries. Within the group of developing countries, the open economies grew at 4.49 percent per year, and the closed economies grew at 0.69 percent per year. Within the group of developed economies, the open economies grew at 2.29 percent per year, and the closed economies grew at 0.74 percent per year.[16]

A study by Wacziarg and Welch updated the Sachs and Warner data through the late 1990s. They found that from 1950 to 1998, countries that liberalized their trade regimes experienced, on average, increases in their annual growth rates of 1.5 percent compared to preliberalization times.[17]

The message of these studies seems clear: Adopt an open economy and embrace free trade, and your nation will be rewarded with higher economic growth rates.

Country FOCUS

Moving U.S. White Collar Jobs Offshore

Economists have long argued that free trade produces gains for all countries that participate in a free trading system, but as the next wave of globalization sweeps through the U.S. economy, many people are wondering if this is true, particularly those who stand to lose their jobs because of this wave of globalization. In the popular imagination for much of the past quarter century, free trade was associated with the movement of low-skill, blue-collar manufacturing jobs out of rich countries such as the United States and toward low-wage countries—textiles to Costa Rica, athletic shoes to the Philippines, steel to Brazil, electronic products to Malaysia, and so on. While many observers bemoaned the "hollowing out" of U.S. manufacturing, economists stated that high-skilled and high-wage, white-collar jobs associated with the knowledge-based economy would stay in the United States. Computers might be assembled in Malaysia, so the argument went, but they would continue to be designed in Silicon Valley by high-skilled U.S. engineers.

Recent developments have some people questioning this assumption. As the global economy slowed after 2000 and corporate profits slumped, many American companies responded by moving white-collar "knowledge-based" jobs to developing nations where they could be performed for a fraction of the cost. During the long economic boom of the 1990s, Bank of America had to compete with other organizations for the scarce talents of information technology specialists, driving annual salaries to more than $100,000. However, with business under pressure, between 2002 and early 2003 the bank cut nearly 5,000 jobs from its 25,000-strong, U.S.-based information technology workforce. Some of these jobs were transferred to India, where work that costs $100 an hour in the United States can be done for $20 an hour.

One beneficiary of Bank of America's downsizing is Infosys Technologies Ltd., a Bangalore, India, information technology firm where 250 engineers now develop information

technology applications for the bank. Other Infosys employees are busy processing home loan applications for Greenpoint Mortgage of Novato, California. Nearby in the offices of another Indian firm, Wipro Ltd., five radiologists interpret 30 CT scans a day for Massachusetts General Hospital that are sent over the Internet. At yet another Bangalore business, engineers earn $10,000 a year designing leading-edge semiconductor chips for Texas Instruments. Nor is India the only beneficiary of these changes. Accenture, a large U.S. management consulting and information technology firm, moved 5,000 jobs in software development and accounting to the Philippines. Also in the Philippines, Procter & Gamble employs 650 professionals who prepare the company's global tax returns. The work used to be done in the United States, but now it is done in Manila, with just final submission to local tax authorities in the United States and other countries handled locally.

Some architectural work also is being outsourced to lower-cost locations. Flour Corp., a California-based construction company, employs some 1,200 engineers and draftsmen in the Philippines, Poland, and India to turn layouts of industrial facilities into detailed specifications. For a Saudi Arabian chemical plant Flour is designing, 200 young engineers based in the Philippines earning less than $3,000 a year collaborate in real time over the Internet with elite U.S. and British engineers who make up to $90,000 a year. Why does Flour do this? According to the company, the answer is simple. Doing so reduces the prices of a project by 15 percent, giving the company a cost-based competitive advantage in the global market for construction design.

Sources: P. Engardio, A. Bernstein, and M. Kripalani, "Is Your Job Next?" *BusinessWeek*, February 3, 2003, pp. 50–60; "America's Pain, India's Gain," *The Economist*, January 11, 2003, p. 57; and M. Schroeder and T. Aeppel, "Skilled Workers Mount Opposition to Free Trade, Swaying Politicians," *The Wall Street Journal*, October 10, 2003, pp. A1, A11.

Higher growth will raise income levels and living standards. This last point has been confirmed by a study that looked at the relationship between trade and growth in incomes. The study, undertaken by Jeffrey Frankel and David Romer, found that on average, a one percentage point increase in the ratio of a country's trade to its gross domestic product increases income per person by at least one-half percent.[18] For every 10 percent increase in the importance of international trade in an economy, average income levels will rise by at least 5 percent. Despite the short-term adjustment costs associated with adopting a free trade regime, trade would seem to produce greater economic growth and higher living standards in the long run, just as the theory of Ricardo would lead us to expect.[19]

Heckscher-Ohlin Theory

LEARNING OBJECTIVE 2
Be familiar with the different theories explaining trade flows between nations.

Factor Endowments
The extent to which a country is endowed with such resources as land, labor, and capital.

Ricardo's theory stresses that comparative advantage arises from differences in productivity. Thus, whether Ghana is more efficient than South Korea in the production of cocoa depends on how productively it uses its resources. Ricardo stressed labor productivity and argued that differences in labor productivity between nations underlie the notion of comparative advantage. Swedish economists Eli Heckscher (in 1919) and Bertil Ohlin (in 1933) put forward a different explanation of comparative advantage. They argued that comparative advantage arises from differences in national factor endowments.[20] By **factor endowments** they meant the extent to which a country is endowed with such resources as land, labor, and capital. Nations have varying factor endowments, and different factor endowments explain differences in factor costs; specifically, the more abundant a factor, the lower its cost. The Heckscher-Ohlin theory predicts that countries will export those goods that make intensive use of factors that are locally abundant, while importing goods that make intensive use of factors that are locally scarce. Thus, the Heckscher-Ohlin theory attempts to explain the pattern of international trade that we observe in the world economy. Like Ricardo's theory, the Heckscher-Ohlin theory argues that free trade is beneficial. Unlike Ricardo's theory, however, the Heckscher-Ohlin theory argues that the pattern of international trade is determined by differences in factor endowments, rather than differences in productivity.

The Heckscher-Ohlin theory has commonsense appeal. For example, the United States has long been a substantial exporter of agricultural goods, reflecting in part its unusual abundance of arable land. In contrast, China excels in the export of goods produced in labor-intensive manufacturing industries, such as textiles and footwear. This reflects China's relative abundance of low-cost labor. The United States, which lacks abundant low-cost labor, has been a primary importer of these goods. Note that it is relative, not absolute, endowments that are important; a country may have larger absolute amounts of land and labor than another country, but be relatively abundant in one of them.

THE LEONTIEF PARADOX

The Heckscher-Ohlin theory has been one of the most influential theoretical ideas in international economics. Most economists prefer the Heckscher-Ohlin theo ry to Ricardo's theory because it makes fewer simplifying assumptions. Because of its influence, the theory has been subjected to many empirical tests. Beginning with a famous study published in 1953 by Wassily Leontief (winner of the Nobel Prize in economics in 1973), many of these tests have raised questions about the validity of the Heckscher-Ohlin theory.[21] Using the Heckscher-Ohlin theory, Leontief postulated that since the United States was relatively abundant in capital compared to other nations, the United States would be an exporter of capital-intensive goods and an importer of labor-intensive goods. To his surprise, however, he found that U.S. exports were less capital intensive than U.S. imports. Since this result was at variance with the predictions of the theory, it has become known as the Leontief paradox.

No one is quite sure why we observe the Leontief paradox. One possible explanation is that the United States has a special advantage in producing new products or goods made with innovative technologies. Such products may be less capital intensive than products whose technology has had time to mature and become suitable for mass production. Thus, the United States may be exporting goods that heavily use skilled labor and innovative entrepreneurship, such as computer software, while importing heavy manufacturing products that use large amounts of capital. Some empirical studies tend to confirm this.[22] Still, tests of the Heckscher-Ohlin theory using data for a large number of countries tend to confirm the existence of the Leontief paradox.[23]

This leaves economists with a difficult dilemma. They prefer the Heckscher-Ohlin theory on theoretical grounds, but it is a relatively poor predictor of real-world international trade patterns. On the other hand, the theory they regard as being too limited, Ricardo's theory of comparative advantage, actually predicts trade patterns with greater accuracy. The best solution to this dilemma may be to return to the Ricardian idea that trade patterns are largely driven by international differences in productivity. Thus, one might argue that the United States exports commercial aircraft and imports textiles not because its factor endowments are especially suited to aircraft manufacture and not suited to textile manufacture, but because the United States is relatively more efficient at producing aircraft than textiles. A key assumption in the Heckscher-Ohlin theory is that technologies are the same across countries. This may not be the case. Differences in technology may lead to differences in productivity, which, in turn, drives international trade patterns.[24] Thus, Japan's success in exporting automobiles in the 1970s and 1980s was based not just on the relative abundance of capital, but also on its development of innovative manufacturing technology that enabled it to achieve higher productivity levels in automobile production than other countries that also had abundant capital. More recent empirical work suggests that this theoretical explanation may be correct.[25] The new research shows that once differences in technology across countries are controlled for, countries do indeed export those goods that make intensive use of factors that are locally abundant, while importing goods that make intensive use of factors that are locally scarce. In other words, once the impact of differences of technology on productivity is controlled for, the Heckscher-Ohlin theory seems to gain predictive power.

The Product Life-Cycle Theory

Raymond Vernon initially proposed the product life-cycle theory in the mid-1960s.[26] Vernon's theory was based on the observation that for most of the 20th century a very large proportion of the world's new products had been developed by U.S. firms and sold first in the U.S. market (e.g., mass-produced automobiles, televisions, instant cameras, photocopiers, personal computers, and semiconductor chips). To explain this, Vernon argued that the wealth and size of the U.S. market gave U.S. firms a strong incentive to develop new consumer products. In addition, the high cost of U.S. labor gave U.S. firms an incentive to develop cost-saving process innovations.

Just because a new product is developed by a U.S. firm and first sold in the U.S. market, it does not follow that the product must be produced in the United States. It could be produced abroad at some low-cost location and then exported back into the United States. However, Vernon argued that most new products were initially produced in America. Apparently, the pioneering firms believed it was better to keep production facilities close to the market and to the firm's center of decision making, given the uncertainty and risks inherent in introducing new products. Also, the demand for most new products tends to be based on non-price factors. Consequently, firms can charge relatively high prices for new products, which obviates the need to look for low-cost production sites in other countries.

Vernon went on to argue that early in the life cycle of a typical new product, while demand is starting to grow rapidly in the United States, demand in other advanced countries is limited to high-income groups. The limited initial demand in other advanced countries does not make it worthwhile for firms in those countries to start producing the new product, but it does necessitate some exports from the United States to those countries.

Over time, demand for the new product grows in other advanced countries (e.g., Great Britain, France, Germany, and Japan). As it does, it becomes worthwhile for foreign producers to begin producing for their home markets. In addition, U.S. firms might set up production facilities in those advanced countries where demand is growing.

LEARNING OBJECTIVE 2
Be familiar with the different theories explaining trade flows between nations.

Consequently, production within other advanced countries begins to limit the potential for exports from the United States.

As the market in the United States and other advanced nations matures, the product becomes more standardized, and price becomes the main competitive weapon. As this occurs, cost considerations play a greater role in the competitive process. Producers based in advanced countries where labor costs are lower than in the United States (e.g., Italy, Spain) might now be able to export to the United States. If cost pressures become intense, the process might not stop there. The cycle by which the United States lost its advantage to other advanced countries might be repeated once more, as developing countries (e.g., Thailand) begin to acquire a production advantage over advanced countries. Thus, the locus of global production initially switches from the United States to other advanced nations and then from those nations to developing countries.

The consequence of these trends for the pattern of world trade is that the United States switches from being an exporter of the product to an importer of the product as production becomes concentrated in lower-cost foreign locations. Figure 5.5 shows the growth of production and consumption over time in the United States, other advanced countries, and developing countries.

EVALUATING THE PRODUCT LIFE-CYCLE THEORY

Historically, the product life-cycle theory seems to be an accurate explanation of international trade patterns. Consider photocopiers; the product was developed in the early 1960s by Xerox in the United States and sold initially to U.S. users. Originally Xerox exported photocopiers from the United States, primarily to Japan and the advanced countries of Western Europe. As demand began to grow in those countries, Xerox entered into joint ventures to set up production in Japan (Fuji-Xerox) and Great Britain (Rank-Xerox). In addition, once Xerox's patents on the photocopier process expired, other foreign competitors began to enter the market (e.g., Canon in Japan, Olivetti in Italy). As a consequence, exports from the United States declined, and U.S. users began to buy some of their photocopiers from lower-cost foreign sources, particularly Japan. More recently, Japanese companies have found that manufacturing costs are too high in their own country, so they have begun to switch production to developing countries such as Singapore and Thailand. Thus, initially the United States and now other advanced countries (e.g., Japan and Great Britain) have switched from being exporters of photocopiers to importers. This evolution in the pattern of international trade in photocopiers is consistent with the predictions of the product life-cycle theory that mature industries tend to go out of the United States and into low-cost assembly locations.

However, the product life-cycle theory is not without weaknesses. Viewed from an Asian or European perspective, Vernon's argument that most new products are developed and introduced in the United States seems ethnocentric. Although it may be true that during U.S. dominance of the global economy (from 1945 to 1975), most new products were introduced in the United States, there have always been important exceptions. These exceptions appear to have become more common in recent years. Many new products are now first introduced in Japan (e.g., videogame consoles) or Europe (new wireless phones). Also, with the increased globalization and integration of the world economy discussed in Chapter 1, a growing number of new products (e.g., laptop computers, compact disks, and digital cameras) are now introduced simultaneously in the United States, Japan, and the advanced European nations. This may be accompanied by globally dispersed production, with particular components of a new product being produced in those locations around the globe where the mix of factor costs and skills is most favorable (as predicted by the theory of comparative advantage). In sum, although Vernon's theory may be useful for explaining the pattern of international trade during the brief period of American global dominance, its relevance in the modern world seems more limited.

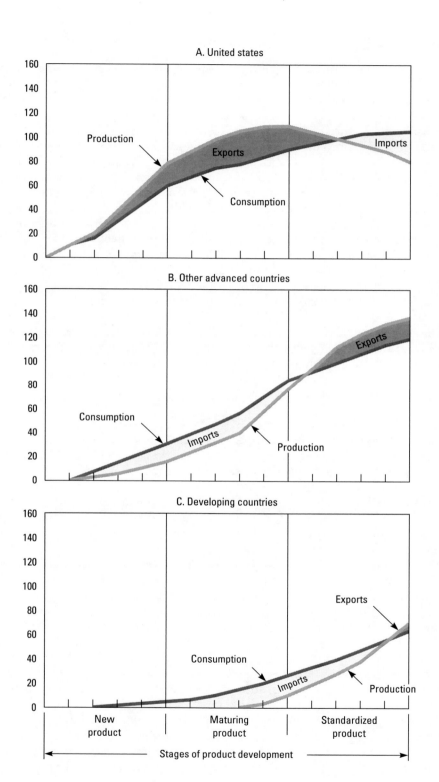

A. United states

B. Other advanced countries

C. Developing countries

New product   Maturing product   Standardized product

Stages of product development

5.5 figure

The Product Life-Cycle Theory

Source: Adapted from R. Vernon and L.T. Wells, *The Economic Environment of International Business*. 4th ed., © 1986. Reprinted by permission of Pearson Education, Inc., Upper Saddle River, N.J.

New Trade Theory

LEARNING OBJECTIVE 2
Be familiar with the different theories explaining trade flows between nations.

The new trade theory began to emerge in the 1970s when a number of economists pointed out that the ability of firms to attain economies of scale might have important implications for international trade.[27] **Economies of scale** are unit cost reductions associated with a large scale of output. Economies of scale have a number of sources, including the ability to spread fixed costs over a large volume, and the ability of large-volume producers to utilize specialized employees and equipment that are more productive than less specialized employees and equipment. Economies of scale are a major source of cost reductions in many industries, from computer software to automobiles, and from pharmaceuticals to aerospace. For example, Microsoft realizes economies of scale by spreading the fixed costs of developing new versions of its Windows operating system, which runs to about $5 billion, over the 250 million or so personal computers upon which each new system is ultimately installed. Similarly, automobile companies realize economies of scale by producing a high volume of automobiles from an assembly line where each employee has a specialized task.

Economies of Scale
Unit cost reductions associated with a large scale of output.

New trade theory makes two important points: First, through its impact on economies of scale, trade can increase the variety of goods available to consumers and decrease the average costs of those goods. Second, in those industries when the output required to attain economies of scale represents a significant proportion of total world demand, the global market may be able to support only a small number of enterprises. Thus, world trade in certain products may be dominated by countries whose firms were first movers in their production.

LEARNING OBJECTIVE 3
Understand why many economists believe that unrestricted free trade between nations will raise the economic welfare of countries that participate in a free trade system.

INCREASING PRODUCT VARIETY AND REDUCING COSTS

Imagine first a world without trade. In industries where economies of scale are important, both the variety of goods that a country can produce and the scale of production are limited by the size of the market. If a national market is small, there may not be enough demand to enable producers to realize economies of scale for certain products. Accordingly, those products may not be produced, thereby limiting the variety of products available to consumers. Alternatively, they may be produced, but at such low volumes that unit costs and prices are considerably higher than they might be if economies of scale could be realized.

Now consider what happens when nations trade with each other. Individual national markets are combined into a larger world market. As the size of the market expands due to trade, individual firms may be able to better attain economies of scale. The implication, according to new trade theory, is that each nation may be able to specialize in producing a narrower range of products than it would in the absence of trade, yet by buying goods that it does not make from other countries, each nation can simultaneously increase the *variety* of goods available to its consumers and *lower the costs* of those goods—thus trade offers an opportunity for mutual gain even when countries do not differ in their resource endowments or technology.

Suppose there are two countries, each with an annual market for 1 million automobiles. By trading with each other, these countries can create a combined market for 2 million cars. In this combined market, due to the ability to better realize economies of scale, more varieties (models) of cars can be produced, and cars can be produced at a lower average cost, than in either market alone. For example, demand for a sports car may be limited to 55,000 units in each national market, while a total output of at least 100,000 per year may be required to realize significant scale economies. Similarly, demand for a minivan may be 80,000 units in each national market, and again a total output of at least 100,000 per year may be required to realize significant scale economies. Faced with limited domestic market demand, firms in each nation may decide not to produce a sports car, since the costs of doing so at such low volume are too great. Although they may produce minivans, the cost of doing so will be higher, as will prices, than if significant economies of scale had been attained. Once the two countries decide to trade, however, a firm in one nation may specialize in producing sports cars, while a firm in the other nation may produce minivans. The combined demand for 110,000 sports cars and 160,000 minivans allows each firm to realize scale economies. Consumers benefit from having access to a product (sports cars) that was not available before international trade and from the lower price for a product (minivans) that could not be produced at the most efficient scale before international trade. Trade is thus mutually beneficial because it allows for the specialization of production, the realization of scale economies, the production of a greater variety of products, and lower prices.

ECONOMIES OF SCALE, FIRST-MOVER ADVANTAGES, AND THE PATTERN OF TRADE

A second theme in new trade theory is that the pattern of trade we observe in the world economy may be the result of economies of scale and first-mover advantages. **First-mover advantages** are the economic and strategic advantages that accrue to early entrants into an industry.[28] The ability to capture scale economies ahead of later entrants, and thus benefit from a lower cost structure, is an important first-mover advantage. New trade theory argues that for those products where economies of scale are significant and represent a substantial proportion of world demand, the first movers in an industry can gain a scale-based cost advantage that later entrants find almost impossible to match. Thus, the pattern of trade that we observe for such products may reflect first-mover advantages. Countries may dominate in the export of certain goods because economies of scale are important in their production and because firms located in those countries were the first to capture scale economies, giving them a first-mover advantage.

First-Mover Advantages
The economic and strategic advantages that accrue to early entrants into an industry.

The European Union might come to dominate in the export of super-jumbo jets primarily because Airbus, a European-based firm, was the first to produce a 550-seat aircraft and realize economies of scale.

For example, consider the commercial aerospace industry. In aerospace there are substantial scale economies that come from the ability to spread the fixed costs of developing a new jet aircraft over a large number of sales. It has cost Airbus some $14 billion to develop its new super-jumbo jet, the 550 seat A380. To recoup those costs and break even, Airbus will have to sell at least 250 A380 planes. If Airbus can sell over 350 A380 planes, it will apparently be a profitable venture. However, total demand over the next 20 years for this class of aircraft is estimated to be somewhere between 400 and 600 units. Thus, the global market can probably only profitably support one producer of jet aircraft in the super-jumbo category. It follows that the European Union might come to dominate in the export of very large jet aircraft, primarily because a European-based firm, Airbus, was the first to produce a super-jumbo jet aircraft and realize scale economies. Other potential producers, such as Boeing, might be shut out of the market because they will lack the scale economies that Airbus will enjoy. By pioneering this market category, Airbus may have captured a *first-mover advantage* based on *scale economies* that will be difficult for rivals to match, and that will result in the European Union becoming the *leading exporter* of very large jet aircraft. (Boeing does not believe the market to be large enough to even profitably support one producer, hence its decision not to build a similar aircraft and instead focus on its super-efficient 787).

IMPLICATIONS OF NEW TRADE THEORY

New trade theory has important implications. The theory suggests that nations may benefit from trade even when they do not differ in resource endowments or technology. Trade allows a nation to specialize in the production of certain products, attaining scale economies and lowering the costs of producing those products, while buying products that it does not produce from other nations that specialize in the production of other products. By this mechanism, the variety of products available to consumers in each nation is increased, while the average costs of those products should fall, as should their price, freeing resources to produce other goods and services.

The theory also suggests that a country may predominate in the export of a good simply because it was lucky enough to have one or more firms among the first to produce that good. Because they are able to gain economies of scale, the first movers in an industry may get a lock on the world market that discourages subsequent entry. First movers' ability to benefit from increasing returns creates a barrier to entry. In the commercial aircraft industry, the fact that Boeing and Airbus are already in the industry and have the benefits of economies of scale discourages new entry and reinforces the dominance of America and Europe in the trade of midsized and large jet aircraft. This dominance is further reinforced because global demand may not be sufficient to profitably support another producer of midsized and large jet aircraft in the industry. So although Japanese firms might be able to compete in the market, they have decided not to enter the industry but to ally themselves as major subcontractors with primary producers (e.g., Mitsubishi Heavy Industries is a major subcontractor for Boeing on the 777 and 787 programs).

New trade theory is at variance with the Heckscher-Ohlin theory, which suggests that a country will predominate in the export of a product when it is particularly well endowed with those factors used intensively in its manufacture. New trade theorists argue that the United States is a major exporter of commercial jet aircraft not because it is better endowed with the factors of production required to manufacture aircraft, but because one of the first movers in the industry, Boeing, was a U.S. firm. The new trade theory is not at variance with the theory of comparative advantage. Economies of scale increases productivity. Thus, the new trade theory identifies an important source of comparative advantage.

This theory is quite useful in explaining trade patterns. Empirical studies seem to support the predictions of the theory that trade increases the specialization of production within an industry, increases the variety of products available to consumers, and results in lower average prices.[29] With regard to first-mover advantages and international trade, a study by Harvard business historian Alfred Chandler suggests the existence of first-mover advantages is an important factor in explaining the dominance of firms from certain nations in specific industries.[30] The number of firms is very limited in many global industries, including the chemical industry, the heavy construction-equipment industry, the heavy truck industry, the tire industry, the consumer electronics industry, the jet engine industry, and the computer software industry.

Perhaps the most contentious implication of the new trade theory is the argument that it generates for government intervention and strategic trade policy.[31] New trade theorists stress the role of luck, entrepreneurship, and innovation in giving a firm first-mover advantages. According to this argument, the reason Boeing was the first mover in commercial jet aircraft manufacture—rather than firms like Great Britain's DeHavilland and Hawker Siddley, or Holland's Fokker, all of which could have been— was that Boeing was both lucky and innovative. One way Boeing was lucky is that DeHavilland shot itself in the foot when its Comet jet airliner, introduced two years earlier than Boeing's first jet airliner, the 707, was found to be full of serious technological flaws. Had DeHavilland not made some serious technological mistakes, Great Britain might have become the world's leading exporter of commercial jet aircraft. Boeing's innovativeness was demonstrated by its independent development of the technological know-how required to build a commercial jet airliner. Several new trade theorists have pointed out, however, that Boeing's R&D was largely paid for by the U.S. government; the 707 was a spin-off from a government-funded military program (the entry of Airbus into the industry was also supported by significant government subsidies). Herein is a rationale for government intervention; by the sophisticated and judicious use of subsidies, could a government increase the chances of its domestic firms becoming first movers in newly emerging industries, as the U.S. government apparently did with Boeing (and the European Union did with Airbus)? If this is possible, and the new trade theory suggests it might be, we have an economic rationale for a proactive trade policy that is at variance with the free trade prescriptions of the trade theories we have reviewed so far. We will consider the policy implications of this issue in Chapter 6.

LEARNING OBJECTIVE 4
Be familiar with the arguments of those who maintain that government can play a proactive role in promoting national competitive advantage in certain industries.

National Competitive Advantage: Porter's Diamond

LEARNING OBJECTIVE 2
Be familiar with the different theories explaining trade flows between nations.

In 1990 Michael Porter of the Harvard Business School published the results of an intensive research effort that attempted to determine why some nations succeed and others fail in international competition.[32] Porter and his team looked at 100 industries in 10 nations. Like the work of the new trade theorists, Porter's work was driven by a belief that existing theories of international trade told only part of the story. For Porter, the essential task was to explain why a nation achieves international success in a particular industry. Why does Japan do so well in the automobile industry? Why does Switzerland excel in the production and export of precision instruments and pharmaceuticals? Why do Germany and the United States do so well in the chemical industry? These questions cannot be answered easily by the Heckscher-Ohlin theory, and the theory of comparative advantage offers only a partial explanation. The theory of comparative advantage would say that Switzerland excels in the production and export of precision instruments

figure 5.6

Determinants of National Competitive Advantage: Porter's Diamond

Source: Reprinted by permission of the *Harvard Business Review.* "The Competitive Advantage of Nations" by Michael E. Porter, March–April 1990, p. 77. Copyright © 1990 by The President and Fellows of Harvard College; all rights reserved.

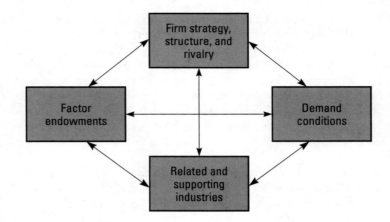

because it uses its resources very productively in these industries. Although this may be correct, this does not explain why Switzerland is more productive in this industry than Great Britain, Germany, or Spain. Porter tries to solve this puzzle.

Porter theorizes that four broad attributes of a nation shape the environment in which local firms compete, and these attributes promote or impede the creation of competitive advantage (see Figure 5.6). These attributes are

- *Factor endowments*—a nation's position in factors of production such as skilled labor or the infrastructure necessary to compete in a given industry.
- *Demand conditions*—the nature of home demand for the industry's product or service.
- *Relating and supporting industries*—the presence or absence of supplier industries and related industries that are internationally competitive.
- *Firm strategy, structure, and rivalry*—the conditions governing how companies are created, organized, and managed and the nature of domestic rivalry.

 Another Perspective

Dubai: From Oil to Glitz
When it comes to making the most of its factor endowments, Dubai may take the prize. Part of the United Arab Emirates, Dubai built its economy on its rich petroleum and natural gas reserves. Today, however, it has reinvented itself as a finance capital and tourist destination. Nearly all of the world's major banks and many major corporations now have operations in Dubai. In 2007, oil-industry giant Halliburton moved its world headquarters there.

Though a Muslim city, Dubai resembles Las Vegas, with opulent hotels and nightclubs, massive shopping malls with built-in amusement parks, and an array of recreation from golf and boating to horse racing. Adding to its allure are low import duties and a currency tied to the U.S. dollar. ("Dubai: Wall Street in the Desert?" *BusinessWeek,* October 8, 2007, www.businessweek.com; and "Surprising Dubai," *BusinessWeek,* April 30, 2007, www.businessweek.com)

Porter speaks of these four attributes as constituting the *diamond.* He argues that firms are most likely to succeed in industries or industry segments where the diamond is most favorable. He also argues that the diamond is a mutually reinforcing system. The effect of one attribute is contingent on the state of others. For example, Porter argues favorable demand conditions will not result in competitive advantage unless the state of rivalry is sufficient to cause firms to respond to them.

Porter maintains that two additional variables can influence the national diamond in important ways: chance and government. Chance events, such as major innovations, can reshape industry structure and provide the opportunity for one nation's firms to supplant another's. Government, by its choice of policies, can detract from or improve national advantage. For example, regulation can alter home demand conditions, antitrust policies can influence the intensity of rivalry within an industry, and government investments in education can change factor endowments.

FACTOR ENDOWMENTS   Factor endowments lie at the center of the Heckscher-Ohlin theory. While Porter does not propose anything radically new, he does analyze the characteristics of factors of production. He recognizes hierarchies among factors, distinguishing between *basic factors* (e.g., natural resources, climate, location, and demographics) and *advanced factors* (e.g., communication infrastructure, sophisticated and skilled labor, research facilities, and technological know-how). He argues that advanced factors are the most significant for competitive advantage. Unlike the naturally endowed basic factors, advanced factors are a product of investment by individuals, companies, and governments. Thus, government investments in basic and higher education, by improving the general skill and knowledge level of the population and by stimulating advanced research at higher education institutions, can upgrade a nation's advanced factors.

Another Perspective

The relationship between advanced and basic factors is complex. Basic factors can provide an initial advantage that is subsequently reinforced and extended by investment in advanced factors. Conversely, disadvantages in basic factors can create pressures to invest in advanced factors. An obvious example of this phenomenon is Japan, a country that lacks arable land and mineral deposits and yet through investment has built a substantial endowment of advanced factors. Porter notes that Japan's large pool of engineers (reflecting a much higher number of engineering graduates per capita than almost any other nation) has been vital to Japan's success in many manufacturing industries.

DEMAND CONDITIONS   Porter emphasizes the role home demand plays in upgrading competitive advantage. Firms are typically most sensitive to the needs of their closest customers. Thus, the characteristics of home demand are particularly important in shaping the attributes of domestically made products and in creating pressures for innovation and quality. Porter argues that a nation's firms gain competitive advantage if their domestic consumers are sophisticated and demanding. Such consumers pressure local firms to meet high standards of product quality and to produce innovative products. Porter notes that Japan's sophisticated and knowledgeable buyers of cameras helped stimulate the Japanese camera industry to improve product quality and to introduce innovative models. A similar example can be found in the wireless telephone equipment industry, where sophisticated and demanding local customers in Scandinavia helped push Nokia of Finland and Ericsson of Sweden to invest in cellular phone technology long before demand for cellular phones took off in other developed nations. The case of Nokia is reviewed in more depth in the accompanying Management Focus.

RELATED AND SUPPORTING INDUSTRIES   The third broad attribute of national advantage in an industry is the presence of suppliers or related industries that are internationally competitive. The benefits of investments in advanced factors

Management FOCUS

The Rise of Finland's Nokia

The wireless phone market is one of the great growth stories of the last decade. Starting from a very low base in 1990, annual global sales of wireless phones surged to about 1.1 billion units in 2007. By the end of 2007, the number of wireless subscribers worldwide was around 2 billion, up from less than 10 million in 1990. Nokia is one of the dominant players in the world market for mobile phones with a 39 percent market share at the end of 2007. Nokia's roots are in Finland, not normally a country that comes to mind when one talks about leading-edge technology companies. In the 1980s, Nokia was a rambling Finnish conglomerate with activities that embraced tire manufacturing, paper production, consumer electronics, and telecommunications equipment. By 2007, it had transformed itself into a focused telecommunications equipment manufacturer with a global reach and sales of over $42 billion. How has this former conglomerate emerged to take a global leadership position in wireless telecommunications equipment? Much of the answer lies in the history, geography, and political economy of Finland and its Nordic neighbors.

In 1981 the Nordic nations cooperated to create the world's first international wireless telephone network. They had good reason to become pioneers: It cost far too much to lay a traditional wire-line telephone service in those sparsely populated and inhospitably cold countries. The same features made telecommunications all the more valuable: People driving through the Arctic winter and owners of remote northern houses needed a telephone to summon help if things went wrong. As a result, Sweden, Norway, and Finland became the first nations in the world to take wireless telecommunications seriously. They found, for example, that although it cost up to $800 per subscriber to bring traditional wire-line service to remote locations, the same locations could be linked by wireless cellular for only $500 per person. As a consequence, 12 percent of people in Scandinavia owned cellular phones by 1994, compared with less than 6 percent in the United States, the world's second most developed market. This lead continued over the next decade. By 2007, 90 percent of the population in Finland owned a wireless phone, compared with 70 percent in the United States.

Nokia, a longtime telecommunications equipment supplier, was positioned to take advantage of this development from the start, but other forces also helped Nokia develop its competitive edge. Unlike virtually every other developed nation, Finland has never had a national telephone monopoly. Instead, the country's telephone services have long been provided by about 50 autonomous local telephone companies whose elected boards set prices by referendum (which naturally means low prices). This army of independent and cost-conscious telephone service providers prevented Nokia from taking anything for granted in its home country. With typical Finnish pragmatism, its customers were willing to buy from the lowest-cost supplier, whether that was Nokia, Ericsson, Motorola, or some other company. This situation contrasted sharply with that prevailing in most developed nations until the late 1980s and early 1990s, where domestic telephone monopolies typically purchased equipment from a dominant local supplier or made it themselves. Nokia responded to this competitive pressure by doing everything possible to drive down its manufacturing costs while staying at the leading edge of wireless technology.

The consequences of these forces are clear. Nokia is now a leader in digital wireless technology. Many now regard Finland as the lead market for wireless telephone services. If you want to see the future of wireless, you don't go to New York or San Francisco; you go to Helsinki, where Finns use their wireless handsets not just to talk to each other but also to browse the Web, execute e-commerce transactions, control household heating and lighting systems, or purchase Coke from a wireless-enabled vending machine. Nokia has gained this lead because Scandinavia started switching to digital technology five years before the rest of the world.

Sources: "Lessons from the Frozen North," *The Economist,* October 8, 1994, pp. 76–77; "A Finnish Fable," *The Economist,* October 14, 2000; D. O'Shea and K. Fitchard, "The First 3 Billion Is Always the Hardest," *Wireless Review* 22 (September 2005), pp. 25–31; P. Taylor, "Big Names Dominate in Mobile Phones," *Financial Times,* September 29, 2006, p. 26; and Nokia Web site at **www.nokia.com**.

of production by related and supporting industries can spill over into an industry, thereby helping it achieve a strong competitive position internationally. Swedish strength in fabricated steel products (e.g., ball bearings and cutting tools) has drawn on strengths in Sweden's specialty steel industry. Technological leadership in the U.S. semiconductor industry provided the basis for U.S. success in personal computers and several other technically advanced electronic products. Similarly, Switzerland's success in pharmaceuticals is closely related to its previous international success in the technologically related dye industry.

One consequence of this process is that successful industries within a country tend to be grouped into clusters of related industries. This was one of the most pervasive findings of Porter's study. One such cluster Porter identified was in the German textile and apparel sector, which included high-quality cotton, wool, synthetic fibers, sewing machine needles, and a wide range of textile machinery. Such clusters are important because valuable knowledge can flow between the firms within a geographic cluster, benefiting all within that cluster. Knowledge flows occur when employees move between firms within a region and when national industry associations bring employees from different companies together for regular conferences or workshops.[33]

FIRM STRATEGY, STRUCTURE, AND RIVALRY The fourth broad attribute of national competitive advantage in Porter's model is the strategy, structure, and rivalry of firms within a nation. Porter makes two important points here. First, different nations are characterized by different management ideologies, which either help them or do not help them to build national competitive advantage. For example, Porter noted the predominance of engineers in top management at German and Japanese firms. He attributed this to these firms' emphasis on improving manufacturing processes and product design. In contrast, Porter noted a predominance of people with finance backgrounds leading many U.S. firms. He linked this to U.S. firms' lack of attention to improving manufacturing processes and product design. He argued that the dominance of finance led to an overemphasis on maximizing short-term financial returns. According to Porter, one consequence of these different management ideologies was a relative loss of U.S. competitiveness in those engineering-based industries where manufacturing processes and product design issues are all-important (e.g., the automobile industry).

Porter's second point is that there is a strong association between vigorous domestic rivalry and the creation and persistence of competitive advantage in an industry. Vigorous domestic rivalry induces firms to look for ways to improve efficiency, which makes them better international competitors. Domestic rivalry creates pressures to innovate, to improve quality, to reduce costs, and to invest in upgrading advanced factors. All this helps to create world-class competitors. Porter cites the case of Japan:

> Nowhere is the role of domestic rivalry more evident than in Japan, where it is all-out warfare in which many companies fail to achieve profitability. With goals that stress market share, Japanese companies engage in a continuing struggle to outdo each other. Shares fluctuate markedly. The process is prominently covered in the business press. Elaborate rankings measure which companies are most popular with university graduates. The rate of new product and process development is breathtaking.[34]

A similar point about the stimulating effects of strong domestic competition can be made with regard to the rise of Nokia of Finland to global preeminence in the market for cellular telephone equipment. For details, see the Management Focus.

EVALUATING PORTER'S THEORY Porter contends that the degree to which a nation is likely to achieve international success in a certain industry is a function of the combined impact of factor endowments, domestic demand conditions, related and supporting industries, and domestic rivalry. He argues that the presence of

LEARNING OBJECTIVE 4
Be familiar with the arguments of those who maintain that government can play a proactive role in promoting national competitive advantage in certain industries.

all four components is usually required for this diamond to boost competitive performance (although there are exceptions). Porter also contends that government can influence each of the four components of the diamond—either positively or negatively. Factor endowments can be affected by subsidies, policies toward capital markets, policies toward education, and so on. Government can shape domestic demand through local product standards or with regulations that mandate or influence buyer needs. Government policy can influence supporting and related industries through regulation and influence firm rivalry through such devices as capital market regulation, tax policy, and antitrust laws.

If Porter is correct, we would expect his model to predict the pattern of international trade that we observe in the real world. Countries should be exporting products from those industries where all four components of the diamond are favorable, while importing in those areas where the components are not favorable. Is he correct? We simply do not know. Porter's theory has not been subjected to detailed empirical testing. Much about the theory rings true, but the same can be said for the new trade theory, the theory of comparative advantage, and the Heckscher-Ohlin theory. It may be that each of these theories, which complement each other, explains something about the pattern of international trade.

Focus on Managerial Implications

LEARNING OBJECTIVE 5
Understand the important implications that international trade theory holds for business practice.

Why does all this matter for business? There are at least three main implications for international businesses of the material discussed in this chapter: location implications, first-mover implications, and policy implications.

Location

Underlying most of the theories we have discussed is the notion that different countries have particular advantages in different productive activities. Thus, from a profit perspective, it makes sense for a firm to disperse its productive activities to those countries where, according to the theory of international trade, they can be performed most efficiently. If design can be performed most efficiently in France, that is where design facilities should be located; if the manufacture of basic components can be performed most efficiently in Singapore, that is where they should be manufactured; and if final assembly can be performed most efficiently in China, that is where final assembly should be performed. The result is a global web of productive activities, with different activities being performed in different locations around the globe depending on considerations of comparative advantage, factor endowments, and the like. If the firm does not do this, it may find itself at a competitive disadvantage relative to firms that do.

Consider the production of a laptop computer, a process with four major stages: (1) basic research and development of the product design, (2) manufacture of standard electronic components (e.g., memory chips), (3) manufacture of advanced components (e.g., flat-top color display screens and microprocessors), and (4) final assembly. Basic R&D requires a pool of highly skilled and educated workers with good backgrounds in microelectronics. The two countries with a comparative advantage in basic microelectronics R&D and design are Japan and the United States, so most producers of laptop computers locate their R&D facilities in one, or both, of these countries. (Apple, Motorola, Texas Instruments, Toshiba, and Sony all have major R&D facilities in both Japan and the United States.)

The manufacture of standard electronic components is a capital-intensive process requiring semiskilled labor, and cost pressures are intense. The best locations for such activities today are places such as Taiwan, Malaysia, and South Korea. These countries have pools of relatively skilled, moderate-cost labor. Thus, many producers of laptop computers have standard components, such as memory chips, produced at these locations.

The manufacture of advanced components such as microprocessors is a capital-intensive process requiring skilled labor. Because cost pressures are not so intense at this stage, these components can be—and are—manufactured in countries with high labor costs that also have pools of highly skilled labor (e.g., Japan and the United States).

Finally, assembly is a relatively labor-intensive process requiring only low-skill labor, and cost pressures are intense. As a result, final assembly may be carried out in a country such as Mexico, which has an abundance of low-cost, low-skill labor. A laptop computer produced by a U.S. manufacturer may be designed in California, have its standard components produced in Taiwan and Singapore, its advanced components produced in Japan and the United States, its final assembly in Mexico, and be sold in the United States or elsewhere in the world. By dispersing production activities to different locations around the globe, the U.S. manufacturer is taking advantage of the differences between countries identified by the various theories of international trade.

First-Mover Advantages

According to the new trade theory, firms that establish a first-mover advantage with regard to the production of a particular new product may subsequently dominate global trade in that product. This is particularly true in industries where the global market can profitably support only a limited number of firms, such as the aerospace market, but early commitments also seem to be important in less concentrated industries such as the market for cellular telephone equipment (see the Management Focus on Nokia). For the individual firm, the clear message is that it pays to invest substantial financial resources in trying to build a first-mover, or early-mover, advantage, even if that means several years of losses before a new venture becomes profitable. The idea is to preempt the available demand, gain cost advantages related to volume, build an enduring brand ahead of later competitors, and, consequently, establish a long-term sustainable competitive advantage. Although the details of how to achieve this are beyond the scope of this book, many publications offer strategies for exploiting first-mover advantages, and for avoiding the traps associated with pioneering a market (first-mover disadvantages).[35]

Government Policy

The theories of international trade also matter to international businesses because firms are major players on the international trade scene. Business firms produce exports, and business firms import the products of other countries. Because of their pivotal role in international trade, businesses can exert a strong influence on government trade policy, lobbying to promote free trade or trade restrictions. The theories of international trade claim that promoting free trade is generally in the best interests of a country, although it may not always be in the best interest of an individual firm. Many firms recognize this and lobby for open markets.

For example, when the U.S. government announced its intention to place a tariff on Japanese imports of liquid crystal display (LCD) screens in the 1990s, IBM and

Apple Computer protested strongly. Both IBM and Apple pointed out that (1) Japan was the lowest-cost source of LCD screens; (2) they used these screens in their own laptop computers; and (3) the proposed tariff, by increasing the cost of LCD screens, would increase the cost of laptop computers produced by IBM and Apple, thus making them less competitive in the world market. In other words, the tariff, designed to protect U.S. firms, would be self-defeating. In response to these pressures, the U.S. government reversed its posture.

Unlike IBM and Apple, however, businesses do not always lobby for free trade. In the United States, for example, restrictions on imports of steel are the result of direct pressure by U.S. firms on the government. In some cases, the government has responded to pressure by getting foreign companies to agree to "voluntary" restrictions on their imports, using the implicit threat of more comprehensive formal trade barriers to get them to adhere to these agreements (historically, this has occurred in the automobile industry). In other cases, the government used what are called "anti-dumping" actions to justify tariffs on imports from other nations (these mechanisms will be discussed in detail in the next chapter).

As predicted by international trade theory, many of these agreements have been self-defeating, such as the voluntary restriction on machine tool imports agreed to in 1985. Due to limited import competition from more efficient foreign suppliers, the prices of machine tools in the United States rose to higher levels than would have prevailed under free trade. Because machine tools are used throughout the manufacturing industry, the result was to increase the costs of U.S. manufacturing in general, creating a corresponding loss in world market competitiveness. Shielded from international competition by import barriers, the U.S. machine tool industry had no incentive to increase its efficiency. Consequently, it lost many of its export markets to more efficient foreign competitors. Because of this misguided action, the U.S. machine tool industry shrunk during the period when the agreement was in force. For anyone schooled in international trade theory, this was not surprising.[36] A similar scenario unfolded in the U.S. steel industry, where tariff barriers erected by the government in 2001 raised the cost of steel to important U.S. users, such as automobile companies and appliance makers, making their products more uncompetitive.

Finally, Porter's theory of national competitive advantage also contains policy implications. Porter's theory suggests that it is in the best interest of business for a firm to invest in upgrading advanced factors of production; for example, to invest in better training for its employees and to increase its commitment to research and development. It is also in the best interests of business to lobby the government to adopt policies that have a favorable impact on each component of the national diamond. Thus, according to Porter, businesses should urge government to increase investment in education, infrastructure, and basic research (since all these enhance advanced factors) and to adopt policies that promote strong competition within domestic markets (since this makes firms stronger international competitors, according to Porter's findings).

Key Terms

free trade, p. 161	zero-sum game, p. 165	factor endowments, p. 176
new trade theory, p. 163	absolute advantage, p. 165	economies of scale, p. 180
mercantilism, p. 164	constant returns to specialization, p. 171	first-mover advantages, p. 181

Summary

This chapter has reviewed a number of theories that explain why it is beneficial for a country to engage in international trade and has explained the pattern of international trade observed in the world economy. We have seen how the theories of Smith, Ricardo, and Heckscher-Ohlin all make strong cases for unrestricted free trade. In contrast, the mercantilist doctrine and, to a lesser extent, the new trade theory can be interpreted to support government intervention to promote exports through subsidies and to limit imports through tariffs and quotas.

In explaining the pattern of international trade, the second objective of this chapter, we have seen that with the exception of mercantilism, which is silent on this issue, the different theories offer largely complementary explanations. Although no one theory may explain the apparent pattern of international trade, taken together, the theory of comparative advantage, the Heckscher-Ohlin theory, the product life-cycle theory, the new trade theory, and Porter's theory of national competitive advantage do suggest which factors are important. Comparative advantage tells us that productivity differences are important; Heckscher-Ohlin tells us that factor endowments matter; the product life-cycle theory tells us that where a new product is introduced is important; the new trade theory tells us that increasing returns to specialization and first-mover advantages matter; and Porter tells us that all these factors may be important insofar as they impact the four components of the national diamond. The chapter made these major points:

1. Mercantilists argued that it was in a country's best interests to run a balance-of-trade surplus. They viewed trade as a zero-sum game, in which one country's gains cause losses for other countries.

2. The theory of absolute advantage suggests that countries differ in their ability to produce goods efficiently. The theory suggests that a country should specialize in producing goods in areas where it has an absolute advantage and import goods in areas where other countries have absolute advantages.

3. The theory of comparative advantage suggests that it makes sense for a country to specialize in producing those goods that it can produce most efficiently, while buying goods that it can produce relatively less efficiently from other countries—even if that means buying goods from other countries that it could produce more efficiently itself.

4. The theory of comparative advantage suggests that unrestricted free trade brings about increased world production; that is, that trade is a positive-sum game.

5. The theory of comparative advantage also suggests that opening a country to free trade stimulates economic growth, which creates dynamic gains from trade. The empirical evidence seems to be consistent with this claim.

6. The Heckscher-Ohlin theory argues that the pattern of international trade is determined by differences in factor endowments. It predicts that countries will export those goods that make intensive use of locally abundant factors and will import goods that make intensive use of factors that are locally scarce.

7. The product life-cycle theory suggests that trade patterns are influenced by where a new product is introduced. In an increasingly integrated global economy, the product life-cycle theory seems to be less predictive than it once was.

8. New trade theory states that trade allows a nation to specialize in the production of certain goods, attaining scale economies and lowering the costs of producing those goods, while buying goods that it does not produce from other nations that are similarly specialized. By this mechanism, the variety of goods available to consumers in each nation is increased, while the average costs of those goods should fall.

9. New trade theory also states that in those industries where substantial economies of scale imply that the world market will profitably support only a few firms, countries may predominate in the export of certain products simply because they had a firm that was a first mover in that industry.

10. Some new trade theorists have promoted the idea of strategic trade policy. The argument is that government, by the sophisticated and judicious use of subsidies, might be able to increase the chances of domestic firms becoming first movers in newly emerging industries.

11. Porter's theory of national competitive advantage suggests that the pattern of trade is influenced by four attributes of a nation: (*a*) factor endowments, (*b*) domestic demand conditions, (*c*) relating and supporting industries, and (*d*) firm strategy, structure, and rivalry.

12. Theories of international trade are important to an individual business firm primarily because they can help the firm decide where to locate its various production activities.

13. Firms involved in international trade can and do exert a strong influence on government policy toward trade. By lobbying government, business firms can promote free trade or trade restrictions.

Critical Thinking and Discussion Questions

1. Mercantilism is a bankrupt theory that has no place in the modern world. Discuss.

2. Is free trade fair? Discuss.

3. Unions in developed nations often oppose imports from low-wage countries and advocate trade barriers to protect jobs from what they often characterize as "unfair" import competition. Is such competition "unfair"? Do you think that this argument is in the best interests of (*a*) the unions, (*b*) the people they represent, and/or (*c*) the country as a whole?

4. What are the potential costs of adopting a free trade regime? Do you think governments should do anything to reduce these costs? What?

5. Reread the Country Focus on China as a neo-mercantilist nation.
   a. Do you think China is pursing an economic policy that can be characterized as neo-mercantilist?
   b. What should the United States, and other countries, do about this?

6. Reread the Country Focus on moving white-collar jobs offshore.
   a. Who benefits from the outsourcing of skilled white-color jobs to developing nations? Who are the losers?
   b. Will developed nations like the United States suffer from the loss of high skilled and high paying jobs to developing nations?
   c. Is there a difference between the transference of high-paying white-collar jobs, such as computer programming and accounting, to developing nations and low-paying blue-collar jobs? If so, what is the difference, and should government do anything to stop the flow of white-collar jobs out of the country to countries like India?

7. Drawing upon the new trade theory and Porter's theory of national competitive advantage, outline the case for government policies that would build national competitive advantage in biotechnology. What kinds of policies would you recommend that the government adopt? Are these policies at variance with the basic free trade philosophy?

8. The world's poorest countries are at a competitive disadvantage in every sector of their economies. They have little to export. They have no capital; their land is of poor quality; they often have too many people given available work opportunities; and they are poorly educated. Free trade cannot possibly be in the interests of such nations. Discuss.

Research Task 🌐 globalEDGE http://globalEDGE.msu.edu

Use the globalEDGE Resource Desk (http://globalEDGE.msu.edu/ResourceDesk/) to complete the following exercises:

1. You work for a rice production company and your current project is to determine the ten countries which—in your estimation—should have an advantage in producing rice. Using a resource that tracks *statistics on economic factors* like worldwide rice production, develop a list and brief report about the top 10 rice producing countries with data from the most recent year. Were you surprised by any countries listed? Why (or, why not)?

2. Your coffee firm is looking to find new locations to source coffee from in order to sustain growth as it internationalizes. Currently, your company only purchases green coffee beans from South America and is hoping to begin purchasing coffee from the Central American countries of Costa Rica, El Salvador, Guatemala, Honduras, and Panama. Applying the most current information from *FAOSTAT*, a United Nations agency website that gathers data on food and agricultural trade flows, determine which three countries have the highest export value of green coffee as well as growth of export value over the last year of data available.

closing case

Trade in Information Technology and U.S. Economic Growth

Entrepreneurial enterprises in the United States invented most of the information technology that we use today, including computer and communications hardware, software, and services. In the 1960s and 1970s, the information technology sector was led by companies such as IBM and DEC, which developed first mainframe and then midrange computers. In the 1980s, the locus of growth in the sector shifted to personal computers, and the innovations of companies such as Intel, Apple, IBM, Dell, and Compaq helped develop the mass market for the product. Along the way, however, something happened to this uniquely American industry—it started to move the production of hardware offshore.

In the early 1980s production of "commodity components" for computers such as DRAMs (memory chips) migrated to low-cost producers in Japan and then later to Taiwan and Korea. Soon hard disk drives, display screens, keyboards, computer mice, and a host of other components were outsourced to foreign manufacturers. By the early 2000s, American factories were specializing in making only the highest value components, such as the microprocessors made by Intel, and in final assembly (Dell, for example, assembles PCs at two North American facilities). Just about every other component was made overseas because it cost less to do so. There was a lot of hand-wringing among politicians and journalists about the possible negative implication for the U.S. economy of this trend. According to the critics, high-paying manufacturing jobs in the information technology sector were being exported to foreign producers.

Was this trend bad for the U.S. economy, as the critics claimed? According to research, the globalization of production made information technology hardware about 20 per-

cent less expensive than it would otherwise have been. The price declines supported additional investments in information technology by businesses and households. Because they were getting cheaper, computers diffused throughout the United States faster. In turn, the rapid diffusion of information technology translated into faster productivity growth as businesses used computers to streamline process. Between 1995 and 2002 productivity grew by 2.8 percent per annum in the United States, well above the historic norm. According to calculations by academic researchers, some 0.3 percent per annum of this growth could be attributed directly to the reduced prices of information technology hardware made possible by the move to offshore production. In turn, the 0.3 percent annual gain in productivity from 1995 to 2002 resulted in an additional $230 billion in accumulated gross domestic product in the United States. In short, some argue that the American economy grew at a faster rate precisely because production of information technology hardware was shifted to foreigners.

There is also evidence that the reduced price for hardware made possible by international trade created a boom in jobs in two related industries—computer software and services. During the 1990s the number of information technology jobs in the United States grew by 22 percent, twice the rate of job creation in the economy as a whole, and this at a time when manufacturing information technology jobs were moving offshore. The growth could partly be attributed to robust demand for computer software and services within the United States, and partly due to demand for software and services from foreigners, including those same foreigners who were now making much of the hardware. In sum, some argue that buying computer hardware from foreigners, as opposed to making it in the United States, had a significant *positive* impact upon the U.S. economy that outweighed any adverse effects from job losses in the manufacturing sector.

Sources: C.L. Mann, "Globalization of IT Services and White Collar Jobs," International Economic Policy Briefs, *Institute of International Economics,* December 2003; A. Bernstein, "Shaking up Trade Theory," *BusinessWeek,* December 6, 2004, pp. 116–20; "Semiconductor Trade: A Wafer Thin Case," *The Economist,* July 27, 1996, pp. 53–54; and K.J. Stiroh, "Information Technology and the U.S. Productivity Revival," Federal Reserve Bank of New York, January 2001.

Case Discussion Questions

1. During the 1990s and 2000s, computer hardware companies in certain developed nations progressively moved the production of hardware components offshore, often outsourcing them to producers in developing nations. What does international trade theory suggest about the implications of this trend for economic growth in those developed nations?

2. Is the experience of the United States, as described in the case, consistent with the predictions of international trade theory?

3. What are the implications of the theory and data for (*a*) government policy in advanced nations such as the United States, and (*b*) the strategy of a firm in the computer industry, such as Dell or Apple Computer?

INTERNATIONAL TRADE AND THE BALANCE OF PAYMENTS

International trade involves the sale of goods and services to residents in other countries (exports) and the purchase of goods and services from residents in other countries (imports). A country's **balance-of-payments accounts** keep track of the payments to and receipts from other countries for a particular time period. These include payments to foreigners for imports of goods and service and receipts from foreigners for goods and services exported to them. A summary copy of the U.S. balance-of-payments accounts for 2006 is given in Table A1. Any transaction resulting in a payment to other countries is entered in the balance-of-payments accounts as a debit and given a negative (−) sign. Any transaction resulting in a receipt from other countries is entered as a credit and given a positive (+) sign. In this appendix we briefly describe the form of the balance-of-payments accounts, and we discuss whether a current account deficit, often a cause of much concern in the popular press, is something to worry about.

Balance-of-Payments Accounts Keep track of the payments to and receipts from other countries.

Balance-of-Payments Accounts

Balance-of-payments accounts are divided into three main sections: the current account, the capital account, and the financial account (to confuse matters, what is now called the *capital account* was until recently part of the current account, and the financial account used to be called the capital account). The **current account** records transactions that pertain to three categories, all of which can be seen in Table A1. The first category, *goods*, refers to the export or import of physical goods (e.g., agricultural food stuffs, autos, computers, chemicals). The second category is the export or import of *services* (e.g., intangible products such as banking and insurance services). The third category, *income receipts and payments*, refers to income from foreign investments and payments that have to be made to foreigners investing in a country. For example, if a

Current Account Records the economic transactions with other countries in a given time period.

Table A1

United States Balance of Payments Accounts, 2006 ($ millions)

Source: Bureau of Economic Analysis.

Current Account	$ Millions
Exports of goods, services, and income receipts	$2,058,836
Goods	1,023,689
Services	413,127
Income receipts	622,020
Imports of Goods, Services, and Income Payments	**−2,831,369**
Goods	−1,859,655
Services	−342,428
Income payments	−629,286
Unilateral current transfers (net)	**−84,122**
Current Account Balance	**−856,655**
Capital Account	
Capital account transactions (net)	−3,914
Financial Account	
U.S. owned assets abroad, net	−1,045,760
U.S. official reserve assets	2,374
U.S. government assets	5,219
U.S. private assets	−1,053,353
Foreign-Owned Assets in the United States	**1,764,909**
Foreign official assets in the United States	300,510
Other foreign assets in the United States	1,464,399
Statistical Discrepancy	**141,419**

U.S. citizen owns a share of a Finnish company and receives a dividend payment of $5, that payment shows up on the U.S. current account as the receipt of $5 of investment income. Also included in the current account are unilateral current transfers, such as U.S. government grants to foreigners (including foreign aid), and private payments to foreigners (such as when a foreign worker in the United States sends money to his or her home country).

Current Account Deficit

Occurs when a country imports more goods, services and income than it exports.

Current Account Surplus

Occurs when a country exports more goods and services than it imports

A **current account deficit** occurs when a country imports more goods, services, and income than it exports. A **current account surplus** occurs when a country exports more goods, services, and income than it imports. Table A1 shows that in 2006 the United States ran a current account deficit of −$856,655,000,000. This is often a headline-grabbing figure and is widely reported in the news media. In recent years the U.S. current account deficit has been getting steadily larger, primarily due to the fact that America imports far more physical goods than it exports (you will notice that America actually runs a surplus on trade in services and is close to balance on income payments).

Figure A1 shows how the U.S. current account position has changed in recent years. The 2006 current account deficit was the largest on record and was equivalent to around 6.5 percent of the country's GDP. Many people find this figure to be

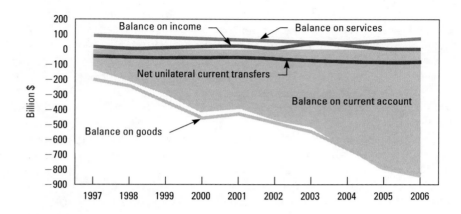

figure

Current Account Balance and Its Components

Source: U.S. Bureau of Economic Analysis (www.bea.gov/international/index.htm).

disturbing, the common assumption being that growing imports of goods displaces domestic production, causes unemployment, and reduces the growth of the United States economy. For example, the *New York Times* responded to the record current account deficit in 2006 by stating:

> A growing trade deficit acts as a drag on overall economic growth. Economists said that they expect that, in light of the new numbers, the government will have to revise its estimate of the nation's fourth quarter gross domestic product to show slightly slower expansion.[37]

However, the issue is somewhat more complex than implied by statements like this. Fully understanding the implications of a large and persistent deficit requires that we look at the rest of the balance-of-payments accounts.

The **capital account** records onetime changes in the stock of assets. As noted above, until recently this item was included in the current account. The capital account includes capital transfers, such as debt forgiveness and migrant transfers (the goods and financial assets that accompany migrants as they enter or leave the country). In the big scheme of things, this is a relatively small figure amounting to $3.914 billion in 2006.

The **financial account** (formally the capital account) records transactions that involve the purchase or sale of assets. Thus, when a German firm purchases stock in a U.S. company, or buys a U.S. bond, the transaction enters the U.S. balance of payments as a credit on the capital account. This is because capital is flowing into the country. When capital flows out of the United States, it enters the capital account as a debit.

The financial account is comprised of a number of elements. The net change in U.S.-owned assets abroad includes the change in assets owned by the U.S. government (U.S. official reserve assets and U.S. government assets) and the change in assets owned by private individuals and corporations. As can be seen from Table A1, in 2006 there was a −$1,045 billion reduction in U.S.-owned assets owned abroad, primarily due to a $1,053 billion fall in the amount of foreign assets owned by U.S. corporations and individuals. In other words, private entities in the United States were net sellers of foreign assets in 2006, including foreign stocks, bonds, and real estate.

Capital Account
Records one time changes in the stock of capital assets.

Financial Account
Records international transactions that involve the purchase or sale of assets.

Also included in the financial account are foreign-owned assets in the United States. These are divided into assets owned by foreign governments (foreign official assets) and assets owned by other foreign entities such as corporations and individuals (other foreign assets in the United States). As can be seen, in 2006 foreigners increased their holdings of U.S. assets, including treasury bills, corporate stocks and bonds, and direct investments in the United States, by $1,765 billion. Some $301 billion of this was due to an increase in the holding of U.S. assets by foreign governments, with the remainder being due to investments by private corporations and individuals in U.S. assets.

A basic principle of balance-of-payments accounting is double-entry bookkeeping. Every international transaction automatically enters the balance of payments twice—once as a credit and once as a debit. Imagine that you purchase a car produced in Japan by Toyota for $20,000. Since your purchase represents a payment to another country for goods, it will enter the balance of payments as a debit on the current account. Toyota now has the $20,000 and must do something with it. If Toyota deposits the money at a U.S. bank, Toyota has purchased a U.S. asset—a bank deposit worth $20,000—and the transaction will show up as a $20,000 credit on the financial account. Or Toyota might deposit the cash in a Japanese bank in return for Japanese yen. Now the Japanese bank must decide what to do with the $20,000. Any action that it takes will ultimately result in a credit for the U.S. balance of payments. For example, if the bank lends the $20,000 to a Japanese firm that uses it to import personal computers from the United States, then the $20,000 must be credited to the U.S. balance-of-payments current account. Or the Japanese bank might use the $20,000 to purchase U.S. government bonds, in which case it will show up as a credit on the U.S. balance-of-payments financial account.

Thus, any international transaction automatically gives rise to two offsetting entries in the balance of payments. Because of this, *the sum of the current account balance, the capital account, and the financial account balance should always add up to zero*. In practice, this does not always occur due to the existence of "statistical discrepancies," the source of which need not concern us here (note that in 2006 the statistical discrepancy amounted to $141 billion).

Does the Current Account Deficit Matter?

As discussed earlier, there is some concern when a country is running a deficit on the current account of its balance of payments.[38] In recent years a number of rich countries, including most notably the United States, have run persistent and growing current account deficits. When a country runs a current account deficit, the money that flows to other countries can then be used by those countries to purchase assets in the deficit country. Thus, when the United States runs a trade deficit with China, the Chinese use the money received from U.S. consumers to purchase U.S. assets such as stocks, bonds, and the like. Put another way, a deficit on the current account is financed by selling assets to other countries; that is, by a surplus on the financial account. Thus, the persistent U.S. current account deficit is being financed by a steady sale of U.S. assets (stocks, bonds, real estate, and whole corporations) to other countries. In short, countries that run current account deficits become net debtors.

For example, as a result of financing its current account deficit through asset sales, the United States must deliver a stream of interest payments to foreign bondholders, rents to foreign landowners, and dividends to foreign stockholders. One might argue that such payments to foreigners drain resources from a country and limit the funds available for investment within the country. Since investment within a country is necessary to stimulate economic growth, a persistent current account deficit can choke off a country's future economic growth. This is the basis of the argument that persistent deficits are bad for an economy.

However, things are not this simple. For one thing, in an era of global capital markets, money is efficiently directed toward its highest value uses; and over the last quarter of a century many of the highest value uses of capital have been in the United States. So even though capital is flowing out of the United States in the form of payments to foreigners, much of that capital finds its way right back into the country to fund productive investments in the United States. In short, it is not clear that the current account deficit chokes off U.S. economic growth. In fact, the U.S. economy has grown at an impressive rate over the last 25 years, despite running a persistent current account deficit, and despite financing that deficit by selling U.S. assets to foreigners. This is precisely because foreigners reinvest much of the income earned from U.S. assets, and from exports to the United States, right back into the United States. This revisionist view, which has gained in popularity in recent years, suggests that a persistent current account deficit might not be the drag on economic growth it was once thought to be.[39]

Having said this, there is still a nagging fear that at some point the appetite that foreigners have for U.S. assets might decline. If foreigners suddenly reduce their investments in the United States, what would happen? In short, instead of reinvesting the dollars that they earn from exports and investment in the United States back into the country, they would sell those dollars for another currency, European euros or Japanese yen, for example, and invest in euro- and yen-denominated assets instead. This would lead to a fall in the value of the dollar on foreign exchange markets, and that in turn would increase the price of imports, and lower the price of U.S. exports making them more competitive, which should reduce the overall level of the current account deficit. Thus in the long run, the persistent U.S. current account deficit could be corrected via a reduction in the value of the U.S. dollar. The concern is that such adjustments may not be smooth. Rather than a controlled decline in the value of the dollar, the dollar might suddenly lose a significant amount of its value in a very short time, precipitating a "dollar crisis."[40] Since the U.S. dollar is the world's major reserve currency and is held by many foreign governments and banks, any dollar crisis could deliver a body blow to the world economy and at the very least trigger a global economic slowdown. That would not be a good thing.

Key Terms

balance-of-payments accounts, p. 195
current account, p. 195

current account deficit, p. 196
current account surplus, p. 196

capital account, p. 197
financial account, p. 197

Part 3 Cross-Border Trade and Investment

LEARNING OBJECTIVES

After you have read this chapter you should:

1 Describe the policy instruments used by governments to influence international trade flows.

2 Understand why governments sometimes intervene in international trade.

3 Articulate the arguments against strategic trade policy.

4 Describe the development of the world trading system and the current trade issue.

5 Explain the implications for managers of developments in the world trading system.

chapter 6

The Political Economy of International Trade

opening case

For the last 25 years global food prices have been falling, driven by the increased productivity and output of the farm sector worldwide. In 2007, this came to an abrupt end as global food prices soared. By September 2007, the world price of wheat rose to over $400 a ton—the highest price ever recorded and up from $200 a ton in May. The price of corn (maize) surged to $175 a ton, some 60 percent above its average for 2006. An index of food prices, which *The Economist* magazine has kept since 1845 and which is adjusted for inflation, hit its highest level ever in December 2007! What is driving this surge in food prices, and is it here to stay?

There are two explanations for rising food prices: increased demand and the trade-distorting effects of tariff barriers and subsidies for biofuels. The increased demand has been driven by greater food consumption in rapidly developing nations, most notably China and India. Rising consumption of meat, in particular, has driven up demand for grains; it takes eight kilograms of cereals to produce one kilogram of beef, so as demand for meat rises, consumption of grains by cattle surges. Farmers now feed 200 million to 250 million more tons of grain to their animals than they did 20 years ago, driving up grain prices.

As for biofuel subsidies, both the United States and the European Union have adopted policies to increase production of ethanol and biodiesel to slow global warming (both products are argued to produce fewer CO_2 emissions, although exactly how effective they are at doing this is actively debated). In 2000, about 15 million tons of American corn was turned into ethanol; in 2007 the figure reached 85 million tons. To promote increased production, governments have given subsidies to farmers. In the United States, subsidies amount to between $0.29 and $0.36 per liter of ethanol. In Europe the subsidies are as high as $1 a liter. Not surprisingly, the subsidies have created an incentive for farmers to plant more crops that can be turned into biofuels (primarily corn and soybeans). This has diverted land away from production of corn and soy for food and reduced the supply of land devoted to growing crops that don't receive biofuel subsidies, such as wheat. This highly subsidized source of demand seems to be having a dramatic effect on demand for corn and soybeans. In 2007, for example, the U.S. increase in demand for corn-based ethanol accounted for more than half of the global increase in demand for corn.

The situation is aggravated by shutting alternative products that can be turned into biofuels, most notably sugarcane, out of the American and EU markets through high tariffs, thereby keeping prices of corn, soybeans, and other food products high. Brazil, the world's most efficient producer of sugarcane, confronts import tariffs of at least 25 percent by value in the United States and 50 percent in the EU, raising the price of imported sugarcane and making it uncompetitive with subsidized corn and soybeans. Sugarcane is widely seen as a more environmentally friendly raw material for biofuels than either corn or soy. Sugarcane uses less fertilizer than corn or soybeans and produces a higher yield per hectare in terms of its energy content. Ethanol is also produced from what used to be considered a waste product—the fiber removed from the cane during processing.

Looking forward, however, if policy makers have their way the situation may get even worse. Plans in both the United States and EU call for an increase in the production of biofuels, but neither political entity has agreed to reduce tariff barriers on sugarcane nor to remove the trade-distorting subsidies given to those who produce corn and soy for biofuels. Brazil is not sitting on the sidelines; in 2007 it asked the World Trade Organization to probe U.S. subsidies to corn farmers for ethanol production. An initial ruling was expected in late 2008.

Who benefits from these policies? In a word, producers, most notably farmers in the EU and United States, where farm incomes are surging. The losers include consumers who now have to pay more for food; and hardest hit are some of the world's poorest people. One estimate suggests that if food prices rise by one-third, they will reduce living standards in rich countries by about 3 percent, but in very poor ones by about 10 percent. According to the International Food Policy Research Institute, unless policies change, cereal prices will rise by 10 to 20 percent by 2015, and the expansion of biofuel production could reduce calorie intake by 2 to 8 percent by 2020 in many of the world's poorest nations. ●

Sources: "Cheap No More: Food Prices," *The Economist,* December 8, 2007, p. 84; "Brazil Seeks WTO Probe of U.S. Farm Subsidies," *Journal of Commerce,* September 13, 2007, p. 1; M. Wolf, "Biofuels: An Everyday Story of Special Interests and Subsidies," *Financial Times,* October 31, 2007, p. 11; and J. Von Braun and R.K. Pachauri, "The Promises and Challenges of Biofuels for the Poor in Developing Countries: IFPRI 2005–2006 Annual Report Essay," (Washington, DC: International Food Policy Research Institute, 2007).

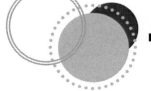

Introduction

Our review of the classical trade theories of Smith, Ricardo, and Heckscher-Ohlin in Chapter 5 showed us that in a world without trade barriers, trade patterns are determined by the relative productivity of different factors of production in different countries. Countries will specialize in products that they can make most efficiently, while importing products that they can produce less efficiently. Chapter 5 also laid out the intellectual case for free trade. Remember, **free trade** refers to a situation in which a government does not attempt to restrict what its citizens can buy from or sell to another country. As we saw in Chapter 5, the theories of Smith, Ricardo, and Heckscher-Ohlin predict that the consequences of free trade include both static economic gains (because free trade supports a higher level of domestic consumption and more efficient utilization of resources) and dynamic economic gains (because free trade stimulates economic growth and the creation of wealth).

Another Perspective

Rankings of the World Economic Forum
The World Economic Forum (WEF) is an independent economic organization whose mission is to improve the state of the world. Based in Geneva, Switzerland, it hosts meetings that serve as a forum for the collaboration of international leaders. The WEF also conducts global economic research and annually publishes country competitive rankings. In the latest report (2007–08), the top countries in competitiveness were the United States, Switzerland, and Denmark, followed by Sweden, Germany, Finland, and Singapore. If you review the report's complete list of rankings, you'll note a strong correlation between a country's ranking and its political system. Visit www.gcr.weforum.org/.

In this chapter, we look at the political reality of international trade. Although many nations are nominally committed to free trade, they tend to intervene in international trade to protect the interests of politically important groups or promote the interests of key domestic producers. The opening case illustrates the nature of such political realities. In the United States, subsidies have promoted the production of ethanol from a relatively inefficient source, corn, while tariffs placed on sugarcane imports have created an incentive not to use this more efficient raw material for biofuel production. While these policies are pro-producer (grain prices and farm incomes have been surging), they harm consumers who must now pay more for food. The removal of subsidies and tariffs would promote the production of ethanol from sugarcane and divert valuable land back to the business of growing grains for food, driving down food prices.

Free Trade
The absence of barriers to the free flow of goods and services between countries.

In this chapter, we explore the political and economic reasons that governments have for intervening in international trade. When governments intervene, they often do so by restricting imports of goods and services into their nation, while adopting policies that promote domestic production and exports. Normally their motives are to protect domestic producers and jobs from foreign competition while increasing the foreign market for products of domestic producers. However, in recent years, social issues have intruded into the decision-making calculus. In the United States, for example, a movement is growing to ban imports of goods from countries that do not abide by the same labor, health, and environmental regulations as the United States.

We start this chapter by describing the range of policy instruments that governments use to intervene in international trade. This is followed by a detailed review of the various political and economic motives that governments have for intervention. In the third section of this chapter, we consider how the case for free trade stands up in view of the various justifications given for government intervention in international trade. Then we look at the emergence of the modern international trading system, which is based on the General Agreement on Tariffs and Trade and its successor, the WTO. The GATT and WTO are the creations of a series of multinational treaties. The most recent was completed in 1995, involved more than 120 countries, and resulted in the creation of the WTO. The purpose of these treaties has been to lower barriers to the free flow of goods and services between nations. Like the GATT before it, the WTO promotes free trade by limiting the ability of national governments to adopt policies that restrict imports into their nations. In the final section of this chapter, we discuss the implications of this material for management practice.

Instruments of Trade Policy

LEARNING OBJECTIVE 1
Describe the policy instruments used by governments to influence international trade flows.

Trade policy uses seven main instruments: tariffs, subsidies, import quotas, voluntary export restraints, local content requirements, administrative policies, and antidumping duties. Tariffs are the oldest and simplest instrument of trade policy. As we shall see later in this chapter, they are also the instrument that the GATT and WTO have been most successful in limiting. A fall in tariff barriers in recent decades has been accompanied by a rise in nontariff barriers, such as subsidies, quotas, voluntary export restraints, and antidumping duties.

Tariff
A tax levied by governments on imports or exports.

Specific Tariff
Levied as a fixed charge for each unit of good imported.

Ad Valorem Tariff
Levied as a proportion of the value of the imported good.

TARIFFS A **tariff** is a tax levied on imports (or exports). Tariffs fall into two categories. **Specific tariffs** are levied as a fixed charge for each unit of a good imported (e.g., $3 per barrel of oil). **Ad valorem tariffs** are levied as a proportion of the value of the imported good. In most cases, tariffs are placed on imports to protect domestic producers from foreign competition by raising the price of imported goods. However, tariffs also produce revenue for the government. Until the income tax was introduced, for example, the U.S. government received most of its revenues from tariffs.

The important thing to understand about an import tariff is who suffers and who gains. The government gains because the tariff increases government revenues. Domestic producers gain because the tariff affords them some protection against foreign competitors by increasing the cost of imported foreign goods. Consumers lose because they must pay more for certain imports. For example, in March 2002 the U.S. government placed an ad valorem tariff of 8 percent to 30 percent on imports of foreign steel. The idea was to protect domestic steel producers from cheap imports of foreign steel. The effect, however, was to raise the price of steel products in the United States by between 30 and 50 percent. A number of U.S. steel consumers, ranging from appliance makers to automobile companies, objected that the steel tariffs would raise their costs of production and make it more difficult for them to compete in the global marketplace. Whether the gains to the government and domestic producers exceed the loss to consumers depends on various factors such as the amount of the tariff, the importance of the imported good to domestic consumers, the number of jobs saved in the protected industry, and so on. In the steel case, many argued that the losses to steel consumers apparently outweighed the gains to steel producers. In November 2003, the World Trade Organization declared that the tariffs represented a violation of the WTO treaty, and the United States removed them in December of that year.

 **Another Perspective**

U.S. Tariff Rates
Because the United States takes a free trade public position, many people assume the U.S. government has few tariffs. Information about U.S. trade is readily available online. For example, you can review the U.S. government's current tariffs at the U.S. Office of Tariff Affairs and Trade Agreements site (www.usitc.gov/tata/index.htm). However, with many schedules and fine distinctions made within product groups, this site can be a challenge to browse. For interesting statistics on imports and exports of the United States, as well of as other nations, check out the World Trade Organization Web site at www.wto.org.

In general, two conclusions can be derived from economic analysis of the effect of import tariffs.[1] First, tariffs are unambiguously pro-producer and anti-consumer. While they protect producers from foreign competitors, this restriction of supply also raises domestic prices. For example, a study by Japanese economists calculated that tariffs on imports of foodstuffs, cosmetics, and chemicals into Japan cost the average Japanese consumer about $890 per year in the form of higher prices.[2] Almost all studies find that import tariffs impose significant costs on domestic consumers in the form of higher prices.[3]

Second, import tariffs reduce the overall efficiency of the world economy. They reduce efficiency because a protective tariff encourages domestic firms

Hill: Global Business
Today, Sixth Edition

6. The Political Economy of
International Trade

Text

© The McGraw−Hill
Companies, 2009

215

to produce products at home that, in theory, could be produced more efficiently abroad. The consequence is an inefficient utilization of resources. For example, tariffs on the importation of rice into South Korea have led to an increase in rice production in that country; however, rice farming is an unproductive use of land in South Korea. It would make more sense for the South Koreans to purchase their rice from lower-cost foreign producers and to utilize the land now employed in rice production in some other way, such as growing foodstuffs that cannot be produced more efficiently elsewhere or for residential and industrial purposes.

Sometimes tariffs are levied on exports of a product from a country. Export tariffs are far less common than import tariffs. In general, export tariffs have two objectives: first, to raise revenue for the government, and second, to reduce exports from a sector, often for political reasons. For example, in 2004 China imposed a tariff on textile exports. The primary objective was to moderate the growth in exports of textiles from China, thereby alleviating tensions with other trading partners.

SUBSIDIES   A **subsidy** is a government payment to a domestic producer. Subsidies take many forms, including cash grants, low-interest loans, tax breaks, and government equity participation in domestic firms. By lowering production costs, subsidies help domestic producers in two ways: (1) competing against foreign imports and (2) gaining export markets. According to the World Trade Organization, in the mid-2000s, countries spent some $300 billion on subsidies, $250 billion of which was spent by 21 developed nations.[4]

Subsidy
Government financial assistance to a domestic producer.

Agriculture tends to be one of the largest beneficiaries of subsidies in most countries (see the opening case for an example). In the mid-2000s, the European Union was paying around €44 billion annually ($55 billion) in farm subsidies. Not to be outdone, in May 2002 President George W. Bush signed into law a bill that contained subsidies of more than $180 billion for U.S. farmers spread out over 10 years. This was followed in 2007 by a farm bill that contained $286 billion in subsidies for the next 10 years. The Japanese also have a long history of supporting inefficient domestic producers with farm subsidies. The accompanying Country Focus looks at subsidies to wheat producers in Japan.

Nonagricultural subsidies are much lower, but they are still significant. For example, subsidies historically were given to Boeing and Airbus to help them lower the cost of developing new commercial jet aircraft. In Boeing's case, subsidies came in the form of tax credits for R&D spending or Pentagon money that was used to develop military technology, which then was transferred to civil aviation projects. In the case of Airbus, subsidies took the form of government loans at below-market interest rates.

The main gains from subsidies accrue to domestic producers, whose international competitiveness is increased as a result. Advocates of strategic trade policy (which, as you will recall from Chapter 5, is an outgrowth of the new trade theory) favor subsidies to help domestic firms achieve a dominant position in those industries in which economies of scale are important and the world market is not large enough to profitably support more than a few firms (aerospace and semiconductors are two such industries). According to this argument, subsidies can help a firm achieve a first-mover advantage in an emerging industry (just as U.S. government subsidies, in the form of substantial R&D grants, allegedly helped Boeing). If this is achieved, further gains to the domestic economy arise from the employment and tax revenues that a major global company can generate. However, government subsidies must be paid for, typically by taxing individuals and corporations.

Whether subsidies generate national benefits that exceed their national costs is debatable. In practice, many subsidies are not that successful at increasing the international competitiveness of domestic producers. Rather, they tend to protect the

Country FOCUS

Subsidized Wheat Production in Japan

Japan is not a particularly good environment for growing wheat. Wheat produced on large fields in the dry climates of North America, Australia, and Argentina is far cheaper and of much higher quality than anything produced in Japan. Indeed, Japan imports some 80 percent of its wheat from foreign producers. Yet tens of thousands of farmers in Japan still grow wheat, usually on small fields where yields are low and costs high, and production is rising. The reason is government subsidies designed to keep inefficient Japanese wheat producers in business. In 2004, Japanese farmers were selling their output at market prices, which were running at $9 per bushel, but they received an average of at least $35 per bushel for their 2004 production! The difference—$26 a bushel—was government subsidies paid to producers. The estimated costs of these subsidies were more than $700 million in 2004.

To finance its production subsidy, Japan operates a tariff rate quota on wheat imports in which a higher tariff rate is imposed once wheat imports exceed the quota level. The in-quota rate tariff is zero, while the over-quota tariff rate for wheat is $500 a ton. The tariff raises the cost so much that it deters over-quota imports, essentially restricting supply and raising the price for wheat inside Japan. The Japanese Ministry of Agriculture, Forestry and Fisheries (MAFF) has the sole right to purchase wheat imports within the quota (and since there are very few over-quota imports, the MAFF is a monopoly buyer on wheat imports into Japan). The MAFF buys wheat at world prices then resells it to millers in Japan at the artificially high prices that arise

due to the restriction on supply engineered by the tariff rate quota. Estimates suggest that in 2003, the world market price for wheat was $5.96 per bushel, but within Japan the average price for imported wheat was $10.23 a bushel. The markup of $4.27 a bushel yielded the MAFF in excess of $450 million in profit. This "profit" was then used to help cover the $700 million cost of subsidies to inefficient wheat farmers, with the rest of the funds coming from general government tax revenues.

Thanks to these policies, the price of wheat in Japan can be anything from 80 to 120 percent higher than the world price, and Japanese wheat production, which exceeded 850,000 tons in 2004, is significantly greater than it would be if a free market was allowed to operate. Indeed, under free market conditions, there would be virtually no wheat production in Japan since the costs of production are simply too high. The beneficiaries of this policy are the thousands of small farmers in Japan who grow wheat. The losers include Japanese consumers, who must pay more for products containing wheat and who must finance wheat subsidies through taxes, and foreign producers, who are denied access to a chunk of the Japanese market by the over-quota tariff rate. Why then does the Japanese government continue to pursue this policy? It continues because small farmers are an important constituency and Japanese politicians want their votes.

Sources: J. Dyck and H. Fukuda, "Taxes on Imports Subsidize Wheat Production in Japan," *Amber Waves,* February 2005, p. 2; and H. Fukuda, J. Dyck, and J. Stout, "Wheat and Barley Policies in Japan," U.S. Department of Agriculture research report, WHS-04i-01, November 2004.

inefficient and promote excess production. For example, agricultural subsidies (1) allow inefficient farmers to stay in business, (2) encourage countries to overproduce heavily subsidized agricultural products, (3) encourage countries to produce products that could be grown more cheaply elsewhere and imported, and therefore (4) reduce international trade in agricultural products. One study estimated that if advanced countries abandoned subsidies to farmers, global trade in agricultural products would be 50 percent higher and the world as a whole would be better off by $160 billion.[5] Another study estimated that removing all barriers to trade in agriculture (both subsidies and tariffs) would raise world income by $182 billion.[6] This increase in wealth arises from the more efficient use of agricultural land. For a specific example, see the Country Focus on wheat subsidies in Japan.

Import Quota
A direct restriction on the quantity of some good that can be imported into a country.

IMPORT QUOTAS AND VOLUNTARY EXPORT RESTRAINTS An **import quota** is a direct restriction on the quantity of some good that may be imported into a country. The restriction is usually enforced by issuing import licenses to a group of individuals or firms. For example, the United States has a quota on

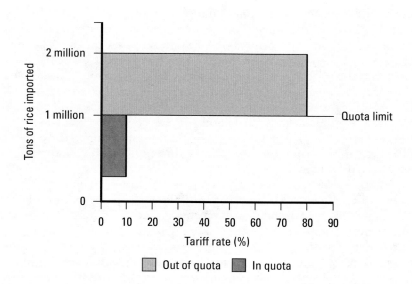

6.1 figure

Hypothetical Tariff Rate Quote

cheese imports. The only firms allowed to import cheese are certain trading companies, each of which is allocated the right to import a maximum number of pounds of cheese each year. In some cases, the right to sell is given directly to the governments of exporting countries. Historically this is the case for sugar and textile imports in the United States. However, the international agreement governing the imposition of import quotas on textiles, the Multi-Fiber Agreement, expired in December 2004.

A common hybrid of a quota and a tariff is known as a tariff rate quota. Under a **tariff rate quota,** a lower tariff rate is applied to imports within the quota than those over the quota. For example, as illustrated in Figure 6.1, an ad valorem tariff rate of 10 percent might be levied on rice imports into South Korea of 1 million tons, after which an out-of-quota rate of 80 percent might be applied. Thus, South Korea might import 2 million tons of rice, 1 million at a 10 percent tariff rate and another 1 million at an 80 percent tariff. Tariff rate quotas are common in agriculture, where their goal is to limit imports over quota. An example is given in the Country Focus that looks at how Japan uses the combination of a tariff rate quota and subsidies to protect inefficient Japanese wheat farmers from foreign competition.

A variant on the import quota is the voluntary export restraint. A **voluntary export restraint (VER)** is a quota on trade imposed by the exporting country, typically at the request of the importing country's government. One of the most famous historical examples is the limitation on auto exports to the United States enforced by Japanese automobile producers in 1981. A response to direct pressure from the U.S. government, this VER limited Japanese imports to no more than 1.68 million vehicles per year. The agreement was revised in 1984 to allow 1.85 million Japanese vehicles per year. The agreement was allowed to lapse in 1985, but the Japanese government indicated its intentions at that time to continue to restrict exports to the United States to 1.85 million vehicles per year.[7] Foreign producers agree to VERs because they fear more damaging punitive tariffs or import quotas might follow if they do not. Agreeing to a VER is seen as a way to make the best of a bad situation by appeasing protectionist pressures in a country.

Tariff Rate Quota
The process of applying a lower tariff rate to imports within the import quota than those over the quota.

Voluntary Export Restraint (VER)
A quota on trade imposed by the exporting country, typically at the request of the importing country's government.

As with tariffs and subsidies, both import quotas and VERs benefit domestic producers by limiting import competition. As with all restrictions on trade, quotas do not benefit consumers. An import quota or VER always raises the domestic price of an imported good. When imports are limited to a low percentage of the market by a quota or VER, the price is bid up for that limited foreign supply. The automobile industry VER mentioned earlier increased the price of the limited supply of Japanese imports. According to a study by the U.S. Federal Trade Commission, the automobile VER cost U.S. consumers about $1 billion per year between 1981 and 1985. That $1 billion per year went to Japanese producers in the form of higher prices.[8] The extra profit that producers make when supply is artificially limited by an import quota is referred to as a **quota rent.**

If a domestic industry lacks the capacity to meet demand, an import quota can raise prices for *both* the domestically produced and the imported good. This happened in the U.S. sugar industry, in which a tariff rate quota system has long limited the amount foreign producers can sell in the U.S. market. According to one study, import quotas have caused the price of sugar in the United States to be as much as 40 percent greater than the world price.[9] These higher prices have translated into greater profits for U.S. sugar producers, which have lobbied politicians to keep the lucrative agreement. They argue U.S. jobs in the sugar industry will be lost to foreign producers if the quota system is scrapped.

Quota Rent
The extra profit producers make when supply is artificially limited by an import quota.

LOCAL CONTENT REQUIREMENTS

A **local content requirement** is a requirement that some specific fraction of a good be produced domestically. The requirement can be expressed either in physical terms (e.g., 75 percent of component parts for this product must be produced locally) or in value terms (e.g., 75 percent of the value of this product must be produced locally). Local content regulations have been widely used by developing countries to shift their manufacturing base from the simple assembly of products whose parts are manufactured elsewhere into the local manufacture of component parts. They have also been used in developed countries to try to protect local jobs and industry from foreign competition. For example, a little-known law in the United States, the Buy America Act, specifies that government agencies must give preference to American products when putting contracts for equipment out to bid unless the foreign products have a significant price advantage. The law specifies a product as "American" if 51 percent of the materials by value are produced domestically. This amounts to a local content requirement. If a foreign company, or an American one for that matter, wishes to win a contract from a U.S. government agency to provide some equipment, it must ensure that at least 51 percent of the product by value is manufactured in the United States.

Local Content Requirement
A requirement that some specific fraction of a good be produced domestically.

Local content regulations provide protection for a domestic producer of parts in the same way an import quota does: by limiting foreign competition. The aggregate economic effects are also the same; domestic producers benefit, but the restrictions on imports raise the prices of imported components. In turn, higher prices for imported components are passed on to consumers of the final product in the form of higher final prices. So as with all trade policies, local content regulations tend to benefit producers and not consumers.

ADMINISTRATIVE POLICIES

In addition to the formal instruments of trade policy, governments of all types sometimes use informal or administrative policies to restrict imports and boost exports. **Administrative trade policies** are bureaucratic rules designed to make it difficult for imports to enter a country. It has been argued

Administrative Trade Policies
Rules adopted by governments that can be used to restrict imports or boost exports.

Hill: Global Business
Today, Sixth Edition

6. The Political Economy of
International Trade

Text

© The McGraw–Hill
Companies, 2009

219

that the Japanese are the masters of this trade barrier. In recent decades Japan's formal tariff and nontariff barriers have been among the lowest in the world. However, critics charge that the country's informal administrative barriers to imports more than compensate for this. For example, at one point the Netherlands exported tulip bulbs to almost every country in the world except Japan. In Japan, customs inspectors insisted on checking every tulip bulb by cutting it vertically down the middle, and even Japanese ingenuity could not put them back together. Federal Express also initially had a tough time expanding its global express shipping services into Japan because Japanese customs inspectors insist on opening a large proportion of express packages to check for pornography, a process that delayed an "express" package for days. Japan is not the only country that engages in such policies. France once required that all imported videotape recorders arrive through a small customs entry point that was both remote and poorly staffed. The resulting delays kept Japanese VCRs out of the French market until a VER agreement was negotiated.[10] As with all instruments of trade policy, administrative instruments benefit producers and hurt consumers, who are denied access to possibly superior foreign products.

ANTIDUMPING POLICIES   In the context of international trade, **dumping** is variously defined as selling goods in a foreign market at below their costs of production or as selling goods in a foreign market at below their "fair" market value. There is a difference between these two definitions; the fair market value of a good is normally judged to be greater than the costs of producing that good because the former includes a "fair" profit margin. Dumping is viewed as a method by which firms unload excess production in foreign markets. Some dumping may be the result of predatory behavior, with producers using substantial profits from their home markets to subsidize prices in a foreign market with a view to driving indigenous competitors out of that market. Once this has been achieved, so the argument goes, the predatory firm can raise prices and earn substantial profits.

> **Dumping**
> Selling goods in a foreign market for less than their cost of production or below their fair market value.

An alleged example of dumping occurred in 1997, when two South Korean manufacturers of semiconductors, LG Semicon and Hyundai Electronics, were accused of selling dynamic random access memory chips (DRAMs) in the U.S. market at below their costs of production. This action occurred in the middle of a worldwide glut of chip-making capacity. It was alleged that the firms were trying to unload their excess production in the United States.

Antidumping policies are designed to punish foreign firms that engage in dumping. The ultimate objective is to protect domestic producers from unfair foreign competition. Although antidumping policies vary somewhat from country to country, the majority are similar to those used in the United States. If a domestic producer believes that a foreign firm is dumping production in the U.S. market, it can file a petition with two government agencies, the Commerce Department and the International Trade Commission. In the Korean DRAM case, Micron Technology, a U.S. manufacturer of DRAMs, filed the petition. The government agencies then investigate the complaint. If a complaint has merit, the Commerce Department may impose an antidumping duty on the offending foreign imports (antidumping duties are often called **countervailing duties**). These duties, which represent a special tariff, can be fairly substantial and stay in place for up to five years. For example, after reviewing Micron's complaint, the Commerce Department imposed 9 percent and 4 percent countervailing duties on LG Semicon and Hyundai DRAM chips, respectively. The accompanying Management Focus discusses another example of how a firm, U.S. Magnesium, used antidumping legislation to gain protection from unfair foreign competitors.

> **Antidumping Policies**
> Rules designed to punish foreign firms that engage in dumping and thus protect domestic producers from unfair foreign competition.

> **Countervailing Duties**
> Antidumping duties.

Management FOCUS

U.S. Magnesium Seeks Protection

In February 2004, U.S. Magnesium, the sole surviving U.S. producer of magnesium, a metal that is primarily used in the manufacture of certain automobile parts and aluminum cans, filed a petition with the U.S. International Trade Commission (ITC) contending that a surge in imports had caused material damage to the U.S. industry's employment, sales, market share, and profitability. According to U.S. Magnesium, Russian and Chinese producers had been selling the metal at prices significantly below market value. During 2002 and 2003, imports of magnesium into the United States rose 70 percent, while prices fell by 40 percent and the market share accounted for by imports jumped to 50 percent from 25 percent.

"The United States used to be the largest producer of magnesium in the world," a U.S. Magnesium spokesman said at the time of the filing. "What's really sad is that you can be state of the art and have modern technology, and if the Chinese, who pay people less than 90 cents an hour, want to run you out of business, they can do it. And that's why we are seeking relief."

During a yearlong investigation, the ITC solicited input from various sides in the dispute. Foreign producers and consumers of magnesium in the United States argued that falling prices for magnesium during 2002 and 2003 simply reflected an imbalance between supply and demand due to additional capacity coming on stream not from Russia or China but from a new Canadian plant that opened in 2001 and from a planned Australian plant. The Canadian plant shut down in 2003, the Australian plant never came on stream, and prices for magnesium rose again in 2004.

Magnesium consumers in the United States also argued to the ITC that imposing antidumping duties on foreign imports of magnesium would raise prices in the United States significantly above world levels. A spokesman for Alcoa, which mixes magnesium with aluminum to make alloys for cans, predicted that if antidumping duties were imposed, high magnesium prices in the United States would force Alcoa to move some production out of the United States. Alcoa also noted that in 2003, U.S. Magnesium was unable to supply all of Alcoa's needs, forcing the company to turn to imports. Consumers of magnesium in the automobile industry asserted that high prices in the United States would drive engineers to design magnesium out of automobiles, or force manufacturing elsewhere, which would ultimately hurt everyone.

The six members of the ITC were not convinced by these arguments. In March 2005, the ITC ruled that both China and Russia had been dumping magnesium in the United States. The government decided to impose duties ranging from 50 percent to more than 140 percent on imports of magnesium from China. Russian producers face duties ranging from 19 percent to 22 percent. The duties will be levied for five years, after which the ITC will revisit the situation.

According to U.S. Magnesium, the favorable ruling will allow the company to reap the benefits of nearly $50 million in investments made in its manufacturing plant and enable the company to boost its capacity by 28 percent by the end of 2005. Commenting on the favorable ruling, a U.S. Magnesium spokesman noted, "Once unfair trade is removed from the marketplace we'll be able to compete with anyone." U.S. Magnesium's customers and competitors, however, did not view the situation in the 2002–03 period as one of unfair trade. While the imposition of antidumping duties no doubt will help to protect U.S. Magnesium and the 400 people it employs from foreign competition, magnesium consumers in the United States are left wondering if they will be the ultimate losers.

Sources: D. Anderton, "U.S. Magnesium Lands Ruling on Unfair Imports," *Desert News,* October 1, 2004, p. D10; "U.S. Magnesium and Its Largest Consumers Debate before U.S. ITC," *Platt's Metals Week,* February 28, 2005, p. 2; and S. Oberbeck, "U.S. Magnesium Plans Big Utah Production Expansion," *Salt Lake Tribune,* March 30, 2005.

The Case for Government Intervention

LEARNING OBJECTIVE 2
Understand why governments sometimes intervene in international trade.

Now that we have reviewed the various instruments of trade policy that governments can use, it is time to look at the case for government intervention in international trade. Arguments for government intervention take two paths: political and economic. Political arguments for intervention are concerned with protecting the interests of certain groups within a nation (normally producers), often at the expense of other groups (normally consumers). Economic arguments for intervention are typically concerned with boosting the overall wealth of a nation (to the benefit of all, both producers and consumers).

Hill: Global Business
Today, Sixth Edition

6. The Political Economy of
International Trade

Text

© The McGraw–Hill
Companies, 2009

221

POLITICAL ARGUMENTS FOR INTERVENTION   Political arguments for government intervention cover a range of issues, including preserving jobs, protecting industries deemed important for national security, retaliating against unfair foreign competition, protecting consumers from "dangerous" products, furthering the goals of foreign policy, and advancing the human rights of individuals in exporting countries.

Protecting Jobs and Industries   Perhaps the most common political argument for government intervention is that it is necessary for protecting jobs and industries from unfair foreign competition. The tariffs placed on imports of foreign steel by President George W. Bush in March 2002 were designed to do this. (Many steel producers were located in states that Bush needed to win reelection in 2004.) A political motive also underlay establishment of the Common Agricultural Policy (CAP) by the European Union. The CAP was designed to protect the jobs of Europe's politically powerful farmers by restricting imports and guaranteeing prices. However, the higher prices that resulted from the CAP have cost Europe's consumers dearly. This is true of many attempts to protect jobs and industries through government intervention. For example, the imposition of steel tariffs in 2002 raised steel prices for American consumers, such as automobile companies, making them less competitive in the global marketplace.

National Security   Countries sometimes argue that it is necessary to protect certain industries because they are important for national security. Defense-related industries often get this kind of attention (e.g., aerospace, advanced electronics, semiconductors, etc.). Although not as common as it used to be, this argument is still made. Those in favor of protecting the U.S. semiconductor industry from foreign competition, for example, argue that semiconductors are now such important components of defense products that it would be dangerous to rely primarily on foreign producers for them. In 1986, this argument helped persuade the federal government to support Sematech, a consortium of 14 U.S. semiconductor companies that accounted for 90 percent of the U.S. industry's revenues. Sematech's mission was to conduct joint research into manufacturing techniques that can be parceled out to members. The government saw the venture as so critical that Sematech was specially protected from antitrust laws. Initially, the U.S. government provided Sematech with $100 million per year in subsidies. By the mid-1990s, however, the U.S. semiconductor industry had regained its leading market position, largely through the personal computer boom and demand for microprocessor chips made by Intel. In 1994, the consortium's board voted to seek an end to federal funding, and since 1996 the consortium has been funded entirely by private money.[11]

Retaliation   Some argue that governments should use the threat to intervene in trade policy as a bargaining tool to help open foreign markets and force trading partners to "play by the rules of the game." The U.S. government has used the threat of punitive trade sanctions to try to get the Chinese government to enforce its intellectual property laws. Lax enforcement of these laws had given rise to massive copyright infringements in China that had been costing U.S. companies such as Microsoft hundreds of millions of dollars per year in lost sales revenues. After the United States threatened to impose 100 percent tariffs on a range of Chinese imports, and after harsh words between officials from the two countries, the Chinese agreed to tighter enforcement of intellectual property regulations.[12]

If it works, such a politically motivated rationale for government intervention may liberalize trade and bring with it resulting economic gains. It is a risky strategy, however. A country that is being pressured may not back down and instead may respond to the imposition of punitive tariffs by raising trade barriers of its own. This is exactly what the Chinese government threatened to do when pressured by the United States, although it ultimately did back down. If a government does not back down, however, the results could be higher trade barriers all around and an economic loss to all involved.

Protecting Consumers   Many governments have long had regulations to protect consumers from unsafe products. The indirect effect of such regulations often is to limit or ban the importation of such products. For example, in 2003 several countries, including Japan and South Korea, decided to ban imports of American beef after a single case of mad cow disease was found in Washington State. The ban was motivated to protect consumers from what was seen to be an unsafe product. Together, Japan and South Korea accounted for about $2 billion of U.S. beef sales, so the ban had a significant impact on U.S. beef producers. After two years, both countries lifted the ban, although they placed stringent requirements on U.S. beef imports to reduce the risk of importing beef that might be tainted by mad cow disease (e.g., Japan required that all beef must come from cattle under 21 months of age).[13]

The accompanying Country Focus describes how the European Union banned the sale and importation of hormone-treated beef. The ban was motivated by a desire to protect European consumers from the possible health consequences of eating meat from animals treated with growth hormones. The conflict over the importation of hormone-treated beef into the EU may prove to be a taste of things to come. In addition to the use of hormones to promote animal growth and meat production, biotechnology has made it possible to genetically alter many crops so that they resist common herbicides, produce proteins that are natural insecticides, grow dramatically improved yields, or withstand inclement weather conditions. A new breed of genetically modified tomatoes has an antifreeze gene inserted into its genome and can thus be grown in colder climates than hitherto possible. Another example is a genetically engineered cotton seed produced by Monsanto. The seed has been engineered to express a protein that protects against three common insect pests: the cotton bollworm, tobacco budworm, and pink bollworm. Use of this seed reduces or eliminates the need for traditional pesticide applications for these pests.

A genetically engineered cotton seed that protects against three common insects has been met with resistance in Europe due to a fear that these genetically altered seeds could potentially be harmful to humans.

Country FOCUS

Trade in Hormone-Treated Beef

In the 1970s, scientists discovered how to synthesize certain hormones and use them to accelerate the growth rate of livestock animals, reduce the fat content of meat, and increase milk production. Bovine somatotropin (BST), a growth hormone produced by cattle, was first synthesized by the biotechnology firm Genentech. Injections of BST could be used to supplement an animal's own hormone production and increase its growth rate. These hormones soon became popular among farmers, who found that they could cut costs and help satisfy consumer demands for leaner meat. Although these hormones occurred naturally in animals, consumer groups in several countries soon raised concerns about the practice. They argued that the use of hormone supplements was unnatural and that the health consequences of consuming hormone-treated meat were unknown but might include hormonal irregularities and cancer.

The European Union responded to these concerns in 1989 by banning the use of growth-promoting hormones in the production of livestock and the importation of hormone-treated meat. The ban was controversial because a reasonable consensus existed among scientists that the hormones posed no health risk. Although the EU banned hormone-treated meat, many other countries did not, including big meat-producing countries such as Australia, Canada, New Zealand, and the United States. The use of hormones soon became widespread in these countries. According to trade officials outside the EU, the European ban constituted an unfair restraint on trade. As a result of this ban, exports of meat to the EU fell. For example, U.S. red meat exports to the EU declined from $231 million in 1988 to $98 million in 1994. The complaints of meat exporters were bolstered in 1995 when Codex Alimentarius, the international food standards body of the UN's Food and Agriculture Organization and the World Health Organization, approved the use of growth hormones. In making this decision, Codex reviewed the scientific literature and found no evidence of a link between the consumption of

hormone-treated meat and human health problems, such as cancer.

Fortified by such decisions, in 1995 the United States pressed the EU to drop the import ban on hormone-treated beef. The EU refused, citing "consumer concerns about food safety." In response, both Canada and the United States independently filed formal complaints with the World Trade Organization. The United States was joined in its complaint by a number of other countries, including Australia and New Zealand. The WTO created a trade panel of three independent experts. After reviewing evidence and hearing from a range of experts and representatives of both parties, the panel in May 1997 ruled that the EU ban on hormone-treated beef was illegal because it had no scientific justification. The EU immediately indicated it would appeal the finding to the WTO court of appeals. The WTO court heard the appeal in November 1997 and in February 1998 agreed with the findings of the trade panel that the EU had not presented any scientific evidence to justify the hormone ban.

This ruling left the EU in a difficult position. Legally, the EU had to lift the ban or face punitive sanctions, but the ban had wide public support in Europe. The EU feared that lifting the ban could produce a consumer backlash. Instead the EU did nothing, so in February 1999 the United States asked the WTO for permission to impose punitive sanctions on the EU. The WTO responded by allowing the United States to impose punitive tariffs valued at $120 million on EU exports to the United States. The EU decided to accept these tariffs rather than lift the ban on hormone-treated beef, and as of 2008, the ban and punitive tariffs were still in place.

Sources: C. Southey, "Hormones Fuel a Meaty EU Row," *Financial Times,* September 7, 1995, p. 2; E.L. Andrews, "In Victory for U.S., European Ban on Treated Beef Is Ruled Illegal," *The New York Times,* May 9, 1997, p. A1; F. Williams and G. de Jonquieres, "WTO's Beef Rulings Give Europe Food for Thought," *Financial Times,* February 13, 1998, p. 5; R. Baily, "Food and Trade: EU Fear Mongers' Lethal Harvest," *Los Angeles Times,* August 18, 2002, p. M3; "The US-EU Dispute over Hormone Treated Beef," *The Kiplinger Agricultural Letter,* January 10, 2003; and Scott Miller, "EU Trade Sanctions Have Duel Edge," *The Wall Street Journal,* February 26, 2004, p. A3.

As enticing as such innovations sound, they have met with intense resistance from consumer groups, particularly in Europe. The fear is that the widespread use of genetically altered seed corn could have unanticipated and harmful effects on human health and may result in "genetic pollution." (An example of genetic pollution would be when the widespread use of crops that produce natural pesticides stimulates the evolution of "superbugs" that are resistant to those pesticides.) Such concerns have led Austria and Luxembourg to outlaw the importation, sale, or use of genetically altered organisms. Sentiment against genetically altered organisms also runs strong in several other European countries, most notably Germany and Switzerland. It seems likely, therefore, that the World Trade Organization will be drawn into the conflict between those that want

Beijing's Tiananmen Square, a tangible reminder of China's history of human rights abuses.

to expand the global market for genetically altered organisms, such as Monsanto, and those that want to limit it, such as Austria and Luxembourg.[14]

Furthering Foreign Policy Objectives

Governments sometimes use trade policy to support their foreign policy objectives.[15] A government may grant preferential trade terms to a country with which it wants to build strong relations. Trade policy has also been used several times to pressure or punish rogue states that do not abide by international law or norms. Iraq labored under extensive trade sanctions after the UN coalition defeated the country in the 1991 Gulf War until the 2003 invasion of Iraq by U.S.-led forces. The theory is that such pressure might persuade the rogue state to mend its ways, or it might hasten a change of government. In the case of Iraq, the sanctions were seen as a way of forcing that country to comply with several UN resolutions. The United States has maintained long-running trade sanctions against Cuba. Their principal function is to impoverish Cuba in the hope that the resulting economic hardship will lead to the downfall of Cuba's Communist government and its replacement with a more democratically inclined (and pro-U.S.) regime. The United States also has had trade sanctions in place against Libya and Iran, both of which it accuses of supporting terrorist action against U.S. interests and building weapons of mass destruction. In late 2003, the sanctions against Libya seemed to yield some returns when that country announced it would terminate a program to build nuclear weapons, and the U.S. government responded by relaxing those sanctions.

Other countries can undermine unilateral trade sanctions. The U.S. sanctions against Cuba, for example, have not stopped other Western countries from trading with Cuba. The U.S. sanctions have done little more than help create a vacuum into which other trading nations, such as Canada and Germany, have stepped. In an attempt to halt this and further tighten the screws on Cuba, in 1996 the U.S. Congress passed the **Helms-Burton Act.** This act allows Americans to sue foreign firms that use property in Cuba confiscated from them after the 1959 revolution. Later in 1996, Congress passed a similar law, the **D'Amato Act,** aimed at Libya and Iran.

The passage of Helms-Burton elicited protests from America's trading partners, including the European Union, Canada, and Mexico, all of which claim the law violates their sovereignty and is illegal under World Trade Organization rules. For example, Canadian companies that have been doing business in Cuba for years see no reason they should suddenly be sued in U.S. courts when Canada does not restrict trade with Cuba. They are not violating Canadian law, and they are not U.S. companies, so why should they be subject to U.S. law? Despite such protests, the law is still on the books in the United States, although the U.S. government has not enforced this act—probably because it is unenforceable.

Protecting Human Rights

Protecting and promoting human rights in other countries is an important element of foreign policy for many democracies. Governments sometimes use trade policy to try to improve the human rights policies of trading partners. For years, the most obvious example of this was the annual debate in the United States over whether to grant most favored nation (MFN) status to China. MFN status allows countries to export goods to the United States under favorable terms. Under MFN rules, the average tariff on Chinese goods imported into the United States was 8 percent. If China's MFN status were rescinded, tariffs could have risen to about 40 percent. Trading partners who are signatories of the World Trade Organization, as

Helms-Burton Act
Passed in 1996, this law allows Americans to sue foreign firms that use Cuban property confiscated from them during Cuba's 1959 revolution.

D'Amato Act
Passed in 1996, this law allows Americans to sue foreign firms that use property in Libya or Iran confiscated from Americans.

most are, automatically receive MFN status. However, China did not join the WTO until 2001, so historically the decision of whether to grant MFN status to China was a real one. The decision was made more difficult by the perception that China had a poor human rights record. As indications of the country's disregard for human rights, critics of China often point to the 1989 Tiananmen Square massacre, China's continuing subjugation of Tibet (which China occupied in the 1950s), and the squashing of political dissent in China.[16] These critics argue that it was wrong for the United States to grant MFN status to China, and that instead, the United States should withhold MFN status until China showed measurable improvement in its human rights record. The critics argue that trade policy should be used as a political weapon to force China to change its internal policies toward human rights.

Others contend that limiting trade with such countries would make matters worse, not better. They argue that the best way to change the internal human rights stance of a country is to engage it through international trade. At its core, the argument is simple: Growing bilateral trade raises the income levels of both countries, and as a state becomes richer, its people begin to demand, and generally receive, better treatment with regard to their human rights. This is a variant of the argument in Chapter 2 that economic progress begets political progress (if political progress is measured by the adoption of a democratic government that respects human rights). This argument ultimately won the day in 1999 when the Clinton administration blessed China's application to join the WTO and announced that trade and human rights issues should be decoupled.

ECONOMIC ARGUMENTS FOR INTERVENTION

With the development of the new trade theory and strategic trade policy (see Chapter 5), the economic arguments for government intervention have undergone a renaissance in recent years. Until the early 1980s, most economists saw little benefit in government intervention and strongly advocated a free trade policy. This position has changed at the margins with the development of strategic trade policy, although as we will see in the next section, there are still strong economic arguments for sticking to a free trade stance.

The Infant Industry Argument

The **infant industry argument** is by far the oldest economic argument for government intervention. Alexander Hamilton proposed it in 1792. According to this argument, many developing countries have a potential comparative advantage in manufacturing, but new manufacturing industries cannot initially compete with established industries in developed countries. To allow manufacturing to get a toehold, the argument is that governments should temporarily support new industries (with tariffs, import quotas, and subsidies) until they have grown strong enough to meet international competition.

Infant Industry Argument
Proposed by Alexander Hamilton in 1792, this oldest economic argument for government intervention states that developing countries have a comparative advantage in manufacturing.

This argument has had substantial appeal for the governments of developing nations during the past 50 years, and the GATT has recognized the infant industry argument as a legitimate reason for protectionism. Nevertheless, many economists remain critical of this argument for two main reasons. First, protection of manufacturing from foreign competition does no good unless the protection helps make the industry efficient. In case after case, however, protection seems to have done little more than foster the development of inefficient industries that have little hope of ever competing in the world market. Brazil, for example, built the world's 10th largest auto industry behind tariff barriers and quotas. Once those barriers were removed in the late 1980s, however, foreign imports soared, and the industry was forced to face up to the fact that after 30 years of protection, the Brazilian industry was one of the world's most inefficient.[17]

Second, the infant industry argument relies on an assumption that firms are unable to make efficient long-term investments by borrowing money from the domestic or international capital market. Consequently, governments have been required to subsidize long-term investments. Given the development of global capital markets over the past 20 years, this assumption no longer looks as valid as it once did. Today, if a developing country has a potential comparative advantage in a manufacturing industry, firms in that country should be able to borrow money from the capital markets to finance the required investments. Given financial support, firms based in countries with a potential comparative advantage have an incentive to endure the necessary initial losses in order to make long-run gains without requiring government protection. Many Taiwanese and South Korean firms did this in industries such as textiles, semiconductors, machine tools, steel, and shipping. Thus, given efficient global capital markets, the only industries that would require government protection would be those that are not worthwhile.

Strategic Trade Policy   Some new trade theorists have proposed the strategic trade policy argument.[18] We reviewed the basic argument in Chapter 5 when we considered the new trade theory. The new trade theory argues that in industries in which the existence of substantial economies of scale implies that the world market will profitably support only a few firms, countries may predominate in the export of certain products simply because they had firms that were able to capture first-mover advantages. The long-term dominance of Boeing in the commercial aircraft industry has been attributed to such factors.

The **strategic trade policy** argument has two components. First, it is argued that by appropriate actions, a government can help raise national income if it can somehow ensure that the firm or firms that gain first-mover advantages in an industry are domestic rather than foreign enterprises. Thus, according to the strategic trade policy argument, a government should use subsidies to support promising firms that are active in newly emerging industries. Advocates of this argument point out that the substantial R&D grants that the U.S. government gave Boeing in the 1950s and 1960s probably helped tilt the field of competition in the newly emerging market for passenger jets in Boeing's favor. (Boeing's first commercial jet airliner, the 707, was derived from a military plane.) Similar arguments have been made with regard to Japan's dominance in the production of liquid crystal display screens (used in laptop computers). Although these screens were invented in the United States, the Japanese government, in cooperation with major electronics companies, targeted this industry for research support in the late 1970s and early 1980s. The result was that Japanese firms, not U.S. firms, subsequently captured first-mover advantages in this market.

The second component of the strategic trade policy argument is that it might pay a government to intervene in an industry by helping domestic firms overcome the barriers to entry created by foreign firms that have already reaped first-mover advantages. This argument underlies government support of Airbus Industrie, Boeing's major competitor. Formed in 1966 as a consortium of four companies from Great Britain, France, Germany, and Spain, Airbus had less than 5 percent of the world commercial aircraft market when it began production in the mid-1970s. By 2006, it had increased its share to 45 percent, threatening Boeing's long-term dominance of the market. How did Airbus achieve this? According to the U.S. government, the answer is a $15 billion subsidy from the governments of Great Britain, France, Germany, and Spain.[19] Without this subsidy, Airbus would never have been able to break into the world market.

If these arguments are correct, they support a rationale for government intervention in international trade. Governments should target technologies that may be important in the future and use subsidies to support development work aimed at commercializing those technologies. Furthermore, government should provide export subsidies until the domestic firms have established first-mover advantages in the world market. Government support may also be justified if it can help domestic firms overcome the first-mover advantages enjoyed by foreign competitors and emerge as viable competitors in the world market (as in the Airbus and LCD examples). In this case, a combination of home-market protection and export-promoting subsidies may be needed.

The Revised Case for Free Trade

The strategic trade policy arguments of the new trade theorists suggest an economic justification for government intervention in international trade. This justification challenges the rationale for unrestricted free trade found in the work of classic trade theorists such as Adam Smith and David Ricardo. In response to this challenge to economic orthodoxy, a number of economists—including some of those responsible for the development of the new trade theory, such as Paul Krugman—point out that although strategic trade policy looks appealing in theory, in practice it may be unworkable. This response to the strategic trade policy argument constitutes the revised case for free trade.[20]

LEARNING OBJECTIVE 3
Articulate the arguments against strategic trade policy.

RETALIATION AND TRADE WAR Krugman argues that a strategic trade policy aimed at establishing domestic firms in a dominant position in a global industry is a beggar-thy-neighbor policy that boosts national income at the expense of other countries. A country that attempts to use such policies will probably provoke retaliation. In many cases, the resulting trade war between two or more interventionist governments will leave all countries involved worse off than if a hands-off approach had been adopted in the first place. If the U.S. government were to respond to the Airbus subsidy by increasing its own subsidies to Boeing, for example, the result might be that the subsidies would cancel each other out. In the process, both European and U.S. taxpayers would end up supporting an expensive and pointless trade war, and both Europe and the United States would be worse off.

Krugman may be right about the danger of a strategic trade policy leading to a trade war. The problem, however, is how to respond when one's competitors are already being supported by government subsidies; that is, how should Boeing and the United States respond to the subsidization of Airbus? According to Krugman, the answer is probably not to engage in retaliatory action but to help establish rules of the game that minimize the use of trade-distorting subsidies. This is what the World Trade Organization seeks to do.

DOMESTIC POLICIES Governments do not always act in the national interest when they intervene in the economy; politically important interest groups often influence them. The European Union's support for the Common Agricultural Policy (CAP), which arose because of the political power of French and German farmers, is an example. The CAP benefited inefficient farmers and the politicians who relied on the farm vote, but not consumers in the EU, who end up paying more for their foodstuffs. Thus, a further reason for not embracing strategic trade policy, according to Krugman, is that such a policy is almost certain to be captured by special-interest groups within the economy, who will distort it to their own ends. Krugman concludes that in the United States,

> To ask the Commerce Department to ignore special-interest politics while formulating detailed policy for many industries is not realistic: To establish a blanket policy of free trade, with exceptions granted only under extreme pressure, may not be the optimal policy according to the theory but may be the best policy that the country is likely to get.[21]

Development of the World Trading System

LEARNING OBJECTIVE 4
Describe the development of the world trading system and the current trade issues.

Strong economic arguments support unrestricted free trade. While many governments have recognized the value of these arguments, they have been unwilling to unilaterally lower their trade barriers for fear that other nations might not follow suit. Consider the problem that two neighboring countries, say, Brazil and Argentina, face when deciding whether to lower trade barriers between them. In principle, the government of Brazil might favor lowering trade barriers, but it might be unwilling to do so for fear that Argentina will not do the same. Instead, the government might fear that the Argentineans will take advantage of Brazil's low barriers to enter the Brazilian market, while at the same time continuing to shut Brazilian products out of their market through high trade barriers. The Argentinean government might believe that it faces the same dilemma. The essence of the problem is a lack of trust. Both governments recognize that their respective nations will benefit from lower trade barriers between them, but neither government is willing to lower barriers for fear that the other might not follow.[22]

Such a deadlock can be resolved if both countries negotiate a set of rules to govern cross-border trade and lower trade barriers. But who is to monitor the governments to make sure they are playing by the trade rules? And who is to impose sanctions on a government that cheats? Both governments could set up an independent body to act as a referee. This referee could monitor trade between the countries, make sure that no side cheats, and impose sanctions on a country if it does cheat in the trade game.

While it might sound unlikely that any government would compromise its national sovereignty by submitting to such an arrangement, since World War II an international trading framework has evolved that has exactly these features. For its first 50 years, this framework was known as the General Agreement on Tariffs and Trade. Since 1995, it has been known as the World Trade Organization. Here we look at the evolution and workings of the GATT and WTO.

FROM SMITH TO THE GREAT DEPRESSION

As noted in Chapter 5, the theoretical case for free trade dates to the late 18th century and the work of Adam Smith and David Ricardo. Free trade as a government policy was first officially embraced by Great Britain in 1846, when the British Parliament repealed the Corn Laws. The Corn Laws placed a high tariff on imports of foreign corn. The objectives of the Corn Laws tariff were to raise government revenues and to protect British corn producers. There had been annual motions in Parliament in favor of free trade since the 1820s when David Ricardo was a member. However, agricultural protection was withdrawn only as a result of a protracted debate when the effects of a harvest failure in Great Britain were compounded by the imminent threat of famine in Ireland. Faced with considerable hardship and suffering among the populace, Parliament narrowly reversed its long-held position.

During the next 80 years or so, Great Britain, as one of the world's dominant trading powers, pushed the case for trade liberalization; but the British government was a voice in the wilderness. Its major trading partners did not reciprocate the British policy of unilateral free trade. The only reason Britain kept this policy for so long was that as the world's largest exporting nation, it had far more to lose from a trade war than did any other country.

By the 1930s, the British attempt to stimulate free trade was buried under the economic rubble of the Great Depression. The Great Depression had roots in the failure of the world economy to mount a sustained economic recovery after the end of World War I in 1918. Things got worse in 1929 with the U.S. stock market collapse and the subsequent run on the U.S. banking system. Economic problems were compounded

Hill: Global Business
Today, Sixth Edition

6. The Political Economy of
International Trade

Text

© The McGraw–Hill
Companies, 2009

229

in 1930 when the U.S. Congress passed the Smoot-Hawley tariff. Aimed at avoiding rising unemployment by protecting domestic industries and diverting consumer demand away from foreign products, the **Smoot-Hawley Act** erected an enormous wall of tariff barriers. Almost every industry was rewarded with its "made-to-order" tariff. A particularly odd aspect of the Smoot-Hawley tariff-raising binge was that the United States was running a balance-of-payment surplus at the time and it was the world's largest creditor nation. The Smoot-Hawley Act had a damaging effect on employment abroad. Other countries reacted to the U.S. action by raising their own tariff barriers. U.S. exports tumbled in response, and the world slid further into the Great Depression.[23]

Smoot-Hawley Act
Passed in 1930, this U.S. law erected a wall of tariff barriers against imports.

1947–1979: GATT, TRADE LIBERALIZATION, AND ECONOMIC GROWTH
Economic damage caused by the beggar-thy-neighbor trade policies that the Smoot-Hawley Act ushered in exerted a profound influence on the economic institutions and ideology of the post-World War II world. The United States emerged from the war both victorious and economically dominant. After the debacle of the Great Depression, opinion in the U.S. Congress had swung strongly in favor of free trade. Under U.S. leadership, the GATT was established in 1947.

The GATT was a multilateral agreement whose objective was to liberalize trade by eliminating tariffs, subsidies, import quotas, and the like. From its foundation in 1947 until it was superseded by the WTO, the GATT's membership grew from 19 to more than 120 nations. The GATT did not attempt to liberalize trade restrictions in one fell swoop; that would have been impossible. Rather, tariff reduction was spread over eight rounds. The last, the Uruguay Round, was launched in 1986 and completed in December 1993. In these rounds, mutual tariff reductions were negotiated among all members, who then committed themselves not to raise import tariffs above negotiated rates. GATT regulations were enforced by a mutual monitoring mechanism. If a country believed that one of its trading partners was violating a GATT regulation, it could ask the Geneva-based bureaucracy that administered the GATT to investigate. If GATT investigators found the complaints to be valid, member countries could be asked to pressure the offending party to change its policies. In general, such pressure was sufficient to get an offending country to change its policies. If it were not, the offending country could be expelled from the GATT.

In its early years, the GATT was by most measures very successful. For example, the average tariff declined by nearly 92 percent in the United States between the Geneva Round of 1947 and the Tokyo Round of 1973–79. Consistent with the theoretical arguments first advanced by Ricardo and reviewed in Chapter 5, the move toward free trade under the GATT appeared to stimulate economic growth. From 1953 to 1963, world trade grew at an annual rate of 6.1 percent, and world income grew at an annual rate of 4.3 percent. Performance from 1963 to 1973 was even better; world trade grew at 8.9 percent annually, and world income grew at 5.1 percent annually.[24]

1980–1993: PROTECTIONIST TRENDS
During the 1980s and early 1990s, the world trading system erected by the GATT came under strain as pressures for greater protectionism increased around the world. Three reasons caused the rise in such pressures during the 1980s. First, the economic success of Japan strained the world trading system. Japan was in ruins when the GATT was created. By the early 1980s, however, it had become the world's second largest economy and its largest exporter. Japan's success in such industries as automobiles and semiconductors might have been enough to strain the world trading system. Things were made worse by the widespread perception in the West that despite low tariff rates and subsidies, Japanese markets were closed to imports and foreign investment by administrative trade barriers.

Second, the world trading system was strained by the persistent trade deficit in the world's largest economy, the United States. Although the deficit peaked in 1987 at more than $170 billion, by the end of 1992 the annual rate was still running about $80 billion. From a political perspective, the matter was worsened in 1992 by the $45 billion U.S. trade deficit with Japan, a country perceived as not playing by the rules. The consequences of the U.S. deficit included painful adjustments in industries such as automobiles, machine tools, semiconductors, steel, and textiles, where domestic producers steadily lost market share to foreign competitors. The resulting unemployment gave rise to renewed demands in the U.S. Congress for protection against imports.

A third reason for the trend toward greater protectionism was that many countries found ways to get around GATT regulations. Bilateral voluntary export restraints, or VERs, circumvent GATT agreements, because neither the importing country nor the exporting country complain to the GATT bureaucracy in Geneva—and without a complaint, the GATT bureaucracy can do nothing. Exporting countries agree to VERs to avoid more damaging punitive tariffs. One of the best-known examples is the automobile VER between Japan and the United States, under which Japanese producers promised to limit their auto imports into the United States as a way of defusing growing trade tensions. According to a World Bank study, 13 percent of the imports of industrialized countries in 1981 were subjected to nontariff trade barriers such as VERs. By 1986, this figure had increased to 16 percent. The most rapid rise was in the United States, where the value of imports affected by nontariff barriers (primarily VERs) increased by 23 percent between 1981 and 1986.[25]

THE URUGUAY ROUND AND THE WORLD TRADE ORGANIZATION

Against the background of rising pressures for protectionism, in 1986 GATT members embarked on their eighth round of negotiations to reduce tariffs, the Uruguay Round (so named because it occurred in Uruguay). This was the most difficult round of negotiations yet, primarily because it was also the most ambitious. Until then, GATT rules had applied only to trade in manufactured goods and commodities. In the Uruguay Round, member countries sought to extend GATT rules to cover trade in services. They also sought to write rules governing the protection of intellectual property, to reduce agricultural subsidies, and to strengthen the GATT's monitoring and enforcement mechanisms.

The Uruguay Round dragged on for seven years before an agreement was reached December 15, 1993. It went into effect July 1, 1995. The Uruguay Round contained the following provisions:

1. Tariffs on industrial goods were to be reduced by more than one-third, and tariffs were to be scrapped on more than 40 percent of manufactured goods.
2. Average tariff rates imposed by developed nations on manufactured goods were to be reduced to less than 4 percent of value, the lowest level in modern history.
3. Agricultural subsidies were to be substantially reduced.
4. GATT fair trade and market access rules were to be extended to cover a wide range of services.
5. GATT rules also were to be extended to provide enhanced protection for patents, copyrights, and trademarks (intellectual property).
6. Barriers on trade in textiles were to be significantly reduced over 10 years.
7. The World Trade Organization was to be created to implement the GATT agreement.

Services and Intellectual Property   In the long run, the extension of GATT rules to cover services and intellectual property may be particularly significant. Until 1995, GATT rules applied only to industrial goods (i.e., manufactured goods and commodities). In 2006, world trade in services amounted to $2,710 billion (compared to world trade in goods of $12,762 billion).[26] Ultimately, extension of GATT rules to this important trading arena could significantly increase both the total share of world trade accounted for by services and the overall volume of world trade. The extension of GATT rules to cover intellectual property will make it much easier for high-technology companies to do business in developing nations where intellectual property rules historically have been poorly enforced (see Chapter 2 for details).

The World Trade Organization   The clarification and strengthening of GATT rules and the creation of the World Trade Organization also hold out the promise of more effective policing and enforcement of GATT rules. The WTO acts as an umbrella organization that encompasses the GATT along with two new sister bodies, one on services and the other on intellectual property. The WTO's General Agreement on Trade in Services (GATS) has taken the lead to extending free trade agreements to services. The WTO's Agreement on Trade-Related Aspects of Intellectual Property Rights (TRIPS) is an attempt to narrow the gaps in the way intellectual property rights are protected around the world and to bring them under common international rules. WTO has taken over responsibility for arbitrating trade disputes and monitoring the trade policies of member countries. While the WTO operates on the basis of consensus as the GATT did, in the area of dispute settlement, member countries are no longer able to block adoption of arbitration reports. Arbitration panel reports on trade disputes between member countries are automatically adopted by the WTO unless there is a consensus to reject them. Countries that have been found by the arbitration panel to violate GATT rules may appeal to a permanent appellate body, but its verdict is binding. If offenders fail to comply with the recommendations of the arbitration panel, trading partners have the right to compensation or, in the last resort, to impose (commensurate) trade sanctions. Every stage of the procedure is subject to strict time limits. Thus, the WTO has something that the GATT never had—teeth.[27]

WTO: Experience to Date   By 2008, the WTO had 151 members, including China, which joined at the end of 2001. Another 25 countries, including the Russian Federation and the Ukraine were negotiating for membership into the organization. Since its formation, the WTO has remained at the forefront of efforts to promote global free trade. Its creators expressed the hope that the enforcement mechanisms granted to the WTO would make it more effective at policing global trade rules than the GATT had been. The great hope was that the WTO might emerge as an effective advocate and facilitator of future trade deals, particularly in areas such as services. The experience so far has been encouraging, although the collapse of WTO talks in Seattle in late 1999 and slow progress with the next round of trade talks, the Doha Round, have raised a number of questions about the future direction of the WTO.

WTO as Global Police   The first decade in the life of the WTO suggests that its policing and enforcement mechanisms are having a positive effect.[28] Between 1995 and early 2008, more than 370 trade disputes between member countries were brought to the WTO.[29] This record compares with a total of 196 cases handled by the GATT over almost half a century. Of the cases brought to the WTO, three-fourths had been resolved by informal consultations between the disputing countries. Resolving the remainder has involved more formal procedures, but these have been largely successful. In general, countries involved have adopted the WTO's recommendations. The fact that countries are using the WTO represents an important vote of confidence in the organization's dispute resolution procedures.

Expanding Trade Agreements   As explained earlier, the Uruguay Round of GATT negotiations extended global trading rules to cover trade in services. The WTO was given the role of brokering future agreements to open up global trade in services. The WTO was also encouraged to extend its reach to encompass regulations governing foreign direct investment, something the GATT had never done. Two of the first industries targeted for reform were the global telecommunication and financial services industries.

In February 1997, the WTO brokered a deal to get countries to agree to open their telecommunication markets to competition, allowing foreign operators to purchase ownership stakes in domestic telecommunication providers and establishing a set of common rules for fair competition. Under the pact, 68 countries accounting for more than 90 percent of world telecommunication revenues pledged to start opening their markets to foreign competition and to abide by common rules for fair competition in telecommunications. Most of the world's biggest markets, including the United States, European Union, and Japan, were fully liberalized by January 1, 1998, when the pact went into effect. All forms of basic telecommunication service are covered, including voice telephony, data and fax transmissions, and satellite and radio communications. Many telecommunication companies responded positively to the deal, pointing out that it would give them a much greater ability to offer their business customers one-stop shopping—a global, seamless service for all their corporate needs and a single bill.[30]

This was followed in December 1997 with an agreement to liberalize cross-border trade in financial services.[31] The deal covers more than 95 percent of the world's financial services market. Under the agreement, which took effect at the beginning of March 1999, 102 countries pledged to open to varying degrees their banking, securities, and insurance sectors to foreign competition. In common with the telecommunication deal, the accord covers not just cross-border trade but also foreign direct investment. Seventy countries agreed to dramatically lower or eradicate barriers to foreign direct investment in their financial services sector. The United States and the European Union, with minor exceptions, are fully open to inward investment by foreign banks, insurance, and securities companies. As part of the deal, many Asian countries made important concessions that allow significant foreign participation in their financial services sectors for the first time.

The WTO in Seattle: A Watershed?   At the end of November 1999, representatives from the WTO's member states met in Seattle, Washington. The goal of the meeting was to launch a new round of talks—dubbed the millennium round—aimed at further reducing barriers to cross-border trade and investment. Prominent on the agenda was an attempt to get the assembled countries to agree to work toward the reduction of barriers to cross-border trade in agricultural products and trade and investment in services.

These expectations were dashed on the rocks of a hard and unexpected reality. The talks ended December 3, 1999, without any agreement being reached. Inside the meeting rooms, the problem was an inability to reach consensus on the primary goals for the next round of talks. A major stumbling block was friction between the United States and the European Union over whether to endorse the aim of ultimately eliminating subsidies to agricultural exporters. The United States wanted the elimination of such

WTO protesters gather in front of the Niketown store at Fifth Avenue and Pike Street in downtown Seattle before the opening of the WTO sessions in Seattle.

subsidies to be a priority. The EU, with its politically powerful farm lobby and long history of farm subsidies, was unwilling to take this step. Another stumbling block was related to efforts by the United States to write "basic labor rights" into the law of the world trading system. The United States wanted the WTO to allow governments to impose tariffs on goods imported from countries that did not abide by what the United States saw as fair labor practices. Representatives from developing nations reacted angrily to this proposal, suggesting it was simply an attempt by the United States to find a legal way of restricting imports from poorer nations.

While the disputes inside the meeting rooms were acrimonious, it was events outside that captured the attention of the world press. The WTO talks proved to be a lightning rod for a diverse collection of organizations from environmentalists and human rights groups to labor unions. For various reasons, these groups oppose free trade. All these organizations argued that the WTO is an undemocratic institution that was usurping the national sovereignty of member states and making decisions of great importance behind closed doors. They took advantage of the Seattle meetings to voice their opposition, which the world press recorded. Environmentalists expressed concern about the impact that free trade in agricultural products might have on the rate of global deforestation. They argued that lower tariffs on imports of lumber from developing nations will stimulate demand and accelerate the rate at which virgin forests are logged, particularly in nations such as Malaysia and Indonesia. They also pointed to the adverse impact that some WTO rulings have had on environmental policies. For example, the WTO had recently blocked a U.S. rule that ordered shrimp nets be equipped with a device that allows endangered sea turtles to escape. The WTO found the rule discriminated against foreign importers who lacked such nets.[32] Environmentalists argued that the rule was necessary to protect the turtles from extinction.

Human rights activists see WTO rules as outlawing the ability of nations to stop imports from countries where child labor is used or working conditions are hazardous. Similarly, labor unions oppose trade laws that allow imports from low-wage countries and result in a loss of jobs in high-wage countries. They buttress their position by arguing that American workers are losing their jobs to imports from developing nations that do not have adequate labor standards.

Supporters of the WTO and free trade dismiss these concerns. They have repeatedly pointed out that the WTO exists to serve the interests of its member states, not subvert them. The WTO lacks the ability to force any member nation to take an action to which it is opposed. The WTO can allow member nations to impose retaliatory tariffs on countries that do not abide by WTO rules, but that is the limit of its power. Furthermore, supporters argue, it is rich countries that pass strict environmental laws and laws governing labor standards, not poor ones. In their view, free trade, by raising living standards in developing nations, will be followed by the passage of such laws in these nations. Using trade regulations to try to impose such practices on developing nations, they believe, will produce a self-defeating backlash.

Many representatives from developing nations, which make up about 110 of the WTO's 150 members, also reject the position taken by environmentalists and advocates of human and labor rights. Poor countries, which depend on exports to boost their economic growth rates and work their way out of poverty, fear that rich countries will use environmental concerns, human rights, and labor-related issues to erect barriers to the products of the developing world. They believe that attempts to incorporate language about the environment or labor standards in future trade agreements will amount to little more than trade barriers by another name.[33] If this were to occur, they argue that the effect would be to trap the developing nations of the world in a grinding cycle of poverty and debt.

These pro-trade arguments fell on deaf ears. As the WTO representatives gathered in Seattle, environmentalists, human rights activists, and labor unions marched in the streets. Some of the more radical elements in these organizations, together with groups of anarchists who were philosophically opposed to "global capitalism" and "the rape of the world by multinationals," succeeded not only in shutting down the opening ceremonies of the WTO but also in sparking violence in the normally peaceful streets of Seattle. A number of demonstrators damaged property and looted; and the police responded with tear gas, rubber bullets, pepper spray, and baton charges. When it was over, 600 demonstrators had been arrested, millions of dollars in property had been damaged in downtown Seattle, and the global news media had their headline: "WTO Talks Collapse amid Violent Demonstrations."

What happened in Seattle is notable because it may have been a watershed of sorts. In the past, previous trade talks were pursued in relative obscurity with only interested economists, politicians, and businesspeople paying much attention. Seattle demonstrated that the issues surrounding the global trend toward free trade have moved to center stage in the popular consciousness. The debate on the merits of free trade and globalization has become mainstream. Whether further liberalization occurs, therefore, may depend on the importance that popular opinion in countries such as the United States attaches to issues such as human rights and labor standards, job security, environmental policies, and national sovereignty. It will also depend on the ability of advocates of free trade to articulate in a clear and compelling manner the argument that, in the long run, free trade is the best way of promoting adequate labor standards, of providing more jobs, and of protecting the environment.

THE FUTURE OF THE WTO: UNRESOLVED ISSUES AND THE DOHA ROUND

Much remains to be done on the international trade front. Four issues at the forefront of the current agenda of the WTO are the increase in antidumping policies, the high level of protectionism in agriculture, the lack of strong protection for intellectual property rights in many nations, and continued high tariff rates on nonagricultural goods and services in many nations. We shall look at each in turn before discussing the latest round of talks between WTO members aimed at reducing trade barriers, the Doha Round, which began in 2001 and were still ongoing as of 2007.

Antidumping Actions

Antidumping actions proliferated during the 1990s. WTO rules allow countries to impose antidumping duties on foreign goods that are being sold cheaper than at home, or below their cost of production, when domestic producers can show that they are being harmed. Unfortunately, the rather vague definition of what constitutes "dumping" has proved to be a loophole that many countries are exploiting to pursue protectionism.

Between January 1995 and mid-2007, WTO members had reported implementation of some 3,097 antidumping actions to the WTO. India initiated the largest number of antidumping actions, some 474; the EU initiated 363 over the same period, and the United States 375 (see Figure 6.2). Antidumping actions seem to be concentrated in certain sectors of the economy such as basic metal industries (e.g., aluminum and steel), chemicals, plastics, and machinery and electrical equipment.[34] These sectors account for some 70 percent of all antidumping actions reported to the WTO. These four sectors since 1995 have been characterized by periods of intense competition and excess productive capacity, which have led to low prices and profits (or losses) for firms in those industries. It is not unreasonable, therefore, to hypothesize that the high level of antidumping actions in these industries represents an attempt by beleaguered manufacturers to use the political process in their nations to seek protection from foreign competitors, who they claim are engaging in unfair competition. While some of these

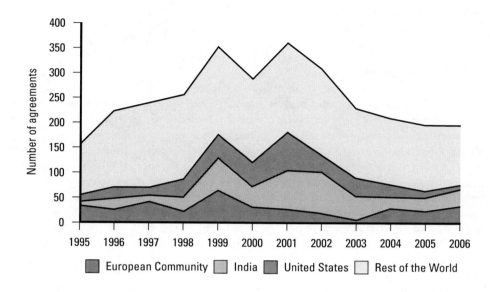

6.2 figure

Antidumping Agreements, 1995–2006

Source: Constructed by author from WTO data.

claims may have merit, the process can become very politicized as representatives of businesses and their employees lobby government officials to "protect domestic jobs from unfair foreign competition," and government officials, mindful of the need to get votes in future elections, oblige by pushing for antidumping actions. The WTO is clearly worried by this trend, suggesting that it reflects persistent protectionist tendencies and pushing members to strengthen the regulations governing the imposition of antidumping duties. On the other hand, since the WTO signaled that antidumping would be a focus of the Doha Round, the number of antidumping actions has declined somewhat (see Figure 6.2).

Protectionism in Agriculture   Another recent focus of the WTO has been the high level of tariffs and subsidies in the agricultural sector of many economies. Tariff rates on agricultural products are generally much higher than tariff rates on manufactured products or services. For example, in the mid-2000s the average tariff rates on nonagricultural products were 4.2 percent for Canada, 3.8 percent for the European Union, 3.9 percent for Japan, and 4.4 percent for the United States. On agricultural products, however, the average tariff rates were 21.2 percent for Canada, 15.9 percent for the European Union, 18.6 percent for Japan, and 10.3 percent for the United States.[35] The implication is that consumers in these countries are paying significantly higher prices than necessary for agricultural products imported from abroad, which leaves them with less money to spend on other goods and services.

The historically high tariff rates on agricultural products reflect a desire to protect domestic agriculture and traditional farming communities from foreign competition. In addition to high tariffs, agricultural producers also benefit from

Another Perspective

A Global Food Crisis

Tariffs on agriculture may have taken an unexpected turn, with the emergence of the first world food crisis since World War II. According to the World Bank, world food prices have risen over 80 percent between 2005 and 2008. American consumers began to feel the pinch in 2007, when the price of many staple goods increased—milk, for example, rose nearly 20 percent in a single year. Observers say government subsidies, rising fuel prices, and an emphasis on biofuel production have exacerbated the problem. For people in developing countries, the situation may be catastrophic, global economists say. (Sallie James, "Food Fight," *Free Trade Bulletin 31,* January 31, 2008; www.freetrade.org; and David Stringer, "World Food Program Warns of 'Silent Tsunami' of Hunger," *Chicago Tribune,* April 22, 2008, www.chicagotribune.com)

substantial subsidies. According to estimates from the OECD, government subsidies on average account for some 17 percent of the cost of agricultural production in Canada, 21 percent in the United States, 35 percent in the European Union, and 59 percent in Japan.[36] In total, OECD countries spend more than $300 billion a year in subsidies to agricultural producers.

Not surprising, the combination of high tariff barriers and significant subsidies introduces significant distortions into the production of agricultural products and international trade of those products. The net effect is to raise prices to consumers, reduce the volume of agricultural trade, and encourage the overproduction of products that are heavily subsidized (with the government typically buying the surplus). Because global trade in agriculture currently amounts to 10.5 percent of total merchandized trade, or about $750 billion per year, the WTO argues that removing tariff barriers and subsidies could significantly boost the overall level of trade, lower prices to consumers, and raise global economic growth by freeing consumption and investment resources for more productive uses. According to estimates from the International Monetary Fund, removal of tariffs and subsidies on agricultural products would raise global economic welfare by $128 billion annually.[37] Others suggest gains as high as $182 billion.[38]

The biggest defenders of the existing system have been the advanced nations of the world, which want to protect their agricultural sectors from competition by low-cost producers in developing nations. In contrast, developing nations have been pushing hard for reforms that would allow their producers greater access to the protected markets of the developed nations. Estimates suggest that removing all subsidies on agricultural production alone in OECD countries could return to the developing nations of the world three times more than all the foreign aid they currently receive from the OECD nations.[39] In other words, free trade in agriculture could help to jump-start economic growth among the world's poorer nations and alleviate global poverty.

Protecting Intellectual Property   Another issue that has become increasingly important to the WTO has been protecting intellectual property. The 1995 Uruguay agreement that established the WTO also contained an agreement to protect intellectual property (the Trade-Related Aspects of Intellectual Property Rights, or TRIPS, agreement). The TRIPS regulations oblige WTO members to grant and enforce patents lasting at least 20 years and copyrights lasting 50 years. Rich countries had to comply with the rules within a year. Poor countries, in which such protection generally was much weaker, had five years' grace, and the very poorest had 10 years. The basis for this agreement was a strong belief among signatory nations that the protection of intellectual property through patents, trademarks, and copyrights must be an essential element of the international trading system. Inadequate protections for intellectual property reduce the incentive for innovation. Because innovation is a central engine of economic growth and rising living standards, the argument has been that a multilateral agreement is needed to protect intellectual property.

Without such an agreement it is feared that producers in a country, let's say India, might market imitations of patented innovations pioneered in a different country, say the United States. This can affect international trade in two ways. First, it reduces the export opportunities in India for the original innovator in the United States. Second, to the extent that the Indian producer is able to export its pirated imitation to additional countries, it also reduces the export opportunities in those countries for the U.S. inventor. Also, one can argue that because the size of the total world market for the innovator is reduced, its incentive to pursue risky and expensive innovations is also reduced. The net effect would be less innovation in the world economy and less economic growth.

Something very similar to this has been occurring in the pharmaceutical industry, with Indian drug companies making copies of patented drugs discovered elsewhere. In 1970, the Indian government stopped recognizing product patents on drugs, but it elected to continue respecting process patents. This permitted Indian companies to reverse-engineer Western pharmaceuticals without paying licensing fees. As a result, foreigners' share of the Indian drug market fell from 75 percent in 1970 to 30 percent in 2000. For example, an Indian company sells a version of Bayer's patented antibiotic Cipro for $0.12 a pill, versus the $5.50 it costs in the United States. Under the WTO TRIPS agreement, India agreed to adopt and enforce the international drug patent regime by 2005.[40]

As noted in Chapter 2, intellectual property rights violation is also an endemic problem in several other industries, most notably computer software and music. The WTO believes that reducing piracy rates in areas such as drugs, software, and music recordings would have a significant impact on the volume of world trade and increase the incentive for producers to invest in the creation of intellectual property. A world without piracy would have more new drugs, computer software, and music recordings produced every year. In turn, this would boost economic and social welfare, and global economic growth rates. It is thus in the interests of WTO members to make sure that intellectual property rights are respected and enforced. While the 1995 Uruguay agreement that created the WTO did make headway with the TRIPS agreement, some believe these requirements do not go far enough and further commitments are necessary.

Market Access for Nonagricultural Goods and Services   Although the WTO and the GATT have made big strides in reducing the tariff rates on nonagricultural products, much work remains. Most developed nations have brought their tariff rates on industrial products down to an *average* of 3.8 percent of value, but exceptions still remain. In particular, while average tariffs are low, high tariff rates persist on certain imports into developed nations, which limit market access and economic growth. For example, Australia and South Korea, both OECD countries, still have bound tariff rates of 15.1 percent and 24.6 percent, respectively, on imports of transportation equipment (*bound tariff rates* are the highest rate that can be charged, which is often, but not always, the rate that is charged). In contrast, the bound tariff rates on imports of transportation equipment into the United States, EU, and Japan are 2.7 percent, 4.8 percent, and 0 percent, respectively (see Table 6.1). A particular

Country	Metals	Transportation Equipment	Electric Machinery
Canada	2.8%	6.8%	5.2%
United States	1.8	2.7	2.1
Brazil	33.4	33.6	31.9
Mexico	34.7	35.8	34.1
European Union	1.6	4.7	3.3
Australia	4.5	15.1	13.3
Japan	0.9	0.0	0.2
South Korea	7.7	24.6	16.1

6.1 table

Bound Tariffs on Select Industrial Products— Simple Averages

Source: WTO.

area for concern is high tariff rates on imports of selected goods from developing nations into developed nations.

In addition, tariffs on services remain higher than on industrial goods. The average tariff on business and financial services imported into United States, for example, is 8.2 percent, into the EU it is 8.5 percent, and into Japan it is 19.7 percent.[41] Given the rising value of cross-border trade in services, reducing these figures can be expected to yield substantial gains.

The WTO would like to bring down tariff rates still further and reduce the scope for the selective use of high tariff rates. The ultimate aim is to reduce tariff rates to zero. Although this might sound ambitious, 40 nations have already moved to zero tariffs on information technology goods, so a precedent exists. Empirical work suggests that further reductions in average tariff rates toward zero would yield substantial gains. One estimate by economists at the World Bank suggests that a broad global trade agreement coming out of the current Doha negotiations could increase world income by $263 billion annually by 2015, of which $109 billion would go to poor countries.[42] Another estimate from the OECD suggests a figure closer to $300 billion annually.[43] See the accompanying Country Focus for estimates of the benefits to the American economy from free trade.

Looking further out, the WTO would like to bring down tariff rates on imports of nonagricultural goods into developing nations. Many of these nations use the infant industry argument to justify the continued imposition of high tariff rates; however, ultimately these rates need to come down for these nations to reap the full benefits of international trade. For example, the bound tariff rates of 53.9 percent on imports of transportation equipment into India and 33.6 percent on imports into Brazil, by

Country FOCUS

Estimating the Gains from Trade for America

A study published by the Institute for International Economics tried to estimate the gains to the American economy from free trade. According to the study, due to reductions in tariff barriers under the GATT and WTO since 1947, the GDP of the United States was 7.3 percent higher by 2003 than would otherwise have been the case. That amounts to roughly $1 trillion a year, or $9,000 extra income for each American household per year.

The same study tried to estimate what would happen if America reached free trade deals with all its trading partners, reducing tariff barriers on all goods and services to zero. Using several methods to estimate the impact, the study concluded that additional annual gains of between $450 billion and $1.3 trillion could be realized. This final march to free trade, according to the study's authors, could safely be expected to raise incomes of the average American household by an additional $4,500 per year.

The authors also tried to estimate the scale and cost of employment disruption that would be caused by a move to universal free trade. Jobs would be lost in certain sectors and gained in others if the country abolished all tariff barriers. Using historical data as a guide, they estimated that 226,000 jobs would be lost every year due to expanded trade, although some two-thirds of those losing jobs would find reemployment after a year. Reemployment, however, would be at a wage that was 13 to 14 percent lower. The study concluded that the disruption costs would total some $54 billion annually, primarily in the form of lower lifetime wages to those whose jobs were disrupted as a result of free trade. Offset against this, however, must be the higher economic growth resulting from free trade, which creates many new jobs and raises household incomes, creating another $450 billion to $1.3 trillion annually in *net* gains to the economy. In other words, the estimated annual gains from trade are far greater than the estimated annual costs associated with job disruption, and more people benefit than lose as result of shift to a universal free trade regime.

Source: S.C. Bradford, P.L.E. Grieco, and G.C. Hufbauer, "The Payoff to America from Global Integration," in *The United States and the World Economy: Foreign Policy for the Next Decade,* C.F. Bergsten, ed. (Washington, DC: Institute for International Economics, 2005).

raising domestic prices, help to protect inefficient domestic producers and limit economic growth by reducing the real income of consumers who must pay more for transportation equipment and related services.

A New Round of Talks: Doha   Antidumping actions, trade in agricultural products, better enforcement of intellectual property laws, and expanded market access were four of the issues the WTO wanted to tackle at the 1999 meetings in Seattle, but those meetings were derailed. In late 2001, the WTO tried again to launch a new round of talks between member states aimed at further liberalizing the global trade and investment framework. For this meeting, it picked the remote location of Doha in the Persian Gulf state of Qatar, no doubt with an eye on the difficulties that antiglobalization protesters would have in getting there. Unlike the Seattle meetings, at Doha, the member states of the WTO agreed to launch a new round of talks and staked out an agenda. The talks were originally scheduled to last three years, although they have already gone on longer and may not be concluded for a while.

The agenda agreed upon at Doha should be seen as a game plan for negotiations over the next few years. The agenda includes cutting tariffs on industrial goods and services, phasing out subsidies to agricultural producers, reducing barriers to cross-border investment, and limiting the use of antidumping laws. Some difficult compromises were made to reach agreement on this agenda. The EU and Japan had to give significant ground on the issue of agricultural subsidies, which are used extensively by both entities to support politically powerful farmers. The United States bowed to pressure from virtually every other nation to negotiate revisions of antidumping rules, which the United States has used extensively to protect its steel producers from foreign competition. Europe had to scale back its efforts to include environmental policy in the trade talks, primarily because of pressure from developing nations that see environmental protection policies as trade barriers by another name. Excluded from the agenda was any language pertaining to attempts to tie trade to labor standards in a country.

Countries with big pharmaceutical sectors acquiesced to demands from African, Asian, and Latin American nations on the issue of drug patents. Specifically, the language in the agreement declares that WTO regulation on intellectual property "does not and should not prevent members from taking measures to protect public health." This language was meant to assure the world's poorer nations that they can make or buy generic equivalents to fight such killers as AIDS and malaria.

Clearly, it is one thing to agree to an agenda and quite another to reach a consensus on a new treaty. Nevertheless, this agreement yields some potential winners. These include low-cost agricultural producers in the developing world and developed nations such as Australia and the United States. If the talks are successful, agricultural producers in these nations will ultimately see the global markets for their goods expand. Developing nations also gain from the lack of language on labor standards, which many saw as an attempt by rich nations to erect trade barriers. The sick and poor of the world also benefit from guaranteed access to cheaper medicines. There are also clear losers in this agreement, including EU and Japanese farmers, U.S. steelmakers, environmental activists, and pharmaceutical firms in the developed world. These losers can be expected to lobby their governments hard during the ensuing years to make sure that the final agreement is more in their favor.[44] In general, though, if successful, the Doha Round of negotiations could significantly raise global economic welfare. As noted earlier, estimates suggest that a successful Doha Round would raise global incomes by as much as $300 billion annually, with 60 percent of the gain going to the world's poorer nations, which would help to pull 150 million people out of poverty.[45]

The talks are currently ongoing, and as seems normal in these cases, they are characterized by halting progress punctuated by significant setbacks and missed deadlines. A September 2003 meeting in Cancun, Mexico, broke down, primarily because there was no agreement on how to proceed with reducing agricultural subsidies and tariffs; the EU, United States, and India, among others, proved less than willing to reduce tariffs and subsidies to their politically important farmers, while countries such as Brazil and certain West African nations wanted free trade as quickly as possible. In early 2004, both the United States and the EU made a determined push to start the talks again, and in mid-2004 both seemed to commit themselves to sweeping reductions in agricultural tariffs and subsidies. However, since then little progress has been made and the talks are in deadlock, primarily because of disagreements over how deep the cuts in subsidies to agricultural produces should be. As of early 2008, the goal was to reduce tariffs for manufactured and agricultural goods by 60 to 70 percent, and to cut subsidies to half of their current level, but getting nations to agree to these goals was proving exceedingly difficult.

Focus on Managerial Implications

LEARNING OBJECTIVE 5
Explain the implications for managers of developments in the world trading system.

What are the implications of all this for business practice? Why should the international manager care about the political economy of free trade or about the relative merits of arguments for free trade and protectionism? There are two answers to this question. The first concerns the impact of trade barriers on a firm's strategy. The second concerns the role that business firms can play in promoting free trade or trade barriers.

Trade Barriers and Firm Strategy

To understand how trade barriers affect a firm's strategy, consider first the material in Chapter 5. Drawing on the theories of international trade, we discussed how it makes sense for the firm to disperse its various production activities to those countries around the globe where they can be performed most efficiently. Thus, it may make sense for a firm to design and engineer its product in one country, to manufacture components in another, to perform final assembly operations in yet another country, and then export the finished product to the rest of the world.

Clearly, trade barriers constrain a firm's ability to disperse its productive activities in such a manner. First and most obvious, tariff barriers raise the costs of exporting products to a country (or of exporting partly finished products between countries). This may put the firm at a competitive disadvantage to indigenous competitors in that country. In response, the firm may then find it economical to locate production facilities in that country so that it can compete on an even footing. Second, quotas may limit a firm's ability to serve a country from locations outside of that country. Again, the response by the firm might be to set up production facilities in that country—even though it may result in higher production costs. Such reasoning was one of the factors behind the rapid expansion of Japanese automaking capacity in the United States during the 1980s and 1990s. This followed the establishment of a VER agreement between the United States and Japan that limited U.S. imports of Japanese automobiles.

Third, to conform to local content regulations, a firm may have to locate more production activities in a given market than it would otherwise. Again, from the firm's perspective, the consequence might be to raise costs above the level that could be achieved if each production activity was dispersed to the optimal location for that activity. And finally, even when trade barriers do not exist, the firm may still want to locate some production activities in a given country to reduce the threat of trade barriers being imposed in the future.

All these effects are likely to raise the firm's costs above the level that could be achieved in a world without trade barriers. The higher costs that result need not translate into a significant competitive disadvantage relative to other foreign firms, however, if the countries imposing trade barriers do so to the imported products of all foreign firms, irrespective of their national origin. But when trade barriers are targeted at exports from a particular nation, firms based in that nation are at a competitive disadvantage to firms of other nations. The firm may deal with such targeted trade barriers by moving production into the country imposing barriers. Another strategy may be to move production to countries whose exports are not targeted by the specific trade barrier.

Finally, the threat of antidumping action limits the ability of a firm to use aggressive pricing to gain market share in a country. Firms in a country also can make strategic use of antidumping measures to limit aggressive competition from low-cost foreign producers. For example, the U.S. steel industry has been very aggressive in bringing antidumping actions against foreign steelmakers, particularly in times of weak global demand for steel and excess capacity. In 1998 and 1999, the United States faced a surge in low-cost steel imports as a severe recession in Asia left producers there with excess capacity. The U.S. producers filed several complaints with the International Trade Commission. One argued that Japanese producers of hot rolled steel were selling it at below cost in the United States. The ITC agreed and levied tariffs ranging from 18 percent to 67 percent on imports of certain steel products from Japan (these tariffs are separate from the steel tariffs discussed earlier).[46]

Policy Implications

As noted in Chapter 5, business firms are major players on the international trade scene. Because of their pivotal role in international trade, firms can and do exert a strong influence on government policy toward trade. This influence can encourage protectionism or it can encourage the government to support the WTO and push for open markets and freer trade among all nations. Government policies with regard to international trade can have a direct impact on business.

Consistent with strategic trade policy, examples can be found of government intervention in the form of tariffs, quotas, antidumping actions, and subsidies helping firms and industries establish a competitive advantage in the world economy. In general, however, the arguments contained in this chapter and in Chapter 5 suggest that government intervention has three drawbacks. Intervention can be self-defeating because it tends to protect the inefficient rather than help firms become efficient global competitors. Intervention is dangerous; it may invite retaliation and trigger a trade war. Finally, intervention is unlikely to be well executed, given the opportunity for such a policy to be captured by special-interest groups. Does this mean that business should simply encourage government to adopt a laissez-faire free trade policy?

Most economists would probably argue that the best interests of international business are served by a free trade stance, but not a laissez-faire stance. It is probably in the best long-run interests of the business community to encourage the government to aggressively promote greater free trade by, for example, strengthening the WTO. Business probably has much more to gain from government efforts to open protected markets to imports and foreign direct investment than from government efforts to support certain domestic industries in a manner consistent with the recommendations of strategic trade policy.

This conclusion is reinforced by a phenomenon we touched on in Chapter 1—the increasing integration of the world economy and internationalization of production that has occurred over the past two decades. We live in a world where many firms of all national origins increasingly depend for their competitive advantage on globally dispersed production systems. Such systems are the result of freer trade. Freer trade has brought great advantages to firms that have exploited it and to consumers who benefit from the resulting lower prices. Given the danger of retaliatory action, business firms that lobby their governments to engage in protectionism must realize that by doing so they may be denying themselves the opportunity to build a competitive advantage by constructing a globally dispersed production system. By encouraging their governments to engage in protectionism, their own activities and sales overseas may be jeopardized if other governments retaliate. This does not mean a firm should never seek protection in the form of antidumping actions and the like, but it should review its options carefully and think through the larger consequences.

Key Terms

free trade, p. 203

tariff, p. 204

specific tariff, p. 204

ad valorem tariff, p. 204

subsidy, p. 205

import quota, p. 206

tariff rate quota, p. 207

voluntary export restraint (VER), p. 207

quota rent, p. 208

local content requirement, p. 208

administrative trade policies, p. 208

dumping, p. 209

antidumping policies, p. 209

countervailing duties, p. 209

Helms-Burton Act, p. 214

D'Amato Act, p. 214

infant industry argument, p. 215

strategic trade policy, p. 216

Smoot Hawley Act, p. 219

Summary

The goal of this chapter was to describe how the reality of international trade deviates from the theoretical ideal of unrestricted free trade reviewed in Chapter 5. In this chapter, we have reported the various instruments of trade policy, reviewed the political and economic arguments for government intervention in international trade, reexamined the economic case for free trade in light of the strategic trade policy argument, and looked at the evolution of the world trading framework. While a policy of free trade may not always be the theoretically optimal policy (given the arguments of the new trade theorists), in practice it is probably the best policy for a government to pursue. In particular, the long-run interests of business and consumers may be best served by strengthening international institutions such as the WTO. Given the danger that isolated protectionism might escalate into a trade war, business probably has far more to gain from government efforts to open protected markets to imports and foreign direct investment (through the WTO) than from government efforts to protect domestic industries from foreign competition. The chapter made the following points:

1. Trade policies, such as tariffs, subsidies, antidumping regulations, and local content requirements tend to be pro-producer and anti-consumer. Gains accrue to producers (who are protected from foreign competitors), but consumers lose because they must pay more for imports.

2. There are two types of arguments for government intervention in international trade: political and economic. Political arguments for intervention are concerned with protecting the interests of certain groups, often at the expense of other groups, or with promoting goals with

regard to foreign policy, human rights, consumer protection, and the like. Economic arguments for intervention are about boosting the overall wealth of a nation.

3. A common political argument for intervention is that it is necessary to protect jobs. However, political intervention often hurts consumers and it can be self-defeating. Countries sometimes argue that it is important to protect certain industries for reasons of national security. Some argue that government should use the threat to intervene in trade policy as a bargaining tool to open foreign markets. This can be a risky policy; if it fails, the result can be higher trade barriers.

4. The infant industry argument for government intervention contends that to let manufacturing get a toehold, governments should temporarily support new industries. In practice, however, governments often end up protecting the inefficient.

5. Strategic trade policy suggests that with subsidies, government can help domestic firms gain first-mover advantages in global industries where economies of scale are important. Government subsidies may also help domestic firms overcome barriers to entry into such industries.

6. The problems with strategic trade policy are twofold: (a) such a policy may invite

retaliation, in which case all will lose, and (b) strategic trade policy may be captured by special-interest groups, which will distort it to their own ends.

7. The GATT was a product of the postwar free trade movement. The GATT was successful in lowering trade barriers on manufactured goods and commodities. The move toward greater free trade under the GATT appeared to stimulate economic growth.

8. The completion of the Uruguay Round of GATT talks and the establishment of the World Trade Organization have strengthened the world trading system by extending GATT rules to services, increasing protection for intellectual property, reducing agricultural subsidies, and enhancing monitoring and enforcement mechanisms.

9. Trade barriers act as a constraint on a firm's ability to disperse its various production activities to optimal locations around the globe. One response to trade barriers is to establish more production activities in the protected country.

10. Business may have more to gain from government efforts to open protected markets to imports and foreign direct investment than from government efforts to protect domestic industries from foreign competition.

Critical Thinking and Discussion Questions

1. Do you think governments should consider human rights when granting preferential trading rights to countries? What are the arguments for and against taking such a position?

2. Whose interests should be the paramount concern of government trade policy—the interests of producers (businesses and their employees) or those of consumers?

3. Given the arguments relating to the new trade theory and strategic trade policy, what kind of trade policy should business be pressuring government to adopt?

4. You are an employee of a U.S. firm that produces personal computers in Thailand and then exports them to the United States and other countries for sale. The personal computers were originally produced in Thailand to take

advantage of relatively low labor costs and a skilled workforce. Other possible locations considered at the time were Malaysia and Hong Kong. The U.S. government decides to impose punitive 100 percent ad valorem tariffs on imports of computers from Thailand to punish the country for administrative trade barriers that restrict U.S. exports to Thailand. How should your firm respond? What does this tell you about the use of targeted trade barriers?

5. Reread the Management Focus "U.S. Magnesium Seeks Protection." Who gains most from the antidumping duties levied by the United States on imports of magnesium from China and Russia? Who are the losers? Are these duties in the best national interests of the United States?

Use the globalEDGE Resource Desk (http://globalEDGE.msu.edu/ResourceDesk/) to complete the following exercises:

1. Your company is considering exporting its pharmaceutical products to Japan, but management's current knowledge of the country's trade policies and barriers for this sector is limited. Conduct the appropriate level of research in a *trade barriers database* to identify any information on Japan's current standards and technical requirements for pharmaceutical

products. Prepare an executive summary of your findings.

2. You work for a national chain of clothing stores that is considering importing textiles from India into the U.S. You want to determine whether the goods are subject to import quotas. Using information provided by the *U.S. Customs and Border Protections*, prepare a report highlighting the elements that determine whether a shipment is subject to this type of trade restriction.

closing case

Agricultural Subsidies

In the 1930s in the middle of the Great Depression, the U.S. government passed an act that provided subsidies to farmers. They have been receiving them ever since. The subsidies are currently running about $20 billion annually (in December 2007 Congress passed bills raising this total to $29 billion for the next 10 years). The largest single recipients have been cotton farmers. In 2005, U.S. cotton farmers received $5 billion in subsidies—and that on a crop that was worth only $4 billion! In total, subsidies to cotton farmers amounted to $19.1 billion between 1995 and 2005. These payments are skewed toward large farmers. Between 1995 and 2005, the top 10 percent of recipients received some 81 percent of all payments, or $15.5 billion.

The subsidies garnered by cotton farmers are a testament to the political lobbying power of the National Cotton Council of America, which represents farmers in cotton-producing states. Without the subsidies there is little doubt that many American cotton farmers would not be able to compete in world markets. According to recent data, the average cost to produce a pound of cotton in the United States is almost three times higher than in other major cotton-producing countries, such as China, Brazil, and the African nations of Benin and Mali. By shielding U.S. farmers from international competition, critics argue that U.S. cotton subsidies result in over production, which depresses the world price for cotton. In the past 10 years, a persistent global surplus of cotton has driven down the average price per pound from as high as $1.20 in

mid-1995 to only $0.65 a pound in mid-2006, lower than the costs of production of many U.S. cotton farmers.

The impact of falling prices on developing countries such as Benin and Mali can be particularly harsh. One study estimated that in Benin, where 95 percent of rural households live on less than $1 a day, a 40 percent reduction in the price of cotton reduces income to cotton growers by 21 percent, which in turn would cause an estimated 334,000 people in Benin to fall below the poverty line. Since the world price of cotton has fallen by almost half since 1995, and assuming that U.S. cotton subsidies caused at least some of that reduction, the data suggest that U.S. subsidies contributed significantly to economic devastation in very poor producing nations. Some estimates suggest that the loss suffered by Benin due to low cotton prices caused by U.S. subsidies and excess production exceeded the foreign aid that the country received from the United States.

In the early 2000s, Brazil decided to file a complaint against the United States in the World Trade Organization of which both the United States and Brazil are members (Benin was a third party to the dispute). The Brazilians claimed that U.S. subsidies distorted world trade in cotton and caused harm to efficient producers in Brazil and elsewhere. In a landmark ruling, in March 2005 the World Trade Organization condemned U.S. subsidies and required the U.S. government to remove them. The U.S. responded by removing a scheme that compensated U.S. cotton mills and exporters for buying U.S.

cotton, but the majority of subsidies were left intact. According to Oxfam, the U.K.-based development charity, the U.S. reforms touched programs accounting for less than 10 percent of all the subsidies received by U.S. cotton farmers.

In late 2006, Brazil requested that the WTO establish a compliance panel to investigate whether the United States failed to scrap its subsidies as required by the March 2005 ruling. If the WTO finds against the United States, Brazil could seek retaliatory sanctions, imposing duties of up to $3 billion on U.S. goods exported to Brazil. The United States immediately went on the defensive, arguing that "The United States has gone to extraordinary lengths to implement recommendations and rulings. Given all of these changes, there is no basis for Brazil's request for a compliance panel." The WTO, however, overruled American objections and started a formal investigation.

Sources: K.H. Cross, "King Cotton, Developing Countries and the Peace Clause," *Journal of International Economics and Law* 9, no. 1 (2006), pp. 149–95; F. Williams, "WTO Plans to Probe US Farm Subsidies," *Financial Times,* September 29, 2006, p. 12; "A Tangle of Troubles: Cotton," *The Economist,* July 22, 2006, p. 53; www.unctad.org/infocomm/anglais/cotton/prices.htm, accessed March 23, 2007; and "The No Farmer Left Behind Act," *The Wall Street Journal,* November 14, 2007, p. A16.

Case Discussion Questions

1. Why do you think that the U.S. government pays subsidies to farmers?

2. What is the impact of farm subsidies on the price of agricultural products in the United States, and on prices elsewhere?

3. Who benefits from U.S. farm subsidies, and who are the losers?

4. What would happen if the United States (and other countries) stopped paying subsidies to farmers to grow certain crops? Who would benefit, and who would lose?

Part 3 Cross-Border Trade and Investment

LEARNING OBJECTIVES

After you have read this chapter you should:

1 Be familiar with current trends regarding FDI in the world economy.

2 Understand the different theories of foreign direct investment.

3 Appreciate how political ideology shapes a government's attitudes toward FDI.

4 Understand the benefits and costs of FDI to home and host countries.

5 Be able to discuss the range of policy instruments that governments use to influence FDI.

6 Be able to articulate the implications for management practice of the theory and government policies associated with FDI.

chapter 7

Foreign Direct Investment

Lakshmi Mittal and the Growth of Mittal Steel

opening case

In 2007 ArcelorMittal was created in a controversial merger between Mittal Steel and Arcelor. The merger was the brainchild of Mittal CEO Lakshmi Mittal and his son, Aditya. Under Lakshmi's leadership, the family-owned Mittal Steel had grown from obscure origins in India to become the largest steel company in the world. The story dates to the early 1970s. At that time, the company was facing limited growth opportunities in India. Regulations constrained expansion opportunities, and Mittal competed with both a state-owned rival, SAIL, and a private national champion, Tata Steel. So Lakshmi's father financed the start-up of a steelmaking plant in Indonesia in 1975.

To reduce costs in his Indonesian plant, Mittal did not smelt iron ore, but instead purchased direct reduced iron pellets. The supplier was a struggling state-owned steel firm in Trinidad. Impressed by Mittal's success in Indonesia, the Trinidadians asked him to turn their firm around under a contract. Mittal set up another company to run the Trinidad plant. In 1989, after a successful turnaround, Mittal purchased the Trinidadian plant.

Now the company that had been born in India had two major foreign operations, but it was just the beginning. The global steel industry had been in a slump for 25 years due to excess capacity and slow demand growth as substitute materials replaced steel in a number of applications, but Mittal saw opportunity in purchasing the assets of distressed companies on the cheap. He believed that the global steel industry was about to turn a corner, driven in large part not only by sustained economic growth in developed nations, but also by growing demand in newly industrializing nations including China and his own native India. He saw all sorts of opportunities for buying poorly run companies as they came up for sale, injecting them with capital, improving their efficiency by getting them to adopt modern production technology, and taking advantage of the coming boom in steel demand. He also saw the opportunity to use the purchasing power of a global steel company to drive down the price it would have to pay for raw material inputs.

In 1992 Mittal made his next move, buying Sibalsa of Mexico, a state-owned steel company that was being privatized. This was followed in 1994 by the purchase of the fourth largest Canadian steelmaker from the government of Quebec. Then in 1995 Mittal Steel purchased a midsized German steelmaker and Kazakhstan's largest steelmaker, which was at the time in something of a shambles as the country transitioned from a socialist system to a more market-based economy. By this time, Mittal was hungry for more international growth, but his company was capital-constrained. So he decided to take it public, but not in his native India or Indonesia, where the liquidity of the capital markets was limited. Instead, in 1997 he moved the company's headquarters to Rotterdam, and then offered stock in Mittal Steel for sale to the public through both the Amsterdam and New York stock exchanges, raising $776 million in the process.

With capital from the initial public offering (IPO), Mittal purchased two more German steelmakers in 1997. This was followed in 1998 by the acquisition of Inland Steel Company, a U.S. steelmaker. Over the next few years, more acquisitions followed in France, Algeria, and Poland among other nations. In 2005, Mittal Steel purchased International Steel, a company formed from the integration of troubled U.S. steelmakers that had been in bankruptcy. By this time Mittal's prediction had come true; global demand for steel was booming again for the first time in a generation, driven in large part by demand in China, and steel prices were hitting record highs. Mittal Steel was now the world's largest steelmaker. This set the scene for Mittal Steel's $32 billion hostile acquisition of Arcelor, a European firm formed from the merger of steelmakers from Luxembourg, France, and Spain. The acquisition was bitterly contested, with the management of Arcelor and many European politicians opposing the acquisition of a European company by an Indian enterprise (although Mittal Steel was legally a Dutch company). Arcelor's shareholders, however, saw value in the deal and ultimately approved it in late 2006. In 2007 the new firm, now headquartered in Luxembourg, generated sales of $110 billion and net income of $10.2 billion, making it by far the world's largest steel company. ●

Sources: "Mittalic Magic," *The Economist,* February 16, 2008, p. 80; K. Gopalan, "Steel Czar," *Business Today,* January 13, 2008, pp. 102–06; S. Daneskhu, "FDI into Richest Country's Set to Rise 20% This Year," *Financial Times,* June 22, 2007, p. 7; and historical information archived at ArcelorMittal Web site, www.arcelormittal.com/, accessed March 17, 2008.

Introduction

Foreign direct investment (FDI) occurs when a firm invests directly in facilities to produce or market a product in a foreign country. According to the U.S. Department of Commerce, FDI occurs whenever a U.S. citizen, organization, or affiliated group takes an interest of 10 percent or more in a foreign business entity. Once a firm undertakes FDI, it becomes a *multinational enterprise.* An example of FDI is given in the opening case. Starting from small beginnings in India, Mittal Steel (now ArcelorMittal) made multiple foreign direct investments over 30 years to become the world's largest steelmaker.

FDI takes on two main forms. The first is a **greenfield investment,** which involves the establishment of a new operation in a foreign country. The second involves acquiring or merging with an existing firm in the foreign country (most of Mittal Steel's expansion

Greenfield Investment
Establishing a new operation in a foreign country.

has been in the form of acquisitions, although it has made some substantial green investments in recent years). Acquisitions can be a minority (where the foreign firm takes a 10 percent to 49 percent interest in the firm's voting stock), majority (foreign interest of 50 percent to 99 percent), or full outright stake (foreign interest of 100 percent).[1]

We begin this chapter by looking at the importance of foreign direct investment in the world economy. Next, we review the theories that have been used to explain foreign direct investment. The chapter then moves on to look at government policy toward foreign direct investment and closes with a section on implications for business.

Foreign Direct Investment in the World Economy

When discussing foreign direct investment, it is important to distinguish between the flow of FDI and the stock of FDI. The **flow of FDI** refers to the amount of FDI undertaken over a given time period (normally a year). The **stock of FDI** refers to the total accumulated value of foreign-owned assets at a given time. We also talk of **outflows of FDI,** meaning the flow of FDI out of a country, and **inflows of FDI,** the flow of FDI into a country.

TRENDS IN FDI The past 30 years have seen a marked increase in both the flow and stock of FDI in the world economy. The average yearly outflow of FDI increased from $25 billion in 1975 to a record $1.4 trillion in 2000. It fell back in the early 2000s, but by 2007 FDI flows were again around $1.5 trillion (see Figure 7.1).[2] Over this period, the flow of FDI accelerated faster than the growth in world trade and world output. For example, between 1992 and 2007, the total flow of FDI from all countries increased more than eightfold while world trade by value grew by some 150 percent and world output by around 45 percent.[3] As a result of the strong FDI flow, by 2006 the global stock of FDI exceeded $12 trillion. At least 78,000 parent companies had 780,000 affiliates in foreign markets that collectively employed more than 70 million people abroad and generated value accounting for about one-tenth of global GDP. The foreign affiliates of multinationals had an estimated $25 trillion in global sales, much higher than the value of global exports, which stood at close to $14.1 trillion.[4]

FDI has grown more rapidly than world trade and world output for several reasons. First, despite the general decline in trade barriers over the past 30 years, business firms still fear protectionist pressures. Executives see FDI as a way of circumventing future trade barriers. Second, much of the recent increase in FDI is being driven by the political and economic changes that have been occurring in many of the world's developing nations. The general shift toward democratic political institutions and free market economies that we discussed in Chapter 2 has encouraged FDI. Across much of Asia, Eastern Europe, and Latin America, economic growth, economic deregulation, privatization programs that are open to foreign investors, and removal of many restrictions on FDI have made these countries more attractive to foreign multinationals. According to the United Nations, some 90 percent of the 2,444 changes made worldwide between 1992 and 2006 in the laws governing foreign direct investment created a more favorable environment for FDI (see Figure 7.2).[5] However, since 2002 the number of regulations that are less favorable toward FDI has increased, suggesting the pendulum may be starting to swing the other way. Latin America in particular has recorded a marked increase in regulations that are less favorable to FDI; two-thirds of the reported changes in 2005 and 2006 made the environment for direct investment less welcome. Most of these unfavorable changes were focused on extractive industries, such as oil and gas, where governments seemed to focus on limiting

LEARNING OBJECTIVE 1
Be familiar with current trends regarding FDI in the world economy.

Flow of FDI
The amount of FDI undertaken over a given time.

Stock of FDI
The total accumulated value of foreign-owned assets at a given time.

Outflows of FDI
The flow of FDI out of a country.

Inflows of FDI
The flow of FDI into a country.

figure **7.1**

FDI Outflows, 1982–2007 ($ billions)

Source: Constructed by the author from data in United Nations, *World Investment Report, 2007* (New York and Geneva. United Nations, 2007).

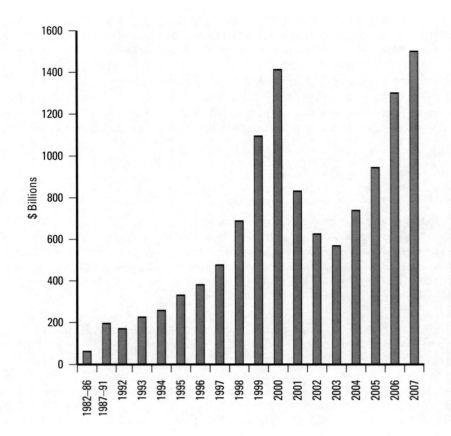

figure **7.2**

National Regulatory Changes Governing FDI, 1992–2006

Source: Constructed by the author from data in United Nations, *World Investment Report, 2007.* (New York and Geneva: United Nations, 2007).

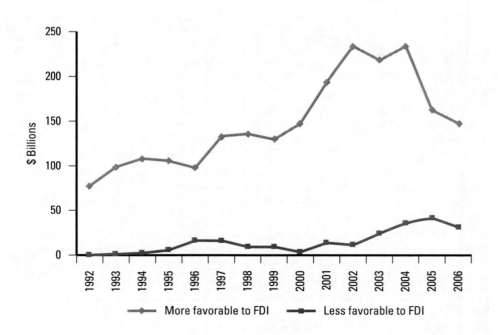

FDI and capturing more of the economic value from FDI through, for example, higher taxes and royalty rates applied to foreign enterprises.

Notwithstanding recent adverse developments in some nations, the general desire of governments to facilitate FDI also has been reflected in a dramatic increase in the number of bilateral investment treaties designed to protect and promote investment between two countries. As of 2006, 2,573 such treaties involved more than 160 countries, a 12-fold increase from the 181 treaties that existed in 1980.[6]

The globalization of the world economy is also having a positive impact on the volume of FDI. Firms such as ArscelorMittal now see the whole world as their market, and they are undertaking FDI in an attempt to make sure they have a significant presence in many regions of the world. For reasons that we shall explore later in this book, many firms now believe it is important to have production facilities based close to their major customers. This, too, creates pressure for greater FDI.

THE DIRECTION OF FDI Historically, most FDI has been directed at the developed nations of the world as firms based in advanced countries invested in the others' markets (see Figure 7.3). During the 1980s and 1990s, the United States was often the favorite target for FDI inflows. The United States has been an attractive target for FDI because of its large and wealthy domestic markets, its dynamic and stable economy, a favorable political environment, and the openness of the country to FDI. Investors include firms based in Great Britain, Japan, Germany, Holland, and France. Inward investment into the United States remained high during the early 2000s, totaling $192 billion in 2007. The developed nations of the European Union have also been recipients of significant FDI inflows, principally from U.S. and Japanese enterprises and from other member states of the EU. In 2007, inward investment into

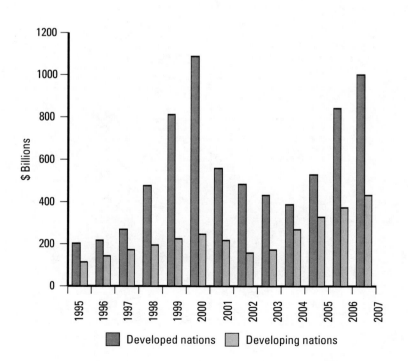

7.3 figure

FDI Inflows by Region, 1995–2007 ($ billions)

Source: Constructed by the author from data in United Nations, *World Investment Report, 2007* (New York and Geneva: United Nations, 2007).

the EU reached a record $610 billion. The United Kingdom was the largest national recipient, with inward investments of some $171 billion.[7]

Even though developed nations still account for the largest share of FDI inflows, FDI into developing nations has increased (see Figure 7.3). From 1985 to 1990, the annual inflow of FDI into developing nations averaged $27.4 billion, or 17.4 percent of the total global flow. In the mid- to late 1990s, the inflow into developing nations was generally between 35 and 40 percent of the total, before falling back to account for about 25 percent of the total in the 2000–02 period and then rising to 31 to 40 percent between 2004 and 2007. Most recent inflows into developing nations have been targeted at the emerging economies of South, East, and Southeast Asia. Driving much of the increase has been the growing importance of China as a recipient of FDI, which attracted around $60 billion of FDI in 2004 and close to $70 billion in 2005 to 2007.[8] The reasons for the strong flow of investment into China are discussed in the accompanying Country Focus.

Latin America emerged as the next most important region in the developing world for FDI inflows. In 2007, total inward investments into this region reached about $126 billion. Mexico and Brazil have historically been the two top recipients of inward FDI in Latin America, a trend that continued in 2007. At the other end of the scale, Africa has long received the smallest amount of inward investment, about $36 billion in 2006 and 2007. The inability of Africa to attract greater investment is in part a reflection of the political unrest, armed conflict, and frequent changes in economic policy in the region.[9]

Another way of looking at the importance of FDI inflows is to express them as a percentage of gross fixed capital formation. **Gross fixed capital formation** summarizes the total amount of capital invested in factories, stores, office buildings, and the like. Other things being equal, the greater the capital investment in an economy, the more favorable its future growth prospects are likely to be. Viewed this way, FDI can be seen as an important source of capital investment and a determinant of the future growth rate of an economy. Figure 7.4 summarizes inward flows of FDI as a percentage of gross fixed capital formation for developed and developing economies for 1992–2006. During

Gross Fixed Capital Formation The summary of the total amount of capital invested in factories, stores, office buildings, and the like.

figure **7.4**

Inward FDI as a Percent of Gross Fixed Capital Formation, 1992–2006

Source: Constructed by the author from data in United Nations, *World Investment Report, 2007* (New York and Geneva: United Nations, 2007).

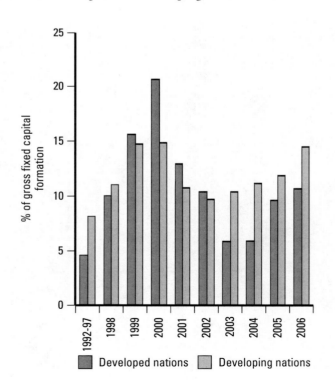

Country FOCUS

Foreign Direct Investment in China

Beginning in late 1978, China's leadership decided to move the economy away from a centrally planned socialist system to one that was more market driven. The result has been close to three decades of sustained high economic growth rates of around 10 percent annually compounded. This rapid growth has attracted substantial foreign investment. Starting from a tiny base, foreign investment increased to an annual average rate of $2.7 billion between 1985 and 1990 and then surged to $40 billion annually in the late 1990s, making China the second biggest recipient of FDI inflows in the world after the United States. By the mid-2000s, China was attracting about $65 billion to $70 billion of FDI annually, with another $35 billion to $40 billion a year going into Hong Kong.

Over the past 20 years, this inflow has resulted in establishment of 280,000 foreign-funded enterprises in China. The total stock of FDI in mainland China grew from effectively zero in 1978 to $300 billion in 2006 (another $750 billion of FDI stock was in Hong Kong). FDI amounted to about 8 to 10 percent of annualized gross fixed capital formation in China between 1998 and 2006, suggesting that FDI is an important source of economic growth in China.

The reasons for the investment are fairly obvious. With a population of more than 1 billion people, China represents the largest market in the world. Historically, import tariffs made it difficult to serve this market via exports, so FDI was required if a company wanted to tap into the country's huge potential. Although China joined the World Trade Organization in 2001, which will ultimately mean a reduction in import tariffs, this will occur slowly, so this motive for investing in China will persist. Also, many foreign firms believe that doing business in China requires a substantial presence in the country to build *guanxi,* the crucial relationship networks (see Chapter 3 for details). Furthermore, a combination of cheap labor and tax incentives, particularly for enterprises that establish themselves in special economic zones, makes China an attractive base from which to serve Asian or world markets with exports.

Less obvious, at least to begin with, was how difficult it would be for foreign firms to do business in China. Blinded by the size and potential of China's market, many firms may not have paid enough attention to the complexities of operating a business in this country until after the investment has been made. China may have a huge population, but despite two decades of rapid growth, it is still relatively poor. The lack of purchasing power translates into relative weak

markets for many Western consumer goods. Another problem is the lack of a well-developed transportation infrastructure or distribution system outside of major urban areas. PepsiCo discovered this problem at its subsidiary in Chongqing. Perched above the Yangtze River in southwest Sichuan province, Chongqing lies at the heart of China's massive hinterland. The Chongqing municipality, which includes the city and its surrounding regions, contains more than 30 million people, but according to Steve Chen, the manager of the PepsiCo subsidiary, the lack of well-developed road and distribution systems means he can reach only about half of this population with his product.

Other problems include a highly regulated environment, which can make it problematic to conduct business transactions, and shifting tax and regulatory regimes. For example, a few years ago, the Chinese government suddenly scrapped a tax credit scheme that had made it attractive to import capital equipment into China. This immediately made it more expensive to set up operations in the country. Then there are problems with local joint-venture partners that are inexperienced, opportunistic, or simply operate according to different goals. One U.S. manager explained that when he laid off 200 people to reduce costs, his Chinese partner hired them all back the next day. When he inquired why they had been hired back, the executive of the Chinese partner, which was government-owned, explained that as an agency of the government, it had an "obligation" to reduce unemployment.

To continue to attract foreign investment, the Chinese government has committed itself to invest more than $800 billion in infrastructure projects over the next 10 years. This should improve the nation's poor highway system. By giving preferential tax breaks to companies that invest in special regions, such as that around Chongqing, the Chinese have created incentives for foreign companies to invest in China's vast interior where markets are underserved. They have been pursuing a macroeconomic policy that includes an emphasis on maintaining steady economic growth, low inflation, and a stable currency, all of which are attractive to foreign investors. Given these developments, it seems likely that the country will continue to be an important magnet for foreign investors well into the future.

Sources: Interviews by the author while in China; United Nations, *World Investment Report, 2007* (New York and Geneva: United Nations, 2007); Linda Ng and C. Tuan, "Building a Favorable Investment Environment: Evidence for the Facilitation of FDI in China," *The World Economy,* 2002, pp. 1095–114; and S. Chan and G. Qingyang, "Investment in China Migrates Inland," *Far Eastern Economic Review,* May 2006, pp. 52–57.

Another Perspective

P&G's Greenfield Investment

The world's largest consumer products company, Procter & Gamble has been making foreign direct investments since the 1940s. But it wasn't until 2007 that it opened a plant in Singapore. The fragrance manufacturing plant is also the region's first perfume factory to be established by a multinational.

The plant is part of a P&G global restructuring to improve productivity. The new strategy shifts P&G's regional operations to a hub-and-spoke business model from the single-country approach that led its global expansion. Projected to supply over 3 million kilograms of perfume annually for P&G throughout Asia, the plant also serves as an innovation hub for its perfume business. ("P&G Opens First Singapore Plant," *Foreign Direct Investment,* April 10, 2008, www.fdimagazine.com)

1992–97, FDI flows accounted for about 4 percent of gross fixed capital formation in developed nations and 8 percent in developing nations. By 1998–2006, the figure was 11.3 percent worldwide, suggesting that FDI had become an increasingly important source of investment in the world's economies.

These gross figures hide important individual country differences. For example, in 2006, inward FDI accounted for some 34 percent of gross fixed capital formation in Britain and 40 percent in Sweden, but –2 percent in Venezuela and –0.6 percent in Japan—suggesting that FDI is an important source of investment capital, and thus economic growth, in the first two countries but not the latter two where foreign investors actually reduced their overall stake in the economy. These differences can be explained by several factors, including the perceived ease and attractiveness of investing in a nation. To the extent that burdensome regulations limit the opportunities for foreign investment in countries such as Japan and Venezuela, these nations may be hurting themselves by limiting their access to needed capital investments.

THE SOURCE OF FDI Since World War II, the United States has been the largest source country for FDI, a position it retained during the late 1990s and early 2000s. Other important source countries include the United Kingdom, France, Germany, the Netherlands, and Japan. Collectively, these six countries accounted for 56 percent of all FDI outflows for the 1998–2006 period and 61 percent of the total global stock of FDI in 2006 (see Figure 7.5). As might be expected, these countries also predominate in rankings of the world's largest multinationals.[10] These nations dominate primarily because they were the most developed nations with the largest economies during much of the postwar period and therefore home to many of the largest and best-capitalized enterprises. Many of these countries also had a long history as trading nations and naturally looked to foreign markets to fuel their economic expansion. Thus,

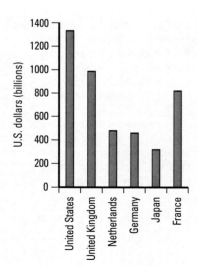

figure 7.5

Cumulative FDI Outflows, 1998–2006 ($ billions)

Note: Share accounted for by the United States would have been larger were it not for significant one-time investment inflows in 2005 due to changes in the U.S. tax laws.

Source: Constructed by the author from data in United Nations, *World Investment Report, 2006* (New York and Geneva: United Nations, 2006).

it is no surprise that enterprises based there have been at the forefront of foreign investment trends.

THE FORM OF FDI: ACQUISITIONS VERSUS GREENFIELD INVESTMENTS

FDI can take the form of a greenfield investment in a new facility or an acquisition of or a merger with an existing local firm. The data suggest the majority of cross-border investment is in the form of mergers and acquisitions rather than greenfield investments. UN estimates indicate that some 40 to 80 percent of all FDI inflows were in the form of mergers and acquisitions between 1998 and 2006. In 2001, for example, mergers and acquisitions accounted for some 78 percent of all FDI inflows. In 2004, the figure was 59 percent, while in 2006 it was back up to 61 percent.[11] However, FDI flows into developed nations differ markedly from those into developing nations. In the case of developing nations, only about one-third of FDI is in the form of cross-border mergers and acquisitions. The lower percentage of mergers and acquisitions may simply reflect the fact that there are fewer target firms to acquire in developing nations.

When you see a BP gas station as you are driving down the road, do you realize that the company is British owned? BP = British Petroleum.

When contemplating FDI, why do firms apparently prefer to acquire existing assets rather than undertake greenfield investments? We shall consider it in greater depth in Chapter 12; for now we will make only a few basic observations. First, mergers and acquisitions are quicker to execute than greenfield investments. This is an important consideration in the modern business world where markets evolve very rapidly. Many firms apparently believe that if they do not acquire a desirable target firm, then their global rivals will. Second, foreign firms are acquired because those firms have valuable strategic assets, such as brand loyalty, customer relationships, trademarks or patents, distribution systems, production systems, and the like. It is easier and perhaps less risky for a firm to acquire those assets than to build them from the ground up through a greenfield investment. Third, firms make acquisitions because they believe they can increase the efficiency of the acquired unit by transferring capital, technology, or management skills. However, there is evidence that many mergers and acquisitions fail to realize their anticipated gains.[12] Chapter 12 further studies this issue.

THE SHIFT TO SERVICES

In the past two decades, the sector composition of FDI has shifted sharply away from extractive industries and manufacturing and toward services. In 1990, some 47 percent of FDI stock was in service industries; by 2005, this figure had increased to 61 percent. Similar trends can be seen in the composition of cross-border mergers and acquisitions, in which services are playing a much larger role. The composition of FDI in services has also changed. Until recently it was concentrated in trade and financial services. However, industries such as electricity, water, telecommunications, and business services (such as information technology consulting services) are becoming more prominent.

The shift to services is being driven by four factors that will probably stay in place for some time. First, the shift reflects the general move in many developed economies away from manufacturing and toward service industries. By the early 2000s, services accounted for 72 percent of the GDP in developed economies and 52 percent in developing economies. Second, many services cannot be traded internationally. They need to be produced where they are consumed. Starbucks, which is a service business, cannot sell hot lattes to Japanese consumers from its Seattle stores—it has to set up shops in Japan. FDI is the principal way to bring services to foreign markets. Third, many countries have liberalized their regimes governing FDI in services (Chapter 6 revealed that the WTO engineered global deals to remove barriers to cross-border investment in telecommunications and financial services during the late 1990s). This liberalization has made large inflows possible. After Brazil privatized its telecommunications company in the late 1990s and removed restrictions on investment by foreigners in this sector, FDI surged into the Brazilian telecommunications sector.

Finally, the rise of Internet-based global telecommunications networks has allowed some service enterprises to relocate some of their value-creation activities to different nations to take advantage of favorable factor costs. Procter & Gamble, for example, has shifted some of its back-office accounting functions to the Philippines where accountants trained in U.S. accounting rules can be hired at a much lower salary. Dell has call-answering centers in India for the same reason. Similarly, both Microsoft and IBM now have some software development and testing facilities located in India. Software code written at Microsoft during the day can now be transmitted instantly to India and then tested while the code writers at Microsoft sleep. By the time the U.S. code writers arrive for work the next morning, the code has been tested, bugs have been identified, and they can start working on corrections. By locating testing facilities in India, Microsoft can work on its code 24 hours a day, reducing the time it takes to develop new software products.

Theories of Foreign Direct Investment

LEARNING OBJECTIVE 2
Understand the different theories of foreign direct investment.

In this section, we review several theories of foreign direct investment. These theories approach the various phenomena of foreign direct investment from three complementary perspectives. One set of theories seeks to explain why a firm will favor direct investment as a means of entering a foreign market when two other alternatives, exporting and licensing, are open to it. Another set of theories seeks to explain why firms in the same industry often undertake foreign direct investment at the same time, and why they favor certain locations over others as targets for foreign direct investment. Put differently, these theories attempt to explain the observed *pattern* of foreign direct investment flows. A third theoretical perspective, known as the **eclectic paradigm,** attempts to combine the two other perspectives into a single holistic explanation of foreign direct investment (this theoretical perspective is *eclectic* because the best aspects of other theories are taken and combined into a single explanation).

Eclectic Paradigm
The theory that combining location-specific assets or resource endowments and the firm's own unique assets often requires FDI; it requires the firm to establish production facilities where those foreign assets or resource endowments are located.

WHY FOREIGN DIRECT INVESTMENT? Why do firms go to all of the trouble of establishing operations abroad through foreign direct investment when two alternatives, exporting and licensing, are available to them for exploiting the profit opportunities in a foreign market? **Exporting** involves producing goods at home and then shipping them to the receiving country for sale. **Licensing** involves granting a foreign entity (the licensee) the right to produce and sell the firm's product in return for a royalty fee on every unit sold. The question is important, given that a cursory examination of the topic suggests that foreign direct investment may be both expensive and risky compared with exporting and licensing. FDI is expensive because a firm must bear the costs of establishing production facilities in a foreign country or of acquiring a foreign enterprise. FDI is risky because of the problems associated with doing business in a different culture where the rules of the game may be very different. Relative to indigenous firms, a foreign firm undertaking FDI in a country for the first time is more likely to make costly mistakes due to its ignorance. When a firm exports,

Exporting
Sale of products produced in one country to residents of another country.

Licensing
Occurs when a firm (the licensor) grants a foreign entity (the licensee) the right to produce its product, use its production processes, or use its brand name or trademark in return for a royalty fee on every unit sold.

it need not bear the costs of associated with FDI, and it can reduce the risks associated with selling abroad by using a native sales agent. Similarly, when a firm allows another enterprise to produce its products under license, the licensee bears the costs or risks. So why do so many firms apparently prefer FDI over either exporting or licensing? The answer can be found by examining the limitations of exporting and licensing as means for capitalizing on foreign market opportunities.

Limitations of Exporting   The viability of an exporting strategy is often constrained by transportation costs and trade barriers. When transportation costs are added to production costs, it becomes unprofitable to ship some products over a large distance. This is particularly true of products that have a low value-to-weight ratio and that can be produced in almost any location. For such products, the attractiveness of exporting decreases, relative to either FDI or licensing. This is the case, for example, with cement. Thus Cemex, the large Mexican cement maker, has expanded internationally by pursuing FDI, rather than exporting (see the Management Focus feature on Cemex). For products with a high value-to-weight ratio, however, transportation costs are normally a minor component of total landed cost (e.g., electronic components, personal computers, medical equipment, computer software, etc.) and have little impact on the relative attractiveness of exporting, licensing, and FDI.

Transportation costs aside, some firms undertake foreign direct investment as a response to actual or threatened trade barriers such as import tariffs or quotas. By placing tariffs on imported goods, governments can increase the cost of exporting relative to foreign direct investment and licensing. Similarly, by limiting imports through quotas, governments increase the attractiveness of FDI and licensing. For example, the wave of FDI by Japanese auto companies in the United States during the 1980s and 1990s was partly driven by protectionist threats from Congress and by quotas on the importation of Japanese cars. For Japanese auto companies, these factors decreased the profitability of exporting and increased that of foreign direct investment. In this context, it is important to understand that trade barriers do not have to be physically in place for FDI to be favored over exporting. Often, the desire to reduce the threat that trade barriers might be imposed is enough to justify foreign direct investment as an alternative to exporting.

Limitations of Licensing   There is a branch of economic theory known as **internalization theory** that seeks to explain why firms often prefer foreign direct investment over licensing as a strategy for entering foreign markets (this approach is also known as the **market imperfections** approach).[13] According to internalization theory, licensing has three major drawbacks as a strategy for exploiting foreign market opportunities. First, *licensing may result in a firm's giving away valuable technological know-how to a potential foreign competitor.* For example, in the 1960s, RCA licensed its leading-edge color television technology to a number of Japanese companies, including Matsushita and Sony. At the time, RCA saw licensing as a way to earn a good return from its technological know-how in the Japanese market without the costs and risks associated with foreign direct investment. However, Matsushita and Sony quickly assimilated RCA's technology and used it to enter the U.S. market to compete directly against RCA. As a result, RCA is now a minor player in its home market, while Matsushita and Sony have a much bigger market share.

A second problem is that licensing does not give a firm the tight control over manufacturing, marketing, and strategy in a foreign country that may be required to maximize its profitability. With licensing, control over manufacturing, marketing, and strategy is granted to a licensee in return for a royalty fee. However, for both strategic and operational reasons, a firm may want to retain control over these functions. The rationale for wanting control over the strategy of a foreign entity

Internalization Theory
The argument that firms prefer FDI over licensing in order to retain control over know-how, manufacturing, marketing, and strategy or because some firm capabilities are not amenable to licensing.

Market Imperfections
Another name for Internalization theory (see above).

Management FOCUS

Foreign Direct Investment by Cemax

In little more than a decade, Mexico's largest cement manufacturer, Cemex, has transformed itself from a primarily Mexican operation into the third largest cement company in the world behind Holcim of Switzerland and Lafarge Group of France. Cemex has long been a powerhouse in Mexico and currently controls more than 60 percent of the market for cement in that country. Cemex's domestic success has been based in large part on an obsession with efficient manufacturing and a focus on customer service that is tops in the industry.

Cemex is a leader in using information technology to match production with consumer demand. The company sells ready-mixed cement that can survive for only about 90 minutes before solidifying, so precise delivery is important. But Cemex can never predict with total certainty what demand will be on any given day, week, or month. To better manage unpredictable demand patterns, Cemex developed a system of seamless information technology, including truck-mounted global positioning systems, radio transmitters, satellites, and computer hardware, that allows it to control the production and distribution of cement like no other company can, responding quickly to unanticipated changes in demand and reducing waste. The results are lower costs and superior customer service, both differentiating factors for Cemex.

The company also pays lavish attention to its distributors—some 5,000 in Mexico alone—who can earn points toward rewards for hitting sales targets. The distributors can then convert those points into Cemex stock. High-volume distributors can purchase trucks and other supplies through Cemex at significant discounts. Cemex also is known for its marketing drives that focus on end users, the builders themselves. For example, Cemex trucks drive around Mexican building sites, and if Cemex cement is being used, the construction crews win soccer balls, caps, and T-shirts.

Cemex's international expansion strategy was driven by a number of factors. First, the company wished to reduce its reliance on the Mexican construction market, which was characterized by very volatile demand. Second, the company realized there was tremendous demand for cement in many developing countries, where significant construction was being undertaken or needed. Third, the company believed that it understood the needs of construction businesses in developing nations better than the established multinational cement companies, all of which were from developed nations. Fourth, Cemex believed that it could create significant value by acquiring inefficient cement companies in other markets and transferring its skills in customer service, marketing, information technology, and production management to those units.

The company embarked in earnest on its international expansion strategy in the early 1990s. Initially, Cemex targeted other developing nations, acquiring established cement makers in Venezuela, Colombia, Indonesia, the Philippines, Egypt, and several other countries. It also purchased two stagnant companies in Spain and turned them around. Bolstered by the success of its Spanish ventures, Cemex began to look for expansion opportunities in developed nations. In 2000, Cemex purchased Houston-based Southland, one of the largest cement companies in the United States, for $2.5 billion. Following the Southland acquisition, Cemex had 56 cement plants in 30 countries, most of which were gained through acquisitions. In all cases, Cemex devoted great attention to transferring its technological, management, and marketing know-how to acquired units, thereby improving their performance.

In 2004, Cemex made another major foreign investment move, purchasing RMC of Great Britain for $5.8 billion. RMC was a huge multinational cement firm with sales of $8 billion, only 22 percent of which were in the United Kingdom, and operations in more than 20 other nations, including many European nations where Cemex had no presence. Finalized in March 2005, the RMC acquisition has transformed Cemex into a global powerhouse in the cement industry with more than $15 billion in annual sales and operations in 50 countries. Only about 15 percent of the company's sales are now generated in Mexico. Following the acquisition of RMC, Cemex found that the RMC plant in Rugby, England, was running at only 70 percent of capacity, partly because repeated production problems kept causing a kiln shutdown. Cemex brought in an international team of specialists to fix the problem and quickly increased production to 90 percent of capacity.

Going forward, Cemex has made it clear that it will continue to expand and is eyeing opportunities in the fast-growing economies of China and India where currently it lacks a presence, and where its global rivals are already expanding.

Not all of Cemex's expansions have worked out as planned. In 2006, Cemex announced that it would exit Indonesia after a long-running dispute with the government there. Cemex entered Indonesia in 1998 as part of an IMF-sponsored privatization program by purchasing a 25 percent stake in a government-owned Indonesian cement maker, Semen Gresik. At the time, Indonesia promised to allow Cemex to acquire a majority stake in Semen Gresik in 2001. However, the country never granted that permission, as local vested interests, including politicians and unions, voiced worries about "Indonesian assets falling into foreign hands" and lobbied the central government to block the deal. A frustrated Cemex eventually reached an agreement to sell its 25 percent stake to another Indonesian enterprise.

Sources: C. Piggott, "Cemex's Stratospheric Rise," *Latin Finance*, March 2001, p. 76; J.F. Smith, "Making Cement a Household Word," *Los Angeles Times*, January 16, 2000, p. C1; D. Helft, "Cemex Attempts to Cement Its Future," *The Industry Standard*, November 6, 2000; Diane Lindquist, "From Cement to Services," *Chief Executive*, November 2002, pp. 48–50; "Cementing Global Success," *Strategic Direct Investor*, March 2003, p. 1; M.T. Derham, "The Cemex Surprise," *Latin Finance*, November 2004, pp. 1–2; "Holcim Seeks to Acquire Aggregate," *The Wall Street Journal*, January 13, 2005, p. 1; J. Lyons, "Cemex Prowls for Deals in Both China and India," *The Wall Street Journal*, January 27, 2006, p. C4; and S. Donnan, "Cemex Sells 25 Percent Stake in Semen Gresik," *FT.com*, May 4, 2006, p. 1.

is that a firm might want its foreign subsidiary to price and market very aggressively as a way of keeping a foreign competitor in check. Unlike a wholly owned subsidiary, a licensee would probably not accept such an imposition, because it would likely reduce the licensee's profit, or it might even cause the licensee to take a loss.

The rationale for wanting control over the operations of a foreign entity is that the firm might wish to take advantage of differences in factor costs across countries, producing only part of its final product in a given country, while importing other parts from where they can be produced at lower cost. Again, a licensee would be unlikely to accept such an arrangement, since it would limit the licensee's autonomy. Thus, for these reasons, when tight control over a foreign entity is desirable, foreign direct investment is preferable to licensing.

A third problem with licensing arises when the firm's competitive advantage is based not as much on its products as on the management, marketing, and manufacturing capabilities that produce those products. The problem here is that *such capabilities are often not amenable to licensing*. While a foreign licensee may be able to physically reproduce the firm's product under license, it often may not be able to do so as efficiently as the firm could itself. As a result, the licensee may not be able to fully exploit the profit potential inherent in a foreign market.

For example, consider Toyota, a company whose competitive advantage in the global auto industry is acknowledged to come from its superior ability to manage the overall process of designing, engineering, manufacturing, and selling automobiles; that is, from its management and organizational capabilities. Toyota is credited with pioneering the development of a new production process, known as *lean production*, that enables it to produce higher quality automobiles at a lower cost than its global rivals.[14] Although Toyota could license certain products, its real competitive advantage comes from its management and process capabilities. These kinds of skills are difficult to articulate or codify; they certainly cannot be written down in a simple licensing contract. They are organization-wide and have been developed over the years. They are not embodied in any one individual but instead are widely dispersed throughout the company. Put another way, Toyota's skills are embedded in its organizational culture, and culture is something that cannot be licensed. Thus, if Toyota were to allow a foreign entity to produce its cars under license, the chances are that the entity could not do so as efficiently as could Toyota. In turn, this would limit the ability of the foreign entity to fully develop the market potential of that product. Such reasoning underlies Toyota's preference for direct investment in foreign markets, as opposed to allowing foreign automobile companies to produce its cars under license.

All of this suggests that when one or more of the following conditions holds, markets fail as a mechanism for selling know-how and FDI is more profitable than licensing: (1) when the firm has valuable know-how that cannot be adequately protected by a licensing contract; (2) when the firm needs tight control over a foreign entity to maximize its market share and earnings in that country; and (3) when a firm's skills and know-how are not amenable to licensing.

Advantages of Foreign Direct Investment   It follows that a firm will favor foreign direct investment over exporting as an entry strategy when transportation costs or trade barriers make exporting unattractive. Furthermore, the firm will favor foreign direct investment over licensing (or franchising) when it wishes to maintain control over its technological know-how, or over its operations and business strategy, or when the firm's capabilities are simply not amenable to licensing, as may often be the case.

THE PATTERN OF FOREIGN DIRECT INVESTMENT

Observation suggests that firms in the same industry often undertaken foreign direct investment at around the same time. Also, firms tend to direct their investment activities toward certain locations. The two theories we consider in this section attempt to explain the patterns that we observe in FDI flows.

Strategic Behavior

One theory is based on the idea that FDI flows are a reflection of strategic rivalry between firms in the global marketplace. An early variant of this argument was expounded by F. T. Knickerbocker, who looked at the relationship between FDI and rivalry in oligopolistic industries.[15] An **oligopoly** is an industry composed of a limited number of large firms (e.g., an industry in which four firms control 80 percent of a domestic market would be defined as an oligopoly). A critical competitive feature of such industries is interdependence of the major players: What one firm does can have an immediate impact on the major competitors, forcing a response in kind. By cutting prices, one firm in an oligopoly can take market share away from its competitors, forcing them to respond with similar price cuts to retain their market share. Thus, the interdependence between firms in an oligopoly leads to imitative behavior; rivals often quickly imitate what a firm does in an oligopoly.

Oligopoly
An industry composed of a limited number of large firms.

Imitative behavior can take many forms in an oligopoly. One firm raises prices, the others follow; one expands capacity, and the rivals imitate lest they be left at a disadvantage in the future. Knickerbocker argued that the same kind of imitative behavior characterizes FDI. Consider an oligopoly in the United States in which three firms—A, B, and C—dominate the market. Firm A establishes a subsidiary in France. Firms B and C decide that if successful, this new subsidiary may knock out their export business to France and give firm A a first-mover advantage. Furthermore, firm A might discover some competitive asset in France that it could repatriate to the United States to torment firms B and C on their native soil. Given these possibilities, firms B and C decide to follow firm A and establish operations in France.

Studies that looked at FDI by U.S. firms during the 1950s and 60s show that firms based in oligopolistic industries tended to imitate each other's FDI.[16] The same phenomenon has been observed with regard to FDI undertaken by Japanese firms during the 1980s.[17] For example, Toyota and Nissan responded to investments by Honda in the United States and Europe by undertaking their own FDI in the United States and Europe. More recently, research has shown that models of strategic behavior in a global oligopoly can explain the pattern of FDI in the global tire industry.[18]

Knickerbocker's theory can be extended to embrace the concept of multipoint competition. **Multipoint competition** arises when two or more enterprises encounter each other in different regional markets, national markets, or industries.[19] Economic theory suggests that rather like chess players jockeying for advantage, firms will try to match each other's moves in different markets to try to hold each other in check. The idea is to ensure that a rival does not gain a commanding position in one market and then use the profits generated there to subsidize competitive attacks in other markets. Kodak and Fuji Photo Film Co., for example, compete against each other around the world. If Kodak enters a particular foreign market, Fuji will not be far behind. Fuji feels compelled to follow Kodak to ensure that Kodak does not gain a dominant position in the foreign market that it could then leverage to gain a competitive advantage elsewhere. The converse also holds, with Kodak following Fuji when the Japanese firm is the first to enter a foreign market.

Multipoint Competition
When two or more enterprises encounter each other in different regional markets, national markets, or industries.

Although Knickerbocker's theory and its extensions can help to explain imitative FDI behavior by firms in oligopolistic industries, it does not explain why the first firm in an oligopoly decides to undertake FDI rather than to export or license. Internalization theory addresses this phenomenon. The imitative theory also does not address the issue of whether FDI is more efficient than exporting or licensing for expanding abroad. Again, internalization theory addresses the efficiency issue. For these reasons, many economists favor internalization theory as an explanation for FDI, although most would agree that the imitative explanation tells an important part of the story.

The Product Life Cycle   Raymond Vernon's product life-cycle theory, described in Chapter 5, also is used to explain FDI. Vernon argued that often the same firms that pioneer a product in their home markets undertake FDI to produce a product for consumption in foreign markets. Thus, Xerox introduced the photocopier in the United States, and it was Xerox that set up production facilities in Japan (Fuji–Xerox) and Great Britain (Rank–Xerox) to serve those markets. Vernon's view is that firms undertake FDI at particular stages in the life cycle of a product they have pioneered. They invest in other advanced countries when local demand in those countries grows large enough to support local production (as Xerox did). They subsequently shift production to developing countries when product standardization and market saturation give rise to price competition and cost pressures. Investment in developing countries, where labor costs are lower, is seen as the best way to reduce costs.

Vernon's theory has merit. Firms do invest in a foreign country when demand in that country will support local production, and they do invest in low-cost locations (e.g., developing countries) when cost pressures become intense.[20] However, Vernon's theory fails to explain why it is profitable for a firm to undertake FDI at such times, rather than continuing to export from its home base or licensing a foreign firm to produce its product. Just because demand in a foreign country is large enough to support local production, it does not necessarily follow that local production is the most profitable option. It may still be more profitable to produce at home and export to that country (to realize the economies of scale that arise from serving the global market from one location). Alternatively, it may be more profitable for the firm to license a foreign company to produce its product for sale in that country. The product life-cycle theory ignores these options and, instead, simply argues that once a foreign market is large enough to support local production, FDI will occur. This limits its explanatory power and its usefulness to business in that it fails to identify when it is profitable to invest abroad.

THE ECLECTIC PARADIGM   The eclectic paradigm has been championed by the British economist John Dunning.[21] Dunning argues that in addition to the various factors discussed above, location-specific advantages are also of considerable importance in explaining both the rationale for and the direction of foreign direct investment. By **location-specific advantages,** Dunning means the advantages that arise from utilizing resource endowments or assets that are tied to a particular foreign location and that a firm finds valuable to combine with its own unique assets (such as the firm's technological, marketing, or management capabilities). Dunning accepts the argument of internalization theory that it is difficult for a firm to license its own unique capabilities and know-how. Therefore, he argues that combining location-specific assets or resource endowments with the firm's own unique capabilities often requires foreign direct investment. That is, it requires the firm to establish production facilities where those foreign assets or resource endowments are located.

An obvious example of Dunning's arguments are natural resources, such as oil and other minerals, which are by their character specific to certain locations. Dunning suggests that to exploit such foreign resources, a firm must undertake FDI. Clearly, this explains the FDI undertaken by many of the world's oil companies, which have to invest where oil is located in order to combine their technological and managerial capabilities with this valuable location-specific resource. Another obvious example is

Location-Specific Advantages
Advantages that arise from utilizing resource endowments or assets that are tied to a particular foreign location and that a firm finds valuable to combine with its own unique assets, such as technological, marketing, or management capabilities.

Silicon Valley has long been known as the epicenter of the computer and semiconductor industry.

valuable human resources, such as low-cost, highly skilled labor. The cost and skill of labor varies from country to country. Since labor is not internationally mobile, according to Dunning it makes sense for a firm to locate production facilities in those countries where the cost and skills of local labor are most suited to its particular production processes.

However, Dunning's theory has implications that go beyond basic resources such as minerals and labor. Consider Silicon Valley, which is the world center for the computer and semiconductor industry. Many of the world's major computer and semiconductor companies, such as Apple Computer, Hewlett-Packard, and Intel, are located close to each other in the Silicon Valley region of California. As a result, much of the cutting-edge research and product development in computers and semiconductors takes place there. According to Dunning's arguments, knowledge is generated in Silicon Valley with regard to the design and manufacture of computers and semiconductors that is available nowhere else in the world. As it is commercialized that knowledge diffuses throughout the world, but the leading edge of knowledge generation in the computer and semiconductor industries is to be found in Silicon Valley. In Dunning's language, this means that Silicon Valley has a *location-specific advantage* in the generation of knowledge related to the computer and semiconductor industries. In part, this advantage comes from the sheer concentration of intellectual talent in this area, and in part it arises from a network of informal contacts that allows firms to benefit from each others' knowledge

Externalities
Knowledge spillovers.

generation. Economists refer to such knowledge spillovers as **externalities,** and there is a well-established theory suggesting that firms can benefit from such externalities by locating close to their source.[22]

In so far as this is the case, it makes sense for foreign computer and semiconductor firms to invest in research and, perhaps, production facilities so they too can learn about and utilize valuable new knowledge before those based elsewhere, thereby giving them a competitive advantage in the global marketplace.[23] Evidence suggests that European, Japanese, South Korean, and Taiwanese computer and semiconductor firms are investing in the Silicon Valley region, precisely because they wish to benefit from the externalities that arise there.[24] Others have argued that direct investment by foreign firms in the U.S. biotechnology industry has been motivated by desires to gain access to the unique location-specific technological knowledge of U.S. biotechnology firms.[25] Dunning's theory, therefore, seems to be a useful addition to those outlined above, for it helps explain how location factors affect the direction of FDI.[26]

Political Ideology and Foreign Direct Investment

LEARNING OBJECTIVE 3
Appreciate how political ideology shapes a government's attitudes toward FDI.

Historically, political ideology toward FDI within a nation has ranged from a dogmatic radical stance that is hostile to all inward FDI at one extreme to an adherence to the noninterventionist principle of free market economics at the other. Between these two extremes is an approach that might be called *pragmatic nationalism.*

THE RADICAL VIEW

The radical view traces its roots to Marxist political and economic theory. Radical writers argue that the multinational enterprise (MNE) is an instrument of imperialist domination. They see the MNE as a tool for exploiting host countries to the exclusive benefit of their capitalist-imperialist home countries. They argue that MNEs extract profits from the host country and take them to their home country, giving nothing of value to the host country in exchange. They note, for example, that key technology is tightly controlled by the MNE, and that important jobs in the foreign subsidiaries of MNEs go to home-country nationals rather than to citizens of the host country. Because of this, according to the radical view, FDI by the MNEs of advanced capitalist nations keeps the less developed countries of the world relatively backward and dependent on advanced capitalist nations for investment, jobs, and technology. Thus, according to the extreme version of this view, no country should ever permit foreign corporations to undertake FDI, since they can never be instruments of economic development, only of economic domination. Where MNEs already exist in a country, they should be immediately nationalized.[27]

From 1945 until the 1980s, the radical view was very influential in the world economy. Until the collapse of communism between 1989 and 1991, the countries of Eastern Europe were opposed to FDI. Similarly, communist countries elsewhere, such as China, Cambodia, and Cuba, were all opposed in principle to FDI (although in practice the Chinese started to allow FDI in mainland China in the 1970s). Many socialist countries, particularly in Africa where one of the first actions of many newly independent states was to nationalize foreign-owned enterprises, also embraced the radical position. Countries whose political ideology was more nationalistic than socialistic further embraced the radical position. This was true in Iran and India, for example, both of which adopted tough policies restricting FDI and nationalized many foreign-owned enterprises. Iran is a particularly interesting case because its Islamic government, while rejecting Marxist theory, has essentially embraced the radical view that FDI by MNEs is an instrument of imperialism.

By the end of the 1980s, the radical position was in retreat almost everywhere. There seem to be three reasons for this: (1) the collapse of communism in Eastern Europe; (2) the generally abysmal economic performance of those countries that embraced the radical position, and a growing belief by many of these countries that FDI can be an important source of technology and jobs and can stimulate economic growth; and (3) the strong economic performance of those developing countries that embraced capitalism rather than radical ideology (e.g., Singapore, Hong Kong, and Taiwan).

THE FREE MARKET VIEW

The free market view traces its roots to classical economics and the international trade theories of Adam Smith and David Ricardo (see Chapter 5). The intellectual case for this view has been strengthened by the internalization explanation of FDI. The free market view argues that international production should be distributed among countries according to the theory of comparative advantage. Countries should specialize in the production of those goods and services that they can produce most efficiently. Within this framework, the MNE is an instrument for dispersing the production of goods and services to the most efficient locations around the globe. Viewed this way, FDI by the MNE increases the overall efficiency of the world economy.

Imagine that Dell decided to move assembly operations for many of its personal computers from the United States to Mexico to take advantage of lower labor costs in Mexico. According to the free market view, moves such as this can be seen as increasing the overall efficiency of resource utilization in the world economy. Mexico, due to its lower labor costs, has a comparative advantage in the assembly of PCs. By moving the production of PCs from the United States to Mexico, Dell frees U.S. resources for use in activities in which the United States has a comparative advantage (e.g., the design of computer software, the manufacture of high-value-added components such as microprocessors, or basic R&D). Also, consumers benefit because the PCs cost less than they would if they were produced domestically. In addition, Mexico gains from the technology, skills, and capital that the PC company transfers with its FDI. Contrary to the radical view, the free market view stresses that such resource transfers benefit the host country and stimulate its economic growth. Thus, the free market view argues that FDI is a benefit to both the source country and the host country.

For reasons explored earlier in this book (see Chapter 2), the free market view has been ascendant worldwide in recent years, spurring a global move toward the removal of restrictions on inward and outward foreign direct investment. However, in practice no country has adopted the free market view in its pure form (just as no country has adopted the radical view in its pure form). Countries such as Great Britain and the United States are among the most open to FDI, but the governments of these countries both have still reserved the right to intervene. Britain does so by reserving the right to block foreign takeovers of domestic firms if the takeovers are seen as "contrary to national security interests" or if they have the potential for "reducing competition." (In practice, the U.K. government has rarely exercised this right.) U.S. controls on FDI are more limited and largely informal. For political reasons, the United States will occasionally restrict U.S. firms from undertaking FDI in certain countries (e.g., Cuba and Iran). In addition, inward FDI meets some limited restrictions. For example, foreigners are prohibited from purchasing more than 25 percent of any U.S. airline or from acquiring a controlling interest in a U.S. television broadcast network. Since 1988, the government has had the right to review the acquisition of a U.S. enterprise by a foreign firm on the grounds of national security. However, of the 1,500 bids reviewed by the Committee on Foreign Investment in the United States under this law by 2005, only one has been nullified: the sale of a Seattle-based aircraft parts manufacturer to a Chinese enterprise in the early 1990s.[28]

PRAGMATIC NATIONALISM   In practice, many countries have adopted neither a radical policy nor a free market policy toward FDI, but instead a policy that can best be described as pragmatic nationalism.[29] The pragmatic nationalist view is that FDI has both benefits and costs. FDI can benefit a host country by bringing capital, skills, technology, and jobs, but those benefits come at a cost. When a foreign company rather than a domestic company produces products, the profits from that investment go abroad. Many countries are also concerned that a foreign-owned manufacturing plant may import many components from its home country, which has negative implications for the host country's balance-of-payments position.

Recognizing this, countries adopting a pragmatic stance pursue policies designed to maximize the national benefits and minimize the national costs. According to this view, FDI should be allowed so long as the benefits outweigh the costs. Japan offers an example of pragmatic nationalism. Until the 1980s, Japan's policy was probably one of the most restrictive among countries adopting a pragmatic nationalist stance. This was due to Japan's perception that direct entry of foreign (especially U.S.) firms with ample managerial resources into the Japanese markets could hamper the development and growth of their own industry and technology.[30] This belief led Japan to block the majority of applications to invest in Japan. However, there were always exceptions to this policy. Firms that had important technology were often permitted to undertake FDI if they insisted that they would neither license their technology to a Japanese firm nor enter into a joint venture with a Japanese enterprise. IBM and Texas Instruments were able to set up wholly owned subsidiaries in Japan by adopting this negotiating position. From the perspective of the Japanese government, the benefits of FDI in such cases—the stimulus that these firms might impart to the Japanese economy—outweighed the perceived costs.

Another aspect of pragmatic nationalism is the tendency to aggressively court FDI believed to be in the national interest by, for example, offering subsidies to foreign MNEs in the form of tax breaks or grants. The countries of the European Union often seem to be competing with each other to attract U.S. and Japanese FDI by offering large tax breaks and subsidies. Britain has been the most successful at attracting Japanese investment in the automobile industry. Nissan, Toyota, and Honda now have major assembly plants in Britain and use the country as their base for serving the rest of Europe—with obvious employment and balance-of-payments benefits for Britain.

SHIFTING IDEOLOGY   Recent years have seen a marked decline in the number of countries that adhere to a radical ideology. Although few countries have adopted a pure free market policy stance, an increasing number of countries are gravitating toward the free market end of the spectrum and have liberalized their foreign investment regime. This includes many countries that less than two decades ago were firmly in the radical camp (e.g., the former communist countries of Eastern Europe and many of the socialist countries of Africa) and several countries that until recently could best be described as pragmatic nationalists with regard to FDI (e.g., Japan, South Korea, Italy, Spain, and most Latin American countries). One result has been the surge in the volume of FDI worldwide, which, as we noted earlier, has been growing twice as fast as the growth in world trade. Another result has been an increase in the volume of FDI directed at countries that have recently liberalized their FDI regimes, such as China, India, and Vietnam.

As a counterpoint, there is recent evidence of the beginnings of what might become a shift to a more hostile approach to foreign direct investment. Venezuela and Bolivia have become increasingly hostile to foreign direct investment. In 2005 and 2006, the governments of both nations unilaterally rewrote contracts for oil and gas exploration, raising the royalty rate that foreign enterprises had to pay the government for oil and gas extracted in their territories. Following his election victory, in 2006 Bolivian President Evo Morales nationalized the nation's gas fields and stated that he would evict foreign firms unless they agreed to pay about 80 percent of their revenues to the state and relinquish production oversight. In some developed nations too, evidence of hostile reactions to inward FDI is increasing. In Europe in 2006, there was a hostile political reaction to the attempted takeover of Europe's largest steel company, Arcelor, by Mittal Steel, a global company controlled by an Indian entrepreneur, Lakshmi Mittal (see the opening case). In mid-2005 China National Offshore Oil Company withdrew a takeover bid for Unocal of the United States after highly negative reaction in Congress about the proposed takeover of a "strategic asset" by a Chinese company. Similarly, as detailed in the accompanying Management Focus, in 2006 a Dubai-owned company withdrew its planned takeover of some operations at six U.S. ports after negative political reactions. So far, these countertrends are nothing more than isolated incidents, but if they become more widespread, the 30-year-long movement toward lower barriers to cross-border investment could be in jeopardy.

Management FOCUS

DP World and the United States

In February 2006, DP World, a ports operator with global reach owned by the government of Dubai, a member of the United Arab Emirates and a staunch U.S. ally, paid $6.8 billion to acquire P&O, a British firm that runs a global network of marine terminals. With P&O came the management operations of six U.S. ports: Miami, Philadelphia, Baltimore, New Orleans, New Jersey, and New York. The acquisition had already been approved by U.S. regulators when it suddenly became front-page news. Upon hearing about the deal, several prominent U.S. senators raised concerns about the acquisition. Their objections were twofold. First, they raised questions about the security risks associated with management operations in key U.S. ports being owned by a foreign enterprise that was based in the Middle East. The implication was that terrorists could somehow take advantage of the ownership arrangement to infiltrate U.S. ports. Second, they were concerned that DP World was a state-owned enterprise and argued that foreign governments should not be in a position of owning key "U.S. strategic assets."

The Bush administration was quick to defend the takeover, stating that it posed no threat to national security. Others noted that DP World was a respected global firm with an American chief operating officer and an American-educated chairman; the head of the global ports management operation would also be an American. DP World would not own the U.S. ports in question, just manage them, while security issues would remain in the hands of U.S. customs officials and the U.S. Coast Guard. Dubai was also a member of America's Container Security Initiative, which allows U.S. customs officials to inspect cargo in foreign ports before it leaves for the United States. Most of the DP World employees at American ports would be U.S. citizens, and any UAE citizen transferred to DP World would be subject to American visa approval.

These arguments fell on deaf ears. With several U.S. senators threatening to pass legislation to prohibit foreign ownership of U.S. port operations, DP World bowed to the inevitable and announced that it would sell the right to manage the six U.S. ports for about $750 million. Looking forward, however, DP World stated it would seek an initial public offering in 2007, and that the then-private firm would in all probability continue to look for ways to enter the United States. In the words of the firm's CEO, "This is the world's largest economy. How can you just ignore it?"

Sources: "Trouble at the Waterfront," *The Economist*, February 25, 2006, p. 48; "Paranoia about Dubai Ports Deals Is Needless," *Financial Times*, February 21, 2006, p. 16; and "DP World: We'll Be Back," *Traffic World*, May 29, 2006, p. 1.

Benefits and Costs of FDI

LEARNING OBJECTIVE 4
Understand the benefits and costs of FDI to home and host countries.

To a greater or lesser degree, many governments can be considered pragmatic nationalists when it comes to FDI. Accordingly, their policy is shaped by a consideration of the costs and benefits of FDI. Here we explore the benefits and costs of FDI, first from the perspective of a host (receiving) country, and then from the perspective of the home (source) country. In the next section, we look at the policy instruments governments use to manage FDI.

HOST-COUNTRY BENEFITS
The main benefits of inward FDI for a host country arise from resource-transfer effects, employment effects, balance-of-payments effects, and effects on competition and economic growth.

Resource-Transfer Effects
Foreign direct investment can make a positive contribution to a host economy by supplying capital, technology, and management resources that would otherwise not be available and thus boost that country's economic growth rate.[31]

With regard to capital, many MNEs, by virtue of their large size and financial strength, have access to financial resources not available to host-country firms. These funds may be available from internal company sources, or, because of their reputation, large MNEs may find it easier to borrow money from capital markets than host-country firms would.

As for technology, you will recall from Chapter 2 that technology can stimulate economic development and industrialization. Technology can take two forms, both of which are valuable. Technology can be incorporated in a production process (e.g., the technology for discovering, extracting, and refining oil) or it can be incorporated in a product (e.g., personal computers). However, many countries lack the research and development resources and skills required to develop their own indigenous product and process technology. This is particularly true in less developed nations. Such countries must rely on advanced industrialized nations for much of the technology required to stimulate economic growth, and FDI can provide it.

Research supports the view that multinational firms often transfer significant technology when they invest in a foreign country.[32] For example, a study of FDI in Sweden found that foreign firms increased both the labor and total factor productivity of Swedish firms that they acquired, suggesting that significant technology transfers had occurred (technology typically boosts productivity).[33] Also, a study of FDI by the Organization for Economic Cooperation and Development (OECD) found that foreign investors invested significant amounts of capital in R&D, suggesting that not only were they transferring technology to those countries, but they may also have been upgrading existing technology or creating new technology.[34]

Foreign management skills acquired through FDI may also produce important benefits for the host country. Foreign managers trained in the latest management techniques can often help to improve the efficiency of operations in the host country, whether those operations are acquired or greenfield developments. Beneficial spin-off effects may also arise when local personnel who are trained to occupy managerial, financial, and technical posts in the subsidiary of a foreign MNE leave the firm and help to establish indigenous firms. Similar benefits may arise if the superior management skills of a foreign MNE stimulate local suppliers, distributors, and competitors to improve their own management skills.

Employment Effects Another beneficial employment effect claimed for FDI is that it brings jobs to a host country that would otherwise not be created there. The effects of FDI on employment are both direct and indirect. Direct effects arise when a foreign MNE employs a number of host-country citizens. Indirect effects arise when jobs are created in local suppliers as a result of the investment and when jobs are created because of increased local spending by employees of the MNE. The indirect employment effects are often as large as, if not larger than, the direct effects. For example, when Toyota decided to open a new auto plant in France in 1997, estimates suggested the plant would create 2,000 direct jobs and perhaps another 2,000 jobs in support industries.[35]

Cynics argue that not all the "new jobs" created by FDI represent net additions in employment. In the case of FDI by Japanese auto companies in the United States, some argue that the jobs created by this investment have been more than offset by the jobs lost in U.S.-owned auto companies, which have lost market share to their Japanese competitors. As a consequence of

Another Perspective

Alabama Courts FDI from Korea
When South Korean automaker Hyundai decided to invest in its first auto plant in the United States, it used accounting firm KPMG to narrow the choices to four states: Alabama, Kentucky, Mississippi, and Ohio. Alabama began a full-court press on the Koreans, offering them $76.7 million in tax breaks, $61.8 million in training grants, and $34 million in land purchase assistance—in all, a package valued at $252.8 million.

Opening in Montgomery in 2005, Hyundai's $1.4 billion plant created 3,300 jobs. To support Hyundai's U.S. operations, some 70 suppliers have established locations in North America, creating about 5,500 additional jobs. (www.hyundai.com)

such substitution effects, the net number of new jobs created by FDI may not be as great as initially claimed by an MNE. The issue of the likely net gain in employment may be a major negotiating point between an MNE wishing to undertake FDI and the host government.

When FDI takes the form of an acquisition of an established enterprise in the host economy as opposed to a greenfield investment, the immediate effect may be to reduce employment as the multinational tries to restructure the operations of the acquired unit to improve its operating efficiency. However, even in such cases, research suggests that once the initial period of restructuring is over, enterprises acquired by foreign firms tend to grow their employment base at a faster rate than domestic rivals. For example, an OECD study found that between 1989 and 1996 foreign firms created new jobs at a faster rate than their domestic counterparts.[36] In America, the workforce of foreign firms grew by 1.4 percent per year in that time period, compared with 0.8 percent per year for domestic firms. In Britain and France, the workforce of foreign firms grew at 1.7 percent per year, while employment at domestic firms fell by 2.7 percent. The same study found that foreign firms tended to pay higher wage rates than domestic firms, suggesting that the quality of employment was better. Another study looking at FDI in Eastern European transition economies found that although employment fell following the acquisition of an enterprise by a foreign firm, often those enterprises were in competitive difficulties and would not have survived if they had not been acquired. Also, after an initial period of adjustment and retrenchment, employment downsizing was often followed by new investments, and employment either remained stable or increased.[37]

Balance-of-Payments Effects   FDI's effect on a country's balance-of-payments accounts is an important policy issue for most host governments. A country's **balance-of-payments accounts** track both its payments to and its receipts from other countries. Governments normally are concerned when their country is running a deficit on the current account of their balance of payments. The **current account** tracks the export and import of goods and services. A current account deficit, or trade deficit as it is often called, arises when a country is importing more goods and services than it is exporting. Governments typically prefer to see a current account surplus than a deficit. The only way in which a current account deficit can be supported in the long run is by selling assets to foreigners (for a detailed explanation of why this is the case, see the appendix to Chapter 5). For example, the persistent U.S. current account deficit since the 1980s has been financed by a steady sale of U.S. assets (stocks, bonds, real estate, and whole corporations) to foreigners. Since national governments invariably dislike seeing the assets of their country fall into foreign hands, they prefer their nation to run a current account surplus. There are two ways in which FDI can help a country to achieve this goal.

First, if the FDI is a substitute for imports of goods or services, the effect can be to improve the current account of the host country's balance of payments. Much of the FDI by Japanese automobile companies in the United States and Europe, for example, can be seen as substituting for imports from Japan. Thus, the current account of the U.S. balance of payments has improved somewhat because many Japanese companies are now supplying the U.S. market from production facilities in the United States, as opposed to facilities in Japan. Insofar as this has reduced the need to finance a current account deficit by asset sales to foreigners, the United States has clearly benefited.

A second potential benefit arises when the MNE uses a foreign subsidiary to export goods and services to other countries. According to a UN report, inward FDI by foreign multinationals has been a major driver of export-led economic

Balance-of-Payments Accounts
National accounts that track both payments to and receipts from foreigners.

Current Account
In the balance of payments, this records transactions involving the export or import of goods and services.

growth in a number of developing and developed nations over the last decade.[38] For example, in China exports increased from $26 billion in 1985 to more than $250 billion by 2001 and to $969 billion in 2006. Much of this dramatic export growth was due to the presence of foreign multinationals that invested heavily in China during the 1990s. The subsidiaries of foreign multinationals accounted for 50 percent of all exports from that country in 2001, up from 17 percent in 1991. In mobile phones, for example, the Chinese subsidiaries of foreign multinationals—primarily Nokia, Motorola, Ericsson, and Siemens—accounted for 95 percent of China's exports.

Effect on Competition and Economic Growth   Economic theory tells us that the efficient functioning of markets depends on an adequate level of competition between producers. When FDI takes the form of a greenfield investment, the result is to establish a new enterprise, increasing the number of players in a market and thus consumer choice. In turn, this can increase the level of competition in a national market, thereby driving down prices and increasing the economic welfare of consumers. Increased competition tends to stimulate capital investments by firms in plant, equipment, and R&D as they struggle to gain an edge over their rivals. The long-term results may include increased productivity growth, product and process innovations, and greater economic growth.[39] Such beneficial effects seem to have occurred in the South Korean retail sector following the liberalization of FDI regulations in 1996. FDI by large Western discount stores, including Wal-Mart, Costco, Carrefour, and Tesco, seems to have encouraged indigenous discounters such as E-Mart to improve the efficiency of their own operations. The results have included more competition and lower prices, which benefit South Korean consumers.

FDI's impact on competition in domestic markets may be particularly important in the case of services, such as telecommunications, retailing, and many financial services, where exporting is often not an option because the service has to be produced where it is delivered.[40] For example, under a 1997 agreement sponsored by the World Trade Organization, 68 countries accounting for more than 90 percent of world telecommunications revenues pledged to start opening their markets to foreign investment and competition and to abide by common rules for fair competition in telecommunications. Before this agreement, most of the world's telecommunications markets were closed to foreign competitors, and in most countries the market was monopolized by a single carrier, which was often a state-owned enterprise. The agreement has dramatically increased the level of competition in many national telecommunications markets producing two major benefits. First, inward investment has increased competition and stimulated investment in the modernization of telephone networks around the world, leading to better service. Second, the increased competition has resulted in lower prices.

HOST-COUNTRY COSTS   Three costs of FDI concern host countries. They arise from possible adverse effects on competition within the host nation, adverse effects on the balance of payments, and the perceived loss of national sovereignty and autonomy.

Adverse Effects on Competition   Host governments sometimes worry that the subsidiaries of foreign MNEs may have greater economic power than indigenous competitors. If it is part of a larger international organization, the foreign MNE may be able to draw on funds generated elsewhere to subsidize its costs in the host market, which could drive indigenous companies out of business and allow the firm to monopolize the market. Once the market is monopolized, the foreign MNE could raise prices above those that would prevail in competitive markets, with harmful effects on the economic welfare of the host nation. This concern tends to be greater in countries that have few large firms of their own (generally less developed countries). It tends to be a relatively minor concern in most advanced industrialized nations.

In general, while FDI in the form of greenfield investments should increase competition, it is less clear that this is the case when the FDI takes the form of acquisition of an established enterprise in the host nation, as was the case when Cemex acquired RMC is Britain (see the Management Focus). Because an acquisition does not result in a net increase in the number of players in a market, the effect on competition may be neutral. When a foreign investor acquires two or more firms in a host country, and subsequently merges them, the effect may be to reduce the level of competition in that market, create monopoly power for the foreign firm, reduce consumer choice, and raise prices. For example, in India, Hindustan Lever Ltd., the Indian subsidiary of Unilever, acquired its main local rival, Tata Oil Mills, to assume a dominant position in the bath soap (75 percent) and detergents (30 percent) markets. Hindustan Lever also acquired several local companies in other markets, such as the ice cream makers Dollops, Kwality, and Milkfood. By combining these companies, Hindustan Lever's share of the Indian ice cream market went from zero in 1992 to 74 percent in 1997.[41] However, although such cases are of obvious concern, there is little evidence that such developments are widespread. In many nations, authorities have the right to review and block any mergers or acquisitions that they view as having a detrimental impact on competition. If such institutions are operating effectively, this should be sufficient to make sure that foreign entities do not monopolize a country's markets.

Adverse Effects on the Balance of Payments

The possible adverse effects of FDI on a host country's balance-of-payments position are twofold. First, set against the initial capital inflow that comes with FDI must be the subsequent outflow of earnings from the foreign subsidiary to its parent company. Such outflows show up as capital outflow on balance of payments accounts. Some governments have responded to such outflows by restricting the amount of earnings that can be repatriated to a foreign subsidiary's home country. A second concern arises when a foreign subsidiary imports a substantial number of its inputs from abroad, which results in a debit on the current account of the host country's balance of payments. One criticism leveled against Japanese-owned auto assembly operations in the United States, for example, is that they tend to import many component parts from Japan. Because of this, the favorable impact of this FDI on the current account of the U.S. balance-of-payments position may not be as great as initially supposed. The Japanese auto companies have responded to these criticisms by pledging to purchase 75 percent of their component parts from U.S.-based manufacturers (but not necessarily U.S.-owned manufacturers). When the Japanese auto company Nissan invested in the United Kingdom, Nissan responded to concerns about local content by pledging to increase the proportion of local content to 60 percent and subsequently raising it to more than 80 percent.

National Sovereignty and Autonomy

Some host governments worry that FDI is accompanied by some loss of economic independence. The concern is that key decisions that can affect the host country's economy will be made by a foreign parent that has no real commitment to the host country, and over which the host country's government has no real control. Most economists dismiss such concerns as groundless and irrational. Political scientist Robert Reich has noted that such concerns are the product of outmoded thinking because they fail to account for the growing interdependence of the world economy.[42] In a world in which firms from all advanced nations are increasingly investing in each other's markets, it is not possible for one country to hold another to "economic ransom" without hurting itself.

HOME-COUNTRY BENEFITS

The benefits of FDI to the home (source) country arise from three sources. First, the home country's balance of payments benefits from the inward flow of foreign earnings. FDI can also benefit the home country's balance of payments if the foreign subsidiary creates demands for home-country exports of capital equipment, intermediate goods, complementary products, and the like.

Second, benefits to the home country from outward FDI arise from employment effects. As with the balance of payments, positive employment effects arise when the foreign subsidiary creates demand for home-country exports. Thus, Toyota's investment in auto assembly operations in Europe has benefited both the Japanese balance-of-payments position and employment in Japan, because Toyota imports some component parts for its European-based auto assembly operations directly from Japan.

Third, benefits arise when the home-country MNE learns valuable skills from its exposure to foreign markets that can subsequently be transferred back to the home country. This amounts to a reverse resource-transfer effect. Through its exposure to a foreign market, an MNE can learn about superior management techniques and superior product and process technologies. These resources can then be transferred back to the home country, contributing to the home country's economic growth rate.[43] For example, one reason General Motors and Ford invested in Japanese automobile companies (GM owns part of Isuzu, and Ford owns part of Mazda) was to learn about their production processes. If GM and Ford are successful in transferring this know-how back to their U.S. operations, the result may be a net gain for the U.S. economy.

HOME-COUNTRY COSTS

Against these benefits must be set the apparent costs of FDI for the home (source) country. The most important concerns center on the balance-of-payments and employment effects of outward FDI. The home country's balance of payments may suffer in three ways. First, the balance of payments suffers from the initial capital outflow required to finance the FDI. This effect, however, is usually more than offset by the subsequent inflow of foreign earnings. Second, the current account of the balance of payments suffers if the purpose of the foreign investment is to serve the home market from a low-cost production location. Third, the current account of the balance of payments suffers if the FDI is a substitute for

Another Perspective

FDI Effects: Look at the Whole Picture

Some critics of globalization suggest that FDI is an advanced form of colonialism that destroys local cultures in developing countries. What these critics say may have some limited validity, but it isn't the whole picture. Take Freeport McMoRan, a U.S.-based mining company with operations in West Papua, the former Irian Jaya, Indonesia, where the world's largest gold, mineral, and copper reserves have been found. Freeport formed a joint-venture with the Indonesian government to mine a concession, an isolated tract of land the size of Massachusetts on a remote island, half of which is the country of Papua New Guinea.

Freeport has brought education, Internet-connections, world-class health care, and the modern world to the isolated local tribes in West Papua, nomadic peoples who wear loincloths and hunt in the forest. Their traditional, subsistence way of life is threatened, while at the same time, they gain from their share of the operation's profits, from their increased health care and education, and from local employment opportunities with FCX. Is this colonialism or a kind of ethical investing? See more on this issue at www.FCX.com and www.corpwatch.org.

direct exports. Thus, insofar as Toyota's assembly operations in the United States are intended to substitute for direct exports from Japan, the current account position of Japan will deteriorate.

With regard to employment effects, the most serious concerns arise when FDI is seen as a substitute for domestic production. This was the case with Toyota's investments in the United States and Europe. One obvious result of such FDI is reduced home-country employment. If the labor market in the home country is already tight, with little unemployment, this concern may not be that great. However, if the home country is suffering from unemployment, concern about the export of jobs may arise. For example, one objection frequently raised by U.S. labor leaders to the free trade pact between the United States, Mexico, and Canada (see the next chapter) is that the United States will lose hundreds of thousands of jobs as U.S. firms invest in Mexico to take advantage of cheaper labor and then export back to the United States.[44]

INTERNATIONAL TRADE THEORY AND FDI   When assessing the costs and benefits of FDI to the home country, keep in mind the lessons of international trade theory (see Chapter 5). International trade theory tells us that home-country concerns about the negative economic effects of offshore production may be misplaced. The term **offshore production** refers to FDI undertaken to serve the home market. Far from reducing home-country employment, such FDI may actually stimulate economic growth (and hence employment) in the home country by freeing home-country resources to concentrate on activities where the home country has a comparative advantage. In addition, home-country consumers benefit if the price of the particular product falls as a result of the FDI. Also, if a company were prohibited from making such investments on the grounds of negative employment effects while its international competitors reaped the benefits of low-cost production locations, it would undoubtedly lose market share to its international competitors. Under such a scenario, the adverse long-run economic effects for a country would probably outweigh the relatively minor balance-of-payments and employment effects associated with offshore production.

Offshore Production
FDI undertaken to serve the home market.

Government Policy Instruments and FDI

LEARNING OBJECTIVE 5
Be able to discuss the range of policy instruments that governments use to influence FDI.

We have reviewed the costs and benefits of FDI from the perspective of both home country and host country. We now turn our attention to the policy instruments that home (source) countries and host countries can use to regulate FDI.

HOME-COUNTRY POLICIES   Through their choice of policies, home countries can both encourage and restrict FDI by local firms. We look at policies designed to encourage outward FDI first. These include foreign risk insurance, capital assistance, tax incentives, and political pressure. Then we will look at policies designed to restrict outward FDI.

Encouraging Outward FDI   Many investor nations now have government-backed insurance programs to cover major types of foreign investment risk. The types of risks insurable through these programs include the risks of expropriation (nationalization), war losses, and the inability to transfer profits back home. Such programs are particularly useful in encouraging firms to undertake investments in politically unstable countries.[45] In addition, several advanced countries also have special funds or banks that make government loans to firms wishing to invest in developing countries. As a further incentive to encourage domestic firms to under-take FDI, many countries have eliminated double taxation of foreign income (i.e., taxation of income in both the host country and the home country). Last, and per-haps most significant, a number of investor countries (including the United States) have used their political influence to persuade host countries to relax their restrictions on inbound FDI. For example, in response to direct U.S. pressure, Japan relaxed many of its formal restrictions on inward FDI in the 1980s. Now, in response to further U.S. pressure, Japan moved toward relaxing its informal barriers to inward FDI. One beneficiary of this trend has been Toys "R" Us, which, after five years of intensive lobbying by company and U.S. government officials, opened its first retail stores in Japan in December 1991. By 2008, Toys "R" Us had more 170 stores in Japan, and its Japanese operation, in which Toys "R" Us retained a controlling stake, had a listing on the Japanese stock market.

Restricting Outward FDI   Virtually all investor countries, including the United States, have exercised some control over outward FDI from time to time. One policy has been to limit capital outflows out of concern for the country's balance of payments. From the early 1960s until 1979, for example, Britain had exchange-control regulations that limited the amount of capital a firm could take out of the country. Although the main intent of such policies was to improve the British balance of payments, an important secondary intent was to make it more difficult for British firms to undertake FDI.

In addition, countries have occasionally manipulated tax rules to try to encourage their firms to invest at home. The objective behind such policies is to create jobs at home rather than in other nations. At one time, Britain adopted such policies. The British advanced corporation tax system taxed British companies' foreign earnings at a higher rate than their domestic earnings. This tax code created an incentive for British companies to invest at home.

Finally, countries sometimes prohibit national firms from investing in certain countries for political reasons. Such restrictions can be formal or informal. For example, formal U.S. rules prohibit U.S. firms from investing in countries such as Cuba and Iran, whose political ideology and actions are judged to be contrary to U.S. interests. Similarly, during the 1980s, informal pressure was applied to dissuade U.S. firms from investing in South Africa. In this case, the objective was to pressure South Africa to change its apartheid laws, which happened during the early 1990s.

HOST-COUNTRY POLICIES   Host countries adopt policies designed both to restrict and to encourage inward FDI. As noted earlier in this chapter, political ideology has determined the type and scope of these policies in the past. In the last decade of the 20th century, many countries moved quickly away from a situation where they adhered to some version of the radical stance and prohibited much FDI, and toward a situation where a combination of free market objectives and pragmatic nationalism took hold.

Encouraging Inward FDI   It is common for governments to offer incentives to foreign firms to invest in their countries. Such incentives take many forms, but the most common are tax concessions, low-interest loans, and grants or subsidies. Incentives are motivated by a desire to gain from the resource-transfer and employment effects of FDI. They are also motivated by a desire to capture FDI away from other potential host countries. For example, in the mid-1990s, the governments of Britain and France competed with each other on the incentives they offered Toyota to invest in their respective countries. In the United States, state governments often compete with

Often, governments provide incentives to attract foreign firms. For example, Kentucky offered Toyota an incentive package worth $112 million to build its assembly plant there.

each other to attract FDI. For example, Kentucky offered Toyota an incentive package worth $112 million to persuade it to build its U.S. automobile assembly plants there. The package included tax breaks, new state spending on infrastructure, and low-interest loans.[46]

Restricting Inward FDI Host governments use a wide range of controls to restrict FDI in one way or another. The two most common are ownership restraints and performance requirements. Ownership restraints can take several forms. In some countries, foreign companies are excluded from specific fields. They are excluded from tobacco and mining in Sweden and from the development of certain natural resources in Brazil, Finland, and Morocco. In other industries, foreign ownership may be permitted although a significant proportion of the equity of the subsidiary must be owned by local investors. Foreign ownership is restricted to 25 percent or less of an airline in the United States. In India, foreign firms were prohibited from owning media businesses until 2001, when the rules were relaxed, allowing foreign firms to purchase up to 26 percent of a foreign newspaper.[47]

The rationale underlying ownership restraints seems to be twofold. First, foreign firms are often excluded from certain sectors on the grounds of national security or competition. Particularly in less developed countries, the feeling seems to be that local firms might not be able to develop unless foreign competition is restricted by a combination of import tariffs and controls on FDI. This is a variant of the infant industry argument discussed in Chapter 6.

Second, ownership restraints seem to be based on a belief that local owners can help to maximize the resource-transfer and employment benefits of FDI for the host country. Until the early 1980s, the Japanese government prohibited most FDI but allowed joint ventures between Japanese firms and foreign MNEs if the MNE had a valuable technology. The Japanese government clearly believed such an arrangement would speed up the subsequent diffusion of the MNE's valuable technology throughout the Japanese economy.

Performance requirements can also take several forms. Performance requirements are controls over the behavior of the MNE's local subsidiary. The most common performance requirements are related to local content, exports, technology transfer, and local participation in top management. As with certain ownership restrictions, the logic underlying performance requirements is that such rules help to maximize the benefits and minimize the costs of FDI for the host country. Many countries employ some form of performance requirements when it suits their objectives. However, performance requirements tend to be more common in less developed countries than in advanced industrialized nations.[48]

INTERNATIONAL INSTITUTIONS AND THE LIBERALIZATION OF FDI

Until the 1990s, there was no consistent involvement by multinational institutions in the governing of FDI. This changed with the formation of the World Trade Organization in 1995. The WTO embraces the promotion of international trade in services. Since many services have to be produced where they are sold, exporting is not an option (for example, one cannot export McDonald's hamburgers or consumer banking services). Given this, the WTO has become involved in regulations governing FDI. As might be expected for an institution created to promote free trade, the thrust of the WTO's efforts has been to push for the liberalization of regulations governing FDI, particularly in services. Under the auspices of the WTO, two extensive multinational agreements were reached in 1997 to liberalize trade in telecommunications and financial services. Both these agreements contained detailed clauses that require signatories to liberalize their regulations governing inward FDI, essentially opening their markets to foreign telecommunications and financial services companies.

The WTO has had less success trying to initiate talks aimed at establishing a universal set of rules designed to promote the liberalization of FDI. Led by Malaysia and India, developing nations have so far rejected efforts by the WTO to start such discussions. In an attempt to make some progress on this issue, the Organization for Economic Cooperation and Development in 1995 initiated talks between its members. (The OECD is a Paris-based intergovernmental organization of "wealthy" nations whose purpose is to provide its 29 member states with a forum in which governments can compare their experiences, discuss the problems they share, and seek solutions that can then be applied within their own national contexts. The members include most EU countries, the United States, Canada, Japan, and South Korea.) The aim of the talks was to draft a multilateral agreement on investment (MAI) that would make it illegal for signatory states to discriminate against foreign investors. This would liberalize rules governing FDI between OECD states.

These talks broke down in early 1998, primarily because the United States refused to sign the agreement. According to the United States, the proposed agreement contained too many exceptions that would weaken its powers. For example, the proposed agreement would not have barred discriminatory taxation of foreign-owned companies, and it would have allowed countries to restrict foreign television programs and music in the name of preserving culture. Environmental and labor groups also campaigned against the MAI, criticizing the proposed agreement because it contained no binding environmental or labor agreements. Despite such setbacks, negotiations on a revised MAI treaty might restart in the future. Also, as noted earlier, many individual nations have continued to liberalize their policies governing FDI to encourage foreign firms to invest in their economies.[49]

Focus on Managerial Implications

LEARNING OBJECTIVE 6
Be able to articulate the implications for management practice of the theory and government policies associated with FDI.

Several implications for business are inherent in the material discussed in this chapter. In this section, we deal first with the implications of the theory and then turn our attention to the implications of government policy.

The Theory of FDI

The implications of the theories of FDI for business practice are straightforward. First, the location-specific advantages argument associated with John Dunning does help explain the *direction* of FDI. However, the location-specific advantages argument does not explain *why* firms prefer FDI to licensing or to exporting. In this regard, from both an explanatory and a business perspective perhaps the most useful theories are those that focus on the limitations of exporting and licensing; that is, internalization theories. These theories are useful because they identify with some precision how the relative profitability of foreign direct investment, exporting, and licensing vary with circumstances. The theories suggest that exporting is preferable to licensing and FDI so long as transportation costs are minor and trade barriers are trivial. As transportation costs or trade barriers increase, exporting becomes unprofitable, and the choice is between FDI and licensing. Since FDI is more costly and more risky than licensing, other things being equal, the theories argue that licensing is preferable to FDI. Other things are seldom equal, however. Although licensing may work, it is not an attractive option when one or more of the following conditions exist: (1) the firm has valuable know-how that cannot be adequately protected by a licensing contract, (2) the firm needs tight control over a foreign entity in order to maximize its market share and earnings in that country, and (3) a firm's skills and capabilities are not amenable to licensing. Figure 7.6 presents these considerations as a decision tree.

Firms for which licensing is not a good option tend to be clustered in three types of industries:

1. High-technology industries in which protecting firm-specific expertise is of paramount importance and licensing is hazardous.
2. Global oligopolies, in which competitive interdependence requires that multinational firms maintain tight control over foreign operations so that they have the ability to launch coordinated attacks against their global competitors (as Kodak has done with Fuji).
3. Industries in which intense cost pressures require that multinational firms maintain tight control over foreign operations (so that they can disperse manufacturing to locations around the globe where factor costs are most favorable in order to minimize costs).

Although empirical evidence is limited, the majority of the evidence seems to support these conjectures.[50] In addition, licensing is not a good option if the competitive advantage of a firm is based upon managerial or marketing knowledge that is embedded in the routines of the firm or the skills of its managers, and that is difficult to codify in a "book of blueprints." This would seem to be the case for firms based in a fairly wide range of industries.

Firms for which licensing is a good option tend to be in industries whose conditions are opposite to those specified above. That is, licensing tends to be more common, and more profitable, in fragmented, low-technology industries in which globally dispersed

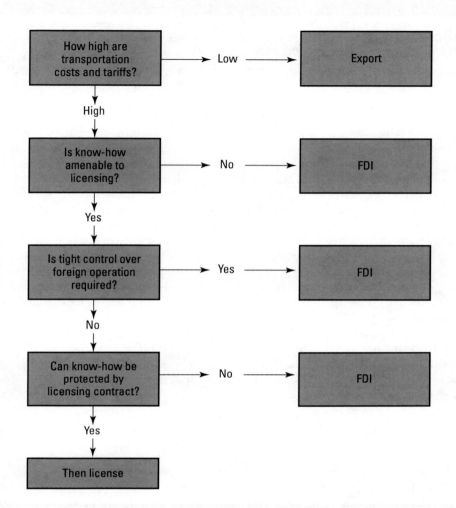

7.6 figure

A Decision Framework

manufacturing is not an option. A good example is the fast-food industry. McDonald's has expanded globally by using a franchising strategy. Franchising is essentially the service-industry version of licensing, although it normally involves much longer term commitments than licensing. With franchising, the firm licenses its brand name to a foreign firm in return for a percentage of the franchisee's profits. The franchising contract specifies the conditions that the franchisee must fulfill if it is to use the franchisor's brand name. Thus, McDonald's allows foreign firms to use its brand name so long as they agree to run their restaurants on exactly the same lines as McDonald's restaurants elsewhere in the world. This strategy makes sense for McDonald's because (1) like many services, fast food cannot be exported, (2) franchising economizes the costs and risks associated with opening up foreign markets, (3) unlike technological know-how, brand names are relatively easy to protect using a contract, (4) there is no compelling reason for McDonald's to have tight control over franchisees, and (5) McDonald's know-how, in terms of how to run a fast-food restaurant, is amenable to being specified in a written contract (e.g., the contract specifies the details of how to run a McDonald's restaurant).

Finally, it should be noted that the product life-cycle theory and Knickerbocker's theory of FDI tend to be less useful from a business perspective. The problem with these two theories is that they are descriptive rather than analytical. They do a good job of describing the historical evolution of FDI, but they do a relatively poor job of identifying the factors that influence the relative profitability of FDI, licensing, and exporting. Indeed, the issue of licensing as an alternative to FDI is ignored by both of these theories.

Government Policy

A host government's attitude toward FDI should be an important variable in decisions about where to locate foreign production facilities and where to make a foreign direct investment. Other things being equal, investing in countries that have permissive policies toward FDI is clearly preferable to investing in countries that restrict FDI.

However, often the issue is not this straightforward. Despite the move toward a free market stance in recent years, many countries still have a rather pragmatic stance toward FDI. In such cases, a firm considering FDI must often negotiate the specific terms of the investment with the country's government. Such negotiations center on two broad issues. If the host government is trying to attract FDI, the central issue is likely to be the kind of incentives the host government is prepared to offer to the MNE and what the firm will commit in exchange. If the host government is uncertain about the benefits of FDI and might choose to restrict access, the central issue is likely to be the concessions that the firm must make to be allowed to go forward with a proposed investment.

To a large degree, the outcome of any negotiated agreement depends on the relative bargaining power of both parties. Each side's bargaining power depends on three factors:

- The value each side places on what the other has to offer.
- The number of comparable alternatives available to each side.
- Each party's time horizon.

From the perspective of a firm negotiating the terms of an investment with a host government, the firm's bargaining power is high when the host government places a high value on what the firm has to offer, the number of comparable alternatives open to the firm is greater, and the firm has a long time in which to complete the negotiations. The converse also holds. The firm's bargaining power is low when the host government places a low value on what the firm has to offer, the number of comparable alternatives open to the firm is fewer, and the firm has a short time in which to complete the negotiations.[51]

Key Terms

Summary

The objectives of this chapter were to review theories that attempt to explain the pattern of FDI between countries and to examine the influence of governments on firms' decisions to invest in foreign countries. The following points were made:

1. Any theory seeking to explain FDI must explain why firms go to the trouble of acquiring or establishing operations abroad, when the alternatives of exporting and licensing are available to them.

2. High transportation costs or tariffs imposed on imports help explain why many firms prefer FDI or licensing over exporting.

3. Firms often prefer FDI to licensing when: (*a*) a firm has valuable know-how that cannot be adequately protected by a licensing contract, (*b*) a firm needs tight control over a foreign entity to maximize its market share and earnings in that country, and (*c*) a firm's skills and capabilities are not amenable to licensing.

4. Knickerbocker's theory suggests that much FDI is explained by imitative behavior by rival firms in an oligopolistic industry.

5. Vernon's product life-cycle theory suggests that firms undertake FDI at particular stages in the life cycle of products they have pioneered. However, Vernon's theory does not address the issue of whether FDI is more efficient than exporting or licensing for expanding abroad.

6. Dunning has argued that location-specific advantages are of considerable importance in explaining the nature and direction of FDI. According to Dunning, firms undertake FDI to exploit resource endowments or assets that are location-specific.

7. Political ideology is an important determinant of government policy toward FDI. Ideology ranges from a radical stance that is hostile to FDI to a noninterventionist, free market stance. Between the two extremes is an approach best described as pragmatic nationalism.

8. Benefits of FDI to a host country arise from resource transfer effects, employment effects, and balance-of-payments effects.

9. The costs of FDI to a host country include adverse effects on competition and balance of payments and a perceived loss of national sovereignty.

10. The benefits of FDI to the home (source) country include improvement in the balance of payments as a result of the inward flow of foreign earnings, positive employment effects when the foreign subsidiary creates demand for home-country exports, and benefits from a reverse resource-transfer effect. A reverse resource-transfer effect arises when the foreign subsidiary learns valuable skills abroad that can be transferred back to the home country.

11. The costs of FDI to the home country include adverse balance-of-payments effects that arise from the initial capital outflow and from the export substitution effects of FDI. Costs also arise when FDI exports jobs abroad.

12. Home countries can adopt policies designed to both encourage and restrict FDI. Host countries try to attract FDI by offering incentives and try to restrict FDI by dictating ownership restraints and requiring that foreign MNEs meet specific performance requirements.

Critical Thinking and Discussion Questions

1. In 2004, inward FDI accounted for some 24 percent of gross fixed capital formation in Ireland, but only 0.6 percent in Japan. What do you think explains this difference in FDI inflows into the two countries?

2. Compare and contrast these explanations of FDI: internalization theory, Vernon's product life-cycle theory, and Knickerbocker's theory of FDI. Which theory do you think offers the best explanation of the historical pattern of FDI? Why?

3. Read the Management Focus on Cemex and then answer the following questions:
   a. Which theoretical explanation, or explanations, of FDI best explains Cemex's FDI?

b. What is the value that Cemex brings to the host economy? Can you see any potential drawbacks of inward investment by Cemex in an economy?

c. Cemex has a strong preference for acquisitions over greenfield ventures as an entry mode. Why?

d. Why do you think Cemex decided to exit Indonesia after failing to gain majority control of Semen Gresik? Why is majority control so important to Cemex?

e. Why do you think politicians in Indonesia tried to block Cemex's attempt to gain majority control over Semen Gresik? Do you think Indonesia's best interests were served by limiting Cemex's FDI in the country?

4. You are the international manager of a U.S. business that has just developed a revolutionary new personal computer that can perform the same functions as existing PCs but costs only half as much to manufacture. Several patents protect the unique design of this computer. Your CEO has asked you to formulate a recommendation for how to expand into Western Europe. Your options are (*a*) to export from the United States, (*b*) to license a European firm to manufacture and market the computer in Europe, or (*c*) to set up a wholly owned subsidiary in Europe. Evaluate the pros and cons of each alternative and suggest a course of action to your CEO.

Research Task globalEDGE http://globalEDGE.msu.edu

Use the globalEDGE Resource Desk (http://globalEDGE.msu.edu/ResourceDesk/) to complete the following exercises:

1. You are working for a company that is considering investing in a foreign country. Management has requested a report regarding the attractiveness of alternative countries based on the potential return of FDI. Accordingly, the ranking of the top 25 countries in terms of FDI attractiveness is a crucial ingredient for your report. A colleague mentioned a potentially useful tool called the *"FDI Confidence Index"* which is updated periodically. Find this

index and provide additional information regarding how the index is constructed.

2. Your company is considering opening a new factory in Latin America and management is evaluating the specific country locations for this direct investment. The pool of candidate countries has been narrowed to Argentina, Brazil, and Mexico. Prepare a short report comparing the foreign direct investment (*FDI*) climate and regulations of these three countries, using the *Country Commercial Guides* prepared by the U.S. Department of Commerce.

---

closing case

Starbucks' Foreign Direct Investment

Thirty years ago, Starbucks was a single store in Seattle's Pike Place Market selling premium roasted coffee. Today it is a global roaster and retailer of coffee with some 13,000 stores, more than 3,750 of which are to be found in 38 foreign countries. Starbucks Corporation set out on its current course in the 1980s when the company's director of marketing, Howard Schultz, came back from a trip to Italy enchanted with the Italian coffeehouse experience. Schultz, who later became CEO, persuaded the company's owners to experiment with the coffeehouse format—and the Starbucks experience was born. The strategy was to sell the

company's own premium roasted coffee and freshly brewed espresso-style coffee beverages, along with a variety of pastries, coffee accessories, teas, and other products, in a tastefully designed coffeehouse setting. The company also focused on providing superior customer service. Reasoning that motivated employees provide the best customer service, Starbucks' executives devoted a lot of attention to employee hiring and training programs and progressive compensation policies that gave even part-time employees stock option grants and medical benefits. The formula led to spectacular success in the United States, where Starbucks went from obscurity to one of the best-known brands in the country in a decade.

In 1995, with 700 stores across the United States, Starbucks began exploring foreign opportunities. Its first target market was Japan. Although Starbucks had resisted a franchising strategy in North America, where its stores are company-owned, Starbucks initially decided to license its format in Japan. However, the company also realized that a pure licensing agreement would not give it the control needed to ensure that the Japanese licensees closely followed Starbucks' successful formula. So the company established a joint venture with a local retailer, Sazaby Inc. Each company held a 50 percent stake in the venture, Starbucks Coffee of Japan. Starbucks initially invested $10 million in this venture, its first foreign direct investment. The Starbucks format was then licensed to the venture, which was charged with taking over responsibility for growing Starbucks' presence in Japan.

To make sure the Japanese operations replicated the "Starbucks experience" in North America, Starbucks transferred some employees to the Japanese operation. The licensing agreement required all Japanese store managers and employees to attend training classes similar to those given to U.S. employees. The agreement also required that stores adhere to the design parameters established in the United States. In 2001, the company introduced a stock option plan for all Japanese employees, making it the first company in Japan to do so. Skeptics doubted that Starbucks would be able to replicate its North American success overseas, but by the end of 2007 Starbucks had over 700 stores in Japan and planed to continue opening them at a brisk pace.

After Japan, the company embarked on an aggressive foreign investment program. In 1998, it purchased Seattle Coffee, a British coffee chain with 60 retail stores, for $84 million. An American couple, originally from Seattle, had started Seattle Coffee with the intention of establishing a Starbucks-like chain in Britain. In the late 1990s, Starbucks opened stores in Taiwan, China, Singapore, Thailand, New Zealand, South Korea, and Malaysia.

In Asia, Starbucks' most common strategy was to license its format to a local operator in return for initial licensing fees and royalties on store revenues. As in Japan, Starbucks insisted on an intensive employee training program and strict specifications regarding the format and layout of the store. However, Starbucks became disenchanted with some of the straight licensing arrangements and converted several into joint-venture arrangements or wholly owned subsidiaries. In Thailand, for example, Starbucks initially entered into a licensing agreement with Coffee Partners, a local Thai company. Under the terms of the licensing agreement, Coffee Partners was required to open at least 20 Starbucks coffee stores in Thailand within five years. However, Coffee Partners found it difficult to raise funds from Thai banks to finance this expansion. In July 2000, Starbucks acquired Coffee Partners for about $12 million. Its goal was to gain tighter control over the expansion strategy in Thailand. By the end of 2007 the company had 103 stores in Thailand.

By 2002, Starbucks was pursuing an aggressive expansion in mainland Europe. As its first entry point, Starbucks chose Switzerland. Drawing on its experience in Asia, the company entered into a joint venture with a Swiss company, Bon Appetit Group, Switzerland's largest food service company. Bon Appetit was to hold a majority stake in the venture, and Starbucks would license its format to the Swiss company under an agreement similar to those it had used successfully in Asia. This was followed by a joint venture in other countries. In 2006, Starbucks announced that it believed there was the potential for up to 15,000 stores outside of the United States, with major opportunities in China, which the company now views as the largest single market opportunity outside of the United States. Currently the company only has 350 stores in China.

Sources: Starbucks 10K, various years; C. McLean, "Starbucks Set to Invade Coffee-Loving Continent," *Seattle Times,* October 4, 2000, p. E1; J. Ordonez, "Starbucks to Start Major Expansion in Overseas Market," *The Wall Street Journal,* October 27, 2000, p. B10; S. Homes and D. Bennett, "Planet Starbucks," *BusinessWeek,* September 9, 2002, pp. 99–110; "Starbucks Outlines International Growth Strategy," *Business Wire,* October 14, 2004; and A. Yeh, "Starbucks Aims for New Tier in China," *Financial Times,* February 14, 2006, p. 17.

Case Discussion Questions

1. Initially Starbucks expanded internationally by licensing its format to foreign operators. It soon became disenchanted with this strategy. Why?

2. Why do you think Starbucks has now elected to expand internationally primarily through local joint ventures, to whom it licenses its format, as opposed to using to a pure licensing strategy?

3. What are the advantages of a joint-venture entry mode for Starbucks over entering through wholly owned subsidiaries? On occasion, Starbucks has chosen a wholly owned subsidiary to control its foreign expansion (e.g., in Britain and Thailand). Why?

4. Which theory of FDI best explains the international expansion strategy adopted by Starbucks?

Part 3 Cross-Border Trade and Investment

LEARNING OBJECTIVES

After you have read this chapter you should:

1 Be able to explain the different levels of regional economic integration.

2 Understand the economic and political arguments for regional economic integration.

3 Understand the economic and political arguments against regional economic integration.

4 Be familiar with the history, current scope, and future prospects of the world's most important regional economic agreements.

5 Understand the implications for business that are inherent in regional economic integration agreements.

Hill: Global Business
Today, Sixth Edition

8. Regional Economic
Integration

Text

© The McGraw–Hill
Companies, 2009

283

c h a p t e r   8

Regional Economic Integration

The European Energy Market

For several years now the European Union, the largest regional trading bloc in the world, has been trying to liberalize its energy market, replacing the markets of its 27 member states with a single continent-wide market for electricity and gas. The first phase of liberalization took effect in June 2007. When fully implemented, the ability of energy producers to sell electricity and gas across national borders will increase competition, which should lower energy prices, forcing utilities to become more efficient, and boost economic growth across the region. The road toward the creation of a single EU energy market has been anything but easy. Many national markets are dominated by a single enterprise, often a former state-owned utility. Electricitie de France, for example, has an 87 percent share of that country's electricity market. Injecting competition into such concentrated markets will prove difficult.

To complicate matters, most of these utilities are vertically integrated, producing, transmitting, and selling power. These vertically integrated producers have little interest in letting other utilities use their transmission grids to sell power to end users or in buying power from other producers. For the full benefits of competition to take hold, the EU recognizes that utilities need to be split into generation, transmission, and marketing companies so that the business of selling energy can be separated from the businesses of producing it and transmitting it. Only then, so the thinking goes, will independent power marketing companies be able to buy energy from the cheapest source, whether it is within national borders or elsewhere in the EU, and resell it to consumers, thereby promoting competition. For now, efforts to mandate the de-integration of utilities are some way off. Indeed, in February 2007 national energy ministers from the different EU states rejected a call from the European Commission, the top competition body in the EU, to break apart utilities. Instead, the energy ministers asked the commission for more details about what such a move would accomplish, thereby effectively delaying any attempt to de-integrate national power companies.

The response of established utilities to the creation of a single continent-wide market for energy has been to try to acquire utilities in other EU nations in an effort to build systems that serve more than one country. The underlying logic is that larger utilities should be able to realize economies of scale, and this would enable them to compete more effectively in a liberalized market. However, some cross-border takeover bids have run into fierce opposition from local politicians who resent their "national energy companies" being taken over by foreign entities. Most notably, when E.ON, the largest German utility, made a bid to acquire Endesa, Spain's largest utility, in 2006, Spanish politicians sought to block the acquisition and keep ownership of Endesa in Spanish hands, imposing conditions that were designed to stop the Germans from acquiring the Spanish company. In response to this outburst of nationalism, the European Commission took the Spanish government to the European Union's highest court, arguing that Madrid had violated the commission's exclusive powers within the EU to scrutinize and approve big cross-border mergers in Europe. Subsequently, Enel, Italy's biggest power company, stepped in and purchased Endesa. ●

Sources: "Power Struggles: European Utilities," *The Economist,* December 2, 2006, p. 74; "Anger Management in Brussels," *Petroleum Economist,* April 2006, pp. 1–3; R. Bream, "Liberalization of EU Market Accelerates Deal-making," *Financial Times,* February 28, 2007, p. 4; and "Twists and Turns: Energy Liberalization in Europe," *The Economist,* December 8, 2007, p. 76.

Introduction

In this chapter we will take a close look at the arguments for regional economic integration through the establishment of trading blocs such as the European Union and the North American Free Trade Agreement. We will discuss the difficult process of forming such blocs and using them as an institutional means for lowering the barriers to cross-border trade and investment between member states. The opening case illustrates some of the promise and problems associated with integrating the economies of different nations into regional trading blocs. By promoting free trade in energy across national borders, the EU hopes to increase competition and lower energy prices to consumers. However, as described in the case, political opposition and the realities of the existing industry structure have made this a difficult goal to attain.

Regional Economic Integration
Agreements among countries in a geographic region to reduce, and ultimately remove, tariff and nontariff barriers to the free flow of goods, services, and factors of production between each other.

By **regional economic integration** we mean agreements among countries in a geographic region to reduce, and ultimately remove, tariff and nontariff barriers to the free flow of goods, services, and factors of production between each other. The last two decades have witnessed an unprecedented proliferation of regional trade blocs that promote economic integration. World Trade Organization members are required to notify the WTO of any regional trade agreements in which they participate. By 2008, nearly all of the WTO's members had notified the organization of participation in one or more regional trade agreements. The total number of regional trade agreements currently in force is around 205.[1]

Consistent with the predictions of international trade theory and particularly the theory of comparative advantage (see Chapter 5) agreements designed to promote freer trade within regions are believed to produce gains from trade for all member countries. As we saw in Chapter 6, the General Agreement on Tariffs and Trade and its successor, the World Trade Organization, also seek to reduce trade barriers. With 151 member states, the WTO has a worldwide perspective. By entering into regional agreements, groups of countries aim to reduce trade barriers more rapidly than can be achieved under the auspices of the WTO. Thus, while a global market for electricity and gas is a long way off, the EU hopes to have a regional market established and functioning relatively soon.

Nowhere has the movement toward regional economic integration been more successful than in Europe. On January 1, 1993, the European Union (EU) formally removed many barriers to doing business across borders within the EU in an attempt to create a single market with 340 million consumers. However, the EU did not stop there. The member states of the EU have launched a single currency, the euro; they are moving toward a closer political union. On May 1, 2004, the EU expanded from 15 to 25 countries and in 2007 two more countries joined, Bulgaria and Romania. Today, the EU has a population of almost 500 million and a gross domestic product of €11 trillion, making it larger than the United States in economic terms.

Similar moves toward regional integration are being pursued elsewhere in the world. Canada, Mexico, and the United States have implemented the North American Free Trade Agreement (NAFTA). Ultimately, this promises to remove all barriers to the free flow of goods and services between the three countries. While the implementation of NAFTA has resulted in job losses in some sectors of the American economy, in aggregate and consistent with the predications of international trade theory, the benefits of greater regional trade are argued to outweigh any costs. South America, too, is moving toward regional integration. In 1991, Argentina, Brazil, Paraguay, and Uruguay implemented an agreement known as MERCOSUR to start reducing barriers to trade between each other, and although progress within MERCOSUR has been halting, the institution is still in place. There are also active attempts at regional economic integration in Central America, the Andean region of South America, Southeast Asia, and parts of Africa.

While the move toward regional economic integration is generally seen as a good thing, some observers worry that it will lead to a world in which regional trade blocs compete against each other. In this possible future scenario, free trade will exist within each bloc, but each bloc will protect its market from outside competition with high tariffs. The specter of the EU and NAFTA turning into economic fortresses that shut out foreign producers with high tariff barriers is worrisome to those who believe in unrestricted free trade. If such a situation were to materialize, the resulting decline in trade between blocs could more than offset the gains from free trade within blocs.

With these issues in mind, this chapter will explore the economic and political debate surrounding regional economic integration, paying particular attention to the economic and political benefits and costs of integration; review progress toward regional

Another Perspective

Economic Integration in the Classical World
Traditionally, the success of the Roman Empire has been explained by economic historians as an example of centralized, forced reallocation of goods. Recent scholarship, though, suggests that there was not a single empire-wide, centralized market for all goods, but that local markets were connected and that most exchanges were voluntary, based on reciprocity and exchange. Ancient Rome had an economic system that was an enormous, integrated conglomeration of interdependent markets. Transportation and communication took time, and the discipline of the market was loose. But there were many voluntary economic connections between even far-flung parts of the early Roman Empire. (Karl Polanyi, *The Livelihood of Man*; and Peter Temin, "Market Economy in the Early Roman Empire," University of Oxford, Discussion Papers in Economic and Social History)

economic integration around the world; and map the important implications of regional economic integration for the practice of international business. Before tackling these objectives, we first need to examine the levels of integration that are theoretically possible.

Levels of Economic Integration

LEARNING OBJECTIVE 1
Be able to explain the different levels of regional economic integration.

Free Trade Area
An area in which all barriers to the trade of goods and services among member countries are removed.

European Free Trade Association (EFTA)
The most enduring free trade area in the world, which focuses on free trade in industrial goods and currently includes Norway, Iceland, Liechtenstein, and Switzerland.

Several levels of economic integration are possible in theory (see Figure 8.1). From least integrated to most integrated, they are a free trade area, a customs union, a common market, an economic union, and, finally, a full political union.

In a **free trade area,** all barriers to the trade of goods and services among member countries are removed. In the theoretically ideal free trade area, no discriminatory tariffs, quotas, subsidies, or administrative impediments are allowed to distort trade between members. Each country, however, is allowed to determine its own trade policies with regard to nonmembers. Thus, for example, the tariffs placed on the products of nonmember countries may vary from member to member. Free trade agreements are the most popular form of regional economic integration, accounting for almost 90 percent of regional agreements.[2]

The most enduring free trade area in the world is the **European Free Trade Association (EFTA).** Established in January 1960, EFTA currently joins four countries—Norway, Iceland, Liechtenstein, and Switzerland—down from seven in 1995 (three EFTA members, Austria, Finland, and Sweden, joined the EU on January 1, 1996). EFTA was founded by those Western European countries that initially decided not to be part of the European Community (the forerunner of the EU). Its original members included Austria, Great Britain, Denmark, Finland, and Sweden, all of which are now members of the EU. The emphasis of EFTA has been on free trade in industrial goods. Agriculture was left out of the arrangement, each member being allowed to determine its own level of support. Members are also free to determine the level

figure 8.1

Levels of Economic Integration

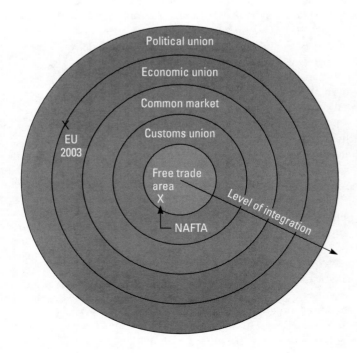

of protection applied to goods coming from outside EFTA. Other free trade areas include the North American Free Trade Agreement, which we shall discuss in depth later in the chapter.

The customs union is one step farther along the road to full economic and political integration. A **customs union** eliminates trade barriers between member countries and adopts a common external trade policy. Establishment of a common external trade policy necessitates significant administrative machinery to oversee trade relations with non-members. Most countries that enter into a customs union desire even greater economic integration down the road. The EU began as a customs union, but has now moved beyond this stage. Another customs union is the current version of the Andean Community (formally known as the Andean Pact) between Bolivia, Colombia, Ecuador, Peru, and Venezuela. The Andean Community established free trade between member countries and imposes a common tariff, of 5 to 20 percent, on products imported from outside.[3]

The next level of economic integration, a **common market** has no barriers to trade between member countries, includes a common external trade policy, and allows factors of production to move freely between members. Labor and capital are free to move because there are no restrictions on immigration, emigration, or cross-border flows of capital between member countries. Establishing a common market demands a significant degree of harmony and cooperation on fiscal, monetary, and employment policies. Achieving this degree of cooperation has proven very difficult. For years, the European Union functioned as a common market, although it has now moved beyond this stage. MERCOSUR, the South American grouping of Argentina, Brazil, Paraguay, Uruguay, and (as of 2006) Venezuela, hopes to eventually establish itself as a common market.

An economic union entails even closer economic integration and cooperation than a common market. Like the common market, an **economic union** involves the free flow of products and factors of production between member countries and the adoption of a common external trade policy, but it also requires a common currency, harmonization of members' tax rates, and a common monetary and fiscal policy. Such a high degree of integration demands a coordinating bureaucracy and the sacrifice of significant amounts of national sovereignty to that bureaucracy. The EU is an economic union, although an imperfect one since not all members of the EU have adopted the euro, the currency of the EU, differences in tax rates and regulations across countries still remain, and some markets, such as the market for energy, are still not fully deregulated.

The move toward economic union raises the issue of how to make a coordinating bureaucracy accountable to the citizens of member nations. The answer is through **political union** in which a central political apparatus coordinates the economic, social, and foreign policy of the member states. The EU is on the road toward at least partial political union. The European Parliament, which is playing an ever more important role in the EU, has been directly elected by citizens of the EU countries since the late 1970s. In addition, the Council of Ministers (the controlling, decision-making body of the EU) is composed of government ministers from each EU member. The United States provides an example of even closer political union; in the United States, independent states are effectively combined into a single nation. Ultimately, the EU may move toward a similar federal structure.

Customs Union
A group of countries committed to eliminating trade barriers and adopting a common external trade policy.

Common Market
A group of countries committed to eliminating trade barriers, adopting a common external trade policy, and allowing factors of production to move freely between members.

Economic Union
A group of countries committed to removing trade barriers, adopting a common currency, harmonizing tax rates, and pursuing a common external trade policy.

Political Union
A central political apparatus coordinating the economic, social, and foreign policy of its member states.

The Case for Regional Integration

The case for regional integration is both economic and political. The case for integration is typically not accepted by many groups within a country, which explains why most attempts to achieve regional economic integration have been contentious and halting. In this section, we examine the economic and political cases for integration and two impediments to integration. In the next section, we look at the case against integration.

LEARNING OBJECTIVE 2
Understand the economic and political arguments for regional economic integration.

Another Perspective

Economic Integration and the EU Worker

Being a citizen of a country that is regionally integrated, such as the countries of the EU, may have benefits related to career development. From an employer's perspective, workers are more mobile. They can move from Spain to Finland, Latvia to France, and never have to think about work permits and, depending on the countries, currencies. In addition, labor and commercial law is becoming integrated across the EU. The mobility and flexibility of such employees may be attractive to a U.S. MNE as well, because it could use them in many markets.

THE ECONOMIC CASE FOR INTEGRATION

The economic case for regional integration is straightforward. We saw in Chapter 5 how economic theories of international trade predict that unrestricted free trade will allow countries to specialize in the production of goods and services that they can produce most efficiently. The result is greater world production than would be possible with trade restrictions. That chapter also revealed how opening a country to free trade stimulates economic growth, which creates dynamic gains from trade. Chapter 7 detailed how foreign direct investment (FDI) can transfer technological, marketing, and managerial know-how to host nations. Given the central role of knowledge in stimulating economic growth, opening a country to FDI also is likely to stimulate economic growth. In sum, economic theories suggest that free trade and investment is a positive-sum game, in which all participating countries stand to gain.

Given this, the theoretical ideal is an absence of barriers to the free flow of goods, services, and factors of production among nations. However, as we saw in Chapters 6 and 7, a case can be made for government intervention in international trade and FDI. Because many governments have accepted part or all of the case for intervention, unrestricted free trade and FDI have proved to be only an ideal. Although international institutions such as the WTO have been moving the world toward a free trade regime, success has been less than total. In a world of many nations and many political ideologies, it is very difficult to get all countries to agree to a common set of rules.

Against this background, regional economic integration can be seen as an attempt to achieve additional gains from the free flow of trade and investment between countries beyond those attainable under international agreements such as the WTO. It is easier to establish a free trade and investment regime among a limited number of adjacent countries than among the world community. Coordination and policy harmonization problems are largely a function of the number of countries that seek agreement. The greater the number of countries involved, the more perspectives that must be reconciled, and the harder it will be to reach agreement. Thus, attempts at regional economic integration are motivated by a desire to exploit the gains from free trade and investment.

THE POLITICAL CASE FOR INTEGRATION

The political case for regional economic integration also has loomed large in several attempts to establish free trade areas, customs unions, and the like. Linking neighboring economies and making them increasingly dependent on each other creates incentives for political cooperation between the neighboring states and reduces the potential for violent conflict. In addition, by grouping their economies, the countries can enhance their political weight in the world.

These considerations underlay the 1957 establishment of the European Community (EC), the forerunner of the EU. Europe had suffered two devastating wars in the first half of the 20th century, both arising out of the unbridled ambitions of nation-states. Those who have sought a united Europe have always had a desire to make another war in Europe unthinkable. Many Europeans also believed that after World War II, the European nation-states were no longer large enough to hold their own in world markets and politics. The need for a united Europe to deal with the United States and the politically alien Soviet Union loomed large in the minds of many of the

EC's founders.[4] A long-standing joke in Europe is that the European Commission should erect a statue to Joseph Stalin, for without the aggressive policies of the former dictator of the old Soviet Union, the countries of Western Europe may have lacked the incentive to cooperate and form the EC.

IMPEDIMENTS TO INTEGRATION   Despite the strong economic and political arguments in support, integration has never been easy to achieve or sustain for two main reasons. First, although economic integration aids the majority, it has its costs. While a nation as a whole may benefit significantly from a regional free trade agreement, certain groups may lose. Moving to a free trade regime involves painful adjustments. For example, due to the 1994 establishment of NAFTA, some Canadian and U.S. workers in such industries as textiles, which employ low-cost, low-skilled labor, lost their jobs as Canadian and U.S. firms moved production to Mexico. The promise of significant net benefits to the Canadian and U.S. economies as a whole is little comfort to those who lose as a result of NAFTA. Such groups have been at the forefront of opposition to NAFTA and will continue to oppose any widening of the agreement.

A second impediment to integration arises from concerns over national sovereignty. For example, Mexico's concerns about maintaining control of its oil interests resulted in an agreement with Canada and the United States to exempt the Mexican oil industry from any liberalization of foreign investment regulations achieved under NAFTA. Concerns about national sovereignty arise because close economic integration demands that countries give up some degree of control over such key issues as monetary policy, fiscal policy (e.g., tax policy), and trade policy. This has been a major stumbling block in the EU. To achieve full economic union, the EU introduced a common currency, the euro, controlled by a central EU bank. Although most member states have signed on, Great Britain remains an important holdout. A politically important segment of public opinion in that country opposes a common currency on the grounds that it would require relinquishing control of the country's monetary policy to the EU, which many British perceive as a bureaucracy run by foreigners. In 1992, the British won the right to opt out of any single currency agreement, and as of 2008, the British government had yet to reverse its decision.

The Case against Regional Integration

Although the tide has been running strongly in favor of regional free trade agreements in recent years, some economists have expressed concern that the benefits of regional integration have been oversold, while the costs have often been ignored.[5] They point out that the benefits of regional integration are determined by the extent of trade creation, as opposed to trade diversion. **Trade creation** occurs when high-cost domestic producers are replaced by low-cost producers within the free trade area. It may also occur when higher cost external producers are replaced by lower cost external producers within the free trade area. **Trade diversion** occurs when lower cost external suppliers are replaced by higher cost suppliers within the free trade area. A regional free trade agreement will benefit the world only if the amount of trade it creates exceeds the amount it diverts.

Suppose the United States and Mexico imposed tariffs on imports from all countries, and then they set up a free trade area, scrapping all trade barriers between themselves but maintaining tariffs on imports from the rest of the world. If the United States began to import textiles from Mexico, would this change be for the better? If the United States previously produced all its own textiles at a higher cost than Mexico, then the free trade agreement has shifted production to the cheaper source. According to the theory of

LEARNING OBJECTIVE 2
Understand the economic and political arguments against regional economic integration.

Trade Creation
Trade created within a free trade area due to the replacement of high-cost domestic or external producers by low-cost external producers.

Trade Diversion
Trade diverted within a free trade area when lower-cost external suppliers are replaced by higher-cost external suppliers.

comparative advantage, trade has been created within the regional grouping, and there would be no decrease in trade with the rest of the world. Clearly, the change would be for the better. If, however, the United States previously imported textiles from Costa Rica, which produced them more cheaply than either Mexico or the United States, then trade has been diverted from a low-cost source—a change for the worse.

In theory, WTO rules should ensure that a free trade agreement does not result in trade diversion. These rules allow free trade areas to be formed only if the members set tariffs that are not higher or more restrictive to outsiders than the ones previously in effect. However, as we saw in Chapter 6, GATT and the WTO do not cover some nontariff barriers. As a result, regional trade blocs could emerge whose markets are protected from outside competition by high nontariff barriers. In such cases, the trade diversion effects might outweigh the trade creation effects. The only way to guard against this possibility, according to those concerned about this potential, is to increase the scope of the WTO so it covers nontariff barriers to trade. There is no sign that this is going to occur anytime soon, however; so the risk remains that regional economic integration will result in trade diversion.

Regional Economic Integration in Europe

LEARNING OBJECTIVE 3
Be familiar with the history, current scope, and future prospects of the world's most important regional economic agreements.

Europe has two trade blocs—the European Union and the European Free Trade Association. Of the two, the EU is by far the more significant, not just in terms of membership (the EU currently has 27 members; the EFTA has 4), but also in terms of economic and political influence in the world economy. Many now see the EU as an emerging economic and political superpower of the same order as the United States. Accordingly, we will concentrate our attention on the EU.[6]

European Union (EU)
The regional economical union of most European countries, formed as a result of the two world wars and the European nations' desire to hold their own in the world's political and economic stage.

EVOLUTION OF THE EUROPEAN UNION The **European Union** (EU) is the product of two political factors: (1) the devastation of Western Europe during two world wars and the desire for a lasting peace, and (2) the European nations' desire to hold their own on the world's political and economic stage. In addition, many Europeans were aware of the potential economic benefits of closer economic integration of the countries.

The forerunner of the EU, the European Coal and Steel Community, was formed in 1951 by Belgium, France, West Germany, Italy, Luxembourg, and the Netherlands. Its objective was to remove barriers to intragroup shipments of coal, iron, steel, and scrap metal. With the signing of the **Treaty of Rome** in 1957, the European Community was established. The name changed again in 1994 when the European Community became the European Union following the ratification of the Maastricht Treaty (discussed later).

Treaty of Rome
Signed in 1957, this established the European Community, a forerunner to the European Union, and created the common European market.

The Treaty of Rome provided for the creation of a common market. Article 3 of the treaty laid down the key objectives of the new community, calling for the elimination of internal trade barriers and the creation of a common external tariff and requiring member states to abolish obstacles to the free movement of factors of production among the members. To facilitate the free movement of goods, services, and factors of production, the treaty provided for any necessary harmonization of the member states' laws. Furthermore, the treaty committed the EC to establish common policies in agriculture and transportation.

The community grew in 1973, when Great Britain, Ireland, and Denmark joined. These three were followed in 1981 by Greece, in 1986 by Spain and Portugal, and in 1996 by Austria, Finland, and Sweden, bringing the total membership to 15 (East Germany became part of the EC after the reunification of Germany in 1990). Another 10 countries joined the EU on May 1, 2004, 8 of them from Eastern Europe plus the small Mediterranean nations of Malta and Cyprus, and Bulgaria and Romania joined

8.1 map

Member States of the European Union in 2008

Source: The European Union, http://europa.eu/abc/european_countries/index_en.htm.

in 2007, bringing the total number of member states to 27 (see Map 8.1). With a population of almost 500 million and a GDP of €11 trillion, larger than that of the United States, the EU through these enlargements has become a global superpower.[7]

POLITICAL STRUCTURE OF THE EUROPEAN UNION   The economic policies of the EU are formulated and implemented by a complex and still-evolving political structure. The four main institutions in this structure are the European Commission, the Council of the European Union, the European Parliament, and the Court of Justice.[8]

The **European Commission** is responsible for proposing EU legislation, implementing it, and monitoring compliance with EU laws by member states. Headquartered in Brussels, Belgium, the commission has more than 24,000 employees. It is run by a group of

European Commission
Responsible for proposing, implementing, and monitoring compliance with EU legislation; run by a group of commissioners appointed by each member country.

L'Oreal chief executive officer Lindsay Owen-Jones (L) and L'Oreal deputy chief executive officer Jean-Paul Agon attend a press conference to announce that L'Oreal is buying Body Shop International, renowned for its ethical hair and skin products, 17 March 2006 in Clichy. L'Oreal, the world's leading cosmetics company, is buying Body Shop International for 652 million pounds (940 million euros, 1.143 billion dollars). L'Oreal will pay 300.0 pence a share for Body Shop, which will be maintained as a separate entity and continue to be led by its current management team, the French firm said in a statement.

commissioners appointed by each member country for five-year renewable terms. There are 27 commissioners, one from each member state. A president of the commission is chosen by member states, and the president then chooses other members in consultation with the states. The entire commission has to be approved by the European Parliament before it can begin work. The commission has a monopoly in proposing European Union legislation. The commission makes a proposal, which goes to the Council of the European Union and then to the European Parliament. The council cannot legislate without a commission proposal in front of it. The commission is also responsible for implementing aspects of EU law, although in practice much of this must be delegated to member states. Another responsibility of the commission is to monitor member states to make sure they are complying with EU laws. In this policing role, the commission will normally ask a state to comply with any EU laws that are being broken. If this persuasion is not sufficient, the commission can refer a case to the Court of Justice.

The European Commission's role in competition policy has become increasingly important to business in recent years. Since 1990 when the office was formally assigned a role in competition policy, the EU's competition commissioner has been steadily gaining influence as the chief regulator of competition policy in the member nations of the EU. As with antitrust authorities in the United States, which include the Federal Trade Commission and the Department of Justice, the role of the competition commissioner is to ensure that no one enterprise uses its market power to drive out competitors and monopolize markets. The commissioner also reviews proposed mergers and acquisitions to make sure they do not create a dominant enterprise with substantial market power.[9] For example, in 2000 a proposed merger between Time Warner of the United States and EMI of the United Kingdom, both music recording companies, was withdrawn after the commission expressed concerns that the merger would reduce the number of major record companies from five to four and create a dominant player in the $40 billion global music industry. Similarly, the commission blocked a proposed merger between two U.S. telecommunication companies, World-Com and Sprint, because their combined holdings of Internet infrastructure in Europe would give the merged companies so much market power that the commission argued the combined company would dominate that market. Another example of the commission's influence over business combinations is given in the accompanying Management Focus, which looks at the commission's role in shaping mergers and joint ventures in the media industry.

European Council
The ultimate decision-making body of the EU, it passes legislation from the commission into law and is comprised of one representative from each member state's government.

The **European Council** represents the interests of member states. It is clearly the ultimate controlling authority within the EU since draft legislation from the commission can become EU law only if the council agrees. The council is composed of one representative from the government of each member state. The membership, however, varies depending on the topic being discussed. When agricultural issues are being discussed, the agriculture ministers from each state attend council meetings; when transportation is being discussed, transportation ministers attend, and so on. Before 1993, all council issues had to be decided by unanimous agreement between member states. This often led to marathon council sessions and a failure to make progress or reach agreement on commission proposals. In an attempt to clear the resulting logjams,

Management FOCUS

The European Commission and Media Industry Mergers

In late 1999, U.S. Internet giant AOL announced it would merge with the music and publishing conglomerate Time Warner. Both the U.S. companies had substantial operations in Europe. The European commissioner for competition, Mario Monti, announced the commission would investigate the impact of the merger on competition in Europe.

The investigation took on a new twist when Time Warner subsequently announced it would form a joint venture with British-based EMI. Time Warner and EMI are two of the top five music publishing companies in the world. The proposed joint venture would have been three times as large as its nearest global competitor. The European Commission now had two concerns. The first was that the joint venture between EMI and Time Warner would reduce the level of competition in the music publishing industry. The second was that a combined AOL–Time Warner would dominate the emerging market for downloading music over the Internet, particularly given the fact that AOL would be able to gain preferential access to the music libraries of both Warner and EMI. This would potentially put other online service providers at a disadvantage. The commission was also concerned that AOL Europe was a joint venture between AOL and Bertelsmann, a German media company that also had considerable music publishing interests. Accordingly, the commission announced it would undertake a separate investigation of the proposed deal between Time Warner and EMI.

These investigations continued into late 2000 and were resolved by a series of concessions extracted by the European Commission. First, under pressure from the commission, Time Warner and EMI agreed to drop their proposed joint venture, thereby maintaining the level of competition in the music publishing business. Second, AOL and Time Warner agreed to allow rival Internet service providers access to online music on the same terms as AOL would receive from Warner Music Group for the next five years. Third, AOL agreed to sever all ties with Bertelsmann, and the German company agreed to withdraw from AOL Europe. These developments alleviated the commission's concern that the AOL–Time Warner combination would dominate the emerging market for the digital download of music. With these concessions in hand, the commission approved the AOL–Time Warner merger in early October 2000.

By late 2000 the AOL-Timer Warner merger had been completed. The shape of the media business, both in Europe and worldwide, now looked very different, and the European Commission had played a pivotal role in determining the outcome. Its demand for concessions altered the strategy of several companies, led to somewhat different combinations from those originally planned, and, the commission believed, preserved competition in the global media business.

Sources: W. Drozdiak, "EU Allows Vivendi Media Deal," *Washington Post,* October 14, 2000, p. E2; D. Hargreaves, "Business as Usual in the New Economy," *Financial Times,* October 6, 2000, p. 1; and D. Hargreaves, "Brussels Clears AOL-Time Warner Deal," *Financial Times,* October 12, 2000, p. 12.

---

the Single European Act formalized the use of majority voting rules on issues "which have as their object the establishment and functioning of a single market." Most other issues, however, such as tax regulations and immigration policy, still require unanimity among council members if they are to become law. The votes that a country gets in the council are related to the size of the country. For example, Britain, a large country, has 29 votes, whereas Denmark, a much smaller state, has 7 votes.

The **European Parliament,** which now has 732 members, is directly elected by the populations of the member states. The parliament, which meets in Strasbourg, France, is primarily a consultative rather than legislative body. It debates legislation proposed by the commission and forwarded to it by the council. It can propose amendments to that legislation, which the commission and ultimately the council are not obliged to take up but often will. The power of the parliament recently has been increasing, although not by as much as parliamentarians would like. The European Parliament now has the right to vote on the appointment of commissioners as well as veto some laws (such as the EU budget and single-market legislation).

One major debate waged in Europe over the last few years is whether the council or the parliament should ultimately be the most powerful body in the EU. Some in Europe expressed concern over the democratic accountability of the EU bureaucracy. One

European Parliament
Made up of 732 members directly elected by member states' populations, it serves as a consultative body to debate and propose amendments to the legislation forwarded from the council.

side argued that the answer to this apparent democratic deficit lay in increasing the power of the parliament, while others think that true democratic legitimacy lies with elected governments, acting through the Council of the European Union.[10] After significant debate, in December 2007 the member states signed a new treaty, The **Treaty of Lisbon,** which increases the power of the European Parliament. If ratified by all member states, a process that is scheduled to be completed by the end of 2008, for the first time in history the European Parliament will become the co-equal legislator for almost all European laws.[11] The Treaty of Lisbon also creates a new position, a president of the European Council, who will serve a 30-month term and represent the nation-states that make up the EU. Under the treaty, the European Commission will be reduced to 18 members, with a rotation system that ensures that every member state has regular and equal membership.

The **Court of Justice,** which is comprised of one judge from each country, is the supreme appeals court for EU law. Like commissioners, the judges are required to act as independent officials, rather than as representatives of national interests. The commission or a member country can bring other members to the court for failing to meet treaty obligations. Similarly, member countries, companies, or institutions can bring the commission or council to the court for failure to act according to an EU treaty.

THE SINGLE EUROPEAN ACT

Two revolutions occurred in Europe in the late 1980s. The first was the collapse of communism in Eastern Europe. The second revolution was much quieter, but its impact on Europe and the world may have been just as profound as the first. It was the adoption of the **Single European Act** by the member nations of the European Community (EC) in 1987. This act committed member countries to work toward establishment of a single market by December 31, 1992.

The Single European Act was born of a frustration among members that the community was not living up to its promise. By the early 1980s, it was clear that the EC had fallen short of its objectives to remove barriers to the free flow of trade and investment between member countries and to harmonize the wide range of technical and legal standards for doing business. Against this background, many of the EC's prominent businesspeople mounted an energetic campaign in the early 1980s to end the EC's economic divisions. The EC responded by creating the Delors Commission. Under the chairmanship of Jacques Delors, the commission proposed that all impediments to the formation of a single market be eliminated by December 31, 1992. The result was the Single European Act, which was independently ratified by the parliaments of each member country and became EC law in 1987.

The Objectives of the Act

The purpose of the Single European Act was to have one market in place by December 31, 1992. The act proposed the following changes:[12]

- Remove all frontier controls between EC countries, thereby abolishing delays and reducing the resources required for complying with trade bureaucracy.
- Apply the principle of "mutual recognition" to product standards. A standard developed in one EC country should be accepted in another, provided it meets basic requirements in such matters as health and safety.
- Open public procurement to nonnational suppliers, reducing costs directly by allowing lower-cost suppliers into national economies and indirectly by forcing national suppliers to compete.
- Lift barriers to competition in the retail banking and insurance businesses, which should drive down the costs of financial services, including borrowing, throughout the EC.

Treaty of Lisbon
2007 treaty designed to increase the power of the European Parliament.

Court of Justice
Comprised of one judge from each member state, this is the supreme appeals court for EU law.

Single European Act
Adopted by members of the European Community in 1987, this act committed member countries to establish a single market by the end of 1992.

- Remove all restrictions on foreign exchange transactions between member countries by the end of 1992.
- Abolish restrictions on cabotage—the right of foreign truckers to pick up and deliver goods within another member state's borders—by the end of 1992. Estimates suggested this would reduce the cost of haulage within the EC by 10 to 15 percent.

The creation of a single financial services market in the EU has taken longer than expected due to member states differing regulations and the significant amount of inertia involved in getting people to accept this change.

All those changes were predicted to lower the costs of doing business in the EC, but the single-market program was also expected to have more complicated supply-side effects. For example, the expanded market was predicted to give EC firms greater opportunities to exploit economies of scale. In addition, it was thought that the increase in competitive intensity brought about by removing internal barriers to trade and investment would force EC firms to become more efficient. To signify the importance of the Single European Act, the European Community also decided to change its name to the European Union once the act took effect.

Impact   The Single European Act has had a significant impact on the EU economy.[13] The act provided the impetus for the restructuring of substantial sections of European industry. Many firms have shifted from national to pan-European production and distribution systems in an attempt to realize scale economies and better compete in a single market. The results have included faster economic growth than would otherwise have been the case.

However, 15 years after the formation of a single market, the reality still falls short of the ideal. For example, as described in the accompanying Country Focus, as of 2007 the EU still lacked a fully functioning single market for financial services (although much of the groundwork was in place). Thus, although the EU is undoubtedly moving toward a single marketplace, established legal, cultural, and language differences between nations mean that implementation has been uneven.

THE ESTABLISHMENT OF THE EURO   In December 1991, EC members signed a treaty (the **Maastricht Treaty**) that committed them to adopting a common currency by January 1, 1999.[14] The euro is now used by 15 of the 27 member states of the European Union; these 15 states are members of what is often referred to as the euro zone. It encompasses 320 million EU citizens and includes the powerful economies of Germany and France. Many of the countries that joined the EU on May 1, 2004, and the two that joined in 2007 will adopt the euro when they fulfill certain economic criteria—a high degree of price stability, a sound fiscal situation, stable exchange rates, and converged long-term interest rates. The current members had to meet the same criteria.

Establishment of the euro has rightly been described as an amazing political feat with few historical precedents. Establishing the euro required participating national governments not only to give up their own currencies, but also to give up control over monetary policy. Governments do not routinely sacrifice national sovereignty for the greater good, indicating the importance that the Europeans attach to the euro. By adopting the euro, the EU has created the second most widely traded currency in the

Maastricht Treaty
A 1991 treaty committing members of the EC to adopt a common currency by 1999.

Country FOCUS

Creating a Single European Market in Financial Services

The European Union in 1999 embarked upon an ambitious action plan to create a single market in financial services by January 1, 2005. Launched a few months after the euro, the EU's single currency, the goal was to dismantle barriers to cross-border activity in financial services, creating a continent-wide market for banking service, insurance services, and investment products. In this vision of a single Europe, a citizen of France might use a German firm for basic banking services, borrow a home mortgage from an Italian institution, buy auto insurance from a Dutch enterprise, and keep her savings in mutual funds managed by a British company. Similarly, an Italian firm might raise capital from investors across Europe, using a German firm as its lead underwriter to issue stock for sale through stock exchanges in London and Frankfurt.

One main benefit of a single market, according to its advocates, would be greater competition for financial services, which would give consumers more choices, lower prices, and require financial service firms in the EU to become more efficient, thereby increasing their global competitiveness. Another major benefit would be the creation of a single European capital market. The increased liquidity of a larger capital market would make it easier for firms to borrow funds, lowering their cost of capital (the price of money) and stimulating business investment in Europe, which would create more jobs. A European Commission study suggested that the creation of a single market in financial services would increase the EU's gross domestic product by 1.1 percent a year, creating an additional 130 billion euros (€) in wealth over a decade. Total business investment would increase by 6 percent annually in the long run, private consumption by 0.8 percent, and total employment by 0.5 percent a year.

Creating a single market, however, has been anything but easy. The financial markets of different EU member states have historically been segmented from each other, and each has its own regulatory framework. In the past, EU financial services firms rarely did business across national borders because of a host of different national regulations with regard to taxation, oversight, accounting information, cross-border takeovers, and the like, all of which had to be harmonized. To complicate matters, longstanding cultural and linguistic barriers complicated the move toward a single market. While in theory an Italian might benefit by being able to purchase homeowners' insurance from a British company, in practice he might be predisposed to purchase it from a local enterprise, even if the price were higher.

By 2007 the EU had made significant progress. Some 41 measures designed to create a single market in financial services had become EU law and others were in the pipeline. The new rules embraced issues as diverse as the conduct of business by investment firms, stock exchanges, and banks; disclosure standards for listing companies on public exchanges; and the harmonization of accounting standards across nations. However, there had also been significant setbacks. Most notably, legislation designed to make it easier for firms to make hostile cross-border acquisitions was defeated, primarily due to opposition from German members of the European Parliament, making it more difficult for financial service firms to build pan-European operations. In addition, national governments have still reserved the right to block even friendly cross-border mergers between financial service firms. For example, Italian banking law still requires the governor of the Bank of Italy to give permission to any foreign enterprise that wishes to purchase more than 5 percent of an Italian bank—and no foreigners have yet to acquire a majority position in an Italian bank, primarily, critics say, due to nationalistic concerns on the part of the Italians.

The critical issue now is enforcement of the rules. Some believe that it will be at least another decade before the benefits of the new regulations become apparent. In the meantime, the changes may impose significant costs on financial institutions as they attempt to deal with the new raft of regulations.

Sources: C. Randzio-Plath, "Europe Prepares for a Single Financial Market," *Intereconomic,* May–June 2004, pp. 142–46; T. Buck, D. Hargreaves, and P. Norman, "Europe's Single Financial Market," *Financial Times,* January 18, 2005, p. 17; "The Gate-keeper," *The Economist,* February 19, 2005, p. 79; P. Hofheinz, "A Capital Idea: The European Union Has a Grand Plan to Make Its Financial Markets More Efficient," *The Wall Street Journal,* October 14, 2002, p. R4; and "Banking on McCreevy: Europe's Single Market," *The Economist,* November 26, 2005, p. 91.

world after that of the U.S. dollar. Some believe that ultimately the euro could come to rival the dollar as the most important currency in the world.

Three long-term EU members, Great Britain, Denmark, and Sweden, are still sitting on the sidelines. The countries agreeing to the euro locked their exchange rates against each other January 1, 1999. Euro notes and coins were not actually issued until January 1, 2002. In the interim, national currencies circulated in each of the 12 countries.

However, in each participating state, the national currency stood for a defined amount of euros. After January 1, 2002, euro notes and coins were issued and the national currencies were taken out of circulation. By mid-2002, all prices and routine economic transactions within the euro zone were in euros.

Benefits of the Euro   Europeans decided to establish a single currency in the EU for a number of reasons. First, they believe that businesses and individuals will realize significant savings from having to handle one currency, rather than many. These savings come from lower foreign exchange and hedging costs. For example, people going from Germany to France will no longer have to pay a commission to a bank to change German deutsche marks into French francs. Instead, they will be able to use euros. According to the European Commission, such savings should amount to 0.5 percent of the European Union's GDP, or about $45 billion a year.

Second, and perhaps more importantly, the adoption of a common currency makes it easier to compare prices across Europe. This should increase competition because it will be much easier for consumers to shop around. For example, if a German finds that cars sell for less in France than Germany, he may be tempted to purchase from a French car dealer rather than his local car dealer. Alternatively, traders may engage in arbitrage to exploit such price differentials, buying cars in France and reselling them in Germany. The only way that German car dealers will be able to hold on to business in the face of such competitive pressures will be to reduce the prices they charge for cars. As a consequence of such pressures, the introduction of a common currency should lead to lower prices. This should translate into substantial gains for European consumers.

Third, faced with lower prices, European producers will be forced to look for ways to reduce their production costs to maintain their profit margins. The introduction of a common currency, by increasing competition, should ultimately produce long-run gains in the economic efficiency of European companies.

Fourth, the introduction of a common currency should give a strong boost to the development of a highly liquid pan-European capital market. The development of such a capital market should lower the cost of capital and lead to an increase in both the level of investment and the efficiency with which investment funds are allocated. This could be especially helpful to smaller companies that have historically had difficulty borrowing money from domestic banks. For example, the capital market of Portugal is very small and illiquid, which makes it extremely difficult for bright Portuguese entrepreneurs with a good idea to borrow money at a reasonable price. However, in theory, such companies should soon be able to tap a much more liquid pan-European capital market. Currently Europe has no continent-wide capital market, such as the NASDAQ market in the United States, that funnels investment capital to dynamic young growth companies. The euro's introduction could facilitate establishment of such a market, particularly when coupled with regulations designed to create a single market in financial services (see the Country Focus). The long-run benefits of such a development should not be underestimated.

Finally, the development of a pan-European, euro-denominated capital market will increase the range of investment options open to both individuals and institutions. For example, it will now be much easier for individuals and institutions based in, let's say, Holland to invest in Italian or French companies. This will enable European investors to better diversify their risk, which again lowers the cost of capital, and should also increase the efficiency with which capital resources are allocated.[15]

Costs of the Euro   The drawback, for some, of a single currency is that national authorities have lost control over monetary policy. Thus, it is crucial to ensure that the EU's monetary policy is well managed. The Maastricht Treaty called for establishment of the independent European Central Bank (ECB), similar in some respects to the U.S. Federal Reserve, with a clear mandate to manage monetary policy so as to ensure price stability. The ECB, based in Frankfurt, is meant to be independent from political pressure—although critics question this. Among other things, the ECB sets interest rates and determines monetary policy across the euro zone.

The implied loss of national sovereignty to the ECB underlies the decision by Great Britain, Denmark, and Sweden to stay out of the euro zone for now. Many in these countries are suspicious of the ECB's ability to remain free from political pressure and to keep inflation under tight control.

In theory, the design of the ECB should ensure that it remains free of political pressure. The ECB is modeled on the German Bundesbank, which historically has been the most independent and successful central bank in Europe. The Maastricht Treaty prohibits the ECB from taking orders from politicians. The executive board of the bank, which consists of a president, vice president, and four other members, carries out policy by issuing instructions to national central banks. The policy itself is determined by the governing council, which consists of the executive board plus the central bank governors from the 15 euro zone countries. The governing council votes on interest rate changes. Members of the executive board are appointed for eight-year nonrenewable terms, insulating them from political pressures to get reappointed. Nevertheless, the jury is still out on the issue of the ECB's independence, and it will take some time for the bank to establish its credentials.

Optimal Currency Area
An area of countries where similarities in the underlying economic activity structure make it feasible to adopt a single currency and use a single exchange rate.

According to critics, another drawback of the euro is that the EU is not what economists would call an optimal currency area. In an **optimal currency area,** similarities in the underlying structure of economic activity make it feasible to adopt a single currency and use a single exchange rate as an instrument of macroeconomic policy. Many of the European economies in the euro zone, however, are very dissimilar. For example, Finland and Portugal have different wage rates, tax regimes, and business cycles, and they may react very differently to external economic shocks. A change in the euro exchange rate that helps Finland may hurt Portugal. Obviously, such differences complicate macroeconomic policy. For example, when euro economies are not growing in unison, a common monetary policy may mean that interest rates are too high for depressed regions and too low for booming regions. It will be interesting to see how the EU copes with the strains caused by such divergent economic performance.

One way of dealing with such divergent effects within the euro zone might be for the EU to engage in fiscal transfers, taking money from prosperous regions and pumping it into depressed regions. Such a move, however, would open a political can of worms. Would the citizens of Germany forgo their "fair share" of EU funds to create jobs for underemployed Portuguese workers?

Several critics believe that the euro puts the economic cart before the political horse. In their view, a single currency should follow, not precede, political union. They argue that the euro will unleash enormous pressures for tax harmonization and fiscal transfers from the center, both policies that cannot be pursued without the appropriate political structure. The most apocalyptic vision that flows from these negative views is that far from stimulating economic growth, as its advocates claim, the euro will lead to lower economic growth and higher inflation within Europe. To quote one critic:

Imposing a single exchange rate and an inflexible exchange rate on countries that are characterized by different economic shocks, inflexible wages, low labor mobility, and separate national fiscal systems without significant cross-border fiscal transfers will raise the overall level of cyclical unemployment among EMU members. The shift from national monetary policies dominated by the (German) Bundesbank within the European Monetary System to a European Central Bank governed by majority voting with a politically determined exchange rate policy will almost certainly raise the average future rate of inflation.[16]

The Early Experience   Since its establishment January 1, 1999, the euro has had a volatile trading history against the world's major currency, the U.S. dollar. After starting life in 1999 at €1 = $1.17, the euro steadily fell until it reached a low of €1 = $0.83 in October 2000, leading critics to claim the euro was a failure. A major reason for the fall in the euro's value was that international investors were investing money in booming U.S. stocks and bonds and taking money out of Europe to finance this investment. In other words, they were selling euros to buy dollars so that they could invest in dollar-denominated assets. This increased the demand for dollars and decreased the demand for the euro, driving the value of the euro down against the dollar.

The fortunes of the euro began improving in late 2001 when the dollar weakened, and the currency stood at a robust all-time high of €1 = $1.54 in early March 2008. One reason for the rise in the value of the euro was that the flow of capital into the United States had stalled as the U.S. financial markets fell.[17] Many investors were now taking money out of the United States, selling dollar-denominated assets such as U.S. stocks and bonds, and purchasing euro-denominated assets. Falling demand for U.S. dollars and rising demand for euros translated into a fall in the value of the dollar against the euro. Furthermore, in a vote of confidence in both the euro and the ability of the ECB to manage monetary policy within the euro zone, many foreign central banks added more euros to their supply of foreign currencies. In the first three years of its life, the euro never reached the 13 percent of global reserves made up by the deutsche mark and other former euro zone currencies. The euro didn't jump that hurdle until early 2002, but by 2004 it made up 20 percent of global reserves. Currency specialists expected the growing U.S. current account deficit, which reached 7 percent of GDP in 2005, to drive the dollar down further, and the euro still higher.[18] In 2007 this started to occur, with the euro appreciating steadily against the dollar from 2005 until early 2008. While the strong euro is a source of pride for Europeans, it does make it harder for euro zone exporters to sell their goods abroad.

ENLARGEMENT OF THE EUROPEAN UNION

A major issue facing the EU over the past few years has been that of enlargement. Enlargement of the EU into Eastern Europe has been a possibility since the collapse of communism at the end of the 1980s, and by the end of the 1990s, 13 countries had applied to become EU members. To qualify for EU membership the applicants had to privatize state assets, deregulate markets, restructure industries, and tame inflation. They also had to enshrine complex EU laws into their own systems, establish stable democratic governments, and respect human rights.[19] In December 2002, the EU formally agreed to accept the applications of 10 countries, and they joined

Another Perspective

The EU and Free Movement of Labor

The free movement of labor was touted as one advantage of forming the European Union. And yet, since 2004, when the EU added 10 member countries to its original 15, some Western European members have worried about the influx of cheap labor to their countries.

The United Kingdom, Ireland, and Sweden refrained from instituting labor restrictions when the EU was formed. Finland, Greece, Italy, Portugal, and Spain lifted their barriers in 2006, and the Netherlands followed suit in 2007. Austria and Germany, on the other hand, planned to extend their labor restrictions to 2011, the maximum transition period. (Lucia Kubosova, "Germany to Keep Immigrant Labor Limits," *BusinessWeek*, May 1, 2007, www.businessweek.com; and Klaus Prettner and Alfred Stiglbauer, "Effects of the Full Opening of the Austrian Labor Market to EU-8 Citizens," Austrian National Bank, *Monetary Policy and the Economy*, Q4 07, www.oenb.at)

May 1, 2004. The new members include the Baltic countries, the Czech Republic, and the larger nations of Hungary and Poland. The only new members not in Eastern Europe are the Mediterranean island nations of Malta and Cyprus. Their inclusion in the EU expanded the union to 25 states, stretching from the Atlantic to the borders of Russia; added 23 percent to the landmass of the EU; brought 75 million new citizens into the EU, building an EU with a population of 450 million people; and created a single continental economy with a GDP of close to €11 trillion. In 2007, Bulgaria and Romania joined, bringing total membership to 27 nations.

The new members were not able to adopt the euro until at least 2007 (and 2010 in the case of the latest entrants), and free movement of labor between the new and existing members was not allowed until then. Consistent with theories of free trade, the enlargement should create added benefits for all members. However, given the small size of the Eastern European economies (together they amount to only 5 percent of the GDP of current EU members) the initial impact will probably be small. The biggest notable change might be in the EU bureaucracy and decision-making processes, where budget negotiations among 27 nations are bound to prove more problematic than negotiations among 15 nations.

Left standing at the door is Turkey. Turkey, which has long lobbied to join the union, presents the EU with some difficult issues. The country has had a customs union with the EU since 1995, and about half of its international trade is already with the EU. However, full membership has been denied because of concerns over human rights issues (particularly Turkish policies toward its Kurdish minority). In addition, some on the Turk side suspect the EU is not eager to let a primarily Muslim nation of 66 million people, which has one foot in Asia, join the EU. The EU formally indicated in December 2002 that it would allow the Turkish application to proceed with no further delay in December 2004 if the country improved its human rights record to the satisfaction of the EU. In December 2004, the EU agreed to allow Turkey to start accession talks in October 2005, but those talks are not moving along rapidly, and the nation might not join until 2010, if at all.

Regional Economic Integration in the Americas

LEARNING OBJECTIVE 4
Be familiar with the history, current scope, and future prospects of the world's most important regional economic agreements.

No other attempt at regional economic integration comes close to the EU in its boldness or its potential implications for the world economy, but regional economic integration is on the rise in the Americas. The most significant attempt is the North American Free Trade Agreement. In addition to NAFTA, several other trade blocs are in the offing in the Americas (see Map 8.2), the most significant of which appear to be the Andean Community and MERCOSUR. Also, negotiations are under way to establish a hemisphere-wide Free Trade Area of the Americas (FTAA), although currently they seem to be stalled.

THE NORTH AMERICAN FREE TRADE AGREEMENT The governments of the United States and Canada in 1988 agreed to enter into a free trade agreement, which took effect January 1, 1989. The goal of the agreement was to eliminate all tariffs on bilateral trade between Canada and the United States by 1998. This was followed in 1991 by talks among the United States, Canada, and Mexico aimed at establishing a **North American Free Trade Agreement** for the three countries. The talks concluded in August 1992 with an agreement in principle, and the following year the agreement was ratified by the governments of all three countries. The agreement became law January 1, 1994.[20]

North American Free Trade Agreement (NAFTA)
The free trade agreement among Canada, Mexico, and the United States, officially implemented in 1994.

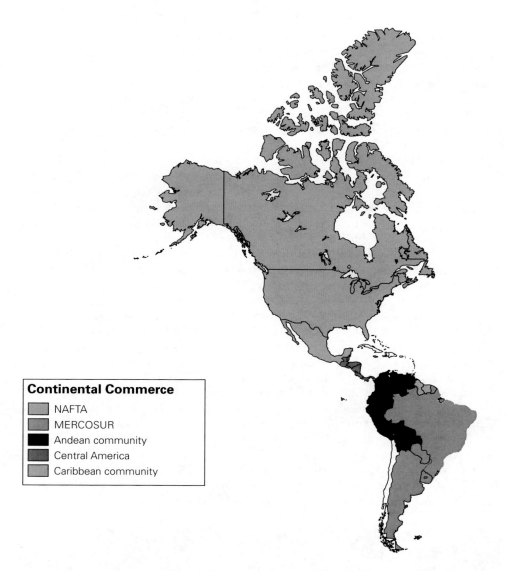

8.2 map

Economic Integration in the Americas

Source: *The Economist*, April 21, 2001, p. 20. Copyright © 2001 The Economist Newspaper Ltd. All rights reserved. Reprinted with permission. Further reproduction prohibited. www.economist.com.

Continental Commerce

- NAFTA
- MERCOSUR
- Andean community
- Central America
- Caribbean community

NAFTA's Contents The contents of NAFTA include the following:

- Abolition by 2004 of tariffs on 99 percent of the goods traded among Mexico, Canada, and the United States.
- Removal of most barriers on the cross-border flow of services, allowing financial institutions, for example, unrestricted access to the Mexican market by 2000.
- Protection of intellectual property rights.
- Removal of most restrictions on foreign direct investment between the three member countries, although special treatment (protection) will be given to Mexican energy and railway industries, American airline and radio communications industries, and Canadian culture.
- Application of national environmental standards, provided such standards have a scientific basis. Lowering of standards to lure investment is described as being inappropriate.
- Establishment of two commissions with the power to impose fines and remove trade privileges when environmental standards or legislation involving health and safety, minimum wages, or child labor are ignored.

The Case for NAFTA Proponents of NAFTA have argued that the free trade area should be viewed as an opportunity to create an enlarged and more efficient productive base for the entire region. Advocates acknowledge that one effect of NAFTA would be that some U.S. and Canadian firms would move production to Mexico to take advantage of lower labor costs. (In 2004, the average hourly labor cost in Mexico was still one-tenth of that in the United States and Canada.) Movement of production to Mexico, they argued, was most likely to occur in low-skilled, labor-intensive manufacturing industries where Mexico might have a comparative advantage. Advocates of NAFTA argued that many would benefit from such a trend. Mexico would benefit from much-needed inward investment and employment. The United States and Canada would benefit because the increased incomes of the Mexicans would allow them to import more U.S. and Canadian goods, thereby increasing demand and making up for the jobs lost in industries that moved production to Mexico. U.S. and Canadian consumers would benefit from the lower prices of products made in Mexico. In addition, the international competitiveness of U.S. and Canadian firms that move production to Mexico to take advantage of lower labor costs would be enhanced, enabling them to better compete with Asian and European rivals.

The Case against NAFTA Those who opposed NAFTA claimed that ratification would be followed by a mass exodus of jobs from the United States and Canada into Mexico as employers sought to profit from Mexico's lower wages and less strict environmental and labor laws. According to one extreme opponent, Ross Perot, up to 5.9 million U.S. jobs would be lost to Mexico after NAFTA in what he famously characterized as a "giant sucking sound." Most economists, however, dismissed these numbers as being absurd and alarmist. They argued that Mexico would have to run a bilateral trade surplus with the United States of close to $300 billion for job loss on such a scale to occur—and $300 billion was the size of Mexico's GDP. In other words, such a scenario seemed implausible.

More sober estimates of the impact of NAFTA ranged from a net creation of 170,000 jobs in the United States (due to increased Mexican demand for U.S. goods and services) and an increase of $15 billion per year to the joint U.S. and Mexican GDP, to a net loss of

Many workers in the United States initially felt that NAFTA would take away their jobs as employers looked for cheaper labor in Mexico. However, a 1996 study by researchers at the University of California–Los Angeles concluded the impact on jobs was a net gain of 3,000 for the United States in the first two years of the NAFTA regime.

490,000 U.S. jobs. To put these numbers in perspective, employment in the U.S. economy was predicted to grow by 18 million from 1993 to 2003. As most economists repeatedly stressed, NAFTA would have a small impact on both Canada and the United States. It could hardly be any other way, since the Mexican economy was only 5 percent of the size of the U.S. economy. Signing NAFTA required the largest leap of economic faith from Mexico rather than Canada or the United States. Falling trade barriers would expose Mexican firms to highly efficient U.S. and Canadian competitors that, when compared to the average Mexican firm, had far greater capital resources, access to highly educated and skilled workforces, and much greater technological sophistication. The short-run outcome was likely to be painful economic restructuring and unemployment in Mexico. But advocates of NAFTA claimed there would be long-run dynamic gains in the efficiency of Mexican firms as they adjusted to the rigors of a more competitive marketplace. To the extent that this occurred, they argued, Mexico's economic growth rate would accelerate, and Mexico might become a major market for Canadian and U.S. firms.[21]

Environmentalists also voiced concerns about NAFTA. They pointed to the sludge in the Rio Grande and the smog in the air over Mexico City and warned that Mexico could degrade clean air and toxic waste standards across the continent. They pointed out that the lower Rio Grande was the most polluted river in the United States, and that with NAFTA, chemical waste and sewage would increase along its course from El Paso, Texas, to the Gulf of Mexico.

There was also opposition in Mexico to NAFTA from those who feared a loss of national sovereignty. Mexican critics argued that their country would be dominated by U.S. firms that would not really contribute to Mexico's economic growth, but instead would use Mexico as a low-cost assembly site, while keeping their high-paying, high-skilled jobs north of the border.

NAFTA: The Results so Far   Studies of NAFTA's impact to date suggest its initial effects were at best muted, and both advocates and detractors may have been guilty of exaggeration.[22] On average, studies indicate that NAFTA's overall impact has been small but positive.[23] From 1993 to 2005, trade between NAFTA's partners grew by 250 percent.[24] Canada and Mexico are now the number one and two trade partners of the United States, suggesting the economies of the three NAFTA nations have become more closely integrated. In 1990, U.S. trade with Canada and Mexico accounted for about a quarter of total U.S. trade. By 2005, the figure was close to one-third. Canada's trade with its NAFTA partners increased from about 70 percent to more than 80 percent of all Canadian foreign trade between 1993 and 2005, while Mexico's trade with NAFTA increased from 66 percent to 80 percent over the same period. All three countries also experienced strong productivity growth over this period. In Mexico, labor productivity has increased by 50 percent since 1993, and the passage of NAFTA may have contributed to this. However, estimates suggest that employment effects of NAFTA have been small. The most pessimistic estimates suggest the United States lost 110,000 jobs per year due to NAFTA between 1994 and 2000—and many economists dispute this figure—which is tiny compared to the more than 2 million jobs a year created in the United States during the same period. Perhaps the most significant impact of NAFTA has not been economic, but political. Many observers credit NAFTA with helping to create the background for increased political stability in Mexico. Mexico is now viewed as a stable democratic nation with a steadily growing economy, something that is beneficial to the United States, which shares a 2,000-mile border with the country.[25]

Enlargement   One issue confronting NAFTA is that of enlargement. A number of other Latin American countries have indicated their desire to eventually join NAFTA. The governments of both Canada and the United States are adopting a wait-and-see attitude with regard to most countries. Getting NAFTA approved was a bruising political experience, and neither government is eager to repeat the process soon. Nevertheless, the Canadian, Mexican, and U.S. governments began talks in 1995 regarding Chile's possible entry into NAFTA. As of 2008, however, these talks had yielded little progress, partly because of political opposition in the U.S. Congress to expanding NAFTA. In December 2002, however, the United States and Chile did sign a bilateral free trade pact.

THE ANDEAN COMMUNITY

Andean Pact
Based on the EU model and begun in 1969, this agreement unites Bolivia, Chile, Ecuador, Colombia, and Peru in free trade, but it has been unsuccessful at achieving its stated goals; renamed the Andean Community in 1997.

Bolivia, Chile, Ecuador, Colombia, and Peru signed an agreement in 1969 to create the Andean Pact. The **Andean Pact** was largely based on the EU model, but was far less successful at achieving its stated goals. The integration steps begun in 1969 included an internal tariff reduction program, a common external tariff, a transportation policy, a common industrial policy, and special concessions for the smallest members, Bolivia and Ecuador.

By the mid-1980s, the Andean Pact had all but collapsed and had failed to achieve any of its stated objectives. There was no tariff-free trade between member countries, no common external tariff, and no harmonization of economic policies. Political and economic problems seem to have hindered cooperation between member countries. The countries of the Andean Pact have had to deal with low economic growth, hyperinflation, high unemployment, political unrest, and crushing debt burdens. In addition, the dominant political ideology in many of the Andean countries during this period tended toward the radical/socialist end of the political spectrum. Since such an ideology is hostile to the free market economic principles on which the Andean Pact was based, progress toward closer integration could not be expected.

The tide began to turn in the late 1980s when, after years of economic decline, the governments of Latin America began to adopt free market economic policies. In 1990, the heads of Bolivia, Ecuador, Peru, Colombia, and Venezuela met in the Galápagos Islands. The resulting Galápagos Declaration effectively relaunched the Andean Pact, which was renamed the Andean Community in 1997. The declaration's objectives included the establishment of a free trade area by 1992, a customs union by 1994, and a common market by 1995. This last milestone has not been reached. A customs union was implemented in 1995, although until 2003 Peru opted out and Bolivia received preferential treatment. The Andean Community now operates as a customs union. In December 2003, it signed an agreement with MERCOSUR to restart stalled negotiations on the creation of a free trade area between the two trading blocs. Those negotiations are currently proceeding at a slow pace. In late 2006, Venezuela withdrew from the Andean Community as part of that country's attempts to join MERCOSUR.

MERCOSUR

MERCOSUR
The free trade pact among Brazil, Argentina, Paraguay, Uruguay, and Venezuela, originating in 1988.

MERCOSUR originated in 1988 as a free trade pact between Brazil and Argentina. The modest reductions in tariffs and quotas accompanying this pact reportedly helped bring about an 80 percent increase in trade between the two countries in the late 1980s.[26] This success encouraged the expansion of the pact in March 1990 to include Paraguay and Uruguay. In 2005, the pact was further expanded when Venezuela joined MERCOSUR, although it may take years for Venezuela to become fully integrated into the pact.

The initial aim of MERCOSUR was to establish a full free trade area by the end of 1994 and a common market sometime thereafter. In December 1995, MERCOSUR's members agreed to a five-year program under which they hoped to perfect their free trade area and move toward a full customs union—something that has yet to be achieved.[27] For its first eight years or so, MERCOSUR seemed to be making a positive contribution to the economic growth rates of its member states. Trade between MERCOSUR's four core members quadrupled between 1990 and 1998. The combined GDP of the four member states grew at an annual average rate of 3.5 percent between 1990 and 1996, a performance that is significantly better than the four attained during the 1980s.[28]

However, MERCOSUR had its critics, including Alexander Yeats, a senior economist at the World Bank, who wrote a stinging critique of MERCOSUR.[29] According to Yeats, the trade diversion effects of MERCOSUR outweigh its trade creation effects. Yeats pointed out that the fastest growing items in intra-MERCOSUR trade were cars, buses, agricultural equipment, and other capital-intensive goods that are produced relatively inefficiently in the four member countries. In other words, MERCOSUR countries, insulated from outside competition by tariffs that run as high as 70 percent of value on motor vehicles, are investing in factories that build products that are too expensive to sell to anyone but themselves. The result, according to Yeats, is that MERCOSUR countries might not be able to compete globally once the group's external trade barriers come down. In the meantime, capital is being drawn away from more efficient enterprises. In the near term, countries with more efficient manufacturing enterprises lose because MERCOSUR's external trade barriers keep them out of the market.

MERCOSUR hit a significant roadblock in 1998, when its member states slipped into recession and intrabloc trade slumped. Trade fell further in 1999 following a financial crisis in Brazil that led to the devaluation of the Brazilian real, which immediately made the goods of other MERCOSUR members 40 percent more expensive in Brazil, their largest export market. At this point, progress toward establishing a full customs union all but stopped. Things deteriorated further in 2001 when Argentina, beset by economic stresses, suggested the customs union be temporarily suspended. Argentina wanted to suspend MERCOSUR's tariff so that it could abolish duties on imports of capital equipment, while raising those on consumer goods to 35 percent (MERCOSUR had established a 14 percent import tariff on both sets of goods). Brazil agreed to this request, effectively halting MERCOSUR's quest to become a fully functioning customs union.[30] Hope for a revival arose in 2003 when new Brazilian President Lula da Silva announced his support for a revitalized and expanded MERCOSUR modeled after the EU with a larger membership, a common currency, and a democratically elected MERCOSUR parliament.[31] As of 2008, however, little progress had been made in moving MERCOSUR down that road, and critics felt that the customs union was becoming more imperfect over time.[32]

CENTRAL AMERICAN COMMON MARKET, CAFTA, AND CARICOM

Two other trade pacts in the Americas have not made much progress. In the early 1960s, Costa Rica, El Salvador, Guatemala, Honduras, and Nicaragua attempted to set up a **Central American Common Market.** It collapsed in 1969 when war broke out between Honduras and El Salvador after a riot at a soccer match between teams from the two countries. Since then the six member countries have made some progress toward reviving their agreement (the five founding members were joined by the Dominican Republic). The proposed common market was given a boost in 2003 when the United States signaled its intention to enter into bilateral free trade negotiations with the group. These negotiations cumulated in a 2005 agreement to establish a free trade agreement between the six countries and the United States. Known as the **Central America Free Trade Agreement,** or **CAFTA,** the aim is to lower trade barriers between the United States and the six countries for most goods and services.

Central American Common Market
A trade pact among Costa Rica, El Salvador, Guatemala, Honduras, and Nicaragua, which began in the early 1960s but collapsed in 1969 due to war.

Central America Free Trade Agreement (CAFTA)
The agreement of the member states of the Central American Common Market joined by the Dominican Republic to trade freely with the United States.

CARICOM
Established in 1973 to promote a customs union between the English-speaking Caribbean countries by 1991, but it failed.

A customs union was to have been created in 1991 between the English-speaking Caribbean countries under the auspices of the Caribbean Community. Referred to as **CARICOM,** it was established in 1973. However, it repeatedly failed to progress toward economic integration. A formal commitment to economic and monetary union was adopted by CARICOM's member states in 1984, but since then little progress has been made. In October 1991, the CARICOM governments failed, for the third consecutive time, to meet a deadline for establishing a common external tariff. Despite this, CARICOM expanded to 15 members by 2005. In early 2006, six CARICOM members established the **Caribbean Single Market and Economy (CSME).** Modeled on the EU's single market, the goal of CSME is to lower trade barriers and harmonize macroeconomic and monetary policy between member states.[33]

Caribbean Single Market and Economy (CSME)
Unites six CARICOM members in agreeing to lower trade barriers and harmonize macroeconomic and monetary policies.

FREE TRADE AREA OF THE AMERICAS

At a hemisphere-wide Summit of the Americas in December 1994, a Free Trade Area of the Americas (FTAA) was proposed. It took more than three years for the talks to start, but in April 1998, 34 heads of state traveled to Santiago, Chile, for the second Summit of the Americas where they formally inaugurated talks to establish an FTAA by January 1, 2005—something that didn't occur. The continuing talks have addressed a wide range of economic, political, and environmental issues related to cross-border trade and investment. Although both the United States and Brazil were early advocates of the FTAA, support from both countries seems to be mixed at this point. Because the United States and Brazil have the largest economies in North and South America, respectively, strong U.S. and Brazilian support is a precondition for establishment of the free trade area.

The major stumbling blocks so far have been twofold. First, the United States wants its southern neighbors to agree to tougher enforcement of intellectual property rights and lower manufacturing tariffs, which they do not seem eager to embrace. Second, Brazil and Argentina want the United States to reduce its subsidies to U.S. agricultural producers and scrap tariffs on agricultural imports, which the U.S. government does not seem inclined to do. For progress to be made, most observers agree that the United States and Brazil have to first reach an agreement on these crucial issues.[34] If the FTAA is eventually established, it will have major implications for cross-border trade and investment flows within the hemisphere. The FTAA would open a free trade umbrella over 850 million people who accounted for some $16 trillion in GDP in 2007.

Currently, however, FTAA is very much a work in progress, and the progress has been slow. A November 2005 attempt at a summit of 34 heads of state from North and South America to resume talks failed when opponents, led by Venezuela President Hugo Chavez, blocked efforts by the Bush administration to set an agenda for further talks on FTAA. In voicing his opposition, Chavez condemned the U.S. free trade model as a "perversion" that would unduly benefit the United States, to the detriment of poor people in Latin America whom Chavez claims have not benefited from free trade details.[35] Such views make progress on establishing a FTAA in the near term unlikely.

LEARNING OBJECTIVE 4
Be familiar with the history, current scope, and future prospects of the world's most important regional economic agreements.

Regional Economic Integration Elsewhere

Numerous attempts at regional economic integration have been tried throughout Asia and Africa. However, few exist in anything other than name. Perhaps the most significant is the Association of Southeast Asian Nations (ASEAN). In addition, the

Asia-Pacific Economic Cooperation (APEC) forum has recently emerged as the seed of a potential free trade region.

ASSOCIATION OF SOUTHEAST ASIAN NATIONS
Formed in 1967, the **Association of Southeast Asian Nations (ASEAN)** includes Brunei, Cambodia, Indonesia, Laos, Malaysia, Myanmar, Philippines, Singapore, Thailand, and Vietnam. Laos, Myanmar, Vietnam, and Cambodia have all joined recently, creating a regional grouping of 500 million people with a combined GDP of some $740 billion (see Map 8.3). The basic objective of ASEAN is to foster freer trade between member countries and to achieve cooperation in their industrial policies. Progress so far has been limited, however.

Until recently only 5 percent of intra-ASEAN trade consisted of goods whose tariffs had been reduced through an ASEAN preferential trade arrangement. This may be changing. In 2003, an ASEAN Free Trade Area (AFTA) between the six original members of ASEAN came into full effect. The AFTA has cut tariffs on manufacturing and agricultural products to less than 5 percent. However, there are some significant exceptions to this tariff reduction. Malaysia, for example, refused to bring down tariffs on imported cars until 2005 and then agreed to lower the tariff to 20 percent, not the 5 percent called for under the AFTA. Malaysia wants to protect automaker Proton and inefficient local carmakers from foreign competition. Similarly, the Philippines has refused to lower tariff rates on petrochemicals, and rice, the largest agricultural product in the region, will remain subject to higher tariff rates until at least 2020.[36]

Notwithstanding such issues, ASEAN and AFTA are at least progressing toward establishing a free trade zone. Vietnam joined the AFTA in 2006, Laos and Myanmar in 2008, and Cambodia is scheduled to in 2010. The goal is to reduce import tariffs among the six original members to zero by 2010, and to do so by 2015 for the newer members (although important exceptions to that goal, such as tariffs on rice, will no doubt persist). ASEAN is also pushing for free trade agreements with China, Japan, and South Korea.

ASIA-PACIFIC ECONOMIC COOPERATION
Asia-Pacific Economic Cooperation (APEC) was founded in 1990 at the suggestion of Australia. **APEC** currently has 21 member states including such economic powerhouses as the United States, Japan, and China (see Map 8.4). Collectively, the member states account for about 55 percent of the world's GNP, 49 percent of world trade, and much of the growth in the world economy. The stated aim of APEC is to increase multilateral cooperation in view of the economic rise of the Pacific nations and the growing interdependence within the region. U.S. support for APEC was also based on the belief that it might prove a viable strategy for heading off any moves to create Asian groupings from which it would be excluded.

Interest in APEC was heightened considerably in November 1993 when the heads of APEC member states met for the first time at a two-day conference in Seattle. Debate before the meeting speculated on the likely future role of APEC. One view was that APEC should commit itself to the ultimate formation of a free trade area. Such a move would transform the Pacific Rim from a geographical expression into the world's largest free trade area. Another view was that APEC would produce no more than hot air and lots of photo opportunities for the leaders involved. As it turned out, the APEC meeting produced little more than some vague commitments from member states to work together for greater economic integration and a general lowering of trade barriers. However, significantly, member states did not rule out the possibility of closer economic cooperation in the future.[37]

Association of Southeast Asian Nations (ASEAN)
An attempt at regional economic integration among Brunei, Cambodia, Indonesia, Laos, Malaysia, Myanmar, the Philippines, Singapore, Thailand, and Vietnam.

APEC
An organization designed to increases multilateral economic cooperation between nations bordering the Pacific Ocean.

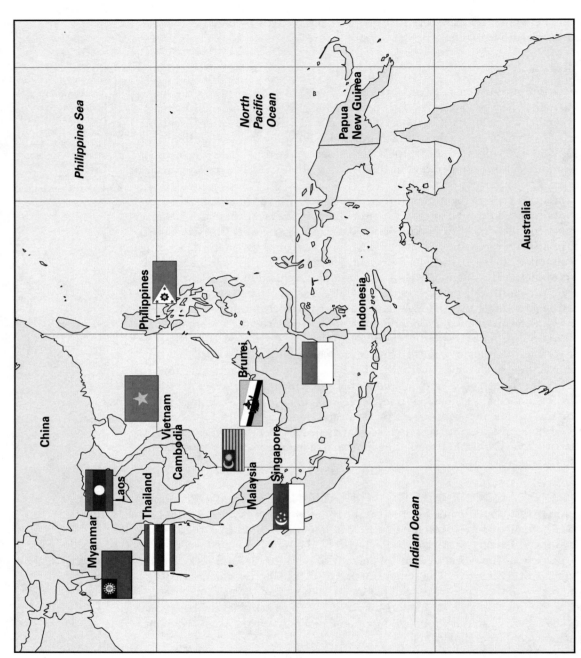

China

Myanmar

Laos

Thailand

Vietnam

Cambodia

Malaysia

Singapore

Brunei

Philippines

Philippine Sea

North Pacific Ocean

Papua New Guinea

Indonesia

Australia

Indian Ocean

8.3 map ASEAN Countries

Source: www.aseansec.org/69.htm.

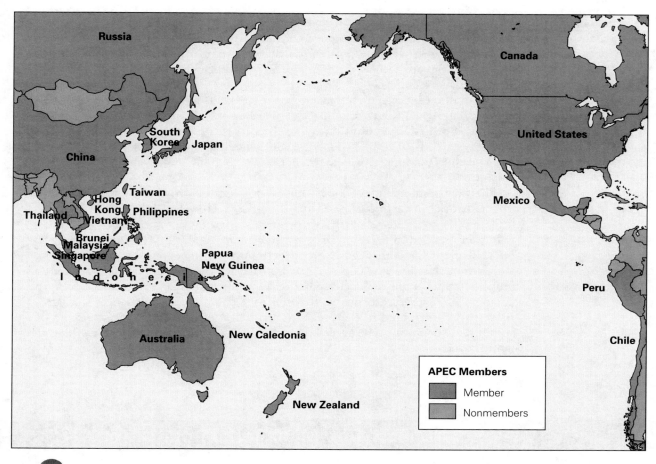

8.4 map

APEC Members

Source: APEC Web site, www.apec.org.

The heads of state have met again on a number of occasions, most recently in 2007. At a 1997 meeting, member states formally endorsed proposals designed to remove trade barriers in 15 sectors, ranging from fish to toys. However, the vague plan committed APEC members to doing no more than holding further talks, which is all that they have done to date. Commenting on the vagueness of APEC pronouncements, the influential Brookings Institution, a U.S.-based economic policy institution, noted that APEC "is in grave danger of shrinking into irrelevance as a serious forum." Despite the slow progress, APEC is worth watching. If it eventually does transform itself into a free trade area, it will probably be the world's largest.[38]

REGIONAL TRADE BLOCS IN AFRICA   African countries have been experimenting with regional trade blocs for half a century. There are now nine trade blocs on the African continent. Many countries are members of more than one group. Although the number of trade groups is impressive, progress toward the establishment of meaningful trade blocs has been slow.

Many of these groups have been dormant for years. Significant political turmoil in several African nations has persistently impeded any meaningful progress. Also, deep suspicion of free trade exists in several African countries. The argument most frequently heard is that because these countries have less developed and less diversified economies, they need to be "protected" by tariff barriers from unfair foreign competition. Given the prevalence of this argument, it has been hard to establish free trade areas or customs unions.

The most recent attempt to reenergize the free trade movement in Africa occurred in early 2001, when Kenya, Uganda, and Tanzania, member states of the East African Community (EAC), committed themselves to relaunching their bloc, 24 years after it collapsed. The three countries, with 80 million inhabitants, intend to establish a customs union, regional court, legislative assembly, and, eventually, a political federation.

Their program includes cooperation on immigration, road and telecommunication networks, investment, and capital markets. However, while local business leaders welcomed the relaunch as a positive step, they were critical of the EAC's failure in practice to make progress on free trade. At the EAC treaty's signing in November 1999, members gave themselves four years to negotiate a customs union, with a draft slated for the end of 2001. But that fell far short of earlier plans for an immediate free trade zone, shelved after Tanzania and Uganda, fearful of Kenyan competition, expressed concerns that the zone could create imbalances similar to those that contributed to the breakup of the first community.[39] It remains to be seen if these countries can succeed this time, but if history is any guide, it will be an uphill road.

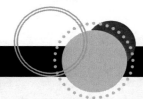

Focus on Managerial Implications

LEARNING OBJECTIVE 5
Understand the implications for business that are inherent in regional economic integration agreements.

Currently the most significant developments in regional economic integration are occurring in the EU and NAFTA. Although some of the Latin American trade blocs, ASEAN, and the proposed FTAA may have economic significance in the future, the EU and NAFTA currently have more profound and immediate implications for business practice. Accordingly, in this section we will concentrate on the business implications of those two groups. Similar conclusions, however, could be drawn with regard to the creation of a single market anywhere in the world.

Opportunities

The creation of a single market through regional economic integration offers significant opportunities because markets that were formerly protected from foreign competition are increasingly open. For example, in Europe before 1992 the large French and Italian markets were among the most protected. These markets are now much more open to foreign competition in the form of both exports and direct investment. Nonetheless, to fully exploit such opportunities, it may pay non-EU firms to set up EU subsidiaries. Many major U.S. firms have long had subsidiaries in Europe. Those that do not would be advised to consider establishing them now, lest they run the risk of being shut out of the EU by nontariff barriers.

Additional opportunities arise from the inherent lower costs of doing business in a single market—as opposed to 27 national markets in the case of the EU or 3 national markets in the case of NAFTA. Free movement of goods across borders, harmonized product standards, and simplified tax regimes make it possible for firms based in the EU and the NAFTA countries to realize potentially significant cost economies by centralizing production in those EU and NAFTA locations where the mix of factor costs and skills is optimal. Rather than producing a product in each of the 27 EU countries or the 3 NAFTA countries, a firm may be able to serve the whole EU or North American market from a single location. This location must be chosen carefully, of course, with an eye on local factor costs and skills.

For example, in response to the changes created by EU after 1992, the St. Paul–based 3M Company consolidated its European manufacturing and distribution facilities to take advantage of economies of scale. Thus, a plant in Great Britain now produces 3M's printing products and a German factory its reflective traffic control materials for the entire EU. In each case, 3M chose a location for centralized production after carefully considering the likely production costs in alternative locations within the EU. The ultimate goal of 3M is to dispense with all national distinctions, directing R&D, manufacturing, distribution, and marketing for each product group from an EU headquarters.[40] Similarly, Unilever, one of Europe's largest companies, began rationalizing its production in advance of 1992 to attain scale economies. Unilever concentrated its production of dishwashing powder for the EU in one plant, bath soap in another, and so on.[41]

Even after the removal of barriers to trade and investment, enduring differences in culture and competitive practices often limit the ability of companies to realize cost economies by centralizing production in key locations and producing a standardized product for a single multicountry market. Consider the case of Atag Holdings NV, a Dutch maker of kitchen appliances.[42] Atag thought it was well placed to benefit from the single market, but found it tough going. Atag's plant is just one mile from the German border and near the center of the EU's population. The company thought it could cater to both the "potato" and "spaghetti" belts—marketers' terms for consumers in Northern and Southern Europe—by producing two main product lines and selling these standardized "euro-products" to "euro-consumers." The main benefit of doing so is the economy of scale derived from mass production of a standardized range of products. Atag quickly discovered that the "euro-consumer" was a myth. Consumer preferences vary much more across nations than Atag had thought. Consider ceramic cooktops; Atag planned to market just 2 varieties throughout the EU but has found it needs 11. Belgians, who cook in huge pots, require extra-large burners. Germans like oval pots and burners to fit. The French need small burners and very low temperatures for simmering sauces and broths. Germans like oven knobs on the top; the French want them on the front. Most Germans and French prefer black and white ranges; the British demand a range of colors including peach, pigeon blue, and mint green.

Threats

Just as the emergence of single markets creates opportunities for business, it also presents a number of threats. For one thing, the business environment within each grouping will become more competitive. The lowering of barriers to trade and investment between countries is likely to lead to increased price competition throughout the EU and NAFTA. For example, before 1992 a Volkswagen Golf cost 55 percent more in Great Britain than in Denmark and 29 percent more in Ireland than in Greece.[43] Over time, such price differentials will vanish in a single market. This is a direct threat to any firm doing business in EU or NAFTA countries. To survive in the tougher single-market environment, firms must take advantage of the opportunities offered by the creation of a single market to rationalize their production and reduce their costs. Otherwise, they will be at a severe disadvantage.

A further threat to firms outside these trading blocs arises from the likely long-term improvement in the competitive position of many firms within the areas. This is particularly relevant in the EU, where many firms have historically been limited by a high-cost structure in their ability to compete globally with North American and Asian firms. The creation of a single market and the resulting increased competition in the EU is beginning to produce serious attempts by many EU firms to reduce their cost structure by rationalizing production. This is transforming many EU companies into efficient global competitors. The message for non-EU businesses is that they need to prepare for the emergence of more capable European competitors by reducing their own cost structures.

Another threat to firms outside of trading areas is the threat of being shut out of the single market by the creation of a "trade fortress." The charge that regional economic integration might lead to a fortress mentality is most often leveled at the EU. Although the free trade philosophy underpinning the EU theoretically argues against the creation of any fortress in Europe, occasional signs indicate the EU may raise barriers to imports and investment in certain "politically sensitive" areas, such as autos. Non-EU firms might be well advised, therefore, to set up their own EU operations. This could also occur in the NAFTA countries, but it seems less likely.

Finally, the emerging role of the European Commission in competition policy suggests the EU is increasingly willing and able to intervene and impose conditions on companies proposing mergers and acquisitions. This is a threat insofar as it limits the ability of firms to pursue the corporate strategy of their choice. The commission may require significant concessions from businesses as a precondition for allowing proposed mergers and acquisitions to proceed. While this constrains the strategic options for firms, it should be remembered that in taking such action, the commission is trying to maintain the level of competition in Europe's single market, which should benefit consumers.

Key Terms

regional economic integration, p. 274

free trade area, p. 276

European Free Trade Association, p. 276

customs union, p. 277

common market, p. 277

economic union, p. 277

political union, p. 277

trade creation, p. 279

trade diversion, p. 279

European Union, p. 280

Treaty of Rome, p. 280

European Commission, p. 281

European Council, p. 282

European Parliament, p. 283

Treaty of Lisbon, p. 284

Court of Justice, p. 284

Single European Act, p. 284

Maastricht Treaty, p. 285

optimal currency area, p. 288

North American Free Trade Agreement, p. 290

Andean Pact, p. 294

MERCOSUR, p. 294

Central American Common Market, p. 295

Central American Free Trade Agreement (CAFTA), p. 295

CARICOM, p. 296

Caribbean Single Market and Economy (CSME), p. 296

Association of Southeast Asian Nations (ASEAN), p. 297

Summary

This chapter pursued three main objectives: to examine the economic and political debate surrounding regional economic integration; to review the progress toward regional economic integration in Europe, the Americas, and elsewhere; and to distinguish the important implications of regional economic integration for the practice of international business. The chapter made the following points:

1. A number of levels of economic integration are possible in theory. In order of increasing integration, they include a free trade area, a customs union, a common market, an economic union, and full political union.

2. In a free trade area, barriers to trade between member countries are removed, but each country determines its own external trade policy. In a customs union, internal barriers to trade are removed and a common external trade policy is adopted. A common market is similar to a customs union, except that a common market also allows factors of production to move freely between countries. An economic union involves even closer integration, including the establishment of a common currency and the harmonization of tax rates. A political union is the logical culmination of attempts to achieve ever closer economic integration.

3. Regional economic integration is an attempt to achieve economic gains from the free flow of trade and investment between neighboring countries.

4. Integration is not easily achieved or sustained. Although integration brings benefits to the majority, it is never without costs for the minority. Concerns over national sovereignty often slow or stop integration attempts.

5. Regional integration will not increase economic welfare if the trade creation effects in the free trade area are outweighed by the trade diversion effects.

6. The Single European Act sought to create a true single market by abolishing administrative barriers to the free flow of trade and investment between EU countries.

7. Twelve EU members now use a common currency, the euro. The economic gains from a common currency come from reduced exchange costs, reduced risk associated with currency fluctuations, and increased price competition within the EU.

8. Increasingly, the European Commission is taking an activist stance with regard to competition policy, intervening to restrict mergers and acquisitions that it believes will reduce competition in the EU.

9. Although no other attempt at regional economic integration comes close to the EU in terms of potential economic and political significance, various other attempts are being made in the world. The most notable include NAFTA in North America, the Andean Pact and MERCOSUR in Latin America, ASEAN in Southeast Asia, and perhaps APEC.

10. The creation of single markets in the EU and North America means that many markets that were formerly protected from foreign competition are now more open. This creates major investment and export opportunities for firms within and outside these regions.

11. The free movement of goods across borders, the harmonization of product standards, and the simplification of tax regimes make it possible for firms based in a free trade area to realize potentially enormous cost economies by centralizing production in those locations within the area where the mix of factor costs and skills is optimal.

12. The lowering of barriers to trade and investment between countries within a trade group will probably be followed by increased price competition.

Critical Thinking and Discussion Questions

1. NAFTA has produced significant net benefits for the Canadian, Mexican, and U.S. economies. Discuss.

2. What are the economic and political arguments for regional economic integration? Given these arguments, why don't we see more substantial examples of integration in the world economy?

3. What effect is creation of a single market and a single currency within the EU likely to have on competition within the EU? Why?

4. Do you think it is correct for the European Commission to restrict mergers between American companies that do business in Europe? (For example, the European Commission vetoed the proposed merger between WorldCom and Sprint, both U.S. companies, and it carefully reviewed the merger between AOL and Time Warner, again both U.S. companies.)

5. How should a U.S. firm that currently exports only to ASEAN countries respond to the creation of a single market in this regional grouping?

6. How should a firm with self-sufficient production facilities in several ASEAN countries respond to the creation of a single market? What are the constraints on its ability to respond in a manner that minimizes production costs?

7. After a promising start, MERCOSUR, the major Latin American trade agreement, has faltered and made little progress since 2000. What problems are hurting

MERCOSUR? What can be done to solve these problems?

8. Would establishment of a Free Trade Area of the Americas (FTAA) be good for the two most advanced economies in the hemisphere, the United States and Canada? How might the establishment of the FTAA impact the strategy of North American firms?

9. Reread the Management Focus on the European Commission and media industry mergers, then answer the following questions:
   a. Given that both AOL and Time Warner are U.S.-based companies, do you think the European Commission had a right to review and regulate their planned merger?
   b. Were the concessions extracted by the European Commission from AOL and Time Warner reasonable? Whose interests was the commission trying to protect?
   c. What precedent do the actions of the European Commission in this case set? What are the implications for managers of foreign enterprises with substantial operations in Europe?

Research Task globalEDGE http://globalEDGE.msu.edu

Use the globalEDGE Resource Desk (http://globalEDGE.msu.edu/ResourceDesk/) to complete the following exercises:

1. The enlargement of European Union into Eastern Europe has brought together countries with different levels of economic development. Choose two long-term EU member countries and two newer members. Compare and contrast the macroeconomic situation in these countries by analyzing each country's primary economic indicators, available from "Eurostatistics—Data

for short-term economic analysis," a statistical book, published by *Eurostat*. Prepare a short report describing the similarities and differences between the two groups of countries.

2. The establishment of the Free Trade Area of the Americas could be a threat as well as an opportunity for your company. Identify the countries participating in the negotiations for the *FTAA*. Are there any countries in the Americas not participating in the negotiations? What are the main issues covered in the negotiation process?

closing case

NAFTA and the U.S. Textile Industry

When the North American Free Trade Agreement (NAFTA) took effect in 1994, many expressed fears that large job losses in the U.S. textile industry would occur as companies moved production from the United States to Mexico. NAFTA

opponents argued passionately, but unsuccessfully, that the treaty should not be adopted because of the negative impact it would have on U.S. employment.

A quick glance at the data available 10 years after the passage of NAFTA suggests the critics had a point. Between 1994 and 2004, production of apparel fell by 40 percent and production of textiles by 20 percent and this during a period when overall U.S. demand for apparel grew by almost 60 percent. During the same time frame, employment in textile mills in the United Stated dropped from 478,000 to 239,000, employment in apparel manufacturing plummeted from 858,000 to 296,000, while exports of apparel from Mexico to the United States surged from $1.26 billion to $3.84 billion. Such data seem to indicate that the job losses have been due to apparel production migrating from the United States to Mexico.

There is anecdotal evidence to support this assertion. For example, in 1995, Fruit of the Loom Inc., the largest manufacturer of underwear in the United States, said it would close six of its domestic plants and cut back operations at two others, laying off about 3,200 workers, or 12 percent of its U.S. workforce. The company announced the closures were part of its drive to move its operations to cheaper plants abroad, particularly in Mexico. Before the closures, less than 30 percent of its sewing was done outside the United States, but Fruit of the Loom planned to move the majority of that work to Mexico. For textile manufacturers, the advantages of locating in Mexico include cheap labor and inputs. Labor rates in Mexico average between $10 and $20 a day, compared to $10 to $12 an hour for U.S. textile workers.

However, job losses in the U.S. textile industry do not mean that the overall effects of NAFTA have been negative. Clothing prices in the United States have also fallen since 1994 as textile production shifted from high-cost U.S. producers to lower-cost Mexican producers. This benefits consumers, who now have more money to spend on other items. The cost of a typical pair of designer jeans, for example, fell from $55 in 1994 to about $48 today. In 1994, blank T-shirts wholesaled for $24 a dozen. Now they sell for $14 a dozen.

In addition to lower prices, the shift in textile production to Mexico also benefited the U.S. economy in other ways. Despite the move of fabric and apparel production to Mexico, exports have surged for U.S. yarn makers, many of which are in the chemical industry. Before the passage of NAFTA, U.S. yarn producers, such as E. I. du Pont, supplied only small amounts of product to Mexico. However, as apparel production moved to Mexico, exports of fabric and yarn to that country have surged. U.S. producers supply 70 percent of the raw material going to Mexican sewing shops. Between 1994 and 2004, U.S. cotton and yarn exports to Mexico grew from $293 million to $1.21 billion. Although the U.S. textile industry has lost jobs, advocates of NAFTA argue that the U.S. economy has benefited in the form of lower clothing prices and an increase in exports from fabric and yarn producers. NAFTA supporters argue that trade has been created because of NAFTA. The gains from trade are being captured by U.S. consumers and by producers in certain sectors. As always, the establishment of a free trade area creates winners and losers—and the losers have been employees in the textile industry—but advocates of free trade argue that the gains outweigh the losses.

Sources: C. Burritt, "Seven Years into NAFTA, Textile Makers Seek a Payoff in Mexico," *Atlanta Journal-Constitution,* December 17, 2000, p. Q1; I. McAllister, "Trade Agreements: How They Affect U.S. Textile," *Textile World,* March 2000, pp. 50–54; J. Millman, "Mexico Weaves More Ties," *The Wall Street Journal,* August 21, 2000, p. A12; J.R. Giermanski, "A Fresh Look at NAFTA: What Really Happened?" *Logistics,* September 2002, pp. 43–46; G.C. Hufbauer and J.C. Schott, *NAFTA Revisited: Achievements and Challenges* (Washington, DC: Institute for International Economics, 2005); O. Cadot et al, "Market Access and Welfare under Free Trade Agreements: Textiles under NAFTA," *The World Bank Economic Review* 19 (2005), pp. 379–405; American Textile Manufactures Institute at www.atmi.org/index.asp; and U.S. Department of Commerce Trade Stat Express Web site at http://tse.export.gov/.

Case Discussion Questions

1. Why did many textile jobs apparently migrate out of the United States in the years after the establishment of NAFTA?

2. Who gained from the process of readjustment in the textile industry after NAFTA? Who lost?

3. With hindsight, do you think it is better to protect vulnerable industries such as textiles, or to let them adjust to the painful winds of change that follow entering into free trade agreements? What would the benefits of costs of protection be? What would the costs be?

Part 4 Global Money System

LEARNING OBJECTIVES

After you have read this chapter you should:

1 Be conversant with the functions of the foreign exchange market.

2 Understand what is meant by spot exchange rates.

3 Appreciate the role that forward exchange rates play in insuring against foreign exchange risk.

4 Understand the different theories explaining how currency exchange rates are determined and their relative merits.

5 Be familiar with the merits of different approaches toward exchange rate forecasting.

6 Understand the differences among translation, transaction, and economic exposure, and what managers can do to manage each type of exposure.

chapter **9**

The Foreign Exchange Market

Hyundai and Kia Face a Strong Won

opening case

For several years Hyundai and its affiliate Kia, Korea's fast-growing carmakers, have benefited from export-led growth. Hyundai sells 60 percent and Kia 80 percent of production in foreign markets, particularly the United States, where they have been gaining share recently. By 2006 the two companies had about 4.3 percent of the U.S. market, and they planned to double their market share by 2010. Their success in foreign markets has been attributed to good product quality, reasonable design, and aggressive pricing. In the United States and European Union, Hyundai and Kia price their cars below the prices of both domestic firms and the major Japanese companies, such as Toyota and Honda. This low-price strategy has enabled the two affiliated companies to increase foreign sales, but their profit margins per car are low—as low as 3 percent on cars sold in the United States. This makes them very vulnerable to changes in the value of the Korean currency, the won, against the U.S. dollar.

In 2006, the won rose in value by about 7 percent against the U.S. dollar. It continued to appreciate throughout the first nine months of 2007, hitting a 10-year high against the dollar in October 2007. A stronger won means that Hyundai and Kia vehicles sold in the United States for dollars are recorded at a lower value when translated back into won, which has hurt the financial performance of both companies. In 2006, despite rising unit sales, profits at Hyundai fell 35 percent, and those at Kia fell some 94 percent. Kia had to sell 15 cars on average in the United States in 2006 to make the same amount of revenue and profit that it got from 14 cars in 2005. If the won continues to gain in value against the dollar over the next few years, as many analysts predict, Hyundai and Kia may be forced to raise prices in the United States.

The possibility that the won will continue to strengthen against the dollar and other major currencies is also a spur to increasing output outside of Korea. Hyundai opened its first U.S. automobile plant in Montgomery,

Alabama, in 2005 and recently announced plans to build an engine plant close by. There is speculation that Hyundai will expand its U.S. manufacturing presence in the near future. Kia also is expanding its presence in the United States as a hedge against adverse currency movements. In 2006 the company broke ground on a U.S. manufacturing plant in Georgia, which is expected to open in 2009. ●

Sources: Evan Ramstad, "Won's Rise Hurts Korean Car Makers," *The Wall Street Journal,* December 13, 2006, p. B3; S. Jung, "Call to Cap Strength of Won," *Financial Times,* October 10, 2007, p. 15; and W. Diem, "Hyundai Suffers Growing Pains While Seeking Solutions," *Ward's Auto World,* August 2007, p. 9.

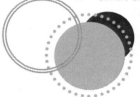

Introduction

Hyundai and its affiliate Kia are affected by changes in the value of currencies on the foreign exchange market. As detailed in the opening case, a rising won has made it more difficult for the two companies to make profits on U.S. sales and forced them to consider changing their long-held low-price strategy. What happens in the foreign exchange market can have a fundamental impact on the sales, profits, and strategy of an enterprise. Accordingly, it is very important for managers to understand the foreign exchange market and how changes in currency exchange rates might affect their enterprise. With this in mind, the current chapter has three main objectives. The first is to explain how the foreign exchange market works. The second is to examine the forces that determine exchange rates and to discuss the degree to which it is possible to predict future exchange rate movements. The third objective is to map the implications for international business of exchange rate movements. This chapter is the first of two that deal with the international monetary system and its relationship to international business. In the next chapter, we will explore the institutional structure of the international monetary system. The institutional structure is the context within which the foreign exchange market functions. As we shall see, changes in the institutional structure of the international monetary system can exert a profound influence on the development of foreign exchange markets.

Foreign Exchange Market
A market for converting the currency of one country into that of another country.

The **foreign exchange market** is a market for converting the currency of one country into that of another country. An **exchange rate** is simply the rate at which one currency is converted into another. For example, Kia uses the foreign exchange market to convert the dollars it earns from selling cars in the United States into Korean won. Without the foreign exchange market, international trade and international investment on the scale that we see today would be impossible; companies would have to resort to barter. The foreign exchange market is the lubricant that enables companies based in countries that use different currencies to trade with each other.

Exchange Rate
The rate at which one currency is converted into another.

We know from earlier chapters that international trade and investment have their risks. As the opening case illustrates, some of these risks exist because future exchange rates cannot be perfectly predicted. The rate at which one currency is converted into another can change over time. For example, in late 2005 one U.S. dollar bought 1,050 Korean won, but by late 2007 one dollar bought only 918 won. The dollar had fallen in value against the won, making Korean goods, such as Kia and Hyundai cars, more expensive in the United States and U.S. goods cheaper in Korea. The change in exchange rates hurt the profitability of Korean exporters such as Kia and Hyundai. One function of the foreign exchange market is to provide some insurance against the risks that arise from such volatile changes in exchange rates, commonly referred to as foreign exchange risk. Although the foreign exchange market offers some insurance against foreign exchange risk, it cannot provide complete insurance. It is not unusual for international businesses to suffer losses because of unpredicted changes in exchange rates. Currency fluctuations can make seemingly profitable trade and investment deals unprofitable, and vice versa.

We begin this chapter by looking at the functions and the form of the foreign exchange market. This includes distinguishing among spot exchanges, forward exchanges, and currency swaps. Then we will consider the factors that determine exchange rates. We will also look at how foreign trade is conducted when a country's currency cannot be exchanged for other currencies; that is, when its currency is not convertible. The chapter closes with a discussion of these things in terms of their implications for business.

The Functions of the Foreign Exchange Market

The foreign exchange market serves two main functions. The first is to convert the currency of one country into the currency of another. The second is to provide some insurance against **foreign exchange risk,** by which we mean the adverse consequences of unpredictable changes in exchange rates.[1]

LEARNING OBJECTIVE 1
Be conversant with the functions of the foreign exchange market.

Foreign Exchange Risk
The risk that changes in exchange rates will hurt the profitability of a business deal.

CURRENCY CONVERSION   Each country has a currency in which the prices of goods and services are quoted. In the United States, it is the dollar ($); in Great Britain, the pound (£); in France, Germany, and other members of the euro zone it is the euro (€); in Japan, the yen (¥); and so on. In general, within the borders of a particular country, one must use the national currency. A U.S. tourist cannot walk into a store in Edinburgh, Scotland, and use U.S. dollars to buy a bottle of Scotch whisky. Dollars are not recognized as legal tender in Scotland; the tourist must use British pounds. Fortunately, the tourist can go to a bank and exchange her dollars for pounds. Then she can buy the whisky.

When a tourist changes one currency into another, she is participating in the foreign exchange market. The exchange rate is the rate at which the market converts one currency into another. For example, an exchange rate of €1 = $1.30 specifies that one euro buys 1.30 U.S. dollars. The exchange rate allows us to compare the relative prices of goods and services in different countries. Our U.S. tourist wishing to buy a bottle of Scotch whisky in Edinburgh may find that she must pay £30 for the bottle, knowing that the same bottle costs $45 in the United States. Is this a good deal? Imagine the current pound/dollar exchange rate is £1.00 = $2.00 (i.e., one British pound buys $2.00). Our intrepid tourist takes out her calculator and converts £30 into dollars. (The calculation is 30 × 2). She finds that the bottle of Scotch costs the equivalent of $60. She is surprised that a bottle of Scotch whisky could cost less in the United States than in Scotland (alcohol is taxed heavily in Great Britain).

Tourists are minor participants in the foreign exchange market; companies engaged in international trade and investment are major ones.

Another Perspective

How Foreign Exchange Challenges Business Travel Ethics
In preparation for a trip to Japan, you exchange U.S. dollars for yen in late May, just before you leave. For $1,000, your bank gives you ¥104,000. During your time in Osaka, the dollar weakens against the yen, to ¥99.5 to the dollar. Meanwhile, you enjoyed Japanese hospitality and spent only ¥10,000. Back home, you take your remaining ¥94,000 to the bank to convert back to dollars. How much have you spent on your trip? Will you list these expenses on your expense report?

International businesses have four main uses of foreign exchange markets. First, the payments a company receives for its exports, the income it receives from foreign investments, or the income it receives from licensing agreements with foreign firms may be in foreign currencies. To use those funds in its home country, the company must convert them to its home country's currency. Consider the Scotch distillery that exports its whisky to the United States. The distillery is paid in dollars, but since those dollars cannot be spent in Great Britain, they must be converted into British pounds. Similarly, when Kia sells cars in the United States for dollars, it must convert those dollars into won to use them in Korea.

Second, international businesses use foreign exchange markets when they must pay a foreign company for its products or services in its country's currency. For example, Dell buys many of the components for its computers from Malaysian firms. The Malaysian companies must be paid in Malaysia's currency, the ringgit, so Dell must convert money from dollars into ringgit to pay them.

Third, international businesses use foreign exchange markets when they have spare cash that they wish to invest for short terms in money markets. For example, consider a U.S. company that has $10 million it wants to invest for three months. The best interest rate it can earn on these funds in the United States may be 4 percent. Investing in a South Korean money market account, however, may earn 12 percent. Thus, the company may change its $10 million into Korean won and invest it in South Korea. Note, however, that the rate of return it earns on this investment depends not only on the Korean interest rate, but also on the changes in the value of the Korean won against the dollar in the intervening period.

Currency Speculation
Moving funds from one currency to another over the short term in hopes of profiting from shifts in exchange rates.

Finally, currency speculation is another use of foreign exchange markets. **Currency speculation** typically involves the short-term movement of funds from one currency to another in the hopes of profiting from shifts in exchange rates. Consider again a U.S. company with $10 million to invest for three months. Suppose the company suspects that the U.S. dollar is overvalued against the Japanese yen. That is, the company expects the value of the dollar to depreciate (fall) against that of the yen. Imagine the current dollar/yen exchange rate is $1 = ¥120. The company exchanges its $10 million into yen, receiving ¥1.2 billion ($10 million × 120 = ¥1.2 billion). Over the next three months, the value of the dollar depreciates against the yen until $1 = ¥100. Now the company exchanges its ¥1.2 billion back into dollars and finds that it has $12 million. The company has made a $2 million profit on currency speculation in three months on an initial investment of $10 million! In general, however, companies should beware, for speculation by definition is a very risky business. The company cannot know for sure what will happen to exchange rates. While a speculator may profit handsomely if his speculation about future currency movements turns out to be correct, he can also lose vast amounts of money if it turns out to be wrong.

Hedging
The process of insuring one's business against foreign exchange risk by using forward exchanges or currency swaps.

INSURING AGAINST FOREIGN EXCHANGE RISK

A second function of the foreign exchange market is to provide insurance against foreign exchange risk, which is the possibility that unpredicted changes in future exchange rates will have adverse consequences for the firm. When a firm insures itself against foreign exchange risk, we say that is it engaging in **hedging.** To explain how the market performs this function, we must first distinguish among spot exchange rates, forward exchange rates, and currency swaps.

LEARNING OBJECTIVE 2
Understand what is meant by spot exchange rates.

Spot Exchange Rates

When two parties agree to exchange currency and execute the deal immediately, the transaction is referred to as a spot exchange. Exchange rates governing such "on the spot" trades are referred to as spot exchange rates. The

spot exchange rate is the rate at which a foreign exchange dealer converts one currency into another currency on a particular day. Thus, when our U.S. tourist in Edinburgh goes to a bank to convert her dollars into pounds, the exchange rate is the spot rate for that day.

Spot exchange rates are reported on a real-time basis on many financial Web sites.

Table 9.1 shows the exchange rates for a selection of currencies traded in the New York foreign exchange market as of 1:22 p.m. February 27, 2008. An exchange rate can be quoted in two ways: as the amount of foreign currency one U.S. dollar will buy, or as the value of a dollar for one unit of foreign currency. Thus, one U.S. dollar bought €0.611 on February 27, 2008, and one euro bought $1.5126.

Using insurance to protect against forward exchange rates helps companies hedge against financial risk.

Spot rates change continually, often on a minute-by-minute basis (although the magnitude of changes over such short periods is usually small). The value of a currency is determined by the interaction between the demand and supply of that currency relative to the demand and supply of other currencies. For example, if lots of people want U.S. dollars and dollars are in short supply, and few people want British pounds and pounds are in plentiful supply, the spot exchange rate for converting dollars into pounds will change. The dollar is likely to appreciate against the pound (or, the pound will depreciate against the dollar). Imagine the spot exchange rate is £1 = $2.00 when the market opens. As the day progresses, dealers demand more dollars and fewer pounds. By the end of the day, the spot exchange rate might be £1 = $1.98. Each pound now buys fewer dollars than at the start of the day. The dollar has appreciated, and the pound has depreciated.

Spot Exchange Rate
The rate at which a foreign exchange dealer converts currency on any particular day.

Forward Exchange Rates   Changes in spot exchange rates can be problematic for an international business. For example, a U.S. company that imports laptop computers from Japan knows that in 30 days it must pay yen to a Japanese supplier when a

LEARNING OBJECTIVE 3
Appreciate the role that forward exchange rates play in insuring against foreign exchange risk.

Major Currency Cross Rates							
Currency **Last Trade**	**U.S. $** N/A	**¥en** 1:22 pm ET	**Euro** 1:22 pm ET	**Can $** 1:22 pm ET	**U.K. £** 1:22 pm ET	**AU $** 1:20 pm ET	**Swiss Franc** 1:22 pm ET
1 U.S. $ =	1	106.4600	0.6611	0.9782	0.5028	1.0619	1.0642
1 ¥en =	0.009393	1	0.006210	0.009188	0.004723	0.009975	0.009997
1 Euro =	1.5126	161.0312	1	1.4795	0.7606	1.6062	1.6098
1 Can $ =	1.0223	108.8381	0.6759	1	0.5140	1.0856	1.0880
1 U.K. £ =	1.9888	211.7280	1.3148	1.9453	1	2.1119	2.1166
1 AU $ =	0.9417	100.2533	0.6226	0.9211	0.4735	1	1.0022
1 Swiss Franc =	0.9396	100.0329	0.6212	0.9191	0.4725	0.9978	1

table **9.1**

Value of the U.S. Dollar against Other Currencies, February 27, 2008

Source: Yahoo! Finance.

shipment arrives. The company will pay the Japanese supplier ¥200,000 for each laptop computer, and the current dollar/yen spot exchange rate is $1 = ¥120. At this rate, each computer costs the importer $1,667 (i.e., 1,667 = 200,000/120). The importer knows she can sell the computers the day they arrive for $2,000 each, which yields a gross profit of $333 on each computer ($2,000 − $1,667). However, the importer will not have the funds to pay the Japanese supplier until the computers have been sold. If over the next 30 days the dollar unexpectedly depreciates against the yen, say, to $1 = ¥95, the importer will still have to pay the Japanese company ¥200,000 per computer, but in dollar terms that would be equivalent to $2,105 per computer, which is more than she can sell the computers for. A depreciation in the value of the dollar against the yen from $1 = ¥120 to $1 = ¥95 would transform a profitable deal into an unprofitable one.

Forward Exchange
When two parties agree to exchange currency and execute a deal at some specific date in the future.

To *insure* or *hedge* against this risk, the U.S. importer might want to engage in a forward exchange. A **forward exchange** occurs when two parties agree to exchange currency and execute the deal at some specific date in the future. Exchange rates governing such future transactions are referred to as **forward exchange rates.** For most major currencies, forward exchange rates are quoted for 30 days, 90 days, and 180 days into the future. In some cases, it is possible to get forward exchange rates for several years into the future. Returning to our computer importer example, let us assume the 30-day forward exchange rate for converting dollars into yen is $1 = ¥110. The importer enters into a 30-day forward exchange transaction with a foreign exchange dealer at this rate and is guaranteed that she will have to pay no more than $1,818 for each computer (1,818 = 200,000/110). This guarantees her a profit of $182 per computer ($2,000 − $1,818). She also insures herself against the possibility that an unanticipated change in the dollar/yen exchange rate will turn a profitable deal into an unprofitable one.

Forward Exchange Rate
The exchange rate governing forward exchange transactions, calculated at the time of the exchange but based on future expectations.

In this example, the spot exchange rate ($1 = ¥120) and the 30-day forward rate ($1 = ¥110) differ. Such differences are normal; they reflect the expectations of the foreign exchange market about future currency movements. In our example, the fact that $1 bought more yen with a spot exchange than with a 30-day forward exchange indicates foreign exchange dealers expected the dollar to depreciate against the yen in the next 30 days. When this occurs, we say the dollar is selling at a discount on the 30-day forward market (i.e., it is worth less than on the spot market). Of course, the opposite can also occur. If the 30-day forward exchange rate were $1 = ¥130, for example, $1 would buy more yen with a forward exchange than with a spot exchange. In such a case, we say the dollar is selling at a premium on the 30-day forward market. This reflects the foreign exchange dealers' expectations that the dollar will appreciate against the yen over the next 30 days.

In sum, when a firm enters into a forward exchange contract, it is taking out insurance against the possibility that future exchange rate movements will make a transaction unprofitable by the time that transaction has been executed. Although many firms routinely enter into forward exchange contracts to hedge their foreign exchange risk, there are some spectacular examples of what happens when firms don't take out this insurance. An example is given in the accompanying Management Focus, which explains how a failure to fully insure against foreign exchange risk cost Volkswagen dearly.

Currency Swaps   The preceding discussion of spot and forward exchange rates might lead you to conclude that the option to buy forward is very important to companies engaged in international trade—and you would be right. By April 2007, the latest date for which information is available, forward instruments accounted for some 69 percent of all foreign exchange transactions, while spot exchanges accounted for 31 percent.[2] However, the vast majority of these forward exchanges were not forward

Management FOCUS

Volkswagen's Hedging Strategy

In January 2004, Volkswagen, Europe's largest carmaker, reported a 95 percent drop in 2003 fourth-quarter profits, which slumped from €1.05 billion to a mere €50 million. For all of 2003 Volkswagen's operating profit fell by 50 percent from the record levels attained in 2002. Although the profit slump had multiple causes, two factors were the focus of much attention—the sharp rise in the value of the euro against the dollar during 2003, and Volkswagen's decision to hedge only 30 percent of its foreign currency exposure, as opposed to the 70 percent it had traditionally hedged. In total, currency losses due to the dollar's rise are estimated to have reduced Volkswagen's operating profits by some €1.2 billion ($1.5 billion).

The rise in the value of the euro during 2003 took many companies by surprise. Since its introduction January 1, 1999, when it became the currency unit of 12 members of the European Union, the euro had recorded a volatile trading history against the U.S. dollar. In early 1999 the exchange rate stood at €1 = $1.17, but by October 2000 it had slumped to €1 = $0.83. Although it recovered, reaching parity of €1 = $1.00 in late 2002, few analysts predicted a rapid rise in the value of the euro against the dollar during 2003. As so often happens in the foreign exchange markets, the experts were wrong; by late 2003 the exchange rate stood at €1 = $1.25.

For Volkswagen, which made cars in Germany and exported them to the United States, the fall in the value of the dollar against the euro during 2003 was devastating. To understand what happened, consider a Volkswagen Jetta built in Germany for export to the United States. The Jetta costs €14,000 to make in Germany and ship to a dealer in the United States, where it sells for $15,000. With the exchange rate standing at around €1 = $1.00, the $15,000 earned from the sale of a Jetta in the United States could be converted into €15,000, giving Volkswagen a profit of €1,000 on every Jetta sold. But if the exchange rate

changes during the year, ending up at €1 = $1.25 as it did during 2003, each dollar of revenue will now only buy €0.80 (€1/$1.25 = €0.80), and Volkswagen is squeezed. At an exchange rate of €1=$1.25, the $15,000 Volkswagen gets for the Jetta is now worth only €12,000, meaning the company will lose €2,000 on every Jetta sold (when the exchange rate is €1 = $1.25, $15,000/1.25 = €12,000).

Volkswagen could have insured against this adverse movement in exchange rates by entering the foreign exchange market in late 2002 and buying a *forward contract* for dollars at an exchange rate of around $1 = €1 (a *forward contract* gives the holder the right to exchange one currency for another at some point in the future at a predetermined exchange rate). Called *hedging*, the financial strategy of buying forward guarantees that at some future point, such as 180 days, Volkswagen would have been able to exchange the dollars it got from selling Jettas in the United States into euros at $1 = €1, *irrespective of what the actual exchange rate was at that time*. In 2003 such a strategy would have been good for Volkswagen. However, hedging is not without its costs. For one thing, if the euro had declined in value against the dollar, instead of appreciating as it did, Volkswagen would have made even more profit per car in euros by not hedging (a dollar at the end of 2003 would have bought more euros than a dollar at the end of 2002). For another thing, hedging is expensive since foreign exchange dealers will charge a high commission for selling currency forward. Volkswagen decided to hedge just 30 percent of its anticipated U.S. sales in 2003 through forward contracts, rather than the 70 percent it had historically hedged. The decision cost the company over a €1 billion. For 2004, the company announced it would revert back to hedging 70 percent of its foreign currency exposure.

Sources: Mark Landler, "As Exchange Rates Swing, Car Makers Try to Duck," *The New York Times,* January 17, 2004, pp. B1, B4; N. Boudette, "Volkswagen Posts 95% Drop in Net," *The Wall Street Journal,* Februray 19, 2004, p. A3; and "Volkswagen's Financial Mechanic," *Corporate Finance,* June 2003, p. 1.

exchanges of the type we have been discussing, but a more sophisticated instrument known as currency swaps.

A **currency swap** is the simultaneous purchase and sale of a given amount of foreign exchange for two different value dates. Swaps are transacted between international businesses and their banks, between banks, and between governments when it is desirable to move out of one currency into another for a limited period without incurring foreign exchange risk. A common kind of swap is spot against forward. Consider a company such as Apple Computer. Apple assembles laptop computers in the United States, but the screens are made in Japan. Apple also sells some of the finished laptops in Japan. So, like many companies, Apple both buys from and sells to Japan. Imagine

Currency Swap
The simultaneous purchase and sale of a given amount of foreign exchange for two different value dates.

Another Perspective

Key into Exchange Rate Language

The language used to describe exchange rates can be confusing, even though the ideas themselves are simple. Here's why: Any given observation describes a changing relationship (the movement in the currencies) that itself describes two relationships (the exchange rates for both currencies). The important thing to remember is that an exchange rate is described in terms of other exchange rates.

The language we use to describe these moving phenomena works in a similar, dual way: The euro gains against the dollar, so the euro is strengthening, or becoming dearer, from a dollar perspective. Meanwhile, the same observation indicates its mirror image, that the dollar is weakening, becoming cheaper against the euro, from a euro perspective.

Apple needs to change $1 million into yen to pay its supplier of laptop screens today. Apple knows that in 90 days it will be paid ¥120 million by the Japanese importer that buys its finished laptops. It will want to convert these yen into dollars for use in the United States. Let us say today's spot exchange rate is $1 = ¥120 and the 90-day forward exchange rate is $1 = ¥110. Apple sells $1 million to its bank in return for ¥120 million. Now Apple can pay its Japanese supplier. At the same time, Apple enters into a 90-day forward exchange deal with its bank for converting ¥120 million into dollars. Thus, in 90 days Apple will receive $1.09 million (¥120 million/110 = $1.09 million). Since the yen is trading at a premium on the 90-day forward market, Apple ends up with more dollars than it started with (although the opposite could also occur). The swap deal is just like a conventional forward deal in one important respect: It enables Apple to insure itself against foreign exchange risk. By engaging in a swap, Apple knows today that the ¥120 million payment it will receive in 90 days will yield $1.09 million.

The Nature of the Foreign Exchange Market

The foreign exchange market is not located in any one place. It is a global network of banks, brokers, and foreign exchange dealers connected by electronic communications systems. When companies wish to convert currencies, they typically go through their own banks rather than entering the market directly. The foreign exchange market has been growing at a rapid pace, reflecting a general growth in the volume of cross-border trade and investment (see Chapter 1). In March 1986, the average total value of global foreign exchange trading was about $200 billion per day. By April 1995, it was more than $1,200 billion per day, and by April 2004 it had reached $1.8 trillion per day, and by April 2007 it had surged to $3.21 trillion per day.[3] The most important trading centers are London (34 percent of activity), New York (16 percent of activity), and Zurich, Tokyo, and Singapore (each with about 6 percent of activity).[4] Major secondary trading centers include Frankfurt, Paris, Hong Kong, and Sydney.

London's dominance in the foreign exchange market is due to both history and geography. As the capital of the world's first major industrial trading nation, London had become the world's largest center for international banking by the end of the 19th century, a position it has retained. Today London's central position between Tokyo and Singapore to the east and New York to the west has made it the critical link between the East Asian and New York markets. Due to the particular differences in time zones, London opens soon after Tokyo closes for the night and is still open for the first few hours of trading in New York.[5]

Two features of the foreign exchange market are of particular note. The first is that the market never sleeps. Tokyo, London, and New York are all shut

Even though the British pound has declined in its importance as a vehicle currency, London remains the key location for global foreign exchange.

for only 3 hours out of every 24. During these three hours, trading continues in a number of minor centers, particularly San Francisco and Sydney, Australia. The second feature of the market is the integration of the various trading centers. High-speed computer linkages between trading centers around the globe have effectively created a single market. The integration of financial centers implies there can be no significant difference in exchange rates quoted in the trading centers. For example, if the yen/dollar exchange rate quoted in London at 3 p.m. is ¥120 = $1, the yen/dollar exchange rate quoted in New York at the same time (10 a.m. New York time) will be identical. If the New York yen/dollar exchange rate were ¥125 = $1, a dealer could make a profit through **arbitrage,** buying a currency low and selling it high. For example, if the prices differed in London and New York as given, a dealer in New York could take $1 million and use that to purchase ¥125 million. She could then immediately sell the ¥125 million for dollars in London, where the transaction would yield $1.046666 million, allowing the trader to book a profit of $46,666 on the transaction. If all dealers tried to cash in on the opportunity, however, the demand for yen in New York would rise, resulting in an appreciation of the yen against the dollar such that the price differential between New York and London would quickly disappear. Because foreign exchange dealers are always watching their computer screens for arbitrage opportunities, the few that arise tend to be small, and they disappear in minutes.

Arbitrage
The purchase of securities in one market for immediate resale in another market to profit from a price discrepancy.

Another feature of the foreign exchange market is the important role played by the U.S. dollar. Although a foreign exchange transaction can involve any two currencies, most transactions involve dollars on one side. This is true even when a dealer wants to sell a nondollar currency and buy another. A dealer wishing to sell Korean won for Brazilian real, for example, will usually sell the won for dollars and then use the dollars to buy real. Although this may seem a roundabout way of doing things, it is actually cheaper than trying to find a holder of real who wants to buy won. Because the volume of international transactions involving dollars is so great, it is not hard to find dealers who wish to trade dollars for won or real.

Due to its central role in so many foreign exchange deals, the dollar is a vehicle currency. In 2007, 86 percent of all foreign exchange transactions involved dollars on one side of the transaction. After the dollar, the most important vehicle currencies were the euro (37 percent), the Japanese yen (16.5 percent), and the British pound (15 percent), reflecting the importance of these trading entities in the world economy. The euro has replaced the Germany mark as the world's second most important vehicle currency. The British pound used to be second in importance to the dollar as a vehicle currency, but its importance has diminished in recent years. Despite this, London has retained its leading position in the global foreign exchange market.

Economic Theories of Exchange Rate Determination

At the most basic level, exchange rates are determined by the demand and supply of one currency relative to the demand and supply of another. For example, if the demand for dollars outstrips the supply of them and if the supply of Japanese yen is greater than the demand for them, the dollar/yen exchange rate will change. The dollar will appreciate against the yen (or the yen will depreciate against the dollar). However, while differences in relative demand and supply explain the determination of exchange rates, they do so only in a superficial sense. This simple explanation does not tell us what factors underlie the demand for and supply of a currency. Nor does it tell us when the demand for dollars will exceed the supply (and vice versa) or when the supply of Japanese yen will exceed demand for them (and vice versa).

LEARNING OBJECTIVE 4
Understand the different theories explaining how currency exchange rates are determined and their relative merits.

Neither does it tell us under what conditions a currency is in demand or under what conditions it is not demanded. In this section, we will review economic theory's answers to these questions. This will give us a deeper understanding of how exchange rates are determined.

If we understand how exchange rates are determined, we may be able to forecast exchange rate movements. Because future exchange rate movements influence export opportunities, the profitability of international trade and investment deals, and the price competitiveness of foreign imports, this is valuable information for an international business. Unfortunately, there is no simple explanation. The forces that determine exchange rates are complex, and no theoretical consensus exists, even among academic economists who study the phenomenon every day. Nonetheless, most economic theories of exchange rate movements seem to agree that three factors have an important impact on future exchange rate movements in a country's currency: the country's price inflation, its interest rate, and market psychology.[6]

PRICES AND EXCHANGE RATES

To understand how prices are related to exchange rate movements, we first need to discuss an economic proposition known as the law of one price. Then we will discuss the theory of purchasing power parity (PPP), which links changes in the exchange rate between two countries' currencies to changes in the countries' price levels.

Law of One Price
The principle that in competitive markets free of transportation costs and barriers to trade, identical products sold in different countries must sell for the same price when their price is expressed in the same currency.

The Law of One Price

The **law of one price** states that in competitive markets free of transportation costs and barriers to trade (such as tariffs), identical products sold in different countries must sell for the same price when their price is expressed in terms of the same currency.[7] For example, if the exchange rate between the British pound and the dollar is £1 = $2.00, a jacket that retails for $80 in New York should sell for £40 in London (since $80/2.00 = £40). Consider what would happen if the jacket cost £30 in London ($60 in U.S. currency). At this price, it would pay a trader to buy jackets in London and sell them in New York (an example of arbitrage). The company initially could make a profit of $20 on each jacket by purchasing it for £30 ($60) in London and selling it for $80 in New York (we are assuming away transportation costs and trade barriers). However, the increased demand for jackets in London would raise their price in London, and the increased supply of jackets in New York would lower their price there. This would continue until prices were equalized. Thus, prices might equalize when the jacket cost £35 ($70) in London and $70 in New York (assuming no change in the exchange rate of £1 = $2.00).

Efficient Market
A market in which prices reflect all available information and trade is not restricted.

Purchasing Power Parity

If the law of one price were true for all goods and services, the purchasing power parity (PPP) exchange rate could be found from any individual set of prices. By comparing the prices of identical products in different currencies, it would be possible to determine the "real" or PPP exchange rate that would exist if markets were efficient. (An **efficient market** has no impediments to the free flow of goods and services, such as trade barriers.)

A less extreme version of the PPP theory states that given relatively efficient markets—that is, markets in which few impediments to international trade exist—the price of a "basket of goods" should be roughly equivalent in each country. To express the PPP theory in symbols, let P$ be the U.S. dollar price of a basket of particular goods and P¥ be the price of the same basket of goods in Japanese yen. The PPP theory predicts that the dollar/yen exchange rate, E$/¥, should be equivalent to:

$$E_{\$/¥} = P_\$/P_¥$$

Thus, if a basket of goods costs $200 in the United States and ¥20,000 in Japan, PPP theory predicts that the dollar/yen exchange rate should be $200/¥20,000 or $0.01 per Japanese yen (i.e., $1 = ¥100).

Every year, the newsmagazine *The Economist* publishes its own version of the PPP theorem, which it refers to as the "Big Mac Index." *The Economist* has selected McDonald's Big Mac as a proxy for a "basket of goods" because it is produced according to more or less the same recipe in about 120 countries. The Big Mac PPP is the exchange rate that would have hamburgers costing the same in each country. According to *The Economist*, comparing a country's actual exchange

rate with the one predicted by the PPP theorem based on relative prices of Big Macs is a test on whether a currency is undervalued or not. This is not a totally serious exercise, as *The Economist* admits, but it does provide us with a useful illustration of the PPP theorem.

The Big Mac index for July 2, 2007, is reproduced in Table 9.2. To calculate the index, *The Economist* converts the price of a Big Mac in a country into dollars at current exchange rates and divides that by the average price of a Big Mac in America (which was $3.41). According to the PPP theorem, the prices should be the same. If they are not, it implies that the currency is either overvalued against the dollar or undervalued. For example, the average price of a Big Mac in the euro area was $4.17 at the euro/dollar exchange rate prevailing on July 2, 2007. Dividing this by the average price of a Big Mac in the United States gives 1.22 (i.e., 4.17/3.41), which suggests that the euro was overvalued by 22 percent against the U.S. dollar.

The next step in the PPP theory is to argue that the exchange rate will change if relative prices change. For example, imagine there is no price inflation in the United States, while prices in Japan are increasing by 10 percent a year. At the beginning of the year, a basket of goods costs $200 in the United States and ¥20,000 in Japan, so the dollar/yen exchange rate, according to PPP theory, should be $1 = ¥100. At the end of the year, the basket of goods still costs $200 in the United States, but it costs ¥22,000 in Japan. PPP theory predicts that the exchange rate should change as a result. More precisely, by the end of the year:

$$E_{\$/\text{¥}} = \$200/\text{¥}22{,}000$$

Thus, ¥1 = $0.0091 (or $1 = ¥110). Because of 10 percent price inflation, the Japanese yen has depreciated by 10 percent against the dollar. One dollar will buy 10 percent more yen at the end of the year than at the beginning.

Money Supply and Price Inflation   In essence, PPP theory predicts that changes in relative prices will result in a change in exchange rates. Theoretically, a country in which price inflation is running wild should expect to see its currency

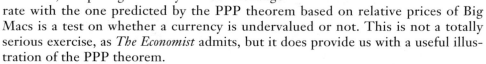

table 9.2

The Big Mac Index, July 2, 2007

†Purchasing-power parity; local price divided by price in United States
‡Average of New York, Chicago, Atlanta, and San Francisco.
§Dollars per pound.
**Weighted average of prices in euro area
††Dollars per euro.

Source: *The Economist*, July 5, 2007, www.economist.com/finance/displaystory.cfm?story_id=9448015.

Cash and carry
The hamburger standard

	Big Mac prices				
	In Local Currency	In Dollars	Implied PPP† of the Dollar	Actual Dollar Exchange Rate July 2	Under (−)/Over (+) Valuation Against the Dollar, %
United States‡	$3.41	3.41			
Argentina	Peso 8.25	2.67	2.42	3.09	−22
Australia	A$3.45	2.95	1.01	1.17	−14
Brazil	Real 6.90	3.61	2.02	1.91	+6
Britain	£1.99	4.01	1.71§	2.01§	+18
Canada	C$3.88	3.68	1.41	1.05	+8
Chile	Peso 1,565	2.97	459	527	−13
China	Yuan 11.0	1.45	3.23	7.60	−58
Czech Republic	Koruna 52.9	2.51	15.5	21.1	−27
Denmark	Dkr 27.75	5.08	8.14	5.45	+49
Egypt	Pound 9.54	1.68	2.80	5.69	−51
Euro area**	€3.05	4.17	1.12††	1.36††	+22
Hong Kong	HK$12.0	1.54	3.52	7.82	−55
Hungary	Forint 600	3.33	176	180	−2
Indonesia	Rupiah 15,900	1.76	4,663	9,015	−48
Japan	¥280	2.29	82.1	122	−33
Malaysia	Ringgit 5.50	1.60	1.61	3.43	−53
Mexico	Peso 29.0	2.69	8.50	10.8	−21
New Zealand	NZ$4.60	3.59	1.35	1.28	+5
Peru	New Sol 9.50	3.00	2.79	3.17	−12
Philippines	Peso 85.0	1.85	24.9	45.9	−46
Poland	Zloty 6.90	2.51	2.02	2.75	−26
Russia	Rouble 52.0	2.03	15.2	25.6	−41
Singapore	S$3.95	2.59	1.16	1.52	−24
South Africa	Rand 15.5	2.22	4.55	6.97	−35
South Korea	Won 2.900	3.14	850	923	−8
Sweden	SKr33.0	4.86	9.68	6.79	+42
Switzerland	SFr6.30	5.20	1.85	1.21	+53
Taiwan	NT$75.0	2.29	22.0	32.8	−33
Thailand	Baht 62.0	1.80	18.2	34.5	−47
Turkey	Lire 4.75	3.66	1.39	1.30	+7
Venezuela	Bolivar 7.400	3.45	2,170	2,147	+1

9.2 table

The Big Mac Index, July 2, 2007 *(continued)*

Cash and carry The hamburger standard **Big Mac prices**					
	In Local Currency	In Dollars	Implied PPP† of the Dollar	Actual Dollar Exchange Rate July 2	Under (−)/Over (+) Valuation Against the Dollar, %
Colombia	Peso 6,900	3.53	2,023	1,956	+3
Costa Rica	Colon 1,130	2.18	331	519	−36
Estonia	Kroon 30.0	2.61	8.80	11.5	−23
Iceland	Kronur 469	7.61	138	61.7	+123
Latvia	Lats 1.39	2.72	0.41	0.51	−20
Lithuania	Litas 6.60	2.61	1.94	2.53	−24
Norway	Kroner 40.0	6.88	11.7	5.81	+102
Pakistan	Rupee 140	2.32	41.1	60.4	−32
Paraguay	Guarani 10,500	2.04	3,079	5,145	−40
Saudi Arabia	Riyal 9.00	2.40	2.64	3.75	−30
Slovakia	Koruna 61.3	2.49	18.0	24.6	−27
Sri Lanka	Rupee 210	1.89	61.6	111	−45
UAE	Dirhams 10.0	2.72	2.93	3.67	−20
Ukraine	Hryvnia 9.25	1.84	2.71	5.03	−46
Uruguay	Peso 62.0	2.59	18.2	23.9	−24

depreciate against that of countries in which inflation rates are lower. If we can predict what a country's future inflation rate is likely to be, we can also predict how the value of its currency relative to other currencies—its exchange rate—is likely to change. The growth rate of a country's money supply determines its likely future inflation rate.[8] Thus, in theory at least, we can use information about the growth in money supply to forecast exchange rate movements.

Inflation is a monetary phenomenon. It occurs when the quantity of money in circulation rises faster than the stock of goods and services; that is, when the money supply increases faster than output increases. Imagine what would happen if everyone in the country was suddenly given $10,000 by the government. Many people would rush out to spend their extra money on those things they had always wanted—new cars, new furniture, better clothes, and so on. There would be a surge in demand for goods and services. Car dealers, department stores, and other providers of goods and services would respond to this upsurge in demand by raising prices. The result would be price inflation.

A government increasing the money supply is analogous to giving people more money. An increase in the money supply makes it easier for banks to borrow from the government and for individuals and companies to borrow from banks. The resulting increase in credit causes increases in demand for goods and services. Unless the output of goods and services is growing at a rate similar to that of the money supply, the result will be inflation. This relationship has been observed time after time in country after country.

table 9.3

Macroeconomic Data for Bolivia, April 1984–October 1985

Source: Juan-Antino Morales, "Inflation Stabilization in Bolivia," in *Inflation Stabilization: The Experience of Israel, Argentina, Brazil, Bolivia, and Mexico,* ed. Michael Bruno et al. (Cambridge, MA: MIT Press, 1988).

Month	Money Supply (billions of pesos)	Price Level Relative to 1982 (average = 1)	Exchange Rate (pesos per dollar)
1984			
April	270	21.1	3,576
May	330	31.1	3,512
June	440	32.3	3,342
July	599	34.0	3,570
August	718	39.1	7,038
September	889	53.7	13,685
October	1,194	85.5	15,205
November	1,495	112.4	18,469
December	3,296	180.9	24,515
1985			
January	4,630	305.3	73,016
February	6,455	863.3	141,101
March	9,089	1,078.6	128,137
April	12,885	1,205.7	167,428
May	21,309	1,635.7	272,375
June	27,778	2,919.1	481,756
July	47,341	4,854.6	885,476
August	74,306	8,081.0	1,182,300
September	103,272	12,647.6	1,087,440
October	132,550	12,411.8	1,120,210

So now we have a connection between the growth in a country's money supply, price inflation, and exchange rate movements. Put simply, *when the growth in a country's money supply is faster than the growth in its output, price inflation is fueled.* The PPP theory tells us that a country with a high inflation rate will see depreciation in its currency exchange rate. In one of the clearest historical examples, in the mid-1980s, Bolivia experienced hyperinflation—an explosive and seemingly uncontrollable price inflation in which money loses value very rapidly. Table 9.3 presents data on Bolivia's money supply, inflation rate, and its peso's exchange rate with the U.S. dollar during the period of hyperinflation. The exchange rate is actually the "black market" exchange rate, as the Bolivian government prohibited converting the peso to other currencies during the period. The data show that the growth in money supply, the rate of price inflation, and the depreciation of the peso against the dollar all moved in step with each other. This is just what PPP theory and monetary economics predict. Between April 1984 and July 1985, Bolivia's money supply increased by 17,433 percent, prices increased by 22,908 percent, and the value of the peso against the dollar fell by 24,662 percent! In October 1985, the Bolivian government instituted a dramatic stabilization plan—which included the introduction of a new currency and tight control of the money supply—and by 1987 the country's annual inflation rate was down to 16 percent.[9]

Another way of looking at the same phenomenon is that an increase in a country's money supply, which increases the amount of currency available, changes the relative demand and supply conditions in the foreign exchange market. If the U.S. money supply is growing more rapidly than U.S. output, dollars will be relatively more plentiful than the currencies of countries where monetary growth is closer to output growth. As a result of this relative increase in the supply of dollars, the dollar will depreciate on the foreign exchange market against the currencies of countries with slower monetary growth.

Government policy determines whether the rate of growth in a country's money supply is greater than the rate of growth in output. A government can increase the money supply simply by telling the country's central bank to issue more money. Governments tend to do this to finance public expenditure (building roads, paying government workers, paying for defense, etc.). A government could finance public expenditure by raising taxes, but since nobody likes paying more taxes and since politicians do not like to be unpopular, they have a natural preference for expanding the money supply. Unfortunately, there is no magic money tree. The inevitable result of excessive growth in money supply is price inflation. However, this has not stopped governments around the world from expanding the money supply, with predictable results. If an international business is attempting to predict future movements in the value of a country's currency on the foreign exchange market, it should examine that country's policy toward monetary growth. If the government seems committed to controlling the rate of growth in money supply, the country's future inflation rate may be low (even if the current rate is high) and its currency should not depreciate too much on the foreign exchange market. If the government seems to lack the political will to control the rate of growth in money supply, the future inflation rate may be high, which is likely to cause its currency to depreciate. Historically, many Latin American governments have fallen into this latter category, including Argentina, Bolivia, and Brazil. More recently, many of the newly democratic states of Eastern Europe made the same mistake.

Empirical Tests of PPP Theory   PPP theory predicts that exchange rates are determined by relative prices, and that changes in relative prices will result in a change in exchange rates. A country in which price inflation is running wild should expect to see its currency depreciate against that of countries with lower inflation rates. This is intuitively appealing, but is it true in practice? There are several good examples of the connection between a country's price inflation and exchange rate position (such as Bolivia). However, extensive empirical testing of PPP theory has yielded mixed results.[10] While PPP theory seems to yield relatively accurate predictions in the long run, it does not appear to be a strong predictor of short-run movements in exchange rates covering time spans of five years or less.[11] In addition, the theory seems to best predict exchange rate changes for countries with high rates of inflation and underdeveloped capital markets. The theory is less useful for predicting short-term exchange rate movements between the currencies of advanced industrialized nations that have relatively small differentials in inflation rates.

The failure to find a strong link between relative inflation rates and exchange rate movements has been referred to as the purchasing power parity puzzle. Several factors may explain the failure of PPP theory to predict exchange rates more accurately.[12] PPP theory assumes away transportation costs and barriers to trade. In practice, these factors are significant and they tend to create significant price differentials between countries. Transportation costs are certainly not trivial for many goods. Plus, as we saw in Chapter 6, governments routinely intervene in international trade, creating tariff and nontariff barriers to cross-border trade. Barriers to trade limit the ability of traders to use arbitrage to equalize prices for the same product in different countries, which is required for the law of one price to hold. Government intervention in cross-border trade, by violating the assumption of efficient markets, weakens the link between relative price changes and changes in exchange rates predicted by PPP theory.

In addition, the PPP theory may not hold if many national markets are dominated by a handful of multinational enterprises that have sufficient market power to be able to exercise some influence over prices, control distribution channels, and differentiate their product offerings between nations.[13] In fact, this situation seems to prevail in a number of industries. In the detergent industry, two companies, Unilever and Procter & Gamble, dominate the market in nation after nation. In heavy earth-moving equipment, Caterpillar Inc. and Komatsu are global market leaders. In the market for semiconductor equipment, Applied Materials has a commanding market share lead in almost every important national market. Microsoft dominates the market for personal computer operating systems and applications systems around the world, and so on. In such cases, dominant enterprises may be able to exercise a degree of pricing power, setting different prices in different markets to reflect varying demand conditions. This is referred to as price discrimination. For price discrimination to work, arbitrage must be limited. According to this argument, enterprises with some market power may be able to control distribution channels and therefore limit the unauthorized resale (arbitrage) of products purchased in another national market. They may also be able to limit resale (arbitrage) by differentiating otherwise identical products among nations along some line, such as design or packaging.

For example, even though the version of Microsoft Office sold in China may be less expensive than the version sold in the United States, the use of arbitrage to equalize prices may be limited because few Americans would want a version that was based on Chinese characters. The design differentiation between Microsoft Office for China and for the United States means that the law of one price would not work for Microsoft Office, even if transportation costs were trivial and tariff barriers between the United States and China did not exist. If the inability to practice arbitrage were widespread enough, it would break the connection between changes in relative prices and exchange rates predicted by the PPP theorem and help explain the limited empirical support for this theory.

Another factor of some importance is that governments also intervene in the foreign exchange market in attempting to influence the value of their currencies. We will look at why and how they do this in Chapter 10. For now, the important thing to note is that governments regularly intervene in the foreign exchange market, and this further weakens the link between price changes and changes in exchange rates. One more factor explaining the failure of PPP theory to predict short-term movements in foreign exchange rates is the impact of investor psychology and other factors on currency purchasing decisions and exchange rate movements. We will discuss this issue in more detail later in this chapter.

INTEREST RATES AND EXCHANGE RATES Economic theory tells us that interest rates reflect expectations about likely future inflation rates. In countries where inflation is expected to be high, interest rates also will be high, because investors want compensation for the decline in the value of their money. This relationship was first formalized by economist Irvin Fisher and is referred to as the Fisher Effect.

The **Fisher Effect** states that a country's "nominal" interest rate (i) is the sum of the required "real" rate of interest (r) and the expected rate of inflation over the period for which the funds are to be lent (I). More formally,

$$i = r + I$$

For example, if the real rate of interest in a country is 5 percent and annual inflation is expected to be 10 percent, the nominal interest rate will be 15 percent. As predicted by the Fisher Effect, a strong relationship seems to exist between inflation rates and interest rates.[14]

We can take this one step further and consider how it applies in a world of many countries and unrestricted capital flows. When investors are free to transfer capital between countries, real interest rates will be the same in every country. If differences in real interest rates did emerge between countries, arbitrage would soon equalize them. For example, if the real interest rate in Japan was 10 percent and only 6 percent in the United States, it would pay investors to borrow money in the United States and invest it in Japan. The resulting increase in the demand for money in the United States would raise the real interest rate there, while the increase in the supply of foreign money in Japan would lower the real interest rate there. This would continue until the two sets of real interest rates were equalized.

It follows from the Fisher Effect that if the real interest rate is the same worldwide, any difference in interest rates between countries reflects differing expectations about inflation rates. Thus, if the expected rate of inflation in the United States is greater than that in Japan, U.S. nominal interest rates will be greater than Japanese nominal interest rates.

Since we know from PPP theory that there is a link (in theory at least) between inflation and exchange rates, and since interest rates reflect expectations about inflation, it follows that there must also be a link between interest rates and exchange rates. This link is known as the International Fisher Effect (IFE). The **International Fisher Effect** states that for any two countries, the spot exchange rate should change in an equal amount but in the opposite direction to the difference in nominal interest rates between the two countries. Stated more formally, the change in the spot exchange rate between the United States and Japan, for example, can be modeled as follows:

$$[(S_1 - S_2)/S_2] \times 100 = i_\$ - i_¥$$

where $i_\$$ and $i_¥$ are the respective nominal interest rates in the United States and Japan, S_1 is the spot exchange rate at the beginning of the period, and S_2 is the spot exchange rate at the end of the period. If the U.S. nominal interest rate is higher than Japan's, reflecting greater expected inflation rates, the value of the dollar against the yen should fall by that interest rate differential in the future. So if the interest rate in the United States is 10 percent and in Japan it is 6 percent, we would expect the value of the dollar to depreciate by 4 percent against the Japanese yen.

Do interest rate differentials help predict future currency movements? The evidence is mixed; as in the case of PPP theory, in the long run, there seems to be a relationship between interest rate differentials and subsequent changes in spot exchange rates. However, considerable short-run deviations occur. Like PPP, the International Fisher Effect is not a good predictor of short-run changes in spot exchange rates.[15]

INVESTOR PSYCHOLOGY AND BANDWAGON EFFECTS Empirical evidence suggests that neither PPP theory nor the International Fisher Effect are particularly good at explaining short-term movements in exchange rates. One reason may

Fisher Effect
The theory that nominal interest rates (i) in each country equal the required real rate of interest (r) and expected rate of inflation (I) over the time period for which the funds are to be lent. That is, $i = r + I$.

International Fisher Effect
The theory that for any two countries, the spot exchange rate should change in an equal amount but in the opposite direction to the difference in normal interest rates between countries.

George Soros, whose Quantum Fund has been fantastically successful in managing hedge funds, has been criticized by world leaders for being able to cause huge changes in currency markets by his actions.

Bandwagon Effect
When traders move like a herd, all in the same direction and at the same time, in response to each others' perceived actions.

be the impact of investor psychology on short-run exchange rate movements. Evidence accumulated over 10 years reveals that various psychological factors play an important role in determining the expectations of market traders as to likely future exchange rates.[16] In turn, expectations have a tendency to become self-fulfilling prophecies.

A good example of this mechanism occurred in September 1992 when the famous international financier George Soros made a huge bet against the British pound. Soros borrowed billions of pounds, using the assets of his investment funds as collateral, and immediately sold those pounds for German deutsche marks (this was before the advent of the euro). This technique, known as short selling, can earn the speculator enormous profits if he can subsequently buy back the pounds he sold at a much better exchange rate, and then use those pounds, purchased cheaply, to repay his loan. By selling pounds and buying deutsche marks, Soros helped to start pushing down the value of the pound on the foreign exchange markets. More importantly, when Soros started shorting the British pound, many foreign exchange traders, knowing Soros's reputation, jumped on the bandwagon and did likewise. This triggered a classic **bandwagon effect** with traders moving as a herd in the same direction at the same time. As the bandwagon effect gained momentum, with more traders selling British pounds and purchasing deutsche marks in expectation of a decline in the pound, their expectations became a self-fulfilling prophecy. Massive selling forced down the value of the pound against the deutsche mark. In other words, the pound declined in value not so much because of any major shift in macroeconomic fundamentals, but because investors followed a bet placed by a major speculator, George Soros.

According to a number of studies, investor psychology and bandwagon effects play a major role in determining short-run exchange rate movements.[17] However, these effects can be hard to predict. Investor psychology can be influenced by political factors and by microeconomic events, such as the investment decisions of individual firms, many of which are only loosely linked to macroeconomic fundamentals, such as relative inflation rates. Also, bandwagon effects can be both triggered and exacerbated by the idiosyncratic behavior of politicians. Something like this seems to have occurred in Southeast Asia during 1997 when, one after another, the currencies of Thailand, Malaysia, South Korea, and Indonesia lost between 50 percent and 70 percent of their value against the U.S. dollar in a few months. For a detailed look at what occurred in South Korea, see the accompanying Country Focus. The collapse in the value of the Korean currency did not occur because South Korea had a higher inflation rate than the United States. It occurred because of an excessive buildup of dollar-denominated debt among South Korean firms. By mid-1997 it was clear that these companies were having trouble servicing this debt. Foreign investors, fearing a wave of corporate bankruptcies, took their money out of the country, exchanging won for U.S. dollars. As this began to depress the exchange rate, currency traders jumped on the bandwagon and speculated against the won (selling it short), and it was this that produced a collapse in the value of the won.

SUMMARY Relative monetary growth, relative inflation rates, and nominal interest rate differentials are all moderately good predictors of long-run changes in exchange rates. They are poor predictors of short-run changes in exchange rates,

Country FOCUS

Anatomy of a Currency Crisis

In early 1997, South Korea could look back with pride on a 30-year "economic miracle" that had raised the country from the ranks of the poor and given it the world's 11th largest economy. By the end of 1997, the Korean currency, the won, had lost a staggering 67 percent of its value against the U.S. dollar, the South Korean economy lay in tatters, and the International Monetary Fund was overseeing a $55 billion rescue package. This sudden turn of events had its roots in investments made by South Korea's large industrial conglomerates, or *chaebol,* during the 1990s, often at the bequest of politicians. In 1993, Kim Young-Sam, a populist politician, became president of South Korea. Mr. Kim took office during a mild recession and promised to boost economic growth by encouraging investment in export-oriented industries. He urged the *chaebol* to invest in new factories. South Korea enjoyed an investment-led economic boom in 1994–1995, but at a cost. The *chaebol,* always reliant on heavy borrowing, built up massive debts that were equivalent, on average, to four times their equity.

As the volume of investments ballooned during the 1990s, the quality of many of these investments declined significantly. The investments often were made on the basis of unrealistic projections about future demand conditions. This resulted in significant excess capacity and falling prices. An example is investments made by South Korean *chaebol* in semiconductor factories. Investments in such facilities surged in 1994 and 1995 when a temporary global shortage of dynamic random access memory chips (DRAMs) led to sharp price increases for this product. However, supply shortages had disappeared by 1996 and excess capacity was beginning to make itself felt, just as the South Koreans started to bring new DRAM factories on stream. The results were predictable; prices for DRAMs plunged and the earnings of South Korean DRAM manufacturers fell by 90 percent, which meant it was difficult for them to make scheduled payments on the debt they had acquired to build the extra capacity. The risk of corporate bankruptcy increased significantly, and not just in the semiconductor industry. South Korean companies were also investing heavily in a wide range of other industries, including automobiles and steel.

Matters were complicated further because much of the borrowing had been in U.S. dollars, as opposed to Korean won. This had seemed like a smart move at the time. The dollar/won exchange rate had been stable at around $1 = won 850. Interest rates on dollar borrowings were two to three percentage points lower than rates on borrowings in Korean won. Much of this borrowing was in the form of short-term, dollar-denominated debt that had to be paid back to the lending institution within one year. While the borrowing strategy seemed to make sense, it involved risk. If the won were to depreciate against the dollar, the size of the debt burden that South Korean companies would have to service would increase when measured in the local currency. Currency depreciation would raise borrowing costs, depress corporate earnings, and increase the risk of bankruptcy. This is exactly what happened.

By mid-1997, foreign investors had become alarmed at the rising debt levels of South Korean companies, particularly given the emergence of excess capacity and plunging prices in several areas where the companies had made huge investments, including semiconductors, automobiles, and steel. Given increasing speculation that many South Korean companies would not be able to service their debt payments, foreign investors began to withdraw their money from the Korean stock and bond markets. In the process, they sold Korean won and purchased U.S. dollars. The selling of won accelerated in mid-1997 when two of the smaller *chaebol* filed for bankruptcy, citing their inability to meet scheduled debt payments. The increased supply of won and the increased demand for U.S. dollars pushed down the price of won in dollar terms from around won 840 = $1 to won 900 = $1.

At this point, the South Korean central bank stepped into the foreign exchange market to try to keep the exchange rate above won 1,000 = $1. It used dollars that it held in reserve to purchase won. The idea was to try to push up the price of the won in dollar terms and restore investor confidence in the stability of the exchange rate. This action, however, did not address the underlying debt problem faced by South Korean companies. Against a backdrop of more corporate bankruptcies in South Korea, and the government's stated intentions to take some troubled companies into state ownership, Standard & Poor's, the U.S. credit rating agency, downgraded South Korea's sovereign debt. This caused the Korean stock market to plunge 5.5 percent, and the Korean won to fall to won 930 = $1. According to S&P, "The downgrade of . . . ratings reflects the escalating cost to the government of supporting the country's ailing corporate and financial sectors."

The S&P downgrade triggered a sharp sale of the Korean won. In an attempt to protect the won against what was fast becoming a classic bandwagon effect, the South Korean central bank raised short-term interest rates to over 12 percent, more than double the inflation rate. The bank also stepped up its intervention in the currency exchange markets, selling dollars and purchasing won in an attempt to keep the exchange rate above won 1,000 = $1.

(continued)

The main effect of this action, however, was to rapidly deplete South Korea's foreign exchange reserves. These stood at $30 billion on November 1, but fell to only $15 billion two weeks later. With its foreign exchange reserves almost exhausted, the South Korean central bank gave up its defense of the won November 17. Immediately, the price of won in dollars plunged to around won 1,500 = $1, effectively increasing by 60 to 70 percent the amount of won heavily indebted Korean companies had to pay to meet scheduled payments on their dollar-denominated debt.

These losses, due to adverse changes in foreign exchange rates, depressed the profits of many firms. South Korean firms suffered foreign exchange losses of more than $15 billion in 1997.

Sources: J. Burton and G. Baker, "The Country That Invested Its Way into Trouble," *Financial Times*, January 15, 1998, p. 8; J. Burton, "South Korea's Credit Rating Is Lowered," *Financial Times*, October 25, 1997, p. 3; J. Burton, "Currency Losses Hit Samsung Electronics," *Financial Times*, March 20, 1998, p. 24; and "Korean Firms' Foreign Exchange Losses Exceed US $15 Billion," *Business Korea*, February 1998, p. 55.

however, perhaps because of the impact of psychological factors, investor expectations, and bandwagon effects on short-term currency movements. This information is useful for an international business. Insofar as the long-term profitability of foreign investments, export opportunities, and the price competitiveness of foreign imports are all influenced by long-term movements in exchange rates, international businesses would be advised to pay attention to countries' differing monetary growth, inflation, and interest rates. International businesses that engage in foreign exchange transactions on a day-to-day basis could benefit by knowing some predictors of short-term foreign exchange rate movements. Unfortunately, short-term exchange rate movements are difficult to predict.

Exchange Rate Forecasting

LEARNING OBJECTIVE 5
Be familiar with the merits of different approaches toward exchange rate forecasting.

A company's need to predict future exchange rate variations raises the issue of whether it is worthwhile for the company to invest in exchange rate forecasting services to aid decision making. Two schools of thought address this issue. The efficient market school argues that forward exchange rates do the best possible job of forecasting future spot exchange rates, and, therefore, investing in forecasting services would be a waste of money. The other school of thought, the inefficient market school, argues that companies can improve the foreign exchange market's estimate of future exchange rates (as contained in the forward rate) by investing in forecasting services. In other words, this school of thought does not believe the forward exchange rates are the best possible predictors of future spot exchange rates.

THE EFFICIENT MARKET SCHOOL   Forward exchange rates represent market participants' collective predictions of likely spot exchange rates at specified future dates. If forward exchange rates are the best possible predictor of future spot rates, it would make no sense for companies to spend additional money trying to forecast short-run exchange rate movements. Many economists believe the foreign exchange market is efficient at setting forward rates.[18] An **efficient market** is one in which prices reflect all available public information. (If forward rates reflect all available information about likely future changes in exchange rates, a company cannot beat the market by investing in forecasting services.)

Efficient Market
One in which prices reflect all available public information.

If the foreign exchange market is efficient, forward exchange rates should be unbiased predictors of future spot rates. This does not mean the predictions will be accurate in any specific situation. It means inaccuracies will not be consistently above or below future spot rates; they will be random. Many empirical tests have addressed the efficient market hypothesis. Although most of the early work seems to confirm the hypothesis (suggesting that companies should not waste their money on forecasting services) some recent studies have challenged it.[19] There is some evidence that forward rates are not unbiased predictors of future spot rates, and that more accurate predictions of future spot rates can be calculated from publicly available information.[20]

THE INEFFICIENT MARKET SCHOOL
Citing evidence against the efficient market hypothesis, some economists believe the foreign exchange market is inefficient. An **inefficient market** is one in which prices do not reflect all available information. In an inefficient market, forward exchange rates will not be the best possible predictors of future spot exchange rates.

Inefficient Market
A market in which prices do not reflect all available information.

If this is true, it may be worthwhile for international businesses to invest in forecasting services (as many do). The belief is that professional exchange rate forecasts might provide better predictions of future spot rates than forward exchange rates do. However, the track record of professional forecasting services is not that good.[21] For example, forecasting services did not predict the 1997 currency crisis that swept through Southeast Asia.

APPROACHES TO FORECASTING
Assuming the inefficient market school is correct that the foreign exchange market's estimate of future spot rates can be improved, on what basis should forecasts be prepared? Here again, there are two schools of thought. One adheres to fundamental analysis, while the other uses technical analysis.

Fundamental Analysis **Fundamental analysis** draws on economic theory to construct sophisticated econometric models for predicting exchange rate movements. The variables contained in these models typically include those we have discussed, such as relative money supply growth rates, inflation rates, and interest rates. In addition, they may include variables related to balance-of-payments positions.

Fundamental Analysis
Draws on economic theory to construct econometric models for predicting exchange rate movements.

Running a deficit on a balance-of-payments current account (a country is importing more goods and services than it is exporting) creates pressures that may result in the depreciation of the country's currency on the foreign exchange market.[22] Consider what might happen if the United States was running a persistent current account balance-of-payments deficit (as it has been). Since the United States would be importing more than it was exporting, people in other countries would be increasing their holdings of U.S. dollars. If these people were willing to hold their dollars, the dollar's exchange rate would not be influenced. However, if these people converted their dollars into other currencies, the supply of dollars in the foreign exchange market would increase (as would demand for the other currencies). This shift in demand and supply would create pressures that could lead to the depreciation of the dollar against other currencies.

This argument hinges on whether people in other countries are willing to hold dollars. This depends on such factors as U.S. interest rates, the return on holding other dollar-denominated assets such as stocks in U.S. companies, and, most importantly, inflation rates. So, in a sense, the balance-of-payments situation is not a fundamental predictor of future exchange rate movements. For example, between 1998 and 2001, the U.S. dollar appreciated against most major currencies despite a growing balance-of-payments deficit. Relatively high real interest rates in the United States, coupled with low inflation and a booming U.S. stock market that attracted inward investment from foreign capital, made the dollar very attractive to foreigners, so they did not convert their dollars into other currencies. On the contrary, they converted other currencies into dollars to invest in U.S. financial assets, such as bonds and stocks, because they believed they could earn a high return by doing so. Capital flows into the United States fueled by foreigners who wanted to buy U.S. stocks and bonds kept the dollar strong despite the current account deficit. But what makes financial assets such as stocks and bonds attractive? The answer is prevailing interest rates and inflation rates, both of which affect underlying economic growth and the real return to holding U.S. financial assets. Given this, we are back to the argument that the fundamental determinants of exchange rates are monetary growth, inflation rates, and interest rates.

Technical Analysis
Uses price and volume data to determine past trends, which are expected to continue into the future.

Technical Analysis **Technical analysis** uses price and volume data to determine past trends, which are expected to continue into the future. This approach does not rely on a consideration of economic fundamentals. Technical analysis is based on the premise that there are analyzable market trends and waves and that previous trends and waves can be used to predict future trends and waves. Since there is no theoretical rationale for this assumption of predictability, many economists compare technical analysis to fortune-telling. Despite this skepticism, technical analysis has gained favor in recent years.[23]

Currency Convertibility

Freely Convertible
When a country's government allows both residents and nonresidents to convert its currency into foreign currency.

Until this point we have invalidly assumed that the currencies of various countries are freely convertible into other currencies. Due to government restrictions, a significant number of currencies are not freely convertible into other currencies. A country's currency is said to be **freely convertible** when the country's government allows both residents and nonresidents to purchase unlimited amounts of a foreign currency with it. A currency is said to be **externally convertible** when only nonresidents may convert it into a foreign currency without any limitations. A currency is **nonconvertible** when neither residents nor nonresidents are allowed to convert it into a foreign currency.

Externally Convertible
When a country's government allows only nonresidents to convert the currency into foreign currency.

Free convertibility is not universal. Many countries place some restrictions on their residents' ability to convert the domestic currency into a foreign currency (a policy of external convertibility). Restrictions range from the relatively minor (such as restricting the amount of foreign currency they may take with them out of the country on trips) to the major (such as restricting domestic businesses' ability to take foreign currency out of the country). External convertibility restrictions can limit domestic companies' ability to invest abroad, but they present few problems for foreign companies wishing to do business in that country. For example, even if the Japanese government tightly controlled the ability of its residents to convert the yen into U.S. dollars, all U.S. businesses with deposits in Japanese banks may at any time convert all their yen into dollars and take them out of the country. Thus, a U.S. company with a subsidiary in Japan is assured that it will be able to convert the profits from its Japanese operation into dollars and take them out of the country.

Nonconvertible
When a country's government allows neither residents nor nonresidents to convert its currency into a foreign currency.

Serious problems arise, however, under a policy of nonconvertibility. This was the practice of the former Soviet Union, and it continued to be the practice in Russia for several years after the collapse of the Soviet Union. When strictly applied, nonconvertibility means that although a U.S. company doing business in a country such as Russia may be able to generate significant ruble profits, it may not convert those rubles into dollars and take them out of the country. Obviously this is not desirable for international business.

To deal with nonconvertibility problems, companies will barter instead. Venezuela traded iron ore for Caterpillar construction equipment. Caterpillar in turn sold the iron ore to Romania for farm products, which it then sold on international markets for dollars.

Governments limit convertibility to preserve their foreign exchange reserves. A country needs an adequate supply of these reserves to service its international debt commitments and to purchase imports. Governments typically impose convertibility restrictions on their currency when they fear that free convertibility will lead to a run on their foreign exchange reserves. This occurs when residents and nonresidents rush to convert their holdings of domestic currency into a foreign currency—a phenomenon generally referred to as **capital flight.** Capital flight is most likely to occur when the value of the domestic currency is depreciating rapidly because of hyperinflation, or when a country's economic prospects are shaky in other respects. Under such circumstances, both residents and nonresidents tend to believe that their money is more likely to hold its value if it is converted into a foreign currency and invested abroad. Not only will a run on foreign exchange reserves limit the country's ability to service its international debt and pay for imports, but it will also lead to a precipitous depreciation in the exchange rate as residents and nonresidents unload their holdings of domestic currency on the foreign exchange markets (thereby increasing the market supply of the country's currency). Governments fear that the rise in import prices resulting from currency depreciation will lead to further increases in inflation. This fear provides another rationale for limiting convertibility.

Companies can deal with the nonconvertibility problem by engaging in countertrade. **Countertrade** refers to a range of barterlike agreements by which goods and services can be traded for other goods and services. Countertrade can make sense when a country's currency is nonconvertible. For example, consider the deal that General Electric struck with the Romanian government when that country's currency was nonconvertible. When General Electric won a contract for a $150 million generator project in Romania, it agreed to take payment in the form of Romanian goods that could be sold for $150 million on international markets. In a similar case, the Venezuelan government negotiated a contract with Caterpillar under which Venezuela would trade 350,000 tons of iron ore for Caterpillar heavy construction equipment. Caterpillar subsequently traded the iron ore to Romania in exchange for Romanian farm products, which it then sold on international markets for dollars.[24] More recently, in a 2003 deal the government of Indonesia entered into a countertrade with Libya under which Libya

Capital Flight
When residents and nonresidents rush to convert their holdings of domestic currency into a foreign currency, usually taking place when domestic currency is depreciating rapidly or a country is facing dim economic prospects.

Countertrade
The trade of goods and services produced in one country for the goods and services of another country.

agreed to purchase $540 million in Indonesian goods, including textiles, tea, coffee, electronics, plastics, and auto parts, in exchange for 50,000 barrels per day of Libyan crude oil.[25]

How important is countertrade? Twenty years ago, a large number of nonconvertible currencies existed in the world, and countertrade was quite significant. However, in recent years many governments have made their currencies freely convertible, and the percentage of world trade that involves countertrade is probably significantly below 10 percent.[26]

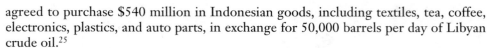

Focus on Managerial Implications

LEARNING OBJECTIVE 6
Understand the differences among translation, transaction, and economic exposure, and what mangers can do to manage each type of exposure.

This chapter contains a number of clear implications for business. First, it is critical that international businesses understand the influence of exchange rates on the profitability of trade and investment deals. Adverse changes in exchange rates can make apparently profitable deals unprofitable. As noted, the risk introduced into international business transactions by changes in exchange rates is referred to as foreign exchange risk. Foreign exchange risk is usually divided into three main categories: transaction exposure, translation exposure, and economic exposure.

Transaction Exposure

Transaction Exposure
The extent to which the income from individual transactions is affected by fluctuations in foreign exchange values.

Transaction exposure is the extent to which the income from individual transactions is affected by fluctuations in foreign exchange values. Such exposure includes obligations for the purchase or sale of goods and services at previously agreed prices and the borrowing or lending of funds in foreign currencies. For example, suppose in 2004 an American airline agreed to purchase 10 Airbus 330 aircraft for €120 million each for a total price of €1.20 billion, with delivery scheduled for 2008 and payment due then. When the contract was signed in 2001 the dollar/euro exchange rate stood at $1 = €1.10 so the American airline anticipated paying $1.09 billion for the 10 aircraft when they were delivered (€1.2 billion/1.1 = $1.09 billion). However, imagine that the value of the dollar depreciated against the euro over the intervening period, so that $1 only bought €0.80 in 2008 when payment was due ($1 = €0.80). Now the total cost is $1.5 billion (€1.2 billion/0.80 = $1.5 billion), an increase of $0.41 billion! The transaction exposure here is $0.41 billion, which is the money lost due to an adverse movement in exchange rates between the time when the deal was signed and when the aircraft were paid for.

Translation Exposure

Translation Exposure
The extent to which the reported consolidated results and balance sheets of a corporation are affected by fluctuations in foreign exchange values.

Translation exposure is the impact of currency exchange rate changes on the reported financial statements of a company. Translation exposure is concerned with the present measurement of past events. The resulting accounting gains or losses are said to be unrealized—they are "paper" gains and losses—but they are still important. Consider a U.S. firm with a subsidiary in Mexico. If the value of the Mexican peso depreciates significantly against the dollar this would substantially reduce the dollar value of the Mexican subsidiary's equity. In turn, this would reduce the total dollar value of the firm's equity reported in its consolidated balance sheet. This would raise the apparent leverage of the firm (its debt ratio), which could increase the firm's cost of borrowing and potentially limit its access to the capital market. Similarly, if an American firm has a subsidiary in the European Union, and if the value of the euro depreciates rapidly against that of the dollar over a year, this will reduce the dollar value of the euro profit made by the European subsidiary, resulting in negative translation exposure. In fact, many U.S. firms suffered from significant negative translation exposure in Europe during 2000, precisely because the euro did depreciate rapidly against the dollar. In 2002–2007, the euro rose in value against the dollar. This positive translation exposure boosted the dollar profits of American multinationals with significant operations in Europe.

Economic Exposure

Economic exposure is the extent to which a firm's future international earning power is affected by changes in exchange rates. Economic exposure is concerned with the long-run effect of changes in exchange rates on future prices, sales, and costs. This is distinct from transaction exposure, which is concerned with the effect of exchange rate changes on individual transactions, most of which are short-term affairs that will be executed within a few weeks or months. Consider the effect of wide swings in the value of the dollar on many U.S. firms' international competitiveness. The rapid rise in the value of the dollar on the foreign exchange market in the 1990s hurt the price competitiveness of many U.S. producers in world markets. U.S. manufacturers that relied heavily on exports (such as Caterpillar) saw their export volume and world market share decline. The reverse phenomenon occurred in 2000–2007, when the dollar declined against most major currencies. The fall in the value of the dollar helped increase the price competitiveness of U.S. manufacturers in world markets.

Economic Exposure
The extent to which a firm's future international earning power is affected by changes in exchange rates.

Reducing Translation and Transaction Exposure

A number of tactics can help firms minimize their transaction and translation exposure. These tactics primarily protect short-term cash flows from adverse changes in exchange rates. We have already discussed two of these tactics at length in the chapter, entering into forward exchange rate contracts and buying swaps. In addition to buying forward and using swaps, firms can minimize their foreign exchange exposure through leading and lagging payables and receivables—that is, paying suppliers and collecting payment from customers early or late depending on expected exchange rate movements. A **lead strategy** involves attempting to collect foreign currency receivables (payments from customers) early when a foreign currency is expected to depreciate and paying foreign currency payables (to suppliers) before they are due when a currency is expected to appreciate. A **lag strategy** involves delaying collection of foreign currency receivables if that currency is expected to appreciate and delaying payables if the currency is expected to depreciate. Leading and lagging involve accelerating payments from weak-currency to strong-currency countries and delaying inflows from strong-currency to weak-currency countries.

Lead and lag strategies can be difficult to implement, however. The firm must be in a position to exercise some control over payment terms. Firms do not always have this kind of bargaining power, particularly when they are dealing with important customers who are in a position to dictate payment terms. Also, because lead and lag strategies can put pressure on a weak currency, many governments limit leads and lags. For example, some countries set 180 days as a limit for receiving payments for exports or making payments for imports.

Lead Strategy
Attempting to collect foreign currency receivables early when a foreign currency is expected to depreciate and paying foreign currency payables before they are due when a currency is expected to appreciate.

Lag Strategy
Delaying collection of foreign currency receivables if that currency is expected to appreciate and delaying payables if that currency is expected to depreciate.

Reducing Economic Exposure

Reducing economic exposure requires strategic choices that go beyond the realm of financial management. The key to reducing economic exposure is to distribute the firm's productive assets to various locations so the firm's long-term financial well-being

Management FOCUS

Dealing with the Rising Euro

Udo Pfeiffer, the CEO of SMS Elotherm, a German manufacturer of machine tools to engineer crankshafts for cars, signed a deal in late November 2004, to supply the U.S. operations of DaimlerChrysler with $1.5 million worth of machines. The machines would be manufactured in Germany and exported to the United States. When the deal was signed, Pfeiffer calculated that at the agreed price, the machines would yield a profit of €30,000 each. Within three days that profit had declined by €8,000! The dollar had slid precipitously against the euro. SMS would be paid in dollars by DaimlerChrysler, but when translated back into euros, the price had declined. Since the company's costs were in euros, the declining revenues when expressed in euros were squeezing profit margins.

With the exchange rate standing at €1 = $1.33 in early December 2004, Pfeiffer was deeply worried. He knew that if the dollar declined further to around €1 = $1.50, SMS would be losing money on its sales to America. He could try to raise the dollar price of his products to compensate for the fall in the value of the dollar, but he knew that was unlikely to work. The market for machine tools was very competitive, and manufacturers were constantly pressuring machine tool companies to lower prices, not raise them.

Another small German supplier to U.S. automobile companies, Keiper, was faring somewhat better. In 2001 Keiper, which manufactures metal frames for automobile seats, opened a plant in London, Ontario, to supply the U.S. operations of DaimlerChrysler. At the time the investment was made, the exchange rate was €1 = $1. Management at Keiper had agonized over whether the investment made sense. Some in the company believed that it was better to continue exporting from Germany. Others argued that Keiper would benefit from being close to a major customer. Now with the euro appreciating every day, it looked like a smart move. Keiper had a real hedge against the rising value of the euro. But the advantages of being based in Canada were tempered by two things; first, the U.S. dollar had also depreciated against the Canadian dollar, although not by as much as its depreciation against the euro. Second, Keiper was still importing parts from Germany, and the euro had also appreciated against the Canadian dollar, raising the costs at Keiper's Ontario plant.

Source: Adapted from M. Landler, "Dollar's Fall Drains Profit of European Small Business," *The New York Times,* December 2, 2004, p. C1.

---

is not severely affected by adverse changes in exchange rates. This is a strategy that firms both large and small sometimes pursue. For example, fearing that the euro will continue to strengthen against the U.S. dollar, some European firms who do significant business in the United States have set up local production facilities in that market to ensure that a rising euro does not put them at a competitive disadvantage relative to their local rivals. Similarly, Toyota has production plants distributed around the world in part to make sure that a rising yen does not price Toyota cars out of local markets. The accompanying Management Focus discusses how two German firms tried to reduce economic exposure.

Other Steps for Managing Foreign Exchange Risk

A firm needs to develop a mechanism for ensuring it maintains an appropriate mix of tactics and strategies for minimizing its foreign exchange exposure. Although there is no universal agreement as to the components of this mechanism, a number of common themes stand out.[27] First, central control of exposure is needed to protect resources efficiently and ensure that each subunit adopts the correct mix of tactics and strategies. Many companies have set up in-house foreign exchange centers. Although such centers may not be able to execute all foreign exchange deals—particularly in large, complex multinationals where myriad transactions may be pursued simultaneously—they should at least set guidelines for the firm's subsidiaries to follow.

Second, firms should distinguish between, on one hand, transaction and translation exposure and, on the other, economic exposure. Many companies seem to focus on reducing their transaction and translation exposure and pay scant attention to economic exposure, which may have more profound long-term implications.[28] Firms need to develop strategies for dealing with economic exposure. For example, Black & Decker, the maker of power tools, has a strategy for actively managing its economic risk. The key to Black & Decker's strategy is flexible sourcing. In response to foreign exchange movements, Black & Decker can move production from one location to another to offer the most competitive pricing. Black & Decker manufactures in more than a dozen locations around the world—in Europe, Australia, Brazil, Mexico, and Japan. More than 50 percent of the company's productive assets are based outside North America. Although each of Black & Decker's factories focuses on one or two products to achieve economies of scale, there is considerable overlap. On average, the company runs its factories at no more than 80 percent capacity, so most are able to switch rapidly from producing one product to producing another or to add a product. This allows a factory's production to be changed in response to foreign exchange movements. For example, if the dollar depreciates against other currencies, the amount of imports into the United States from overseas subsidiaries can be reduced and the amount of exports from U.S. subsidiaries to other locations can be increased.[29]

Third, the need to forecast future exchange rate movements cannot be overstated, though, as we saw earlier in the chapter, this is a tricky business. No model comes close to perfectly predicting future movements in foreign exchange rates. The best that can be said is that in the short run, forward exchange rates provide the best predictors of exchange rate movements, and in the long run, fundamental economic factors—particularly relative inflation rates—should be watched because they influence exchange rate movements. Some firms attempt to forecast exchange rate movements in-house; others rely on outside forecasters. However, all such forecasts are imperfect attempts to predict the future.

Fourth, firms need to establish good reporting systems so the central finance function (or in-house foreign exchange center) can regularly monitor the firm's exposure positions. Such reporting systems should enable the firm to identify any exposed accounts, the exposed position by currency of each account, and the time periods covered.

Finally, on the basis of the information it receives from exchange rate forecasts and its own regular reporting systems, the firm should produce monthly foreign exchange exposure reports. These reports should identify how cash flows and balance sheet elements might be affected by forecasted changes in exchange rates. The reports can then be used by management as a basis for adopting tactics and strategies to hedge against undue foreign exchange risks.

Surprisingly, some of the largest and most sophisticated firms don't take such precautionary steps, exposing themselves to very large foreign exchange risks. Thus, as we have seen in this chapter, Volkswagen suffered significant losses during the early 2000s due to a failure to hedge its foreign exchange exposure.

Key Terms

foreign exchange market, p. 308

exchange rate, p. 308

foreign exchange risk, p. 309

currency speculation, p. 310

hedging, p. 310

spot exchange rate, p. 311

forward exchange, p. 312

forward exchange rate, p. 312

currency swap, p. 313

Summary

This chapter explained how the foreign exchange market works, examined the forces that determine exchange rates, and then discussed the implications of these factors for international business. Given that changes in exchange rates can dramatically alter the profitability of foreign trade and investment deals, this is an area of major interest to international business. The chapter made the following points:

1. One function of the foreign exchange market is to convert the currency of one country into the currency of another. A second function of the foreign exchange market is to provide insurance against foreign exchange risk.

2. The spot exchange rate is the exchange rate at which a dealer converts one currency into another currency on a particular day.

3. Foreign exchange risk can be reduced by using forward exchange rates. A forward exchange rate is an exchange rate governing future transactions. Foreign exchange risk can also be reduced by engaging in currency swaps. A swap is the simultaneous purchase and sale of a given amount of foreign exchange for two different value dates.

4. The law of one price holds that in competitive markets that are free of transportation costs and barriers to trade, identical products sold in different countries must sell for the same price when their price is expressed in the same currency.

5. Purchasing power parity (PPP) theory states the price of a basket of particular goods should be roughly equivalent in each country. PPP theory predicts that the exchange rate will change if relative prices change.

6. The rate of change in countries' relative prices depends on their relative inflation rates. A country's inflation rate seems to be a function of the growth in its money supply.

7. The PPP theory of exchange rate changes yields relatively accurate predictions of long-term trends in exchange rates, but not of short-term movements. The failure of PPP theory to predict exchange rate changes more accurately may be due to transportation costs, barriers to trade and investment, and the impact of psychological factors such as bandwagon effects on market movements and short-run exchange rates.

8. Interest rates reflect expectations about inflation. In countries where inflation is expected to be high, interest rates also will be high.

9. The International Fisher Effect states that for any two countries, the spot exchange rate should change in an equal amount but in the opposite direction to the difference in nominal interest rates.

10. The most common approach to exchange rate forecasting is fundamental analysis. This relies on variables such as money supply growth, inflation rates, nominal interest rates, and balance-of-payments positions to predict future changes in exchange rates.

11. In many countries, the ability of residents and nonresidents to convert local currency into a foreign currency is restricted by government policy. A government restricts the convertibility of its currency to protect the country's foreign exchange reserves and to halt any capital flight.

12. Problematic for international business is a policy of nonconvertibility, which prohibits

Hill: Global Business
Today, Sixth Edition

9. The Foreign Exchange
Market

Text

© The McGraw–Hill
Companies, 2009

345

residents and nonresidents from exchanging local currency for foreign currency. Nonconvertibility makes it very difficult to engage in international trade and investment in the country. One way of coping with the nonconvertibility problem is to engage in countertrade—to trade goods and services for other goods and services.

13. The three types of exposure to foreign exchange risk are transaction exposure, translation exposure, and economic exposure.

14. Tactics that insure against transaction and translation exposure include buying forward, using currency swaps, leading and lagging payables and receivables, manipulating transfer prices, using local debt financing, accelerating

dividend payments, and adjusting capital budgeting to reflect foreign exchange exposure.

15. Reducing a firm's economic exposure requires strategic choices about how the firm's productive assets are distributed around the globe.

16. To manage foreign exchange exposure effectively, the firm must exercise centralized oversight over its foreign exchange hedging activities, recognize the difference between transaction exposure and economic exposure, forecast future exchange rate movements, establish good reporting systems within the firm to monitor exposure positions, and produce regular foreign exchange exposure reports that can be used as a basis for action.

Critical Thinking and Discussion Questions

1. The interest rate on South Korean government securities with one-year maturity is 4 percent, and the expected inflation rate for the coming year is 2 percent. The interest rate on U.S. government securities with one-year maturity is 7 percent, and the expected rate of inflation is 5 percent. The current spot exchange rate for Korean won is $1 = W1,200. Forecast the spot exchange rate one year from today. Explain the logic of your answer.

2. Two countries, Great Britain and the United States, produce just one good: beef. Suppose the price of beef in the United States is $2.80 per pound and in Britain it is £3.70 per pound.
   a. According to PPP theory, what should the dollar/pound spot exchange rate be?
   b. Suppose the price of beef is expected to rise to $3.10 in the United States and to £4.65 in Britain. What should the one-year forward dollar/pound exchange rate be?
   c. Given your answers to parts a and b, and given that the current interest rate in the United States is 10 percent, what would you expect the current interest rate to be in Britain?

3. Reread the Management Focus on Volkswagen, then answer the following questions:
   a. Why do you think management at Volkswagen decided to hedge only

30 percent of the company's foreign currency exposure in 2003? What would have happened if 70 percent of the exposure had been hedged?
   b. Why do you think the value of the U.S. dollar declined against that of the euro in 2003?
   c. Apart from hedging through the foreign exchange market, what else can Volkswagen do to reduce its exposure to future declines in the value of the U.S. dollar against the euro?

4. You manufacture wine goblets. In mid-June you receive an order for 10,000 goblets from Japan. Payment of ¥400,000 is due in mid-December. You expect the yen to rise from its present rate of $1 = ¥130 to $1 = ¥100 by December. You can borrow yen at 6 percent a year. What should you do?

5. You are the CFO of a U.S. firm whose wholly owned subsidiary in Mexico manufactures component parts for your U.S. assembly operations. The subsidiary has been financed by bank borrowings in the United States. One of your analysts told you that the Mexican peso is expected to depreciate by 30 percent against the dollar on the foreign exchange markets over the next year. What actions, if any, should you take?

Research Task globalEDGE   http://globalEDGE.msu.edu

Use the globalEDGE Resource Desk (http://globalEDGE.msu.edu/ResourceDesk/) to complete the following exercises:

1. You are assigned the duty of ensuring the availability of 100 million Japanese Yen for a payment scheduled for tomorrow. Your company possesses only US Dollars, so identify a website that provides *real-time exchange rates*, and find the spot exchange rate for Japanese Yen. How many dollars do you have to spend to acquire the amount of Yen required?

2. Your company imports olive oil from Italy to sell in the U.S. The exchange rate fluctuations over the past year have had significant impact on your bottom line. In preparing an annual report for your company, you would like to include a one-year *currency chart* showing the movement of the U.S. Dollar versus the Euro. Describe the pattern you see. Over the past year, has the Dollar gained or lost ground versus the Euro?

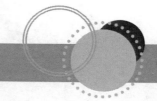

closing case

The Curse of the Strong Dollar at STMicro

Europe's STMicro is the world's sixth largest manufacturer of semiconductor chips with sales of nearly $9 billion. The company makes chips for mobile phones, printers, and cars, among other things. It counts Nokia, the world's largest maker of wireless handsets, among its customers. Formed in 1987 from a merger between and Italian and French firms, the majority of STMicro's operations have long been in Western Europe. During the early 2000s, when the dollar was strong against the euro, this worked in STMicro's favor. Some 70 percent of the company's costs were denominated in euros while semiconductors were priced in U.S. dollars. The combination of a weak euro and a strong dollar translated into robust profits for STMicro.

However, in 2003 the euro began to rise against the dollar, rapidly shifting the profit calculus against STMicro. The euro, which traded as low as €1 = $0.83 in October 2000, had reached parity of €1 = $1.00 in late 2002. Few analysts predicted a rapid rise in the value of the euro against the dollar during 2003. The experts were wrong; by late 2003 the exchange rate stood at €1 = $1.20. The rise continued through 2004, with the exchange rate peaking at €1 = $1.32 in early 2005. It fell back to €1 = $1.20 in early 2006 before rising back to at €1 = $1.30 by late 2006.

One cause of the rise in the value of the euro against the dollar was record U.S. foreign trade deficits in 2002–2006.

The U.S. economy grew rapidly during 2003–2006, sucking in imports from foreign nations while generating anemic export growth. The result was a flow of dollars out of the United States into the hands of foreigners. Historically, foreigners had reinvested those dollars in the United States, and the return flow had kept the dollar strong despite persistent trade deficits. This didn't happen to the same extent in 2003–2006. Instead, many foreigners sold the dollars they received for other currencies, such as the euro, Japanese yen, or British pound. They did this because they had become increasingly pessimistic about the future value of the dollar and were reducing their dollar holdings accordingly. Their pessimism was itself a function of two factors. First, U.S. government officials stated that they would prefer a weaker dollar to increase the competitiveness of U.S. companies in the global marketplace (the theory being that a falling dollar would make U.S. exports more competitive). With the government talking the dollar down, many foreigners decided to reduce their dollar holdings. Second, the U.S. government ran record budget deficits in 2003–2006, and these were projected to remain high for some time. Looking at this, some foreigners concluded that the U.S. government might be forced to finance its spending by expanding the supply of dollars (i.e., by printing money), which would lead to inflation and reduce the value of the dollar even further. Thus, they sold dollars and purchased currencies thought to be less inflation-prone.

For STMicro, the results of these macroeconomic events were serious. The company does very little currency hedging, so as the dollar fell, the euro value of STMicro's sales compressed, while costs, being largely dominated in euros, stayed high. Although strong global chip sales helped to offset the fall in the value of the dollar, STMicro's profits still slumped in 2004 and 2005. In response, STMicro's CEO, Carlo Bozotti, pledged to take some $500 million out of the company's cost structure, primarily by shutting some high-cost European operations, cutting 3,000 jobs, and moving production to Asia where it planned to add 1,500 jobs. Bozotti described the strategy as one of "real hedging" that would allow STMicro to move production from Europe to Asia, and back if necessary, to deal with the consequences of shifts in exchange rates against the dollar.

Sources: M. Pesola, "STMicro Unveils More Job Cuts in Chip Making," *Financial Times,* May 17, 2005, p. 22; B. Lagrotteria and C. Bryan-Low, "Dealing with the Dollar: Strong Euro Bedevils EU Firms," *The Wall Street Journal*, June 21, 2005, p. A14; and H. Schoemaker, "STMicro Profit Slips, but 1st Quarter Looks Upbeat," *The Wall Street Journal*, January 26, 2006, p. B5.

Case Discussion Questions

1. In retrospect, could the fall in the value of the dollar against the euro have been predicted in 2003?

2. What was the fundamental reason for the decline in the value of the dollar against the euro in 2003–2006? To what extent is the decline in the value of the dollar consistent with the theories of exchange rate determination discussed in this chapter?

3. Why do you think STMicro did very little currency hedging? Was this wise?

Part 4 Global Money System

LEARNING OBJECTIVES

After you have read this chapter you should:

1 Be familiar with the historical development of the modern global monetary system.

2 Discuss the role played by the World Bank and the IMF in the international monetary system.

3 Be familiar with the differences between a fixed and floating exchange rate system.

4 Know what exchange rate regimes are used in the world today and why countries adopt different exchange rate regimes.

5 Understand the debate surrounding the role of the IMF in the management of financial crises.

6 Appreciate the implications of the global monetary system for currency management and business strategy.

chapter 10

The International Monetary System

Argentina's Monetary Crisis

In the 1990s Argentina was the darling of the international financial community. The country had fixed the exchange rate for the Argentinean peso to the U.S. dollar at $1 = 1 peso. Maintaining the exchange rate had required Argentina to adopt strict anti-inflationary policies, which had succeeded in bringing down Argentina's historically high inflation rate and stimulated economic growth. By 2001, however, the economy was running into trouble. Global economic growth slumped, and demand for many of the commodities that Argentina exported had fallen in tandem. Argentina's large neighbor and main trading partner, Brazil, was grappling with a financial crisis of its own and had devalued its currency against the dollar, and thus the peso, effectively pricing many Argentinean goods out of its market. To compound matters, the dollar had appreciated against most major currencies, taking the peso up with it, and making Argentinean goods more expensive in other international markets.

Starting in 1999, the Argentinean economy entered a tailspin that was to take unemployment up to 25 percent by 2002. Anticipating that the country would have to devalue the peso against the dollar, corporations and individuals started to pull money out of pesos, placing their funds in dollar accounts. As people sold pesos, the Argentinean government used its foreign exchange reserves to buy them back in an effort to maintain the exchange rate at $1 = 1 peso. The government quickly ran down its reserves, and in 2000, the country negotiated a loan from the International Monetary Fund (IMF) to prop up its currency. In return for the loan, which ultimately reached $15 billion, the Argentinean government agreed to adopt a financial austerity program to balance its budget. However, conditions in the country continued to deteriorate, in no small part, some critics claimed, because the strict IMF policies made an already bad recession worse. By late 2001, with government tax revenues plunging as the economy contracted, the

Argentinean government defaulted on its debt repayments, effectively rendering $80 billion of government-issued bonds worthless. This created a massive crisis of confidence, which put further pressure on the peso. Throughout 2001 the Argentina government had been trying to support the value of the peso with the help of the loan from the IMF, but it was becoming ever more difficult, and the debt default was the final nail in the coffin. In early 2002, the government bowed to the inevitable and decoupled the peso from the dollar, allowing it to float freely. It immediately fell to $1 = 3.5 pesos.

The fall in the value of the peso helped to revive Argentinean commodity exports, which were now much cheaper for foreign buyers. A rebound in global economic growth after 2001 also helped, as did an economic recovery in neighboring Brazil. By 2003, the economy was once more on a growth path and unemployment was falling. In 2005 Argentina repaid its entire debt to the IMF. Commenting on the debt repayment, Argentinean President Nestor Kirchner criticized the IMF for promoting policies that "provoked poverty and pain on the Argentine people." While that view was popular in Argentina, some outside observers worried that, freed from IMF constraints, the Argentinean economy would return to its historic norm of loose monetary policy and high inflation. ●

Sources: Guillermo Nielsen, "Inside Argentina's Financial Crisis," *Euromoney,* March 2006, pp. 21–28; "Nestor Unbounded: The IMF and Argentina," *The Economist,* December 24, 2005, p. 12; and "Which Is the Victim? Argentina and the IMF," *The Economist,* March 6, 2004, pp. 82–83.

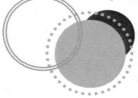

Introduction

International Monetary System
The institutional arrangements countries adopt that govern exchange rates.

Floating Exchange Rate
A system under which the exchange rate for converting one currency into another is continuously adjusted depending on the law of supply and demand.

What happened in Argentina in the early 2000s goes to the heart of the subject matter covered in this chapter. Here we look at the international monetary system, and its role in determining exchange rates. The **international monetary system** refers to the institutional arrangements that govern exchange rates. In Chapter 9 we assumed the foreign exchange market was the primary institution for determining exchange rates, and the impersonal market forces of demand and supply determined the relative value of any two currencies (i.e., their exchange rate). Furthermore, we explained that the demand and supply of currencies is influenced by their respective countries' relative inflation rates and interest rates. When the foreign exchange market determines the relative value of a currency, we say that the country is adhering to a **floating exchange rate** regime. The world's four major trading currencies—the U.S. dollar, the European Union's euro, the Japanese yen, and the British pound—are all free to float against each other. Thus, their exchange rates are determined by market forces and fluctuate against each other day to day, if not minute to minute. However, the exchange rates of many currencies are not determined by the free play of market forces; other institutional arrangements are adopted.

Many of the world's developing nations peg their currencies, primarily to the dollar or the euro. A **pegged exchange rate** means the value of the currency is fixed relative to a reference currency, such as the U.S. dollar, and then the exchange rate between that currency and other currencies is determined by the reference currency exchange rate. Argentina, for example, pegged its exchange rate to the dollar throughout the 1990s, before allowing it to float in 2002 (see the opening case). Similarly, many of the states around the Gulf of Arabia have long pegged their currencies to the dollar.

Other countries, while not adopting a formal pegged rate, try to hold the value of their currency within some range against an important reference currency such as the U.S. dollar, or a "basket" of currencies. This is often referred to as a **dirty float.** It is a float because in theory, the value of the currency is determined by market forces, but it is a *dirty float* (as opposed to a clean float) because the central bank of a country will intervene in the foreign exchange market to try to maintain the value of its currency if it depreciates too rapidly against an important reference currency. This has been the policy adopted by the Chinese since July 2005. The value of the Chinese currency, the yuan, has been linked to a basket of other currencies, including the dollar, yen, and euro, and it is allowed to vary in value against individual currencies, but only within tight limits.

Still other countries have operated with a **fixed exchange rate,** in which the values of a set of currencies are fixed against each other at some mutually agreed on exchange rate. Before the introduction of the euro in 2000, several member states of the European Union operated with fixed exchange rates within the context of the **European Monetary System (EMS).** For a quarter of a century after World War II, the world's major industrial nations participated in a fixed exchange rate system. Although this system collapsed in 1973, some still argue that the world should attempt to reestablish it.

In this chapter, we will explain how the international monetary system works and point out its implications for international business. To understand how the system works, we must review its evolution. We will begin with a discussion of the gold standard and its breakup during the 1930s. Then we will discuss the 1944 Bretton Woods conference. This established the basic framework for the post–World War II international monetary system. The Bretton Woods system called for fixed exchange rates against the U.S. dollar. Under this fixed exchange rate system, the value of most currencies in terms of U.S. dollars was fixed for long periods and allowed to change only under a specific set of circumstances. The Bretton Woods conference also created two major international institutions that play a role in the international monetary system—the International Monetary Fund (IMF) and the World Bank. The IMF was given the task of maintaining order in the international monetary system; the World Bank's role was to promote development.

Today, both these institutions continue to play major roles in the world economy and in the international monetary system. In 1997 and 1998, for example, the IMF helped several Asian countries deal with the dramatic decline in the value of their currencies that occurred during the Asian financial crisis that started in 1997. The IMF was also actively involved in helping Argentina manage its financial crisis in 2001. In late 2007, for example, the IMF had programs in 68 countries, the majority in the developing world, and had some $17 billion in loans to nations.[1] At times of financial crisis, these loan amounts can spike much higher (there were $71 billion in outstanding loans in 2005). There has been a vigorous debate about the role of the IMF and to a lesser extent the World Bank and the appropriateness of their policies for many developing nations. Several prominent critics claim that in some cases, IMF policies make things worse, not better (this was argued to be the case in Argentina, where very restrictive policies may have worsened the crisis). The debate over the role of the IMF took on new urgency given the institution's extensive involvement in the economies of developing countries during the late 1990s and early 2000s. Accordingly, we shall discuss the issue in some depth.

Pegged Exchange Rate
A system under which the value of a country's currency is fixed relative to a reference currency, and then the exchange rate between that currency and other currencies is determined by the reference currency exchange rate.

Dirty Float
A system under which a country's currency is nominally allowed to float freely against other currencies, but in which the government will intervene if it believes the currency has deviated too far from its fair value.

Fixed Exchange Rate
A system under which the exchange rate for converting one currency into another is set at a constant rate.

European Monetary System (EMS)
System for managing exchange rates of EU currencies against each other. Now replaced by the euro.

The Bretton Woods system of fixed exchange rates collapsed in 1973. Since then, the world has operated with a mixed system in which some currencies are allowed to float freely, but many are either managed by government intervention or pegged to another currency. We will explain the reasons for the failure of the Bretton Woods system as well as the nature of the present system. We will also discuss how pegged exchange rate systems work. More than three decades after the breakdown of the Bretton Woods system, the debate continues over what kind of exchange rate regime is best for the world. Some economists advocate a system in which major currencies are allowed to float against each other. Others argue for a return to a fixed exchange rate regime similar to the one established at Bretton Woods. This debate is intense and important, and we will examine the arguments of both sides.

Finally, we will discuss the implications of all this material for international business. We will see how the exchange rate policy adopted by a government can have an important impact on the outlook for business operations in a given country. Pegging the value of the peso to the U.S. dollar, for example, turned out to have serious consequences for the competitiveness of Argentinean businesses. As the dollar appreciated on foreign exchange markets, so did the peso, effectively pricing many Argentinean goods out of world markets and contributing to an economic recession in that nation. If government exchange rate policies result in currency devaluation, for example, exporters based in that country may benefit as their products become more price competitive in foreign markets. This too happened in Argentina after the 2002 devaluation. Alternatively, importers will suffer from an increase in the price of their products, which can trigger inflationary pressure in a nation. We will also look at how the policies adopted by the IMF can have an impact on the economic outlook for a country and, accordingly, on the costs and benefits of doing business in that country.

The Gold Standard

LEARNING OBJECTIVE 1
Be familiar with the historical development of the modern global monetary system.

The gold standard had its origin in the use of gold coins as a medium of exchange, unit of account, and store of value—a practice that dates to ancient times. When international trade was limited in volume, payment for goods purchased from another country was typically made in gold or silver. However, as the volume of international trade expanded in the wake of the Industrial Revolution, a more convenient means of financing international trade was needed. Shipping large quantities of gold and silver around the world to finance international trade seemed impractical. The solution adopted was to arrange for payment in paper currency and for governments to agree to convert the paper currency into gold on demand at a fixed rate.

MECHANICS OF THE GOLD STANDARD Pegging currencies to gold and guaranteeing convertibility is known as the **gold standard.** By 1880, most of the world's major trading nations, including Great Britain, Germany, Japan, and the United States, had adopted the gold standard. Given a common gold standard, the value of any currency in units of any other currency (the exchange rate) was easy to determine.

Gold Standard
The practice of pegging currencies to gold and guaranteeing convertibility.

For example, under the gold standard, one U.S. dollar was defined as equivalent to 23.22 grains of "fine" (pure) gold. Thus, one could, in theory, demand that the U.S. government convert that one dollar into 23.22 grains of gold. Since there are 480 grains in an ounce, one ounce of gold cost $20.67 (480/23.22). The amount of a currency needed to purchase one ounce of gold was referred to as the **gold par value.** The British pound was valued at 113 grains of fine gold. In other words, one ounce of gold cost £4.25 (480/113). From the gold par values of pounds and dollars, we can calculate what the exchange rate was for converting pounds into dollars; it was £1 = $4.87 (i.e., $20.67/£4.25).

Gold Par Value
The amount of currency needed to purchase one ounce of gold.

STRENGTH OF THE GOLD STANDARD The great strength claimed for the gold standard was that it contained a powerful mechanism for achieving balance-of-trade equilibrium by all countries.[2] A country is said to be in **balance-of-trade equilibrium** when the income its residents earn from exports is equal to the money its residents pay to other countries for imports (the current account of its balance of payments is in balance). Suppose there are only two countries in the world, Japan and the United States. Imagine Japan's trade balance is in surplus because it exports more to the United States than it imports from the United States. Japanese exporters are paid in U.S. dollars, which they exchange for Japanese yen at a Japanese bank. The Japanese bank submits the dollars to the U.S. government and demands payment of gold in return. (This is a simplification of what would occur, but it will make our point.)

Under the gold standard, when Japan has a trade surplus, there will be a net flow of gold from the United States to Japan. These gold flows automatically reduce the U.S. money supply and swell Japan's money supply. As we saw in Chapter 9, there is a close connection between money supply growth and price inflation. An increase in money supply will raise prices in Japan, while a decrease in the U.S. money supply will push U.S. prices downward. The rise in the price of Japanese goods will decrease demand for these goods, while the fall in the price of U.S. goods will increase demand for these goods. Thus, Japan will start to buy more from the United States, and the United States will buy less from Japan, until a balance-of-trade equilibrium is achieved.

This adjustment mechanism seems so simple and attractive that even today, almost 70 years after the final collapse of the gold standard, some people believe the world should return to a gold standard.

THE PERIOD BETWEEN THE WARS: 1918–1939 The gold standard worked reasonably well from the 1870s until the start of World War I in 1914, when it was abandoned. During the war, several governments financed part of their massive military expenditures by printing money. This resulted in inflation, and by the war's end in 1918, price levels were higher everywhere. The United States returned to the gold standard in 1919, Great Britain in 1925, and France in 1928.

Great Britain returned to the gold standard by pegging the pound to gold at the pre-war gold parity level of £4.25 per ounce, despite substantial inflation between 1914 and 1925. This priced British goods out of foreign markets, which pushed the country into a deep depression. When foreign holders of pounds lost confidence in Great Britain's commitment to maintaining its currency's value, they began converting their holdings of pounds into gold. The British government saw that it could not satisfy the demand for gold without seriously depleting its gold reserves, so it suspended convertibility in 1931.

The United States followed suit and left the gold standard in 1933 but returned to it in 1934, raising the dollar price of gold from $20.67 per ounce to $35 per ounce. Since more dollars were needed to buy an ounce of gold than before, the implication was that the dollar was worth less. This effectively amounted to a devaluation of the dollar relative to other currencies. Thus, before the devaluation, the pound/dollar exchange rate was £1 = $4.87, but after the devaluation it was £1 = $8.24. By reducing the price of U.S. exports and increasing the price of imports, the government was trying to create employment in the United States by boosting output (the U.S. government was basically using the exchange rate as an instrument of trade policy, something it now accuses China of doing). However, a number of other countries adopted a similar tactic, and in the cycle of competitive devaluations that soon emerged, no country could win.

The net result was the shattering of any remaining confidence in the system. With countries devaluing their currencies at will, one could no longer be certain how much gold a currency could buy. Instead of holding onto another country's currency, people

Balance-of-Trade Equilibrium
Reached when the income a country's residents earned from exports equals the money they pay for imports.

often tried to change it into gold immediately, lest the country devalue its currency in the intervening period. This put pressure on the gold reserves of various countries, forcing them to suspend gold convertibility. By the start of World War II in 1939, the gold standard was dead.

The Bretton Woods System

LEARNING OBJECTIVE 2
Discuss the role played by the World Bank and the IMF in the international monetary system.

In 1944, at the height of World War II, representatives from 44 countries met at Bretton Woods, New Hampshire, to design a new international monetary system. With the collapse of the gold standard and the Great Depression of the 1930s fresh in their minds, these statesmen were determined to build an enduring economic order that would facilitate postwar economic growth. There was consensus that fixed exchange rates were desirable. In addition, the conference participants wanted to avoid the senseless competitive devaluations of the 1930s, and they recognized that the gold standard would not ensure this. The major problem with the gold standard as previously constituted was that no multinational institution could stop countries from engaging in competitive devaluations.

The agreement reached at Bretton Woods established two multinational institutions— the International Monetary Fund (IMF) and the World Bank. The task of the IMF would be to maintain order in the international monetary system and that of the World Bank would be to promote general economic development. The Bretton Woods agreement also called for a system of fixed exchange rates that would be policed by the IMF. Under the agreement, all countries were to fix the value of their currency in terms of gold but were not required to exchange their currencies for gold. Only the dollar remained convertible into gold—at a price of $35 per ounce. Each country decided what it wanted its exchange rate to be vis-à-vis the dollar and then calculated the gold par value of the currency based on that selected dollar exchange rate. All participating countries agreed to try to maintain the value of their currencies within 1 percent of the par value by buying or selling currencies (or gold) as needed. For example, if foreign exchange dealers were selling more of a country's currency than demanded, that country's government would intervene in the foreign exchange markets, buying its currency in an attempt to increase demand and maintain its gold par value.

In 1944, at the height of World War II, representatives from 44 countries met at Bretton Woods, New Hampshire, to design a new international monetary system. Pictured here is Henry Morgenthau, then secretary of the Treasury, addressing the opening meeting of the conference where the IMF and the World Bank were established.

Another aspect of the Bretton Woods agreement was a commitment not to use devaluation as a weapon of competitive trade policy. However, if a currency became too weak to defend, a devaluation of up to 10 percent would be allowed without any formal approval by the IMF. Larger devaluations required IMF approval.

THE ROLE OF THE IMF   The IMF Articles of Agreement were heavily influenced by the worldwide financial collapse, competitive devaluations, trade wars, high unemployment, hyperinflation in Germany and elsewhere, and general economic disintegration that occurred between the two world wars. The aim of the Bretton Woods agreement, of which the IMF was the main custodian, was to try to avoid a repetition of that chaos through a combination of discipline and flexibility.

Discipline   A fixed exchange rate regime imposes discipline in two ways. First, the need to maintain a fixed exchange rate puts a brake on competitive devaluations and brings stability to the world trade environment. Second, a fixed exchange rate regime imposes monetary discipline on countries, thereby curtailing price inflation. For example, consider what would happen under a fixed exchange rate regime if Great Britain rapidly increased its money supply by printing pounds. As explained in Chapter 9, the increase in money supply would lead to price inflation. Given fixed exchange rates, inflation would make British goods uncompetitive in world markets, while the prices of imports would become more attractive in Great Britain. The result would be a widening trade deficit in Great Britain, with the country importing more than it exports. To correct this trade imbalance under a fixed exchange rate regime, Great Britain would be required to restrict the rate of growth in its money supply to bring price inflation back under control. Thus, fixed exchange rates are seen as a mechanism for controlling inflation and imposing economic discipline on countries.

Flexibility   Although monetary discipline was a central objective of the Bretton Woods agreement, a rigid policy of fixed exchange rates was recognized as too inflexible. It would probably break down just as the gold standard had. In some cases, a country's attempts to reduce its money supply growth and correct a persistent balance-of-payments deficit could force the country into recession and create high unemployment. The architects of the Bretton Woods agreement wanted to avoid high unemployment, so they built limited flexibility into the system. Two major features of the IMF Articles of Agreement fostered this flexibility: IMF lending facilities and adjustable parities.

The IMF stood ready to lend foreign currencies to members to tide them over during short periods of balance-of-payments deficits, when a rapid tightening of monetary or fiscal policy would hurt domestic employment. A pool of gold and currencies contributed by IMF members provided the resources for these lending operations. A persistent balance-of-payments deficit can lead to a depletion of a country's reserves of foreign currency, forcing it to devalue its currency. By providing deficit-laden countries with short-term foreign currency loans, IMF funds would buy time for countries to bring down their inflation rates and reduce their balance-of-payments deficits. The belief was that such loans would reduce pressures for devaluation and allow for a more orderly and less painful adjustment.

Countries were to be allowed to borrow a limited amount from the IMF without adhering to any specific agreements. However, extensive drawings from IMF funds would require a country to agree to increasingly stringent IMF supervision of its macroeconomic policies. Heavy borrowers from the IMF must agree to monetary and fiscal conditions set down by the IMF, which typically included IMF-mandated targets on domestic money supply growth, exchange rate policy, tax policy, government spending, and so on.

The system of adjustable parities allowed for the devaluation of a country's currency by more than 10 percent if the IMF agreed that a country's balance of payments was in "fundamental disequilibrium." The term *fundamental disequilibrium* was not defined in the IMF's Articles of Agreement, but it was intended to apply to countries that had suffered permanent adverse shifts in the demand for their products. Without devaluation, such a country would experience high unemployment and a persistent trade deficit until the domestic price level had fallen far enough to restore a balance-of-payments equilibrium. The belief was that devaluation could help sidestep a painful adjustment process in such circumstances.

THE ROLE OF THE WORLD BANK   The official name for the World Bank is the International Bank for Reconstruction and Development (IBRD). When the Bretton Woods participants established the World Bank, the need to reconstruct the war-torn economies of Europe was foremost in their minds. The bank's initial mission was to help finance the building of Europe's economy by providing low-interest loans. As it turned out, the World Bank was overshadowed in this role by the Marshall Plan, under which the United States lent money directly to European nations to help them rebuild. So the bank turned its attention to "development" and began lending money to Third World nations. In the 1950s, the bank concentrated on public-sector projects. Power stations, road building, and other transportation investments were much in favor. During the 1960s, the bank also began to lend heavily in support of agriculture, education, population control, and urban development.

The bank lends money under two schemes. Under the IBRD scheme, money is raised through bond sales in the international capital market. Borrowers pay what the bank calls a market rate of interest—the bank's cost of funds plus a margin for expenses. This "market" rate is lower than commercial banks' market rate. Under the IBRD scheme, the bank offers low-interest loans to risky customers whose credit rating is often poor, such as the governments of underdeveloped nations.

A second scheme is overseen by the International Development Association (IDA), an arm of the bank created in 1960. Resources to fund IDA loans are raised through subscriptions from wealthy members such as the United States, Japan, and Germany. IDA loans go only to the poorest countries. Borrowers have 50 years to repay at an interest rate of 1 percent a year. The world's poorest nations receive grants and noninterest loans.

The Collapse of the Fixed Exchange Rate System

LEARNING OBJECTIVE 1
Be familiar with the historical development of the modern global monetary system.

The system of fixed exchange rates established at Bretton Woods worked well until the late 1960s, when it began to show signs of strain. The system finally collapsed in 1973, and since then we have had a managed-float system. To understand why the system collapsed, one must appreciate the special role of the U.S. dollar in the system. As the only currency that could be converted into gold, and as the currency that served as the reference point for all others, the dollar occupied a central place in the system. Any pressure on the dollar to devalue could wreak havoc with the system, and that is what occurred.

Most economists trace the breakup of the fixed exchange rate system to the U.S. macroeconomic policy package of 1965–1968.[3] To finance both the Vietnam conflict and his welfare programs, President Lyndon Johnson backed an increase in U.S. government spending that was not financed by an increase in taxes. Instead, it was financed by an increase in the money supply, which led to a rise in price inflation from less than 4 percent in 1966 to close to 9 percent by 1968. At the same time, the rise in government spending had stimulated the economy. With more money in their pockets, people spent more—particularly on imports—and the U.S. trade balance began to deteriorate. (Note parallels with the situation prevailing in the United States in 2002–2008 when the government again expanded spending to pay for a foreign war and financed that spending through monetary expansion—in essence, more government borrowing—that stimulated the economy and led to a surge in imports. Some observers worry that the implied expansion in the U.S. money supply may ultimately lead to higher inflation.)

The increase in inflation and the worsening of the U.S. foreign trade position gave rise to speculation in the foreign exchange market that the dollar would be devalued. Things came to a head in the spring of 1971 when U.S. trade figures showed that for the first time since 1945, the United States was importing more than it was exporting. This set off massive purchases of German deutsche marks in the foreign exchange market by speculators who guessed that the mark would be revalued against the dollar. On a single day, May 4, 1971, the Bundesbank (Germany's central bank) had to buy $1 billion to hold the dollar/deutsche mark exchange rate at its fixed exchange rate given the great demand for deutsche marks. On the morning of May 5, the Bundesbank purchased another $1 billion during the first hour of foreign exchange trading! At that point, the Bundesbank faced the inevitable and allowed its currency to float.

In the weeks following the decision to float the deutsche mark, the foreign exchange market became increasingly convinced that the dollar would have to be devalued. However, devaluation of the dollar was no easy matter. Under the Bretton Woods provisions, any other country could change its exchange rates against all currencies simply by fixing its dollar rate at a new level. But as the key currency in the system, the dollar could be devalued only if all countries agreed to simultaneously revalue against the dollar. Many countries did not want this because it would make their products more expensive relative to U.S. products.

To force the issue, President Nixon announced in August 1971 that the dollar was no longer convertible into gold. He also announced that a new 10 percent tax on imports would remain in effect until U.S. trading partners agreed to revalue their currencies against the dollar. This brought the trading partners to the bargaining table, and in December 1971 an agreement was reached to devalue the dollar by about 8 percent against foreign currencies. The import tax was then removed.

The problem was not solved, however. The U.S. balance-of-payments position continued to deteriorate throughout 1972, while the nation's money supply continued to expand at an inflationary rate. Speculation continued to grow that the dollar was still overvalued and that a second devaluation would be necessary. In anticipation, foreign exchange dealers began converting dollars to deutsche marks and other currencies. After a massive wave of speculation in February 1972, which culminated with European central banks spending $3.6 billion on March 1 to try to prevent their currencies from appreciating against the dollar, the foreign exchange market was closed. When the foreign exchange market reopened March 19, the currencies of Japan and most European countries were floating against the dollar, although many developing countries continued to peg their currency to the dollar, and many do to this day. At that time, the switch to a floating system was viewed as a temporary response to unmanageable speculation in the foreign exchange market. But it is now more than 30 years since the Bretton Woods system of fixed exchange rates collapsed, and the temporary solution looks permanent.

Another Perspective

United States off the Gold Standard

When Nixon took the United States off the gold standard in 1971, his decision established the dollar as the standard against which other currencies would be measured. The U.S. gold reserves, which in 1945 had held 80 percent of all gold reserves worldwide, had been under serious pressure since France, under the leadership of Charles De Gaulle, had demanded to convert the French dollar reserves to gold in 1965, the first of many central bank requests. Nixon's decision set up the dollar to be the de facto standard of the new floating system, and it continues that way today.

The Bretton Woods system had an Achilles' heel: The system could not work if its key currency, the U.S. dollar, was under speculative attack. The Bretton Woods system could work only as long as the U.S. inflation rate remained low and the United States did not run a balance-of-payments deficit. Once these things occurred, the system soon became strained to the breaking point.

The Floating Exchange Rate Regime

LEARNING OBJECTIVE 1
Be familiar with the historical development of the modern global monetary system.

The floating exchange rate regime that followed the collapse of the fixed exchange rate system was formalized in January 1976 when IMF members met in Jamaica and agreed to the rules for the international monetary system that are in place today.

THE JAMAICA AGREEMENT
The Jamaica meeting revised the IMF's Articles of Agreement to reflect the new reality of floating exchange rates. The main elements of the Jamaica agreement include the following:

- Floating rates were declared acceptable. IMF members were permitted to enter the foreign exchange market to even out "unwarranted" speculative fluctuations.
- Gold was abandoned as a reserve asset. The IMF returned its gold reserves to members at the current market price, placing the proceeds in a trust fund to help poor nations. IMF members were permitted to sell their own gold reserves at the market price.
- Total annual IMF quotas—the amount member countries contribute to the IMF—were increased to $41 billion. (Since then they have been increased to $311 billion while the membership of the IMF has been expanded to include 184 countries.) Non-oil-exporting, less developed countries were given greater access to IMF funds.

After Jamaica, the IMF continued its role of helping countries cope with macroeconomic and exchange rate problems, albeit within the context of a radically different exchange rate regime.

EXCHANGE RATES SINCE 1973
Since March 1973, exchange rates have become much more volatile and less predictable than they were between 1945 and 1973.[4] This volatility has been partly due to a number of unexpected shocks to the world monetary system, including:

- The oil crisis in 1971, when the Organization of Petroleum Exporting Countries (OPEC) quadrupled the price of oil. The harmful effect of this on the U.S. inflation rate and trade position resulted in a further decline in the value of the dollar.
- The loss of confidence in the dollar that followed a sharp rise in the U.S. inflation rate in 1977–1978.
- The oil crisis of 1979, when OPEC once again increased the price of oil dramatically—this time it was doubled.
- The unexpected rise in the dollar between 1980 and 1985, despite a deteriorating balance-of-payments picture.
- The rapid fall of the U.S. dollar against the Japanese yen and German deutsche mark between 1985 and 1987, and against the yen between 1993 and 1995.
- The partial collapse of the European Monetary System in 1992.
- The 1997 Asian currency crisis, when the Asian currencies of several countries, including South Korea, Indonesia, Malaysia, and Thailand, lost between 50 percent and 80 percent of their value against the U.S. dollar in a few months.
- The decline in the value of the US dollar in the mid to late 2000s.

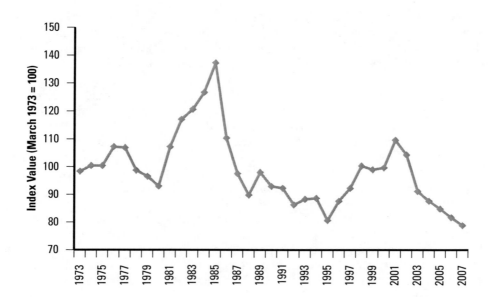

10.1 figure

Major Currencies' Dollar Index, 1973–2007

Source: Constructed by the author from Federal Reserve Board statistics at www.federalreserve.gov/releases/H10/summary/.

Figure 10.1 summarizes how the value of the U.S. dollar has fluctuated against an index of major trading currencies between 1973 and 2007. (The index, which was set equal to 100 in March 1973, is a weighted average of the foreign exchange values of the U.S. dollar against currencies that circulate widely outside the country of issue.) An interesting phenomenon in Figure 10.1 is the rapid rise in the value of the dollar between 1980 and 1985 and its subsequent fall between 1985 and 1988. A similar, though less pronounced, rise and fall in the value of the dollar occurred between 1995 and 2007. We will briefly discuss the rise and fall of the dollar during these periods, since this tells us something about how the international monetary system has operated in recent years.[5]

The rise in the value of the dollar between 1980 and 1985 occurred when the United States was running a large and growing trade deficit, importing substantially more than it exported. Conventional wisdom would suggest that the increased supply of dollars in the foreign exchange market as a result of the trade deficit should lead to a reduction in the value of the dollar, but as shown in Figure 10.1 it increased in value. Why?

A number of favorable factors overcame the unfavorable effect of a trade deficit. Strong economic growth in the United States attracted heavy inflows of capital from foreign investors seeking high returns on capital assets. High real interest rates attracted foreign investors seeking high returns on financial assets. At the same time, political turmoil in other parts of the world, along with relatively slow economic growth in the developed countries of Europe, helped create the view that the United States was a good place to invest. These inflows of capital increased the demand for dollars in the foreign exchange market, which pushed the value of the dollar upward against other currencies.

The fall in the value of the dollar between 1985 and 1988 was caused by a combination of government intervention and market forces. The rise in the dollar, which priced U.S. goods out of foreign markets and made imports relatively cheap, had contributed to a dismal trade picture. In 1985, the United States posted a record-high trade deficit of more than $160 billion. This led to growth in demands for protectionism in the United States. In September 1985, the finance ministers and central bank governors of the so-called Group of Five major industrial countries (Great Britain, France, Japan, Germany, and the United States) met at the Plaza Hotel in New York and reached what was later referred to as the Plaza Accord. They announced that it would be desirable for most major currencies to appreciate vis-à-vis the U.S. dollar and pledged to intervene in the foreign exchange markets, selling dollars, to encourage this objective. The dollar had already begun to weaken in the summer of 1985, and this announcement further accelerated the decline.

The dollar continued to decline until 1987. The governments of the Group of Five began to worry that the dollar might decline too far, so the finance ministers of the Group of Five met in Paris in February 1987 and reached a new agreement known as the Louvre Accord. They agreed that exchange rates had been realigned sufficiently and pledged to support the stability of exchange rates around their current levels by intervening in the foreign exchange markets when necessary to buy and sell currency. Although the dollar continued to decline for a few months after the Louvre Accord, the rate of decline slowed, and by early 1988 the decline had ended.

Except for a brief speculative flurry around the time of the Persian Gulf War in 1991, the dollar was relatively stable for the first half of the 1990s. However, in the late 1990s the dollar again began to appreciate against most major currencies, including the euro after its introduction, even though the United States was still running a significant balance-of-payments deficit. Once again, the driving force for the appreciation in the value of the dollar was that foreigners continued to invest in U.S. financial assets, primarily stocks and bonds, and the inflow of money drove up the value of the dollar on foreign exchange markets. The inward investment was due to a belief that U.S. financial assets offered a favorable rate of return.

By 2002, however, foreigners had started to lose their appetite for U.S. stocks and bonds, and the inflow of money into the United States slowed. Instead of reinvesting dollars earned from exports to the United States in U.S. financial assets, they exchanged those dollars for other currencies, particularly euros, to invest them in non-dollar-denominated assets. One reason for this was the continued growth in the U.S. trade deficit, which hit a record $767 billion in 2005 (by 2007 it had "fallen" to $712 billion). Although the U.S. trade deficits had been hitting records for decades, this deficit was the largest ever when measured as a percentage of the country's GDP (7 percent of GDP in 2005).

The record deficit meant that ever more dollars were flowing out of the United States into foreign hands, and those foreigners were less inclined to reinvest those dollars in the United States at a rate required to keep the dollar stable. This growing reluctance of foreigners to invest in the United States was in turn due to several factors. First, there was a slowdown in U.S. economic activity during 2001–2002, and a somewhat slow recovery thereafter, which made U.S. assets less attractive. Second, the U.S. government's budget deficit expanded rapidly after 2001, hitting a record $318 billion in 2005 before falling back to $158 billion in 2007. This led to fears that ultimately the budget deficit would be financed by an expansionary monetary policy that could lead to higher price inflation. Since inflation would reduce the value of the dollar, foreigners decided to hedge against this risk by holding fewer dollar assets in their investment portfolios. Third, from 2003 onward U.S. government officials began to "talk down" the value of the dollar, in part because the administration believed that a cheaper

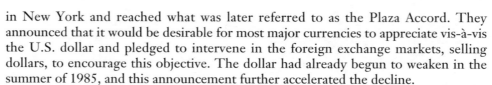

Another Perspective

Floating Dollars and OPEC

In the early 1970s, dollars became the currency for oil trades through an agreement between the United States and OPEC. This commitment of OPEC to dollar oil sales was made secretly by the United States and Saudi Arabia, first, and then the United States and other OPEC countries. The impact of petrodollars, as they are known, is huge. Petrodollars lead oil-producing countries to be likely to invest their dollar surpluses in the United States. In fact, OPEC dollar surpluses help to fund the U.S. trade deficit. Iraq, Iran, and Venezuela have at times initiated a push to move trading in oil to the euro, but so far OPEC has stayed with the dollar. (Peter Dale Scott, *Drugs, Oil, and War: The United States in Afghanistan, Colombia, and Indochina,* 2003, pp. 41–42)

Country FOCUS

The U.S. Dollar, Oil Prices, and Recycling Petrodollars

Between 2004 and 2008 global oil prices surged. They surpassed $100 a barrel in early 2008, up from around $20 in 2001. The rise in oil prices was due to a combination of greater than expected demand for oil, particularly from rapidly developing giants such as China and India; tight supplies; and perceived geopolitical risks in the Middle East, the world's largest oil-producing region. With these conditions predicted to persist for some time, oil prices could remain high for the foreseeable future.

The surge in oil prices has been a windfall for oil-producing countries. Collectively they earned $700 billion in oil revenues in 2005, and well over $1 trillion in 2007, some 64 percent of which went to members of the Organization of Petroleum Exporting Countries (OPEC). Saudi Arabia, the world's largest oil producer, reaped a major share of that. Since oil is priced in U.S. dollars, the rise in oil prices has translated into a substantial increase in the dollar holdings of oil producers (the dollars earned from the sale of oil are often referred to as *petrodollars*). In essence, rising oil prices represent a net transfer of dollars from oil consumers in countries such as the United States, to oil producers in Russia, Saudi Arabia, and Venezuela. The question now being asked is: What will they do with those dollars?

One possibility is that the producing countries will spend their petrodollars on public-sector infrastructure, such as health services, education, roads, and telecommunications systems. This could boost economic growth in those countries and pull in foreign imports, which would help to counterbalance the trade surpluses enjoyed by oil producers and support global economic growth. There is some evidence that spending has picked up in many oil-producing countries. However, according to the IMF, OPEC members only spent about 40 percent of their windfall profits from higher oil prices in 2002–2006. The last time oil prices increased sharply in 1979, oil producers significantly ramped up spending on infrastructure, only to find themselves saddled with excessive debt when oil prices collapsed a few years later. This time they are being more cautious.

Another possibility is that the oil producers will invest a good chunk of the dollars they earn from oil sales in dollar-denominated assets, such as U.S. bonds, stocks, and real estate. So far, this seems to have been happening, with OPEC members in particular funneling dollars back into U.S. assets, mostly bonds and stocks. The implication is that by recycling their petrodollars, oil producers are helping to finance the large and growing current account deficit of the United States, enabling it to pay its growing oil import bills.

A third possibility is that oil producers will invest in non-dollar-denominated assets, such as European and Japanese bonds and stocks. This too has been happening. Some OPEC investors have purchased not just small equity positions, but entire companies. In 2005, for example, Dubai International Capital purchased the Tussauds Group, a British theme-park firm, and DP World of Dubai purchased P&O, Britain's biggest port and ferries group. (P&O held the contract to manage operations at six U.S. ports, and the takeover bid led to a storm of protest in the United States from those who feared that an Arab takeover of P&O might create a security risk.) Despite these examples, between 2005 and 2007, the bulk of petrodollars appear to have been recycled into dollar-denominated assets, in large part because U.S. interest rates increased throughout 2004–2007. If that flow of petrodollars should dry up, the dollar could fall sharply.

Sources: "Recycling the Petrodollars; Oil Producers' Surpluses," *The Economist*, November 12, 2005, pp. 101–02; S. Johnson, "Dollar's Rise Aided by OPEC Holdings," *Financial Times*, December 5, 2005, p. 17; and "The Petrodollar Puzzle," *The Economist*, June 9, 2007, p. 86.

---

dollar would increase exports and reduce imports, thereby improving the U.S. balance of trade position.[6] Foreigners saw this as a signal that the U.S. government would not intervene in the foreign exchange markets to prop up the value of the dollar, which increased their reluctance to reinvest dollars earned from export sales in U.S. financial assets. As a result of these factors, demand for dollars weakened and the value of the dollar slid on the foreign exchange markets, hitting an index value of 80.19 in December 2004, the lowest value since the index began in 1973. Although the dollar strengthened a little in 2005 and 2006, many commentators believe that it could resume its fall in coming years particularly if large holders of U.S. dollars, such as oil-producing states, decide to diversify their foreign exchange holdings (see the accompanying Country Focus for a discussion of this possibility). Indeed, the dollar's fall renewed in 2007, and by November 2007 the dollar index against major currencies stood at 72.5, down from 102.5 in November 2002.

Thus, we see that in recent history the value of the dollar has been determined by both market forces and government intervention. Under a floating exchange rate regime, market forces have produced a volatile dollar exchange rate. Governments have sometimes responded by intervening in the market—buying and selling dollars—in an attempt to limit the market's volatility and to correct what they see as overvaluation (in 1985) or potential undervaluation (in 1987) of the dollar. In addition to direct intervention, the value of the dollar has frequently been influenced by statements from government officials. The dollar may not have declined by as much as it did in 2004, for example, had not U.S. government officials publicly ruled out any action to stop the decline. Paradoxically, a signal not to intervene can affect the market. The frequency of government intervention in the foreign exchange market explains why the current system is sometimes thought of as a **managed-float system** or a dirty-float system.

Managed-Float System
System under which some currencies are allowed to float freely, but the majority are either managed by government intervention or pegged to another currency.

Fixed versus Floating Exchange Rates

LEARNING OBJECTIVE 3
Be familiar with the differences between a fixed and floating exchange rate system.

The breakdown of the Bretton Woods system has not stopped the debate about the relative merits of fixed versus floating exchange rate regimes. Disappointment with the system of floating rates in recent years has led to renewed debate about the merits of fixed exchange rates. In this section, we review the arguments for fixed and floating exchange rate regimes.[7] We will discuss the case for floating rates before discussing why many commentators are disappointed with the experience under floating exchange rates and yearn for a system of fixed rates.

THE CASE FOR FLOATING EXCHANGE RATES   The case in support of floating exchange rates has two main elements: monetary policy autonomy and automatic trade balance adjustments.

Monetary Policy Autonomy   It is argued that under a fixed system, a country's ability to expand or contract its money supply as it sees fit is limited by the need to maintain exchange rate parity. Monetary expansion can lead to inflation, which puts downward pressure on a fixed exchange rate (as predicted by the PPP theory; see Chapter 9). Similarly, monetary contraction requires high interest rates (to reduce the demand for money). Higher interest rates lead to an inflow of money from abroad, which puts upward pressure on a fixed exchange rate. Thus, to maintain exchange rate parity under a fixed system, countries were limited in their ability to use monetary policy to expand or contract their economies.

Advocates of a floating exchange rate regime argue that removal of the obligation to maintain exchange rate parity would restore monetary control to a government. If a government faced with unemployment wanted to increase its money supply to stimulate domestic demand and reduce unemployment, it could do so unencumbered by the need to maintain its exchange rate. While monetary expansion might lead to inflation, this would lead to a depreciation in the country's currency. If PPP theory is correct, the resulting currency depreciation on the foreign exchange markets should offset the effects of inflation. Although under a floating exchange rate regime, domestic inflation would have an impact on the exchange rate, it should have no impact on businesses' international cost competitiveness due to exchange rate depreciation. The rise in domestic costs should be exactly offset by the fall in the value of the country's currency on the foreign exchange markets. Similarly, a government could use monetary policy to contract the economy without worrying about the need to maintain parity.

Trade Balance Adjustments Under the Bretton Woods system, if a country developed a permanent deficit in its balance of trade (importing more than it exported) that could not be corrected by domestic policy, this would require the IMF to agree to a currency devaluation. Critics of this system argue that the adjustment mechanism works much more smoothly under a floating exchange rate regime. They argue that if a country is running a trade deficit, the imbalance between the supply and demand of that country's currency in the foreign exchange markets (supply exceeding demand) will lead to depreciation in its exchange rate. In turn, by making its exports cheaper and its imports more expensive, an exchange rate depreciation should correct the trade deficit.

THE CASE FOR FIXED EXCHANGE RATES
The case for fixed exchange rates rests on arguments about monetary discipline, speculation, uncertainty, and the lack of connection between the trade balance and exchange rates.

Monetary Discipline We discussed the nature of monetary discipline inherent in a fixed exchange rate system when we discussed the Bretton Woods system. The need to maintain a fixed exchange rate parity ensures that governments do not expand their money supplies at inflationary rates. While advocates of floating rates argue that each country should be allowed to choose its own inflation rate (the monetary autonomy argument), advocates of fixed rates argue that governments all too often give in to political pressures and expand the monetary supply far too rapidly, causing unacceptably high price inflation. A fixed exchange rate regime would ensure that this does not occur.

Speculation Critics of a floating exchange rate regime also argue that speculation can cause fluctuations in exchange rates. They point to the dollar's rapid rise and fall during the 1980s, which they claim had nothing to do with comparative inflation rates and the U.S. trade deficit, but everything to do with speculation. They argue that when foreign exchange dealers see a currency depreciating, they tend to sell the currency in the expectation of future depreciation regardless of the currency's longer-term prospects. As more traders jump on the bandwagon, the expectations of depreciation are realized. Such destabilizing speculation tends to accentuate the fluctuations around the exchange rate's long-run value. It can damage a country's economy by distorting export and import prices. Thus, advocates of a fixed exchange rate regime argue that such a system will limit the destabilizing effects of speculation.

Uncertainty Speculation also adds to the uncertainty surrounding future currency movements that characterizes floating exchange rate regimes. The unpredictability of exchange rate movements in the post–Bretton Woods era has made business planning difficult, and it adds risk to exporting, importing, and foreign investment activities. Given a volatile exchange rate, international businesses do not know how to react to the changes—and often they do not react. Why change plans for exporting, importing, or foreign investment after a 6 percent fall in the dollar this month, when the dollar may rise 6 percent next month? This uncertainty, according to the critics, dampens the growth of international trade and investment. They argue that a fixed exchange rate, by eliminating such uncertainty, promotes the growth of international trade and investment. Advocates of a floating system reply that the forward exchange market insures against the risks associated with exchange rate fluctuations (see Chapter 9), so the adverse impact of uncertainty on the growth of international trade and investment has been overstated.

Trade Balance Adjustments   Those in favor of floating exchange rates argue that floating rates help adjust trade imbalances. Critics question the closeness of the link between the exchange rate and the trade balance. They claim trade deficits are determined by the balance between savings and investment in a country, not by the external value of its currency.[8] They argue that depreciation in a currency will lead to inflation (due to the resulting increase in import prices). This inflation will wipe out any apparent gains in cost competitiveness that arise from currency depreciation. In other words, a depreciating exchange rate will not boost exports and reduce imports, as advocates of floating rates claim; it will simply boost price inflation. In support of this argument, those who favor floating rates point out that the 40 percent drop in the value of the dollar between 1985 and 1988 did not correct the U.S. trade deficit. In reply, advocates of a floating exchange rate regime argue that between 1985 and 1992, the U.S. trade deficit fell from more than $160 billion to about $70 billion, and they attribute this in part to the decline in the value of the dollar.

WHO IS RIGHT?   Which side is right in the vigorous debate between those who favor a fixed exchange rate and those who favor a floating exchange rate? Economists cannot agree. Business, as a major player on the international trade and investment scene, has a large stake in the resolution of the debate. Would international business be better off under a fixed regime, or are flexible rates better? The evidence is not clear.

However, we do know that a fixed exchange rate regime modeled along the lines of the Bretton Woods system will not work. Speculation ultimately broke the system, a phenomenon that advocates of fixed rate regimes claim is associated with floating exchange rates! Nevertheless, a different kind of fixed exchange rate system might be more enduring and might foster the stability that would facilitate more rapid growth in international trade and investment. In the next section, we look at potential models for such a system and the problems with such systems.

Exchange Rate Regimes in Practice

LEARNING OBJECTIVE 4
Know what exchange rate regimes are used in the world today, and why countries adopt different exchange rate regimes.

Governments around the world pursue a number of different exchange rate policies. These range from a pure "free float" where the exchange rate is determined by market forces to a pegged system that has some aspects of the pre-1973 Bretton Woods system of fixed exchange rates. Figure 10.2 summarizes the exchange rate policies adopted by member states of the IMF in 2006. Some 14 percent of the IMF's members allow their currency to float freely. Another 26 percent intervene in only a limited way

figure 10.2

Exchange Rate Policies, IMF Members, 2006

Source: Constructed by the author from IMF data.

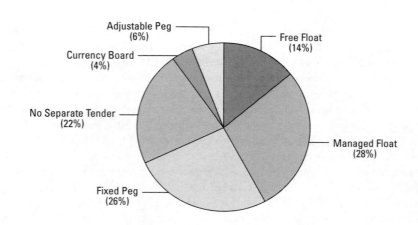

Adjustable Peg (6%)
Currency Board (4%)
No Separate Tender (22%)
Fixed Peg (26%)
Free Float (14%)
Managed Float (28%)

(the so-called managed float). A further 28 percent of IMF members now have no separate legal tender of their own. These include the European Union countries that have adopted the euro, and effectively given up their own currencies, along with smaller states mostly in Africa or the Caribbean that have no domestic currency and have adopted a foreign currency as legal tender within their borders, typically the U.S. dollar or the euro. The remaining countries use more inflexible systems, including a fixed peg arrangement (26 percent) under which they peg their currencies to other currencies, such as the U.S. dollar or the euro, or to a basket of currencies. Other countries have adopted a system under which their exchange rate is allowed to fluctuate against other currencies within a target zone (an adjustable peg system). In this section, we will look more closely at the mechanics and implications of exchange rate regimes that rely on a currency peg or target zone.

PEGGED EXCHANGE RATES   Under a pegged exchange rate regime, a country will peg the value of its currency to that of a major currency so that, for example, as the U.S. dollar rises in value, its own currency rises too. Pegged exchange rates are popular among many of the world's smaller nations. As with a full fixed exchange rate regime, the great virtue claimed for a pegged exchange rate is that it imposes monetary discipline on a country and leads to low inflation. For example, if Belize pegs the value of the Belizean dollar to that of the U.S. dollar so that US$1 = B$1.97 (the peg as of 2007), then the Belizean government must make sure the inflation rate in Belize is similar to that in the United States. If the Belizean inflation rate is greater than the U.S. inflation rate, this will lead to pressure to devalue the Belizean dollar (i.e., to alter the peg). To maintain the peg, the Belizean government would be required to rein in inflation. Of course, for a pegged exchange rate to impose monetary discipline on a country, the country whose currency is chosen for the peg must also pursue sound monetary policy.

Evidence shows that adopting a pegged exchange rate regime moderates inflationary pressures in a country. An IMF study concluded that countries with pegged exchange rates had an average annual inflation rate of 8 percent, compared with 14 percent for intermediate regimes and 16 percent for floating regimes.[9] However, many countries operate with only a nominal peg and in practice are willing to devalue their currency rather than pursue a tight monetary policy. It can be very difficult for a smaller country to maintain a peg against another currency if capital is flowing out of the country and foreign exchange traders are speculating against the currency. Something like this occurred in 1997 when a combination of adverse capital flows and currency speculation forced several Asian countries, including Thailand and Malaysia, to abandon pegs against the U.S. dollar and let their currencies float freely. Malaysia and Thailand would not have been in this position had they dealt with a number of problems that began to arise in their economies during the 1990s, including excessive private-sector debt and expanding current account trade deficits.

CURRENCY BOARDS   Hong Kong's experience during the 1997 Asian currency crisis added a new dimension to the debate over how to manage a pegged exchange rate. During late 1997 when other Asian currencies were collapsing, Hong Kong maintained the value of its currency against the U.S. dollar at about HK$15 = $7.8 despite several concerted speculative attacks. Hong Kong's currency board has been given credit for this success. A country that introduces a **currency board** commits itself to converting its domestic currency on demand into another currency at a fixed exchange rate. To make this commitment credible, the currency board holds reserves of foreign currency equal at the fixed exchange rate to at least 100 percent of the domestic currency issued. The system used in Hong Kong means its currency

Currency Board
A country's currency authority that holds reserves of foreign currency equal at the fixed exchange rate to at least 100 percent of the domestic currency issued in order to keep inflation down.

must be fully backed by the U.S. dollar at the specified exchange rate. This is still not a true fixed exchange rate regime, because the U.S. dollar, and by extension the Hong Kong dollar, floats against other currencies, but it has some features of a fixed exchange rate regime.

Under this arrangement, the currency board can issue additional domestic notes and coins only when there are foreign exchange reserves to back it. This limits the ability of the government to print money and, thereby, create inflationary pressures. Under a strict currency board system, interest rates adjust automatically. If investors want to switch out of domestic currency into, for example, U.S. dollars, the supply of domestic currency will shrink. This will cause interest rates to rise until it eventually becomes attractive for investors to hold the local currency again. In the case of Hong Kong, the interest rate on three-month deposits climbed as high as 20 percent in late 1997, as investors switched out of Hong Kong dollars and into U.S. dollars. The dollar peg held, however, and interest rates declined again.

Since its establishment in 1983, the Hong Kong currency board has weathered several storms. This success persuaded several other countries in the developing world to consider a similar system. Argentina introduced a currency board in 1991 (but abandoned it in 2002) and Bulgaria, Estonia, and Lithuania have all gone down this road in recent years (seven IMF members had currency boards in 2006). Despite interest in the arrangement, however, critics are quick to point out that currency boards have their drawbacks.[10] If local inflation rates remain higher than the inflation rate in the country to which the currency is pegged, the currencies of countries with currency boards can become uncompetitive and overvalued (this is what happened in the case of Argentina, which had a currency board, as detailed in the opening case). Also, under a currency board system, government lacks the ability to set interest rates. Interest rates in Hong Kong, for example, are effectively set by the U.S. Federal Reserve. In addition, economic collapse in Argentina in 2001 and the subsequent decision to abandon its currency board dampened much of the enthusiasm for this mechanism of managing exchange rates.

Crisis Management by the IMF

LEARNING OBJECTIVE 5
Understand the debate surrounding the role of the IMF in the management of financial crises.

Many observers initially believed that the collapse of the Bretton Woods system in 1973 would diminish the role of the IMF within the international monetary system. The IMF's original function was to provide a pool of money from which members could borrow, short term, to adjust their balance-of-payments position and maintain their exchange rate. Some believed the demand for short-term loans would be considerably diminished under a floating exchange rate regime. A trade deficit would presumably lead to a decline in a country's exchange rate, which would help reduce imports and boost exports. No temporary IMF adjustment loan would be needed. Consistent with this, after 1973, most industrialized countries tended to let the foreign exchange market determine exchange rates in response to demand and supply. No major industrial country has borrowed funds from the IMF since the mid-1970s, when Great Britain and Italy did. Since the early 1970s, the rapid development of global capital markets has allowed developed countries such as Great Britain and the United States to finance their deficits by borrowing private money, as opposed to

Another Perspective

IMF: All That Independent?
The IMF promotes global monetary cooperation and economic growth. It was formed at the 1944 Bretton Woods conference where the United Nations began to take shape. Although it exists in relationship with the UN, the IMF operates independently, and today that independence is a source of criticism. Technically speaking, however, the IMF reports to its 185 member countries through its board of governors. U.S. Secretary of the Treasury Henry M. Paulson, Jr., is the U.S. member of the board, and Ben Bernanke, chairman of the U.S. Federal Reserve Board, is the alternate member. They control the U.S. share of the votes on the board of governors, 16.77 percent.

drawing on IMF funds. Despite these developments, the activities of the IMF have expanded over the past 30 years. By 2007, the IMF had 185 members, 68 of which had an IMF program in place. In 1997, the institution implemented its largest rescue packages, committing more than $110 billion in short-term loans to three troubled Asian countries—South Korea, Indonesia, and Thailand. This was followed by additional IMF rescue packages in Turkey, Russia, Argentina, and Brazil.

The IMF's activities have expanded because periodic financial crises have continued to hit many economies in the post–Bretton Woods era, particularly among the world's developing nations. The IMF has repeatedly lent money to nations experiencing financial crises, requesting in return that the governments enact certain macroeconomic policies. Critics of the IMF claim these policies have not always been as beneficial as the IMF might have hoped and in some cases may have made things worse. Following the IMF loans to several Asian economies, these criticisms reached new levels and a vigorous debate was waged as to the appropriate role of the IMF. In this section, we shall discuss some of the main challenges the IMF has had to deal with over the past three decades and review the ongoing debate over the role of the IMF.

FINANCIAL CRISES IN THE POST–BRETTON WOODS ERA

A number of broad types of financial crises have occurred over the past 30 years, many of which have required IMF involvement. A **currency crisis** occurs when a speculative attack on the exchange value of a currency results in a sharp depreciation in the value of the currency or forces authorities to expend large volumes of international currency reserves and sharply increase interest rates to defend the prevailing exchange rate. This is what happened in Brazil in 2002, and the IMF stepped in to help stabilize the value of the Brazilian currency on foreign exchange markets. A **banking crisis** refers to a loss of confidence in the banking system that leads to a run on banks, as individuals and companies withdraw their deposits. A **foreign debt crisis** is a situation in which a country cannot service its foreign debt obligations, whether private-sector or government debt.

These crises tend to have common underlying macroeconomic causes: high relative price inflation rates, a widening current account deficit, excessive expansion of domestic borrowing, and asset price inflation (such as sharp increases in stock and property prices).[11] At times, elements of currency, banking, and debt crises may be present simultaneously, as in the 1997 Asian crisis and the 2000–2002 Argentinean crisis.

To assess the frequency of financial crises, the IMF looked at the macroeconomic performance of a group of 53 countries from 1975 to 1997 (22 of these countries were developed nations, and 31 were developing countries).[12] The IMF found there had been 158 currency crises, including 55 episodes in which a country's currency declined by more than 25 percent. There were also 54 banking crises. The IMF's data suggest that developing nations were more than twice as likely to experience currency and banking crises as developed nations. It is not surprising, therefore, that most of the IMF's loan activities since the mid-1970s have been targeted toward developing nations.

Here we look at two crises that have been of particular significance in terms of IMF involvement since the early 1990s—the 1995 Mexican currency crisis and the 1997 Asian financial crisis. These crises were the result of excessive foreign borrowings, a weak or poorly regulated banking system, and high inflation rates. These factors came together to trigger simultaneous debt and currency crises. Checking the resulting crises required IMF involvement.

MEXICAN CURRENCY CRISIS OF 1995

The Mexican peso had been pegged to the dollar since the early 1980s when the International Monetary Fund made it a condition for lending money to the Mexican government to help bail the

Currency Crisis
When a speculative attack on the exchange value of a currency results in a sharp depreciation of the currency or forces authorities to expend large volumes of international currency reserves and sharply increase interest rates to defend the prevailing exchange rate.

Banking Crisis
When individuals and companies lose confidence in the banking system and withdraw their deposits in what is called a *run on banks*.

Foreign Debt Crisis
A situation in which a country cannot service its foreign debt obligations, whether private-sector or government debt.

country out of a 1982 financial crisis. Under the IMF-brokered arrangement, the peso had been allowed to trade within a tolerance band of plus or minus 3 percent against the dollar. The band was also permitted to "crawl" down daily, allowing for an annual peso depreciation of about 4 percent against the dollar. The IMF believed that the need to maintain the exchange rate within a fairly narrow trading band would force the Mexican government to adopt stringent financial policies to limit the growth in the money supply and contain inflation.

Until the early 1990s, it looked as if the IMF policy had worked. However, the strains were beginning to show by 1994. Since the mid-1980s, Mexican producer prices had risen 45 percent more than prices in the United States, and yet there had not been a corresponding adjustment in the exchange rate. By late 1994, Mexico was running a $17 billion trade deficit, which amounted to some 6 percent of the country's gross domestic product, and there had been an uncomfortably rapid expansion in public- and private-sector debt. Despite these strains, Mexican government officials had been stating publicly that they would support the peso's dollar peg at around $1 = 3.5 pesos by adopting appropriate monetary policies and by intervening in the currency markets if necessary. Encouraged by such statements, $64 billion of foreign investment money poured into Mexico between 1990 and 1994 as corporations and money managers sought to take advantage of the booming economy.

However, many currency traders concluded the peso would have to be devalued, and they began to dump pesos on the foreign exchange market. The government tried to hold the line by buying pesos and selling dollars, but it lacked the foreign currency reserves required to halt the speculative tide (Mexico's foreign exchange reserves fell from $6 billion at the beginning of 1994 to less than $3.5 billion at the end of the year). In mid-December 1994, the Mexican government abruptly announced a devaluation. Immediately, much of the short-term investment money that had flowed into Mexican stocks and bonds over the previous year reversed its course, as foreign investors bailed out of peso-denominated financial assets. This exacerbated the sale of the peso and contributed to the rapid 40 percent drop in its value.

The IMF stepped in again, this time arm in arm with the U.S. government and the Bank for International Settlements. Together the three institutions pledged close to $50 billion to help Mexico stabilize the peso and to redeem $47 billion of public- and private-sector debt that was set to mature in 1995. Of this amount, $20 billion came from the U.S. government and another $18 billion came from the IMF (which made Mexico the largest recipient of IMF aid up to that point). Without the aid package, Mexico would probably have defaulted on its debt obligations, and the peso would have gone into free fall. As is normal in such cases, the IMF insisted on tight monetary policies and further cuts in public spending, both of which helped push the country into a deep recession. However, the recession was relatively short-lived, and by 1997 the country was once more on a growth path, had pared down its debt, and had paid back the $20 billion borrowed from the U.S. government ahead of schedule.[13]

THE ASIAN CRISIS The financial crisis that erupted across Southeast Asia during the fall of 1997 emerged as the biggest challenge to date for the IMF. Holding the crisis in check required IMF loans to help the shattered economies of Indonesia, Thailand, and South Korea stabilize their currencies. In addition, although they did not request IMF loans, the economies of Japan, Malaysia, Singapore, and the Philippines were also hurt by the crisis.

The seeds of this crisis were sown during the previous decade when these countries were experiencing unprecedented economic growth. Although there were and remain important differences between the individual countries, a number of elements were common to most. Exports had long been the engine of economic growth in these countries. From 1990 to 1996, the value of exports from Malaysia had grown by 18 percent annually, Thai exports had grown by 16 percent per year, Singapore's by 15 percent, Hong Kong's by 14 percent, and those of South Korea and Indonesia by 12 percent annually.[14]

The nature of these exports had also shifted in recent years from basic materials and products such as textiles to complex and increasingly high-technology products, such as automobiles, semiconductors, and consumer electronics.

The Investment Boom   The wealth created by export-led growth helped fuel an investment boom in commercial and residential property, industrial assets, and infrastructure. The value of commercial and residential real estate in cities such as Hong Kong and Bangkok started to soar. This fed a building boom the likes of which had never been seen in Asia. Heavy borrowing from banks financed much of this construction. As for industrial assets, the success of Asian exporters encouraged them to make bolder investments in industrial capacity. This was exemplified most clearly by South Korea's giant diversified conglomerates, or *chaebol*, many of which had ambitions to build a major position in the global automobile and semiconductor industries.

An added factor behind the investment boom in most Southeast Asian economies was the government. In many cases, the governments had embarked on huge infrastructure projects. In Malaysia, for example, a new government administrative center was being constructed in Putrajaya for M$20 billion (U.S. $8 billion at the pre-July 1997 exchange rate), and the government was funding the development of a massive high-technology communications corridor and the huge Bakun dam, which at a cost of M$13.6 billion was to be the most expensive power-generation plant in the country.[15] Throughout the region, governments also encouraged private businesses to invest in certain sectors of the economy in accordance with "national goals" and "industrialization strategy." In South Korea, long a country where the government played a proactive role in private-sector investments, President Kim Young-Sam urged the *chaebol* to invest in new factories as a way of boosting economic growth. South Korea enjoyed an investment-led economic boom in 1994–1995, but at a cost. The *chaebol*, always reliant on heavy borrowings, built up massive debts that were equivalent, on average, to four times their equity.[16]

In Indonesia, President Suharto had long supported investments in a network of an estimated 300 businesses owned by his family and friends in a system known as "crony capitalism." Many of these businesses were granted lucrative monopolies by the president. For example, Suharto announced in 1995 that he had decided to manufacture a national car, built by a company owned by one of his sons, Hutomo Mandala Putra, in association with Kia Motors of South Korea. To support the venture, a consortium of Indonesian banks was "ordered" by the government to offer almost $700 million in start-up loans to the company.[17]

By the mid-1990s, Southeast Asia was in the grips of an unprecedented investment boom, much of it financed with borrowed money. Between 1990 and 1995, gross domestic investment grew by 16.3 percent annually in Indonesia, 16 percent in Malaysia, 15.3 percent in Thailand, and 7.2 percent in South Korea. By comparison, investment grew by 4.1 percent annually over the same period in the United States and 0.8 percent in all high-income economies.[18] And the rate of investment accelerated in 1996. In Malaysia, for example, spending on investment accounted for a remarkable 43 percent of GDP in 1996.[19]

Excess Capacity   As the volume of investments ballooned during the 1990s, often at the bequest of national governments, the quality of many of these investments declined significantly. The investments often were made on the basis of unrealistic projections about future demand conditions. The result was significant excess capacity. For example, South Korean *chaebol* investments in semiconductor factories surged in 1994 and 1995 when a temporary global shortage of dynamic random access memory chips (DRAMs) led to sharp price increases for this product. However, supply shortages had disappeared by 1996 and excess capacity was beginning to make itself felt, just as the South Koreans started to bring new DRAM factories on stream. The results were predictable; prices for DRAMs plunged, and the earnings of South Korean DRAM manufacturers fell by 90 percent, which meant it was difficult for them to make scheduled payments on the debt they had taken on to build the extra capacity.[20]

In another example, a building boom in Thailand resulted in excess capacity in residential and commercial property. By early 1997, an estimated 365,000 apartment units were unoccupied in Bangkok. With another 100,000 units scheduled to be completed in 1997, years of excess demand in the Thai property market had been replaced by excess supply. By one estimate, Bangkok's building boom had produced enough excess space by 1997 to meet its residential and commercial needs for five years.[21]

The Debt Bomb By early 1997 what was happening in the South Korean semiconductor industry and the Bangkok property market was being played out elsewhere in the region. Massive investments in industrial assets and property had created excess capacity and plunging prices, while leaving the companies that had made the investments groaning under huge debt burdens that they were now finding it difficult to service.

To make matters worse, much of the borrowing had been in U.S. dollars, as opposed to local currencies. This had originally seemed like a smart move. Throughout the region, local currencies were pegged to the dollar, and interest rates on dollar borrowings were generally lower than rates on borrowings in domestic currency. Thus, it often made economic sense to borrow in dollars if the option was available. However, if the governments could not maintain the dollar peg and their currencies started to depreciate against the dollar, this would increase the size of the debt burden when measured in the local currency. Currency depreciation would raise borrowing costs and could result in companies defaulting on their debt obligations.

Expanding Imports A final complicating factor was that by the mid-1990s, although exports were still expanding across the region, imports were too. The investments in infrastructure, industrial capacity, and commercial real estate were sucking in foreign goods at unprecedented rates. To build infrastructure, factories, and office buildings, Southeast Asian countries were purchasing capital equipment and materials from America, Europe, and Japan. Many Southeast Asian states saw the current accounts of their balance of payments shift strongly into the red during the mid-1990s. By 1995, Indonesia was running a current account deficit that was equivalent to 3.5 percent of its GDP, Malaysia's was 5.9 percent, and Thailand's was 8.1 percent.[22] With deficits like these, it was increasingly difficult for the governments of these countries to maintain their currencies against the U.S. dollar. If that peg could not be held, the local currency value of dollar-denominated debt would increase, raising the specter of large-scale default on debt service payments. The scene was now set for a potentially rapid economic meltdown.

By 1997, years of excess demand in the Thai property market resulted in enough excess space to meet its residential and commercial needs for five years.

The Crisis   The Asian meltdown began in mid-1997 in Thailand when it became clear that several key Thai financial institutions were on the verge of default. These institutions had been borrowing dollars from international banks at low interest rates and lending Thai baht at higher interest rates to local property developers. However, due to speculative overbuilding, these developers could not sell their commercial and residential property, forcing them to default on their debt obligations. In turn, the Thai financial institutions seemed increasingly likely to default on their dollar-denominated debt obligations to international banks. Sensing the beginning of the crisis, foreign investors fled the Thai stock market, selling their positions and converting them into U.S. dollars. The increased demand for dollars and increased supply of Thai baht, pushed down the dollar/Thai baht exchange rate, while the stock market plunged.

Seeing these developments, foreign exchange dealers and hedge funds started speculating against the baht, selling it short. For the previous 13 years, the Thai baht had been pegged to the U.S. dollar at an exchange rate of about $1 = Bt25. The Thai government tried to defend the peg, but only succeeded in depleting its foreign exchange reserves. On July 2, 1997, the Thai government abandoned its defense and announced it would allow the baht to float freely against the dollar. The baht started a slide that would bring the exchange rate down to $1 = Bt55 by January 1998. As the baht declined, the Thai debt bomb exploded. The 55 percent decline in the value of the baht against the dollar doubled the amount of baht required to serve the dollar-denominated debt commitments taken on by Thai financial institutions and businesses. This increased the probability of corporate bankruptcies and further pushed down the battered Thai stock market. The Thailand Set stock market index ultimately declined from 787 in January 1997 to a low of 337 in December of that year, on top of a 45 percent decline in 1996.

On July 28, the Thai government called in the International Monetary Fund. With its foreign exchange reserves depleted, Thailand lacked the foreign currency needed to finance its international trade and service debt commitments and desperately needed the capital the IMF could provide. It also needed to restore international confidence in its currency and needed the credibility associated with gaining access to IMF funds. Without IMF loans, the baht likely would increase its free fall against the U.S. dollar and the whole country might go into default. The IMF agreed to provide the Thai government with $17.2 billion in loans, but the conditions were restrictive.[23] The IMF required the Thai government to increase taxes, cut public spending, privatize several state-owned businesses, and raise interest rates—all steps designed to cool Thailand's overheated economy. The IMF also required Thailand to close illiquid financial institutions. In December 1997, the government shut 56 financial institutions, laying off 16,000 people and further deepening the recession that now gripped the country.

Following the devaluation of the Thai baht, wave after wave of speculation hit other Asian currencies. One after another in a period of weeks, the Malaysian ringgit, Indonesian rupiah, and Singaporean dollar were all marked sharply lower. With its foreign exchange reserves down to $28 billion, Malaysia let the ringgit float on July 14, 1997. Before the devaluation, the ringgit was trading at $1 = 2.525 ringgit. Six months later it had declined to $1 = 4.15 ringgit. Singapore followed on July 17, and the Singaporean dollar quickly dropped in value from $1 = S$1.495 before the devaluation to $1 = S$2.68 a few days later. Next up was Indonesia, whose rupiah was allowed to float August 14. For Indonesia, this was the beginning of a precipitous decline in the value of its currency, which was to fall from $1 = 2,400 rupiah in August 1997 to $1 = 10,000 rupiah on January 6, 1998, a loss of 76 percent.

With the exception of Singapore, whose economy is probably the most stable in the region, these devaluations were driven by factors similar to those behind the earlier devaluation of the Thai baht—a combination of excess investment; high borrowings, much of it in dollar-denominated debt; and a deteriorating balance-of-payments position. Although both Malaysia and Singapore were able to halt the slide in their currencies and stock markets without the help of the IMF, Indonesia was not. Indonesia was struggling with a private-sector, dollar-denominated debt of close to $80 billion. With the rupiah sliding precipitously almost every day, the cost of servicing this debt was exploding, pushing more Indonesian companies into technical default.

On October 31, 1997, the IMF announced it had assembled a $37 billion rescue deal for Indonesia in conjunction with the World Bank and the Asian Development Bank. In return, the Indonesian government agreed to close a number of troubled banks, reduce public spending, remove government subsidies on basic foodstuffs and energy, balance the budget, and unravel the crony capitalism that was so widespread in Indonesia. But the government of President Suharto appeared to backtrack several times on commitments made to the IMF. This precipitated further declines in the Indonesian currency and stock markets. Ultimately, Suharto removed costly government subsidies, only to see the country dissolve into chaos as the populace took to the streets to protest the resulting price increases. This unleashed a chain of events that led to Suharto's removal from power in May 1998.

The final domino to fall was South Korea. During the 1990s, South Korean companies had built up huge debt loads as they invested heavily in new industrial capacity. Now they found they had too much industrial capacity and could not generate the income required to service their debt. South Korean banks and companies had also made the mistake of borrowing in dollars, much of it in the form of short-term loans that would come due within a year. Thus, when the Korean won started to decline in the fall of 1997 in sympathy with the problems elsewhere in Asia, South Korean companies saw their debt obligations balloon. Several large companies were forced to file for bankruptcy. This triggered a decline in the South Korean currency and stock market that was difficult to halt. The South Korean central bank tried to keep the dollar/won exchange rate above $1 = W1,000 but found that this only depleted its foreign exchange reserves. On November 17, the South Korean central bank gave up the defense of the won, which quickly fell to $1 = W1,500.

With its economy on the verge of collapse, the South Korean government on November 21 requested $20 billion in standby loans from the IMF. As the negotiations progressed, it became apparent that South Korea was going to need far more than $20 billion. Among other problems, the country's short-term foreign debt was found to be twice as large as previously thought at close to $100 billion, while the country's foreign exchange reserves were down to less than $6 billion. On December 3, 1997, the IMF and South Korean government reached a deal to lend $55 billion to the country. The agreement with the IMF called for the South Koreans to open their economy and banking system to foreign investors. South Korea also pledged to restrain the *chaebol* by reducing their share of bank financing and requiring them to publish consolidated financial statements and undergo annual independent external audits. On trade liberalization, the IMF said South Korea would comply with its commitments to the World Trade Organization to eliminate trade-related subsidies and restrictive import licensing and would streamline its import certification procedures, all of which should open the South Korean economy to greater foreign competition.[24]

EVALUATING THE IMF'S POLICY PRESCRIPTIONS

By 2006, the IMF was committing loans to some 59 countries that were struggling with economic and currency crises. A detailed example of one such program is given in the accompanying

Country Focus, which looks at IMF loans to Turkey. All IMF loan packages come with conditions attached. In general, the IMF insists on a combination of tight macroeconomic policies, including cuts in public spending, higher interest rates, and tight monetary policy. It also often pushes for the deregulation of sectors formerly protected from domestic and foreign competition, privatization of state-owned assets, and better financial reporting from the banking sector. These policies are designed to cool overheated economies by reining in inflation and reducing government spending and debt. Recently, this set of policy prescriptions has come in for tough criticisms from many observers.[25]

Inappropriate Policies   One criticism is that the IMF's "one-size-fits-all" approach to macroeconomic policy is inappropriate for many countries. In the case of the Asian crisis, critics argue that the tight macroeconomic policies imposed by the IMF are not well suited to countries that are suffering not from excessive government spending and inflation, but from a private-sector debt crisis with deflationary undertones.[26] In South Korea, for example, the government had been running a budget surplus for years (it was 4 percent of South Korea's GDP in 1994–1996) and inflation was low at about 5 percent. South Korea had the second strongest financial position of any country in the Organization for Economic Cooperation and Development. Despite this, critics say, the IMF insisted on applying the same policies that it applies to countries suffering from high inflation. The IMF required South Korea to maintain an inflation rate of 5 percent. However, given the collapse in the value of its currency and the subsequent rise in price for imports such as oil, critics claimed inflationary pressures would inevitably increase in South Korea. So to hit a 5 percent inflation rate, the South Koreans would be forced to apply an unnecessarily tight monetary policy. Short-term interest rates in South Korea did jump from 12.5 percent to 21 percent immediately after the country signed its initial deal with the IMF. Increasing interest rates made it even more difficult for companies to service their already excessive short-term debt obligations, and critics used this as evidence to argue that the cure prescribed by the IMF may actually increase the probability of widespread corporate defaults, not reduce them.

The IMF rejected this criticism. According to the IMF, the central task was to rebuild confidence in the won. Once this was achieved, the won would recover from its oversold levels, reducing the size of South Korea's dollar-denominated debt burden when expressed in won, making it easier for companies to service their debt. The IMF also argued that by requiring South Korea to remove restrictions on foreign direct investment, foreign capital would flow into the country to take advantage of cheap assets. This, too, would increase demand for the Korean currency and help to improve the dollar/won exchange rate.

Korea did recover fairly quickly from the crisis, supporting the position of the IMF. While the economy contracted by 7 percent in 1998, by 2000 it had rebounded and grew at a 9 percent rate (measured by growth in GDP). Inflation, which peaked at 8 percent in 1998, fell to 2 percent by 2000, and unemployment fell from 7 percent to 4 percent over the same period. The won hit a low of $1 = W1,812 in early 1998, but by 2000 was back to an exchange rate of around $1 = W1,200, at which it seems to have stabilized.

Moral Hazard   A second criticism of the IMF is that its rescue efforts are exacerbating a problem known to economists as moral hazard. **Moral hazard** arises when people behave recklessly because they know they will be saved if things go wrong. Critics point out that many Japanese and Western banks were far too willing to lend large amounts of capital to overleveraged Asian companies during the boom years of

Moral Hazard
When people behave recklessly because they know they will be saved if things go wrong.

Country FOCUS

Turkey and the IMF

In May 2001, the International Monetary Fund (IMF) agreed to lend $8 billion to Turkey to help the country stabilize its economy and halt a sharp slide in the value of its currency. This was the third time in two years that the international lending institution had put together a loan program for Turkey, and it was the 18th program since Turkey became a member of the IMF in 1958.

Many of Turkey's problems stemmed from a large and inefficient state sector and heavy subsidies to various private sectors of the economy such as agriculture. Although the Turkish government started to privatize state-owned companies in the late 1980s, the process proceeded at a glacial pace, hamstrung by political opposition within Turkey. Instead of selling state-owned assets to private investors, successive governments increased support to unprofitable state-owned industries and raised the wage rates of state employees. Nor did the government cut subsidies to politically powerful private sectors of the economy, such as agriculture. To support state industries and finance subsidies, Turkey issued significant amounts of government debt. To limit the amount of debt, the government expanded the money supply to finance spending. The result was rampant inflation and high interest rates. During the 1990s, inflation averaged over 80 percent a year while real interest rates rose to more than 50 percent on a number of occasions. Despite this, the Turkish economy continued to grow at a healthy pace of 6 percent annually in real terms, a remarkable achievement given the high inflation rates and interest rates.

By the late 1990s the "Turkish miracle" of sustained growth in the face of high inflation and interest rates was running out of steam. Government debt had risen to 60 percent of gross domestic product, government borrowing was leaving little capital for private enterprises, and the cost of financing government debt was spiraling out of control. Rampant inflation was putting pressure on the Turkish currency, the lira, which at the time was pegged in value to a basket of other currencies. Realizing that it needed to reform its economy, the Turkish government sat down with the IMF in late 1999 to work out a recovery program, adopted in January 2000.

As with most IMF programs, the focus was on bringing down the inflation rate, stabilizing the value of the Turkish currency, and restructuring the economy to reduce government debt. The Turkish government committed itself to reducing government debt by taking a number of steps. These included an accelerated privatization program, using the proceeds to pay down debt; the reduction of agricultural subsidies; reform to make it more difficult for people to qualify for public pension programs; and tax increases. The government also agreed to rein in the growth in the money supply to

better control inflation. To limit the possibility of speculative attacks on the Turkish currency in the foreign exchange markets, the Turkish government and IMF announced that Turkey would peg the value of the lira against a basket of currencies and devalue the lira by a predetermined amount each month throughout 2000, bringing the total devaluation for the year to 25 percent. To ease the pain, the IMF agreed to provide the Turkish government with $5 billion in loans that could be used to support the value of the lira.

Initially the program seemed to be working. Inflation fell to 35 percent in 2000, while the economy grew by 6 percent. By the end of 2000, however, the program was in trouble. Burdened with nonperforming loans, a number of Turkish banks faced default and had been taken into public ownership by the government. When a criminal fraud investigation uncovered evidence that several of these banks had been pressured by politicians into providing loans at below-market interest rates, foreign investors, worried that more banks might be involved, started to pull their money out of Turkey. This sent the Turkish stock market into a tailspin and put enormous pressure on the Turkish lira. The government raised Turkish overnight interbank lending rates to as high as 1,950 percent to try to stem the outflow of capital, but it was clear that Turkey alone could not halt the flow.

The IMF stepped once more into the breach, announcing on December 6, 2000, a quickly arranged $7.5 billion loan program for the country. In return for the loan, the IMF required the Turkish government to close 10 insolvent banks, speed up its privatization plans (which had once more stalled), and cap any pay increases for government workers. The IMF also reportedly urged the Turkish government to let its currency float freely in the foreign exchange markets, but the government refused, arguing that the result would be a rapid devaluation in the lira, which would raise import prices and fuel price inflation. The government insisted that reducing inflation should be its first priority.

This plan started to come apart in February 2001. A surge in inflation and a rapid slowdown in economic growth once more spooked foreign investors. Into this explosive mix waded Turkey's prime minister and president, who engaged in a highly public argument about economic policy and political corruption. This triggered a rapid outflow of capital. The government raised the overnight interbank lending rate to 7,500 percent to try to persuade foreigners to leave their money in the country, but to no avail. Realizing that it would be unable to keep the lira within its planned monthly devaluation range without raising interest rates to absurd levels or seriously depleting the country's foreign exchange reserves, on February 23, 2001, the Turkish government decided to let the lira float freely. The lira immediately dropped

50 percent in value against the U.S. dollar, but ended the day down some 28 percent.

Over the next two months, the Turkish economy continued to weaken as a global economic slowdown affected the nation. Inflation stayed high, and progress at reforming the country's economy remained bogged down by political considerations. By early April, the lira had fallen 40 percent against the dollar since February 23, and the country was teetering on the brink of an economic meltdown. For the third time in 18 months, the IMF stepped in, arranging for another $8 billion in loans. Once more, the IMF insisted that the Turkish government accelerate privatization, close insolvent banks, deregulate its market, and cut government spending. Critics of the IMF, however, claimed this "austerity program" would only slow the Turkish economy and make matters worse, not better. These critics advocated a mix of sound monetary policy and tax cuts to boost Turkey's economic growth.

By 2007 significant progress had been made. Initially the Turkish government failed to fully comply with IMF mandates on economic policy, causing the institution to hold back a scheduled $1.6 billion in IMF loans until the government passed an "austerity budget," which it did reluctantly in March 2003 after months of public hand-wringing. Since then, things have improved. Inflation fell from a peak of 65 percent in December 2000 to about 8.2 percent for 2005 and 9 percent for 2007. Economic growth increased to a robust 9 percent in 2004, followed by 5.9 percent in 2005, 5.2 percent in 2006, and 4 percent in 2007. The pace of the privatization program has increased. The government also generated budget surpluses in 2003–2006.

Sources: P. Blustein, "Turkish Crisis Weakens the Case for Intervention," *Washington Post*, March 2, 2001, p. E1; H. Pope, "Can Turkey Finally Mend Its Economy?" *The Wall Street Journal*, May 22, 2001, p. A18; "Turkish Bath," *The Wall Street Journal*, February 23, 2001, p. A14; E. McBride, "Turkey—Fingers Crossed," *The Economist*, June 10, 2000, pp. SS16–17; "Turkey and the IMF," *The Economist*, December 9, 2000, pp. 81–82; G. Chazan, "Turkey's Decision on Aid Is Sinking In," *The Wall Street Journal*, March 6, 2003, p. A11; S. Fittipaldi, "Markets Keep a Wary Eye on Ankara," *Global Finance*, October 2003, p. 88; "Plumper: Turkey," *The Economist*, December 18, 2004, p. 141; and "Turkey: Country Forecast Summary," *The Economist Intelligence Unit*, January 26, 2006.

the 1990s. These critics argued that the banks should be forced to pay the price for their rash lending policies, even if that meant some banks must close.[27] Only by taking such drastic action, the argument goes, will banks learn the error of their ways and not engage in rash lending in the future. By providing support to these countries, the IMF is reducing the probability of debt default and in effect bailing out the banks whose loans gave rise to this situation.

This argument ignores two critical points. First, if some Japanese or Western banks with heavy exposure to the troubled Asian economies were forced to write off their loans due to widespread debt default, the impact would have been difficult to contain. The failure of large Japanese banks, for example, could have triggered a meltdown in the Japanese financial markets. That would almost inevitably lead to a serious decline in stock markets around the world, which was the very risk the IMF was trying to avoid by stepping in with financial support. Second, it is incorrect to imply that some banks have not had to pay the price for rash lending policies. The IMF has insisted on the closure of banks in South Korea, Thailand, and Indonesia. Foreign banks with short-term loans outstanding to South Korean enterprises have been forced by circumstances to reschedule those loans at interest rates that do not compensate for the extension of the loan maturity.

Lack of Accountability   The final criticism of the IMF is that it has become too powerful for an institution that lacks any real mechanism for accountability.[28] The IMF has determined macroeconomic policies in those countries, yet according to critics such as noted economist Jeffrey Sachs, the IMF, with a staff of less than 1,000, lacks the expertise required to do a good job. Evidence of this, according to Sachs, can be found in the fact that the IMF was singing the praises of the Thai and South Korean governments only months before both countries lurched into crisis. Then the IMF put together a draconian program for South Korea without having deep knowledge of the country. Sachs's solution to this problem is to reform the IMF so it makes greater use of outside experts and its operations are open to greater outside scrutiny.

Observations   As with many debates about international economics, it is not clear which side has the winning hand about the appropriateness of IMF policies. There are cases where one can argue that IMF policies have been counterproductive, or only had limited success. For example, one might question the success of the IMF's involvement in Turkey given that the country has had to implement some 18 IMF programs since 1958 (see the accompanying Country Focus)! But the IMF can also point to some notable accomplishments, including its success in containing the Asian crisis, which could have rocked the global international monetary system to its core. Similarly, many observers give the IMF credit for its deft handling of politically difficult situations, such as the Mexican peso crisis, and for successfully promoting a free market philosophy.

Several years after the IMF's intervention, the economies of Asia and Mexico recovered. Certainly they all averted the kind of catastrophic implosion that might have occurred had the IMF not stepped in, and although some countries still faced considerable problems, it is not clear that the IMF should take much blame for this. The IMF cannot force countries to adopt the policies required to correct economic mismanagement. While a government may commit to taking corrective action in return for an IMF loan, internal political problems may make it difficult for a government to act on that commitment. In such cases, the IMF is caught between a rock and a hard place, for if it decided to withhold money, it might trigger financial collapse and the contagion that it seeks to avoid.

Focus on Managerial Implications

LEARNING OBJECTIVE 6
Understand the implications of the global monetary system for currency management and business strategy.

The implications for international businesses of the material discussed in this chapter fall into three main areas: currency management, business strategy, and corporate–government relations.

Currency Management

An obvious implication with regard to currency management is that companies must recognize that the foreign exchange market does not work quite as depicted in Chapter 9. The current system is a mixed system in which a combination of government intervention and speculative activity can drive the foreign exchange market. Companies engaged in significant foreign exchange activities need to be aware of this and to adjust their foreign exchange transactions accordingly. For example, the currency management unit of Caterpillar claims it made millions of dollars in the hours following the announcement of the Plaza Accord by selling dollars and buying currencies that it expected to appreciate on the foreign exchange market following government intervention.

Under the present system, speculative buying and selling of currencies can create very volatile movements in exchange rates (as exhibited by the rise and fall of the dollar during the 1980s and the Asian currency crisis of the late 1990s). Contrary to the predictions of the purchasing power parity theory (see Chapter 9), exchange rate movements during the 1980s and 1990s often did not seem to be strongly influenced by relative inflation rates. Insofar as volatile exchange rates increase foreign exchange risk, this is not good news for business. On the other hand, as we saw in Chapter 9, the foreign exchange market has developed a number of instruments, such as the forward market and swaps, that can help to insure against foreign exchange risk. Not surprisingly, use of these instruments has increased markedly since the breakdown of the Bretton Woods system in 1973.

Business Strategy

The volatility of the present global exchange rate regime presents a conundrum for international businesses. Exchange rate movements are difficult to predict, and yet their movement can have a major impact on a business's competitive position. For a detailed example, see the accompanying Management Focus on Airbus. Faced with uncertainty about the future value of currencies, firms can utilize the forward exchange market, which Airbus has done. However, the forward exchange market is far from perfect as a predictor of future exchange rates (see Chapter 9). It is also difficult if not impossible to get adequate insurance coverage for exchange rate changes that might occur several years in the future. The forward market tends to offer coverage for exchange rate changes a few months—not years—ahead. Given this, it makes sense to pursue strategies that will increase the company's strategic flexibility in the face of unpredictable exchange rate movements—that is, to pursue strategies that reduce the economic exposure of the firm (which we first discussed in Chapter 9).

Maintaining strategic flexibility can take the form of dispersing production to different locations around the globe as a real hedge against currency fluctuations (this seems to be what Airbus is now considering). Consider the case of Daimler-Benz, Germany's export-oriented automobile and aerospace company. In June 1995, the company stunned the German business community when it announced it expected to post a severe loss in 1995 of about $720 million. The cause was Germany's strong currency, which had appreciated by 4 percent against a basket of major currencies since the beginning of 1995 and had risen by more than 30 percent against the U.S. dollar since late 1994. By mid-1995, the exchange rate against the dollar stood at $1 = DM1.38. Daimler's management believed it could not make money with an exchange rate under $1 = DM1.60. Daimler's senior managers concluded that the appreciation of the mark against the dollar was probably permanent, so they decided to move substantial production outside of Germany and increase purchasing of foreign components. The idea was to reduce the vulnerability of the company to future exchange rate movements. The Mercedes-Benz division has been implementing this move for the last decade. Even before its acquisition of Chrysler Corporation in 1998, Mercedes planned to produce 10 percent of its cars outside of Germany by 2000, mostly in the United States.[29] Similarly, the move by Japanese automobile companies to expand their productive capacity in the United States and Europe can be seen in the context of the increase in the value of the yen between 1985 and 1995, which raised the price of Japanese exports. For the Japanese companies, building production capacity overseas is a hedge against continued appreciation of the yen (as well as against trade barriers).

Another way of building strategic flexibility and reducing economic exposure involves contracting out manufacturing. This allows a company to shift suppliers from country to country in response to changes in relative costs brought about by exchange rate movements. However, this kind of strategy may work only for low-value-added manufacturing (e.g., textiles), in which the individual manufacturers have few if any firm-specific skills that contribute to the value of the product. It may be less appropriate for high-value-added manufacturing, in which firm-specific technology and skills add significant value to the product (e.g., the heavy equipment industry) and in which switching costs are correspondingly high. For high-value-added manufacturing, switching suppliers will lead to a reduction in the value that is added, which may offset any cost gains arising from exchange rate fluctuations.

The roles of the IMF and the World Bank in the present international monetary system also have implications for business strategy. Increasingly, the IMF has been acting as the macroeconomic police of the world economy, insisting that countries seeking significant borrowings adopt IMF-mandated macroeconomic policies. These policies typically include anti-inflationary monetary policies and reductions in government spending. In the short run, such policies usually result in a sharp contraction of

Management FOCUS

Airbus and the Euro

Airbus had reason to celebrate in 2003; for the first time in the company's history it delivered more commercial jet aircraft than longtime rival Boeing. Airbus delivered 305 planes in 2003, compared to Boeing's 281. The celebration, however, was muted, for the strength of the euro against the U.S. dollar was casting a cloud over the company's future. Airbus, which is based in Toulouse, France, prices planes in dollars, just as Boeing has always done. But more than half of Airbus's costs are in euros. So as the dollar drops in value against the euro, and it dropped by over 55 percent between 2002 and the end of 2007, Airbus's costs rise in proportion to its revenue, squeezing profits in the process.

In the short run, the fall in the value of the dollar against the euro did not hurt Airbus. The company fully hedged its dollar exposure until 2005 and was mostly hedged for 2006. However, anticipating that the dollar will stay weak against the euro, Airbus has started to take other steps to reduce its economic exposure to a strong European currency. Recognizing that raising prices is not an option given the strong competition from Boeing, Airbus has decided to focus on reducing its costs. As a step toward doing this, Airbus is giving U.S. suppliers a greater share of work on new aircraft models, such as the A380 super-jumbo and the A350. It is also shifting supply work on some of its older models from European to American-based suppliers. This will increase the proportion of its costs that are in dollars, making profits less vulnerable to a rise in the value of the euro and reducing the costs of building an aircraft when they are converted back into euros.

In addition, Airbus is pushing its European-based suppliers to start pricing in U.S. dollars. Because the costs of many suppliers are in euros, the suppliers are finding that to comply with Airbus's wishes, they too have to move more work to the United States, or to countries whose currency is pegged to the U.S. dollar. Thus, one large French-based supplier, Zodiac, has announced that it was considering acquisitions in the United States. Not only is Airbus pushing suppliers to price components for commercial jet aircraft in dollars, but the company is also requiring suppliers to its A400M program, a military aircraft that will be sold to European governments and priced in euros, to price components in U.S. dollars. Beyond these steps, the CEO of EADS, Airbus's parent company, has publicly stated that it might be prepared to assemble aircraft in the United States if that helps to win important U.S. contracts.

Sources: D. Michaels, "Airbus Deliveries Top Boeing's; But Several Obstacles Remain," *The Wall Street Journal*, January 16, 2004, p. A9; J.L. Gerondeau, "Airbus Eyes U.S. Suppliers as Euro Gains," *Seattle Times*, February 21, 2004, p. C4; "Euro's Gains Create Worries in Europe," *Houston Chronicle.com*, January 13, 2004, p. 3; and K. Done, "Soft Dollar and A380 Hitches Lead to EADS Losses," *Financial Times*, November 9, 2006, p. 32.

demand. International businesses selling or producing in such countries need to be aware of this and plan accordingly. In the long run, the kind of policies imposed by the IMF can promote economic growth and an expansion of demand, which create opportunities for international business.

Corporate–Government Relations

As major players in the international trade and investment environment, businesses can influence government policy toward the international monetary system. For example, intense government lobbying by U.S. exporters helped convince the U.S. government that intervention in the foreign exchange market was necessary. With this in mind, business can and should use its influence to promote an international monetary system that facilitates the growth of international trade and investment. Whether a fixed or floating regime is optimal is a subject for debate. However, exchange rate volatility such as the world experienced during the 1980s and 1990s creates an environment less conducive to international trade and investment than one with more stable exchange rates. Therefore, it would seem to be in the interests of international business to promote an international monetary system that minimizes volatile exchange rate movements, particularly when those movements are unrelated to long-run economic fundamentals.

Key Terms

international monetary system, p. 340

floating exchange rate, p. 340

pegged exchange rate, p. 341

dirty float, p. 341

fixed exchange rate, p. 341

European Monetary System (EMS) , p. 341

gold standard, p. 342

gold par value, p. 342

balance-of-trade equilibrium, p. 343

managed-float system, p. 352

currency board, p. 355

currency crisis, p. 357

banking crisis, p. 357

foreign debt crisis, p. 357

moral hazard, p. 363

Summary

This chapter explained the workings of the international monetary system and pointed out its implications for international business. The chapter made the following points:

1. The gold standard is a monetary standard that pegs currencies to gold and guarantees convertibility to gold. It was thought that the gold standard contained an automatic mechanism that contributed to the simultaneous achievement of a balance-of-payments equilibrium by all countries. The gold standard broke down during the 1930s as countries engaged in competitive devaluations.

2. The Bretton Woods system of fixed exchange rates was established in 1944. The U.S. dollar was the central currency of this system; the value of every other currency was pegged to its value. Significant exchange rate devaluations were allowed only with the permission of the IMF. The role of the IMF was to maintain order in the international monetary system (a) to avoid a repetition of the competitive devaluations of the 1930s and (b) to control price inflation by imposing monetary discipline on countries.

3. The fixed exchange rate system collapsed in 1973, primarily due to speculative pressure on the dollar following a rise in U.S. inflation and a growing U.S. balance-of-trade deficit.

4. Since 1973 the world has operated with a floating exchange rate regime, and exchange rates have become more volatile and far less predictable. Volatile exchange rate movements have helped reopen the debate over the merits of fixed and floating systems.

5. The case for a floating exchange rate regime claims (a) such a system gives countries autonomy regarding their monetary policy and (b) floating exchange rates facilitate smooth adjustment of trade imbalances.

6. The case for a fixed exchange rate regime claims (a) the need to maintain a fixed exchange rate imposes monetary discipline on a country, (b) floating exchange rate regimes are vulnerable to speculative pressure, (c) the uncertainty that accompanies floating exchange rates dampens the growth of international trade and investment, and (d) far from correcting trade imbalances, depreciating a currency on the foreign exchange market tends to cause price inflation.

7. In today's international monetary system, some countries have adopted floating exchange rates, some have pegged their currency to another currency such as the U.S. dollar, and some have pegged their currency to a basket of other currencies, allowing their currency to fluctuate within a zone around the basket.

8. In the post–Bretton Woods era, the IMF has continued to play an important role in helping countries navigate their way through financial crises by lending significant capital to embattled governments and by requiring them to adopt certain macroeconomic policies.

9. An important debate is occurring over the appropriateness of IMF-mandated macroeconomic policies. Critics charge that the IMF often imposes inappropriate conditions on developing nations that are the recipients of its loans.

10. The present managed-float system of exchange rate determination has increased the importance of currency management in international businesses.

11. The volatility of exchange rates under the present managed-float system creates both opportunities and threats. One way of responding to this volatility is for companies to build strategic flexibility and limit their economic exposure by dispersing production to different locations around the globe by contracting out manufacturing (in the case of low-value-added manufacturing) and other means.

Critical Thinking and Discussion Questions

1. Why did the gold standard collapse? Is there a case for returning to some type of gold standard? What is it?

2. What opportunities might current IMF lending policies to developing nations create for international businesses? What threats might they create?

3. Do you think the standard IMF policy prescriptions of tight monetary policy and reduced government spending are always appropriate for developing nations experiencing a currency crisis? How might the IMF change its approach? What would the implications be for international businesses?

4. Debate the relative merits of fixed and floating exchange rate regimes. From the perspective of an international business, what are the most important criteria in a choice between the systems? Which system is the more desirable for an international business?

5. Imagine that Canada, the United States, and Mexico decide to adopt a fixed exchange rate system. What would be the likely consequences of such a system for (*a*) international businesses and (*b*) the flow of trade and investment among the three countries?

6. Reread the Country focus on the U.S. dollar, oil prices and recycling petrodollars, then answer the following questions:

   a. What will happen to the value of the U.S. dollar if oil producers decide to invest most of their earnings from oil sales in domestic infrastructure projects?

   b. What factors determine the relative attractiveness of dollar-, euro-, and yen-denominated assets to oil producers flush with petrodollars? What might lead them to direct more funds toward non-dollar-denominated assets?

   c. What will happen to the value of the U.S. dollar if OPEC members decide to invest more of their petrodollars toward non-dollar assets, such as euro-denominated stocks and bonds?

   d. In addition to oil producers, China is also accumulating a large stock of dollars, currently estimated to total $1.4 trillion. What would happen to the value of the dollar if China and oil-producing nations all shifted out of dollar-denominated assets at the same time? What would be the consequence for the U.S. economy?

Research Task ⬤ globalEDGE http://globalEDGE.msu.edu

Use the globalEDGE Resource Desk (http://globalEDGE.msu.edu/ResourceDesk/) to complete the following exercises:

1. While Latvia has been a member state of the European Union since 2004, it has not completed the third stage of the European Monetary Union and therefore still uses its own currency, the Latvian Lats. Visit the site of the *Bank of Latvia* to get more information about the current monetary policy in Latvia. How is the value of Lats determined? Why?

2. The International Capital Markets division of the International Monetary Fund (IMF) publishes the *Global Financial Stability Report*, a semi-annual report that provides an assessment of the global financial markets. Find the Global Financial Stability Map in the most recent report. Provide a description of the indicators used to construct the map and briefly summarize what the most current map illustrates in terms of changes in financial stability risks.

closing case

China's Managed Float

In 1994, China pegged the value of its currency, the yuan, to the U.S. dollar at an exchange rate of $1 = 8.28 yuan. For the next 11 years, the value of the yuan moved in lockstep with the value of the U.S. dollar against other currencies. By early 2005, however, pressure was building for China to alter its exchange rate policy and let the yuan float freely against the dollar.

Underlying this pressure were claims that after years of rapid economic growth and foreign capital inflows, the pegged exchange rate undervalued the yuan by as much as 40 percent. In turn, the cheap yuan was helping to fuel a boom in Chinese exports to the West, particularly the United States where the trade deficit with China expanded to a record $160 billion in 2004. Job losses among American manufacturing companies created political pressures in the United States for the government to push the Chinese to let the yuan float freely against the dollar. American manufacturers complained that they could not compete against "artificially cheap" Chinese imports. In early 2005, Senators Charles Schumer and Lindsay Graham tried to get the Senate to impose a 27.5 percent tariff on imports from China unless the Chinese agreed to revalue the currency against the U.S. dollar. Although the move was defeated, Schumer and Graham vowed to revisit the issue. For its part, the Bush administration pressured China from 2003 onward, urging the government to adopt a more flexible exchange rate policy.

Keeping the yuan pegged to the dollar was also becoming increasingly problematic for the Chinese. The trade surplus with the United States, coupled with strong inflows of foreign investment, led to a surge of dollars into China. To maintain the exchange rate, the Chinese central bank regularly purchased dollars from commercial banks, issuing them yuan at the official exchange rate. As a result, by mid-2005 China's foreign exchange reserves had risen to more than $700 billion. The Chinese were reportedly buying some $15 billion each month in an attempt to maintain the dollar/yuan exchange rate. When the Chinese central bank issued yuan to mop up excess dollars, the authorities were in effect expanding the domestic money supply, leading to a growing concern that excessive lending could create a financial bubble and a surge in price inflation, which might destabilize the economy.

On July 25, 2005, the Chinese finally bowed to the pressure. The government announced it would abandon the peg against the dollar in favor of a "link" to a basket of currencies, which included the euro, yen, and U.S. dollar. Simultaneously, the government announced it would revalue the yuan against the U.S. dollar by 2.1 percent, and allow that value to move by 0.3 percent a day. The yuan was allowed to move by 1.5 percent a day against other currencies.

Many American observers and politicians thought that the Chinese move was too limited. They called for the Chinese to relax further their control over the dollar/yuan exchange rate. The Chinese resisted. By 2006, pressure was increasing on the Chinese to take action. With the U.S. trade deficit with China hitting a new record of $202 billion in 2005, Senators Schumer and Graham once more crafted a Senate bill that would place a 27.5 percent tariff on Chinese imports unless the Chinese allowed the yuan to depreciate further against the dollar. The Chinese responded by inviting the senators to China and convincing them that the country would move progressively toward a more flexible exchange rate policy.

Over the next year the Chinese appeared to let the yuan continue to appreciate against the dollar. In the last quarter of 2007, for example, the yuan appreciated at an annual rate of 13 percent against the dollar, the fastest pace since the peg to the dollar was abandoned. There seem to be two reasons for this; first, a rising yuan helps the Chinese to keep inflation in check, and second, the costs of holding down the yuan were becoming excessively high.

Sources: B. Bremner et al., "The Yuan Grows Up," *BusinessWeek*, August 8, 2005, p. 44; "Patching the Basket: the Yuan," *The Economist*, October 1, 2005, p. 83; R. McGregor, "Renminbi Revaluation Will Slow Rise in Foreign Exchange Reserves," *Financial Times*, January 1, 2006, p. 3; "Senators Back Off Showdown with China over Yuan," *China Daily*, March 29, 2006 (www.chinadaily.com); and "Revaluation by Stealth: The Chinese Yuan," *The Economist*, January 12, 2008, p. 69.

Case Discussion Questions

1. Why do you think the Chinese government originally pegged the value of the yuan against the U.S. dollar? What were the benefits of doing this for China? What were the costs?

2. Over the last decade, many foreign firms have invested in China and used their Chinese factories to produce goods for export. If the yuan is allowed to float freely against the U.S. dollar on the foreign exchange markets and appreciates in value, how might this affect the fortunes of those enterprises?

3. How might a decision to let the yuan float freely affect future foreign direct investment flows into China?

4. Under what circumstances might a decision to let the yuan float freely destabilize the Chinese economy? What might the global implications of this be?

5. Do you think the U.S. government should push the Chinese to let the yuan float freely? Why?

6. Do you think the Chinese government should let the yuan float, maintain the peg, or change the peg in some way?